PAUL KANE'S FRONTIER

Special Acknowledgment

This book, which contains a new and greatly enriched edition of Paul Kane's classic *Wanderings of an Artist*, has been made possible through the generous aid and cooperation of Mrs. Nelda C. Stark and the Nelda C. and H. J. Lutcher Stark Foundation of Orange, Texas. Original watercolours and paintings from Kane's western travels are reproduced from collections in the Stark Foundation. Two manuscript versions of *Wanderings of an Artist*, also in the Stark Foundation collections, were used by the editor in preparing the present text.

Plate I. Paul Kane, a self-portrait, painted during his western trip, 1846–48. Stark wwc103; crIV-597.

Paul Kane's Frontier

INCLUDING *Wanderings of an Artist among the Indians of North America* BY PAUL KANE

EDITED WITH A BIOGRAPHICAL INTRODUCTION
AND A CATALOGUE RAISONNÉ BY

J. Russell Harper

PUBLISHED FOR THE AMON CARTER MUSEUM, FORT WORTH, AND THE
NATIONAL GALLERY OF CANADA, OTTAWA, BY THE UNIVERSITY OF TEXAS PRESS, AUSTIN & LONDON

The National Gallery of Canada

The National Gallery of Canada was founded in 1880. From 1913 to 1968 it reported through its own Board of Trustees to a Cabinet Minister. In 1968 new legislation placed the Gallery under the Board of the National Museums of Canada, reporting to the Secretary of State with a Visiting Committee to concentrate upon the Gallery.

International Standard Book Number 0–292–70110–1
Library of Congress Catalog Card Number 79–146522
© 1971 by the Amon Carter Museum of Western Art
All Rights Reserved
Manufactured in the United States of America
Composition, Printing, and Binding: Kingsport Press, Kingsport, Tennessee
Illustrations: The Meriden Gravure Company, Meriden, Connecticut
Published in Canada by University of Toronto Press 1971

Amon Carter Museum of Western Art

The Amon Carter Museum was established in 1961 under the will of the late Amon G. Carter for the study and documentation of westering North America. The program of the Museum, expressed in publications, exhibitions, and permanent collections, reflects many aspects of American culture, both historic and contemporary.

CONTENTS

INTRODUCTION

Paul Kane was fortunate enough to receive national acclaim during his own lifetime. It was his large canvases of the western Indians and their romantic land, and his book *Wanderings of an Artist*, which were known then and these have remained the basis of his reputation. But he also left many hundreds of small sketches, which have been virtually unknown for well over a century. This study of Kane and his activities has its origin in the sketches as well as his canvases and his book, and also in his journals, letters and other material not previously made public. The large number of sketches shown here increase his importance immeasurably: they are significant historically, they have a freshness not found in many canvases, and they are altogether more exciting as paintings than his elaborated works. Paul Kane now emerges as a giant among North American artists of his period.

From 1845 to 1848 Kane travelled through the western spaces of America. First he journeyed alone, then in the brigades of the Hudson's Bay Company fur traders, and always he sketched as he went. His trip from Toronto to the Pacific was one of the longest and most adventurous sketching trips in the story of painting. On it he covered many thousands of miles, through high mountain passes in icy weather and across deserts in the blazing sun, hungry and thirsty; he descended torrents in frail canoes; he worked constantly among not always friendly native people. He recorded the Indians in detail, their homes, their ceremonials and their customs, first in the Great Lakes region and then across the western plains, through the Oregon country and along the Pacific northwest coast when these were still unknown regions.

Kane was a remarkable man who lived at a remarkable time. He was very much a man of that time, and his career as an artist-explorer is typical of the story of these years in Canada. Many Canadians, like Kane, were then probing into a variety of facets of their surroundings and seeing their world with a new keenness. Some pursued an interest in natural history, and laid the foundations for the study in Canada of its flora and fauna. Many became restless and dissatisfied with inadequacies in government; the aftermath of rebellion in 1837 was the gradual creation of a whole new political structure. Others, concerned about knowledge for their sons and daughters, instituted new elementary and secondary school systems and founded the great universities of McGill, Queen's and Toronto. Farmers, not content with the results of their labour, organized societies to promote better farming methods and the importation of purebred livestock. Business men saw a need for more means of transportation as an impetus to industrial expansion; they commenced the building of new roads, of canals and railways. Writers became more aware of the society about them and penned the first novels and stories based on the Canadian environment.

Paul Kane gave to the subjects of his brush that same appraising look which other Canadians were giving to many aspects of their life and surroundings. He set out on a search for truth, and it was this determination that he claimed always to be at the centre of his work and art.

This volume has grown out of an idea for a major book on Paul Kane which originated with Mitchell A. Wilder, Director of the Amon Carter Museum of Western Art, Fort Worth, Texas. He secured the co-operation of Mrs. Nelda C. Stark, whose late husband had purchased a superb collection of Kane's sketches and manuscripts; she generously agreed to make all her material available to the public for the first time. Mr. Wilder then approached Dr. Jean Sutherland Boggs, Director of the National Gallery of Canada, Ottawa, who at once agreed that the Gallery would become co-sponsor with the Amon

Carter Museum of a study of Kane and a major exhibition of his paintings. This co-operation between Canada and the United States is particularly appropriate since almost half of Kane's paintings are related to areas in what is now American territory. In all he spent approximately nine years south of the present border.

The research recorded in this volume on Paul Kane and his paintings, which survive in astonishing numbers, was begun by the author late in 1967. It has had much of the excitement of discovery which Kane himself experienced during his four years of seeking subject-matter among the Indians of the frontier. A number of approaches to a study of Kane's life and works suggested themselves. Each was bewildering in its possibilities. From a practical point of view it was necessary to restrict the undertaking to two essential aspects. One would be concerned directly with the artist himself, that is with the events of his career, his philosophical approach as a painter to his subject-matter, and his importance in the world of art. The second aspect would be the recording and documenting of the over eight hundred known paintings and sketches, chiefly from his trips on the western frontier. These works are mainly in several collections. Two large and magnificent accumulations are held by the Royal Ontario Museum, Toronto, and the Nelda C. and H. J. Lutcher Stark Foundation, Orange, Texas. Twelve items each are in the National Gallery of Canada, Ottawa, and the Bushnell Collection of the Peabody Museum, Harvard University; there are smaller numbers in other places. No attempt has been made here to analyse the ethnological significance of Kane's many records of Indian life; the subject would be a study in itself and one that invites exploration now. Even the limited objectives chosen have necessitated protracted detective work. In it has been combined luck, disappointment, sidetracking, and discovery, and it has meant a search that has taken me from Ontario to Victoria on the Pacific, over much of the historic terrain covered by Kane, and even to England.

Kane died nearly a century ago, and the attempt to collect information which would make him into an individual rather than just a name presented problems. During his lifetime he had been particularly reticent in speaking of himself beyond matters relating to his Indian paintings, and as close a friend as Sir Daniel Wilson had the greatest difficulty in compiling a biography at the time of the artist's death. It seemed possible that, despite the lapse of time, descendants of his family or of friends or associates might still have material. This was indeed the case. His grandchildren were found to be living in Winnipeg; they had many personal papers, paintings and sketches, portions of his library, and memorabilia of great value in documenting his career. At an early stage I also compiled a list of the people and places mentioned in Kane's book, *Wanderings of an Artist*, and in other published literature on him. Armed with this list as a starting point, I made a systematic check of the principal archives, manuscript collections and libraries from Ontario to British Columbia in Canada, in the northwestern United States, in Alabama and in England. Inquiries were made about possible papers referring to Kane himself or to men of some historical significance in my list. The co-operation in answer to my queries from archivists and librarians was most generous; many who had nothing relevant suggested other possible sources, and some put me directly in touch with various specialists who were of great assistance. The results were in sum most gratifying. The papers of Sir George Simpson, Kane's first patron, were seen in the Hudson's Bay Company archives; these, and the journals kept at the Company's posts at the time of Kane's visits, yielded many useful references. Papers in the Royal Ontario Museum provided both clarification and further leads. Diaries of several missionaries, such as the Rev. John Hunter of Cumberland House and Mrs. Mary Walker of the Walker and Eells mission in the Oregon Territory, contained interesting observations on the man. Descendants of the Honourable George W. Allan, Kane's second patron, had several paintings, and their papers referred to Kane's trip to Fort Garry in 1849 with Sir Edward Poore. This allusion to Poore led to the unexpected discovery of letters among the Poore family papers which completely documented this episode. Thus each discovery generated its own excitement as the picture of Kane gradually developed, and often also suggested new avenues of research.

During the search for original letters and other manuscript material, several publications about Kane were located which, curiously, had previously missed the attention of art historians. Of particular interest were an informative biography published in the *Anglo-American Magazine* of 1856, a unique printed catalogue of the 1848 exhibition in the Toronto City Hall of Kane's sketches during his four years in the west, personal recollections of Kane published by W. H. G. Kingston in 1856, and two letters from Kane to Lord Strathcona published in the latter's biography by Beckles Willson. Contemporary newspaper articles brought a sense of immediacy and vitality to the story. Toronto papers recorded Kane's visit to the theatre during his youth, devoted several columns to the local reaction to his 1848 exhibition, and gave him an obituary. Papers published in Mobile, Alabama, in 1841 and 1843 and in Oregon City in 1846 added more material. Reviews of Kane's *Wanderings of an Artist* were most illuminating about attitudes then current towards the threatened extinction of the American Indian; a critique in the *Revue des deux mondes*, the most scholarly of all, had not previously been used by writers.

Needless to add, all previously listed publications on Kane were checked, a study was made of the literature of the mid 19th century fur trade and particularly of the Hudson's Bay Company's operations, and publications describing affairs in the Oregon Territory during the crucial 1840s were examined. Reference points for the assessment of Kane's contribution and stature were provided by a study of George Catlin, John Mix Stanley, Henry J. Warre and other painters of Indians and western scenery at the time. One of the most significant discoveries was that of a documented link between Kane and Catlin and various references to his knowledge of Stanley's activities as a painter in the Oregon.

The second aspect of my task, one which appeared to be of formidable complexity, was the preparation of a *catalogue raisonné*. The hundreds of sketches in the Royal Ontario Museum and the Stark Foundation collections, as well as others scattered throughout Canada and the United States were, with but a few exceptions, unknown to the general public and indeed had been seen by comparatively few people. The awesome task of identifying these was simplified in an unexpected way. Many sketches bore numbers, some having as many as seven of these inscribed on them. The numbers appeared to refer to various series. Keys to five of these series were actually discovered, and three series proved to relate to material prepared by Kane himself and thus of primary importance. This first-hand information was in the landscape and portrait logs which the artist kept on his western trip, and in the list of 240 sketches published in the 1848 catalogue. By checking inscribed numbers in these sources, it was possible to identify the bulk of the material. A few items were not clearly identifiable, but most of them seem to be of secondary interest. Some sketches bear ancient identification inscriptions; they proved to be not in Kane's hand and many were quite incorrect. If proof had been needed of the value of Kane's lists, it came when three of the twelve sketches carefully studied by D. I. Bushnell without their aid proved to be misidentified. Surprisingly, most of the sketches listed in the three series have been located. The whole collection, geographically arranged, unites to present a spectacular panorama of the western frontier during the 1840s: the west's celebrated men, its places of historic interest, its way of life which is now strange to us, and an ethnologically rich series of paintings of Indians from a day when their culture was still comparatively pure. A list of the later canvases purchased in 1856 by George W. Allan was in the Royal Ontario Museum collection; by checking it and the subject-matter of the sketches identified, several new identifications of canvases have been made.

Every writer about Kane points out that he was a professional portrait painter before turning to the western landscape and the Indians. Surprisingly little is known of his portraits. As a result of the work for this volume some positive identifications have been possible, some myths have been destroyed, and certain stylistic traits have been isolated. Much remains to be discovered, and it is hoped that the publication of this volume may itself lead to new sources of information.

One gratifying result of this research has been the discovery of Kane as a man with a humanitarian viewpoint unusual in his day and age. His stature as an artist also grows immeasurably from an examination of his field sketches. His journey over many thousands of miles of the difficult western frontier is unequalled by any other artist on the continent of his time, and he had a superb eye for recording the historically important. Certainly he is the equal of and in many respects superior to any other 19th century painter of the North American Indian.

The selection of the illustrations to be included in this book was a delightful exercise since the number of both colour and black-and-white plates to be included permitted generous visual demonstration of Kane's many interests and of various aspects of his work as a creative artist. The choice was guided by several considerations.

The Indians and their life were, of course, Kane's most absorbing interest as an artist. From his western travels it has been possible to include not only portraits of Big Snake, the famous prairie warrior, and of other celebrated chiefs whom he met, but also some of the compelling studies of less exalted Indian men and women from many tribes. Sketches of houses, clothing, canoes, weapons and artefacts from many tribes give a brief look at the material culture of the Indians, and others record such unique ceremonials as the Chualpays scalp dance at Fort Colvile, secret society dances of Vancouver Island, and Blackfoot medicine pipe-stem dances in Saskatchewan. Naturally, with the Hudson's Bay Company as his host, Kane left a visual record of their posts; included is at least one illustration of each of the posts he visited, the tangible symbols of British sovereignty and trade in the wilderness. The westward move of American settlers stirred his imagination; studies of Oregon City, the new metropolis of the west, of mission posts, and of the Puget Sound settlement echo his excitement at this turn of events. Many pure landscape studies have been included; travelling by canoe on rivers and lakes, Kane had full opportunity to appreciate the majesty of the western reaches of the continent. I have included his views of such striking natural phenomena as the Grand Coulee, the Chimney Rocks, waterfalls and erupting Mount St. Helens, as well as quieter autumn pastorals on the North Saskatchewan River and the picturesque Thirty Thousand Islands of Georgian Bay. The illustrations of his journeys have been arranged geographically from east to west, and they are thus a visual travelogue of the area over which he wandered.

A few illustrations of Kane's student works and of portraits painted in Ontario and the midwestern and southern United States are included. No exhaustive research has been done on phases of his career other than his western tour. Hopefully the examples selected will aid in identifying other Kane portraits, particularly in Ontario and Alabama.

On the technical side, illustrations have been selected to demonstrate Kane's procedures and his merits and shortcomings as an artist. Several reproductions demonstrate how *Winter Travelling in Dog Sleds* evolved, originating in small sketch studies, worked out in a pencilled composition, and ending as a canvas. Other illustrations indicate something of the loss of immediacy when he moved from sketch to canvas, his tendancy to fumble in establishing proportions, his occasional reliance on earlier sources. Some of his canvases echo popular taste of the time, but anyone studying these illustrations will be very much aware of the fact that when Kane followed his own inclinations, particularly in working on his small field sketches, he was able to give a freshness and brilliance extraordinary for the years preceding impressionism.

A word should be said here about the structure of this book and how the reader might approach it. It has four main parts, which are both independent and interlocking. The first presents an account of Paul Kane's life and work, with special attention to the significant years of his career and to the period of his travels in the west, including references to information from other sources which give contemporary context to his journey; cross-references are made specifically to plates and figures of this book which reproduce works discussed in this biographical account, and references to *Wanderings of an Artist* are implicit. The second part of the book is a reprinting of the text of the first edition of *Wanderings*, which enables the reader to follow Kane's great journey as told in his own words; in this text have been interpolated references to the illustrations in the present volume and to all the items in sections III and IV of the *catalogue raisonné* so that the reader has constantly available to him a visual and a documentary accompaniment to Kane's narrative of his search for artistic subject-matter. The third part is made up of 205 black-and-white figures; their captions direct the reader to the corresponding items in the fourth part, the *catalogue raisonné*, which lists all Kane's work so far as it is known. Its sections III and IV organize the canvases and sketches of the frontier geographically from east to west, and by kinds of subjects within the various geographical areas; they also provide cross-references to relevant remarks by Kane in *Wanderings*, give background information about places and individuals and Indian tribes which Kane sketched, and indicate which items of the *catalogue* are reproduced in the present volume.

This description will indicate that the reader, depending on his interest, can begin his examination with any one of the four parts and consult the others both simultaneously and later. The appendices provide documents related to the three parts of text, and the index is a guide to the various references in all divisions of the book to individuals, places, and topics.

ACKNOWLEDGMENTS

Generous assistance in preparing this volume has been given by innumerable individuals scattered over two continents. To all I should like to express my warmest thanks. Particular mention must be made first of those who made available the artist's paintings and sketches and hitherto unpublished papers, without which this task would have been redundant. Mrs. Nelda C. Stark has graciously opened for publication the Stark Foundation's unrivalled collection of Kane material; it has made an absolutely essential contribution to the volume. My thanks go also to the artist's descendants: to his grandson's widow, Mrs. Paul Kane III, and to his granddaughters, Mrs. T. M. Willet and Mrs. R. W. Thurston, for the use which they have kindly permitted of their material. Their unflagging interest has been a source of real inspiration. Nothing would have been possible without the planning of Mitchell Wilder of the Amon Carter Museum of Western American Art, Fort Worth, and Jean Sutherland Boggs of the National Gallery of Canada, Ottawa. Their enthusiasm has remained constant, they have put the resources of their institutions behind the project, and both have laboured long in bringing the work to fruition. Through the splendid co-operation of Peter C. Swann and his staff at the Royal Ontario Museum, Toronto, its superb holdings of Kane canvases and sketches were made available for study and reproduction; they have aided in innumerable other ways. The Canada Council has kindly provided assistance so that cleaning of Kane's works in the Museum's collections might be undertaken.

Many other institutions and individuals have helped either by opening their collections for study or by supplying information. My thanks go to the following: Mrs. P. E. Anderson and Mrs. K. B. Edsall, Peabody Museum of Archaeology and Ethnology, Harvard University; David J. Armour, Mackinac Island State Commission; Mrs. Ralph D. Baker; John A. Bovey and Miss E. Blight, Provincial Library and Archives of Manitoba; Clyde N. Bowden, Inland Rivers Library, Cincinnati; Mrs. E. Collard; Alan Cooke, Scott Polar Research Institute, Cambridge, Eng.; Earle Connette, Washington State University Library; Joseph P. Donnelly, S.J.; Mrs. E. Ediger, Glenbow Foundation; John C. Ewers, Smithsonian Institution; Miss Linda Francis, Education Centre Library, Toronto; Miss Edith Firth and A. Suddon, Metropolitan Toronto Central Library; Rev. F. A. Garrett; Mrs. Jas. A. Grant; Frank L. Green, Washington State Historical Society; Edwin C. Guillet; Mr. and Mrs. Leslie Haslett; John Herapath; J. H. Herbert and Richard G. Conn, Manitoba Museum of Science and History; Mrs. Mary Hicky; E. J. Holmgren, Provincial Librarian of Alberta; Mrs. Tom Horst, Historic Mobile Preservation Society; John A. Hussey, Historian, National Park Service, United States Department of the Interior; R. E. Hutchison, Scottish National Portrait Gallery; Willard Ireland and Mrs. Dorothy Blakey Smith, Provincial Archives, British Columbia; the staff of the Hudson's Bay Company Archives, London, Eng. (Miss Alice Johnson was especially helpful); Miss Rosemary Keen, Church Missionary Society Archives, London, Eng.; Kenneth E. Kidd; John H. Kuony, Oshkosh Public Museum; Glenn Lucas, United Church of Canada Archives; C. M. McAllister; P. L. McNair, British Columbia Provincial Museum; Mrs. B. B. McNaughton; Methodist Missionary Society Archives, London, Eng.; H. R. Milner; New York Public Library; Murrough O'Brien; J. E. O'Flaherty, S.J.; Robin Poore; Robert Porter, Peterborough Public Library; Léon Pouliot, S.J.; Mrs. W. Punch, Sault Ste Marie Public Library; M. Ruggles, National Gallery of Canada; Mrs. V. Rust, Henry E. Huntington Library and Art Gallery; Martin Schmitt, University of Oregon; W. I. Smith and staff, Public Archives of Canada; Mrs. Frances K. Smith, Agnes Etherington Art Centre, Kingston,

Ont.; Stuart A. Smith, Beaverbrook Art Gallery; Eric J. Spicer, Parliamentary Librarian, Ottawa; Dr. Jean Stephenson; Franz Stenzel; Wm. E. Taylor and G. M. Day, National Museum of Canada; Peter C. Swann, E. S. Rogers, Mrs. E. A. Phillimore and Mrs. M. Allodi, Royal Ontario Museum; G. P. H. Vernon; Mrs. E. S. Watson; Samuel E. Weir; Wm. J. Withrow and staff, Art Gallery of Ontario; Ross Woodbridge; the Hon. John Yaremko; R. Mackworth Young, Royal Archivist, Windsor. In addition my thanks go to a large number of other people who have generously supplied information.

Finally I should like to express a special debt of gratitude to the staff of the University of Texas Press and the University of Toronto Press, and particularly to Miss Francess Halpenny whose keen observation, depth of perception, and long experience and understanding have prevented many errors and smoothed many rough patches.

J. Russell Harper

Alexandria, Ontario
January 1970

ILLUSTRATIONS

PAUL KANE'S FRONTIER

A NOTE ON NAMES

The names of places, Indian tribes, and individuals as given by Paul Kane in his manuscripts and his published book, by Kane and others in inscriptions on his works, and in catalogues or other records of his paintings, show considerable variation in spelling. Names of tribes and places are also often not those used today. In the reprinting of Kane's *Wanderings* in this book, the spellings of names in his first edition (1859) have been followed faithfully. The forms he gives there to names of particular Indians are used in Part One and in the *catalogue raisonné* of Part Four when sketches are identified. The names of tribes, place names and other personal names are given in Part One, in the notes to Part Two and in Part Four in accepted modern forms. In this connection, guidance has been sought from *Handbook of American Indians North of Mexico*, edited by F. W. Hodge.

PART ONE   Paul Kane: His Life and Career as an Artist

I. Early Years

York was the town in British North America to which Paul Kane came by sailing ship as an Irish immigrant boy about 1819.[1] It was the little capital of Upper Canada,[2] a province which only 28 years earlier had been carved out of the wilderness won by Britain from France during the Seven Years' War. Captain Francis Hall, who visited the province about the time of Kane's arrival, noted a blending of American and British qualities, a character very different from that of older French Quebec:

The system of farming is here altogether English, or American. The low, deep-roofed Canadian dwelling [of older French Canada] gives place to the English farm-house, or Yankey fir-boarded mansion, with a dozen sash windows in its front. Instead of churches, we have taverns; gaols, and assembly-rooms, for convents; and a half sulky nod for a French bow. . . . when the American or Englishman nods, 'tis like the growling salutation of a mastiff, who has not quite leisure enough to turn and quarrel with you.[3]

The province's first English-speaking settlers had been some 7,000 Americans, who in a single year, 1784, were given land within its borders. These were mostly families of soldiers in regiments which had been loyal to the British crown during the Revolutionary War and were disbanded at its end. Former officers originally received up to 1,000 acres and the grants descended to 100 acres for privates. The new settlers formed groups dissatisfied with and dispossessed by the new republican government to the south of the border, and in recognition of their fidelity to the crown the king bestowed on them and their descendants a proud title, United Empire Loyalists. The emergence of a province largely created by the Loyalists was formally recognized in 1791 when Upper Canada was set up as a separate entity and elected a first parliament composed almost entirely of former regimental officers. The prospect of land above the lakes later brought a steady influx of other settlers from the United States and also from England, Scotland and Ireland, men full of optimism for the future and looking forward to a free and full life for themselves and their children. By 1812 the population had increased to 75,000. Then the future of British North America had been threatened by war with the United States and possible disaffection within, but from 1812 to 1814 the militia had supported the British redcoats in defence of the realm and the result had instilled a new feeling of self-confidence. Houses and farms were being built, and the forest back of the lakes and the great river St. Lawrence was gradually changing into a succession of scattered free holdings linked by stage roads with villages and towns at strategic points. Optimism was everywhere, even despite the problems of a post-war depression.[4]

York itself, where the Kanes settled, had only been founded in 1793. Although it was Upper Canada's seat of government, mean buildings, muddy streets and a few precarious sidewalks gave a miserable air to the place. The forest crowded in on every side. Visiting York just three years before the Kanes arrived, Captain Hall had not been complimentary:

[It] is a place of considerable importance in the eyes of its inhabitants; to a stranger, however, it presents little more than about 100 wooden houses, several of them conveniently, and even elegantly built, and I think one, or perhaps two, of brick. The public buildings were destroyed by the Americans [during its capture in 1813]; but as no ruins of them are visible, we must conclude, either, that the destruction exceeded the desolation of Jerusalem, or that the loss to the arts is not quite irreparable: I believe that they did not leave one stone upon another, for they did not find one.[5]

John Howison came the same year as the Kanes, after a visit in Kingston at the eastern end of Lake Ontario. Kingston he had admired but he found the little capital so dull that after walking the streets for about an hour he returned to the comforts of the steamship *Frontenac* on which he was travelling up the lakes.[6]

But there was another side to York's story and this was its prospects for the future. Some of the immigrants who, after the Napoleonic Wars, were crossing the Atlantic in slow, unsanitary

[1] "York" became "Toronto" after its incorporation as a city in 1834.

[2] "Upper Canada" was given a new name, "Canada West," as part of the united province of Canada, 1840–67, and became the province of "Ontario" after Confederation in 1867.

[3] Francis Hall, *Travels in Canada and the United States in 1816 and 1817* (London 1819), pp. 123–24.

[4] Historical background may be found in Gerald M. Craig, *Upper Canada: The Formative Years: 1784–1841* (Toronto 1963), and in J. M. S. Careless, *The Union of the Canadas: 1841–1857* (Toronto 1967).

[5] Hall, *Travels*, pp. 168–69.

[6] John Howison, *Sketches of Upper Canada* (Edinburgh 1821), p. 72.

ships settled in the town instead of a forest clearing and increased its population. Among these newcomers was Michael Kane, the artist's father, with his family.

York was a town with two faces. New legislative buildings were under construction in Simcoe Square near the lakeshore, and the governor's residence close by was being enlarged. Some twenty families, mostly government officials, lived in substantial houses. These were the people who really "mattered." A few, like W. W. Baldwin, had set their homes well back from the waterfront and they had almost the air of estates. Baldwin himself had cut an avenue from his home through the forest so that he could see the harbour shipping. Clustered around these larger houses were the dwellings of the bulk of the citizenry—labourers, tinsmiths, cabinet-makers and tradespeople—men who supported the five York breweries in operation or under construction. It was to this more humble part of the population that Michael Kane belonged. He set up as a "wine and spirits merchant" with his vaults at the corner of present-day Yonge and Adelaide streets. The settlement might be without distinction now, but it would soon be transformed into a city of importance, and the growth of the city would parallel the development of Michael's son Paul from a local amateur into a recognized professional artist.

Mystery shrouds certain aspects of Paul Kane's life. It obscures also some of the life of his father Michael. One fanciful story about the elder Kane, entirely without foundation, describes how he served with Governor Simcoe's troops in Upper Canada in 1794 and helped to lay out York.[7] Certainly he served in the British army, but there is no record that his regiment was ever in America. Michael Kane was born in Preston, Lancashire, and enlisted in the Royal Artillery at Mansfield, Nottinghamshire, in 1793 at the age of 18; almost immediately he transferred to the more glamorous Royal Horse Artillery. He was duly promoted to corporal in 1798 and was discharged from Captain G. W. Dixon's company in 1801.[8] Meanwhile he had been in Ireland. There he married Frances Loach, a girl from Mallow, County Cork, because of "an unfortunate circumstance." Paul's parentage thus combined a conservative and objective English spirit with the spark of a warmer, more romantic Irish temperament. For a year after leaving the army, Michael rented a house in Fermoy, County Cork, but moved from there to Mallow. Tradition says that it was in 1819 that he emigrated with his wife and family to York.[9] There he lived for the balance of his life.

Nothing is known of Michael Kane's personal life and atti-

tudes except what can be gleaned by reading between the lines of a letter to his son.[10] This expresses a fierce adherence to the new world and an aversion to marriage before such a step had been well considered. One senses a practical man. By rumour, he had little interest in the arts or artists. He advanced money several times to his son Paul, but always in the form of loans and not as gifts to subsidize a struggling painter. No one mentions the artist's mother; he had four sisters; one brother died and the others became tradesmen.[11] Michael Kane was buried in 1851 in old St. James's churchyard, Toronto.

Paul Kane himself set up puzzles as if to confuse his biographers. He considered himself very much a Canadian and was determined that he should be remembered as one. On various occasions he stated that he was a native of York, and he wrote in his 1861 census return that he was a Torontonian by birth—but people have for a long time taken liberties in their reports to government. An obituary in a Toronto newspaper, which his grandchildren say was probably composed by his widow, repeats this claim. Friends, all prominent local Toronto citizens, re-echoed his assertion of Canadian origins. He was actually baptized at the parish church, Mallow, Ireland, on September 16, 1810. In the register his surname was written as "Keane" which is how "Kane" is pronounced in that part of Ireland.

The boy was presumably enrolled at one of York's few schools immediately after his arrival in the town; these could have offered little to someone who wanted to become an artist. Most writers assume that he studied in the ugly little frame building of the York District Grammar School, to which the petty government officials sent their sons.[12] If so, the school's much publicized virtue, teaching by a system of constant repeti-

[7] Nicholas Flood Davin, *The Irishman in Canada* (London 1877), p. 211. The statement is repeated by other writers.

[8] British war records show that Michael Kane (enlisted Cane) was recruited to the 1st Battalion, Royal Artillery, 1793. His name was spelled Cain when he transferred to the Royal Horse Artillery in July of that year. His service record (W.O. 69/1) reads: "Gunner Michael Cain, aged 18, height 5.7½. / Enlisted 2 February 1793 at Mansfield [Notts]. / Born Preston, Lancs. / Trade Labourer. / Can read and write. / Colouring dark, hair dark, eyes gray. / Bombardier 6 November 1794. Corporal 5 April 1798. / Discharged 30 September 1801."

[9] Metropolitan Toronto Central Library, Manuscript Division, has lists of early York householders. Kane's name does not appear in the list for 1819. Those for 1820 and 1821 are missing, but in that of 1822 his name is given.

[10] Appendix 10, Letter 1.

[11] The children of Michael Kane are as follows: James, born 1799; Mary 1801; Julia 1803; Frederick 1806; Oliver 1807; Paul 1810; Charlotte 1811; Harriet 1813. Not all of them reached maturity.

[12] The York District Grammar School records are not to be found so that it is impossible to confirm whether Kane attended or the names of instructors he might have had. Kane's association with the school was first mentioned by Davin (*The Irishman in Canada*, p. 611). Davin gives no source. No biography of Kane published during his lifetime makes any reference to the school.

Plate II. Brayley Norton (Mrs. H. R. Norton). ROM L965.1.2; CRI-20.

tion which would bring perfection, had little effect. The diary he wrote while travelling among the Indians is phonetic in its spelling, and he dictated his western letters to Hudson's Bay company scribes. The first draft of *Wanderings of an Artist* is in his wife's hand. His prose is factual and straightforward without any of the Greek and Latin phraseology which would permit colonial graduates to hold their heads high among the cultivated overseas. One wonders if perhaps he attended some more humble school than Bishop John Strachan's renowned establishment. He is alleged to have been a pupil until he was sixteen. This hardly seems likely, but possibly, as a contemporary biographer wrote,[13] he idled away his time in drawing rather than applying himself to the more academic subjects.

York's frontier environment helped to turn Kane's thoughts during boyhood towards the native people and the Northwest. He wrote that the subject of Indians "was one in which I felt a deep interest in my boyhood. I had been accustomed to see hundreds of Indians about my native village, then Little York. . . ."[14] For the town's recalcitrant youths, the Northwest was a romantic goal. Dr. Scadding, an early Toronto antiquarian, recounted, in an often quoted passage, how it beckoned to adventurous souls:

A sporting ramble through the woods, a fishing excursion on the waters, could not be undertaken without communications with Indians and halfbreeds and bad specimens of the French *voyageur*. It was from such sources that a certain idea was derived which, as we remember, was in great vogue among the more fractious of the lads at the school at York. The proposition circulated about, whenever anything went counter to their notions, always was "to run away to the Nor'-West." What the process really involved, or where the "Nor'-West" precisely was, were things vaguely realized. A sort of savage "land of Cockaigne," a region of perfect freedom among the Indians, was imagined; and to reach it Lakes Huron and Superior were to be traversed.[15]

But a curiosity about Indians might have more in it than the restlessness of youth. Kane's boyhood coincided with the rise of an interest in Indians by an increasing number of perceptive people, as part of the new concern with man's surroundings which became apparent at that time. Mists of disinterest after the fierce initial clash between Indians and Europeans during early settlement days along the Atlantic had so hidden the aborigines that many Canadians were only dimly aware that these original residents were still in the background of their life in the east. Now these mists began to roll away, and the Indians to emerge as humans. At the same time philosophers in Europe, and especially in France, were examining Indians and other primitive peoples for lessons to remedy the decadence they felt in their own sophisticated society.

As part of this new interest, Adam Kidd published at Montreal in 1830 a long epic poem *The Huron Chief*.[16] He pictured the Indian as a man with hopes, fears, sorrows and joys—not the cruel warrior who was an ever present threat to the settler's home. In 1836 appeared in Toronto a book by J. Mackintosh dealing with the American Indian tribes and their life and customs.[17] Kane was to own a copy. In New Brunswick, Abraham Gesner, a lawyer, geologist, scientist and inventor, one of the "universal men" found in this age, saw the abject poverty of the Micmac and Malecite Indians of the Saint John River and sought ways to restore them to the dignified, independent life they had known as hunters. He instituted schemes for the sale of Indian handicrafts. He also gathered Indian artefacts so that Canadians generally could appreciate the culture of these forgotten peoples, and from this collection the New Brunswick Museum has grown.

A few Canadian artists also displayed an awakening interest in Indians during the 1820s and 1830s. J. D. Wells, to name one, hung a study of Indians at the exhibition of the Toronto Society of Artists and Amateurs in 1834, a show in which Kane himself was to have paintings. An anonymous New Brunswick or Nova Scotia artist painted superb decorative canvases and water colours of Micmac hunters, with their canoes, trophies of the hunt, wigwams, and unique costumes.[18] Full of detail, these have a feeling of intimacy and the artist seems much more involved with his subjects than in most contemporary paintings in which Indians appear. For instance, J. P. Cockburn, like several British army officers in Canada on garrison duty, regarded the Indians whom he painted merely as curious native peoples in one part of the growing British Empire overseas. Many local painters also introduced them simply as an element in the landscape: in numerous stereotyped views of Halifax Citadel, for example, wigwams are romanticized additions in the foreground

[13] Henry J. Morgan, *Sketches of Celebrated Canadians and Persons Connected with Canada* (Quebec 1862), p. 731.

[14] *Wanderings of an Artist*, p. 51 below.

[15] Henry Scadding, *Toronto of Old* (Toronto 1872), p. 163.

[16] Adam Kidd, *The Huron Chief, and Other Poems* (Montreal 1830).

[17] J. Mackintosh, *The Discovery of America, by Christopher Columbus; and the Origin of the North American Indians* (Toronto 1836).

[18] Typical of paintings by this anonymous artist are one in the National Gallery of Canada, Ottawa, Cat. no. 663, "Micmac Indians," and two in the Beaverbrook Art Gallery, Fredericton, N.B., "Indian Voyageurs: Hunting" and "Indian Voyageurs: Returning from the Hunt." The National Gallery painting is reproduced in J. Russell Harper, *Painting in Canada* (Toronto 1966), Plate 98.

without a hint that the Indians who lived in them might have personalities.[19]

One Canadian commentator, however, went so far as to think of the western Indian as part of the Canadian environment which he was proposing as a central theme in a national art. Kane's paintings seem like the fulfilment of a prophecy made by Philippe Aubert de Gaspé, a Quebec lawyer, politician, and man of letters, whose interests extended to art. In 1833 he recorded his impressions of studios which he had been visiting in Quebec. He was greatly elated with the studio of Joseph Legaré. The exact canvases he saw in it we do not know, but he mentions being excited by paintings of local landscapes and contemporary events. Legaré's canvases generally pictured such newsworthy happenings as rock slides and the fires which were the scourge of 19th century Canadian cities and towns. A cholera epidemic in his native Quebec appears in one canvas, where smudge pots line the streets to kill impure vapours while death wagons and funeral processions circulate through the streets bathed weirdly in moonlight.[20] Such an involvement in his immediate surroundings by a man locally born was a new note in Canadian art.

Aubert de Gaspé's fertile mind was touched by Legaré's renditions of contemporary life and his imagination conjured up other local yet romantic subjects which native Canadians could paint.

> . . . it has often excited my wonder that our native painters have not devoted some part of their time and study to the scenery of Canada—and to their shame be it spoken they have not; and truly they have neglected a field from which rare laurels will yet be won. . . . Our winter views —breaking through the ice—Indian camps by night—the mounted Sioux, Chief of the western wilderness, and the bivouacs on the Prairies—Hillock —and the chase of the buffalo—the council tent—the savage and his forest wigwam.[21]

This is the first recorded suggestion by a Canadian that the Indian could be a major subject for a painter. Kane would concentrate his efforts for four years on the very themes which Aubert de Gaspé had mentioned, and he was to picture the Sioux, chieftains of the west, the buffalo hunt, the prairies and the Rockies, and other scenes of which the Quebecker had no knowledge. This achievement would bring him "rare laurels" as the first Canadian artist really to use the Indian's world. Thus a subject which had presented itself to him as a boy was to become his life's work.

During his younger days Kane is mentioned once in York newspapers, in connection with his attendance at Toronto's first "theatre" just after he had left school. This modest affair was operated in the ballroom on the second floor of Frank's Hotel, King Street, from 1820 to 1829. A single violinist, shade over one eye, substituted for a full orchestra. Dr. Scadding, who often attended, recounted that at the performances

> Pizarro, Barbarossa or the Siege of Algiers, Ali Baba or the Forty Thieves, the Lady of the Lake, the Miller and his Men, were among the pieces here represented. The body-guard of the Dey of Algiers, we remember, consisted of two men, who always came in with military precision just after the hero, and placed themselves in a formal manner at fixed distances behind him, like two sentries. They were in fact soldiers from the garrison, we think. All this appeared very effective.[22]

Dr. Scadding pointed out, however, that this humble place had the same magic as Drury Lane for young Londoners. Here Kane was introduced to the theatre, which seems to have been a life-long interest. In the library he had as an older man was a six-volume set of Shakespeare's plays and an eleven-volume collection of Bell's *British Theatre*. The fact is significant because Kane's years of development coincided with an era when play-acting was enjoying a revival everywhere. Shakespearean drama, stage tableaux, the whole world of make-believe, constituted one aspect of the new romanticism sweeping Europe and America. The theatre was patronized by no group more than artists and became a major factor in directing them towards romantic concepts in painting.

The details of Kane's attendance at the theatre on that night of June 4, 1828, are perhaps of more antiquarian than artistic interest. *Tom and Jerry* or *Life in London* was scheduled for performance at Frank's. The raising of the old baize curtain, called for 7 o'clock, was delayed repeatedly. Near Kane in the pit as the audience waited sat Charles French and several rowdy youths who frequently adjourned to the outside staircase for drinks before the play actually began between 9 and 10 o'clock. They went out again to the tavern in the interval. When they finally left the theatre, they were in such an ugly mood that French picked a quarrel with Isaac Jones, an Uxbridge Quaker, and killed him. Kane saw the fight from across the street and gave evidence at the inquest. A murder conviction was handed down at the October assizes, and the guilty French was hanged

[19] The point is well illustrated in a canvas by John Poad Drake, "Port of Halifax," *c*. 1820; National Gallery of Canada, Cat. no. 9978; it appears in Harper, *Painting in Canada*, as Plate 100.

[20] See Harper, *Painting in Canada*, pp. 80–82 for details of the life and work of Joseph Legaré.

[21] *Quebec Gazette* (Quebec), December 13, 1833.

[22] Scadding, *Toronto of Old*, p. 110.

publicly the following week. He had been an apprentice in the printing house of the controversial William Lyon Mackenzie, soon to lead a rebellion in Upper Canada (a century later his grandson was Canada's prime minister). A spectator in the great crush about the scaffold reported that Mackenzie stood beside the accused at the Court House steps when the noose was lowered, and cried until the tears rolled down his cheeks and made his starched white collar soggy. Assuredly Paul Kane would also have been in that huge crowd.

The incident at the theatre is tantalizingly lonely. Kane's life from 1826, when he was certainly no longer a school boy, until 1836, when he left Canada for the United States and Europe, must be pieced together from fact, tradition and speculation. During these ten years he turned into a young painter with a serious ideal of art as his objective. He was to dedicate himself to a life of artistic work at a time when there were few professionals in the newly emerging Canada although there were numerous amateurs.

For part of this decade Kane worked as a decorative furniture painter. He was apprenticed to W. S. Conger, owner of a furniture factory on Front Street, York. Conger was sympathetic to his ambitions, and is said to have bought him his first canvas, brushes and paints in New York. The date on which Kane ceased to work for the Conger factory is uncertain. Conger moved from York to Cobourg in 1829 although his York shop evidently continued in operation. An entry in the Toronto directory for 1833–34 names Paul "Cane" as a coach, sign and house painter on King Street. Does this indicate that he had gone into business on his own? Sign painting was a customary way for young men on the American frontier to launch themselves into the art world.

The statement has been made several times that Kane studied painting with Toronto's eccentric art master, Thomas Drury, while he was attending the York District Grammar School. This cannot be verified, and there is, in fact, no certain proof that Drury lived in York before 1830.[23] Without instruction, models or any of the other accepted prerequisites of art, Kane had made much headway on his own. Then in 1830, "Having acquired a respectable knowledge of perspective, he felt emboldened to wait upon Mr. Drury, the then drawing master of Upper Canada College, with some of his attempts at delineation. This gentleman at once recognized the marks of original genius, and the germs of future excellence in these essays, and promptly enrolled the young artist in the number of his pupils."[24] Upper Canada College is Toronto's oldest and best-known grammar school for boys. It would seem that Kane must have studied privately with the master for he was now a young adult and certainly would not have been a regular pupil. Drury was a landscape painter who, like Cornelius Krieghoff in Quebec a few years later, taught by having his pupils copy his own works.

A canvas survives from the years when Kane was just beginning to receive instruction. It is a naïve three-quarter length portrait of a young lady, large and ambitious in conception. She sits theatrically, before a background of blue and red drapes, and the canvas is sufficiently "primitive" in style to have a certain appeal. It is the effort of an ambitious youth who wants to run before he can walk. Kane kept it, and it is still the property of a descendant. Did he use Conger's gift of painting supplies for this canvas? Another early portrait is of a young friend, Michael Peter Empey; it has a more accomplished manner and stylistically foreshadows a portrait of Mayor Gurnett of Toronto which seems to have been painted years later (Fig. 8). It is significant that both canvases are portraits, the most difficult of all subject-matter; they are indicative of the young man's practical bent since portrait commissions were the only paintings which had any real commercial sale in Upper Canada.

Kane's development as a painter must have been stimulated by the rapid growth of artistic interest in York, which became the city of Toronto in 1834. Even if standards generally were low, there were enough professional and amateur painters that leading citizens supported formation of the Society of Artists and Amateurs for exhibition purposes. The Society's influential backers were given permission to hold their first show in the province's legislative buildings, and 24 exhibitors hung 196 pictures. There were works by a few professional portrait painters and by architects who sent in architectural and topographical renderings. Military men submitted their coloured drawings, and both lady and gentlemen amateurs a variety of flower studies.[25] Disaster ensued. The cholera epidemic which

[23] The claim that Kane studied at the York District Grammar School under Drury originated in Daniel Wilson's eulogy following Kane's death in 1871 ("Paul Kane, the Canadian Artist," *Canadian Journal*, Toronto, May 1871, p. 67). Wilson realized that he knew little about Kane's early life in spite of their friendship—Kane talked rarely about himself—and had to write to the Hon. George Allan for details. In preparing his text, Wilson in some way altered Kane's contacts with Drury, which had taken place at Upper Canada College, to appear as having occurred at the York District Grammar School.

[24] *Anglo-American Magazine* (Toronto), May 1855, p. 401.

[25] *Catalogue of the First Exhibition of the Society of Artists & Amateurs of Toronto, 1834* (Toronto 1834).

Legaré had painted in Quebec struck Toronto during the exhibition. Few ventured out to pay the admission fee and buy catalogues. Monetary losses were large. John G. Howard, a prominent Toronto architect and art enthusiast, paid much of the deficit from his own pocket, and another decade was to pass before anyone dared suggest a second local art exhibition.

Kane entered nine paintings in the 1834 exhibition. Eight were copies, seven from prints and the eighth after a landscape by his teacher, Drury. A view of John Gamble's house at Mimico was his only original work. Toronto art critics of the time knew little about reviewing exhibitions: the man for the *Patriot* eloquently noted that one of Kane's paintings possessed much truth to nature and was tenderly pencilled; another's merit lay in the fact that the "distances are actually a good way off, and the figures are alive and busy in their several vocations." The reviewer concludes on a moralizing note: "practice and study should make Mr. Kane an artist of name."[26]

Kane had several artists among his friends in Toronto. Samuel Bell Waugh (1814–1885) was one. An American from Mercer, Pennsylvania, and Kane's junior by four years, he lived in Toronto during 1834 and 1835. He then moved on to Montreal for a short time, and by mid-century had become a well-known artist in Philadelphia. James Bowman (1793–1842), another American, was in Toronto at the same time as Waugh, and the two of them made a pact with Kane to study in Italy together at some future date. Bowman had previously been in Lower Canada, where his career had been by no means placid. The artist Antoine Plamondon had almost literally driven him out of Quebec City in 1833, and the next year in Montreal his murals for Notre Dame Church had been much criticized. His reception in Toronto in October 1834 was more cordial. He had arrived with impressive samples of his own canvases for publicity purposes, such as his portrait of the Danish sculptor, Thorwaldsen, a painting of the Capuchin chapel in Rome, and an interior view of the Indian chapel at Two Mountains near Montreal.[27] Bowman had studied in Rome and under Sir Thomas Lawrence. The laudatory editorial in a Toronto newspaper in December 1834 must have appealed to a young artist like Kane: "Mr. Bowman presents a fine subject for moral reflection; he was lately a Backwoods-man of America, and in the recesses of the forest [he] became fired with the noble ambition to rival the first in the Arts. What a stimulus to youthful ambition."[28] Shortly after this notice was published, the governor-general gave Bowman a portrait commission. Certain local "patriots" objected to the choice of an American, but

the *Patriot* saw nothing unusual in it. The paper pointed out in a reply that Mr. Bowman was British by training although "an American artist," and "to use a musty phrase, *'a man is not abase for being born in a stable.'*" The article concludes: "Mr. Bowman could not have attained his excellence in America—who there could have taught him?"[29]

Despite the attractions of friendship, Kane, who seems to have been a restless and impatient youth, followed Conger from Toronto to Cobourg in 1834. Cobourg was an established and prosperous town on Lake Ontario, with many well-known families, and it did not have a resident professional artist. Presumably Kane decorated furniture there. For whom is uncertain. Conger, his old employer, is said to have had a financial interest with Henry Richard Norton in a cabinet-making firm in Cobourg. F. S. Clench, Kane's future father-in-law, was, however, the best cabinet-maker in that town. Clench's staff must have lived in, judging from the number he indicates as dwelling in his house in a census return in the 1830s; if Kane was one of them, he would have had plenty of opportunity to meet the daughter, Harriet. But although there may be some doubt about whether he painted furniture in Cobourg, there is ample evidence that he was spending much time painting portraits of the town's leading citizens. Conger and his wife are said to have been his first Cobourg subjects; their portraits, done about 1834, demonstrate a beginner's clumsiness (Fig. 2). Later came members of the Clench family (Fig. 3), Conger's business partner, Henry Richard Norton, and his wife, and other local people. Kane's portraits are difficult to identify. He never signed them, and his style varied. One group, obviously by the same hand, are primitive in style with the faces treated in broad planes; they have a direct appeal and warm colouring. An example is the portrait of Mrs. Norton (Plate II); photographs of the portraits of Mrs. Clench and of Mrs. Weller, wife of a celebrated early Canadian stage coach operator, show the same characteristics. All of the group must date from his Cobourg days.[30] They rank in quality with many contemporary primitives from Quebec and the Maritimes, and are part of a phase of primitivism which was widely followed in 19th century Canada and

---

[26] *Patriot* (Toronto), July 8, 1834.

[27] *Ibid.*, October 21, 1834. According to the newspaper, the Indians intended to present the picture of the chapel to the Pope.

[28] *Ibid.*, December 5, 1834.

[29] *Ibid.*, December 23, 1834.

[30] For information about Kane's portraits in the Cobourg area and illustrations of a number, see Edwin C. Guillet, *The Valley of the Trent* (Toronto 1957), p. lvii and Figs. 99–104.

which produced some of the most appealing among early Canadian canvases.

Kane left Cobourg because of his friendship with James Bowman, and the move was another turning point in his life. According to the *Patriot*, Bowman and Waugh, "who has given many proofs of much genius," were to go to Rome in the spring of 1835.[31] Instead Bowman went to Detroit, and towards the end of 1836 Kane went there also, expecting to meet his two friends and proceed with them to Rome. At Detroit he met a disappointment. Bowman had just been married and cancelled his trip. Kane apparently wrote to his father about his situation, and Michael Kane, not wholly sympathetic to his son's ambitions, replied on November 4, 1836:

You say that Mr. Bowman has got married and that in all probability will prevent your Italian excursion. This I take to be a fortunate circumstance first in keeping you on the Continent where you ought to remain and Secondly Mr. B. has given you a precedent which you would do well to imitate Viz—acquire long experience before you attempt the blind hazard of marriage.[32]

Waugh went on to Rome alone, where Kane met him several years later. Meanwhile, postponing his own trip, he reported to his father that he was doing well with portrait commissions in the United States; actually he was probably short of money and timid about setting out alone for foreign countries.

Knowledge of Kane's movements for the next five years is sketchy. He painted some portraits in Detroit, where he lived in the American Hotel and had a studio in the Desnoyers Building. At this time he probably met John Mix Stanley, who was then studying with Bowman. Stanley was to become a celebrated painter of Indians and would work in the Oregon country at the same time as Kane. One writer mentions that Kane did some painting in Saint Louis. There is much more information about his activities in Mobile, Alabama, to which he went early in 1840. There he had painting rooms in the town's Corinthian Hall, and his reputation was high enough to prompt a feature article on the fine arts in a local newspaper.[33] The columnist, after proudly describing American progress during his generation in literature, sculpture and other arts, comments on Kane's contribution. He had just finished a striking full-length canvas of Queen Victoria based on one by the English artist, Chalon. Its regal magnificence was enhanced by a brilliance of colour, but sketchily painted areas in it offended the critic's taste; this was a decade when figurative precision and finish were new virtues. Diplomatically, Kane had also painted a portrait of General Harrison immediately preceding his inauguration to a

brief presidency. The writer, like Kane's personal friends in Toronto, Rome, the Oregon, or wherever he travelled, concludes by calling him a "gentleman and very clever fellow."

An article appeared during 1855 in the *Anglo-American Magazine* which, though not always accurate in reporting Kane's activities, gives the most complete summary of these American years which can be found:

Accordingly in 1836, he removed to Detroit, and having there executed some "counterfeit presentments,"—as Hamlet hath it—travelled over the principal cities of the United States, in the exercise of his profession. Sailing down the Mississippi, he landed at New Orleans in the fall of 1838, literally without one shilling in his exchequer, having been robbed on board the steam-boat of everything he possessed, except his garmenture. In order to pay for his passage, he was constrained to transfer the gruff features of the skipper to canvas.

By painting a few portraits in New Orleans, Kane was enabled to accumulate sufficient means to carry him to Mobile, where he became a favourite, and met with considerable success. At the expiration of two years, he had by prudence and unflagging industry, realized funds sufficient to carry him to Italy, a consummation which had long been the cherished dream of his existence.[34]

The only known American canvas, done some time after 1839, pictures the captain or owner of the river steamer *Norma* (Fig. 4). Many others must hang unrecognized on the walls of homes in Mobile and elsewhere. English travellers in the United States in these years noted that portraits were being painted everywhere, and Kane obviously shared in this lucrative activity before photography virtually wiped it out little more than a decade later.

Kane's eagerness for study abroad was that of every young painter on the American continent who wished to advance in his profession. He was expected to make a European tour; on it he would copy Old Masters, contemplate the great canvases of the Renaissance and later painters, and receive instruction in the noted galleries. Many aspiring artists in the United States were accordingly making this European pilgrimage; before Kane, Théophile Hamel had gone from Quebec to Rome, and Antoine Plamondon had studied in Paris. The dream which Kane had cherished for several years presumably became possible with his earnings in Mobile, and he sailed for Europe on June 18, 1841.

[31] *Patriot,* December 5, 1834.
[32] Appendix 10, Letter 1.
[33] For his rooms, see *Mobile Advertiser for the County* (Mobile), April 18, 1843. The article appeared in the *Commercial Register* (Mobile), March 20, 1841, and is given in full below, Appendix 11.
[34] *Anglo-American Magazine,* May 1855, pp. 401–2.

Kane's passport survives. He crossed the Atlantic on the American sailing ship *Paetobus* from New Orleans, and after a voyage of nearly three months arrived at Marseilles on September 14. He hastened to Genoa for his first look at a great European art gallery, then went on to Rome. Through that majestic city passed every young gentleman from England on the Grand Tour; there Keats and other poets of romanticism had lived. Hamel had written home about the gay times he had had dancing with belles from Edinburgh and London, but Kane apparently allowed himself no such frivolities.

The winter in Rome was spent in serious study, copying paintings by Murillo, Andrea del Sarto and Raphael "to improve his colouring." Strangely, portraits painted after his return to North America, such as that of James Richardson (Fig. 9), lack the warmth noticeable in some of his primitives, like that of Mrs. Norton, but they do have a unity of tone which bespeaks acquaintance with the greater sophistication of European painting. Many of the copies Kane made in Italy are of single heads. His portrait of Pope Gregory XV after Busato, for example, is merely the head from the larger composition which had been painted shortly before and was then a local sensation. Again, as a practical man, Kane realized that the single portrait was the prevalent fashion in Canada to which he would return, and the study of these in Europe would eventually be more useful than tackling elaborate and time-consuming compositions. As he worked in Rome's academies alongside students from the British Isles and elsewhere, he made casual friendships with them,[35] but also impressed acquaintances in high places. One gave him an introduction for presentation to the Bishop of Cincinnati after his return home. Another gave him a diamond stick-pin. Generally, however, it was a winter of concentrated hard work. When funds were low, he sold the occasional copy of an Old Master.

The spring of 1842 brought relaxation. Kane and an Edinburgh artist whom he had met in Rome, Hope James Stewart, walked together to Naples. This was a "noisy and *favourite* place" after the quiet of Rome, and they remained during March and April. One writer asserts that they made out-of-town jaunts to see the antiquities at Herculaneum and Pompeii.[36] Another claims that from Naples Kane went much farther afield and crossed the Mediterranean. He

availed himself of an offered passage in a Levantine cruiser, and visited the coasts both of Asia and Africa. He joined a party of Syrian explorers, and was already on his way to Jerusalem, when they were deserted by their Arab guides, and, after being exposed to great danger, were compelled to

return to the coast, and abandon the attempt. This failure to accomplish a visit to the most sacred scenes of the ancient historic world was always a subject of mortifying reflection to him. It was on his return from this unsuccessful pilgrimage that he landed on some part of the African shore; and so was able to say, on regaining his Canadian home, that he had been in every quarter of the globe.[37]

There are no stamps in Kane's passport to indicate that he left Naples for a visit to a foreign state, yet such stamps would have been a legal necessity. How to reconcile this account of his trip with his passport is a conundrum.

The two artist friends left Naples in May 1842 and until October hiked through northern Italy. Their longest stop was in Florence. Kane received permission to draw and to paint in the Pitti Palace and in the Uffizi where he copied Raphael's *Pope Julius II*. He lost his Neapolitan and one of his Roman sketchbooks and notes, but returned home with three volumes of sketches. One has principally views of Rome (Figs. 5, 6). A second contains numerous pencil studies of the self-portraits of Rubens (Fig. 7), Dolci and others and of paintings in the great Florentine collections. Close examination of these copies of Old Masters demonstrates Kane's tendency to misjudge proportions, a weakness he had to struggle against throughout his painting career. Sometimes a neck is seen to be too thick when checked against the original, or heads may be proportionately too large or too small. Years later, when he was painting canvases based on sketches from his western tours in North America, the judging of proportions must have been a constant nightmare; continual adjustments can still be detected through the layers of paint (see Fig. 65). A third surviving sketchbook of that summer, filled in Florence and Venice, has much architectural detail together with sketches of Donatello's statues for Or San Michele, Italian furniture and landscape. Kane's official pass to sketch in the Accademia in Venice still survives, but he seems to have made little use of it; instead he spent much time "scouting" with an English art student named Salter.

The Italian tour ended after thirteen months. Kane's canvases from Rome and Florence were boxed and shipped to London, and Kane himself left the country for Switzerland by way of the Brenner Pass. Another young painter, who was to contribute greatly to the art of Canadian landscape and still life, had crossed the same pass in 1834 after study in Italy; this was

[35] A letter to Kane (Appendix 10, Letter 2) names a number of art students whom he had met in Italy.

[36] *Anglo-American Magazine*, May 1855, p. 402.

[37] Daniel Wilson, "Paul Kane, the Canadian Artist," *Canadian Journal*, May 1871, pp. 68–69.

Daniel Fowler, born, in England, the same year as Kane, who came to Canada in 1843. The brilliance of the sun on the snow in the high Alps unfortunately harmed Kane's eyes, and the effects were to trouble him in later life. A brief stop was made in Paris. On October 20, 1842, he sailed from Calais for a winter in London. His friend Stewart accompanied him but continued on by ship to Edinburgh.[38]

Kane's stay in London proved to be another crucial step in shaping his career. It was at this point that his interests shifted from commissioned portraits to the painting of the western Indians. He was spending a pleasant winter in London with another artist friend, Stewart Watson. The only shadow was illness brought on by the notoriously foul English weather. Then, late that winter, George Catlin reopened his exhibition of American Indian paintings in Piccadilly. It made a profound impression on Kane.

George Catlin had, from 1830 to 1836, lived and painted among no fewer than 48 Indian tribes scattered over the American plains to the foothills of the Rocky Mountains. The clash of cultures between red and white with increasing immigration from the eastern seaboard was then creating an acutely tense situation. Propagandists described the aborigines in darkest terms, but Catlin held them in high regard. He had seen them deprived of their natural life as free hunters on the plains through the expansion of European civilization, and he spoke of them with real anguish of spirit:

I love a people who have always made me welcome to the best they had . . . who are honest without laws, who have no jails and no poor-house . . . who never take the name of God in vain . . . who worship God without a Bible, and I believe that God loves them also . . . who are free from religious animosities . . . who have never raised a hand against me, or stolen my property, where there was no law to punish either . . . who never fought a battle with white men except on their own ground . . . and oh! how I love a people who don't live for the love of money.[39]

With firm devotion to these wronged Indian tribes, Catlin began a crusade on their behalf at Albany during 1837. He visited many eastern American cities where exhibitions of his Indian paintings were held and where he gave lectures on the Red Man. Concurrently he waged a campaign to urge the Congress to purchase his record of a people whom he believed would soon be extinct as a result of its contact with whites. This was unsuccessful. A disappointed man, he packed for overseas 600 canvases and several thousand ethnological items which he had collected, intending to display them in European capitals.

Kane must surely have learned of Catlin's work while he was in the United States, but was in no city there in which the Indian paintings were displayed and certainly could not have seen them. His direct association with the painter could only have been in England.

The London exhibition of Catlin's Indian paintings had opened in Egyptian Hall, Piccadilly, on February 1, 1840, two years before Kane's arrival in the city. The official opening was preceded by three days of private viewing when the Duke of Cambridge, the Duke and Duchess of Sutherland, the Duke of Wellington, the Bishop of London, and many other notables attended. Catlin became a London celebrity, and crowds flocked to see his show. His book, *Letters and Notes on the Manners, Customs, and Condition of the North American Indians,* published in October 1841, was an immediate success.[40] When Kane arrived in London a year later, however, interest had waned to such a point that Catlin was making a provincial tour of Liverpool, Edinburgh and Manchester. He returned to London in the early months of 1843 and formed what was to prove an unhappy partnership with Arthur Rankin, who had brought nine Ojibwa to the city for display. The two men signed a new lease for Egyptian Hall. There was a command performance before Queen Victoria and the Prince Consort in Buckingham Palace; it was widely publicized and the attention it drew must have impressed Kane. The Catlin-Rankin partnership broke up after three months, and ruined the prospect of further financial success. A tragic figure, Catlin wandered around Europe for the next ten years, then slipped away for a long South American tour among almost unknown tribes before returning finally to further travels in the American West. He died in 1872.

Sometime early in 1843 a friendship appears to have developed between Catlin and Kane. The only direct reference to this friendship is in a letter of 1847 from Peter Skene Ogden to Kane in which Ogden speaks of "Catlin, a friend of yours." [41] At no other time than 1843 could the paths of Kane and Catlin have crossed. Kane must have attended an exhibition of Catlin's work either in London or in one of the provincial cities, and undoubtedly had read and familiarized himself that winter with Catlin's

[38] It has been suggested that Stewart emigrated to Canada as a farmer in 1847 but this cannot be confirmed.

[39] George McCracken, *George Catlin and the Old Frontier* (New York 1959), p. 4; ellipses are in the original.

[40] George Catlin, *Letters and Notes on the Manners, Customs, and Condition of the North American Indians* (London 1841). There were a number of reprints, the best known being that of 1876 by Chatto and Windus, London.

[41] Appendix 10, Letter 10.

recently published book. It became a guide to certain phases of his own painting, and indeed portions of his own book, *Wanderings of an Artist*, were obviously inspired by Catlin's volume. An interest in the same subject-matter was felt by Stewart Watson, with whom Kane shared quarters in London; he too wanted to paint North American aborigines, and he wrote to Kane in 1844: "I am still in the determination to come to Canada and to paint Indians, and hope that I'll meet you and work together. . . ."[42] Unquestionably the two must have discussed painting Indians while Kane was still in London; they may have met Catlin together.

There is no clear evidence to explain Kane's almost instant conversion at this time to the cause of painting Indians. A cynic might suggest that he saw a good thing and anticipated fame and fortune coming to him by means of a gallery of Canadian Indians. Or had he unconsciously been rebelling against a career devoted to portraiture, in which he had not so far displayed any outstanding ability, and now found a theme that intrigued him? Did he perhaps foresee what the introduction of cheap, popular photography would do to the kind of portraiture in which he had been engaged? Or was it that his contacts with Catlin and his work suddenly revived and focussed his own interest in Indians, latent since his boyhood? One wonders if, as he turned to them, he realized that he was embarking on a career of such absorption and excitement that it would last his life long.

Kane left London to recross the Atlantic in the early months of 1843, firmly intending to paint a gallery of Canadian Indians which would be similar to Catlin's of Indians in the United States.[43] But there was to be a delay. He sailed from Liverpool for the southern United States and by April 1843 was back in Mobile, advertising his return to his old painting rooms, formerly the parlour of the Corinthian Hall.[44] His name is listed in the Mobile directory for the following year.[45] Stewart Watson addressed a letter to him on June 4, 1844, as "Portrait Painter, Toronto," but at that date he was still in the south. Again the *Anglo-American Magazine* gives the only lucid account of the two-year interval after Kane left London:

[42] Appendix 10, Letter 2.
[43] *Ibid.*
[44] *Mobile Advertiser for the County*, April 18, 1843.
[45] The Mobile *Directory* for 1844 lists Kane at the southeast corner of Royal and Dauphin Streets.
[46] The date should be 1843. Curiously, Kane seems to have attempted deliberately to conceal the two years he spent in Mobile on his return from Europe. He stated repeatedly that he had been overseas for four years when he had actually only been there for two.
[47] *Anglo-American Magazine*, May 1855, p. 402.

Having resolved to return to this continent, Kane repaired to Liverpool, but found when he got there, that he lacked funds sufficient to pay his passage over the Atlantic. He was fortunate enough, however, to fall in with the master of a United States vessel, who consented to give him a berth on credit. Arriving safely at Mobile, in the spring of 1845 [*sic*[46]], after, however, nearly suffering shipwreck, he was enabled to procure a loan from an old acquaintance, and discharged his debt to the honest skipper.

Remaining in Mobile only long enough to accumulate sufficient funds to repay his friend, and furnish the means of locomotion, he returned to Toronto after an absence of nearly nine years.[47]

Kane's card case has survived in his family's collection. It still contains two calling cards of John Warburton Womack. Womack was a remarkable Southerner who was speaker of the Alabama legislature when only 21 and was nominated for the vice-presidency of the United States at 26 (he declined to run because if the president had died in office he could not have succeeded because of his age). He married a wealthy young widow and was known as a kind and generous man. Did he help Kane financially at this time, or was he merely a possibility for a portrait commission?

Kane returned to Toronto in the spring of 1845. He was now 35. His formative years as student and youthful painter were over. He had found his subject-matter and had dedicated himself also to a philosophical ideal. His life's work was about to begin.

II. Sketching among the Indians, 1845–1848

Kane spent little time in his "native" Toronto before leaving for the wide western spaces on June 17, 1845. As he himself tells us, he took no companion but his portfolio, paint box, gun and ammunition. He had no money, no resources, no promises of assistance,[1] knew nothing of the west to which he was going, and had had no contacts with Indians except for casual meetings years earlier. What Paul Kane did have was determination, keenness of spirit supported by an indomitable will, and an intrepid devotion to an ideal. They proved sufficient.

A sense of urgency was not far from the surface despite the calm of Kane's outward manner, which had all the Indian's equanimity. He was convinced that the red man was disappearing everywhere as a result of the disease and dislocation caused

[1] He seems to have made some inquiries about means of travel in the west before he left Toronto; see below for his discussion with Angus Bethune, late of the North West Company.

French River Rapids
Paul Kane 1845

Plate III. French River rapids. Stark POP22; CRIII-25.

by the incursion of whites into all the western reaches of North America. The natives who commonly wandered York's streets in his boyhood had already vanished. He owned John Tanner's story which declared that there would be a speedy and utter extinction of the natives unless a new approach was taken towards them.[2] Like Catlin, Kane felt impelled to preserve for posterity a record of the Indian chieftains, the customs of the tribes and the lands where they lived before change had made such a record impossible.

Kane himself gives an account of his adventurous travels in the great wilderness of the Northwest throughout the next four years. This account is reprinted below, and there is thus no need to follow the route of his journeys in detail here. Briefly, Kane spent the 1845 season around the Great Lakes, chiefly among the Ojibwa. For the next three years he travelled westward among the plains tribes and over the Rockies and western plateau region to the lower Columbia River; from Fort Vancouver on that river he went up the Pacific coast to Vancouver Island. His homeward journey took more than twelve months. The years were full of incident, and he came back with a bulging portfolio of sketches.

A pattern for work was established during the 1845 season and continued in the travels that followed. Kane moved from one centre to another where he knew that Indians congregated. Whenever possible he sketched the principal chiefs—notable men such as the celebrated Menominee of Wisconsin, Oscosh, or a descendant of Tecumseh. His method, he said, was simply to walk up to an Indian, sit down, and begin to sketch his portrait without saying a word. The subject objected quickly if he disapproved. At times Kane was regarded as a medicine man because of his cleverness in producing a "second self"; indeed some were fearful that his possession of this other self could put them in his power. Once he even put such fear to work for him; in his journal for May 20, 1847, appears this anecdote:

A man followed me to-day from lodge to lodge and told the Indians that they would die if I sketched them, which annoyed me very much. I tried to get rid of him but could not until I hit on an expedient, which was to sketch him, which was successful. He told me if I would stop, he would go away and not trouble me more. [See also *Wanderings*, p. 101, below.]

Occasionally he used flattery to overcome qualms, declaring that he intended to show the picture to the Indians' "great mother, the Queen," who would be most anxious to see it. Once he broke off making a sketch because of the chatter of the eight distracted wives of a Vancouver Island chieftain who felt that some harm would befall their husband through the sketch; he himself sat all the while like a "Grand Turk," flattered by the attention paid to him. Kane went further, sketching pipes, ceremonial articles of all kinds, tools of daily life, and houses and villages. Constantly he sought for the strange and uncommon in native customs, such as the more spectacular Indian rituals: medicine pipe ceremonials on the prairies, scalp dances on the upper Columbia River, coffin burials on the lower Columbia. He found few remains of the ancient rites in the Great Lakes region; already acculturation had suppressed many of the old ways and replaced them with a kind of apathy. Finally, Kane recorded the striking features of the landscapes he encountered. His first year he made sketches of Mackinac's tourist attraction of that time, a great natural bridge. Later he would set down the open prairies, swirling fires, towering snow-capped peaks, waterfalls twice the height of Niagara, and the rocky inlets of the far Northwest.

Sketching materials were light and compact. Some of his books for pencil and water colour studies are no more than ten inches across; a larger one, 10 by 14 inches, with marbled cover, contains Whatman paper watermarked 1843. Reference sketches are in pencil; portraits and landscapes in water colour are fresh, direct drawings. For more important works he carried oiled paper (possibly prepared pages from the larger sketchbook) on which he sketched using oil paints. These oil sketches on paper were light and could be packed into a much smaller space than either canvases or paintings on board. A century and a quarter later, they have unfortunately become exceedingly fragile. Many of Kane's oil sketches were taken from life. Preliminary studies in water colour exist for others, and presumably he transcribed them into oil at the first available moment while the immediate mood was still upon him. Sometimes the fur trade brigade with which he travelled halted for so brief a stop that he was forced to work in the faster water colour. Perhaps he had also to conserve his supply of oil colours. Where could they be replenished? Sketches from the last few weeks of travel are all in water colour: had some of the oil pigments been exhausted?

Like any artist, Kane had his less successful moments. Some of the sketches are certainly dull and undistinguished. Yet despite the hardships of travel and the necessity of working under the most trying and difficult circumstances, he returned with an incredible number of sketches in which the quality is generally

[2] *A Narrative of the Captivity and Adventures of John Tanner*, ed. Edwin James (New York 1830), p. 20.

high. In fact the collection is unsurpassed for that period by any other painter of Indians in America.

The first months of travel and sketching were spent around Georgian Bay. From Saugeen village he went to Manitowaning on Manitoulin Island where Ojibwa, Ottawa and Wyandot had gathered for the annual ceremony of the giving of presents by the British government.[3] Here were Indians from the shores of Lakes Huron, Nipissing and Superior and all the adjoining islands. Indeed so many prominent chiefs were available to him as subjects that he went on to similar gatherings at Mackinac Island and on the Fox River of Ojibwa, Menominee and Potawatomi; bands were to receive payment for lands sold to the American government. In no other way could Kane have assembled in one short summer such a varied gallery of Indian personages representative of a number of tribes. Most of his studies are simply portrait busts, a form he preferred. Occasionally he did a full-length work, such as the superb sketch of Mani-tow-wah-bay or "He-Devil" at Mackinac (Plate VII).

At Sault Ste Marie that first summer, Kane's fortunes changed through an unexpected offer of help from John Ballenden, the local Hudson's Bay Company factor. This company has had a history which matches the immensity of the country in which it has performed its operations. It was given exclusive trading privileges in the regions whose waters drained into Hudson Bay in 1670. Thereafter the Company effactually ruled the whole area stretching across to the Pacific, and, at Kane's time, from the Arctic south to the northern American border. For years the Company also controlled the Oregon territory, but this would change with its approaching transfer from British to American jurisdiction.[4]

The real head of the Hudson's Bay Company empire in these years was an energetic Scot, Sir George Simpson. An illegitimate child, he had entered the Company's service at an early age to seek fame and fortune. Forceful, self-confident and shrewd, he had become both governor of Rupert's Land (the Company's territory), and general superintendent of all company affairs in North America. This made him the virtual monarch of vast regions. He travelled from place to place in his special canoe to direct the Company's business transactions and to administer justice. In this canoe Sir George took his own private piper whose skirling bagpipes echoed through the woods and over the plains as he travelled up and down rivers and lakes. Simpson's powers were enormous and no one could travel easily in company territory if he willed otherwise. On the other hand, his

help could make all things possible for visitors to regions under his control.

Kane showed John Ballenden his newly completed sketches and described his hopes for painting a cycle of Indians and also the western landscape. He outlined plans to travel next year with two companions by way of Fort William and the Rainy River to the Red River Settlement. Eventually he hoped to go on to the Pacific. Kane also told Ballenden of his discussion of this project with Angus Bethune in Toronto before setting out. Bethune had discouraged Kane's hopes of receiving help during the trip from Hudson's Bay Company posts, stressing the inhospitality of its local officials. He had helped arrange the merger of the North West Company with the Hudson's Bay Company in 1821 and the former Nor'Wester had little affection for the new masters. This judgment by Bethune may have piqued Ballenden, or he may simply have been impressed with Kane's plans. At any rate he wrote to Sir George Simpson on October 29, 1845, praising Kane's sketches and devotion to his profession and assuring Sir George that Kane was prepared for the hardships of travel in the west.[5] Simpson, impressed, nevertheless wanted assurance that Kane was a British subject before he would even consider helping him.[6] Kane was.

Negotiations between Sir George and Kane continued throughout the ensuing winter after the artist's return to Toronto. Kane arranged to meet Simpson at Montreal, and J. H. Lefroy wrote an introduction for him. Lefroy, a British army officer then doing scientific work at the magnetic observatory in Toronto, was an intimate of leading families both in Canada and in Britain. His name carried respect. He pointed out to Simpson that Kane's pictures would be not only vivid but also "faithful" sketches of the novelties of the west, and that he would prove an interesting visitor for company gentlemen at various posts. Following Kane's visit to Montreal, Lefroy wrote a second time, on March 30, 1846, expressing satisfaction that the superintendent had promised his help. He also assured Sir George that Kane would travel alone the next year, and no doubt would return from the west with a portfolio of sketches not much inferior to Catlin's in variety and greatly superior in

---

[3] For a detailed account of the treaty ceremony at this place in 1838 see Anna Jameson, *Sketches in Canada and Rambles among the Red Men* (London 1852), pp. 276–87.

[4] On the Hudson's Bay Company see E. E. Rich, *The Hudson's Bay Company, 1660–1870*, 3 vols. (Toronto 1960) and *The Fur Trade and the Northwest to 1857* (Toronto 1967).

[5] Hudson's Bay Company Archives, D5/15, Ballenden to Simpson, October 29, 1845.

[6] *Ibid.*, D4/67, Simpson to Ballenden, November 17, 1845.

truth. He assessed Kane as a modest and respectable man.[7]

Sir George Simpson wrote Kane's final letter of authorization only after reaching Rainy River in northern Ontario on May 31, 1846. Simpson and Kane had been travelling west from Toronto at the same time, and Sir George had had an opportunity to gauge the artist's fierce determination. Left behind at Mackinac when he missed the steamboat, Kane had gone to fantastic lengths to overtake Simpson. He set a new and amazing local record for speed by setting off in a skiff with three boys, the eldest an eighteen-year-old stripling, and covering 90 miles of lake and river in less than 24 hours. He had caught up with the amazed Sir George at Sault Ste Marie. At Fort Frances Simpson wrote a circular letter to all Hudson's Bay Company officers in "Ruperts Land and Elsewhere," directing that the artist be given free transportation on company boats and "hospitalities" at all posts (see Appendix 10). Kane, a guest of the Hudson's Bay Company, could go without cost anywhere within the vast territories it controlled.

There were no more colourful men than the crews of the fur trade brigades of the Hudson's Bay Company, who linked all parts of the northern half of the continent. Kane had been introduced to this method of canoe travelling in May when he had joined the brigade going westward from Fort William on Lake Superior to the Red River. He would see much more of it before his return. It was a genuinely romantic experience to be in the great decorated canoes which were like living things as they leaped under the paddles of the voyageurs. Many of these specially selected young men were French-Canadians from the St. Lawrence, others were half-breeds and Indians born in the west. Lithe and bronzed, they were a colourful lot, with handkerchiefs twisted around their heads and sashes at their waists, and spoke in a unique accent. Washington Irving described them in *Astoria:*

The dress of these people is generally half civilized, half savage. They wear a capot or surcoat, made of a blanket, a striped cotton shirt, cloth trowsers, or leather leggins, moccasons of deer-skin, and a belt of variegated worsted, from which are suspended the knife, tobacco-pouch, and other implements. Their language is of the same piebald character, being a French patois, embroidered with Indian and English words and phrases.[8]

These voyageurs, carefree, good-natured, almost always singing, had much of the gaiety and lightness of heart of their French ancestry, were full of anecdote, and were ever ready for a dance. Kane called them amphibious water dogs, for after two thousand miles of paddling they would still wade cheerfully for

sixteen hours at a time in the cold northern Ontario rivers where the rapids were difficult and the task of dragging canoes against the current was formidable. The steersman of the canoe, most experienced of all, stood at the prow, "turning and twisting himself with the lithe agility of a snake, and striking first on one side then on the other, . . . very graceful and picturesque." [9]

The voyageurs travelled by "pipes," pausing to smoke for a brief five minutes and then paddling on at a rate of 50 strokes to the minute which made their canoes "absolutely seem to fly over the water." Normally three pipes marked about twelve miles of travel.[10] They ran even dangerous rapids and, when portages were necessary, carried the canoes and heavy bales often over difficult terrain. Kane meanwhile took advantage of halts to sketch the scenery of northern Ontario or the Columbia River. Day started at three or four o'clock in the morning with some five hours of paddling before breakfast, and camp was made at night only in time for Kane to paint the occasional sunset. It was a gruelling ordeal experienced by these proud and free men of the fur trade brigades.

Sir George Simpson's suggestions were to influence some of Kane's choices of subject-matter. Simpson urged Kane, for example, to go with the half-breeds (or, more correctly, Métis) on the annual buffalo hunt south from the Red River Settlement. That Kane should have made his trip in 1846 is one of the fortunate quirks of fate which repeatedly arranged that he be in the west to record important events at critical moments. The great hunt of 1846 was one of the last on the Winnipeg prairies: wanton slaughter of the buffalo had brought them nearly to extermination. After an hour's chase, Kane writes, 500 dead and dying animals covered from five to six square miles. Up to that time, buffalo had been the bulwark of Fort Garry's economy, and hunters made as much in a few weeks as farmers did in a whole year. Figures give life to this story. The number of carts in the annual hunt had increased from 540 in 1820 to 1,210 in 1840. During the latter year, 620 hunters, 650 women and 360 boys and girls went out in one party.[11] Between 1820 and 1840 hunters had killed an incredible 650,000 buffalo during these annual expeditions in the west, and this was not the total for there was additional slaughter by smaller parties.[12] Little won-

[7] *Ibid.*, D5/15, Lefroy to Simpson, March 30, 1846.

[8] Washington Irving, *Astoria; or, Anecdotes of an Enterprise beyond the Rocky Mountains* (author's rev. ed.; New York 1849), p. 47.

[9] Anna Jameson, *Sketches in Canada*, pp. 296–98.

[10] *Ibid.*

[11] Alexander Begg, *History of the North-West* (Toronto 1894), I, 299.

[12] E. Douglas Branch, *The Hunting of the Buffalo* (Lincoln, Neb., 1962), p. 83.

der that no buffalo herds were found south of Red River after 1847. If Kane had made his western trip two years later, he could not have pencilled his historic panoramas (Plate XVII, Fig. 67) of huntsmen riding pell-mell into a herd of from four to five thousand bulls, an episode of blood and carnage, and of danger as horses tripped in gopher holes and their thrown riders were pursued by wounded animals. It was, as Kane describes it, a scene "of intense excitement" and reckless confusion.

Buffalo would occupy Kane's mind that whole summer during his crossing of the plains, and he was indeed to be the outstanding painter of the vast buffalo herds on the Canadian prairie during their last phase. He sketched the buffalo pound at Fort Carlton, and made studies of an Indian high in a tree waving his feather-decked medicine pipe at the entrance so that its magical powers would send many and fat buffalo into the drive (Figs. 77, 78). Exotic touches delighted him, even if the slaughter was painful. When he was beyond Fort Pitt he was amazed by the vast buffalo herds which covered the prairie "as far as the eye could reach." At Fort Edmonton he saw the mounted Assiniboin chasing buffalo with piercing iron-tipped arrows and spears (Fig. 105). But, strangely, during the homeward trip he completely ignored as subject-matter the largest herd of all, 10,000 buffalo, which he saw wallowing in the snow. All phases of the buffalo hunt as it was practised throughout the seasons were pictured by Kane, except that he did no scenes of the animals struggling through deep snow; by contrast, this phase was one which Catlin seemed to find most picturesque. Kane was only interested during a winter hunt in the fact that he shot one of the largest buffalo bulls he had ever seen. He kept the head, a massive 202 pounds in weight, and repeatedly painted it.

The character of the faces and the dress of Kane's Indians change perceptibly in his sketches as he moves westward. On the prairies they are no longer pictured wearing clothing with European additions or with government medals around their necks. These men of the plains have not the quiet submissive air of the men of Manitowaning who had been in contact with Europeans for generations and foresaw the end of their free native life as hunters. Instead, his Sioux chieftain (Fig. 58), the Assiniboin named Mah-Min (Plate XXVIII, Fig. 109) or the Blackfoot, Big Snake (Fig. 92), are noble beings. Muck-Cranium, the Cree from Fort Carlton (Plate XIX), is above all the haughty Indian looking far out over the plains which are his empire. Here is the proud savage, not beaten down by Europeans, the kind of man for whom Catlin had such regard. Kane finally had

met the Indians he really wanted to paint and through his pictures of them he rendered an unsurpassed tribute to the first residents of this continent.

Kane did paintings of virtually all the Hudson's Bay Company posts he visited, from Fort Frances (Figs. 49, 50) to Fort Victoria (Figs. 188, 189). Fort Garry (Figs. 56, 57), Norway House (Plate XVIII), Fort Carlton (Fig. 75), Fort Pitt (Fig. 83), Fort Edmonton (Plate XXV) and Rocky Mountain House (Fig. 108) were links in the chain across the prairies. Others like Jasper House (Fig. 111), Fort Walla Walla (Fig. 134), and Fort Vancouver (Figs. 150, 151) led across the mountains to the Pacific. These squat bastions in the wilderness spaces spelled safety and comfort when travellers saw them from a distance, and this was the way Kane preferred to sketch them. He could thus present them in their natural surroundings, which close-up studies would not have allowed. Such a panoramic view of the Hudson's Bay Company's empire impressively documents its presence throughout these far-flung regions.

One regret might nevertheless be expressed. Kane painted no close-up of the exterior of Fort Edmonton or of a renowned audience room inside the fort. These features have been graphically described by other travellers:

The fort was painted inside and out, with devices to suit the taste of the savages who frequented it. Over the gateway were a fantastic pair of vanes, and the ceilings and walls of the hall presented gaudy colors and queer sculptures for the admiration of the Indians, the buildings, for the same reason, being painted red.[13]

True, there is a suggestion of the weather-vane over the fort entrance in Kane's canvas, but the exterior must have needed repainting at the time of his visit for there is no suggestion of the appealing red.

Yet a complaint is churlish perhaps. Kane was back at the fort for Christmas in 1847 and as if to atone vividly describes in prose the festive dinner in that same room. Its decorations were the "awe and wonder" of the natives but "were [the artist] to attempt a repetition of the same style in one of the rooms of the Vatican, it might subject him to some severe criticisms from the fastidious." [14] Here at Christmas, with the temperature registering from 40 to 50 degrees below zero outside, the Europeans, including the Rev. Mr. Rundle whose name is commemorated in a mountain peak, ate boiled buffalo hump and buffalo calf,

[13] Begg, *History of the North-West*, I, 212.
[14] *Wanderings of an Artist*, p. 138 below.

dried moose nose, white fish browned in buffalo marrow, buffalo tongue, beaver tails, roast wild goose, and piles of turnips and potatoes. That same evening everyone at the fort, white, Métis and Indians alike, joined in festivities in the "Great House." At the gala ball they dressed with bright sashes and ornamented mocassins, and spoke a babble of tongues. Highland reels were squeaked out by a fiddler. One of Kane's partners was a young Cree girl, "who sported enough beads round her neck to have made a pedlar's fortune," and as they danced she kept jumping up and down with a grave face, both feet off the ground at once "as only an Indian can." Kane painted another girl he met at the dance, a half-breed Cree named Cun-ne-wa-bum (Fig. 107). She looks out demurely enough from beneath a fan made of a white swan's wing, and wears a beaded dress which he later obtained for his ethnological collection.

From Fort Edmonton, Kane had set out on October 6, 1846, for the most harrowing phase of his journey, a crossing of the Rockies in early winter by a pass at over 5,000 feet. It was essential that the Hudson's Bay Company men get through. They carried with them packs of otter skins brought from York Factory which were destined for the Russians on the upper northwest coast of the Pacific: the company's annual rental for trading rights in lands owned by the Russians in that region. Horses stuck in deep snow drifts on the way over, and finally had to be given up for snow-shoes. The party had frequently to wade in rivers choked with floating blocks of ice. When the Columbia was reached, some boats upset in its dangerous rapids. But men and furs reached their destination.

Kane arrived at Fort Vancouver on December 8, 1846, and the relaxation was welcome after the arduous trip across the continent. The fort was the centre of the Hudson's Bay Company's west coast operations, and two of its principal men in that area, James Douglas and Peter Skene Ogden, already famed as fur traders, were hospitable to Kane. The Company needed its shrewdest and most reliable factors for such critical posts. The name "Kane" meant nothing to the men at the fort, however. Thomas Lowe, a company employee, was much more interested in the new bride whom Richard Lane, in charge of the brigade, had brought with him. Kane's intention, to paint the Indians and the local scenery as a record for posterity, was not grasped immediately by the staff despite Simpson's introduction. Lowe wrote:

It is supposed that [he's] taking views and sketches of the most remarkable places on the route, in order to embellish the work about to be published by Sir George Simpson; and it is thought that he intends to go over the same route as Sir George took in the years 1841 and '42, by the Sandwich Islands and through Siberia. . . .[15]

Sir George's book was published in London, the very next year, without illustrations, so that Lowe was evidently wrong in the first of his assumptions.[16]

Kane had arrived at Fort Vancouver in time for the festive Christmas season of 1846 at this far west post. Hudson's Bay Company men on the frontiers kept up their spirits with lusty celebrations and dinners were eaten in the best style. Both Fort Vancouver and Fort Walla Walla had imported English bone china, and the finest of oriental ware was brought carefully to posts which in some ways were havens of English-style living.[17]

Kane made a firm and fast friend of Peter Skene Ogden during these winter months. Ogden had spent most of his life on the Pacific coast from 1818. No man knew the west better than he, and his knowledge of the Indians was unrivalled.[18] He had studied for the law, and on the frontier, where there was no written law and no legal tribunal to appeal to, performed in his own part the acts of "summary legislation, [and] sometimes [. . .] the parts of judge, jury, sheriff, hangman, gallows and all!"[19] He has been presumed to be the anonymous author of *Traits of Indian Life and Character* published in London during 1853. Kane and Ogden passed convivial evenings with married couples at homes in the village area around the fort.[20] Obviously there was much banter about ladies, a good deal of laughter, and general gossip about all and sundry over games of backgammon.

The winter weather was extremely bad for outdoor sketching but Kane dutifully, if without much interest, recorded the fort. He showed more enthusiasm in painting the Indians of the neighbourhood. He mentions particularly the venerable old chief Casanov (Plate XXXVI), who in his days of greatest power could muster 1,000 warriors and had had 10 wives and 18 slaves. During the interlude at Fort Vancouver Kane took time

[15] British Columbia, Provincial Archives, Thomas Lowe's journals kept at Fort Vancouver, Columbia River.

[16] Sir George Simpson, *Narrative of a Journey round the World during the Years 1841 and 1842* (London 1847).

[17] See John A. Hussey, *The History of Fort Vancouver and Its Physical Structure* (Portland, Washington State Historical Society, n.d.), especially Plates XLV, XLVI, XLVII, XLVIII.

[18] On Ogden's life see T. C. Elliott, "Peter Skene Ogden, Fur Trader," *Oregon Historical Quarterly*, 1910, and E. E. Rich, *The Hudson's Bay Company*, II.

[19] Ross Cox, *The Columbia River; or Scenes and Adventures during a Residence of Six Years on the Western Side of the Rocky Mountains among Various Tribes of Indians Hitherto Unknown*, ed. Edgar I. and Jane R. Stewart (Norman, Okla., 1957), p. 308.

[20] See Appendix 10, Letter 10.

for a day's outing, cantering to the plains behind the fort with friends and sketching them in humorous vein while they were resting before the return gallop (Fig. 153). This mood was a relaxation from the serious studies he had been doing for two years. H.M.S. *Modeste* was anchored in the river by the fort and there was a social going and coming between officers and men of the Royal Navy and the Company's gentlemen and other employees. Kane spent much time with the officers in horse-racing and chasing wild calves. But he found himself in Oregon when more serious events were the preoccupation. The ship was there to maintain law and order at a difficult moment and tension was high.

A treaty of June 15, 1846, had fixed the western boundary between British and American territory to the Pacific and decreed that from June 1846 all lands south of the 49th parallel would be United States soil. A first American provisional government had already been established at Champoeg in 1843. The Hudson's Bay Company foresaw an end to its operations on the Columbia and planned a move for its headquarters north to Fort Victoria within continuing British territory. In these years, too, colonists, weary with the roughness and heat of a long journey, were coming in covered wagons over the mountains by the old Oregon trail at an incredible rate. Kane, astonished at their numbers, compiled a table of annual arrivals: 5 people had arrived from the eastern states during 1834; in 1844, it was 1,475 who crossed over the trail; 3,000 in 1845; and in 1846 between 800 and 900 "souls" arrived in the settlement with another 1,000 going to California.[21] The Indians were distraught. The white man's diseases accompanied the settlers and were killing them off in tremendous numbers. So many died in one Columbia River village that no one was left to bury the dead; their bones lay scattered amid its deserted dwellings. Violence would soon erupt at the Whitman Mission (Fig. 137) near Fort Walla Walla. And the appalling destruction of the Indians would continue. In March 1848 Ogden reported the arrival of 4,000 emigrants with "their pleasant travelling companions the Measles, Dysentry and Typhus Fever." Deaths among the whites totalled 119 that year "but the Indian population as usual shared most conspicuous": on the Columbia River alone, 1,500 Indians died during the summer.[22]

Tension, however, did not lessen the camaraderie which came from the presence of H.M.S. *Modeste* in harbour. The ship's officers, like others on ships held fast in the Arctic ice or docked elsewhere for long periods, organized its company into a theatrical group as an aid to morale. A play-bill, probably unique among relics of the west coast's early theatrical events, was kept by Kane (Fig. 152). This handwritten broadside records the company's performance at Fort Vancouver harbour on January 5, 1847. The group offered the farces "High Life below Stairs" and "The Deuce is in him" and as a conclusion "the laughable Comedy of 'The Irish Widow.'" Songs interspersed made it a full evening. That Kane saved this play-bill speaks eloquently of his continuing interest in theatricals, first noted in muddy little York years before. Various pencil doodles among his sketches are obviously theatrical characters: a dandy poses with his cane as he declaims his lines, and there are children dressed in pixy hats. These sketches are mixed in with those from the west coast, although there is nothing definitely to connect them with the performance described in the play-bill.

The theatrical evening attended by Kane actually was only one in a long series by the *Modeste*'s crew during Oregon's first "season." Captain Henry J. Warre, who travelled on the Pacific coast in 1845–46 as part of his mission to investigate defence of the international boundary, attended performances three times and gives more information about them. The first of his visits was on January 8, 1846, and Kane must have witnessed a similar scene when he attended just a year later.

This was the day fixed for the performance of the first Play, ever performed in Oregon—on board the "Modeste" for which great preparations had been for some time going forward—the Stage was rigged on the deck, which was covered in with sails & flags, &c. The façade was really beautifully painted by the sailors themselves. We dined on board. The play commenced at 7 oC. All the H.B. Company's officers & their Ladies attended from the Fort; as also several Americans from the Settlements.— numbering nearly 300 persons, including the Officers & crew of the Ship. The "Mayor of Garrati" & "The deuce is in him" were the pieces selected & were performed inimitably; particularly by the "Ladies" who looked and acted their parts to perfection; the sailor boys made rather large Women & had (as was remarked by a nice little girl of Mr. Douglas) "very red necks." Some of the ladies (nearly all of whom are half-breeds) wondered that they were not before aware that *"any Women lived on board"*—So that the deception was perfect. Between the plays, the Glee Singers gave some excellent songs, which were repeatedly encored, & the play concluded with "God Save the Queen" by the whole Corps Dramatique.

Warre reports that rain nearly ruined the second performance for which a sailor wrote and delivered the prologue: it was undoubtedly earthy but wholesome. Some settlers from the Twality Plains nearby were in the audience and found the

21 Kane family papers.
22 Appendix 10, Letter 14.

man-of-war almost as novel as the plays. Highly excitable nationalism nearly ruined the third evening, in March, when another double bill was enthusiastically received:

Fortunately for the Amateurs on board the Modeste, the 10th March proved a lovely day for the third representation of their Theatricals.—Numbers of Settlers and their families arrived to witness the performance & all the Officers returned to be present.—The Plays chosen were "She Stoops to Conquer" & "Miss in her Teens"—both of which were exceedingly well performed and with great applause.—There were several Americans present who were delighted with the plays, but made some objection to the National Songs for which some of them were nearly fittingly [sic] thrashed by the "Tars"—after they had gone on shore.—However, every thing went off well [&] the Yankees made a sort of apology for their dissent.[23]

New immigrants to Oregon brought other innovations to the west. The *Oregon Spectator* of Oregon City commenced publication in 1846, and Kane seems to have been intrigued with the newspaper. He purchased four issues to send to friends in the east so that they could better understand local conditions. Its editor, awake to everything novel, reported Kane's visit to Oregon City in the issue of February 10, 1847. Kane was then on his way to sketch at Champoeg, and during the visit he had made "faithful and beautiful" pictures of the new town and the falls (Plate XXXVIII; Figs. 161, 162). His paintings captivated the editor, and he saw them as a way of giving a true account of the far west: "Our countrymen on the eastern slope of the Rocky Mountains entertain imperfect notions, doubtless, of the appearance of Oregon and the Settlements, but we can assure them that in the achievements of Mr. Kane, they may behold correct delineations of the country." Kane himself was much concerned throughout his travels that easterners should accept his sketches as being truthful.

A Jesuit, Father Michael Acolti, escorted Kane from Oregon City through the Willamette valley to Champoeg and *en route* they visited two Catholic mission stations. Many early residents in the region were former Hudson's Bay Company employees with French-Canadian Catholic backgrounds, men who had settled on the plains after retirement from company service.[24] Kane was particularly interested in the St. Paul Mission.[25] Here children, red and white, were taught by a staff of nuns from Quebec, timid women, separated from their homes by a continent. Father De Smet had sketched their convent school, but his crude efforts have little historical value. By contrast Kane made a superb rendering of the mission (Plate XXXIX). Prominent is the new church with a steeple which had been built for the

sisters. It is reputedly the first brick building erected on the Pacific coast and no other accurate picture of it seems to exist.

Kane's second sketching expedition from Fort Vancouver was up the Pacific coast in the region of the Canadian northwest then known as New Caledonia. He left on March 25, 1847, with the good wishes of James Douglas who had assured him that he would find much both beautiful and sublime at Nisqually and beyond. The next day Kane met with another of his pieces of luck: when he reached the mouth of the "Kattleputal" (Lewis) River, he saw Mount St. Helens erupting smoke in the distance. This was one of the last of North America's active volcanoes, and had created whole chapters of the Indian myths and legends that fascinated Kane. Many stories linked Mount St. Helens with Mount Hood, which Kane had painted repeatedly from Fort Vancouver. One, for example, described the two peaks as a married couple, Hood being the husband and St. Helens the wife. They quarrelled fiercely and threw fire at each other. St. Helens was victor; Hood, being afraid of her, has since kept quiet and the wife, "having a stout heart, still burned." [26] Kane tried to hire Indian guides to ascend Mount St. Helens with him. It had never been climbed and he was told stories of "Skoocooms," evil genii who had eaten a man visiting it, and of a lake at the base with fish having heads like those of bears. No one would go with him and his only accomplishment was gathering another legend.

Mount St. Helens' most violent eruption had occurred in 1842. A Methodist missionary, Josiah L. Parrish, saw an unusual sight. Smoke and fire shot up, and the smoke spread out at a certain point in a line parallel to the horizon, looking like a vast table supported by immense pillars of flame and smoke. Kane saw and sketched a similar smoke ring, but his picture lacks some of the drama of the more violent eruption five years earlier (Plate XLI). When he painted a canvas of Mount St. Helens (Fig. 164) he chose to show a lurid scene of an eruption by night. After Kane's visit sporadic bursts of activity occurred for some ten years with smoke pouring from crevasses in the ice-capped mountain. Since then the volcano has been completely dormant.

[23] The two descriptions by Warre are in the Henry J. Warre Papers, Public Archives of Canada, MG24F71. See also *Oregon Spectator*, August 20, 1846; January 21, 1847.

[24] See John A. Hussey, *Champoeg: Place of Transition* (Portland, Oregon Historical Society, 1967).

[25] For an account of the mission see [Carl Landerholm], *Notices & Voyages of the Famed Quebec Mission to the Pacific Northwest . . . 1838 to 1847* (Portland, Oregon Historical Society, 1956).

[26] For further details see Kenneth L. Holmes, "Mount St. Helens' Recent Eruptions," *Oregon Historical Quarterly*, 1955, pp. 197–209.

Nearly a hundred sketches survive from the three months during which Kane worked on the southern tip of Vancouver Island, along the adjoining coasts of British Columbia and in the state of Washington. These are of the greatest ethnological and historical interest, and some are among his finest artistic productions. Their subject-matter has no parallel in the work of any other 19th century artist in the same region. Kane was attracted by the number and variety of tribes and no better place existed than Fort Victoria for sketching them. Locally there were Clallam, Sanetch, Makah and others, and farther afield such peoples as the northerly Chimmesyan, Kwakiutl and Haida. Indians from up and down the coast came to the post in large numbers, and a short canoe journey could take him to the homes of others.

Kane was struck by the facial characteristics of the individual tribes and by the head deformations many of them practised. He recorded their boats, both the great decorated war canoes and the less ostentatious craft of the camas-gathering fleet (Figs. 185, 186, 187). He pictured women spinning the wool which they rubbed on their thighs and weaving with primitive looms, the small white dogs raised for wool, and the domestic activities inside the large houses grouped into villages at Fort Victoria, Esquimalt and Suck (for example, Plate XLV, Figs. 196, 197).

In these villages Kane also sketched ornately carved masks with moon-faces and other visages, elaborate rattles, house posts carved to honour ancestral animals, and figures which were grave guardians (Plate XLIV, Figs. 190, 191, 193, 195). Here were the spectacular art forms of a native people whose material culture was more advanced than that of any other Canadian aborigines. Kane does not seem, however, to have been invited to attend the secret society meetings where the elaborately painted ritual masks which he sketched were worn. These ghostly dances were usually held at night when the red of fires piercing its gloom added mystery and drama. Kane's re-creation of such a dance shows masked figures performing in full daylight on a sunny slope, and he omits any suggestion of the excited and often terrified circle of spectators.

No artist of the Victorian period attempted to picture the west coast Indians as Kane had done. In the present century, Emily Carr, who was born in Victoria, in her turn became fascinated with the Indians of this region. She painted various tribes over many years with profound humanity, with humility, understanding and love, and her paintings revealed the religious concepts central in the Indian's art, especially in his great carved totem poles, into which the native sculptor breathed vitality and strength. Hers was a remarkable insight into the simple and honest ways which she found lingering among these once-proud people. Her dedication is one end of a thread which stretches back to Catlin and Kane, even if her painting has the artistic qualities of a later generation.

Events were occurring in this region which would be significant for British Columbia's future, just as farther south in Oregon a future destiny was being worked out. James Douglas had directed the erection of Fort Victoria towards the southern end of Vancouver Island just four years earlier. He named it in honour of Britain's queen, and she was to knight him in 1863 as the virtual founder of a new Canadian province. Kane and Captain Warre, a visitor during 1846, both set down views of this new bastion of British interests on the Pacific.

The Hudson's Bay Company was in these years making a vigorous effort to sell shares in an agricultural development company for Puget Sound where they envisioned a rich new farming community. Promotional circulars were distributed widely, forecasting wealth for investors in this new Pacific Coast enterprise. One went to the bishop at St. Boniface in the Red River Settlement, and he carefully filed it away. As usual alert to history in the making, Kane sketched the newsworthy little village of Nisqually then receiving much attention (Fig. 173).

At last Kane felt his work along the Pacific was finished. He had sketched in all the parts of the far west which were then being talked about and his thoughts turned to his homeward trip. He left Fort Vancouver on July 1, 1847.

It was proposed that Kane would call on the missionaries in the interior of Oregon on his return trip. At the Dalles of the upper Columbia River he was travelling quickly and did not have time to stop at the Methodist mission nearby. It was not, however, so important for him to halt there since he had been able to view numbers of Indians in that particular sector of the Columbia and had made many sketches. His chief interest in the missionaries was really the means of introduction they provided to the Indians in their particular region. Their usefulness is well illustrated by an incident on his westward trek. The fur trade brigade in which he was travelling had stopped at Cumberland House (Le Pas). The Rev. J. Hunter, a local Church of England missionary, wrote on August 25, 1846, in his diary:

The Saskatchewan Brigade arrived here to-day from York Factory in charge of Mr. Rowand. Distributed tracts among the men in the boat. Accompanied Mr. Cain [*sic*], an Artist proceeding with the Brigade, to the tent of Mistahpa'oo to inspect his drums, Medicine Bags, etc. Mr. Cain

Plate IV. Ojibwa Camp (Spider Islands, Georgian Bay). ROM 912.1.3; CRIII-28.

Plate V. Sault Ste Marie (Ojibwa village). ROM912.1.9; CRIII-65.

took a sketch of his drum and the grotesque figures portrayed on it. The principal figure was a man surrounded with a number of tents, over which Mistahpa'oo described him as presiding and protecting.[27]

Although he missed the Methodist mission in 1847, Kane did stop to sketch at Walla Walla as he moved east and also in the strange and romantic Pelouse River valley where the "magnificent scenes" tempted his curiosity. His route led him on July 18 to the American Protestant mission among the Cayuse Indians at Waiilatpu. Evidently he hoped Dr. Marcus Whitman, who was in charge, would introduce him to the local natives. They had a reputation for being aggressive. At this very time they were seething with anger and their bad feelings would soon reach a boiling point. Dr. Whitman, his wife Narcissa, and others had crossed on the Oregon Trail in 1836 to found the first Protestant mission in Oregon. They had laboured among the Cayuse when they first arrived, but had had to undertake additional duties when in 1843 the great wagon trains of immigrants arrived over the Trail. These new arrivals were welcomed and helped at the mission house, a T-shaped adobe building built by the missionaries themselves, who had smoothed and whitewashed the walls with a solution from river mussel shells. Paint bought from the Hudson's Bay Company brightened the building with green doors and window frames, grey interior woodwork, and yellow pine floors.[28] The increasing immigration of succeeding years was reflected in the necessity to give homes to children, half-breed and white, who became orphans on the Trail. Seven Sager children, whose parents had died while coming west, were adopted in 1844.

Kane was at the Whitman mission July 18 to 22, 1847. He describes graphically how the doctor took him to a Cayuse lodge, where he evidently made two sketches of To-ma-kus (Fig. 139). The Indian attempted to throw one sketch in the fire, but Kane snatched it from him. "He glanced at me like a fiend, and appeared greatly enraged, but before he had time to recover from his surprise I left the lodge and mounted my horse, not without occasionally looking back to see if he might not send an arrow after me."[29] Chief Til-au-kite was also sketched here (Fig. 140). Whitman's adopted daughter, one of the Sager children, recalled Kane's visit years later, describing how he had made pictures at the mission. She relates that she and the other children were cleaning up the yard and relaxed from their labour by trying to balance the rake on their finger. Mrs. Whitman reproved them and told them she did not want such frivolity in a picture.[30] Kane's pencil sketch, the only known view of the mission (Fig. 137), omits the children completely,

but in the foreground is a man leading a horse on the old Oregon Trail. When Kane returned to Walla Walla, he undertook to carry a little dog for Mr. Whitman, but in that inhospitable country the heat was so intense that the animal died of prostration on the way.

The second visit of Kane to an Oregon mission, in September, required a detour from Fort Colvile to Tshimakain some seventy miles away. From 1838 to 1849 the Rev. Elkanah Walker and the Rev. Cushing Eells with their wives maintained an establishment among the Spokan Indians. Kane was a guest of the Walkers and visited the Eells for dinner; both had comfortable log houses. One day he and Walker roamed about admiring the impressive scenery. Another day he went with an Indian hoping to visit some celebrated caves but failed to find them. Walker reported to him that there had been fighting at the Dalles between whites and Indians and two on each side had been killed. Tension in the region was obviously mounting. Kane's water-colour sketch (Fig. 131) shows the mission post in its last phase before its abandonment because of the Indian wars which were threatening even during his visit.

The diary of Mrs. Walker under date of September 11 makes a personal reference to Kane. His rough manners after exposure through three years of rugged travel on the frontier, his wild hair and great beard, must have intimidated a woman of the manse. "I think Mr. K[ane] a clever artist but an ungodly man, of not much learning. He gave me considerable information about birds."[31] Her reference to the birds is reinforced by the fact that Kane had several books on nature study in his library, and his son was a great lover of birds in his student days at Trinity College School, Port Hope.

In *Wanderings of an Artist* Kane records for September 21 the arrival of a messenger sent from Walla Walla to Fort Colvile, bringing news of an Indian uprising at the Whitman mission. Kane is curiously in error about the date for the tragedy took place on November 29, and just when he did hear of it is obscure: by November he was up on the Athabasca River. Til-au-kite and To-ma-kus, goaded to fury, had murdered Dr.

---

[27] Church Missionary Society Archives, London, journal of Archdeacon J. Hunter 1844–1865, ref. C C1/037.

[28] For the mission's history and its buildings see Erwin N. Thompson, *Whitman Mission, National Historic Site* (National Park Service Historical Handbook Series no. 37; Washington 1964).

[29] *Wanderings of an Artist*, p. 116 below.

[30] Matilda J. Sager Delaney, *The Whitman Massacre* (Spokane, Ethel Reed Chapter of the Daughters of the American Revolution, 1920).

[31] Henry E. Huntington Library and Art Gallery, diary of Elkanah Walker and Mary Richardson Walker.

Whitman and a general massacre followed. There had been a measles epidemic among the Indians and malcontents spread word that the doctor was poisoning them. Thirteen mission people were killed, several escaped, and 49 were held captive as hostages until released by Peter Skene Ogden who presented the Indians with company guns, blankets and ammunition in exchange for the prisoners.[32] The slayers had split the skulls of the missionaries before abandoning the bodies so that the evil spirits would escape. The mission of Henry Spalding at Lapwai was immediately discontinued, and Walker and Eells closed their mission the following March. The Whitman massacre was one of the most famous and unhappy episodes of the old west.

Though Kane, throughout his wanderings, was greatly concerned that people would later accept his sketches as being true portrayals of the regions he had seen, he was more worried about those of the Northwest coast and the Oregon, then almost unknown in the east, than he was about those of the prairies since Canadians did have some knowledge of the plains. An obvious solution was to secure certificates of authenticity from well-known Hudson's Bay Company men. James Douglas wrote the first of these at Fort Vancouver in June, the day before Kane left for the east.[33] With as much excitement as that grave man could muster, Douglas described the sketches as "faithful and spirited," "masterly" in delineation, an assurance he could give as he had known the places himself for the twenty years he had spent on the Columbia and in the Northwest. Farther up the Columbia, at Walla Walla, William McBean wrote another statement and John Lee Lewes a third at Fort Colvile in September.[34] Kane had been Lewes's guest for six weeks while he had painted portraits (Fig. 122), fishing scenes (Plate XXX; Figs. 123, 124), and the weird Chualpays scalp dance studies (Figs. 127–30). Not to be outdone by Douglas, Lewes pointed out that he had been in the west for forty years among the North American Indians, and emphasized that Kane's pictures of manners and customs had "a correctness, that none but a Master hand could accomplish." No Torontonian was going to think Kane an imposter.

Several other artists were painting in the Oregon and other parts of the regions covered by Kane during that same decade, and some of their pictures are identical in subject-matter with those by Kane. He was thus only one of a group of painters with similar interests. This influx of artists is understandable. The slow but irresistible movement west of American immigrants was taking them across the plains and mountains to the Colum-

bia; "Go west, young man" had become a popular phrase. Inevitably clashes with Indians occurred on the frontier, and word of these went back to the older parts of the United States. The transference of Oregon to the United States and the new provisional governments were feature stories in eastern newspapers. Books on the region were for sale in many stores, a response to the tremendous interest in the newly opening Northwest. In a day when cameras were not yet effective as tourist gadgets, only an artist's sketch could picture these new frontiers for those at home. "Go West" became a fashionable directive for artists as well as immigrants.

John Mix Stanley, the most important of these artists from the eastern United States who painted the Indians and local scenery in the Oregon, arrived during July 1847.[35] It is just possible that he reached Fort Vancouver before Kane left for the east on the first day of the month. Certainly Kane knew of Stanley's arrival shortly after his departure from Fort Vancouver. Kane received sporadic reports of the progress through Oregon of his old friend from the Detroit days of 1836 and followed his work with the greatest interest.

Stanley had first painted Indians on a visit to Galena and Fort Snelling in 1838.[36] Many sketching trips to the plains had followed, in imitation of those of Catlin. He was named official draughtsman for General S. W. Kearny's army expedition to California in 1846. On his discharge, he travelled north to sketch in the Oregon, and began painting Chinook Indians and tribes of the Willamette and Clackamas rivers. Peter Skene Ogden wrote Kane on September 2, 1847, saying that Stanley was then preparing to leave for the interior "in quest of scenery," and that Indian chiefs were "in great demand with him." He went on in the same letter to complain about the changing times on the Columbia with the influx of people: "What with Artists, Archbishops, Bishops, Priests, Nuns, Deacons and Fathers, 22 having lately arrived direct from Brest the country will be lost forever." He refers to one group of religious which had only lately come to Fort Vancouver; it included nuns who "for the salvation of the morals of the Country have been selected with more than usual precautions, being composed of old Women pass'd forty and beauty at a very low discount." However Ogden was

---

[32] See Thompson, *Whitman Mission*, pp. 66, 72.
[33] Appendix 10, Letter 7.
[34] Appendix 10, Letters 9, 11.
[35] Stanley's arrival was reported in the *Oregon Spectator*, July 8, 1847.
[36] For Stanley's career and his Oregon expedition see Nellie B. Pipes, "John Mix Stanley, Indian Painter," *Oregon Historical Quarterly*, 1932, pp. 250–58.

quite willing that one of the artists, Stanley, paint his portrait during the spring of 1847.[37]

Stanley went directly from Fort Vancouver to visit the Walker and Eells Mission, but arrived after Kane's departure. He sketched it from the identical spot at which Kane had sat, but the result is rather more awkward than Kane's sketch. Stanley went on to Fort Colvile and from there retraced his steps down river, intending to paint Dr. Whitman's portrait at Waiilatpu. When he was only a few miles from his destination, he heard of the slaughter on November 29, just two days earlier. He himself nearly lost his life with some Cayuse Indians, but escaped to Walla Walla when an Indian confused his identity, and then returned to Fort Vancouver.[38] He sketched both portraits and scenery in the interior. At Walla Walla he painted Peo-Peo-mox-mox and "Telo-kit," and at Fort Vancouver "Casino"; Kane had painted all three (Figs. 142, 140, Plate XXXVI).[39] Repeatedly Stanley sketched views from the same vantage points as had Kane, for instance Coffin Rock (Fig. 166), the Fort Colvile salmon fisheries (Plate XXX; Figs. 123, 124), the Pelouse and Willamette falls (Plate XXXV; Figs. 132, 162), and others. Stanley then left the Oregon for the Hawaiian Islands. After his return to the United States he exhibited his paintings in New York and throughout the New England area during 1850–51. Efforts were made to persuade the government to buy his collections for the Smithsonian Institution, and Stanley actually deposited all of his Oregon canvases there in 1853. A fire in 1865 unfortunately burned the majority of them, and many of those destroyed were the duplicates in subject-matter of works by Kane. (The collection, incidentally, had not yet been purchased.)

Captain Henry J. Warre shared with Kane more than an interest in the theatre. With his fellow officer on the defence mission, he had taken the same route as Kane from Fort Carlton to Fort Victoria just a year before Kane's arrival in the far west and had also sketched many identical subjects. The captain was a trained observer and set the landscape down in remarkable detail. British army and navy tradition held that sketching should be a gentleman officer's avocation, and indeed many, as did Warre, achieved excellence. In addition to water colours, he made on occasion detailed pencil or pen studies in his journal.[40] Hudson's Bay Company officials apparently pointed out the "tourist sights" to Warre as he passed through, just as they did for Kane and Stanley. Warre travelled up the Willamette valley, saw Indian canoe burials on the lower Columbia, and was impressed by Mount Hood. He sketched the new Fort Victoria, Fort Vancouver, the strange Kutenai canoes, and many views of the Rockies and the plains. Back in England, he took advantage of British concern for the ownership of the Oregon and published his choicest subjects as coloured lithographs.[41] Today they are collector's items.

There were still other artists in the Oregon during those years. Young Gustavus Sohon, who arrived at a slightly later date, deserves mention. A German immigrant, he had joined the American army in 1852 when little more than a boy, and then went with an exploration party to the upper Columbia River. Sohon was referred to by one of the party as "the artist, barometer-carrier, and observer . . . an intelligent German, a clever sketcher, and competent to take instrumental observations." [42] He was at the great Walla Walla council six miles from the site of the Whitman mission when in 1855 the United States negotiated the cession of 60,000 square miles of land by the Indians and set aside reservations for them. The Walla Walla, Cayuse, Nez Percé, Umatilla and other nations were represented by their chieftains and braves, and Sohon sketched the events in detail, adding portraits of the principal participants.

When Kane's work is assessed against that of other artists who worked in Oregon, his is seen to be the most complete of all the records. Similarly, the number and variety of the subjects he painted as he crossed the Canadian prairies are not equalled by any other artist of those times, by Warre or by Peter Rindisbacher, who painted at the Red River twenty years earlier, or by William G. R. Hind in his superb water colours of his trip across the prairies and over the mountains to the Cariboo golddigging with the Overlanders of '62.

A Hudson's Bay Company's autumn brigade left Fort Colvile

---

[37] Appendix 10, Letter 10. The portrait is now in the Provincial Archives of British Columbia, Victoria.

[38] For two versions of this episode see Appendix 10, Letter 14, and Nellie B. Pipes, "John Mix Stanley," p. 252.

[39] For Stanley's Oregon paintings see *Smithsonian Miscellaneous Collections* (Washington), II, 1862, 60–72.

[40] The collections of the Public Archives of Canada include the journals of Warre, in which are drawings and several water colour sketches, and also some individual water colours.

[41] Henry James Warre, *Sketches in North America and the Oregon Territory* (London 1848).

[42] For Sohon and his western sketches see John C. Ewers, *Gustavus Sohon's Portraits of Flathead and Pend d'Oreille Indians, 1854* (Washington, Smithsonian Institution, 1948).

late in September 1847 with Kane in temporary charge until the canoes got to Boat Encampment. They reached the appointed place on October 10, expecting to meet the horses from the east with the furs for the Russians for that year, but one of the delays followed which were especially irritating to brigade men accustomed to fast travel. They waited three weeks. Bored, Kane entered in his daily journal such innocuous memoranda as "Nothing of importance," "Nothing," or "Rained all day." One sunny afternoon he sketched the encampment with his tent and luggage in the foreground, and, to assist him in painting it up later as a canvas, he made a detailed study of the distant mountain peaks (Plate XXIX, Fig. 117). The brigade men varied the monotony on the 12th by paying special tribute to Kane, the "good companion" of the voyage. They made a "lobstick." A tall pine (Kane says in his diary that it was 111 feet high) was trimmed of its lower branches. On one side a smooth surface was cut and he was invited to carve his name on it. The men fired three rounds and gave three hearty cheers in his honour, and the place was thereafter to be named after him.[43] A trapper along the Columbia River rediscovered the tree in 1934. It still bore the carved words: "P. Kane, Oct. 12, 1847," and the section bearing this inscription was cut out and sent to the British Columbia Museum.

"Kane's Encampment" is no longer to be found on the map but the artist's name is commemorated in another way, in the name of a mountain peak to the east of the point where he was camping. Kane, on the arrival of the brigade from the east, went back with a small party and some of the horses to winter east of the Rockies. He says that they left Boat Encampment on October 31, but actually it may have been somewhat later because of his miscalculation of dates. Snow and cold made travelling incredibly difficult. They reached the Committee's Punch Bowl (Fig. 116) on November 2; Kane says about this lake in his journal, "Rather cold punch at present." That night was the coldest on which Kane had ever camped out, the thermometer dropping to more than 56 degrees below zero. As he attempted to wash, the water froze in a solid mass in his hair and beard and he could only thaw it out by standing so close to the fire that it scorched his face. The sun had shone brightly during the afternoon of this day in which he experienced the greatest discomfort in all his years of wanderings. He afterwards blamed the glare of the sun on the snow in the Rockies for contributing to the

weakness of his eyes.[44] Presumably he was so taken up with the hardships of the trail that he did not see or did not bother to mention a mountain peak just northeast of the Committee's Punch Bowl. This was named Mount Kane in his honour by the Canadian government in 1912.

Fort Edmonton was reached early in December. Kane was exhausted from exposure and hunger and was suffering not only from snow blindness but also from *mal de racquet*, the severe muscular pains experienced by those not accustomed to wearing snow-shoes. He had had to wear a pair during the later stages of the journey. But once back in the comfort of the fort, he looked forward to six months of painting on the western prairies centring his activities on Forts Edmonton and Pitt and Rocky Mountain House.

The rule of sketching only Indians was perforce relaxed shortly after he reached Fort Edmonton. A young Hudson's Bay Company man had come from Fort Pitt to claim his bride, the factor's daughter, and a gala occasion was proclaimed. The Reverend Mr. Rundle performed the marriage; the bride's father had forgotten that a minister was necessary until just a few hours before the ceremony and Rundle had been approached at the last minute. He remained to indulge in the sumptuous banquet which Mr. Harriott provided that night. Kane, who went with the couple to Fort Pitt, sketched both the gay turn-out of the teams of dogs (Fig. 101), the bride's having been purchased in Quebec and brought by the groom over thousands of miles for the occasion, and her newly decorated cariole (Fig. 103). From these sketches was painted the well-known canvas of the wedding party's departure, enigmatically titled *Winter Travelling in Dog Sleds* (Plate XXVI). Yet scratch the brusqueness which went to the point of not mentioning that the subject of the painting was a wedding party and Kane would turn out to be a very human person.

The sketches of the Assiniboin Kane was able to make by a trip to Rocky Mountain House in April gave him much satisfaction. The old head chief, Mah-Min (Plate XXVIII, Fig. 109), was so impressed that he took off his great bear's claw collar and presented it to the artist; a second chief, Wah-he-joe-tass-e-neen, feeling rather left out, requested that his portrait be taken; Kane graciously acceded (Plate XXVIII). On their return journey to Edmonton Kane and his companion were counting on a good meal at one of the food caches which, scattered about the prairies, were intended for travellers who found themselves short of supplies. They found inside it a wolverine, so fat from eating food that he could no longer squeeze between the logs to

[43] See note 6 to chapter XXI of *Wanderings of an Artist*, below.
[44] Cox, *The Columbia River*, p. 144, makes the same complaint.

escape. The food was almost destroyed, but Kane sketched the cache in memory of a lost dinner.

Studies of unusual pipe-stems gave him even greater satisfaction. Ritual pipes were smoked by the Plains Indians before going into battle and they regarded them with the greatest awe and respect. A Cree chieftain, Kee-a-kee-ka-sa-coo-way, who arrived at Fort Pitt during Kane's visit, had been elected the tribe's pipe bearer for four years (Fig. 85). His effects in this office were carried by two horses and the pipe-stem itself was in the custody of his favourite wife but was well wrapped since no woman must see it. This was a golden opportunity to sketch just such a Plains ritual as had been suggested by Sir George Simpson. The Cree chief had pipe-stems of other chiefs which he was carrying on a war mission, and with great ceremony each was revealed to Kane who made individual sketches. Largest and finest was one ornamented with both an eagle head and several woodpecker skins attached to the stem (Fig. 88). Kane sketched the chief holding it (Fig. 86), and by some unknown means (such sacred objects were not disposed of lightly) secured an almost identical specimen for his own collection.

The wanderings on the plains were drawing to their close. Kane travelled eastward with the fur brigade down the Saskatchewan River towards Norway House where he would again meet Sir George Simpson before going on to Toronto. Near Fort Pitt came a fitting conclusion to the tour when early in June the brigade met a great party of 1,500 warriors from 1,200 lodges, members of the fierce Blackfoot, the nation best known of all Plains warriors; with them were their allies, the Blood, Sarsi, Gros Ventres and Piegan. One of the leaders of the band was Big Snake himself, a celebrated Blackfoot warrior who strode up and down cracking his whip, singing war songs and spoiling for a fight. Kane's sketch of Big Snake's brother was pronounced so lifelike that he was considered to be a medicine man and was given free entry to all the activities of the Blackfoot camp. He saw a race by naked youth on horseback (Fig. 89). He sketched Big Snake, Little Horn and the other principal chieftains (Figs. 91, 92). A Blood Indian gave his decorated shirt and trousers to his old friend Mr. Harriott, who in turn handed them over to Kane for his collection, not particularly wanting to wear them himself. Kane's final success was receipt of an invitation to attend a medicine pipe-stem dance by the assembled warriors before they continued on their war tour; his own magical powers were expected to increase the ritual's effectiveness. A good viewing place was picked for him and he made an oil sketch of the scene (Plate XXIII). Brilliant sunshine high-lights the Indian dancers who gesticulate with their colourful feather-trimmed pipes, while onlookers, gathered before their tents, are absorbed by the ceremony. This, unique among Kane's field sketches, and the most effective of all, was a noble conclusion to his western Indian series.

Various incidents enlivened the remainder of the journey. Out from Le Pas Kane was able to move ahead in a lighter craft and could sketch the approaching brigade of 24 boats; in one of them he had travelled many miles. Their loads, which had in them pemmican, grease, buffalo skins and other cargo, were less than they should have been because the Blackfoot had done no trading that year.[45] At Le Pas Dr. John Rae and Sir John Richardson had passed them, going to the northwest in search of Sir John Franklin, who was lost in the Arctic, and about whom even Queen Victoria was worrying. They made more impression on Kane then he did on them; Rae's journal mentions meeting the brigade, but has no reference to Kane.[46] Kane's travelling companion at this time was the Rev. J. Hunter who had taken him to visit Indian lodges during the westward trip. There was a delay at Norway House before the final dash through to Upper Canada, and Kane spent his time in shooting and fishing for sturgeon and Winnipeg gold-eye. He did not cook the latter since a company man had said "They eat like mud." He often had with him an 110-year-old Eskimo about whom a strange story was told. Kane repeats it in *Wanderings*. When his wife died during childbirth, the Eskimo gave suck to his starving infant. Milk flowed from his nipple after a few days and the baby was saved. One reader of the 1859 edition of Kane's book has written in the margin: "Cum grano salis." (Fig. 76)

Kane crossed what is now northern Ontario with a swiftly moving band of canoes but had another delay at Fort Frances. He sketched Indians and portages at every opportunity, realizing that he might never again have the opportunity. His last field sketch pictures the old Ojibwa chieftain, Maydoc-game-kin-ungee (Plate XI), proudly wearing the scarlet coat given by the Hudson's Bay Company to those natives whom they wished especially to honour and a chief's medal as the Queen's loyal subject. Sault Ste Marie was reached on October 1, 1848, and Kane went from there to Toronto by comfortable Great Lakes steamer.

No artist ever travelled and lived for three years more cheaply than Kane had done on his 1846–48 wanderings. He

---

[45] Journal of Archdeacon J. Hunter (see note 27), June 12, 1848.
[46] See, however, Earl of Southesk, *Saskatchewan and the Rocky Mountains . . .* (new ed., Edmonton 1969), p. 5.

had had free hospitality and travelling privileges with the Hudson's Bay Company men, but he was nevertheless a frugal man with simple needs. A clay pipe of tobacco and a quart of rum were his occasional concessions to good living. These were drawn from company stores at various posts. Clothes wore out; he needed, for example, two new shirts, a new Scotch bonnet, a pair of blankets, and the combs so necessary for sanitary reasons when living with the Indians. He anticipated the necessity of making small gifts to the Indians as token payment for posing and bartering for specimens to be added to his collection: for these purposes he had glass beads, scarlet and blue cloth, looking glasses and other minor items. For his Babine blanket he paid "five pounds of tobacco, ten charges of ammunition, one blanket, one pound of beads, two check shirts, and one ounce of vermilion." [47] His carved mask cost him a pound of tobacco. Some items were bought from the Company: a northwest coast cedar hat was purchased at Fort Victoria for 1/1; a "raincoat" made from seal intestine by the Aleuts had come from the store at Fort Simpson. A painted buffalo robe to which he refers was bought for him at a price of 15/- from the store at York Factory to which it had been brought from the prairies (Fig. 95). In payment for goods advanced from company stores, he turned in skins of buffalo shot on the prairies at 3/9 each and moose skins at 6/- each. Thus on reaching Toronto he only owed the Company £14/6/9 for his transcontinental journey. He remitted it promptly to Sir George Simpson.

Kane reached Toronto on October 13, 1848. He intended to start painting canvases from his sketches at once but could not since some pictures intended for Sir George Simpson had been damaged in transit and these had to be repaired. Rumours circulated about his remarkable journey and his sketches, and he was induced to exhibit the whole collection publicly in Toronto's "Old" City Hall on Front Street for a small entrance fee. The building was then being used as a market, new quarters having been erected for council meetings in the 1830s. The mayor and city clerk may have backed the exhibition, since Kane had painted a portrait of the mayor, George Gurnett, who was editor of the Toronto *Courier* (Fig. 8). Thomas Daly, the clerk, was an amateur artist and Kane had done a profile drawing of him one day (Fig. 11) while in a discussion with him. The catalogue of the show (see Appendix 3) lists 240 sketches. Indian souvenirs provided another curiosity for the exhibition, which opened on November 9, 1848. Kane regretted that he

[47] *Wanderings of an Artist*, p. 107 below.

had no large canvases; these he felt would have made the show truly a success.

Only visitors who would have been impressed by mere size, however, might have considered that the showing would have been improved by the addition of canvases. Kane had lavished the greatest care on both his water colour and his oil sketches during the western trip. Landscapes bloom with the glow of the clear Canadian atmosphere. Drawings of heads are masterpieces in miniature with a careful expression of character, luminous backgrounds, and appealing colour. All of the sketches in the exhibition were painted with a factual and objective approach which could not fail to speak directly to those who saw them. By contrast, a similar show of Catlin's works would have revealed a nervous, romantic air. Curiously, when Kane painted up his sketches into canvases, he altered his approach, losing the lucid freshness of his first impressions by introducing subjective overtones. These were intended to make his canvases into more profound works of art, but by present-day standards they quite failed to do so.

The newspapers gave the artist an ovation. Hugh Scobie, a local journalist who had published the catalogue, had made a few preliminary references to the show in his *British Colonist* by way of publicity, but printed a more extensive commentary on November 17, 1848. As was typical of mid 19th century reviewers, he paid little attention to the aesthetic qualities in the paintings but much to subject-matter and treatment. His facts were not always strictly accurate, but the review demonstrates the high regard in which Kane's sketches were held by his contemporaries and the sense Torontonians had of the uniqueness of this first great vista of the west. The review is entitled "Kane's Indian Gallery," and reads in part:

The difficulty is, to select a number among so many that are interesting, for the first attention. Perhaps a spirited sketch portrait of a Blackfoot chief, on a grey horse, in all the pride and picturesque splendor of the Indian hunter, is the favorite with most visitors [presumably this is a lost sketch from which was painted Plate XX, "The Man that Always Rides"]; but we do not see that it does more credit to his artistic powers than some very beautiful sketches near it, of scenery on the western prairies, some of which, we are informed, have been requested by Sir George Simpson, than whom there must not be a better judge of the fidelity of Mr. Kane's pencil. A striking characteristic of Mr. Kane's paintings, particularly in their present state, is the truthfulness. Nothing has been sacrificed to effect —no exaggerated examples of costumes—no incredible distortions of features—are permitted to move our wonder, or exalt our conceptions of what is sufficiently wild and striking without improvements. In this respect he contrasts very favorably with Mr. Catlin, who certainly indulged in artistic license to the utmost extent; but in no respect, as an artist, do we think him inferior to his predecessor—in some respects he is superior. There is extraordinary spirit in most of his sketches, whether in water colour or in oil, particularly in the figures, and when we consider that many of them were finished on the spot as we see them, frequently under the most unfavorable circumstances, it is difficult to speak in too high terms of the energy, enterprise and skill of our young fellow townsman. The sketches on the western side of the Rocky Mountains, ground scarcely trodden by any traveller before Mr. Kane, and certainly never before made known to us through the medium of the pencil, are exceedingly interesting. We have here, for the first time, some of the most picturesque scenes of that region; those mysterious "Shining Mountains" of Jonathan Carver, and the older travellers, which are environed to this day by scarcely less romance and interest, than they were invested with by his imagination. We see here the wild natives of Paget's [sic] Sound and its environs, the most barbarous and debased of the Indian tribes, and, at the same time, by a singular anomaly, the most advanced in regular trade, and even manufacture. . . . We think that every mother in this favored city will be interested in a sketch of a poor little infant undergoing the barbarous and preposterous process of having its skull flattened [Fig. 170]. To the portraits of individuals are added sketches of their habitations, their canoes, their methods of the chase, and of the wild scenery of New Caledonia, including the most valuable of our possessions on that coast—Vancouver's Island. Mr. Kane has also made a very extensive and curious collection of specimens of the arts and manufactures of the natives—one, we must say, which gives the visitor a high opinion of their ingenuity and their capabilities of future civilization. The present exhibition contains 240 sketches of persons and scenes belonging to the most interesting regions on both sides of the Rocky Mountains, and these are, we are informed, but part of the contents of Mr. Kane's portfolio. As his absence from the city has not much exceeded two years, in which time he has journeyed many thousands of miles, and twice crossed the Continent, he must have laboured with a degree of diligence and industry deserving of the highest commendation. . . .

Other Toronto newspapers also commented. George Brown's *Globe* for November 15 noted with typical Scottish reticence and scepticism that it had "no doubt" that the Indian portraits and northwestern scenes were "particularly accurate," but its reporter was much more impressed with Kane's large stuffed buffalo head, also on display. The *Christian Guardian* (November 15) and the *Patriot* (November 13) both mentioned individual works. François Lucie's portrait (Plate XXVII), the Blackfoot on horseback, and the view of Mount St. Helens with the smoke cone (Plate XLI) drew their special admiration. One sketch of Mount Hood was described as "perhaps the most perfect picture in the room" (this sketch has not been located).

Toronto in the 1840s lacked an art school and the learning process was almost wholly the copying of available paintings. Most of the newspapers admonished young artists to seize the unusual opportunity of Kane's exhibition to learn something of their craft. Scobie noted:

The sketches are of varied degrees of forwardness from the first outlines in the artist's pocket-book to the more careful and finished oil painting—a circumstance that makes the whole collection particularly interesting to all who study art.

The *Patriot* made a similar recommendation:

Those of our young friends particularly, who may be seeking instruction in the art of drawing, we strongly advise to study these sketches closely, to mark well their simplicity and *elegance*, to note how free they are from exaggeration of tone or colour, and how truly the *perspective* is maintained throughout. We advise the young draftsman or draftswoman to observe all this, and then go, follow Mr. Kane's example, and copy from nature, for there is a harmony in nature not to be found elsewhere.

The philosophy closely parallels that of Emerson and the artists of the Hudson River School south of the border who found in the natural world a perfect harmony.

Kane abruptly closed the exhibition. He was impatient to begin painting his canvases. But the showing had given Torontonians their first comprehensive look at the west and it must have been a factor in turning thoughts in Upper Canada to the promise of that region, then much neglected. But this period of unawareness was coming to an end and men like William Hamilton Merritt would shortly be visiting Chicago and the American west to assess progress there. Kane's exhibition may even have been, ironically, an indirect cause of stirring up the resentment against the Hudson's Bay Company which was the result of the turning of hungry eyes in Canada West towards the great land mass of the prairies as a place for future expansion. There would come a time when the pressure of the Canadian government would result in the Company's having to surrender its control and open the Northwest for development.

So successful had been Kane's Toronto showing that Sir George Simpson offered his patronage for a similar exhibition in Montreal.[48] Kane declined by saying that "unfortunately my circumstances at present do not permit it." His canvases were exhibited at the Art Association of Montreal shortly after 1900. The only time when the sketches seem again to have been put on public view was at the Winnipeg Board of Trade in 1922.

One jarring note resulted from the 1848 exhibition. Captain

[48] Appendix 10, Letter 17.

John O'Brien, whose son was to be the first president of the Royal Canadian Academy, wrote to the newspapers about it and his excess of enthusiasm and praise displeased Sir George Simpson. It caused a first break in the cordial relations between Simpson and Kane. But there were compensations. The artist met his second patron, George W. Allan, probably at the exhibition. Kane had breakfast with Allan on a morning in December and a close friendship between the two persisted thereafter.

Kane's field sketches were split into two groups during his lifetime and many still remain in two collections although items were occasionally sold and have thus become separated from the main bodies. One group, comprising over three hundred pencil and water colour sketches, passed with a number of canvases into the ownership of the Hon. George W. Allan and eventually to a descendant, Major R. Willis. He presented them to the Royal Ontario Museum in 1946 where, with Kane's canvases already in that institution, they formed an amazingly rich collection.

Other sketches, many in oil on paper and others in water colour and pencil, were in Kane's studio at his death and passed to his widow who kept them as poignant reminders of her husband's adventures. A son, Paul Kane II, moved as a homesteader to Manitoba, a part of Canada in which his father had played such an illustrious role as a painter. The sketches were sent to him after his mother's death in 1892. He kept this pictorial record of his father's frontier for years in a small walnut box in the spare bedroom at Rathwell, Manitoba. These western sketches, unmounted and so fragile that they could hardly be handled without damage, were unknown to Canadians generally but on wet Sunday afternoons they were brought out and examined on the parlour table to the delight of Kane's grandchildren. Paul Kane III, in ailing health, sold a group of over two hundred sketches in 1957 to H. J. Lutcher Stark. His wife has turned them over to the Stark Foundation, and this unusual collection is thus available for study for the first time.

III. A Trip to the Red River, 1849

While Kane was working on his final four paintings for Sir George Simpson, an opportunity came for another western trip. Sir Edward Poore, 23 years old, a restless young officer of the Scots Fusilier Guards with a hankering for adventure and excitement, was contemplating a two-year journey through the Rockies and on to the Sandwich Islands. He offered Kane £200 a year plus expenses as "conductor, guide and interpreter" to him and his party.[1] The artist accepted and wrote to Sir George Simpson on the eve of his departure saying that it would afford him "the opportunity of greatly enlarging my present collection." Then, as if with a twinge of conscience about not having completed his undertaking, he promised to take his sketches along with him to the Red River and there finish his copying on canvas for Sir George.[2]

Sir Edward Poore, who signed his letters to his mother as "(the wild) E. Poore," had come from England to America in 1846. It was rumoured that a young English lady had refused his advances. He visited old friends in Cobourg, probably two brothers-in-law; then he hastened to see the wild west at St. Louis where he hunted buffalo, elk, deer, antelope, grouse, raccoons, turkeys, bears and wolves. A month later he was back again in Cobourg; his jacket and money had been stolen on the return journey, he had had to pawn his pistols in Buffalo, and he arrived with just $1 left in his pocket. The young baronet bought a house at nearby Grafton, and there he played polo with friends.[3] But adventure seemed a necessity to him and the far west beckoned again; a trip across the Rockies with some friends was the answer he found this time for a periodic outburst of energy. Companions on the trip were to be a Mr. Franklin and Charles Philips. He had probably met or heard of Kane in Cobourg where the artist was courting Miss Harriet Clench, and he actually purchased a number of his western paintings which were sent home to England. (Their whereabouts today are unknown.) He seems to have had aspirations of becoming a western painter himself since Kane was to be cast in the roles of tutor and guide.

George Allan gave one of his breakfast parties in Kane's honour on April 13, 1849, the day before the departure. Captain and Mrs. J. H. Lefroy (Mrs. Allan's sister), and a Mr. Heath were also guests. The party was, unhappily, a prelude to frustration.

Poore chose to travel through the United States to the Red River rather than by the difficult Lake Superior route. From Buffalo the party went to Sandusky, and then embarked at Cincinnati on the steamer *Dr. Franklin II* which carried them down the Ohio, up the Mississippi through St. Louis, and on to Galena, Illinois, which they reached on May 2. Cholera on

[1] Royal Ontario Museum, Reminiscences of Paul Kane by Mrs. [Allan] Cassels. For letters relating to Sir Edward Poore see Appendix 10.

[2] Hudson's Bay Company Archives, D5/25, Kane to Simpson, April 13, 1849.

[3] Information supplied by Mr. E. C. Guillet.

30

E-dah-wah-Ikaish.

Plate VI. Sketchbook page: Indian youth wearing chief's medal and Indian girl with beads. ROM 946.15.35; CRIII-77.

board the ship gave them a bad scare but they reached Saint Peter unscathed and there they disembarked. They started overland for the Red River on May 15 with one cart, five horses, five mules, and a guide with his own horse. On the way they bought still another cart and horse, and a canoe for crossing the many streams they were likely to meet. Bad luck dogged their heels, and relations grew more and more tense as feelings were aroused by the frustrations from the variety of difficulties they encountered. Poore wrote to his mother:

Philips one morn tied his horse up to the cart with the canoe on it (the canoe is to cross the rivers with, many very bad), some thing frightened him & he threw his head up & broke about 4 ft. off the end of it. All the way we have had mud, water, etc. for it has been a very wet season & the carts would stick & we had to get into the water—Frank, the Guide & myself often up to our waists in water, a thing Kane or Philips would never do if it was possible to avoid.[4]

On another day a cart upset and most of the provisions were lost in the water. Four horses and two pack mules bolted for freedom before it had been righted. Poore and Franklin had to pursue the runaways over treacherous ground, and did not return with the missing animals until late in the evening, only to find that Kane and Philips had eaten the last of their supplies. The two made "supper off *Tea leaves they had used and sugar*." On yet another occasion a horse kicked Poore in the mouth; two teeth were lost, and after this injury he mailed a section of his upper jaw-bone to his mother. Philips almost cut his foot off with an axe. Kane evidently must have considered these young gentlemen as greenhorns and perhaps treated them accordingly.

Furious with the world, Poore dismissed Kane at Fort Garry as impertinent, overbearing and incapable of fulfilling his contract; Kane, he said, could not speak the Indian dialects or act as a guide since he had travelled west before by the easier means of the Hudson's Bay Company's fur brigades. In fact Poore also accused Kane of telling tales to the officials of the Company, with the result that passage was refused to these dashing young gentlemen. Actually Lord Elgin had written Sir George Simpson requesting assistance for Poore before he had set out, and Sir George had granted hospitality at company posts in view of the high quarters from which the request had come, but he had made no promise about passage with the brigades.

The party arrived at Fort Garry on June 18. Philips went to bed, an invalid, and spent two months there recuperating. While they were waiting for Philips, Poore and Franklin went on a three-week buffalo hunt along the Red River, but shot nothing; the buffalo had already vanished from the Winnipeg prairies. The two then departed for the Pacific on July 27, leaving behind Philips and Kane. They hired an Indian and a half-breed, and they took along seven horses and eight mules. At one point Franklin shot a buffalo; Poore had just taken aim at the same animal but his horse had tripped in a gopher hole at that moment and he had not had time to pull the trigger. Poore drew a caricature of the incident in a letter to his mother, seemingly the only art work he attempted on the journey. Hudson's Bay Company officials were much concerned about the inexperienced travellers when they reached Fort Edmonton and decided to allow them to go with the brigade across the Rockies. Poore was involved in an escapade at Mountain Portage during the crossing, and the result was the accidental shooting of a company employee by one of the men in the party.

Poore and Franklin arrived at Fort Vancouver in November; the company officials there found them "harmless creatures [who] take life easily, giving no trouble."[5] Kane had been much perturbed about the whole frustrating trip and wrote about it to his old friend, Peter Skene Ogden. Ogden's reply from Fort Vancouver in March 1851 reads in part:

I was disappointed in not seeing you here with Sir Edward. The latter did not make a *deep* impression with the *Vancouvery Dandys* and still less with the military who often remarked he could be no Gent., having no regard to dress—so you see the external garment is their criterion of a Gent.—although I am not overfond of dress, still I am of opinion that rules of propriety should in all things be strictly observed which I must say Sir Edward lost sight of. What has become of the Man and friend Franklin, truly a free young Man.[6]

Poore, by his own account, wore "*long hair, earrings,* leather trousers fringed & all the other fixings belonging to a half breed" when he was at Fort Garry; evidently the "hippy" garb was retained for the rest of his journey. He and Franklin continued on to Fort Victoria in December. Then word is said to have come from England that the young lady on whom Poore had set his affections was ready to receive his advances.[7] The young baronet hurried home, married, and was back in Cobourg in 1851 where his son was born two years later. Shortly afterwards, Sir Edward took his family back to England. There he left them while he rushed off to Australia; he lived out the rest of his life on the sub-continent as a wandering expatriate, having

[4] Appendix 10, Letter 19.
[5] *Eden Colvile's Letters, 1849–1852,* ed. E. E. Rich (Hudson's Bay Record Society Publications, vol. XIX, 1956), p. 190.
[6] Appendix 10, Letter 22.
[7] Mrs. Cassels, Reminiscences.

completely broken his family ties. He died in Adelaide in 1893, a penniless miner, on his way to the gold fields.[8]

Philips, left behind at Fort Garry in 1849, recovered. He, Kane and the retiring factor, James Sinclair, left the Red River for Canada on August 30, travelling by the United States. John Ballenden, Kane's old friend from Sault Ste Marie, who had been transferred to Fort Garry, kept Sir George Simpson informed about developments. The departure of Philips was advisable, he reported, since he had given indiscreet attentions to ladies who were rather beneath his station, and they might have become troublesome.[9]

No sketches were made by Kane during this visit to Fort Garry, so far as is known. The governor-general, the Earl of Elgin, scion of an ancient Scottish family, whose father had brought the Elgin Marbles to England from the Parthenon, called with the Countess of Elgin at Kane's Toronto studio a year later, on August 16, 1850. They came to see his "pictures taken while travelling in the West with Sir E. Poore."[10] Presumably they actually looked at sketches brought back from the 1845–48 expeditions.

IV. One Hundred Western Canvases

Kane had rented a studio on King Street, Toronto, after he returned from his western wanderings. W. H. G. Kingston, the English novelist, and his bride, on their wedding trip to Canada, found the artist at work in it during 1853, the year of his own marriage, and described him in his studio surroundings. That morning, as they recalled, "We found our way up a steep, high stair to an apartment at the top of the house, more like a poet's chamber than a painter's studio, where we found the artist at work." Here, Kane reminisced genially with his guests about his adventures, and attracted Kingston's goodwill:

His appearance, though roughish from the style of life he had led, much prepossessed me in his favour, and still more did his manners, which were truly pleasing and courteous. He is more like a real old master of the genuine art-loving, gain-scorning, fame-desiring stamp, than one expects to

meet in these utilitarian, gold-seeking days. He works hard, but steadily. . . .[1]

The tools of the artist's craft were around the studio. There was, for instance, a highly prized mahogany paint box. When the top was lifted access could be had to the upper section with its storage for bottles: these square glass bottles were filled with his pigments, ochre, vermilion, blues, lamp black and others, and his mediums.[2] Beneath, sliding from the box's front, was a drawer filled with fine stubble and sable brushes. Among the Kane family papers are receipts of the mid 1850s for his painting supplies—stretching frames for the canvas at 15/- a half dozen, canvas at 5/6 a yard, and sable brushes at 6/3 a dozen. Most of the supplies were bought from A. J. Pell, a famous old Toronto firm of art suppliers. Kane's manual when he needed technical advice was F. T. Burton's *The Artist's Ascunum.*[3]

Kane's method of working up his canvases was discovered only recently during the course of restoration of one of the Hon. George W. Allan's pictures; it was found to be backed by an unfinished painting. Kane had applied a priming coat of white lead on the canvas. This was his usual practice with undercoating for his oils; in a similar way he had applied a coat of white lead to his paper before painting oil sketches during his transcontinental tour.[4] After the priming coat, he had washed in his sky in pale blue and his land area in a greenish tone. He then drew in his subject-matter with a fine brush in burnt umber as a guide for the more detailed painting in richer pigment and full colour.[5]

It was the artist's plan that his studio works should be a cycle of the round number of one hundred, made up of canvases based on his western sketches and covering all phases of Indian life and the landscape in the territories where they lived. The cycle was to provide a panorama from the Great Lakes to the Pacific, and be a memorial to the frontier and its Indian peoples. The preservation of his work for Canadians was Kane's fondest wish, just as Catlin and Stanley in the United States hoped that their paintings would be purchased for posterity.

Kane had commenced painting his western canvases immedi-

[8] An obituary appeared in *The Age* (Melbourne, Australia), December 21, 1893, under the heading "A Strange Career."

[9] Hudson's Bay Company Archives, D5/25, Ballenden to Simpson, August 29, 1849.

[10] Kane family papers, letter from F. A. Grant, aide-de-camp to the Earl of Elgin, to Kane, August 16, 1850.

[1] W. H. G. Kingston, *Western Wanderings; or, A Pleasure Trip in the Canadas* (London 1856), I, 44.

[2] Appendix 8 gives an analysis of these bottles.

[3] F. T. Burton, *The Artist's Ascunum; or, The Essence of a Variety of Useful and Entertaining Arts Carefully and Perspicaciously Laid Down, the Greater Part from Actual Experiment* (Stamford, England, 1812).

[4] Information supplied by F. duPont Cornelius.

[5] Information supplied by Mrs. E. Phillimore, Royal Ontario Museum.

ately after returning to Toronto in 1848. He nevertheless had to regret that his exhibition of sketches at the City Hall that year included no large works; they had not yet been completed. His first duty had been to paint fourteen canvases for Sir George Simpson, but they were only one step towards the hundred works since they were preliminary studies to be copied in replica later. The Simpson group was evidently finished at the close of 1849.[6]

By 1851 Kane had finished some of his planned group and eight canvases were exhibited that autumn at the Upper Canada Provincial Exhibition, in Brockville. He attended in person. Visitors picked him out as a celebrity wherever his striking face was seen in the crowds. The reviews were lengthy and lauded his work. One commented on the unique character of the Indian customs displayed, and on Kane's superb compositions which were sometimes "a little similar to some of Poussins." His inclusion of intriguing details, such as the prairie rose—an unfamiliar and "pretty wild flower"—in the foreground of the picture of the Indian horse race (Fig. 89), was a virtue. Above all, the fact that "there is not a fold of the robe, or plait of the dress, which has not been sketched from nature" was commendable.[7] Another writer, supporting acquisition of these canvases for future viewers, contributed this paragraph: "It is hoped that Canada may at some future day possess the entire collection of this great artist, which must be of great importance in a national point of view, as well as be the means of preserving memorials of these interesting tribes when they have entirely disappeared before the face of the white men."[8] This hope that his canvases would be purchased for the Canadian people was echoed in an article in the *Journal of Education for Upper Canada* the following spring. The author was almost certainly the journal's editor, Egerton Ryerson, a respected educationist who would be known as the father of a new provincial school system. This second comment went even further than had the previous one by suggesting that the paintings should form the nucleus for a "national picture gallery"; it would thus be possible to "secure them to the country, as well as gratify the patriotic desire of the talented artist."[9] The government showed no inclination to make a move in the direction suggested. It was already giving help to Kane.

This assistance by the government involved dealings which were to drag on for years. On July 26, 1850, a petition had been presented to the House of Assembly by Kane asking for financial aid so that he might paint up canvases from his hundreds of sketches; it would eliminate the necessity of his interrupting his painting of the west to undertake commissions and teaching in order to keep solvent.[10] Although such help was rather radical at the time, government subsidy to the arts and letters was not unknown. Kane probably was aware of Théophile Hamel's commission from the Canadian government to prepare portraits of leading legislative figures. It also granted money later to Abbé Léon Provancher to assist him with a first scientific illustrated work on Canadian flora (published in 1862). Similar assistance to scholars in the United States had been given by Congress and almost certainly Kane knew that Henry Schoolcraft had received money to prepare and publish his books on North American Indians. Kane had, indeed, purchased Schoolcraft's first volume. Catlin had made repeated attempts to persuade Congress to buy his Indian paintings. There was thus more than enough precedent for Kane's request for help.

Governments are not noted for hasty action. There was no decision about his petition. Next year it was revived under the joint sponsorship of J.-C. Taché and a Mr. Uniacke, and presented again on June 4, 1851.[11] Taché reported to Kane on the night of August 5 that the petition had been debated that day and he waxed eloquent about the praise which had been heaped on the artist:

This day, mark it, is a day of reward for your exertions as an artist. The Legislature of your country have eulogized you, the most eminent men have praised your talents. Two hours have been expended in exalting your talents and your energy. This is not flattery, this is the truth.[12]

Surely on no other occasion has a Canadian parliament spent two hours in eulogizing an artist. The grant was referred to a committee for consideration, and a parliamentary delegation which then called at Kane's studio was duly impressed by his work. Being of a practical turn characteristic of a legislature where prudent farmers and tradespeople held much power, members were aghast at paying out money without tangible return. (The Canada Council was still a century in the future.)

[6] See Appendix 10, Letter 17. The Simpson collection was later dispersed and the fate of the pictures is not known although it is thought the Coe Collection may have some.

[7] *Anglo-American Magazine* (Toronto), I, July–Dec. 1852, 371–74.

[8] *Canadian Agriculturist* (Toronto), III, 1851, 228.

[9] *Journal of Education for Upper Canada* (Toronto), V, June 1852, 95.

[10] Province of Canada, Legislative Assembly, *Journals*, 1850, p. 194. A letter of 1851 in the Kane family papers refers to his teaching.

[11] Province of Canada, Legislative Assembly, *Journals*, 1851, p. 49.

[12] Appendix 10, Letter 24.

The committee recommended that, instead of making an outright gift, the government should purchase twelve paintings for £500. They actually talked about half of this sum, but finally the larger amount was set aside by the Assembly. Lord Mark Kerr, Lord Elgin's aide, and himself an artist of some ability, called at Kane's studio with two other gentlemen. They chose twelve subjects, evidently from canvases already painted, and it was agreed that the artist should paint replicas for the government. The matter was settled by August 30 and Kane continued painting the hundred canvases of his western cycle without monetary worries.

Delivery of the canvases to the government was, however, delayed repeatedly. These were the years of wandering parliaments in the united province. Shortly after the commission had been given, the whole administration moved to Quebec, and without a reminder on his door step as it were, Kane did nothing about fulfilling his obligations. A note came in 1853 requesting that the canvases be sent to Quebec. Nothing was done. The government returned to Toronto in 1855: still no pictures had been sent. The Canadian commissioners for the great world's fair to be held in Paris during that year wanted the works commissioned by the government to hang in the Canadian displays, but, not having them, they were forced to borrow several from George Allan. He had purchased and received the entire set of one hundred canvases, which Kane had considered his primary task.

The selection of Kane's paintings for the Paris showing gave satisfaction in Canada although the rest of the Canadian display was bitterly criticized. One satirical reviewer pointed out that it might have been more appropriate to send a rural "outhouse" to Paris as a sample of Canada's architecture than to provide a vaunted model of Brock's Monument at Queenston as a sample of her progress in the arts. But the same reviewer felt: "It is a redeeming mercy that Paul Kane's fine pictures, have not been rejected by the 'inquest of taste.' He is almost the only artist, in the proper sense of the word, that Canada boasts of, and I cherish strong hopes that he is destined at once to immortalize himself, and do honour to the land of his nativity." [13] Better still, the canvases were well received by French critics. We do not know which paintings were sent to Paris except for the group portrait of the Blackfoot chiefs, which was singled out for special comment (Fig. 92 is a replica). Kane must have been highly gratified; he secured and kept the book published by the Canadian government which dealt with its participation at the fair and mentioned his canvases. [14]

The government, exasperated at what seemed to be deliberate stalling, now threatened to sue Kane for non-delivery. The artist appeared in person during May 1856 before a committee of the legislature and requested that it not resort to a lawsuit. He repeated his verbal representations in a letter dated May 21, admitting that he had anticipated that the commission would come up again, stating that he had begun the twelve works, and promising that he would soon have them completed. In justification of his actions he wrote that under a private agreement with the committee of 1851 he was excused from delivery of the paintings before he had published his book since any display of them would probably infringe his copyright. [15] Delivery of the canvases was indeed made shortly after this intervention by the government and Kane supplied extensive notes on the paintings. [16]

The twelve canvases hung in the Library of Parliament until 1879, when they were transferred to the Speaker's Chambers. By 1900 the collection was reduced to eleven. [17] Five were delivered to the National Gallery of Canada about that time and the balance were transferred to its collection in 1956. [18] Hamel's paintings have, however, been retained for display in the halls of the Houses of Parliament. The Kane canvases were thus among the first bought for what became the national collection and in a sense their purchase met Egerton Ryerson's suggestion although the group was only given to the National Gallery after many years.

George William Allan, who was Kane's patron and close friend in these years, had first met him in 1848. He was then a young lawyer, son of a leading Canadian capitalist and a man of broad interests. The breakfasts at which he was accustomed to entertain were famous and he indulged his more personal interests at the pleasant morning hour before commencing the day's business activities. He had studied art when he was a boy at Upper Canada College under Thomas Drury, Kane's old master, and his interest in art persisted; he was for a time president of the Ontario Society of Artists. Other activities mark him out as having been a remarkable man. He later became a fellow of the Royal Geographical Society of England, president of the

---

[13] *Anglo-American Magazine* (Toronto), VI, Jan.–June 1855, 298.

[14] *Canada at the Universal Exhibition of 1855*, printed by order of the Legislative Assembly (Toronto 1856).

[15] See Appendix 12.

[16] See Appendix 6.

[17] The canvas showing Boat Encampment had been lost. It has been stated that it was burned in a fire in the Parliament Buildings at Quebec in 1860.

[18] National Gallery of Canada, *Catalogue of Paintings and Sculptures*, III, 152–56.

Horticultural Society of Toronto, the Upper Canada Bible Society, the Toronto Conservatory of Music, and the Historical Society of Ontario. He was a Canadian senator from 1867 and Speaker of the Senate from 1888 to 1891.

Mrs. Allan Cassels, Allan's daughter, recalled Kane had been depressed in 1851 when the government agreed to buy no more than a few canvases, and threatened to set out again for the Pacific; he was only restrained by his coming marriage to Harriet Clench.[19] But his luck was about to change. Allan, who had been abroad for some time and had lost his young wife in Italy, returned to Canada in July 1852. Three months later his father also died and he inherited a sizeable fortune. Alone in the world, Allan now set out to indulge his interests. He commissioned family portraits from George-Théodore Berthon, the respected French painter then living in Toronto; he purchased water colours from Lucius O'Brien, a rising young artist who like Allan had attended Upper Canada College; and he came to Kane's rescue. He bought the entire cycle of one hundred western paintings on which Kane had been working so diligently and which were evidently virtually completed at this time,[20] together with the Indian curiosities which Kane had put in storage. The paintings cost $20,000 and this sum the artist frugally saved; his wife had a small inheritance on which they were able to live.

It was 1853 when Kane married and gave up his roamings. He was 44, and must have felt that he had spent long enough in contemplating his father's instructions not to take such a step until he had considered it thoroughly. His bride, Harriet Clench of Cobourg, was the daughter of F. S. Clench, the cabinet-maker whom Kane had known before he went to the United States in 1836. She must have been sympathetic to his work, since she was herself an artist of some quality who painted flower studies and occasional landscapes illustrating Ontario's pioneer period. With her she brought a substantial dowry, and evidently her father gave the young couple as a wedding present sufficient furniture from the Clench factory for their home. Much of it was black walnut. The artist's house was furnished with it at the time of his death, and it still graces the homes of the Kanes' grandchildren.

The paintings Kane sold to Allan hung at Moss Park, the stately Georgian home in Toronto into which Allan had moved following his father's death. There they remained until after his own death in 1901. Allan maintained a keen interest in Kane's paintings and ethnological material, and he himself gathered a number of objects of natural history and curios. These objects

were all arranged in the hall of his home and a large room known as "The Museum." The Indian artefacts and stuffed birds were a special concern, and when he was away he sent messages back from Ottawa and other places to Wiggins and Hogarth, his gardener and coachman. "Please see that they put camphor in the buffalo case and into the boxes with Paul Kane's things." "I hope the Indian dresses have been thoroughly overhauled. I am very much afraid of those confounded moths getting among my birds." "Has the Museum been smoked yet?" The Museum, as Mrs. Cassels recalls, was a constant source of pleasure to Allan and his family:

The extra fire, blazing in the Museum on a wintry Sunday afternoon, was a treat to all of us. While the elders gathered around the hearth, the children played together, inspecting "things" which were really a fearful joy when faced alone, such as the Indian scalp, or the flathead skull Paul Kane had risked his life to get. I am certain we were far more interested in the Indian portraits than in any of our forebears. And to be told off to "show the Museum" to a visitor was a matter of pride, and when it proved to be a good-natured, long-suffering one, a pleasure, at all events for us.[21]

Financial difficulties for the Allan family following the death of the Hon. George W. forced the sale of many assets. The Kane paintings were purchased by Sir Edmund Osler, who donated them in 1912 to the Royal Ontario Museum; its great collections were then being amassed with extraordinary speed by Dr. C. T. Currelly. Kane's dream that his paintings might be preserved intact in a public collection for the nation was thus partly realized. The ethnological collections were donated later by the Allan family to the Manitoba Museum of Science and History, and so these artefacts are now on the prairies where many of them had been collected.

Of the 100 canvases, 41 are single portraits of Indians representative of tribes scattered from the Great Lakes area to Fort Victoria on the distant Pacific. The heads are those of men and women about whom Kane tells dramatic tales—and they look the part. A second group illustrate Indian life and customs. The more colourful sides of the Indian culture are shown in pictures of the ritual pipe-stem dance on the prairies (Plate XXIII), the chaos of the buffalo hunt (Plate XVII), or the strange incantations of medicine men in the Pacific northwest (Figs. 190, 191). A third group is made up of landscapes, showing majestic scenes of nature and also forts and towns on the wilderness frontier.

[19] Royal Ontario Museum, Reminiscences of Paul Kane by Mrs. Cassels.

[20] Appendix 5 gives a list of the canvases turned over to Allan in 1856. Some substitutions were evidently made later.

[21] Reminiscences by Mrs. Cassels.

Kane's landscapes are never quiet pastorals suitable for dreaming poets, but rather depict settlements made famous by the activities of Hudson's Bay Company fur traders, or places with lively visual interest, such as the Kakabeka Falls portage (Plate XII), the storied rocks of the "Ki-use" maidens (Fig. 135), or Mount St. Helens in mysterious eruption (Plate XLI).

These canvases are based on the sketches completed in his four years of travel. Some are simply enlargements of them. Other, more elaborate compositions are assemblages created from several small sketches re-grouped for a large scene. *Winter Travelling* (Plate XXVI), for example, is based on studies of elaborately decorated dogs and of the new sled, and of trees heavily laden with snow (Figs. 100–103). All these elements were combined into a trial pencil sketch before the canvas was begun.

To appreciate the canvases fully, they must be contrasted with the preliminary studies in the sketches. It will be seen at once that the qualities of the sketches are not the same as those of the canvases painted from them. In the sketches picturesque subject-matter has been rendered with fidelity, and his honesty made a direct and forceful appeal to Kane's contemporaries, as has already been noted. Yet in painting the canvases Kane tried to make improvements over the sketches, and the result was a dichotomy between study and finished work.

The Chualpays scalp dance may serve as an example. The sketch (Fig. 127), despite its dramatic overtones, is handled with great objectivity. It has spontaneity and an immediacy of time and place. The approach is not photographic, but it is direct and perceptive, and results in what must have been an accurate picture of the event. The canvas based on the sketch (Fig. 129) has completely new subjective overtones which dissipate the compelling quality of the original. The many new elements introduced into the finished oil accentuate drama at the expense of truth. Camp fires cast a weird red glow over the ritual. Kane, as in other instances, has turned day into night. Overhead a crescent moon, with a wisp of cloud over its face, looks down on the frenzied dance. The shapes of houses, illuminated by unnatural light, provide an atmospheric stage set. The artist has accentuated stripes painted on the medicine man's body, and highlighted the dresses of the attendant maidens with additional colour touches. At one side is a group of friendly and evidently local Indians, who have brought the scalp of a Blackfoot as a present to the dancer. One of these men wears a Plains Indian jacket. Strangest of all, a beaded medallion on the breast of one man, which certainly accentuates the picturesque effect,

seems to be the design of a medallion of a Blackfoot who should be a thousand miles away from the spot. The ritual is actually celebrating the murder of one of his tribal brothers in a revenge slaying.

Further comparison of field sketches and canvases demonstrates that the fresh colouring which is one of the glories of the former is lost. Several reasons have been suggested for the lowering of the colour key in the transcription. An easy explanation would be that the duller powdered pigment Kane used in his studio could not match the brilliance of the tube colours he presumably carried on his travels. Or, when he was working indoors, did he forget how vivid the light effects could be in the clear Canadian atmosphere? Possibly he could not really credit the brilliance of his own field sketches. The French River canvas (Fig. 22) is dull indeed when placed beside the lively sketch (Plate III). What a sparkling canvas Norway House (Plate XVIII) could have made! Or, again, did Kane perhaps have some preconceived idea that great pictures were solid and dark like those of the old masters he had seen in Italian galleries, their surfaces subdued by layers of varnish? The uninspired colouring of Kakabeka Falls (Fig. 47) may be understandable; it was worked up from a pencil sketch without colour notes. The Allan family certainly regretted sometimes that Kane's trees were not greener and his skies bluer, and also noted that his browns and yellows did not improve with age.

Into many canvases Kane deliberately introduced neutral greys. Did he feel that grey would give a sense of unity and order to the finished canvas, that it would hold every element in its proper place and prevent any one colour from jumping out of the picture frame? We can only wish that he had transcribed to his canvas the colours used in certain portrait sketches so that we could assess the results. He did a series of striking head studies during his first year of field work in the Great Lakes region, and the backgrounds are in stimulating yellow, orange, rich brown and green. These are not backgrounds based on nature directly but are suggestive of sun on landscape. The broken but brilliant splashes of colour have much emotional appeal. The study of Now-on-dhu-go (Plate VIII), an Ottawa Indian from Lake Michigan, is particularly noteworthy. The background sparkles with the pure atmospheric colours of the Impressionists; if the technique had been followed on a large scale, it could have catapulted Kane into the ranks of those preparing for the Impressionist movement soon to sweep France. But instead, in most of his portrait canvases, he preferred to substitute a neutral grey or another dull tone for the colours of his sketches.

And why are there so many cloud banks in the landscape canvases? They hide the clear and exhilarating blue prairie sky. Had Kane seen too many Dutch marines in Europe?

However we must not be too unkind. The Canadian art critic of Kane's day would have found his canvases eminently satisfactory, and indeed an improvement over the field studies. Tastes change, and although today we demand the fresh and colourful, a direct copy of nature was not completely satisfactory to the mid 19th century connoisseur. Then taste demanded that nature should be reconstituted to give a "breadth of effect," an attitude which is well stated by a critic writing about the exhibition of the Ontario Society of Artists held in 1873. He notes:

Some . . . were charming studies, evidently finished on the spot. Though in reference to this it may not be out of place to remark that, while the study of nature cannot be too strongly inculcated, yet a sketch from nature, and a finished picture embodying the earnest and oft renewed study of nature, are not to be confounded without misleading results. . . . But we may remark that some of the larger water-colour drawings betrayed only too much evidence of being done on the spot. They had plenty of accuracy of detail, very valuable as artistic study; but wanted the breadth of effect which is needed to make a picture. Photography will give the detail of the landscape under any light and shade, and from any point of view; but the art of the true artist is required to bring his accumulated study of nature to bear on this subject; just as the poet makes "a thing of beauty" out of what seems homely and prosaic to the common eye.[22]

Kane, by his own standards, felt that his canvases were factually truthful, yet certain embellishments he added to the subject-matter shown in the sketches can cause some dismay. His oil sketch of Coe-coosh or "The Hog" (Plate IX), a Fox River Potawatomi, emphasizes the Indian's painted face, his ugly scowl and his disreputable robes. In the canvas, Coe-coosh has the same red face, but is wearing an elaborate roach on his head (which, indeed, Potawatomi sometimes wore), brooches of trade silver in his hair (and many Indians of the Fox River did wear such brooches), and has a quite respectable buttoned jacket. The old scoundrel has become rather a romantic individual, and his appeal to the eye has been enhanced. Is Kane being completely truthful? Certainly all of the articles added come from the Fox River region, but is this canvas still Coe-coosh?

Variations of this kind between sketches and canvases are numerous. There is an exquisite and refined water colour sketch of a Sioux chieftain (Plate XV). In the canvas (Fig. 58) he dons a handsome embroidered robe which he had not worn in the water colour study. Some stage props came from the artist's ethnological collection and whether this is really a Sioux robe is problematical. Mah-Min, chief of the Assiniboin, met at Rocky Mountain House, is dressed up for the canvas (Fig. 109) with another roach, a club which may not even come from the prairies, a quiver slung over his back, and a beaded jacket. The bear's claw necklace, which was in the sketch and which he gave to Kane, is still around his neck. How does the Otisskun of the canvas acquire his red calumet pipe? Such elaborations add to the picturesque and romantic effect of the larger paintings; yet despite the fact that Kane had seen all these articles at some time in his wanderings, his re-assembly for artistic effect creates conundrums for ethnologists.

Kane's old difficulty in judging proportions correctly reappears in the canvases and was the reason for numerous alterations. One Métis woman in his *Half Breed Encampment* (Fig. 64) he reduced from an eight-foot Amazon to more reasonable proportions. Canvases at Moss Park were retouched frequently. Kane called, usually during breakfast, to take one after another away for alteration; this activity caused continual anxiety to the owner who was apprehensive as to whether the retouching would result in a real improvement.

A number of commentators, including Charles W. Jefferys, have condemned Kane's fine blood horses, descendants of Arabian stallions, suggesting that more lowly beasts would be in keeping with the probable mounts of prairie Indians.[23] On the other hand, some suggest that a certain elegant bearing for prairie horses is correct since they descend from horses imported by the Spanish into Mexico. Indian chiefs were proud of their special horses. Catlin describes how a chief overheard a man criticizing one of his horses in a painting for not having more common lines; the Indian was enraged, saying his horse was of excellent breeding; he would not ride except on the best of steeds.

Kane had constant trouble in sketching moving objects, and so seemed unable to set down wildly charging horses or buffalo while the action occurred. Yet hunting scenes, horseback races, even armed fights, were among the most colourful subjects in the west, and so, feeling obliged to include them, he fell back at times on the ready-made compositions of others. He describes in his book two Assiniboin whom he had seen riding across the prairie in hot pursuit of a buffalo, but apparently he did not sketch them at the time. Back in Toronto he looked at a book of Italian engravings, which had a plate picturing Italian youths

---

[22] *Canadian Magazine and National Review* (Toronto), III, 1873, 545.
[23] See *Wanderings of an Artist* (1968 ed.), pp. xliii–xliv.

on superb steeds chasing an Italian bull, with their lances raised. By transforming the young Italians into Assiniboin Indians, the bull into a buffalo, and putting open prairie beneath the horses' feet, Kane recreated with great *éclat* the hunt he had seen south of Edmonton. (See Figs. 105, 106.) Ironically this apocryphal composition has been the favourite of ethnologists when choosing illustrations demonstrating Indians hunting on the prairie.

A few, possibly not more than half a dozen, other paintings by Kane are based on engravings or paintings of other artists. "The Man that Always Rides" (Plate XX) has a pose used repeatedly by Catlin but whether Catlin's work suggested the rearing horse is uncertain. The same stance was used by Velazquez long before and by Gros and Delacroix in Kane's own era. Most strange and interesting of all Kane's borrowings is his first attempt in the series on the great buffalo hunt. He had not previously dealt with any subject on this scale, and in any case had no time to set down the hunt directly for he was on a horse revelling in the chase. When he did tire of riding and got out his sketchbook, it was to make quick pencil notes of a single dangerously wounded bull, and he nearly lost his life doing so (Fig. 68). He later searched for some kind of precedent to help him record the crowded and busy scene. His first interpretation (Plate XVII), which he must have made on his return to camp that evening, is related to an English sporting print where horses are riding to hounds. This obviously would not quite do! He tried again from another angle. The new sketch (now lost) went off to Sir George Simpson, who wrote to him about it disapprovingly:

In taking the sketch of the buffalo hunt you were good enough to send me last year, you must have stood in the rear of the herd; a side view would have given a better idea of the appearance of the animals, as from the hind view, it required a little explanation to make a stranger understand that the mass of dark objects before him, were intended either for buffalo or any other living animals.[24]

Kane repainted the subject. This time his composition is a detail of the herd viewed from the side (Fig. 67). The whole could be handled more successfully in that way in order to give an immediate feeling of the drama in the swiftly moving mass.

Whatever regrets we may have about Kane's departure from his sketches in painting his canvases, it is still true that they are an important contribution to our knowledge of the frontier of his day. Together, the sketches and canvases form an immense

and striking panorama of the west and present the Indian and his life in all their variety. That panorama made an impression on everyone who saw it: the man in the street, a newspaper editor, a contemporary Canadian artist. The *Anglo-American Magazine* published in 1853 a view by Lucius O'Brien of an Indian scene at Twelve Mile Creek between Hamilton and Niagara Falls. In explanation, the magazine noted: "We give this plate for the double purpose of illustrating a scene in Indian life and of laying before Canadian readers of the present generation a glimpse of the past, a sight which, though now rare to their eyes, was to their fathers common." [25] Kane's depiction of the frontier west fulfilled both these purposes for succeeding generations.

V. *Wanderings of an Artist*

Kane was penniless and hungry for acclaim when he returned to Toronto from his western explorations. He needed money simply for food and he also wanted recognition for his four years of hardship in the wilderness. His paintings would be admired and discussed in due course, but a book about his travels might bring in royalties and would also tell a wider public about his exploits and the Indians whom he held in such high regard. George Catlin's *Letters and Notes on the Manners, Customs, and Condition of the North American Indians* had been a phenomenal success. By 1848 it had already been reprinted several times, had made for Catlin a good deal of money, and had secured his niche in history.

Within a week after reaching home, Kane wrote to Sir George Simpson in Montreal about how best to publish such a book. Presumably one reason for approaching Sir George was that he had recently published an account of his own voyage around the world. Simpson replied, recommending the subscription method as a good one, and promising to persuade his friends to subscribe for copies. He offered some additional practical advice, suggesting that Kane visit nearby towns, obtain portrait commissions to assist with his expenses, and at the same time secure signatures for copies of the projected volume.[1] Kane would have none of this; he was determined to devote all the time he had for painting to completing his Indian canvases.

Sir George went further. By means of a friend, he arranged

[24] Appendix 10, Letter 12.
[25] *Anglo-American Magazine* (Toronto), III, 1853, 17.

[1] Appendix 10, Letter 16.

Plate VII. Mani-tow-wah-bay or "He-Devil," an Ojibwa, Lake Michigan. Glenbow-Alberta Institute, Calgary; crIII-88.

Plate VIII. Now-on-dhu-go, Ottawa chief, Lake Michigan. Stark EOP27; CrIII-89.

for John Russell Bartlett to write to Kane from New York. Bartlett, an American, had spent much time in the southwest and knew many people interested in science. He suggested that Kane approach the Smithsonian Institution in Washington which would probably print his book and engrave the plates for illustrations. The Smithsonian paid nothing for manuscripts but allowed authors a handsome fee for supervising publication of their own books. *Ancient Monuments of the Mississippi Valley*, he said, had been printed in this way. Kane's book would then be distributed free to all parts of the world and he would become a celebrated personality. The Smithsonian even gave the used type to authors for publication of a second edition at the author's expense, and writers often made a good thing out of sale of the reprints.[2] But Kane did nothing about these various proposals. The book after all had not yet even been begun.

The writing of *Wanderings of an Artist* apparently proceeded hand in hand with his painting. The first evidence that part of it had been completed came in 1855 when on March 14 Kane delivered a paper on the Chinook Indians before the Canadian Institute, of which he was a member. This paper, virtually unaltered, became a chapter of his book. Two other papers were read at Institute meetings in 1855 and 1856. The three lectures, and supplementary material for the first one, were published by the Institute in its journal and that on the Chinook Indians also appeared in the *Daily Colonist*.[3]

Kane's narrative is based on his field notes which at times he follows word for word.[4] Personal spellings in the original were, however, corrected judiciously for publication with, for instance, "ice" replacing "ise," "fright" for "frite" and "country" for "cuntry." But the original diary has been expanded with extracts from his field logs of landscapes and portraits and by numerous stories and legends about various Indians he had met. Some of these are involved tales and it seems curious that he made no notes in reference to them while he was travelling; one might even wonder whether a few may have been taken from other books (no borrowings have been traced). Several travel books dealing with the American Indians were gathered by Kane, presumably for research purposes but also probably to give him some idea of the style of writing he should use; a few dealt with tribes he had visited.[5] His book when completed was a straightforward narrative depending for interest on its information and description rather than on literary pretensions. On at least one occasion he seems to have taken liberties with fact. This was in connection with the buffalo hunt near Fort Garry in June 1846, and concerns an incident between the Métis and Sioux. Kane's

field journal puts it two years before his trip, an early manuscript version of the book says that it occurred a year before; in the printed book Kane sees it happen.[6]

Whether Kane approached a publisher before 1858 is uncertain, but in that year he decided to go in person to London. George W. Allan was visiting there at the time, and Allan's brother-in-law, John Henry Lefroy, who had returned from duty in Canada, was in England too. Both offered to assist in arranging details with a publisher. Kane also approached Sir George Simpson at Lachine before he sailed. Sir George sent a letter to William G. Smith, secretary to the Hudson's Bay Company, asking Smith to introduce Kane to various members of its board with the request that they give him all possible help. In doing so, he noted that Kane had not only always been personally grateful for assistance given him, but had also defended the Company against the many attacks being made on it in these years; it could be anticipated that his book, which would likely appeal to a wide audience because of its illustrations, would similarly favour the Company.[7] Board minutes of the Hudson's Bay Company during March 1858 do indeed note that "Mr Paul Kane" should be "cordially received and encouraged."[8] A famous Company man, "Bear" Ellice, formerly a Montrealer, evidently was particularly helpful to him.

Frederick A. Verner, who would later paint the west, and Kane's portrait, and who was an admirer and friend of the

---

[2] Kane family papers, Bartlett to Kane, October 25, 1848.

[3] Paul Kane, "Incidents of Travel on the North-West Coast, Vancouver's Island, Oregon &c.: The Chinook Indians," *Canadian Journal* (Toronto), July 1855, pp. 273–80; "Notes of a Sojourn among the Half-Breeds, Hudson Bay Company's Territory, Red River," *ibid.*, 1856, pp. 128–38; "Notes of Travel among the Walla-Walla Indians," *ibid.*, pp. 417–24; "The Chinook Indians," *ibid.*, 1857, pp. 11–30. "The Chinook Indians," *Daily Colonist* (Toronto), August 6–9, 1855.

[4] Kane kept a journal during his 1846–48 expedition. It commences with an entry dated May 9, 1846, and ends on September 12, 1848. He evidently intended that it should be a daily diary, but there are gaps, some of them for weeks at a time, for instance when he was staying at Fort Vancouver in the winter of 1846–47. This journal contains much of what is now in *Wanderings*, with variations in minor details; significant variations are given below in the notes to the text of that book.

[5] Books which he owned personally include: Ross Cox, *Adventures on the Columbia River* (New York 1832); *A Narrative of the Captivity and Adventures of John Tanner* (New York 1830); J. Mackintosh, *The Discovery of America, by Christopher Columbus; and the Origin of the North American Indians* (Toronto 1836); Henry Schoolcraft, *The Indian and the Wigwam: Personal Memoirs of a Residence of Thirty Years with the Indian Tribes on the American Frontiers* (Philadelphia 1851); Sir George Simpson, *Narrative of a Journey round the World during the Years 1841 and 1842* (London 1847); Sir John Richardson, *An Arctic Searching Expedition* (London 1851); Sir George Back, *Narrative of the Arctic Land Expedition to the Mouth of the Great Fish River . . . 1833, 1834 and 1835* (London 1836); W. L. Stone, *Life of Joseph Brant* (New York 1838).

[6] *Wanderings of an Artist*, p. 70 below.

[7] Hudson's Bay Company Archives, D4/54, Simpson to Smith, February 25, 1858.

[8] L. J. Burpee gives an account of Kane's activities in London in his introduction to the 1925 edition of *Wanderings of an Artist*; see the 1968 reprint, p. xl.

pioneer artist, recalled when himself an old man the troubles which Kane had in arranging publication.[9] It has to be remembered, of course, that he wrote about them more than half a century after the incidents he was recalling and his memory was possibly no longer as sharp as it might have been. Verner asserted that immediately on his arrival in London Kane took his manuscript to the Longman firm. He also said that twelve paintings (perhaps those bought by Sir George Simpson, although the number is neither the fourteen ordered by him nor the ten listed as delivered) were exhibited for the Royal Family at Buckingham Palace during 1858. True, it was quite usual for exhibitions of colonial paintings to be arranged for the monarch. Commander Inglefield's water colours of the Canadian Arctic with his little ship dwarfed by great icebergs were viewed by Queen Victoria at Windsor, the collection being arranged in the corridor for her inspection after lunch. But the daily diary at Buckingham Palace for 1858 contains no reference to such an exhibition and it seems a bit of fantasy.

Verner stated that six months after Kane arrived overseas he was still waiting for a decision about acceptance from the publisher. He then called at the Longman office for what he thought would be the last time. Longman opened a large room, its shelves filled with manuscripts, and remonstrated: " 'How is it that you expect me to look over yours when none in this collection is looked at yet?' Kane's reply was, 'I am independent of the world. Give me my manuscript. I am returning to Canada.' " But the fame of Kane's paintings had now reached high places in London. The publisher had by this time heard independently of his celebrated expedition. Kane was asked to return the following day, and publication was then arranged. The final version of his manuscript was retained by the publishers, only to be burned during the London blitz of 1940. An early version was kept in Toronto and it is this version which is now held by the Stark Foundation.

Wanderings of an Artist among the Indians of North America appeared in 1859, the British price being 25/–. James Bain, Toronto bookseller, was the Canadian agent, and his prospectus, dated January 3, offered copies at $5.50 each. It gave details of the chapter headings and described the twenty-one illustrations, eight of them chromo-lithographs. It suggested that the mass of information on the western Indians would be doubly welcome and valuable "in view of their hunting grounds being broken up by the whistle of the locomotive, as it opens up a highway between East and West." [10]

The book was an immediate success, not least because of the coloured lithographs made from Allan's canvases and the wood engravings from sketches which were scattered through the text. The principal reviews dwelt at length on the assumption that the Indians would soon be extinct through contact with Europeans.

Daniel Wilson praised the volume in a Toronto publication. He commented that although the work was not strictly a literary creation it presented a "soul-stirring journal of adventures and strange perils" recorded in a way which brought out all the writer's striking detail, his "discriminating perception," "the felicitous pencillings of his sketch-book, and all the rich colouring of his portfolio." Naturally, since he was himself interested in ethnology, Wilson emphasized the account of aboriginal characteristics in the life of these primitive peoples as an important aspect of the work. He castigates the publisher, however, for the chromo-lithograph *Half-Breed Cree Girl* which appeared as a frontispiece (this was Cun-ne-wa-bum whom Kane had met in Fort Edmonton at the Christmas dance); he had noted in the original canvas an exceedingly interesting illustration of the blending of white and Indian features, but reproduction removed every trace of the Indian features in a desire to produce the engraver's idea of a pretty face. Wilson adds that it might just as well have been the face of a wax doll.[11]

The London *Athenaeum* noted that the author of the book, an "American," had devoted himself to an American purpose, sketching and recording the deeds and outward form of an unhappily vanishing race.[12] Then this over-romantic reviewer changed to a poetic vein, likening the Indian to the snowdrift which melts and disappears forever. It is a typical touch of heavy Victorian sentiment. The reviewer hoped that Kane's example would be followed: "It is well that ere it fade, some lover of the Red Man who, like Mr. Kane, can strap his portfolio and paint-box on his back, should fill a bullock's horn with powder, and taking his rifle in his firm hand, stride on board the snorting steam-packet at Sturgeon Bay in Lake Huron." Kane's allusions to the Flatheads struck the reviewer as a happy opportunity for criticizing a London monument he evidently disliked: the Flathead chief, he said, must have somewhat resembled the statue of George III in Cockspur Street.

The most scholarly review occupied an impressive twenty-

[9] *Ibid.*, p. xli.
[10] Ontario Archives, *Prospectus of Wanderings of an Artist among the Indians of North America, by Paul Kane* (Toronto, January 3, 1859).
[11] *Canadian Journal* (Toronto), 1859, pp. 186–94.
[12] *Athenaeum* (London), July 2, 1859, pp. 14–15.

three pages in the *Revue des deux mondes*, reflecting the interest of a large number of French scholars and philosophers at this time in primitive peoples.[13] Lavollée, the author of the review, introduced his essay with yet another dissertation on the vanishing American Indian.

One must make haste to visit the Red Men. Their tribes, not long since still masters of a whole world, are disappearing rapidly, driven back and destroyed by the inroads of the white race. Their future is inevitable. Perhaps before a century has passed, the last Indian of North America will have returned to the abode of the Great Spirit: an unfortunate race which, after having lived and multiplied in barbarism, has been stricken to death by contact with civilization! In the United States, the territories assigned to the Indians are being depopulated on a frightening scale; it is the same in British North America. It is not that the white race wishes at any price to dominate and exist alone on these immense regions, which could easily support both the old and the new masters of the American continent. Originally, in the first keenness of conquest, when the European pioneers were bent upon acquiring land, there were undoubtedly numerous acts of violence; but today, inspired by more humane ideas, the administration of the United States and the British government are making praiseworthy efforts to maintain the Red Men, to civilize them by religion and by work. Honour and interest alike bid them protect the tribes, who have been successively deprived of vast spaces, sterile in their hands. Unfortunately there are inexorable laws. The Indians are doomed; their fate will be that of so many primitive races now gone. Let us leave to the ethnographers and the philosophers the task of learned discourse on these great human revolutions and of pronouncing the funeral oration for peoples who have disappeared. On this occasion it is a question simply of describing from nature, while there is still time, some of the features of the life and character of the Red Men, of making a short excursion into the midst of tribes who live, under English rule, in the territories between Canada and the Pacific Ocean.

Lavollée goes on, after a brief reference to Chateaubriand and Cooper, to give a detailed summary of Kane's book, which he describes as not being a literary or scientific work, but valuable as a record of all the artist had seen. The reviewer mentions especially the gathering of the tribes for the treaty ceremonies on the Great Lakes, the portages across to the prairies (with the wistful reminder in their place names of the era of the French), the Métis, the great buffalo hunt, Kane's ways of securing the portraits he wanted, the rigours of the mountain passes, the customs of the Flatheads and Chinooks, the salmon fishing on the Columbia River, the holiday festivities at Fort Edmonton and the wedding, the efforts of a variety of missionaries to spread their faiths. He gives a full rendition of the mournful and romantic tale of the Indian chief who having lost his last

and most loved son asked to be buried alive with him. His abridgement of the book concludes with an elegy for the Indian which, like the one in the *Athenaeum* review, makes use of the snows of the northern world for an analogy. Now that the railway and the search for gold are going to bring more and more whites to the west, he writes, the Indian will be driven far to the north, to the eternal ice of the pole:

there, having cast aside his useless snares and shot his last arrow into empty space, hoping only for the hospitality of the Great Spirit, he will lie down upon the snow, which will soon cover him as with a shroud, and, with him, a whole race will have disappeared forever from the face of the earth.

The English language edition of *Wanderings of an Artist* sold out completely, and within the next four years three foreign language editions appeared. A French edition, evidently pirated, was printed in 1861; it omits Kane's name as author and is without illustrations. A Danish edition was published in Copenhagen in 1861. The most elaborate of the foreign editions, in German, was issued in parts beginning in 1860; later these parts were reissued as a complete volume,[14] with 4 new colour plates and 62 black-and-white illustrations; many of these 62 engravings were fantasies of some romantic European artist's imagination. All the early editions are now collectors' items, with the foreign language copies scarce indeed. The English edition was not reprinted until the twentieth century.[15]

An unfortunate rupture in the friendship of Sir George Simpson and Paul Kane resulted from the publication of his book. The author chose to dedicate *Wanderings of an Artist* to the Honourable George Allan in tribute to his benefactions. Simpson was highly offended, demonstrating a rather petty annoyance and even a certain vindictiveness. In 1861 Kane was considering a sketching trip to the Labrador. Possibly he may have

---

[13] Charles-Hubert Lavollée, "Un artiste chez les Peaux-rouges," *Revue des deux mondes* (Paris), 1859, pp. 963–86; translation by present author. The original French text for the two quotations from Lavollée's review will be found in an addendum at the end of this section of Part One.

[14] *Les Indiens de la baie d'Hudson, promenades d'un artiste parmi les Indiens de l'Amérique du Nord . . .* (Paris, Amyot, 1861), trans. Edouard Delessert. Paul Kane, *En Kunstners Vandringer blandt Indianerne i Nordamerika fra Canada til Vancouvers O og Oregon, gjennem Hudsons-Bai-Kompagniets Territorium* (Kjobenhavn, F. H. Eibes Forlag—Louis Kleins Bogtryferi, 1863), trans. J. K. Paul Kane, *Wanderungen unter den Indianern Nordamerikas von Canada nach der Vancouvers Insel und Oregon* (Leipzig, Schrader, 1860); *Wanderungen eines Kunstlers unter den Indianern Nordamerikas von Canada nach der Vancouvers Insel und nach Oregon* (Leipzig 1862), trans. Luise Hauthal.

[15] See the introductory note to the text of *Wanderings* reprinted below. Some Canadian schoolchildren learned Kane's name. Lesson LXXII on pp. 194–96 of J. Douglas Borthwick's *The British American Reader* (Montreal 1860) was "The Flat-Head Indians" by Paul Kane.

been planning to accompany Henry Youle Hind as artist in his proposed expedition to that region, which took place the next year.[16] Kane's old spirit was revived with the thoughts of sketching other Indian tribes "in their native habitat" and on March 21 he wrote to Donald Smith (later Lord Strathcona), then a Hudson's Bay Company factor at the north shore post of Mingan along the Gulf of St. Lawrence. Kane asked whether Smith would make any facilities available to him, adding that "as I had the misfortune to incur the Governor's displeasure, I understand that he has given orders that I was not to be countenanced by any officers in the service."[17] He explained that his offence was in neither giving paintings to Simpson (actually Simpson had requested an account from Kane for the pictures), nor dedicating his book to him. Kane did not go with Hind; instead Hind took with him next spring his brother, William G. R. Hind, whose superb illustrations decorate the book in which Henry describes the Labrador.

Kane contemplated one further publication: a book of illustrations which would include both landscapes and studies of Indians. The idea probably came again from one of Catlin's volumes, for the latter had brought out a book of magnificently engraved plates of North American Indians in 1844.[18] Kane proposed as his title "Pictorial sketches with Historical notices taken during two journeys across the continent of America to the Columbia River and North West Coast of the Pacific in the years 1845, 1846, 1847 and 1848, by Paul Kane." He started work on the text, which he evidently intended should consist solely of explanatory notes, a paragraph accompanying each plate. Much of the material in the text he prepared is simply a duplication of what had already been published in *Wanderings of an Artist*.[19] The book was never published.

Addendum: Passages from Lavollée's review of *Wanderings of an Artist*

Il faut se hâter de visiter les peaux-rouges. Ces tribus, naguère encore maîtresses de tout un monde, disparaissent rapidement refoulées et anéanties par l'invasion de la race blanche. Leurs destins sont marqués. Avant un siècle peut-être, le dernier Indien de l'Amérique du Nord aura regagné le séjour du Grand-Esprit: race malheureuse qui, après avoir vécu en se multipliant dans la barbarie, s'éteint frappée de mort au contact de la civilisation! Dans les États-Unis, les territoires assignés aux Indiens se dépeuplent dans des proportions effrayantes; il en est de même dans l'Amérique anglaise. Ce n'est point que la race blanche veuille à tout prix dominer et exister seule sur ces immenses régions, qui pourraient aisément nourrir les anciens et les nouveaux maîtres du continent américain. Dans l'origine, aux premières ardeurs de la conquête, lorsque les pionniers européens se sont précipités sur le sol, il y eut sans doute de nombreux actes de violence; mais aujourd'hui, sous l'inspiration d'idées plus humaines, l'administration des États-Unis et le gouvernement britannique tentent de louables efforts pour conserver les peaux-rouges, pour les civiliser par la religion et par le travail. L'honneur et l'intérêt leur commandent de protéger ces tribus, qui ont été successivement expropriées des vastes espaces demeurés stériles entre leurs mains. Malheureusement il y a des lois fatales. Les Indiens sont condamnés; ils auront le destin de tant de races primitives aujourd'hui disparues. Laissons aux ethnographes et aux philosophes le soin de disserter savamment sur ces grandes révolutions humaines et de prononcer l'oraison funèbre des peuples qui s'en vont. Il s'agit simplement ici de décrire d'après nature, quand il en est temps encore, quelques traits de la vie et du caractère des peaux-rouges, de faire une courte excursion au milieu des tribus qui habitent, sous la domination anglaise, les territoires compris entre le Canada et l'Océan-Pacifique.

Repoussé par l'invasion européenne, abruti par les spiritueux que lui apporteront les blancs, l'Indien remontera vers le nord, il fuira jusqu'à ce qu'il se trouve acculé aux glaces éternelles du pôle; là, après avoir jeté ses inutiles filets et lancé dans le vide sa dernière flèche, n'espérant plus que dans l'hospitalité promise par le Grand-Esprit, il se couchera sur la neige, qui l'aura bientôt couvert de son linceul, et, avec lui, toute une race aura disparu à jamais de la surface de la terre.

VI. The Later Years

Kane's days as a wanderer sketching in far places were not to be repeated. He settled down in Toronto, meeting occasionally with friends and leading generally a sedentary life. The Honourable George Allan described him as being at this time 5 feet 11 inches tall, with a particularly keen memory, vivid in description of the curious and distant things he had seen, and with "somewhat of the quiet, unimpressible manner of the Indians, among whom he had spent some of the most eventful years of his life."[1] He had a dignity about him that even a child could

[16] Henry Youle Hind, *Explorations in the Interior of the Labrador Peninsula, the Country of the Montagnais and Nasquapee Indians* (London 1863).

[17] Beckles Willson, *The Life of Lord Strathcona and Mount Royal* (London 1915), pp. 108–09.

[18] George Catlin, *Catlin's North American Indian Portfolio: Hunting Scenes and Amusements of the Rocky Mountains and Prairies of America* (London 1844).

[19] The manuscript which Kane prepared for this second volume is in the collection of the Nelda C. and H. J. Lutcher Stark Foundation. Much of it merely duplicates portions of *Wanderings of an Artist*. An occasional note about sketches is new, and appropriate additions from this new material have been made in Appendices 1 and 2.

[1] Daniel Wilson, "Paul Kane, the Canadian Artist," *Canadian Journal* (Toronto), May 1871, p. 72. This article is based largely on a memorandum supplied by Allan to Wilson.

feel, and he made a strong impression on one of the Allan children. "There was still that look of observation in his eyes, as he turned them upon you, and I remember well the tones of his gentle, rather grunty voice, saying what he had to say, with few words, in a very pleasant cultivated accent."[2] His face, pock-marked since youth, was a kind face. He was much respected by all who met him.

The Kanes lived during their early married years on Jarvis Street in Toronto and then built a house for themselves at 56 Wellesley Street (the location is marked today with an official plaque); it was named "Miss-qua-Kany Lodge," and Mrs Kane lived here until her death in 1892. Across the street lived Captain O'Brien, father of the artist Lucius O'Brien. The Kane home, graced with fine solid furniture, had engravings on the walls, and Kane's own copies of paintings by Murillo, Leonardo da Vinci and Raphael, and of a martyrdom of St. John the Baptist, and a copy too of the portrait of himself by his friend Verner. His large library displayed a remarkable breadth of interest.[3] Kane had become a man of standing in Toronto, then a busy young city. He had four children, two sons and two daughters. The younger boy attended Trinity College School, Port Hope, where Ontario's leading citizens sent their sons. Young Kane and the Honourable George Allan's son were companions, with a common interest in natural history. The older son, Paul, moved to Manitoba in the 1880s.

Remarkably few canvases other than compositions based on his western sketches were painted after Kane's return to the east in 1848. His canvas self-portrait, showing a cultivated young man, has the pinkish flesh tones of a face that has not been exposed for four years in the wilds and it must date from just before he set out for the west. Portraits of James Richardson (Fig. 9), a newspaper editor originally from Cobourg, of Mayor George Gurnett of Toronto (Fig. 8) and of one or two others can be no later than 1851 and must have been painted during the years when he was worrying about finances and before he received the government commission. He considered Joseph Brant's portrait as one of his obligatory hundred subjects; it may be based on an engraving of an A. E. Ames portrait of Brant used as a frontispiece in W. L. Stone's *Life of Brant*[4] (Kane owned this book); on the other hand, it may be based on a portrait by Catlin who in turn seems to have based his work on the engraving. Curiously, Kane copied a Cornelius Krieghoff painting of a French-Canadian notary that had been done in 1848; are there perhaps circulating today other copies by Kane of canvases which masquerade as Krieghoff originals? An oil of

Niagara Falls, probably from some sketch made on a holiday excursion (Fig. 12), is the single known canvas with local subject-matter.

Most unusual of all his later canvases (it can no longer be located) was a re-creation of *Columbus Meeting the Indians on His Landing at San Salvador*. Three ships are in the harbour and the woods are alive with hundreds of Indians peering from every forest tree at the white man as he sets foot on the soil of the New World for the first time.[5] He has departed from his usual factual approach, with his painting based solidly on his own experience, and moved into the realm of imagination. There is one possible explanation for such a radically new direction. Kane had exhibited some paintings of the west at the Upper Canada Provincial Exhibition in 1852. These were entered for competition as "historical" works but the judges contended that on the contrary they were "contemporary" in subject-matter. One reviewer, probably Henry Youle Hind, in discussing the question reiterated the current belief that historical paintings were the highest form of art:

It was clearly a misapprehension of the nature of the subject matter required, and not a want of power, which occasioned this disappointment —we shall hope to see, upon a future occasion, that the spirit stirring incidents of the last war,[6] and the great events which have marked the social progress and constitutional history of the country, have found their fitting expositor in the first native artist of Canada. Considering, however, that historical painting is the highest branch of art, we must remark that the prizes offered are wholly insufficient to tempt an artist capable of executing such a subject to sacrifice time which might be given to easier and more romantic employment.[7]

Is the "Columbus" perhaps Kane's answer to Hind's comments? If so, he remains consistent with his interests by conjuring up a historical painting in which Indians appear, and indeed setting them in the context of the event from which the troubles of the American natives arose.

A remarkable aspect of Kane's later years was the degree of his devotion from 1849 to 1859 to cultivation of his western

[2] Mrs. Cassels, in her Reminiscences of Paul Kane, in the collection of the Royal Ontario Museum.

[3] See Appendix 9.

[4] W. L. Stone, *Life of Joseph Brant—Thayendanegea* (New York 1838), frontispiece.

[5] The painting may be based on a description of the landing of Columbus in a book owned by Kane: J. Mackintosh, *The Discovery of America, by Christopher Columbus; and the Origin of the North American Indians* (Toronto 1836).

[6] The reviewer is presumably referring to the War of 1812–14 rather than the rebellion of 1837 in the Canadas.

[7] *Canadian Journal* (Toronto), 1852, p. 52.

project through painting and writing. Nothing whatever was allowed to interfere. The Toronto Society of Artists, on the president's motion, invited him to become a member in March 1849. Three days later, signing himself somewhat facetiously as "Paolo Canoe," he declined the honour; since "all my time and means are devoted to one particular object, it is impossible for me to give that attention to the interests of the Society which it deserves without great personal inconvenience to myself." [8] Sir Sandford Fleming, inventor of standard time and promoter of intellectual and scientific interests in Toronto, invited him to design a vignette for the new Canadian Institute; he did not reply to the invitation. His only indulgence was to accept an appointment in 1852 as a lieutenant in the Second Toronto Independent Artillery Company of the militia. Paintings were sent to the Upper Canada Provincial Exhibitions from 1850 to 1857, but possibly only to help the promotion of his book and to present to the public some visible results of his travels. Then, with his main body of works completed and his book published, and his eye trouble beginning, he lost interest in promotion and ceased exhibiting. He apparently even refused to talk about subjects that did not interest him, although on matters with which he was familiar he was a lively conversationalist. To be photographed in front of his ethnological specimens delighted him; he even dressed in some of the costumes he had collected and, holding his gun, took up somewhat romantic poses.

This routine of living was interrupted when in 1856 the short-lived lithographic firm, Fuller and Benecke, was established at the Victoria House, Toronto. Kane supervised in that year the colour work for the firm's reproduction of "The Death of Big Snake," said to be the first large coloured lithograph made in Canada (Fig. 90). It was printed at a time when Cornelius Krieghoff was bemoaning the lack of high quality prints in Canada. Krieghoff had sent his own paintings for lithographic reproduction to Munich in 1849, and to Philadelphia in 1866. He complained about the high tariff and wrote to the Canadian minister of finance requesting its removal as an incentive to greater importation of quality prints. He deplored the country's lack of good drawing masters and of collections of good prints and ornaments; as a result, he wrote, no wonder that "our young men should be drunkards and our girls flirts." [9] The lithograph of Kane's work was evidently not a commercial success; the experiment was not repeated.

During these years Kane developed an intimate friendship with Daniel Wilson who in 1853 had been appointed Professor of History and English Literature at University College, To-

ronto. In his native Scotland Wilson had been interested in Scottish archaeology, but in Toronto his attention turned to prehistory in general. Wilson's *Prehistoric Man* is a pioneer Canadian ethnological study.[10] Repeatedly and at length the author drew from Kane's experiences among western primitive peoples, and on them based many of his conclusions. He paid handsome tribute to Kane's help in the book. Throughout it he also introduced illustrations based on Kane's sketches, and on at least one other occasion, in a book on Indian pipes, had used sketches for reproduction.[11] Good friends, Wilson and Kane conversed on matters in which they had "mutual interest."

Tragically, Kane did not develop a new approach to painting with the passage of time. *Wanderings of an Artist* appeared in 1859 and the consuming fire which had burned in him for fifteen years died down. He scarcely touched a brush after that date. Kane had had his due of praise, and without new paintings to maintain their interest, the public gradually began to lose sight of him in the bustle of Canadian expansion. Possibly his thought of a Labrador trip was his last struggle to reawaken his creative urge. He began to complain that "Canada was no place for an artist." It seems quite likely that his health was beginning to fail, and there is a comment that as a result the good companion of the hearthside was beginning to "turn into a bear with a sore head." He gave up his studio in the 1860s. Growing blindness, first noticeable in 1859, began to cut him off from other people. Smallpox had left his eyes weak, but he felt that snow blindness suffered during the crossing of the Brenner Pass in Switzerland and the glare of the sun in the high passes of the Rocky Mountains during his western tour were contributing factors. The loss of sight increased his sense of isolation.

Frederick Verner, who would assume Kane's mantle as a painter of the prairie Indians and the buffalo, was a companion during this time. Years before, when Verner was merely a boy, he had knocked at Kane's studio door; he had requested drawing lessons, and the door closed abruptly in his face without a word of explanation. Now, after Verner had returned to Canada from Italy in 1862, he struck up a friendship with the aging artist. Verner had had his own adventures, as a red shirt in Garibaldi's army assisting in the liberation of Italy. He painted a portrait of Kane and later made two replicas. Kane is pictured

[8] Kane family papers, Kane to John Johnson, March 6, 1849.

[9] J. Russell Harper, *Painting in Canada: A History* (Toronto 1966), pp. 129, 130.

[10] Daniel Wilson, *Prehistoric Man* (Cambridge 1862). Wilson became Sir Daniel in 1888.

[11] *Pipes and Tobacco, an ethnological sketch* (Toronto 1857).

as a rather venerable old man with reddish hair and beard, and wearing the diamond stickpin given to him as a young man by some close friend when he was in Rome. Those who knew Kane declared that he was a much more attractive individual than the rather flat "Cossack" face painted by Verner would indicate. Certainly he is not, in this painting, anything like the colourful man of the Toronto photographs (Fig. 1).

Paul Kane died on February 20, 1871. An obituary preserved by his family has in its conclusion an attractive picture of his later years:

During the last few years Mr. Kane had led a very retiring life. He was very fond, however, of the water, and during the summer months seldom failed to make a daily visit to the island, returning regularly by the last ferry boat in the evening. He was a general favourite with all those who had the pleasure of his acquaintance, and he will be long remembered not only on account of his great talents as an artist, but on account of his goodness of heart and upright character as a man. He was only a few hours ill—having been out of the city on the morning of the day he died.

In her bereavement, his widow borrowed some of her husband's sketches from Mr. Allan, "for sentimental reasons." They were returned later and are a part of those in the Royal Ontario Museum.

Daniel Wilson paid eloquent tribute to Kane in the detailed biographical study which he prepared for the *Canadian Journal*.[12] He mentions how unusual Kane's career had been for its day:

In the midst of this conflict between the artless rudeness of savage life, and the progressive energy of the Anglo-Saxon colonist, young Paul grew up from boyhood, with few external influences calculated in the slightest degree to stimulate artistic tastes, or to direct his attention to the study of Indian manners and customs.

He points out also that despite the fact that the Indian, in debasement, now haunts the new centres of civilization, Kane had felt an intense interest in his life as a free man and had devoted much of his career to recording that life. In conclusion Wilson comes back to the perseverance with which Kane had pursued his laudable ambition:

His published narrative is a modest, but interesting and vivid description of novel scenes and incidents of travel; and his career is a creditable instance of the pursuit of a favourite art, by a self-taught artist, in spite of the most discouraging impediments to success.

In 1882, thirty-two years after Kane's western travels concluded, Lucius O'Brien was travelling with his brother Henry in the foothills of the Rockies. He had become the first president of the new Royal Canadian Academy in 1880. The railway predicted by reviewers of Kane's book in 1859 had not yet completely linked the east with the west but it was under construction. The O'Briens had gone to Chicago by rail and then went on by horseback to the mountains. Lucius had been much interested in Kane during his youth. He himself had painted Indians both as "Lords of the Forest" and in other roles. Here in the Rockies, he and Henry, a mission worker, were travelling from one Indian camp to another. On August 7 they were proceeding up Rosebud Creek when they met an old chief. As they had done at many another such meeting, they inquired whether he had known Paul Kane. The old chief, after a pause, said he remembered the painter of the past and described him correctly.[13] The man with the fierce red beard had made a deep impression on the memory of the Indians, and the sketching hand which had given him in their eyes something of the power of a medicine man had in turn ensured that many of them would not be forgotten far into the future.

---

[12] "Paul Kane, the Canadian Artist," *Canadian Journal* (Toronto), May 1871, pp. 66–72.

[13] Henry O'Brien, manuscript journal for the Rockies, 1882, collection of Mrs. J. A. Grant.

Paul Kane
1846

Coo-Coosh.

a Potawatomie Indian

The Hog- Potawatomie

Plate IX. Coe-coosh or "The Hog," a Potawatomi, Fox River. Stark EOP30; crIII-126.

PART TWO   *Wanderings of an Artist*

A NOTE ON THE TEXT

The text of *Wanderings of an Artist* printed here is that of the original edition published in London, England, in 1859 by Longman, Brown, Green, Longmans, and Roberts, except that it omits the Appendix; this was the only complete edition published in English in Paul Kane's lifetime. A second edition, in which the text differs from that of the first edition in minor details, was published by the Radisson Society of Canada in 1925; it contained an "Editor's Foreword" by John W. Garvin, and Introduction and Notes by Lawrence J. Burpee, and two lists ("Catalogue of Paintings by Paul Kane in the Royal Ontario Museum of Archaeology, in Toronto" and "List of Pictures Purchased for the Legislative Council"). This second edition, reprinted by offset, was published again in 1968 by the Charles E. Tuttle Company, Inc., and M. G. Hurtig Ltd., with an "Introduction to the New Edition" by J. G. MacGregor.

Enclosed within square brackets at relevant points in the text are cross-references to plates and figures printed in the present volume and to entries in its *catalogue raisonné* (thus the reference crIII-2 indicates item 2 in section III of the *catalogue raisonné*). The 1859 edition had 21 illustrations to which Kane refers in his narrative; the *catalogue raisonné* identifies these.

The footnotes to the text are intended to serve two purposes. Some identify persons mentioned by Paul Kane in the text or provide further information about events recorded there. The majority present variations from the printed text of *Wanderings* which are to be found in two manuscripts, in the possession of the Nelda and H. J. Lutcher Stark Foundation of Orange, Texas. These manuscripts are (1) a journal, in Kane's hand, which he kept from 1846 to 1848 and on which a part of the published text is based; (2) a version of the *Wanderings*, in his wife's hand, which was revised further before publication. Both manuscripts show numerous minor variations from the printed version, but only significant ones are recorded here. References to the journal are introduced by the abbreviation "kj" and to the manuscript version of *Wanderings* by "kwms." The 1859 edition of *Wanderings* had three footnotes, and these are incorporated into the present numbering system and identified by the abbreviation "w59." Kane's spelling in kj has been modernized.

Wanderings of an Artist

AMONG THE INDIANS OF NORTH AMERICA
FROM CANADA TO VANCOUVER'S ISLAND
AND OREGON THROUGH THE HUDSON'S
BAY COMPANY'S TERRITORY
AND BACK AGAIN

By Paul Kane

TO

GEORGE WILLIAM ALLAN, ESQ.

OF MOSS PARK, TORONTO, CANADA WEST

This Work

DESIGNED TO ILLUSTRATE THE MANNERS AND CUSTOMS OF THE

INDIAN TRIBES OF BRITISH AMERICA

Is Respectfully Dedicated

AS A TOKEN OF GRATITUDE FOR THE KIND AND GENEROUS INTEREST

HE HAS ALWAYS TAKEN IN THE AUTHOR'S LABOURS,

AS WELL AS A SINCERE EXPRESSION OF ADMIRATION OF THE

LIBERALITY WITH WHICH, AS A NATIVE CANADIAN,

HE IS EVER READY TO FOSTER CANADIAN TALENT AND ENTERPRISE.

Toronto: July 9, 1858.

Preface.

On my return to Canada from the continent of Europe, where I had passed nearly four years in studying my profession as a painter, I determined to devote whatever talents and proficiency I possessed to the painting of a series of pictures illustrative of the North American Indians and scenery. The subject was one in which I felt a deep interest in my boyhood. I had been accustomed to see hundreds of Indians about my native village, then Little York, muddy and dirty, just struggling into existence, now the City of Toronto, bursting forth in all its energy and commercial strength. But the face of the red man is now no longer seen. All traces of his footsteps are fast being obliterated from his once favourite haunts, and those who would see the aborigines of this country in their original state, or seek to study their native manners and customs, must travel far through the pathless forest to find them. To me the wild woods were not altogether unknown, and the Indians but recalled old friends with whom I had associated in my childhood, and though at the commencement of my travels I possessed neither influence nor means for such an undertaking, yet it was with a determined spirit and a light heart that I had made the few preparations which were in my power for my future proceedings.

The principal object in my undertaking was to sketch pictures of the principal chiefs, and their original costumes, to illustrate their manners and customs, and to represent the scenery of an almost unknown country. These paintings, however, would necessarily require explanations and notes, and I accordingly kept a diary of my journey, as being the most easy and familiar form in which I could put such information as I might collect. The following pages are the notes of my daily journey, with little alteration from the original wording, as I jotted them down in pencil at the time; and although without any claim to public approbation as a literary production, still I trust they will possess not only an interest for the curious, but also an intrinsic value to the historian, as they relate not only to that vast tract of country bordering on the great chain of American lakes, the Red River settlement, the valley of Sascatchawan, and its boundless prairies, through which it is proposed to lay the great railway connecting the Atlantic and Pacific Oceans, through the British possessions; but also across the Rocky Mountains down the Columbia River to Oregon, Puget's Sound, and Vancouver's Island, where the recent gold discoveries in the vicinity have drawn thousands of hardy adventurers to those wild scenes amongst which I strayed almost alone, and scarcely meeting a white man or hearing the sound of my own language.

The illustrations—executed from my sketches, or finished paintings, for the purpose of illustrating the present work—constitute only a few specimens of the different classes of subjects which engaged my pencil during a sojourn of nearly four years among the Indians of the North-west. In that period I executed numerous portraits of chiefs, warriors, and medicine-men of the different tribes among whom I sojourned, and also of their wives and daughters. The Indian fishing and hunting scenes, games, dances, and other characteristic customs, also occupied my pencil; while I was not forgetful of the interest which justly attaches to the scenery of a new and unexplored country, and especially to such parts of it as were either intimately associated with native legends and traditions, or otherwise specially connected with the native tribes—as their favourite fishing or hunting grounds, the locations of their villages, or the burying-places of the tribes. The whole of these sketches are now in my possession, and I have already been honoured by a commission to execute a series of paintings from them for the Legislature of the Province of Canada, which now have a place in the Library of the Provincial Parliament. A much more extensive series of oil paintings had been executed by me, from my sketches, for George W. Allan, Esq., of Moss Park, the liberal patron of Canadian art; and I would gladly indulge the hope that the present work will not prove the sole published fruits of my travels among the Indian tribes of North America, but that it will rather be a mere illustration of the novelty and interest which attach to those rarely explored regions, and enable me to publish a much more extensive series of illustrations of the characteristics, habits, and scenery of the country and its occupants.

PAUL KANE

51

Chapter I.

Departure from Toronto.—An Indian Village.—The "Big Pike's" Likeness.—The Chiefs of Saugeen.—An Island Labyrinth.—The Encampment.—An Indian Kettle of Fish.—The Household Drudge. —Manetouawning.—Anecdote of the Chief Sigennok.—The Egyptian Sphynx on Indian Pipes.—A Serenade.—The Conjuror.—The Power of Love.—The Escape.—Heraldic Devices.—Departure for the Sault St. Marie.

I left Toronto on the 17th of June 1845, with no companions but my portfolio and box of paints, my gun, and a stock of ammunition, taking the most direct route to Lake Simcoe. Thence I took the steamboat for Orillia; and crossed over to Sturgeon Bay on Lake Huron, where I had to hire an Indian with a canoe, the packet having left for Penetanguishene a few hours before I reached "Cold Water." After paddling all night, we overtook her the next morning at Penetanguishene, or the "Rolling Sand Bank," which is seated in a deep bay, forming a secure harbour for vessels of any amount of tonnage: it has been so named by the Indians from a high bank of rolling sand at the entrance of the bay. There is a small naval depôt here, and a steamer is employed in making trips of inspection round the lake and its shores. A larger one has been for some years laid up in ordinary, and is no doubt now unfit for use. Besides this depôt, there is a village inhabited by a few whites and half-breeds.

We left Penetanguishene on the 20th, and arrived at Owen's Sound the same evening. I here met with three men bound for Saugeen, about thirty-five or forty miles west of this place, where a council of chiefs was to meet for the purpose of negotiating the sale of a tract of land to the Provincial Government.[1] After engaging an Indian to carry my pack and act as guide, I started in company with them on foot. Our journey was a disagreeable one, through woods and swamps, the rain all the time coming down in torrents. We had to encamp at night supperless, and without shelter of any kind, in our wet clothes, as we had omitted to bring blankets or provisions under the expectation of reaching Saugeen the same evening. We made an early start the next morning, and arrived there about noon, where we found a large assemblage of Indians holding a camp meeting, with its usual accompaniments of boisterous singing and praying, under the superintendence of six or seven Methodist preachers.

The Indian village of Saugeen, meaning "the Mouth of a River," contains about 200 inhabitants (Ojibbeways). It is the site of a former battleground between the Ojibbeways, as usually

pronounced, or Chippawas, and the Mohawks. Of this, the mounds erected over the slain afford abundant evidence in the protrusion of the bones through the surface of the ground. The land hereabouts is excellent, but only a small part is cultivated, as the inhabitants subsist principally on fish, which are taken in great abundance at the entrance of the river. They also kill hundreds of deer by erecting a fence of brushwood many miles in extent, behind which the Indians conceal themselves; and as the deer, in their annual migrations, are seeking an opening through this fence, they fall a prey to the unerring aim of the red man. I sketched the principal chief, named Maticwaub, or "the Bow."[2] [crIII-1] The band of which he is the head chief forms a part of the great nation of the Ojibbeways, which still inhabits the shores of Lakes Huron, Michigan, and Superior. [Fig. 14; crIII-2, 3] There is also another large band of them on the upper Mississippi, 90 or 100 miles above the falls of Saint Anthony; they speak the same language; their medicine dances, called Matayway, and their feasts are in every respect the same, identifying them as one and the same people, although scattered so widely apart. Another branch of them, called the Pilleurs, is found some 200 or 300 miles farther north. They derive their name from their thievish propensities, and richly deserve it, as I unfortunately experienced some few years afterwards on visiting their country.

I also took a sketch of a chief named Maskuhnoonjee, or the "Big Pike." [Figs. 15, 16; crIII-4, 5, 6] This man was very proud of having his likeness taken, and put on his chief's medal presented by the Government to those they acknowledge as chiefs. I have never known a chief to barter away one of these marks of distinction, which they seldom wear on unimportant occasions. An interesting girl, the daughter of a chief from Lake St. Clair, gave me much trouble in prevailing on her to sit for her likeness, although her father insisted upon it; her repugnance proceeded from a superstitious belief that by so doing she would place herself in the power of the possessor of what is regarded by an Indian as a second self. [Fig. 17; crIII-7, 8,

[1] According to the report of the Indian Commissioner for 1845 (in the Public Archives of Canada, RG10, vol. 612), chieftains from St. Clair, Huron, Ontario, Simcoe, Rice and Mud lakes attended the Saugeen meeting; the purpose of the meeting differs from that assigned by Kane. The objective of the Indians is given as formulation of plans by which the Saugeen lands could be held for the sole benefit of the "Ojibwa Nation," the petitioning of the government for aid in establishing a manual labour school, and the sounding out of chieftains about formation of one large settlement at Owen Sound for the various groups. The Bruce Peninsula, in which Saugeen was located, was to be ceded to the British government on October 31, 1854.

[2] KWMS states that Kane sketched not only Maticwaub but also three or four subordinate chiefs and other members of the tribe.

8a] Wāh-pūs, "the Rabbit," also permitted me to take his portrait. [Fig. 18; crIII-9, 10, 11] He resides at Owen's Sound, and was formerly as much renowned for his unconquerable fierceness and intemperance as he is now for his temperance and wisdom. This change in his character is attributable to the influence of the Methodist missionaries, whose church he has joined. He was the first Indian I had seen whose hair had been pulled out, all except the scalp-lock; this custom is common amongst many tribes of Indians, though not universal amongst any.

I remained at Saugeen about ten days,[3] residing in the family of an Indian who had been educated as a Wesleyan missionary.[4] I then returned to Owen's Sound, accompanied by a young man named Dillon, who was extremely desirous of joining in my excursion. [Fig. 19; crIII-12] On arriving at the Sound I bought a canoe and a stock of provisions, and embarked with my new companion for Penetanguishene in our route for the Manitoulin Islands. On the fourth day we passed Christian Island, on which are still standing the ruins of a fort, said to have been built by two Jesuit priests who took refuge on the island with a large band of Hurons, after they had been defeated by the Iroquoisin. They defended the fort until they were nearly all destroyed by hunger and disease, when the missionaries led the survivors to Quebec.[5] The day after passing this island we again reached Penetanguishene, where we obtained a fresh supply of provisions, after which we threaded a labyrinth of islands of every size and form, amounting, as is said, to upwards of 30,-000;[6] and both being strangers to the navigation, we continually lost ourselves in its picturesque mazes, enchanted with the beauty of the ever-varying scenery, as we glided along in our light canoe. We fished and hunted for fouteen days, almost unconscious of the lapse of time so agreeably spent. We saw only two or three Indians, the greater part of them having preceded us to Manetouawning to receive their presents.

Sketch No. 1 [crIII-18] represents an Indian encampment amongst the islands of Lake Huron; the wigwams are made of birch-bark, stripped from the trees in large pieces and sewed together with long fibrous roots; when the birch tree cannot be conveniently had, they weave rushes into mats, called Apuckway, for covering, which are stretched round in the same manner as the bark, upon eight or ten poles tied together at the top, and stuck in the ground at the required circle of the tent, a hole being left at the top to permit the smoke to go out. The fire is made in the centre of the lodge, and the inmates sleep all round with their feet towards it. [Fig. 20; crIII-13 to 21] These lodges are much more comfortable than one would at first suppose from their loose appearance—that is, as far as warmth is considered. The filth, stench, and vermin make them almost intolerable to a white man; but Indians are invariably dirty, and it must be something very terrible indeed which will induce them to take half an hour's trouble in moving their lodge. As to removing the filth, that is never done. Their canoes are also made of birch-bark stretched over a very light frame of split cedar laths; the greatest attention being paid to symmetry and form. [crIII-23] They travel a great deal and are often exposed to rough weather in these boats, which, being extremely light, are carried across "portages" with ease.[7] They make their mohcocks, or kettles, of birch-bark, in which they cook fish and game. This is done by putting red hot stones into the water, and it is astonishing how quickly an Indian woman will boil a fish in this way. The Indians round Lake Huron raise a good deal of corn, which is dried and then pounded in a sort of mortar, made out of a hollow log, as represented in the sketch. [crIII-22]

The Indians in this neighbourhood having a direct communication with the whites, use guns and other weapons of civilized manufacture, bows and arrows being seldom seen except with the children. [Fig. 21; crIII-24] As amongst all other tribes of North American Indians, the women do all the household work, carrying wood, putting up lodges, and cooking. I here noticed a custom amongst the women bearing a curious resemblance to the ancient usages of the Jews. At certain stated periods they are not allowed the slightest intercourse with the rest of the tribe, but are obliged to build a little hut for themselves a short distance from the camp, where they live entirely secluded until their return to health.

[French River: Pl. III, Fig. 22; crIII-25, 26]

Previous to entering the bay of Manetouawning, we put ashore on one of the Spider Islands, to escape from a heavy shower, where we found a single lodge. [Pl. IV; crIII-27 to 31] A woman and her two children were there, but the men were off in the distance fishing, which is the principal occupation

---

[3] KJ says he remained for a week.

[4] This was Richard Conway, an Indian born on the Rice Lake reservation near Peterborough, Ont.

[5] KJ gives what was evidently a local legend: that the Chippewa had been attacked by the Potawatomi and 8,000 Chippewa had gone to the island. The published version has the correct story.

[6] KJ puts the number at 2,700.

[7] W59: "It would be as well to note here that the word *"Portage"* is applied to such places as require the canoes to be taken bodily out of the water and carried up the ascent by the men, and *"Discharge"* to such shallows or rapids as will not allow the canoes to pass without being considerably lightened or entirely emptied, and then pulled or dragged by cord over the difficulty."

of the Indians hereabouts in summer, there being very little game, except occasionally a bear or deer, and, at particular seasons, ducks. The afternoon being clear, I had a fine view of the La Cloche Mountains, and spent the remainder of the evening in sketching. [Fig. 23; cRIII-32 to 37]

Manetouawning is situated at the extremity of a bay six miles long, in the great Manetoulin Island, and is 200 miles distant from Penetanguishene by the route we took.

The word Manetouawning signifies "the Spirit Hole." The village consists of forty or fifty log-houses built by the Provincial Government for the Indians. [cRIII-38] There is a mission, with a church and pastor, an Indian agent, a doctor, and a blacksmith, all paid by the Government. I found nearly 2000 Indians here,[8] waiting the arrival of the vessel that was freighted with their annual presents, comprising guns, ammunition, axes, kettles, and other implements useful to the Indian. [Fig. 24; cRIII-39, 40]

The principal chief here is Sigennok; he is an acute and intelligent Indian; he is appointed to distribute to his tribe their due share of the presents annually consigned to them. [cRIII-42] He receives a salary from the British Government as interpreter. This is paid him from policy, for although useless as an interpreter, from not speaking the English language, his natural eloquence is such that he possesses great influence over his tribe; indeed, it is to the untiring volubility of his tongue that he owes his name, which signifies "The Blackbird." The following anecdote, illustrative of character, was related to me by Captain Anderson, now superintendent of Indian affairs:—Sigennok was, in his younger days, in the continual habit of drinking to excess, and when under the influence of his potations was a perfect maniac, and only to be controlled by main force; but as the attempt to place him under due restraint was attended with no small personal danger, on account of his Herculean strength, it was the custom of his attendants to increase the amount of stimulus, and ply him with it until he became insensible, rather than expose themselves to danger from his ungovernable violence. One day, when in this state of drunken stupor, Captain Anderson—who at that time filled the post of Indian agent,—saw him lying in front of his lodge in one of these fits of oblivion, and bound him hand and foot with strong cords, placing a sickly decrepit boy to watch

over him, with instructions to hasten to him (Captain Anderson) the moment the sleeper should awake, and by no means to let him know who it was that had bound him. After some hours he revived, and angrily demanded of the boy, who had dared to treat him with such indignity. The little fellow, without replying to the inquiry, hobbled away to the captain: he at once hastened to his prisoner, who put the same interrogatory to him as he had before done to the boy, and furiously demanded his instant liberation. The captain replied that the boy had bound him by his own orders, and that he had lain for hours exposed to the derision of the whole camp. He took the opportunity also of commenting forcibly on the disgrace to which so great a warrior had thus subjected himself, merely to gratify a vile and disgusting propensity, which reduced him manifestly beneath the level of the brute beast, which never sacrificed its reason, or the power to protect itself from annoyance or insult from its fellows.

Sigennok, his pride humbled, and greatly mortified at the degraded position in which he had placed himself—in the power, as it were, of the most helpless of his tribe—formed the prompt resolution of at once and for ever abandoning his favourite habit, and promised Captain Anderson that if he would release him from his bonds, he would never again taste ardent spirits. The captain took him at his word, and unbound him. Twenty-three years had elapsed since the occurrence, during which Sigennok had never been known to violate the promise then made.

Sketch No. 2 [Fig. 29] represents Awbonwaishkum. [cRIII-53, 54] This head possesses the characteristics of the Indian to a striking degree: the small piercing eyes, high cheekbones, large mouth, protuberant and hanging lips, are strongly indicative of the race. This chief is a man of great ingenuity and judgment. The sketch No. 3 [Fig. 30] is that of a pipe carved by Awbonwaishkum out of a dark-coloured stone, his only tools being an old knife and broken file. [cRIII-55] I leave it to antiquaries to explain how the bowl of this pipe happens to bear so striking a resemblance to the head of the Egyptian sphinx. I questioned Awbonwaishkum as to whether he knew of any tradition connected with the design, but the only explanation he could offer was, that his forefathers had made similar pipes with the same shaped head for the bowl, and that he therefore supposed the model had always existed among the Indians.

Strolling one evening in the vicinity of the camp, I heard the sound of some musical instrument, and upon approaching the performer, who was lying under a tree, I found that he was playing on an instrument resembling a flageolet in construction,

Plate X. Sioux Scalp Dance (Fort Snelling). ROM912.1.15; crIII-144.

Plate XI. Chief from Fort William (Maydoc-game-kinungee, an Ojibwa). ROM912.1.16; crIV-2.

but much softer in tone. This instrument is principally used by lovers, who play for hours in the vicinity of their mistress's lodge. I have often listened with pleasure to this music, as its simple and plaintive notes stole through the stillness of the forest. The lover made no secret of his object, but conversed with me freely upon the subject of his love.

The Indians assemble annually at Manetouawning from all parts of the shores of Lakes Huron, Nipissing, and Superior, as well as from all the neighbouring islands. [Figs. 27, 28; crIII-43, 46 to 52, 57 to 60] On the arrival of the presents, the Indians, male and female, accompanied by their children, immediately seated themselves in rows on the grass, each chief heading his own little band, and giving in their number and names to Sigennok, who here appears in his proper element, dividing the goods among them with great impartiality. [Fig. 25; crIII-41] He is really a very useful man. His voice is heard everywhere above the universal din of tongues, his native eloquence is unceasing, and seems to have the effect of allaying every envious and unpleasant feeling, and keeping all in good humour and proper order.[9]

Among the numerous Indians assembled here, was one that particularly attracted my attention from his venerable and dignified appearance. In reply to my inquiry, as to who he was, I learned that he was called Shawwanossoway, or "One with his Face towards the West," and that he was a great medicine-man, skilled in the past, present and future. [Fig. 26; crIII-44, 45] As I happened to lose, some days previously, some articles from my tent, I resolved, for the sake of an introduction, and the gratification of my curiosity, to apply to the seer. On laying my case before him, he told me that his power was of no avail wherever the pale faces were concerned, and, notwithstanding my offer of a very liberal remuneration, I could not prevail upon him to put his incantations into practice. He had been, I was told, a celebrated warrior in his youth, but that owing to a romantic incident, he had abandoned the tomahawk and scalping-knife for the peaceable profession of the medicine-man, or, in common parlance, the necromancer or conjuror, in which he has obtained great repute among his people.

[9] According to the report of the Indian commissioner (see note 1), the following presents were handed out on this occasion: 149 yards of blue and grey cloth, 227½ yards of caddies, 942½ yards molton, 747½ yards blue or grey ratteen, 1,975⅓ yards stroud, 102 yards Irish linen, 2,630 yards printed calico, 570 one-point blankets, 240 one and half-point blankets, 250 two-point blankets, 794 two and half-point blankets, 646 three-point blankets, 22 twilled cotton shawls, 1,128 oz. sewing thread, 5,760 sewing needles, 1,440 horn combs, 1,440 awls, 1,440 butcher knives, 1,360 lb. tobacco, 1,326 lb. ball, 4,590 lb. shot, 1,972 lb. gunpowder, 2,652 flints.

There dwelt many years before, on the shores of one of the great lakes, a band of Ojibbeways. Among them was a family consisting of a father and mother, with a grown-up son and daughter, the latter named Awh-mid-way, or, "There is music in her footsteps:" she exceeded in beauty the rest of the tribe, and was eagerly sought in marriage by all the young warriors of her nation. It was not long before Muck-e-tick-enow, or, "Black Eagle," renowned for his prowess in battle and the chase, had, by his assiduities, won her undivided affections; nor did she conceal from him this favourable state of her feelings, but, in accordance with the customs of her people, she had unhesitatingly extinguished the blazing bark which he had sent floating down the stream that glided past her lodge, and thus acknowledged him as her accepted lover. Confident of possessing her heart, he directed all his endeavours to the propitiation of her parents, and eagerly sought how to compensate them for the loss they would undergo in relinquishing a daughter so dearly loved. For this purpose he departed on a long and distant hunt, and while straining every faculty of his mind and body in collecting trophies and presents wherewith to conciliate them, and show his entire devotion to the object of his adoration, their evil destiny brought Shawwanossoway, then a great war chief, in all the pride of manly strength and vigour, to their camp, on his return from a war excursion, in which he had greatly distinguished himself, and spread his fame far and wide, as the terror of his enemies and the boast of his friends.

Having heard of the transcendent charms of Awh-mid-way, he presented himself before her, girded with the scalps of his enemies, and loaded with other trophies of victory. No sooner did he behold her, than, overcome by her charms, he devoted himself to her service and endeavoured, by every art that the most passionate love could dictate, to win her regard. He recounted the numerous battles he had won, the enemies he had slain: he displayed the reeking scalps he had torn from the defeated enemy,—warriors who had been the terror of his nation: he named the many chiefs who had sued to him for peace, and at the same time plied every artifice to win the good-will of her parents, who, proud of what they considered their daughter's superb conquest, listened to him with delight, and urged her, by every persuasive argument, to accept so distinguished a chief as her husband, expatiating on the honour such an alliance would confer on their family. Constant, however, to her first love, she turned a deaf ear to all the protestations of his rival, whose tales of conquest and bloody trophies only excited her abhorrence.

But, nothing daunted, and determined to win her, either by fair means or by foul, Shawwanossoway persevered in his suit, trusting to time and accident to attain his object. The poor girl, now made truly wretched by his undeviating persecution, accompanied by the menaces of her parents, who were determined to conquer what they regarded as the rebellious obstinacy of their child, at length came to the resolution of appealing to the generosity and honour of her persecutor, and, in the hope of propitiating his forbearance, in an evil hour she confessed her long-cherished affection for Muck-e-tick-enow. He no sooner discovered the cause of her rejection of his suit, than rage and jealousy took full possession of his heart, and plans of vengeance rapidly succeeded each other, until he decided on the assassination of his rival. Having learned from his unsuspecting charmer the route her lover had taken, he tracked him, and came up with his camp, and, concealing himself from observation, crawled towards the fire, where his victim sat alone preparing his evening repast, and shot him from behind a tree. Hiding the body among some brushwood, he took possession of the game of his murdered rival as a means of accounting for his own absence, and hastened back to the village, where he renewed his suit more ardently than before, to the utter disappointment and distress of Awh-mid-way who still rejected all his overtures with indignation, until, urged by the positive commands and threats of her parents, she at last, hoping by some artifice still to put off the evil day, consented to name a time when she would receive him as her husband, trusting that her lover would in the meantime return and rescue her from the impending sacrifice, and concealing, as well as she could, her increasing aversion to her persecutor.

The dreaded day at last, however, arrived, but no lover of course returned. Little did she think that his mangled remains had fallen a prey to the ravenous beasts of the forest—for still hope fondly directed her gaze in the direction she had seen him take at his departure, when all was sunshine and prospective happiness. With aching eyes and a bursting heart she saw the evening approach that was to bind her irrevocably to one she abhorred.

The bridal canoe which, according to the Indian custom, had been prepared with all the necessary stores to convey the betrothed pair on a month's excursion together, which is, in fact, the only marriage ceremony, was already lying upon the beach. Night had come—the nuptial feast was prepared—the last she was to partake of in her father's lodge—when lo! the bride was missing, and consternation usurped the place of gaiety in the bridal throng. Eagerly did they seek her with torches and shouts through the neighbouring forests, but no answering sound met their ears, although the search was continued with untiring eagerness till daylight. Then, for the first time, it was discovered that the bridal canoe was gone, and, concluding that the bride had availed herself of it to aid her escape, Shawwanossoway, accompanied by her brother, started in pursuit on foot, following the direction of the shore.

After proceeding for several hours, they caught sight of the canoe and its fair occupant in the distance. Increasing their speed, they reached a point which the canoe must necessarily pass round. Here the lover swam out, hoping to intercept it. In vain did he endeavour, by every means he could devise, to induce her to stop and take him on board. Defeated by her resolute refusal and the vigour and skill with which she plied her paddle, he was obliged to relinquish the pursuit and return to the shore. He had scarcely landed, when a violent storm, accompanied with thunder, lightning, and heavy rain, compelled the pair to encamp for the night. Notwithstanding the tempest, she continued her efforts until the shades of night hid her from their view. The clouds dispersed with the dawning day, and they continued their pursuit until they at length espied the canoe lying on the shore. Thinking they had at last attained their object, they quickened their steps; but, on coming up to it, they encountered a troop of wolves, and their horror may well be conceived on discovering the remains of the being they loved almost wholly devoured, and only to be recognised by her torn and scattered garments. With aching hearts, they carefully gathered her cherished remains, and, placing them in the canoe, returned to the camp, where she was wept and mourned over for many weeks by her disconsolate relatives and friends, and buried with all the ceremonies of her tribe.

It was evident that the heavy storm had driven the canoe ashore, and it is probable that her materials for kindling a fire having become soaked with water, she had been debarred the only means of protecting herself from these ravenous animals.

Shawwanossoway was so much grieved at the misery which his ungovernable passions had brought upon the object of his warmest love, that he formed the resolution of abandoning his warlike pursuits; and, throwing up the tomahawk to the Great Spirit, that it might be employed only as an instrument of justice, he took in its stead the rattle of the medicine-man; nor did he ever after act inconsistently with his altered character.

Six miles from Manetouawning is another village called Wequimecong, comprising fifty or sixty houses, and a Catholic mission with a church.[10] I made a sketch of the principal chief, named Asabonish, "the Racoon," and his daughter. [Fig. 33; crIII-63] He belongs to the tribe of Ahtawwah Indians. This tribe is now scarcely distinct from the Ojibbeways, with whom they have numerously intermarried, and speak the same language. The Indians of this village subsist chiefly on salmon and white fish, which they take in such quantities as to be able to barter away a surplus beyond their own wants for other necessaries. The inhabitants also make abundance of maple sugar, which they sell to the traders; nor are they so very deficient in agricultural skill and industry, having, under the able and kind guidance of the missionary, cultivated many patches of wheat, corn, and potatoes, as well as erected a neat little church.

While I was at Manetouawning, the successor of Mr. Anderson, Captain Ironsides, arrived there; and as he was a half-breed and chief of the Wyandots, I have introduced him among my Indian sketches. [Fig. 31; crIII-56] His name signifies, "Walk in the water:" he is a descendant of Tecumseh, and uses the same *to-tem*, a turtle, each Indian family having a sort of heraldic device, which they use as a signature on important occasions. Sometimes a family passing through the woods will cut a chip out of a tree, and mark their to-tem on the fresh surface, so that the next may know who passed; or should a chief wish to send to a post for any articles, he draws the articles on a piece of birch-bark, and puts his to-tem, a fox, a dog, a bear, or whatever it may be, at the bottom; these are perfectly well understood, and answer every purpose of a written order. [Fig. 32; crIII-61, 62]

I remained at the Manitoulin Island a fortnight, parting with Mr. Dillon, who returned in the schooner that brought the presents. I left for the Sault St. Marie on board the steamer "Experiment," a Government vessel; Captain Harper, who commanded, kindly taking my canoe on board, and giving me a passage. At the Sault St. Marie I made the acquaintance of Mr. Ballantyne, the gentleman in charge of the Hudson Bay Company's Post, who was exceedingly kind.[11] [Pls. V, VI; Fig. 34; crIII-64 to 77] He strongly advised me against attempting to penetrate into the interior, except under the auspices of the Company, representing it as almost impossible and certainly very dangerous; but urged me to apply to Sir George Simpson,

the Governor of the Company at Lachine, who, he thought, when aware of the object I had in view, would send me forward with the spring brigade of canoes next year. Hoping that, by following this advice, I should be able to travel further, and see more of the wilder tribes, I determined upon confining my travels for the present to a mere summer campaign.

Chapter II.

Mackenaw, the "Turtle Island."—Famished Dogs.—The Chief He-Devil.—Green Bay, a Commercial Port.—Consolation in Sorrow.—An Indian Council.—Gambling Habits.—Illicit Traffic in Spirits.—Anecdote of Revenge.—A young Assassin.—Day of Reckoning.—Scenes of Drunkenness.

As it is my intention to speak of the Sault St. Marie in my next trip, I will pass over any mention of it here. After remaining a few days, I embarked on board a steamer [1] for Mackenaw, a distance of ninety miles. There I found a large band of Indians to the number of 2600, who had come from all quarters to receive their pay of $25,000 for land ceded to the United States; [2] these Indians were also Ojibbeways and Ottawas. On arriving among them, I at once pitched my tent in their midst, and commenced to sketch their most remarkable personages. [Pl. VIII; crIII-89 to 94] I soon had to remove my tent, from the circumstance that their famishing dogs, which they keep for the purpose of hunting and drawing their sleds in winter, contrived to carry off all my provisions, and seemed likely to serve me in the same way. This will appear by no means improbable, when I state that, while I was one evening finishing a sketch, sitting on the ground alone in my tent, with my candle stuck in the earth at my side, one of these audacious brutes unceremoniously dashed in through the entrance, seized the burning candle in his jaws and bolted off with it, leaving me in total darkness.

The next day, as I approached my tent, I saw a dog running away from it, and thinking it probably the same rascal that had stolen my candle, I thought to inflict summary justice upon the marauder, and fired the contents of my pistol into his carcase. Beyond my expectations, which had only been to wound, I saw that I had killed him, and was immediately assailed with a

---

[10] According to the report of the Indian commissioner (see note 1), the church maintained a school with a Catholic schoolmaster, Charles Lamorandière. Attendance in 1845 ranged from 32 to 35 boys and 24 to 26 girls.

[11] This is John Ballenden, a well-known Hudson's Bay Company factor, who was subsequently chief factor of the Red River post.

[1] KJ says the vessel was the *General Scott*.

[2] KJ states that nearly 3,000 Indians were waiting to receive payments of $25 each.

demand, from the owner of the dog and his wife, for payment for the loss of his services, which I agreed to liquidate on their paying me for the losses I had sustained in hams and other provisions which their dog had stolen from me. Hereupon they balanced accounts, and considered that we were about even, giving me an invitation to join them at supper, and partake with them of the slaughtered animal, in which operation I afterwards saw them happily engaged.

The Indian name of the island is Mitchi-mac-inum, or, "the Big Turtle," to which animal it bears a strong resemblance in form when seen from a certain point.

It is situated in the straits between Lakes Huron and Michigan [Fig. 37; crIII-84 to 87]; it contains some picturesque spots, one in particular, a natural bridge, which all strangers visit. [Fig. 36; crIII-79 to 83] There is a garrison on the island, consisting of a company of soldiers. [Fig. 35; crIII-78] The inhabitants support themselves chiefly by fishing, the straits here yielding an immense supply of large salmon and white fish. [crIII-97 to 105] Many traders assemble at Mackenaw, at the periods of payment, bringing with them large quantities of spirituous liquors, which they sell clandestinely to these poor creatures, it being prohibited by Government; and many an Indian who travels thither from a long distance returns to his wigwam poorer than he left it, his sole satisfaction being that he and his family have enjoyed a glorious bout of intoxication.

I took the likeness of a chief named Mani-tow-wah-bay, or, "He-Devil." [Pl. VII; crIII-88] He anxiously inquired what I wanted the likenesses for. In order to induce him to sit, I told him that they were going home to his great mother, the Queen. He said that he had often heard of her, and was very desirous of seeing her, and that had he the time and means, he would pay her a visit. It pleased him much that his second self would have an opportunity of seeing her. He told me, with much pride that he had been a successful warrior, and had taken nine scalps in his warfare. He was very fond of liquor, and, when under its influence, was one of the most violent and unmanageable among them.

[Wampum belts: Fig. 38; crIII-95, 96]

Having remained at Mackenaw for three weeks, I left for Green Bay, which is well situated for a commercial port, and must eventually become a place of importance, from the rich farming country in its vicinity; but owing to over speculation in every way in the years 1836 and 1837, it has been paralysed, and houses might now be obtained for the keeping them in repair. Here I amused myself with shooting snipe, which are

met with in abundance. In about a week I left in company with three gentlemen going to Fox River to see the Manōmanee Indians, who were now assembling to receive their payment for lands sold to the United States Government in the vicinity of Lake Winebago. We embarked in my little canoe, and proceeded up stream, arriving on the second night about 11 o'clock at an Indian log-house on the shore of Lake Winebago, or, "Muddy Lake." Two Indian girls, sisters, reside here alone. I remained with them the next day, and took their likenesses; the elder was named Iwa-toke, or, "the Serpent," the younger was called Ke-wah-ten, "the North Wind." [Fig. 39, crIII-107; Fig. 40, crIII-106, 108] We then proceeded up the lake to Fox River, entering which we found an Indian trading-house, round about which a number of idlers were pledging everything they possessed for liquor, under the influence of which dozens were lying about in a state of beastly intoxication.

An Indian called Wah-bannim, or, "the White Dog," sat to me for his likeness. [crIII-109, 110] He was in mourning for his wife, who had died some three months before; the mourning suit consisting of a coat of black paint with which he had smeared his face. He apologised for not appearing in full mourning costume to have his likeness taken, lamenting that a part of the paint had worn off; he was eagerly seeking to obtain whisky to console him for his loss. We gladly quitted this disgusting scene of dissipation, and continued our course up the monotonous stream. After paddling for two days, we reached the Monōmanee camp.

The evening previous to our arrival, we saw some Indians spearing salmon; by night, this has always a very picturesque appearance, the strong red glare of the blazing pine knots and roots in the iron frame, or light-jack, at the bow of the canoe throwing the naked figures of the Indians into wild relief upon the dark water and sombre woods. Great numbers of fish are killed in this manner. As the light is intense, and being above the head of the spearsman, it enables him to see the fish distinctly at a great depth, and at the same time it apparently either dazzles or attracts the fish. In my boyish days I have seen as many as a hundred light-jacks gliding about the Bay of Toronto, and have often joined in the sport. This, I suppose, gave me additional interest in the scene; and although very tired with my long day's paddling, I sat down by the fire, and while my companion was cooking some fish in a moh-cock, Indian fashion (for we had lost our kettle), I made the sketch No. 4. [Fig. 41; crIII-111, 112]

Here we found about 3000 Indians assembled, anxiously

awaiting the arrival of the agent with their money [3] [crIII-124, 130–40]; there was also a large number of traders collected, all busily occupied in the erection of booths for the display of their finery. In about a week the bank of the river wore the aspect of a little town; the booths, placed in rows, presented a scene of bustle and animation: the finery was, of course, all displayed to the best advantage on the outsides of the booths. On the arrival of the Indian agent a council was immediately called in a place erected for the occasion, in which thirty chiefs assembled. I attended in compliance with an invitation I had received from the head chief, Oscosh, or, "the Bravest of the Brave." [Fig. 42; crIII-113, 114]

He opened the council by lighting a pipe, and handing it to all present, each person taking a whiff or two, and passing it to the next. [crIII-116] The mingling clouds of smoke raised by each are supposed to ascend to the Great Spirit, in token of the harmony that pervades the assembly, and to attest the purity of their intentions. After this ceremony the main business of the council began: it almost exclusively consisted of complaints to be forwarded to the Government. After several of the minor chiefs had delivered their sentiments, Oscosh himself rose, and spoke for about an hour, and a finer flow of native eloquence—seasoned with good sense—I never heard, than proceeded from the lips of this untutored savage. Although a small man, his appearance, while speaking, possessed dignity; his attitude was graceful, and free from uncouth gesticulation. He complained of numerous acts of injustice which he supposed their great father, the President, could not possibly know, and which he desired might be represented to him, through the agent, accompanied with a pipe-stem of peace richly ornamented. [crIII-115]

One of the grievances he specified was, that their money passed through too many hands before it reached them, and that a great part of it was thus lost to them. He wound up his long harangue by descanting upon the narrow limits in which they were pent up, which did not allow them sufficient hunting grounds without encroaching upon the rights of other tribes. He said that, like the deer chased by the dogs, they would have to take to the water.

When Oscosh aspired to the dignity of head chief, his election was opposed in the council by another chief, who insisted on contesting the post of honour with him. Oscosh replied, that as there could be only one head chief, he was quite willing on the

instant to settle the dispute with their knives by the destruction of one or the other. This proposal was declined, and his claim has never since been disputed. This tribe is remarkably partial to gaudy decorations, and ornament themselves with great quantities of beads, silver ornaments, and feathers. This passion for display is confined chiefly to the men.

[crIII-118, 119, 121]

They are much addicted to gambling, and I have seen them commence playing, covered with highly-prized decorations, which have gradually changed hands, as the game proceeded, until its close has left the original possessor without a blanket to cover him. The principal despoilers of the Manōmanees are the Pottowattomies, some of whom make it their business to visit the Manōmanee camp on a regular black-leg expedition at the time the latter receive their Government pay, in order to fleece them of whatever they can, and they generally return home laden with booty. Liquor, whenever they can obtain it, is their chief bane, and lays them more open to the fraudulent schemes of their despoilers.

I made a sketch of Coe-coosh, "the Hog," one of these Pottowattomie black-legs, whom I saw intently engaged in gambling. [Pl. IX; crIII-126] The introduction of spirits among the Indians is, as before mentioned, prohibited under severe penalties by the laws of the United States, and with the greatest propriety, as an Indian, when under its influence, is one of the most dangerous animals in existence, and there being so few whites to control them at the period of payment, we should have been in no small danger of losing our lives had it been readily attainable.

I was myself, on this occasion, called up in the dead of the night by the United States' marshal, who had been commissioned to prevent its introduction among them; he required my assistance, in common with all the other whites on the spot, in order to make a search throughout the camp to detect the person who was selling liquor, as some of the Indians were already drunk. Having a suspicion that a half-breed was engaged in the illicit traffic, we all proceeded to his tent. Although we plainly smelt the liquor in his tin pots, not a single keg was to be found in spite of the most vigilant search, carried even to the extent of digging up the earth in his tent. When I was leaving the neighbourhood, I got him to confess that he had sunk several kegs, with buoys attached to them, in the middle of the river. By keeping watch by turns through the night, it fortunately passed over without mischief.

["Pine Tree" (?), crIII-127, 128]

---

[3] In 1845 the United States Treasury provided $6,000 for payments to the Menominee. National Archives, "Letters Sent by the Superintendent and Agent of the Office of Indian Affairs, Mackinac Agency, 1833–1851," letter of July 4, 1845.

Among other Indians whose likeness I took, is that of Kit-chie-ogi-maw, or, "the Great Chief," a Manōmanee, who was celebrated among his tribe for many acts of daring, one of which was narrated to me by his half brother: it occurred eight or ten years previously. [Fig. 43; crIII-117, 120]

His maternal uncle, who was then at Mackenaw, chanced to be present in a grocery store, where ardent spirits were sold, when two soldiers entered, one of whom treated him with so much indignity, that, seizing him in his powerful grasp, and being the stronger and more active man, he threw the soldier down with great violence on the ground upon his back, and planting his knee upon his breast, assured him that he would do him no further injury, if he would behave himself properly. This assurance, given in his own language, was, unfortunately, not understood by either of the soldiers; the second of whom, seeing his comrade in the power of a savage, and his life, as he thought, in peril, instantly drew his side-arms and stabbed the ill-fated Indian to the heart. No punishment of any importance followed the commission of this crime; the offender was merely sent away from Mackenaw to escape the vengeance of the relatives of the murdered man.

A year or two subsequently to this unhappy occurrence, as two white men, a Mr. Clayman and a Mr. Burnett, were coming down the Fox River in a canoe, they chanced to pass the lodge of Kitchie-ogi-maw's father, the brother-in-law of the deceased Indian, who, with his family, was camped on the banks of the river. They were noticed by the squaw, the dead man's sister, who called to her husband that now had arrived the opportunity of revenging her brother's death, and that it was his duty, as a man, not to let so good a chance escape him; but her husband, unwilling to risk so hazardous an encounter without other aid than that of his son, Kitchie-ogi-maw, then a stripling of only fourteen years, hesitated to comply with her request. On which, in order to show her contempt of what she considered his pusillanimity, she hastily divested herself of the breech cloth usually worn by Indian women, and, throwing it insultingly in his face, told him to wear it, for that he was no man. The husband, stung by the opprobrious imputation, caught up his gun, and commanded his son to follow him. The boy declined having any concern in killing the white men, but consented to accompany him for his protection.

The two Americans had now landed and were preparing their camp for the night; one of them was upon his knees engaged in kindling a fire, the other approaching at a distance with an armful of wood; the father raised his gun, but dropped it again to his side in evident agitation; the boy thereupon turned to him, saying, "Father, you tremble too much; give me the gun, and let me do it," and, taking the weapon from his father's hands, he approached the kneeling man from behind, and shot him dead; the other one, hearing the report and catching sight of the Indians, threw down the wood he had collected and ran for his life; the boy seeing a double-barrelled gun lying on the ground near the man he had killed, seized it and followed the fugitive, telling his father to assist in the pursuit, as if this man escaped they might be punished through his evidence for killing the other.

The father was unable to keep up with the boy, who gained on the white man, and, when within twenty or thirty yards of him, took aim and endeavoured to fire; but being unused to the double trigger, and not having cocked both locks, he pulled the wrong one: determined to make sure of his next aim, he cocked both and pulled the two triggers together; part of the charge entered the victim's shoulder, but the recoil of the two barrels going off at once, knocked the boy backwards on the ground. He was, however, only stunned for the moment, and soon recovered his feet; drawing his scalping knife, the young assassin continued his pursuit of the now almost exhausted man, who, in endeavouring to leap over a log lying on the ground, stumbled and fell.

The bloody young wretch now made sure of his victim, and before the latter could recover his feet, had come up within a few yards of him. The white man seeing that the youngster was alone, and the father not within sight, faced his pursuer, armed likewise with a knife, and resolved to grapple with him. But the boy dexterously kept out of his reach, dodging him round the fallen log, until his father should come up when they could unitedly overpower him. The wounded fugitive having now recovered breath, and noticing the father in the distance, took to flight once more, dogged by his indefatigable tormentor, and continued his speed till the morning dawned, when he fell in with some friendly Indians, who protected him and dressed his wounds, none of which were mortal: they supplied all his wants, until he was strong enough to return to his home. Kitchie-ogi-maw now deemed it the safest plan to keep away from any of the White Settlements, and he continues still to observe the same precaution.

I found some Indians of the Winebago tribe at the camp on a visit. The word Winebago signifies "dirty water;" and they are so called from living on the margin of a lake of that name. They are easily distinguished from other tribes, as they have the custom of pulling out their eyebrows.

I took the likeness of their chief, Mauza-pau-Kan, or the "Brave Soldier." [Fig. 46; crIII-129] I remained here for three weeks, and received much kindness and attention from the Manōmanees. Hearing that I was taking sketches of the most noted Indians in the camp, a fellow named Muck-a-ta paid me a visit. He was one of the most ill favoured of any that had been the subjects of my pencil, and by all accounts his physiognomy did not belie his character. [Figs. 44, 45; crIII-122, 123]

The Indians had no sooner received their money than a scene ensued that baffles description. Large quantities of liquor immediately found their way into the camp from some unknown quarter, and the sad effect was almost instantaneous. There was scarcely a man, woman, or child, old enough to lift the vessel to its mouth, that was not wallowing in beastly drunkenness; and we gladly availed ourselves of the arrival of a small steamer that plies on Lake Winebago and the Fox River to make our escape from the disgusting and dangerous scene of singing and dancing and fighting going on around us. We disembarked at a place called "Fond du Lac," where we hired a waggon, and crossed over to the Sheboygan on Lake Michigan, and embarked on board another steamer for Buffalo, which I left again on the 30th of November and arrived the day following at Toronto.

[Fort Snelling: Pl. X; crIII-141 to 144]

Chapter III.

Sir George Simpson.—My Start.—Difficulties of the Route.—The Sault St. Marie.—The "White Fish" and "Thunder Point."—A Day behind the Fair.—Pulling against Stream.—Mangeurs du Lard.—The Lost Men's Portage.—The Blanket of the Dead.—A Compliment from Sir George.—Running from a Bear.

In the ensuing March I repaired to Lachine to seek an interview with Sir George Simpson.[1] Having exhibited to him the sketches which I had made, and explained the nature of the objects which I had in view,[2] Sir George entered cordially into my plans; and, in order to facilitate them, ordered a passage in the spring brigade of canoes.

Accordingly, on the 9th of May, 1846, I left Toronto in company with Governor Simpson for the Sault St. Marie, in order to embark in the brigade of canoes which had left Lachine some time previously, taking the route of the Ottawa and Lake Huron.[3]

On my arrival at Mackenaw in the evening, I was informed by the master of the steamboat that he would not leave until 9 o'clock next morning. Trusting to this assurance, I went on shore for the night; but on coming down to the wharf on the following day, I found that the vessel with Sir George Simpson had departed about twenty minutes previously.[4] This was indeed a damper of no ordinary magnitude, as, should I fail in seeing Sir George before he left the Sault, I should not be able to accompany the canoes. I was aware, likewise, that the governor would not remain longer than a few hours; but how to overtake him was the difficulty, as no boat would leave for four days.

Determined, however, not to be disappointed in my proposed expedition, I used every exertion to procure a mode of conveyance.[5] Walking along the beach, I saw a small skiff lying, and having found the owner, inquired if I could hire it, and whether there was any chance of procuring a crew. The man strongly advised me not to attempt such a perilous voyage, as it was blowing hard, and that it was not in mortal power to reach the Sault by daylight next morning. Resolved, however, to make the attempt, I at length succeeded in chartering the skiff and engaging a crew, consisting of three boys, the eldest being under nineteen years of age.[6] It must be added that they were all well acquainted with boating. The striplings held out no hopes of being able to accomplish the undertaking within the given time, and were only induced to make the attempt by the offer of a high reward. Thus, in a tiny skiff, with a blanket for a sail, and a

[1] kwms states that Kane left Toronto for Lachine on March 25.

[2] kwms reads: "My object in taking this journey was to obtain Sir George's permission to accompany the brigade of canoes which annually leaves Lachine for the North-west passing up the Ottawa into Lake Huron."

[3] kwms reads: "I was apprehensive of not being able to reach this place till the Brigade had passed as I had been informed that they had left Lachine this season five days before the usual period, the ice of the Ottawa having broken up earlier this season than ordinary. I arrived at 4 P.M. at Buffalo on the same day having stopped a short time on our way up to admire for the hundredth time the Falls of Niagara. At Buffalo we embarked at 7 P.M. on board an American steamer bound for Mackinaw, on the 10th at Cleveland, on the 11th at Detroit, and on the 12th landed at Mackinaw."

[4] kwms reads: "As I unwisely decided to breakfast there [the hotel where Kane had spent the night], I found on my arrival at the wharf that I was half an hour too late. The steamer had carried off my baggage."

[5] kwms states that the steamer would not return for two days.

[6] kwms describes how Kane gave a man $10 to find a crew to take him to Sault St. Marie and then promised the boys $20 if they could reach there in time to catch Sir George Simpson.

single loaf of bread along with a little tea and sugar for stores, we launched out in the lake to make a traverse of forty-five miles.[7]

The wind being favourable, the boat shot ahead with tremendous rapidity, but the danger was imminent and continuous from the moment we left the shore until we reached the mouth of the river of St. Marie, which we did at sunset.

Here we remained about twenty minutes, and discussed our tea and bread with appetites sharpened to intensity. But now commenced another difficulty, the navigation of forty-five miles of a river with which we were totally unacquainted, in a dark night against the current and through a channel dotted with numerous islands. All this was to be accomplished by daylight, or the toil and anxiety would be of no avail.

We however set forth unflinchingly; and after a night of the most violent exertion, after running into all sorts of wrong places and backing out again, after giving up half a dozen times in despair, and as often renewing the struggle, our exertions were crowned with success. When morning dawned, there lay the eagerly looked-for steamer not two miles from us.[8]

On getting up in the morning, Sir George Simpson was astonished at seeing me; and his amazement was not lessened when he learned the mode of my conveyance.[9] The voyage on no former occasion had been performed in so short a time under corresponding circumstances, and to this day the undertaking is still talked of as a rather notable adventure in Mackenaw and the Sault.

The Sault St. Marie is situated at the lower extremity of Lake Superior, where it debouches into the river St. Marie, in its course to Lake Huron: having in this part of the river a considerable fall, for about a mile and a half in length, it soon becomes a foaming torrent, down which, however, canoes, steered by practised guides, ordinarily descend safely, although with terrific violence. Sometimes, indeed, the venture is fatal to the bark and its occupants. A short time before our arrival on the present occasion, a canoe, in running down the rapid, had struck upon a sunken rock that made a hole through her bottom. She instantly filled, but, owing to the extreme buoyancy of the

birch-bark these canoes are made of, the men, by balancing themselves adroitly in her, and squatting up to their necks in the water, thereby lessening their weight materially, were enabled to steer her with safety down the foaming billows, and run her on the shore in an eddy at the foot of the rapids.

I took a sketch of the rapids above alluded to, from the American side. [crIII-71] There is a small town called the Sault St. Marie, on the American side, containing 700 or 800 inhabitants, with a well-built garrison, prettily situated on the river's bank. On the Canadian side, about half a mile direct across, the Hudson's Bay Company have a trading establishment, and the Custom House officer, Mr. Wilson, a tolerably handsome house. With these two exceptions, the British side presents to the traveller a collection of poor miserable hovels, occupied solely by half-breeds and Indians. In strolling among these hovels, I made a sketch of a good-looking half-breed girl, whose sudden appearance, emerging from such a wretched neighbourhood, took me by surprise. [crIII-75]

As the brigade of canoes had passed up two days before my arrival at the Sault, and Sir George's canoes were too heavily laden, he was unable to give me a passage. My only alternative was to wait until the "White Fish," a small schooner belonging to the Company, and lying at the upper end of the portage, was unloaded, and trust to the chance of her intercepting the canoes at Fort William. This was very doubtful, depending, as it entirely did, upon the wind; but I had no alternative. Sir George had embarked on the 14th in his canoe, leaving me to follow in the way above named. It took four days to unload the schooner, so that she was not ready to leave before the 20th of May. We had a fair wind at starting, which continued until the night of the 23rd, when it came to blow a gale off "Thunder Point." The night being very dark, we were apprehensive of driving on the rocks at the base of this formidable mountain—Thunder Point, as it is called, being in fact, a perpendicular rock of twelve or fifteen hundred feet high. Seeing it, as I then did, for the first time, by the glare of the almost incessant flashes of lightning, it presented one of the grandest and most terrific spectacles I had ever witnessed. As our crew consisted of only two men, I was under the necessity of assisting to work the vessel, so that all hope of a comfortable sleep in my warm hammock had to be abandoned, and I was obliged to remain the whole night on deck.

At daybreak we succeeded in rounding this dangerous point, and soon passed El Royal, which island is supposed to contain valuable mineral wealth, and cast anchor near the mouth of the

---

[7] KWMS says they left at 10 A.M.

[8] KJ says the voyage was made in 20 hours and KWMS says 21 hours: an example of the many small inconsistencies in the various versions.

[9] KWMS reads: "We encountered Sir George Simpson at the Hudson's Bay Co. post as he was leaving his chamber. As the possibility of our having made the voyage in the way I have described had not once occurred to him, Sir George's first enquiry was 'What other steamer could have arrived?' In explanation I showed him our boat and my three companions all by this time soundly sleeping on the beach."

Plate XII. The Mountain Portage (Kakabeka Falls). ROM 912.1.18; crIV-6.

Kaministaqueah River, which we ascended about two miles to Fort William, in a small boat. This fort, during the existence of the North-west Company, was one of considerable importance as a depôt for all the trade carried on in furs, &c. This importance it has lost, in consequence of the goods which formerly passed by the route of Lake Superior, now passing by Hudson's Bay since the two rival companies have merged into one; but as it possesses the best land in the vicinity of Lake Superior, it might still be made a place of much consideration in an agricultural point of view.

On delivering my letter of introduction to Mr. Mackenzie, the gentleman in charge of the fort, I learned, to my great disappointment, that the brigade had passed up the river the day before. I was compelled, in this dilemma, to trespass on the kindness of this gentleman for the supply of a light canoe and three men, in order to overtake them if possible before they reached the mountain portage, forty miles in advance. In the course of half an hour, thanks to Mr. Mackenzie's kindness, we were straining at the paddles, and, ten hours afterwards, had the satisfaction of coming up with the brigade about thirty-five miles from our starting point.

I found a gentleman named Lane [10] in charge of the brigade, which consisted of three canoes with eight men in each. We all camped immediately, and at 3 o'clock next morning were again *en route* in our canoes. These are constructed of the bark of the birch tree, and are about twenty-eight feet long and four to five feet beam, strong, and capable of carrying, besides their crew of eight men, twenty-five pieces; but at the same time so light as to be easily carried on the shoulders of two men. All goods taken into the interior, and all peltries brought out, are made into packs of 90 lbs. each, for the purpose of easy handling at the frequent *portages* and *discharges*; these packs are called pieces.

After pulling our canoes up a rapid current, we arrived about 8 o'clock at the mountain portage, whose falls surpass even those of Niagara in picturesque beauty; for, although far inferior in volume of water, their height is nearly equal, and the scenery surrounding them infinitely more wild and romantic. Whilst the men were engaged in making the portage, I took advantage of the delay to make a sketch. [Fig. 47; crIV-3, 4, 5]

I have since been informed that the large flat rock which divided the torrent in the centre has fallen in. The interruption thus caused by the falls is about two miles of very steep ascent, up which the men have to carry the canoes and baggage, the

[10] Burpee, in the 1925 edition of *Wanderings,* identifies him as "W. D. Lane." Could he have been W. F. Lane?

former on their shoulders, the latter on their backs, by means of what is technically named a portage-strap, both ends of which are attached to the load of two pieces, while the middle of the strap goes round the forehead, which thus supports the principal part of the burden. [Pl. XII; crIV-6] The men who usually work this brigade of canoes are hired at Lachine, and are called by the uncouth name of *Mangeurs du Lard,* or pork-eaters, among the old hands in the interior, to whom they are unequal in encountering the difficulties incident to a voyage from Lachine to the mouth of the Columbia, whither some of them are sent, and become almost skeletons by the time they reach their destination, through the unavoidable privations and hardships they have to undergo.

Launching our canoes again, we proceeded for about a mile, and made another portage called "The Lost Men's Portage," owing to three men having lost themselves in the woods in crossing it. [crIV-6A] I very nearly met with the same fate myself; for, having gone up to the rapids to take a sketch, I endeavoured, when I had finished, to find my way back, and spent two hours in an unsuccessful attempt to gain the path. I then fortunately thought of discharging my fowling-piece as a signal, and had the pleasure of immediately hearing an answering shot, which guided my steps to the party who were anxiously awaiting my return to embark.

Proceeding a few miles up the stream, we reached the "Pin Portage," so called from the rocks over which we had to carry the canoes being so sharp as actually to cut the feet of the men, who usually go barefooted or only wearing light mocassins. [Fig. 48; crIV-7] We made, in all, six portages in one day, viz., "Ecarté," "Rose Décharge," and "De l'Isle," and the three before named, travelling a distance of forty-three miles: the current was so impetuous, even where we could avail ourselves of our canoes, that the men found the greatest difficulty in forcing up against it with poles.

On the 26th of May we journeyed twenty-six miles, making the following portages and discharges, viz.:—"Recousi Portage," "Couteau Portage," "Belanger Décharge," "Mauvais Décharge," "Tremble Décharge," "Penet Décharge," "Maître Portage," "Little Dog Portage," "Dog Portage [crIV-8]," and the "Big Dog Portage;" the latter affords a splendid view from its summit of the Kaministaqueah river, meandering in the distance, as far as the eye can reach, through one of the loveliest valleys in nature. This view I wished much to have sketched, but time is of so much importance in the movements of these brigades, that I did not consider myself justified in waiting.

The "Big Dog Portage" derives its name from an Indian tradition that a big dog once slept on the summit, and left the impression of his form on the highest point of land, which remains to this present time. The length of this portage is two miles; we camped at the upper end; and while here I made a sketch of the fall, during one of the heaviest showers of rain I ever experienced.

One of our *Mangeurs du Lard* presenting himself at the camp fire in a handsome rabbit-skin blanket, was asked by Mr. Lane where he had obtained it. He replied that he had found it among the bushes. Mr. Lane, knowing that it is customary among the Indians to place offerings of all descriptions upon the graves of their deceased relatives, first rendering them unserviceable to any evil disposed persons in this world, under the idea that the Great Spirit will repair them on the arrival of the deceased in the next, and that they hold in the greatest abhorrence, and never fail to punish, any one who sacrilegiously disturbs them, ordered him immediately to return to the place whence he took it, and replace it exactly as he had found it, unless he wished to have us all murdered. When the man understood what he had done, he replaced the blanket immediately.

On the 27th, Sir George Simpson passed us with his two canoes, accompanied by his secretary Mr. Hopkins. Sir George only stopped a few minutes to congratulate me on my having overcome the difficulties of my starting: he seemed to think that the perseverance and determination I had shown augured well for my future success, and as his canoes were much lighter and better manned than ours, he passed on rapidly in advance. As there were no more currents to overcome, the men this day threw away their poles as useless, and started on a race with their paddles for about fifteen miles through "Dog Lake" and entered "Dog River." We now had to make a long portage of three miles over a high mountain into a small lake.[11] At the upper end of this portage we again overtook Sir George, and were invited to dine with him at the next, some four or five miles further on, but we unluckily could not again come up with him.

On inquiring the cause of some loud shouting that I heard in the woods, I was told that some of our men had surrounded a bear which had given them battle, but that, unarmed as they were, they had deemed discretion the better part of valour, and sounded a retreat. We camped on the banks of a small river. We

[11] KJ names it the "Little Dog Portage" and gives the length as four miles (another example of the minor variations in the various accounts).

had hitherto stemmed against the stream of waters that emptied itself into the Atlantic; but we had now reached streams that flowed at a much more rapid rate, and coursed on to Hudson's Bay. At the close of this day we had accomplished a distance of thirty-three miles, having made the following portages, viz.:— "Barrière Portage," "Joudain Portage," and "Prairie Portage."

Chapter IV.

Four Miles of Swamp.—Lake of a Thousand Isles.—Virtue of a Silver Bullet.—A wild Tale.—Living One upon Another.—The Great Medicine-Man.—A Timid "Little Rat."—A Caterpillar Plague.—Butter in the Wilderness.—A Leap into the Grave.—Going down the Winnipeg.—A novel Viameter.

May 28th.—To-day we passed over one of the largest and most difficult portages in the whole route, it is called the "Savan Portage;" it passes through about four miles of swamp. It formerly had logs laid lengthwise, for the convenience of the men carrying the loads; but they are now for the most part decayed, so that the poor fellows had sometimes to wade up to the middle in mud and water. In all, we made to-day about thirty miles, including the following portages, viz.:—"Milieu Portage" and "Savan Portage," from whence we went twenty miles down the Savan River, and camped near its mouth, where it empties into "Mille Lacs."

On the 29th, we passed through the Lake of the Thousand Islands, thirty-six miles long, a name it well deserves. The scenery surrounding us was truly beautiful; the innumerable rocky islands varying from several miles in length to the smallest proportions, all covered with trees, chiefly pine. [CRIV-9] This lake is filled with innumerable ducks, which the Indians entice in the following curious manner:—A young dog is trained by dragging a piece of meat attached to a string up and down the edge of the shore several times, and putting the dog on the scent, who follows it rapidly, wagging his tail. After the dog has followed it for some time, he is given the meat; this is done repeatedly until the dog will do so whenever he is ordered, and his motions attract the ducks swimming in the distance to within reach of the Indian, who lies concealed on the banks. The flock of ducks is so crowded and numerous, that I have known an Indian kill forty ducks by firing at them whilst in the water, and rapidly loading and firing again whilst the same flock was circling above his head. Our first portage after leaving this lovely lake was "Portage de Pente." We camped at the end of the next portage, called "Little Discharge," having made a distance altogether of fifty-six miles.

May 30th.—We made an early start, reaching the "French Portage" by breakfast-time.[1] Here we lightened the canoes of the principal part of the baggage, and carried it across the portage, a distance of three miles, in order that we might be able to send the canoes round by the river, which had now become very shallow, to meet us at the further end of the portage. We camped this evening at a small lake called Sturgeon Lake, having come a distance of forty-eight miles, passing "French Portage," and "Portage de Morts."

May 31st.—We passed down the "Rivière Maligne"[2] until we came to what are termed the First, Second, and Third portages, and, making the portage "De l'Isle" and "Du Lac," camped near "Lac la Croix Traverse," accomplishing a distance of only twenty-seven miles.

June 1st.—We passed down the river "Macau," where there are some beautiful rapids and falls.[3] Here we fell in with the first Indians we had met since leaving the Lake of the Thousand Islands; they are called "Saulteaux," being a branch of the Ojibbeways, whose language they speak with very slight variation. We purchased from an Indian man and woman some dried sturgeon. The female wore a rabbit-skin dress: they were, as I afterwards learned, considered to be cannibals, the Indian term for which is *Weendigo*, or "One who eats Human Flesh." There is a superstitious belief among Indians that the Weendigo cannot be killed by anything short of a silver bullet. I was informed, on good authority, that a case had occurred here in which a father and daughter had killed and eaten six of their own family from absolute want. The story went on to state, that they then camped at some distance off in the vicinity of an old Indian woman, who happened to be alone in her lodge, her relations having gone out hunting. Seeing the father and daughter arrive unaccompanied by any other members of the family, all of whom she knew, she began to suspect that some foul play had taken place, and to feel apprehensive for her own safety. By way of precaution, she resolved to make the entrance to her lodge very slippery, and as it was winter, and the frost severe, she poured water repeatedly over the ground as fast as it froze, until it was covered with a mass of smooth ice; and instead of going to bed, she remained sitting up in her lodge, watching

with an axe in her hand. When near midnight, she heard steps advancing cautiously over the crackling snow, and looking through the crevices of the lodge, caught sight of the girl in the attitude of listening, as if to ascertain whether the inmate was asleep; this the old woman feigned by snoring aloud. The welcome sound no sooner reached the ears of the wretched girl, than she rushed forward, but, slipping on the ice, fell down at the entrance of the lodge, whereupon the intended victim sprang upon the murderess and buried the axe in her brains: and not doubting but the villainous father was near at hand, she fled with all her speed to a distance, to escape his vengeance. In the meantime, the Weendigo father, who was impatiently watching for the expected signal to his horrid repast, crept up to the lodge, and called to his daughter; hearing no reply, he went on, and, in place of the dead body of the old woman, he saw his own daughter, and hunger overcoming every other feeling, he saved his own life by devouring her remains.

The *Weendigoes* are looked upon with superstitious dread and horror by all Indians, and any one known to have eaten human flesh is shunned by the rest; as it is supposed that, having once tasted it, they would do so again had they an opportunity. They are obliged, therefore, to make their lodges at some distance from the rest of the tribe, and the children are particularly kept out of their way; however, they are not molested or injured in any way, but seem rather to be pitied for the misery they must have endured before they could be brought to this state. I do not think that any Indian, at least none that I have ever seen, would eat his fellow-creature, except under the influence of starvation; nor do I think that there is any tribe of Indians on the North American continent to whom the word "cannibal" can be properly applied.

We traversed to-day a distance of forty-one miles, passing four portages before entering Lake Meican, which is nine miles long, to "Portage Neuf," entering the "Lac la Pluie," where we camped; its name did not seem inappropriate, for we were detained here two days by the incessant torrents of rain that poured down. It took us until the evening of the 4th to reach Fort Francis, at the lower end of the lake, a distance of fifty miles, where I found a letter from Sir George Simpson, enclosing a circular.

There is a beautiful fall of water here within sight of the fort, at the commencement of the river which runs from Lac la Pluie to the Lake of the Woods. Vast quantities of white fish and sturgeon are taken at the foot of the rapids, with which our mess-table at the fort was abundantly supplied; indeed, the

---

[1] In KJ Kane records sketching the French Portage.
[2] In KJ Kane records sketching Rivière Maligne.
[3] In KJ Kane records sketching the falls on the "Macau" River.

chief food here consists of fish and wild rice, with a little grain grown in the vicinity of the fort, this being the first land I had seen fit for agricultural purposes since I had left Fort William. We continued at the fort until the morning of the 5th. There was a large camp of Salteaux Indians in the immediate vicinity: a considerable party of them came to the establishment in the morning to see the "great medicine-man" who made Indians,[4] Mr. Lane having given them to understand that my object in travelling through the country was to paint their likenesses.

I applied to the head chief, Waw-gas-kontz, "the Little Rat," to take his likeness, but was refused, on the grounds that he feared something bad would result to him; but after Iacaway, "the Loud Speaker," had sat for his [crIV-29], Waw-gas-kontz seemed ashamed of his cowardice, and became very anxious to have it done, following me down to the canoe. I had not time, however, to do so; but I could not get rid of him until I promised to take his likeness on my return.

June 5th.—We left the fort at 10 this morning; the rain continued all day, and obliged us to camp at 4 in the afternoon, the distance we went being about thirty miles.

June 6th.—It was a remarkable fact that the trees on each side of the river, and part of the Lake of the Woods, for full 150 miles of our route, were literally stripped of foliage by myriads of green caterpillars, which had left nothing but the bare branches; and I was informed that the scourge extended to more than twice the distance I have named, the whole country wearing the dreary aspect of winter at the commencement of summer.

As it was impossible to take our breakfast on land, unless we made up our minds to eat them, dropping incessantly as they did from the trees among our food, and the ground everywhere covered with them *en masse,* we were compelled to take it in our canoes. We met some Indians, from whom we purchased seven fine sturgeons, each weighing perhaps forty or fifty pounds. We paid for the whole one cotton shirt. We next entered the Lake of the Woods, and camped on a beautiful rocky island, having made fifty-three miles in one day.

June 7th.—We passed through the above lake, sixty-eight miles long. When passing a small island about the middle of it, the steersman of my canoe put ashore on this island, and running to a clump of bushes returned with a small keg of butter, which he told us he had left hidden, or, as they call it, *en cache,* the year before: it proved an acquisition to our larder, although its age had not improved its flavour. We next made the "Rat Portage," at the foot of which is the fort, a small establishment

where they were so badly supplied with provisions as to be able to afford us only two white fish. We consequently thought it advisable to leave the place, although late in the evening, and camped a few miles lower down the Winnipeg River; having travelled to-day a distance of seventy-two miles.

June 8th.—We continued our course down the river Winnipeg, which is broken by numerous beautiful rapids and falls, being indeed one of the most picturesque rivers we had passed in the whole route. Our bowsman caught a pike, which in appearance had two tails, one at each end; but we found on examination that the tail and part of the body of another fish or sucker, nearly as large as himself, which he had tried to swallow, was protruding from his mouth, evidencing the extreme voracity of this species. We passed to-day a Catholic missionary station called "Wabassemmung" (or White Dog) [crIV-13?], which, on my return, two years and a half afterwards, I found deserted, from the circumstance that the Indians of this quarter did not prove very willing converts. We camped for the night a few miles below this station, and still found the caterpillars before alluded to extremely annoying, covering as they did completely our blankets and clothing. We had passed the following places, viz.: "the Dalles," "Grand Décharge," "Terre jaune Portage," "the Charrette Portage," "Terre blanche Portage," "Cave Portage," and Wabassemmung, a distance of seventy-one miles.

June 9th.—We passed the "Chute de Jaques,"[5] so called from a man thus named, who, being dared by one of his companions to run his canoe over a fall of fifteen or twenty feet, an exploit never attempted before or since, unhesitatingly essayed the bold feat, and pushing off his frail bark, jumped into it, and on rounding a small island darted down the main sheet, his companions meanwhile anxiously watching for his safety from the shore. As might have been expected, he was dashed to pieces and no more seen. [crIV-18] We camped this evening, after completing a distance of sixty miles, and making the following portages, viz.: "Portage de l'Isle," "Chute de Jaques," "Point des Bois" (the Indian name of this fall is Ka-mash-aw-aw-sing, or, "the Two Carrying-Places"); "Rochers Boules," "the Slave Falls," which is the highest of all the falls of the Winnipeg River; I never heard the reason of its bearing this name. At "Barrière Portage" we found the black flies and mosquitoes so annoying all night, as to deprive us entirely of sleep.

---

[4] w 59: "The Indians attach a mysterious meaning to the word 'medicine,' applying it to almost everything they cannot clearly understand."

[5] kj records that Kane sketched the Chute de Jacques.

June 10th.—We ran three or four beautiful rapids to-day in our canoes, the men showing great expertness in their management, although so much risk attends it that several canoes have been lost in the attempt. We made about sixty miles to-day down the Winnipeg [Fig. 52; crIV-24, 26–28], passing the following places, viz.: the "Grand Rapid," six portages, all within sight of each other, and about five miles in length inclusively: they are known collectively by the name of "The Six Portages"—the first and second portage of the "Bonnet," "the Grand Bonnet," "Petits Rochers," and "Terre Blanche." We encamped about a couple of miles below the rapids at 5 o'clock —earlier than usual, as our canoes had received some little injury and required repairs. It is usual to start every morning between 3 and 4 o'clock and proceed till 8 for breakfast, then continue steadily on until an hour before dark, just so as to give the men time to prepare for the night. The only rest allowed being at intervals of about an hour, when all hands stop two or three minutes to fill their pipes. It is quite a common way of expressing the distance of one place to another to say that it is so many pipes; and this, amongst those who have travelled in the interior gives a very good idea of the distance. The evening was very beautiful, and soon after we had pitched our tents and lighted our fires, we were visited by some Saulteaux Indians. As I had plenty of time, I sketched the encampment.[6] Our visitors, the clear stream reflecting the brilliant sky so peculiar to North America, the granite rocks backed by the rich foliage of the woods with Indians and voyageurs moving about, made a most pleasing subject. [Pl. XIV; crIV-22, 23]

Chapter V.

Fort Alexander.—Mr. Lane.—A Western Career.—Value of Bark to the Indian.—The Medicine Lodge.—A Double Shot.—Fort Garry. —The nearest Market Town.—Red River Settlement.—White Horse Plain.—Hunting the Buffalo.

June 11th.—We made an early start with a fine breeze, filling our sail,[1] and arrived at Fort Alexander to breakfast, a distance of seventeen or eighteen miles including the three portages: "First Eau Qui Merit," "Second Eau Qui Merit," "Third Eau

Qui Merit." Fort Alexander is situated on Winnipeg River, about three miles above where it disembogues into Lake Winnipeg, and has some good farming land in its vicinity. I here took my farewell of Mr. Lane with great regret, and left the brigade of canoes, which proceeded with him to Norway House, on his route to Mackenzie River. Mr. Lane had entered the Hudson's Bay Company's service when very young, and having served for twenty-six years, he became dissatisfied with the slowness of his promotion, and determined to resign and return to Ireland, his native land. However, on his return home, he found himself lost in civilised life, and quite unable to occupy himself with any business pursuits there; and when I met him, he was again in the employment of the Company, at a lower salary than he had before received, and was going to Mackenzie River, one of the most remote and bleak posts in the whole region, accompanied by his wife, a half-breed. The last that I heard of him was that he had arrived at his post almost starved to death, after travelling about 700 miles on snow shoes through the depth of winter.

Hearing that a camp of Indians lay within a few miles, I requested a Mr. Setler, in charge of the establishment, to procure me a guide to them. I found it indispensably necessary to wear a veil all the way, as a protection from the mosquitoes, which I had never before seen so numerous. I found a very large camp of Saulteaux Indians assembled. [Fig. 54; crIV-32] They have a medicine lodge erected in the centre of their encampment, to which I at once directed my steps. It was rather an oblong structure, composed of poles bent in the form of an arch, and both ends forced into the ground, so as to form, when completed, a long arched chamber, protected from the weather by a covering of birch bark. This bark is one of the most valuable materials that nature supplies to the Red-man, as by its friendly aid he is enabled to brave the inclemency of the weather on land, and float lightly and safely over the vast inland seas that so abound in his wild domain; and when any transient impediments present themselves to his using it on water, so light is its weight, that he easily carries it on his shoulder. Such also is its compactness and closeness of texture, that he forms his culinary and other utensils of it, and, as it is quite impervious to water, he is able, by the aid of heated stones, to boil his fish in them. It also serves for a material or papyrus on which to transmit his hieroglyphic correspondence.

On my first entrance into the medicine lodge—(the reader is already apprised of the mysterious meaning the Indian attaches

---

[6] KWMS has a longer description of the camp site, which is interesting since Kane sketched the camp. It reads: "Mr. Lane's tent and mine are at the edge of the woods. Some of the men are bringing fuel to cook and keep off mosquitoes, while others are putting pitch on the large painted Hudson's Bay canoe."

[1] KJ says they travelled at seven or eight miles an hour.

to the term "medicine")—I found four men, who appeared to be chiefs, sitting upon mats spread upon the ground gesticulating with great violence, and keeping time to the beating of a drum. Something, apparently of a sacred nature was covered up in the centre of the group, which I was not allowed to see. They almost instantly ceased their "pow-wow," or music, and seemed rather displeased at my intrusion, although they approached, and inquiringly felt the legs of my fustian pantaloons,[2] pronouncing me a chief on account of their fineness.

On looking around me, which I now ventured to do, I saw that the interior of their lodge or sanctuary was hung round with mats constructed with rushes, to which were attached various offerings consisting principally of bits of red and blue cloth, calico, &c., strings of beads, scalps of enemies, and sundry other articles beyond my comprehension. Finding they did not proceed with their "pow-wow," I began to think I was intruding, and retired. But no sooner had I emerged from the lodge, than I was surrounded by crowds of women and children, whom nothing would satisfy short of examining me from head to foot, following me in swarms through the camp, not apparently with any hostile intentions, but for the mere gratification of their curiosity. I passed a grave surmounted with a scalp hung on a pole, torn, doubtless, from an enemy by the warrior buried beneath. I now returned to the fort, first engaging six of the Indians to proceed with me to Red River. We left at four o'clock in the afternoon in a small boat, accompanied by Mr. Setler, and camped on the shore of Lake Winnipeg.

June 12*th.*—I wrote this part of my journal by the light of a blazing fire in the above encampment, surrounded by my six painted warriors sleeping in the front of the tent, their hideous faces gleaming in the fire-light: a head wind all day had prevented our making any great progress.

June 13*th.*—We entered the mouth of the Red River about ten this morning. The banks of this river, which here enters the lake, are for five or six miles low and marshy. After proceeding up stream for about twenty miles, we arrived at the Stone Fort, belonging to the Company, where I found Sir George Simpson and several of the gentlemen of the Company, who assemble here annually for the purpose of holding a council for the transaction of business. I remained here until the 15th, and left for the Upper Fort, about twenty miles higher up. We rode on horseback, accompanied by Mr. Peter Jacobs, Wesleyan Indian missionary [Fig. 55; crIV-33, 34], and arrived there in about four hours, after a pleasant ride of eighteen or twenty miles through a considerable part of Red River Settlement. Here

there are a judge and a court house. A Saulteaux Indian was hung here last year for shooting a Sioux Indian and another of his own tribe at one shot, the ball having passed through the Sioux and entered the Saulteaux's body: his intention was to kill the Sioux only, with whom his tribe then was, and had been from time immemorial, at war, so that the killing of the Saulteaux was accidental. The country here is not very beautiful; a dead level plain with very little timber, the landscape wearing more the appearance of the cultivated farms of the old country with scarcely a stick or stump upon it.

This settlement is the chief provision depôt of the Hudson's Bay Company, and it is also here that large quantities of pimmi-kon [pemmican] are procured from the half-breeds, a race who, keeping themselves distinct from both Indians and whites, form a tribe of themselves; and, although they have adopted some of the customs and manners of the French voyageurs, are much more attached to the wild and savage manners of the Red-man. Fort Garry, one of the most important establishments of the Company, is erected on the forks of the Red River and the Assiniboine, in long. 97° W., and in lat. 50° 6′ 20″ N., as will be seen in sketch No. 5. [Figs. 56, 57; crIV-35 to 38] On the opposite side of the river is situated the Roman Catholic church,[3] and two or three miles further down there is a Protestant church.[4] The settlement is formed along the banks of the river for about fifty miles, and extends back from the water, according to the original grant from the Indians, as far as a person can distinguish a man from a horse on a clear day.

Lord Selkirk first attempted to form a settlement here in 1811, but it was speedily abandoned. A few years afterwards several Scotch families, including some from the Orkney Islands, emigrated under the auspices of the Hudson's Bay Company, and now number about 3000, who live as farmers, in great plenty so far as mere food and clothing are concerned.[5] As for the luxuries of life, they are almost unattainable, as they have no market nearer than St. Paul's, on the Mississippi River, a distance of nearly 700 miles over a trackless prairie. The half-

---

[2] KJ states that the trousers are moleskin.

[3] Bishop Joseph-Norbert Provencher built the first Roman Catholic church at the settlement between 1818 and 1820. The church to which Kane refers and shows in the sketch was commenced in 1829 and used until rebuilt in 1908.

[4] The Rev. John West arrived in the 1820s and founded a Protestant church. Services were conducted in a log building from 1831 to 1849 when it was replaced by the present St. Andrews-on-the-Red.

[5] Kane seems to have had trouble in ascertaining the population of the Red River Settlement. KJ gives 1,000 whites and 2,000 half-breeds, and KWMS gives 2,000 whites and 4,000 half-breeds.

breeds are more numerous than the whites, and now amount to 6000. These are the descendants of the white men in the Hudson's Bay Company's employment and the native Indian women. They all speak the Cree language and the Lower Canadian patois; they are governed by a chief named Grant, much after the manner of the Indian tribes. He has presided over them now for a long period, and was implicated in the disturbances which occurred between the Hudson Bay and North-West Companies. He was brought to Canada charged with the murder of Governor Semple, but no sufficient evidence could be produced against him.[6]

The half-breeds are a very hardy race of men, capable of enduring the greatest hardships and fatigues: but their Indian propensities predominate, and consequently they make poor farmers, neglecting their land for the more exciting pleasures of the chase. Their buffalo hunts are conducted by the whole tribe, and take place twice a year, about the middle of June and October, at which periods notice is sent round to all the families to meet at a certain day on the White Horse Plain, about twenty miles from Fort Garry. Here the tribe is divided into three bands, each taking a separate route for the purpose of falling in with the herds of buffaloes. These bands are each accompanied by about 500 carts, drawn by either an ox or a horse. [Fig. 61; crIV-55] Their cart is a curious-looking vehicle, made by themselves with their own axes, and fastened together with wooden pins and leather strings, nails not being procurable. The tire of the wheel is made of buffalo hide, and put on wet; when it becomes dry, it shrinks, and is so tight that it never falls off, and lasts as long as the cart holds together.

Chapter VI.

[6] Cuthbert Grant (1796?–1854) was the colourful half-breed son of a prominent trader of the North West Company, who had assumed leadership of the half-breeds of the Red River during uprisings in 1815 and 1816. Later he co-operated with the Hudson's Bay Company, and was named Warden of the Plains in 1828. Year by year he was appointed leader of the buffalo hunt by the other half-breeds. He was made a member of the Council of Assiniboia. See E. E. Rich, *The Hudson's Bay Company, 1660–1870* (Toronto 1960), vol. II.

I arrived at Fort Garry about three days after the half-breeds had departed; but as I was very anxious to witness buffalo hunting, I procured a guide, a cart for my tent, &c., and a saddle horse for myself, and started after one of the bands.[1] We travelled that day about thirty miles, and encamped in the evening on a beautiful plain covered with innumerable small roses.[2] [Pl. XVI; crIV-52] The next day was anything but pleasant, as our route lay through a marshy tract of country, in which we were obliged to strain through a piece of cloth all the water we drank, on account of the numerous insects, some of which were accounted highly dangerous, and are said to have the power of eating through the coats of the stomach, and causing death even to horses.

The next day I arrived at the Pambinaw River [crIV-53], and found the band cutting poles, which they are obliged to carry with them to dry the meat on [crIV-56], as, after leaving this, no more timbered land is met with until the three bands meet together again at the Turtle Mountain, where the meat they have taken and dried on the route is made into pimmi-kon. This process is as follows:—The thin slices of dried meat are pounded between two stones until the fibres separate; about 50lbs. of this are put into a bag of buffalo skin, with about 40lbs. of melted fat, and mixed together while hot, and sewed up, forming a hard and compact mass; hence its name in the Cree language, *pimmi* signifying meat, and *kon*, fat. Each cart brings home ten of these bags, and all that the half-breeds do not require for themselves is eagerly bought by the Company, for the purpose of sending to the more distant posts, where food is scarce. One pound of this is considered equal to four pounds of ordinary meat, and the pimmi-kon keeps for years perfectly good exposed to any weather.[3]

I was received by the band with the greatest cordiality. They numbered about two hundred hunters, besides women and children.[4] [Fig. 62; crIV-57 to 62] They live, during these hunting excursions, in lodges formed of dressed buffalo skins. They

[1] KJ states that he had trouble in securing a man to go with him since the Sioux and half-breeds were then at war. He left Fort Garry on June 18.

[2] KJ refers to Kane's sketching the sight.

[3] KJ states that the Hudson's Bay Company took part of the dried meat and all of the fat after it was rendered.

[4] KJ describes the party of hunters more fully, stating that they were divided into two parties, of 250 men each, with their wives and children. In all there were about 1,500 carts, drawn by oxen or horses, to carry the meat home. When it was dried, each cart could carry 1,000 pounds. It took 10 buffalo to load a cart. There were about 2,000 half-breeds in all. "They are a distinct class of themselves. They live at the Red River, speak the Indian language, and live by hunting, going out to the Plains twice a year to hunt the buffalo."

are always accompanied by an immense number of dogs, which follow them from the settlements for the purpose of feeding on the offal and remains of the slain buffaloes. These dogs are very like wolves, both in appearance and disposition, and, no doubt, a cross breed between the wolf and dog. A great many of them acknowledge no particular master, and are sometimes dangerous in times of scarcity. I have myself known them to attack the horses and eat them.[5]

Our camp broke up on the following morning, and proceeded on their route to the open plains.[6] [Fig. 60; crIV-54] The carts containing the women and children, and each decorated with some flag, or other conspicuous emblem, on a pole, so that the hunters might recognise their own from a distance, wound off in one continuous line, extending for miles, accompanied by the hunters on horseback. During the forenoon, whilst the line of mounted hunters and carts were winding round the margin of a small lake, I took the opportunity of making a sketch of the singular cavalcade. [crIV-63, 64]

The following day we passed the Dry Dance Mountain, where the Indians, before going on a war party, have a custom of dancing and fasting for three days and nights. This practice is always observed by young warriors going to battle for the first time, to accustom them to the privations and fatigues which they must expect to undergo, and to prove their strength and endurance. Should any sink under the fatigue and fasting of this ceremony, they are invariably sent back to the camp where the women and children remain.[7] [Figs. 63, 64, 65; crIV-65 to 68]

After leaving this mountain, we proceeded on our route without meeting any buffalo, although we saw plenty of indications of their having been in the neighbourhood a short time previously. On the evening of the second day we were visited by twelve Sioux chiefs, with whom the half-breeds had been at war for several years. [Pl. XV; Fig. 58; crIV-40 to 42] They came for the purpose of negotiating a permanent peace, but, whilst smoking the pipe of peace in the council lodge, the dead body of a half-breed, who had gone to a short distance from the camp,

was brought in newly scalped, and his death was at once attributed to the Sioux. The half-breeds, not being at war with any other nation, a general feeling of rage at once sprang up in the young men, and they would have taken instant vengeance, for the supposed act of treachery, upon the twelve chiefs in their power, but for the interference of the old and more temperate of the body, who, deprecating so flagrant a breach of the laws of hospitality, escorted them out of danger, but, at the same time, told them that no peace could be concluded until satisfaction was had for the murder of their friend.[8]

Exposed, as the half-breeds thus are, to all the vicissitudes of wild Indian life, their camps, while on the move, are always preceded by scouts, for the purpose of reconnoitring either for enemies or buffaloes. If they see the latter, they give signal of such being the case, by throwing up handfuls of dust; and, if the former, by running their horses to and fro.

Three days after the departure of the Sioux chiefs, our scouts were observed by their companions to make the signal of enemies being in sight. Immediately a hundred of the best mounted hastened to the spot, and, concealing themselves behind the shelter of the bank of a small stream, sent out two as decoys, who exposed themselves to the view of the Sioux. The latter, supposing them to be alone, rushed upon them, whereupon the concealed half-breeds sprang up, and poured in a volley amongst them, which brought down eight. The others escaped, although several must have been wounded, as much blood was afterwards discovered on their track.[9] Though differing in very few respects from the pure Indians, they [the half-breeds] do not adopt the practice of scalping; and, in this case, being satisfied with their revenge, they abandoned the dead bodies to the malice of a small party of Saulteaux who accompanied them.

The Saulteaux are a band of the great Ojibbeway nation, both words signifying "the Jumpers," and derive the name from their expertness in leaping their canoes over the numerous rapids which occur in the rivers of their vicinity. [Fig. 59; cr-IV-43, 44 and 48–51?]

I took a sketch of one of them, Peccothis, "the Man with a Lump on his Navel." [crIV-45, 46, 47] He appeared delighted with it at first; but the others laughed so much at the likeness, and made so many jokes about it, that he became quite irritated, and insisted that I should destroy it, or, at least, not show it as long as I remained with the tribe.

The Saulteaux, although numerous, are not a warlike tribe, and the Sioux, who are noted for their daring and courage, have long waged a savage war on them, in consequence of which the

---

[5] kj notes that on this day the party did not move since it was Sunday.

[6] kj for June 22 refers to sketching the break-up of the camp and the manner of "catching refractory horses."

[7] kj for June 23 refers to his seeing "a beautiful antelope."

[8] kj for June 18 describes the incident reported here as occurring two years earlier when twelve Sioux came to a half-breed camp to make peace. If it did not occur during Kane's visit, he seems to have been attempting to make the printed book more vivid by changing the time to the present. However, if the incident had indeed occurred two years earlier, one wonders if Kane actually met, and sketched, Sioux when he was on this hunting trip.

[9] According to the sense of kj, Kane is again intimating that this next incident occurred two years earlier; it also says that not two decoys but one were sent out.

Paul Kane 1846

White Mud Portage Winnipeg R.

Plate XIII. White Mud Portage, Winnipeg River. Stark PWC7; CRIV-19.

Encampment River Winnipeg   Paul Kane 1846

Plate XIV. Encampment, Winnipeg River. Stark POP15;CRIV-22.

Saulteaux do not venture to hunt in the plains except in company with the half-breeds. Immediately on their getting possession of the bodies, they commenced a scalp dance, during which they mutilated the bodies in a most horrible manner. One old woman, who had lost several relations by the Sioux, rendered herself particularly conspicuous by digging out their eyes and otherwise dismembering them.

The following afternoon, we arrived at the margin of a small lake, where we encamped rather earlier than usual, for the sake of the water. Next day [10] I was gratified with the sight of a band of about forty buffalo cows in the distance, and our hunters in full chase; they were the first I had seen, but were too far off for me to join in the sport. [11] They succeeded in killing twenty-five, which were distributed through the camp, and proved most welcome to all of us, as our provisions were getting rather short, and I was abundantly tired of pimmi-kon and dried meat. The fires being lighted with the wood we had brought with us in the carts, the whole party commenced feasting with a voracity which appeared perfectly astonishing to me, until I tried myself, and found by experience how much hunting on the plains stimulates the appetite.

The upper part of the hunch of the buffalo, weighing four or five pounds, is called by the Indians the little hunch. This is of a harder and more compact nature than the rest, though very tender, and is usually put aside for keeping. The lower and larger part is streaked with fat and is very juicy and delicious. These, with the tongues, are considered the delicacies of the buffalo. After the party had gorged themselves with as much as they could devour, they passed the evening in roasting the marrow bones and regaling themselves with their contents.

For the next two or three days we fell in with only a single buffalo, or small herds of them; but as we proceeded they became more frequent. [12] At last our scouts brought in word of an immense herd of buffalo bulls about two miles in advance of us. They are known in the distance from the cows, by their feeding singly, and being scattered wider over the plain, whereas the cows keep together for the protection of the calves, which are always kept in the centre of the herd. A half-breed, of the name of Hallett, who was exceedingly attentive to me, woke me in the morning, to accompany him in advance of the party, that I might have the opportunity of examining the buffalo whilst feeding, before the commencement of the hunt. Six hours' hard riding brought us within a quarter of a mile of the nearest of the herd. The main body stretched over the plains as far as the eye could reach. Fortunately the wind blew in our faces: had it blown towards the buffaloes, they would have scented us miles off. I wished to have attacked them at once, but my companion would not allow me until the rest of the party came up, as it was contrary to the law of the tribe. We, therefore, sheltered ourselves from the observation of the herd behind a mound, relieving our horses of their saddles to cool them. In about an hour the hunters came up to us, numbering about one hundred and thirty, and immediate preparations were made for the chase. Every man loaded his gun, looked to his priming, and examined the efficiency of his saddle-girths. [Fig. 66; crIV-69, 70]

The elder men strongly cautioned the less experienced not to shoot each other; a caution by no means unnecessary, as such accidents frequently occur. Each hunter then filled his mouth with balls, which he drops into the gun without wadding; by this means loading much quicker and being enabled to do so whilst his horse is at full speed. It is true, that the gun is more liable to burst, but that they do not seem to mind. Nor does the gun carry so far, or so true; but that is of less consequence, as they always fire quite close to the animal.

Everything being adjusted, we all walked our horses towards the herd. By the time we had gone about two hundred yards, the herd perceived us, and started off in the opposite direction at the top of their speed. We now put our horses to the full gallop, and in twenty minutes were in their midst. There could not have been less than four or five thousand in our immediate vicinity, all bulls, not a single cow amongst them.

The scene now became one of intense excitement; the huge bulls thundering over the plain in headlong confusion, whilst the fearless hunters rode recklessly in their midst, keeping up an incessant fire at but a few yards' distance from their victims. [Pl. XVII; Fig. 67; crIV-71 to 75] Upon the fall of each buffalo, the successful hunter merely threw some article of his apparel—

[10] KJ for June 24 reads: "Made a sketch of the carts in motion. Got ahead of the party when an Indian called out that there were buffalo to the right of me. I ascended a small hill when I" etc.

[11] KJ records that Kane himself joined the chase: "I was not long in turning my horse's head in the direction of the chase. After running about 3 miles, I came nearly up to a cow. My horse became afraid. After beating for about 2 miles more, I came close enough for a shot when I found I had no ball. I fired a shot but without effect."

[12] KJ for June 25 reads: "This morning I took good care that I had plenty of balls. Left with Mr. Hallet [*sic*] and the hunters. All started ahead of the carts hearing that there were buffalo not far off. Saw the buffalo about 7 miles ahead but when we came up within a short distance, we found that they were on the other side of the lake (Lake de Roche), so I did not get a chance to run them. Some of the hunters got across and killed about 60." He continues by noting that the hunt when the immense herd was sighted was the next day.

often carried by him solely for that purpose—to denote his own prey, and then rushed on to another. These marks are scarcely ever disputed, but should a doubt arise as to the ownership, the carcase is equally divided among the claimants.

The chase continued only about one hour, and extended over an area of from five to six square miles, where might be seen the dead and dying buffaloes, to the number of five hundred. In the meantime my horse, which had started at a good run, was suddenly confronted by a large bull that made his appearance from behind a knoll, within a few yards of him, and being thus taken by surprise, he sprung to one side, and getting his foot into one of the innumerable badger holes, with which the plains abound, he fell at once, and I was thrown over his head with such violence, that I was completely stunned, but soon recovered my recollection. Some of the men caught my horse, and I was speedily remounted, and soon saw reason to congratulate myself on my good fortune, for I found a man who had been thrown in a similar way, lying a short distance from me quite senseless, in which state he was carried back to the camp.

I again joined in the pursuit; and coming up with a large bull, I had the satisfaction of bringing him down at the first fire. Excited by my success, I threw down my cap and galloping on, soon put a bullet through another enormous animal. He did not, however, fall, but stopped and faced me, pawing the earth, bellowing and glaring savagely at me. The blood was streaming profusely from his mouth, and I thought he would soon drop. The position in which he stood was so fine that I could not resist the desire of making a sketch. I accordingly dismounted, and had just commenced, when he suddenly made a dash at me.[13] I had hardly time to spring on my horse and get away from him, leaving my gun and everything else behind. [Figs. 68, 69; crIV-76 to 80]

When he came up to where I had been standing, he turned over the articles I had dropped, pawing fiercely as he tossed them about, and then retreated towards the herd. I immediately recovered my gun, and having reloaded, again pursued him, and soon planted another shot in him; and this time he remained on his legs long enough for me to make a sketch. This done I returned with it to the camp, carrying the tongues of the animals I had killed, according to custom, as trophies of my success as a hunter.

I have often witnessed an Indian buffalo hunt since, but never

[13] KJ states that he laid his gun on the pommel of his saddle before dismounting, and took out his sketchbook.

[14] Here again Kane seems to have moved the past to the present. KJ states that the buffalo's rampage had taken place the previous spring.

one on so large a scale. In returning to the camp, I fell in with one of the hunters coolly driving a wounded buffalo before him. In answer to my inquiry why he did not shoot him, he said he would not do so until he got him close to the lodges, as it would save the trouble of bringing a cart for the meat. He had already driven him seven miles, and afterwards killed him within two hundred yards of the tents. That evening, while the hunters were still absent, a buffalo, bewildered by the hunt, got amongst the tents, and at last got into one, after having terrified all the women and children, who precipitately took to flight. When the men returned they found him there still, and being unable to dislodge him, they shot him down from the opening in the top.[14]

Chapter VII.

Camping amongst the Slain.—Wholesale Slaughter.—A Sick Guide. —Parting from the Half-breeds.—A False Alarm.—Dismal Night's Lodging.—Dreadful Position.—Stinking River.—Death of the Guide.—Paternal Government.—The Fire-Water Curse.

Our camp was now moved to the field of slaughter, for the greater convenience of collecting the meat. However lightly I wished to think of my fall, I found myself the next day suffering considerably from the effects of it, and the fatigue I had undergone. The man whom I had brought with me as a guide was also suffering much from an attack of the measles. Next day our hunters sighted and chased another large band of bulls with good success. At night we were annoyed by the incessant howling and fighting of innumerable dogs and wolves that had followed us to the hunt, seemingly as well aware of the feast that was preparing for them as we could be ourselves. The plain now resembled one vast shambles: the women, whose business it is, being all busily employed in cutting the flesh into slices, and hanging them in the sun on racks, made of poles tied together. In reference to the immense number of buffaloes killed, I may mention that it is calculated that the half-breeds alone destroy thirty thousand annually.

Having satisfied myself with buffalo hunting amongst the half-breeds, I was anxious to return to the settlement, in order to prosecute my journey. On proposing to set out I found my guide so unwell, that I feared he would not be able to travel. I tried to procure one of the hunters to take his place and return with me, but none of them would consent to travel alone over so large a tract of country, from fear of the Sioux, in whose territory we then were; and who they dreaded, from the late occurrence, would be watching to cut off any stragglers. Being unable to procure a fresh man, I was about to start alone, when my guide, who thought himself better, proposed to accompany me, on condition that he should ride in the cart, and not be expected to attend to the horses or cooking. This I readily agreed to, as his services as guide were of the utmost importance.

We started next morning for the settlement,[1] a distance which I supposed to be somewhat over two hundred miles. A party of twenty of the hunters escorted us for eight or ten miles, to see that there were no Sioux in the immediate vicinity. We then parted, after taking the customary smoke on separating from friends. I could not avoid a strong feeling of regret at leaving them, having experienced many acts of kindness at their hands, hardly to be expected from so wild and uncultivated a people. We found a great scarcity of water on our return, most of the swamps that had supplied us on our way out being now dried up by the heat of the season.

We fell in with a great many stray dogs and wolves, which appeared to be led on by the scent of the dead carcasses. After hobbling the horses, putting up my tent, and cooking the supper, I then turned in for the night, not without some apprehensions of a hostile visit from the Sioux, as we were still on their hunting grounds, and in the territory of the United States, being still a few miles south of the boundary line. During the night my guide, who was very ill and feverish, cried out that the Sioux were upon us. I started up with my gun in my hand, for I slept with it by my side, and rushing out in the dark, was near shooting my own horse, which, by stumbling over one of the tent pins, had alarmed my companion.

We travelled on the next day with as great rapidity as the ill health of my guide would permit, and on the evening of the 30th of June, we encamped on the bank of the Pambinaw. I lost considerable time next morning in catching the horses, as they are able from habit to run a considerable distance, and pretty fast, in spite of their hobbles.[2] In the afternoon we arrived at the Swampy Lake, about fourteen miles across. A little before sunset we reached about the middle of it, but my guide complained so much that I could not proceed further.

I succeeded in finding a small dry spot above water large enough for me to sit on, but not affording room for my legs,

---

[1] KJ states that they left on June 29.
[2] KJ states that here Kane saw a large wolf, tried to get a shot at it, but found it too wild.

which had to remain in the water, there being no more room in the small cart than was necessary for the sick man. Having no means for cooking, I was compelled to eat my dried meat raw. I tried to compose myself to sleep, but found it impossible, from the myriads of mosquitoes which appeared determined to extract the last drop of blood from my body. After battling with them until 4 o'clock next morning, my eyes almost blinded by their stings, I went in search of the horses, which had strayed away to some distance into deeper water, tempted by some sort of flags growing there. I had to wade up to my middle in pursuit of them, and it was not until 9 o'clock that we were able to proceed.

After leaving this dismal swamp we were within a day's march of the settlement; and my guide, believing himself to be much better, insisted upon my leaving him to drive the cart, whilst I proceeded at a more rapid rate on horseback. This, however, I would not do until I had seen him safe across Stinking River, which the horses had almost to swim in crossing. Having got him over safely, I left him, and proceeded onwards in the direction of the fort. But I had not gone far before I encountered one of the numerous swampy lakes that abound in this region, and render travelling extremely difficult. I had no doubt got on a wrong track, for in endeavouring to cross, my horse quickly sank up to his neck in mud and water. Seeing that I could neither advance nor recede, I dismounted, and found myself in the same predicament, scarcely able to keep my head above the surface. I managed, however, to reach the dry land; and, with the lasso, or long line, which every voyageur in these parts invariably has attached to his horse's neck, succeeded in getting the animal out. I remounted, and endeavoured to cross in another direction, but with no better success. I now found myself surrounded on all sides, as far as I could see, with nothing but swamp. My horse refused to be ridden any further. I had therefore, to dismount, and drag him along as best I could, wading up to my very middle in mud and water abounding with reptiles.

That I had lost my way was now certain; and as it was raining hard, I could not see the sun, nor had I a compass. I, however, determined to fix upon one certain course, and keep that at all hazards, in hopes that I might reach the Assiniboine River, by following which I could not fail to reach the settlement. After travelling in uncertainty for ten or twelve miles, I had at length the satisfaction of reaching the river, and in two hours afterwards I arrived safe at Fort Garry. The next morning I learned that my guide had been brought in by two men who were looking for stray horses. The poor fellow had got rapidly worse after my leaving, and had only proceeded a short distance when he was compelled to stop. He only survived two days after his arrival.[3]

Fort Garry is one of the best built forts in the Hudson's Bay territory. It has a stone wall, with bastions mounted with cannon, inclosing large storehouses and handsome residences for the gentlemen of the establishment. Its strength is such that it has nothing to fear from the surrounding half-breeds or Indians. The gentleman in charge was Mr. Christie, whose many acts of kindness and attention I must ever remember with feelings of grateful respect.[4]

The office of Governor of the Red River Settlement is one of great responsibility and trouble, as the happiness and comfort of the whole settlement depend to a great extent upon the manner in which he carries out his instructions. The half-breeds are much inclined to grumbling, and although the Company treat them with great liberality, they still ask almost for impossibilities; indeed, as far as the Company is concerned, I cannot conceive a more just and strict course than that which they pursue in the conduct of the whole of their immense traffic. In times of scarcity they help all around them, in sickness they furnish them with medicines, and even try to act as mediators between hostile bands of Indians. No drunkenness or debauchery is seen around their posts, and so strict is their prohibition of liquor, that even their officers can only procure a small allowance, which is given as part of their annual outfit on voyages.

Without entering into the general question of the policy of giving a monopoly of the fur trade to one company, I cannot but record, as the firm conviction which I formed from a comparison between the Indians in the Hudson's Bay Company territories and those in the United States, that opening up the trade with the Indians to all who wish indiscriminately to engage in it, must lead to their annihilation. For while it is the interest of such a body as the Hudson's Bay Company to improve the Indians and encourage them to industry, according to their own native habits in hunting and the chase, even with a view to their own profit, it is as obviously the interest of small companies and private adventurers to draw as much wealth as they possibly can from the country in the shortest possible time, although in doing so the very source from which the wealth springs should

be destroyed. The unfortunate craving for intoxicating liquor which characterises all the tribes of Indians, and the terrible effects thereby produced upon them, render it a deadly instrument in the hands of designing men.

It is well known that, although the laws of the United States strictly prohibit the sale of liquor to the Indians, it is impossible to enforce them, and whilst many traders are making rapid fortunes in their territories, the Indians are fast declining in character, numbers, and wealth, whilst those in contact with the Hudson's Bay Company maintain their numbers, retain native characteristics unimpaired, and in some degree share in the advantages which civilisation places within their reach.

Chapter VIII.

Catching the Boat.—Queer Fish.—Fatal Thunder-bolt.—Killing Portraits.—Raising the Wind.—An Island with Wings.—Norway House.—Playgreen Lake.—Bound to the Rock.—A Model Athlete. —Shooting a Buck Moose.—Luxury of a Clean Shirt.—Life for Life. —A Violent Puss.—Buffalo Pounds.—A Perfect Centaur.

Hearing that two small sloops belonging to the Company which ply between the Red River and Norway House would leave the Lower, or Stone Fort, immediately, I rode down on the 5th of July, in company with Mr. W. Simpson, a brother-in-law of Sir George's, and reached our destination in about three hours. This establishment is larger than the Upper Fort, and built with still greater strength, but not so neatly arranged in the interior. We rested about an hour, and then embarked in one of the sloops; two Catholic missionaries, Mr. Le Fleck and Mr. Taché, who were bound for Isle La Croix, occupying the other.[1] We dropped down the river a few miles, and cast anchor in front of the residence of Mr. Smithers, the Episcopalian missionary,[2] and his larder and cellar being well supplied, we passed a most agreeable evening, notwithstanding the mosquitoes, which were very troublesome. Early next morning we went round his very

---

[3] KJ states that the name of his guide who died was Francis de Gourlay (or Gurlay).

[4] This is Alexander Christie (fl. 1809–1849), member of a family prominent in the fur trade. He was governor of Assiniboia in 1833–39 and 1844–48, then he retired and returned to his native Scotland.

[1] Kane refers to the Rev. Louis-François-Richer Laflèche (1818–1898) who had gone to the Red River mission in 1844 and who with Father Taché organized the Isle-à-la-Crosse mission. He was coadjutor Bishop of St. Boniface before returning to Canada in 1854. The Rev. Alexandre-Antonin Taché (1823–1894) went to St. Boniface in 1845. He later became first archbishop of St. Boniface.

[2] The Rev. John Smithurst (1807–1867), to whom Kane refers as "Smithers," was a cousin of Florence Nightingale. He was engaged to her but their marriage was forbidden because of their relationship. He went as a Church of England missionary to the Saulteaux and Swampy Cree at the Indian settlement below Selkirk, Man., where he served from 1839 to 1851.

extensive farm, which seemed to be in a high state of cultivation. He works it principally by Indians, who receive a share of the produce according to their labour.

After a hearty breakfast, we bid a reluctant farewell to our kind host, and drifted down the current, there not being enough wind to fill our sails. When night had set in, I distinctly heard the noise made by the Red River sun-fish, which I have only noticed in this river. The fish resemble our Canadian black bass, weighing from two to three pounds, and during the night they make a singular noise, resembling a person groaning; how they produced these sounds, I was unable to ascertain. We proceeded only a short distance to-day, the current running very slow. After casting anchor for the night, the mosquitoes became so troublesome on board, that Mr. Simpson and I took our blankets on shore and went to an Indian lodge within a short distance of the river, the smoke which pervades these places generally keeping them free from the nuisance. There were three or four families of women and children in the lodge, but the men were all absent hunting. They cleared a corner for us to sleep in, but one of the most awful thunder storms, accompanied by heavy rain, that I had ever witnessed, set in, and effectually prevented our repose. Such tempests are here of frequent occurrence; so vivid was the lightning, and so near the rattling and crashing of the thunder, that I fancied several times during the night that I heard our vessels dashed to pieces by it. The missionaries on board were much terrified, and spent, I believe, the whole night in prayer. A short time previously a lodge containing seven persons was struck by the electric fluid; four of them were immediately killed, the other three were much injured, but recovered. These accidents are of very frequent occurrence about Red River.

July 7th.—We embarked in the morning, and proceeded at a slow rate. On arriving at the mouth of the river we were obliged to cast anchor, as it still remained a dead calm.

July 8th.—This morning we had a strong head wind, putting a stop to our further progress for the present. Mr. Simpson and I took a small boat, and returned up the river to an Indian camp of Saulteaux which we had passed the day before. The Indians crowded round the boat on our arrival, inquiring what we wanted. Our interpreter told them that I had come to take their likenesses. One of them, a huge ugly-looking fellow, entirely naked, stepped up telling me to take his, as he was just as the Great Spirit had made him. I declined, however, as I wanted to sketch one of the females, but she refused, as she could not dress herself suitably for such an occasion, being in mourning for

some friends she had lost, and therefore only wearing her oldest and dirtiest clothes.

After some difficulty, I succeeded in getting a young girl to sit in the costume of this tribe, although her mother was very much afraid it might shorten her life. But on my assuring her that it was more likely to prolong it, she seemed quite satisfied. [Fig. 72; crIV-86] After finishing my sketch, which they all looked at with great astonishment, a medicine-man stepped up and told us that he would give us three days' fair wind for a pound of tobacco. As the demand was so enormous for so small a supply of wind, we declined the bargain, whereupon he hesitatingly reduced his price, offering a greater quantity of wind for a smaller amount of tobacco, till at length, having reduced his price to a small plug for six days, we closed the bargain, declining his invitation to stay and partake of a large roasted dog, which we had seen slaughtered on our arrival. We returned to our vessel to pass another uncomfortable night, tormented by the mosquitoes, which all our efforts at smoking failed to drive out of our hot little cabin.

July 9th.—Hauled up our anchor and left the mouth of the river with a fair wind, and proceeded up Lake Winnipeg.

July 10th.—To-day we were wind-bound under the lee of a low rocky island, and although the surf ran very high on the beach, we determined to explore it as a relief to the monotony of our voyage. [crIV-81?] The attempt furnished us with plenty of excitement, as the boat filled before we reached the shore. We, however, arrived safe, and walked across the island about half a mile. It was literally covered with gulls and pelicans, which were hatching, and all rose in one body on our approach in such a dense mass as to give the appearance of the island itself taking wings.[3] The rocks were so covered with eggs and young birds, that it was difficult to tread without crushing them. Wearied with the discordant screeching of the birds over our heads, and the smell from their dung being very offensive, we soon returned to our vessels. Large quantities of eggs are collected on this island by the voyageurs and Indians, gull's eggs being considered a great delicacy at certain seasons. There did not appear to be any considerable collection of guano here, as probably the island is washed almost clean by the high water and heavy rains in the spring of the year.

July 11th.—We entered the Straits between Lake Winnipeg and Playgreen Lake. The lake derives its name from a green plain which the Indians frequent to play their great game of

---

[3] KJ notes the Indian saying that the pelicans are the birds that make the thunder.

ball. We cast anchor here, and having a small net on board, we set it, and caught a great number of jack-fish or pike, which we found excellent eating.

July 12th.—Sailed on through Playgreen Lake, a distance of twenty-five miles, the channel lying between numerous small rocky islands, some of them so near that we could easily have sprung on shore from the vessel; from Playgreen Lake we entered Jack-fish River, and the current soon carried us to Norway House, a distance of nine miles, where we arrived in the afternoon. [Pl. XVIII; crIV-82, 83] Mr. Ross, the gentleman in charge, received us with great kindness and hospitality. [Fig. 70; crIV-89] Notwithstanding the barrenness of the soil and the severity of the cold in this region, which prevents all hope of deriving any advantage from agricultural pursuits, a Wesleyan Methodist mission is established within a few miles of the fort. [Fig. 71; crIV-84, 85] It is under the superintendence of the Reverend Mr. Mason, and consists of about thirty small log houses, with a church and dwelling-house for the minister. It is supported by the Company with the hope of improving the Indians; but, to judge from appearances, with but small success, as they are decidedly the dirtiest Indians I have met with, and the less that is said about their morality the better.

The Indians belong to the Mas-ka-gau tribe, or "Swamp Indians," so called from their inhabiting the low swampy land which extends the whole way from Norway House to Hudson's Bay. This race is rather diminutive in comparison with those who inhabit the plains, probably from their suffering often for want of food; and instances of their being compelled by hunger to eat one another are not uncommon. Their language somewhat resembles the Cree, but is not so agreeable in sound. I made a sketch of one of them, called the I-ac-a-way, "the Man who is gone on a Hunt without raising his Camp." [4]

I remained at Norway House until the 14th of August, waiting for the brigade of boats which had gone down in the Spring to York Factory, in Hudson's Bay, with the furs, and was now expected back on their return with the outfit of goods for the interior trade.[5] Our time passed very monotonously until the 13th, when Mr. Rowand, chief factor, arrived with six boats: one of the boats under the charge of a clerk, Mr. Lane,

was entirely devoted to the carriage of the furs paid annually by the Hudson's Bay Company to the Russian Government, for the privilege of trading in their territory.[6] These consisted of seventy pieces or packs, each containing seventy-five otter skins of the very best description. They are principally collected on the Mackenzie River, from whence they are carried to York Factory, where they are culled and packed with the greatest care; they have then to be carried up the Saskatchawan, across the Rocky Mountains, down the Columbia River, to Vancouver's Island, and then shipped to Sitka. I mention these furs particularly here, as they were the source of much trouble to us in our future progress.

On the morning of the 14th we left Norway House, in the boats, for Playgreen Lake. These boats are about twenty-eight feet long, and strongly built, so as to be able to stand a heavy press of sail and rough weather, which they often encounter in the lakes: they carry about eighty or ninety packs of 90 lbs. each, and have a crew of seven men, a steersman and six rowers. Mr. Lane was accompanied by his wife, a half-breed, who travelled with us all the way to Fort Vancouver, on the Columbia. We had scarcely got into Playgreen Lake when a heavy gale separated the boats and drove ours on to a rock in the lake. Here we were compelled to remain two nights and a day, without a stick to make a fire, and exposed to the incessant rain, as it was not possible to raise our tents. In the distance we could perceive our more fortunate companions, who had succeeded in gaining the mainland, comfortably under canvas, with blazing fires; but so terrific was the gale that we dared not venture to leave the shelter of the rock.

On the 16th, the wind having somewhat abated, we were enabled to join the rest of the party, when the blazing fires and comfortably cooked food soon restored our spirits. Being sufficiently recruited, and the wind being fair, we again embarked, although the lake was still very rough.

This lake is about 300 miles long, but so shallow, that in high winds the mud at the bottom is stirred up, from which it derives the name of Winnipeg, or Muddy Lake. On the present occasion the waves rose so high that some of the men became sick, and we were obliged to put into a lee shore, not being able to find a landing-place. On nearing the shore some of the men jumped into the water and held the boats off, whilst the others unloaded them and carried the goods on their heads through the dashing surf. When the boats were emptied, they were then enabled to drag them up on the beach. Here we were compelled to remain until the 18th, occupying ourselves in shooting ducks and gulls,

---

[4] This would seem to be the sketch, unlocated, referred to in item 8 of Kane's portrait log. The name "I-ac-a-way" also appears for another Indian; see crIV-29.

[5] KJ refers here specifically to Mr. Ross, factor at Norway House, as a "very kind and good man."

[6] This is Richard Lane. See *Dictionary of Canadian Biography*, vol. X.

which we found in great abundance, and which proved capital eating.

The waves having abated on the morning of the 18th, we made an early start, and arrived in the afternoon at the mouth of the Saskatchawan River. The navigation is here interrupted by what is called the Grand Rapid, which is about three miles long, one mile of which runs with great rapidity, and presents a continual foamy appearance, down which boats are able to descend, but in going up are obliged to make a portage.

I was told a story of one of the steersmen of our brigade, named Paulet Paul, who in steering his boat down by an oar passed through a ring in the stern of the boat, fell overboard, from the oar, on which he was leaning with his whole force, suddenly breaking. His great bodily strength enabled him to gain a footing, and to stand against the rapid until the boat following came past, into which he sprang, and urging the men to pull, he eventually succeeded in jumping into his own boat and guiding her safely down, thereby saving the valuable cargo which might have otherwise been lost. He was a half-breed, and certainly one of the finest formed men I ever saw, and when naked, no painter could desire a finer model. We encamped on the shore, and were obliged to remain here till the third day, for the purpose of getting the goods across, as it required the crews of all the boats to haul each over in succession. There are usually Indians to be met at this portage, who assist the men for a small consideration, but on this occasion they were unfortunately absent.

August 21*st.*—Embarked in the afternoon, and on the 22nd passed through Cedar Lake, and again entered the Saskatchawan River; the land in the neighbourhood of which is very flat and marshy, innumerable small lakes being scattered over the whole region. We met with nothing worth recording till the 25th, when we arrived at the "Pau," a Church of England missionary station, occupied by the Rev. Mr. Hunter.[7] He resides in a neat house most brilliantly decorated inside with blue and red paint, much to the admiration of his flock, which consists of only a small band of the same tribe of Indians as are met with about Norway House. Mr. Hunter and his amiable lady invited us to their table, where we found some bread made from wheat of their own raising, ground in a hand-mill, and they spared no exertions to make us as comfortable as possible.[8]

Mr. Hunter accompanied me to a medicine-man's lodge, a short distance from his own residence. Seeing a very handsomely worked otter-skin bag, apparently well filled, hanging up in the lodge, I inquired as to its purpose, when the Indian informed me it was his medicine-bag, but would not let me examine its contents until he had seen some of my sketches, and was informed that I was a great medicine-man myself, upon which he opened it for my inspection. The contents consisted of bits of bones, shells, minerals, red earth, and other heterogeneous accumulations, perfectly incomprehensible to my uninitiated capacity.

Aug. 26*th.*[9]—We left the hospitable mansion of Mr. Hunter with many kind wishes for our safety and success, and continued our journey along the low and swampy banks of the river. On the 28th, we passed the mouth of the Cumberland River. Here the men had to harness themselves to the boats with their portage straps and drag the boats up the river for several days. We passed a large quantity of the bones of buffaloes which had been drowned in the preceding winter in attempting to cross the ice. The wolves had picked them all clean.

On the 29th I fired both barrels loaded with ball at a large buck moose, which was swimming across the river. He, however, arrived at the other side and trotted up the bank. Thinking I had missed him, I went on, but on my return the following year, two Indians, who had been attracted by the shots, told me that he had dropped 200 yards from the river.

Aug. 30*th.*—We this day fell in with a small band of Crees, from whom we procured some buffalo meat, tongues, and beaver tails; the last is considered a great delicacy. It is a fat, gristly substance, but to me by no means palatable; the rest of our party, however, seemed to enjoy it much. The tongues were decidedly delicious; they are cured by drying them in the smoke of the lodges.

The river as we ascended presented a more inviting appearance, the banks becoming bolder and covered principally with pine and poplar, the latter trees springing up wherever the former are burned off. The men suffered severely from the heat, which was very oppressive.

September 6*th.*—We were within about eighteen or twenty miles of Carlton, when about dark in the evening we heard a tremendous splashing in the water, but so far off that we could not see the cause. Mr. Rowand at once conjectured it to be a large party of Blackfeet swimming their horses across the river, which they do by driving the horse into the water till he loses

[7] James Hunter had taken over Cumberland Station mission in 1844 and, with the co-operation of the Hudson's Bay Company, it was speedily enlarged to a place of importance.

[8] KJ records that Hunter "killed a small pig which we feasted on for a day." The missionary evidently regarded the arrival of the brigade as a gala occasion.

[9] KJ records the date as August 28, not 26.

his footing, when the rider slips off and seizes the tail of the animal, and is thus towed to the opposite shore. We were somewhat alarmed, and immediately loaded our guns, the Blackfeet being the most hostile tribe on the continent; but on coming up to the spot, we found it was the horsekeeper of Fort Carlton, who was swimming his horses across to an island in the middle of the river to save them from the wolves, which had killed several of them, owing to the scarcity of buffaloes. As we had but a short distance to travel next day we encamped for the night.

Sept. 7th.—When we arrived within a couple of miles of Carlton, we halted for the purpose of arranging our toilets previous to presenting ourselves at the establishment. This consisted chiefly of a thorough washing; some, indeed, put on clean shirts, but few, however, could boast of such a luxury. This compliment to the inhabitants was by no means unnecessary, as we were in a most ragged and dirty condition.

The country in the vicinity of Carlton, which is situated between the wooded country and the other plains, varies much from that through which we had been travelling. Instead of dense masses of unbroken forest, it presents more the appearance of a park; the gently undulating plains being dotted here and there with clumps of small trees. The banks of the river rise to the height of 150 or 200 feet in smooth rolling hills covered with verdure. The fort, which is situated about a quarter of a mile back from the river, is enclosed with wooden pickets, and is fortified with blunderbusses on swivels mounted in the bastion. [Fig. 75; crIV-96] This fort is in greater danger from the Blackfeet than any of the Company's establishments, being feebly manned and not capable of offering much resistance to an attack. Their horses have frequently been driven off without the inmates of the fort daring to leave it for their rescue. The buffaloes are here abundant, as is evident from the immense accumulation of their bones which strew the plains in every direction. [Saskatchewan River: Fig. 81; crIV-110 to 119, 178, 179]

The whole of the boats not having yet arrived, we remained here for several days. On the second evening after our arrival we were rather alarmed by the rapid approach of fire, which had originated far off to the west on the prairies. Fortunately, when within about half a mile of the fort, the wind changed, and it turned to the south. We, however, remained up nearly all night for fear of accidents. There were some Cree Indians about the fort, which is one of the trading ports of that nation who extend along the Saskatchawan to the Rocky Mountains, and is one of

the largest tribes of Indians in the Hudson's Bay Company's dominions. [Pl. XIX; Fig. 80; crIV-103, 106 to 109] This tribe has been from time immemorial at war with the Blackfeet, whom they at one time conquered and held in subjection: even now the Crees call the Blackfeet slaves, although they have gained their independence, and are a fierce and warlike tribe. These wars are kept up with unremitting perseverance from year to year; and were they as destructive in proportion to the numbers engaged as the wars of civilised nations, the continent would soon be depopulated of the whole Indian race; but, luckily, Indians are satisfied with small victories, and a few scalps and horses taken from the enemy are quite sufficient to entitle the warriors to return to their friends in triumph and glory. [Pl. XX; crIV-105?]

I made a sketch of Us-koos-koosish, "Young Grass," a Cree brave.[10] [crIV-102] He was very proud of showing his many wounds, and expressed himself rather dissatisfied with my picture, as I had not delineated all the scars, no matter what was their locality. He had a younger brother killed by one of his own tribe in a quarrel; this he considered incumbent on him to revenge, and tracked the offender for upwards of six months before he found an opportunity of killing him, which he however effected at last.

This custom of taking life for life is universal amongst all Indians; and the first death often leads to many, until the feud is stayed either by the intervention of powerful friends, or by one party paying the other a satisfaction in horses or other Indian valuables. An Indian, however, in taking revenge for the death of a relative does not in all cases seek the actual offender; as should the party be one of his own tribe any relative will do, however distant. Should he be a white man, the Indian would most probably kill the first white man he could find.

Mr. Rundell,[11] a missionary, whose station was at Edmonton, was at Carlton awaiting our arrival, for the purpose of returning in company with us. He had with him a favourite cat which he had brought with him in the canoes from Edmonton, being afraid to leave her behind him, as there was some danger of her being eaten during his absence. This cat was the object of a good deal of amusement among the party, of great curiosity amongst

---

[10] KJ states that Kane made a sketch of Fort Carlton and of two Cree Indians, one being a great warrior who had been wounded by the Blackfoot. The latter was evidently Us-koos-koosish.

[11] The Rev. Robert Terrill Rundle (1811–1896), a Methodist, was the first Protestant missionary in Alberta (1840–48). Mount Rundle in Banff National Park is named after him.

Plate XV. Two portrait heads, Sioux; south of Fort Garry(?). ROM946.15.57; CRIV-40.

the Indians, and of a good deal of anxiety and trouble to its kind master.

Mr. Rowand, myself, and Mr. Rundell, having determined to proceed to Edmonton on horseback, as being the shortest and most agreeable route, we procured horses and a guide and, on the morning of the 12th September, we arose early for our start. The Indians had collected in numbers round the fort to see us off, and shake hands with us, a practice which they seem to have taken a particular fancy for. No sooner had we mounted our rather skittish animals than the Indians crowded around, and Mr. Rundell, who was rather a favourite amongst them, came in for a large share of their attentions, which seemed to be rather annoying to his horse. His cat he had tied to the pummel of his saddle by a string, about four feet long, round her neck, and had her safely, as he thought, concealed in the breast of his capote. She, however, did not relish the plunging of the horse, and made a spring out, utterly astonishing the Indians, who could not conceive where she had come from. The string brought her up against the horse's legs, which she immediately attacked. The horse now became furious, kicking violently, and at last threw Mr. Rundell over his head, but fortunately without much injury. All present were convulsed with laughter, to which the Indians added screeching and yelling as an accompaniment, rendering the whole scene indescribably ludicrous. Puss's life was saved by the string breaking; but we left her behind for the men to bring in the boats, evidently to the regret of her master, notwithstanding the hearty laugh which we had had at his expense.

We were accompanied by a party of hunters proceeding to a buffalo pound about six miles off. These pounds can only be made in the vicinity of forests, as they are composed of logs piled up roughly, five feet high, and enclose about two acres. At one side an entrance is left, about ten feet wide, and from each side of this, to the distance of half a mile, a row of posts or short stumps, called dead men, are planted, at the distance of twenty feet each, gradually widening out into the plain from the entrance. [crIV-97] When we arrived at the pound we found a party there anxiously awaiting the arrival of the buffaloes, which their companions were driving in. This is accomplished as follows:—A man, mounted on a fleet horse, usually rides forward till he sees a band of buffaloes. This may be sixteen or eighteen miles distant from the ground, but of course the nearer to it the better. The hunter immediately strikes a light with a flint and steel, and places the lighted spunk in a handful of dried grass, the smoke arising from which the buffaloes soon

smell and start away from it at the top of their speed. The man now rides up alongside of the herd, which, from some unaccountable propensity, invariably endeavour to cross in front of his horse. I have had them follow me for miles in order to do so. The hunter thus possesses an unfailing means, wherever the pound may be situated, of conducting them to it by the dexterous management of his horse. Indians are stationed at intervals behind the posts, or dead men, provided with buffalo robes, who, when the herd are once in the avenue, rise up and shake the robes, yelling and urging them on until they get into the enclosure, the spot usually selected for which is one with a tree in the centre. On this they hang offerings to propitiate the Great Spirit to direct the herd towards it. A man is also placed in the tree with a medicine pipe-stem in his hand, which he waves continually, chaunting a sort of prayer to the Great Spirit, the burden of which is that the buffaloes may be numerous and fat. [Figs. 77, 78; crIV-98 to 101]

As soon as all the herd are within the pound, the entrance is immediately closed with logs, the buffaloes running round and round one after another, and very rarely attempting to break out, which would not be difficult, from the insufficiency of the structure. Should one succeed in doing so the whole herd immediately follow. When once in the enclosure the Indians soon despatch them with their arrows and spears.

Whilst the buffaloes were being driven in, the scene was certainly exciting and picturesque; but the slaughter in the enclosure was more painful than pleasing. This had been the third herd that had been driven into this pound within the last ten or twelve days, and the putrefying carcases tainted the air all round. The Indians in this manner destroy innumerable buffaloes, apparently for the mere pleasure of the thing. I have myself seen a pound so filled up with their dead carcases that I could scarcely imagine how the enclosure could have contained them while living. It is not unusual to drive in so many that their aggregate bulk forces down the barriers. There are thousands of them annually killed in this manner; but not one in twenty is used in any way by the Indians, so that thousands are left to rot where they fall. I heard of a pound, too far out of my direct road to visit, formed entirely of the bones of dead buffaloes that had been killed in a former pound on the same spot, piled up in a circle similarly to the logs above described. This improvidence, in not saving the meat, often exposes them to great hardships during the seasons of the year in which the buffalo migrates to the south.

As is frequently the case on buffalo hunts, a large band of

wolves hovered round us in expectation of a feast, and a young Indian, for the purpose of showing his dexterity, galloped off towards them mounted on a small Indian horse. He succeeded in separating one from the pack, and notwithstanding all the dodging of the wolf, managed to drive him quite close to us. As he approached he entirely abandoned his bridle, and to look at them, one would imagine, from the rapid turnings of the horse without the apparent direction of the rider, that he was as eager in the pursuit as his master. When he had succeeded in getting the wolf close to us, he transfixed him with an arrow at the first shot. [Fig. 79; crIV-104?] We selected a comfortable place on the banks of the river, and, on the boats coming up, we formed our encampment for the night.

Sept. 13*th.*—In the morning we passed a small island on which we saw a herd of eighteen deer. [crIV-125] Our hunter went round to the other side, the water being shallow enough to wade across, and, getting behind the bushes, fired twice at them before they could escape, and brought down two. The rest crossed over to our side of the river, and, as a noble buck was ascending the bank, we all fired at him. He escaped, notwithstanding, into the woods, and I hobbled my horse and pursued him on foot, tracking him readily by the blood which flowed from his wounds. I soon saw him lying down, apparently so exhausted that I forbore to fire again. This forbearance cost me the deer, for on my coming up, he made a sudden plunge into the thicket and escaped. I followed his track a long distance, but could not come up to him. On my return I found two wolves making a dead set at my poor horse, who was trembling with fear. One of them was in the act of springing at him. It was impossible for him to get away, as his fore feet were tied together. I instantly levelled my double-barrelled gun and killed both, one after the other.

Chapter IX.

Beautiful Valley.—Crossing the Water.—The curious Cabree.—A shouting Aide-de-Camp.—Strange Memento Mori.—The Love of Indian Mothers.—No Coat, no Fire.—The "Little Slave."—A Voyageur's Trust.—Surrounded by Beef.—A spirited Cow.

On my coming back to the party, I found them hanging up the two deer for the use of the crews of the boats, having taken what they wanted for themselves. This they did by forming a triangle with poles about twelve feet high in a conspicuous place on the bank, so that the wolves could not reach the meat, and fastening a red handkerchief above it to keep off the crows. Towards evening, as we were approaching the place where we were to cross the river, I saw some buffaloes idly grazing in a valley, and as I wished to give a general idea of the beauty of the scenery which lies all along the banks of the Saskatchawan from this point to Edmonton, I sat down to make a sketch, the rest of the party promising to wait for me at the crossing place. It was the commencement of Indian summer; the evening was very fine, and threw that peculiar soft, warm haziness over the landscape, which is supposed to proceed from the burning of the immense prairies. The sleepy buffaloes grazing upon the undulating hills, here and there relieved by clumps of small trees, the unbroken stillness, and the approaching evening, rendered it altogether a scene of most enchanting repose. [crIV-165 to 170]

On coming up to Mr. Rowand, we prepared to cross for the purpose of avoiding a strong bend in the river. Our ammunition, and other things that required to be kept dry, were put into a sort of basket made of a few willow twigs, with a buffalo skin drawn by a running string over them, something in the form of large bowls. This basket was floated in the water, and dragged by a string held in the teeth. The horse was then driven in, and the traveller, holding on by his tail, was safely ferried to the other side with his baggage.

Sept. 14*th.*—Saw an immense number of cabrees, or prairie antelopes. [Fig. 84; crIV-123] These are the smallest of the deer tribe, amazingly fleet, and very shy, but, strange to say, possessed of great curiosity, apparently determined to look at everything they do not understand, so long as they do not scent it. Our hunter set off into the valley, to show me the manner of shooting them, while I made a sketch. A small stream wound its way through this most beautiful and picturesque valley in a course unusually tortuous, and was fringed on each side by a border of small, dense, and intensely green and purple bushes, contrasting beautifully with the rich yellow grass of the gradually sloping banks, about 200 feet in height, and the golden hues of the few poplars which had just begun to assume the autumnal tints. [Fig. 82; crIV-120, 121]

The hunter stole forward and hid himself behind a small bush, so as to have the wind blowing from them, and gently waved a piece of rag tied to his ramrod; as soon as the cabrees perceived this, they gradually came up to him, until within shot, when he knocked one over; this was of course all he could expect, as the rest were off in an instant.

In the evening we saw smoke in the distance, which we supposed to proceed from a camp of Indians; we waited, therefore, till the boats arrived, with a view to our mutual protection, should they prove to be a hostile tribe. The boats arrived after a short time, and we remained with them all night without molestation.

Sept. 15th.—About an hour after leaving our encampment, we crossed the river again in our boat, and found a large camp of Cree Indians. They came down to us in great numbers. Mr. Rowand, being acquainted with their chiefs, they were very friendly with us, and we bought a large quantity of dried meat from them. About a year and a half after this, on my return, I met the head chief, Kee-a-kee-ka-sa-coo-way, or the "Man who gives the War-whoop," and learned something of his history, which will be introduced in the latter part of my journal. When I was in his company for some time at Fort Pitt, in January 1848, the second chief, Muck-e-too, or "Powder," acted as a sort of aide-de-camp to the other, the head chief issuing his commands in a low tone, while the other mounted his horse and delivered them to the rest of the camp in a loud commanding manner. Muck-e-too is a great warrior and horse thief, the two most important qualifications for a chief, skill in stealing horses being regarded with as much respect as taking scalps. We had much difficulty in getting away from them, as they wished to have a long talk, but our time not permitting, we resumed our journey. They, however, adroitly detained a boat that had not yet come up, and the persons in charge had to give them some tobacco before they would allow them to proceed.

Sept. 16th.—We rode on till the middle of the day through a most delightful country, covered with luxuriant herbage, the plains being enamelled with flowers of various kinds, presenting more the aspect of a garden than of uncultivated land. While roasting some meat before the fire for our breakfast, and allowing our horses to feed, we espied a party of Indians on the opposite side of the river, who were evidently making signals to another party in our rear whom we did not see.[1] Upon this, eight of their young men came down to reconnoitre, and finding we were friends, kindly conducted us to their camp. We bartered with them for some horses.

I made a sketch of one of their chiefs, Otisskun, or "The Horn," or rather I made a sketch of his back. I did this for the purpose of showing his war-cap, and also to delineate the bag

[1] KJ refers to the Indians sketched here as Assiniboin; a list of canvases given by Burpee in the 1925 edition of *Wanderings* refers to Otisskun, one of several men whom Kane sketched here, as a Cree; see also CRIV-127.

which he carries at his back. [Pl. XXI; CRIV-127, 128, 129] These bags are constantly worn, and contain some of the bones or hair of their deceased relatives. These relics they regard with the greatest veneration, and make them their constant companions, whether riding, walking, or sleeping. They are generally worn for a period of three years. Not only amongst this tribe, but also amongst others, the affection for their relatives is very remarkable, though of course sometimes exhibited in a strange manner, as appears to us. As an instance of this, I may mention the universal custom of Indian mothers eagerly seeking another child, although it may be of an enemy, to replace one of her own, whom she may have lost, no matter how many other children she may have. This child is always treated with as great, if not greater, kindness than the rest; but all the mother's care evidently arises from, and has reference to, the love which she bore to the departed.

I had an unexpected trouble to catch my horse, which had got loose, in consequence of the hungry Indian dogs having eaten the lasso of raw hide with which I had fastened him.

Sept. 17th.—We were aroused in the night by our hunter, who told us that the horses were stolen, and as he would not leave the fire unless we accompanied him, we all started in pursuit. After a run of about a mile, we came up with the horses pursued by a band of wolves; the billets of wood attached to their lassoes having retarded their further escape; the wolves were loth to leave their expected prey, but after a shot or two they took to flight. The horses were evidently much terrified, as they showed by remaining close to the camp-fires all night afterwards. [CRIV-124]

In the course of our ride to-day we killed a cabree, which was fortunate, as Mr. and Mrs. Lane arrived at our camp fire in the evening in a state of severe exhaustion, having left the boats in the morning and walked the whole day without tasting food. The boats had reached the other side of the river, and, for want of a channel, had been unable to cross over and take them in. It was unfortunately a very cold night, and very little wood could be procured; besides which, we were unprovided with either tents or blankets, having dispensed with these luxuries since we left Carlton, where we began our journey on horseback. The greatest sufferer probably from the cold of the night was a young clerk who had walked with them, and left his coat and waistcoat in the boat.

Sept. 19th.—The boats this morning found a channel and crossed over to take in the party, who had left them the morning before. We reached Fort Pitt in the evening. It is a neat and compact little fort, and is, like all the rest of the forts except those at Red River, constructed of wood. [Fig. 83; crIV-122] The country here abounds in buffalo; grain and other produce might be raised plentifully here if cultivated. We remained till the 23rd, and I took a sketch of Chimaza, the "Little Slave," a Chippewayeen Indian. [crIV-126] He was the only one of that tribe I ever saw, as they live far north of Fort Pitt, on the Athabasca Lake; his prowess and dexterity in hunting won him a degree of notoriety amongst the traders. He had, when I saw him, upwards of a hundred moose skins, besides furs to a considerable amount, which he had brought to the fort to trade with.

Sept. 23rd.—I left the fort on horseback, accompanied by Mr. Rowand, Mr. Rundell, an Indian boy, and a fresh hunter; on reaching the river we crossed in a boat, and swam our horses by the bridle. We left this establishment in true voyageur style, unburthened with food of any kind, and, although contemplating a journey of 200 miles, trusting solely to our guns, having not even a grain of salt. After leaving the boat, we saddled our horses, and had not proceeded more than ten miles, when we fell in with immense numbers of buffaloes.

During the whole of the three days that it took us to reach Edmonton House, we saw nothing else but these animals covering the plains as far as the eye could reach, and so numerous were they, that at times they impeded our progress, filling the air with dust almost to suffocation. We killed one whenever we required a supply of food, selecting the fattest of the cows, taking only the tongues and boss, or hump, for our present meal, and not burdening ourselves unnecessarily with more. Mr. Rowand fired and wounded a cow, which made immediately for a clump of bushes; he followed it, when the animal turned upon him, and bore him and his horse to the ground, leaping over them, and escaping among the rest. Fortunately, he received no hurt beyond the mortification of being thrown down and run over by an animal which he felt assured he should see roasting at our evening camp fire.

Chapter X.

Long Grass Prairie.—An obstinate Bear.—Abandoning a tired Horse.
—Dried-up Lakes.—Shooting wild Geese.—A dangerous Swim.—
Boat-building.—The blazing Prairie.—Setting Fire to fight Fire.—A
cool Confession.—Indian want of Gallantry.—An Indian Strongbow.

Sept. 24th.—We passed through what is called the Long Grass

Prairie. [crIV-172] The bones of a whole camp of Indians, who were carried off by that fatal scourge of their race, the small-pox, were here bleaching on the plains, having fallen from the platforms and trees on which it is their custom to suspend their dead, covered with skins,—which latter, as well as the supports, time had destroyed. An immense grisly bear was drinking out of a pond, and our hunter went ahead of the party to try and get a shot at him. The bear quietly awaited his attack, and the Indian, seeing him so cool, rather hesitated to advance, not deeming it prudent or safe to depend on the fleetness of his horse unless he had a good start of the bear. He fired, therefore, at too great a distance for his shot to tell. The bear rose up very composedly on his hind legs, and regarding the hunter for a moment, turned about and walked away. I then determined to try my luck. As I was very well mounted, I rode up to within forty or fifty yards of him, and as he turned to look at me, I discharged both barrels; one wounded him in the shoulder, and, with a savage growl, he turned and pursued me. I set off at full gallop towards Mr. Rowand, who waited till he came within shot, when he put another ball into him,—but still the bear advanced.

In the meantime, the Indian and I had both managed to reload, and, as the bear came forward, the Indian fired, and must have hit, as the bear again rose on his hind legs; when, taking deliberate aim, I lodged a ball in his heart, and the huge monster fell to the ground. The Indian now skinned him and cut off his paws, which we found most delicious picking when roasted in the evening. The claws, which I preserved, measured four and a half inches. There is no animal on the whole continent that the Indians hold in so much dread as the grisly bear, and few will attack one of them when alone, unless with a very fleet horse under him.

We had much difficulty that evening in finding a place to encamp away from the immense number of buffaloes that surrounded us, and we found it necessary to fire off our guns during the night to keep them away. [Figs. 96, 97, 98; crIV-171, 173 to 177] We passed through a spot covered with great quantities of shed antlers of the deer. We had ridden so fast as to knock up Mr. Rowand's horse, but, having driven several loose horses with us, to provide against such emergencies, we were not inconvenienced, leaving the poor brute a prey to the wolves, which were constantly hovering about us.

We encamped this evening on the borders of a very beautiful fresh water lake. [Pl. XXIV; crIV-181?] We had passed in our route daily many *dried-up* lakes, principally small, the basins covered with an incrustation of sub-carbonate of soda. [crIV-180] Many of these are bordered with a dense growth of plants resembling in structure the well-known marine production called samphire, but of a rich purple colour. So unbroken is the incrustation of soda, as to give the spots the appearance of being covered with snow.

[Prairie landscapes: crIV-182, 183, 184]

Sept. 26th.—Mr. Rundell remained at the encampment this morning with the Indian boy, being completely knocked up by the hard riding of the preceding days. We were reluctant to leave him, but were under the necessity of going on as fast as possible, as I had still a long journey before me, and the season was drawing to a close. Mr. Rowand and myself, therefore, left the camp at half-past 3 A.M., and pursued our journey almost at a gallop the whole way, having stopped only once for about an hour, for breakfast and to breathe our horses.

About 5 o'clock in the afternoon, when about eight or ten miles from Fort Edmonton, we were met by a party of gentlemen from the fort, who were out shooting wild geese, in which they had been very successful, and on seeing the jaded condition of our horses, they were kind enough to exchange with us, so that we started off for the remaining distance at a round gallop.

On getting to the edge of the river, which it was necessary to cross to reach the fort, Mr. Rowand, having a fine large horse under him, plunged in. Though my horse was very small, I did not hesitate in following him. Mr. Rowand's horse carried him over in fine style, but mine, not being equal to the task, sank under me; still, however, I held firmly on to him, till, drifting into the rapid, he struck a sunken rock in striving to obtain a footing, on which he nearly brought me under him; but, on drifting a little further down, he fortunately found footing in a more shallow part, and was able to ford across, Mr. Rowand appearing greatly to enjoy the scene from his safe position on the shore. We were greeted by the occupants of the fort in their gayest attire, the day being Sunday.

Edmonton is a large establishment: as it has to furnish many other districts with provisions, a large supply is always kept on hand, consisting entirely of dried meat, tongues, and pimmi-kon. There are usually here a chief factor and a clerk, with forty or fifty men with their wives and children, amounting altogether to about 130, who all live within the pickets of the fort. [Pl. XXV; crIV-188 to 191] Their employment consists chiefly in building boats for the trade, sawing timber, most of which they raft down the river from ninety miles higher up, cutting up the small poplar which abounds on the margin of the river for

fire-wood, 800 cords of which are consumed every winter, to supply the numerous fires in the establishment. The employment of the women, who are all, without a single exception, either squaws or half-breeds, consists in making moccasins and clothing for the men, and converting the dried meat into pimmi-kon.

On the night of our arrival at Edmonton, the wind increased to a perfect hurricane, and we had reason to be thankful to Providence for our timely escape from the awful scene we now witnessed from our present place of safety, for, had we been one day later, we might have been involved in its fiery embrace. The scene on which our attention was now riveted, was the conflagration of the prairie through which we had passed but a few hours before. The scene was terrific in the extreme; the night being intensely dark gave increased effect to the brilliancy of the flames. [Fig. 99; crIV-185, 186, 187] We were apprehensive at one time of its crossing the river to the side on which the fort is situated, which must in that case have been destroyed. Our fears, too, for Mr. Rundell, whom we had left behind with the boys, were only relieved three days afterwards, when he arrived in safety. It appeared that he had noticed the fire at a long distance off, and immediately started for the nearest bend in the river, which with great exertions he reached in time, and succeeded in crossing. The mode resorted to by the Indians, when in the immediate vicinity of a prairie on fire, is to set fire to a long patch in front of them, which they follow up, and thus depriving the fire in the rear of fuel, escape all but the smoke, which, however, nearly suffocates them.

[Saskatchewan River: crIV-192, 193]

As we had to remain here until the arrival of the boat with Mr. Lane and the Russian packs of otters, I took a sketch of the fort, and having leisure, I went a good deal amongst the Indians, who are constantly about the fort for the purpose of trading; they were principally Crees [crIV-211] and Assiniboines: Potika-poo-tis, the "Little Round Man," an Assiniboine chief, sat for me. He was well known about the fort, and was commonly called the Duke of Wellington, I suppose from his small person and his warlike feats. [crIV-207] He was on one occasion set upon by a party of Blackfeet, and, while in the act of discharging his gun, received a wound, which he showed me, of rather a remarkable nature. The ball entered his wrist, passed through the arm, entered the neck, and came out near the upper part of the spine. He had received several wounds, but none that seemed seriously to endanger his life, as at the time I saw him he was in good health.

After relating various stories of his war and hunting exploits, he, to my great astonishment, told me that he had killed his own mother. It appears that, while travelling, she told him that she felt too old and feeble to sustain the hardships of life, and too lame to travel any further, and asked him to take pity on her, and end her misery, on which he unhesitatingly shot her on the spot. I asked him whereabouts he had directed his ball. His reply was, "Do you think I would shoot her in a bad place? I hit her there;" pointing his finger to the region of the heart. "She died instantly, and I cried at first; but after I had buried her, the impression wore off."

It must not be supposed that Indians look on the softer sex with feelings at all resembling those entertained towards them in civilised life; in fact, they regard them more in the light of slaves than as companionable beings. As might be expected, this is most evident in their treatment of aged women, whom they consider as scarcely fit to live.

Some of the Company's servants were going up the Saskatchawan river on the ice in the winter, with a sledge of dogs drawing a load, comprising, among other things, an eight-gallon keg of spirits; and in crossing over a piece of bad ice, the dogs went through sledge and all, and were instantly carried under by the force of the current. In the following summer, some Indians, while bathing near the shore, picked up the cask safe and sound; and finding, on examination, that it was full of rum, made up their minds to have a booze. One of them, however, suggested the possibility that the white men had put poison in it, to be revenged on them for having fired on the inland brigade of canoes while going up the river the year before. This deterred them from drinking any until they had tested its quality. For this purpose they selected eight of the oldest women in the camp to try the experiment on. The women fell into the snare; and, becoming intoxicated, commenced singing with great glee. But an old chief soon put a stop to their potations, saying there could be no poison in it, and that it was far too good to be thrown away upon old women. The whole tribe then set to, and were not long in draining the cask.

One day, whilst wandering some distance to the south of the fort, I saw two Assiniboine Indians hunting buffaloes. One was armed with a spear, formed of an ashpole about ten feet long, ornamented with tufts of hair, and having an iron head, which is procured from the trading posts; the other with a bow formed of ash, with the sinews of a buffalo gummed to the back of it. These they use with great dexterity and force; I have known an instance of the arrows passing through the body of the animal,

and sticking in the ground at the opposite side. [Fig. 105; crIV-208, 209, 210]

[Indian studies: crIV-228 to 239]

Chapter XI.

Leaving Fort Edmonton.—The Last of the Buffaloes.—Sir George's Highland Piper.—An Indian Delicacy.—Freak of an Evil Spirit.—Singular Cradle.—Jasper's House.—The Snow and the Cold.—First-steps in Snow Shoes.—Nearly Roasted Aive.—Going down Hill.—Wading an Icy Torrent.—Making up for lost Time.—Shooting the Dalle de Mort.—A Narrow Escape.—A Wet Voyage.

We remained at Edmonton till the morning of the 6th, preparing for the arduous journey which now lay before us. On that morning we started at daybreak. Our party consisted of Mr. Lane and his wife, a young man named Charles, a clerk, who was going to a post on the west side of the Rocky Mountains, a person of the name of M'Gillveray, and sixteen men. We had with us sixty-five horses to carry our baggage and provisions. This seems a large supply of horses for so small a party; but it must be taken into consideration that Edmonton is the last post at which we could get a supply of provisions on this side of the mountains; so that we were necessarily obliged to carry a large quantity with us, owing to the difficulty which always arises in getting the men away from comfortable quarters to commence a long and difficult journey, coupled with the wildness of the horses on a first day's march. We only succeeded in reaching Sturgeon Creek, a distance of about sixteen miles, on the first day. Seeing a group of buffaloes reposing near a small lake, I took a sketch (No. 6). They were the last that I should see for some time; and it was easy for me to keep up with the party at the slow rate at which they proceeded. [Fig. 110; crIV-240 to 244]

Oct. 7th.—The prairies were now fast receding behind us, our course lying to the northward. The track became almost impassable, being wet and swampy; and the horses often stuck fast, and threw off their loads in their struggles to extricate themselves from the mire. We were lucky enough to vary our provisions by killing a great many geese of the kind called "wavy." Could we have procured a little salt, I should have found them more palatable.

Oct. 8th.—The tremendous hurricane above alluded to had torn up immense trees by the roots, and scattered them in piles one on another in all directions, detaining us sometimes for hours, while the men cut a path through them for the horses. Our progress through the thick woods, which we had now fairly entered, was necessarily very slow and fatiguing.

Oct. 9th.—The track still continued bad, and we saw no game; so that our time passed very monotonously, as we had to keep pace with the loaded horses. A Highlander of the name of Colin Frazer had joined our party. He was on his way to a small post, of which he had the charge, at the head of the Athabasca River, in the Rocky Mountains, where he had resided for the last eleven years. He had been brought to the country by Sir George Simpson, in the capacity of his piper, at the time when he explored Frazer's River, and made an extensive voyage through a country hitherto little known, and among Indians who had seen few or no white men. He carried the pipes with him, dressed in his Highland costume; and when stopping at forts, or wherever he found Indians, the bagpipes were put in requisition, much to the astonishment of the natives, who supposed him to be a relation of the Great Spirit, having, of course, never beheld so extraordinary a looking man, or such a musical instrument, which astonished them as much as the sound produced. One of the Indians asked him to intercede with the Great Spirit for him; but Frazer remarked, the petitioner little thought how limited his influence was in that quarter.

Oct. 10th.—I left the party this morning and proceeded on, and at two o'clock in the afternoon, after a smart ride, I arrived at Fort Assiniboine, on the Athabasca River. This establishment, although honoured with the name of a fort, is a mere post used for taking care of horses, a common man or horsekeeper being in charge of it. The rest of the party arrived late the same evening.

Oct. 11th.—We found two boats here, which our men immediately overhauled and set to work to repair and pitch. At 2 o'clock P.M. we embarked, and continued travelling slowly on, against a very strong current, for five days. The water was very low, which added greatly to our difficulties. We saw no game nor Indians to break the monotony of our labour, and the nights and mornings were becoming very cold.

Oct. 15th.—When we stopped to take breakfast, it was very cold and snowing. We held a council, and it was determined that, as the weather had set in so bad, five men and one boat, with the clerk Charles, should return back to Fort Assiniboine with the Russian packs of otter skins.[1] We were now all obliged to crowd into one boat, the others having gone back; and were frequently obliged to disembark and lighten the boat, owing to the unusual lowness of the river. We had almost continually to drag the boat onwards with a line, the men waist deep in the water. One of them slipped off a log into deep water, and it was with no small difficulty we saved him from being drowned. We had not extricated him from the river five minutes before his clothes were stiff with ice. I asked him if he was not cold, and his reply was characteristic of the hardihood of the Iroquois, of which tribe our party principally consisted, "My clothes are cold, but I am not."

Oct. 16th.—The weather had now set in so cold that we began to doubt the possibility of crossing the mountains this season. The line by which the men dragged the boat broke twice to-day in the rapids, and our boat was nearly dashed to pieces among the rocks. Had this misfortune happened, we should have lost all our provisions, and had a great chance of perishing with hunger.

Oct. 17th and 18th.—Weather fine. This is the most monotonous river that ever I have met with in my travels. Nothing but point after point appearing, all thickly covered with pine, any extensive view being entirely out of the question. The course of the river, although tortuous, is rapid, but unbroken by falls, running at the rate of six or seven miles an hour on an average.

Oct. 19th.—We fell in with an Indian hunter and his family. He had two bark canoes; he sold one of them to Colin Frazer, in which he embarked with four men, for the purpose of lightening our boat, and proceeded on in advance of us. We traded with them for some beaver meat and moose noses; the latter is the most delicate eating I ever met with, and is valued amongst the Indians beyond all other food.

Oct. 20th and 21st.—The weather was fine, and we made good progress.

Oct. 22nd.—The men were in extraordinarily good spirits.[2] I measured a tree lying on the ground, which had been cut down by the beaver; it was seven feet in circumference. We found three bears left *en cache* by Colin Frazer, an old one and two cubs. He told me afterwards that he had killed the two cubs at one shot, while one was climbing over the back of the other to ascend a bank. The cubs proved fine eating, and were much relished, as our fresh provisions had been long exhausted.

Oct. 23rd.—We passed a camp fire still burning that had been left by Frazer the night previously.

---

[1] KJ mentions 40 packs of otter, and notes that at the meeting of the men to decide what they should do because of the bad travelling conditions it was agreed that 4 men should go back and 12 go on. Kane says that as a mere passenger he did not have a vote.

[2] KJ notes the men's exuberance: "Men singing. Had for breakfast moose meat and beaver tails."

Oct. 24th.—We passed the Rapids de Mort. The men had great difficulty in getting the boat up; we, of course, had all to walk. All the ponds and still water were frozen hard enough to bear. The rapidity of the current, however, prevented ice forming in the river. A small bag of pimmi-kon made in the usual way, except that it contained Sasketome berries, was stolen, and a search being made for its recovery, a part of it was found in one of the men's bags. The only temptation to the theft could have been that it was more palatable than his own. M'Gillveray, being one of the most powerful men of the party, was called upon to administer the punishment, which he did by repeatedly knocking the delinquent down. This severity of punishment was called for by the fact, that the most disastrous consequences might arise on a journey through these desolate regions, if the most rigid care were not taken of the provisions.

Oct. 25th to 27th.—There was no change in the general aspect of the country; the same monotonous scenery still surrounded us.

Oct. 28th.—We passed the mouth of the Old Man's River. The Indians say that an evil spirit once came down this river—which is so rapid that no canoe can ascend it—and that having reached its mouth, where it enters the Athabasca, he made five steps down, leaving a rapid at every step. These rapids are a mile apart. After which he returned and went up his own river, and has not since been heard of. The river now became so shallow, that we were obliged to make two discharges.

Oct. 29th.—The bank of the river being very high, I ascended it, and saw for the first time the sublime and apparently endless chain of the Rocky Mountains. The outline was scarcely perceptible in the distance through the intervening smoky atmosphere, which is caused by the almost invariable conflagration of the woods at this season of the year. M'Gillveray wounded a moose while out with his gun. The deer took to the water, and swam across to the opposite side. I took the boat and followed him, and brought him down at the first shot. He was a fine large buck. It being nearly night, we encamped on the spot, and supped heartily off him, carrying his remains with us next morning.

Oct. 30th.—We had a fine view of the mountains from the boat for the first time; the men greeted them with a hearty cheer.

Oct. 31st.—The atmosphere clear but very cold. I made a sketch of the river and the mountains in the distance. [crIV-245, 246, 247]

Nov. 1st.—We entered Jasper's Lake in the morning. This lake is about twelve miles long, and from three to four miles wide, but at this season of the year very shallow, on account of its sources in the mountains being frozen. We had to land three men on the south shore for the purpose of decreasing the draft of our boat; but even then we proceeded with great difficulty. Shortly after we had put them on shore, it began to blow a perfect hurricane, which drove us to the north side, and a snow storm coming on, we were compelled to encamp. This was unfortunate, as it was impossible to communicate with the men whom we had left at the other side, and who were without either provisions or blankets, and we knew from the intense cold that they must be suffering severely.

Nov. 2nd.—We were now close upon the mountains, and it is scarcely possible to conceive the intense force with which the wind howled through a gap formed by the perpendicular rock called "Miëtte's Rock," 1500 feet high, on the one side, and a lofty mountain on the other. [crIV-249] The former derives its appellation from a French voyageur, who climbed its summit and sat smoking his pipe with his legs hanging over the fearful abyss. M'Gillveray and the guide went on to Colin Frazer's, distant about fourteen or fifteen miles, to procure horses, as we found that further progress in the boat was impossible, both on account of the shallowness of the water and the violence of the wind.

Nov. 3rd.—The hurricane still continued, accompanied by very heavy snow; indeed, from what I heard, I believe it is always blowing at this place. The forest is composed entirely of very high pine trees, small in circumference, and growing thickly together; these had a very curious appearance in the storm, as they waved in the wind like a field of grain. The immense long roots seemed to be especially provided them by nature to prevent their being blown over; and, as the soil is very light, and upon a rocky foundation, these roots formed a net work near the surface, which was in constant motion, and rocked us to sleep as we lay round our camp fires.

Meanwhile, our guide returned from Jasper's House with several horses. We found our boat blown out of the water, and lying fifteen feet distant from it on the shore although its weight was so great, that the strength of our remaining nine men could not return it to its element.

I selected a horse, and, taking the guide with me, started for the establishment in advance of the rest of the party. After a severe ride of four hours, and having forded the river four times, dangerously crowded with drift ice borne down by a rapid current, sometimes coming over the saddle, I arrived at Jasper's

Plate XVI. Camping on the prairies (Kane and a companion). Stark POP18; CRIV-52.

Paul Kane 1846

Halfbreeds running Buffalo

Plate XVII. Métis chasing a buffalo herd. Stark PWC16; CRIV-71.

House cold, wet, and famished. [crIV-248] But I was soon cheered by a blazing fire and five or six pounds of mountain sheep, which I certainly then thought far more delicious than any domestic animal of the same species. About 10 o'clock that evening, to our great joy, the three men whom we had left on the south shore, came in. Their sufferings had been very great, as they had been wandering through the woods for three days without food, endeavouring to find the house, which none of them had been at before. One of them had not even taken his coat with him, and it was only by lying huddled together at night that they escaped being frozen. Another suffered dreadfully from the swelled state of his legs, caused by the strings usually tied round their leggings being too tight, and which, owing to his benumbed condition, he did not perceive. We had some difficulty in cutting them off, as they were buried in the swollen flesh.

Nov. 4th.—Mr. Lane and party arrived safe in the evening with the loaded horses. Jasper's House consists of only three miserable log huts. The dwelling-house is composed of two rooms, of about fourteen or fifteen feet square each. One of them is used by all comers and goers: Indians, voyageurs, and traders, men, women, and children being huddled together indiscriminately; the other room being devoted to the exclusive occupation of Colin and his family, consisting of a Cree squaw, and nine interesting half-breed children. One of the other huts is used for storing provision in, when they can get any, and the other I should have thought a dog-kennel had I seen many of the canine species about. This post is only kept up for the purpose of supplying horses to parties crossing the mountains. I made a sketch of the establishment (No. 7). [Fig. 111; crIV-250]

Nov. 5th.—We started with a cavalcade of thirteen loaded horses, but as we did not expect to be able to get the horses across the mountains, I got an Indian to make me a pair of snow shoes. The Indians about here do not number above fifteen or twenty; they are the Shoo-Schawp[3] tribe, and their chief, of whom I made a sketch, is called "Capote Blanc" by the voyageurs—in their own language it is Assannitchay, but means the same. [crIV-251] His proper location is a long distance to the north-east; but he had been treacherously entrapped, whilst travelling with thirty-seven of his people, by a hostile tribe, which met him and invited him to sit down and smoke the pipe of peace. They unsuspectingly laid down their arms, but before they had time to smoke, their treacherous hosts seized their

[3] The "Shoo-Schawp" or Shuswap Indians lived to the southwest rather than the northeast of this spot, their lands lying between the Columbia and Fraser rivers.

arms and murdered them all except eleven, who managed to escape, and fled to Jasper's House, where they remained, never daring to return to their own country through the hostile tribe. Capote Blanc was a very simple, kind-hearted old man, with whom I became very friendly.

[Carrier Indian: crIV-252]

We left this inhospitable spot about noon, and crossed the river in a small canoe to where the men were waiting for us, with the horses, which they had swam across the river in the morning. [Figs. 112, 115; crIV-253, 254, 264, 265] We rode on till 4 o'clock, and encamped in a small prairie, of which I made a sketch. [crIV-263?]

Nov. 6th.—We made but few miles of progress to-day, being obliged to encamp at La Row's [LaRocque's] Prairie in order to pasture our horses, our next stopping place being too distant to reach that evening. [crIV-255]

Nov. 7th.—We made a *long day*; our route lay sometimes over almost inaccessible crags, and at others through gloomy and tangled forest; as we ascended, the snow increased in depth, and we began to feel the effects of the increasing cold and rarefaction of the atmosphere.

Nov. 8th.—We saw two mountain goats looking down on us from a lofty and precipitous ledge of rock, not exceeding, to all appearance, a few inches in width. [Fig. 114; crIV-258 to 262] One of the Indians who accompanied us from Jasper's House to take back the horses, started to attain a crag above them, as these animals cannot be approached near enough to shoot them from below, their gaze being always directed downwards. They chanced, however, to see him going up, and immediately escaped to an inaccessible height.

Nov. 9th.—Finding the snow so deep, and knowing, not only that we were late, but that our further progress must be slow, we became apprehensive that the party who should be waiting for us with boats and provisions from Fort Vancouver, at the other side of the mountains, would give up all hopes of meeting us and might leave. This would have entailed the most fearful hardships upon us, if it did not produce actual destruction, as we should have had to recross the mountains with scarcely any or no provisions. We, therefore, despatched the guide and M'Gillveray, to hasten on to Boat Encampment. We encamped at the "Grand Batteur," where we found some snow shoes, which had been hidden by the party that had come out in the spring.

Nov. 10th.—We had not proceeded far before the horses stuck fast in the snow, and we were obliged to encamp on the spot to give those men who were unprovided time to make snow shoes, without which they could not proceed. [crIV-266, 267, 268] We remained here all day, and sent the horses back with everything we could dispense with, our provisions and blankets being quite as much as the men could carry; and some of the new hands, who had only come into the country that year, were now so knocked up by their long and fatiguing voyage from Montreal, which they had left in the spring, as to be quite useless.

Nov. 11th.—We sent two experienced men in advance to beat the track for the new beginners, and made our first essay on snow shoes. Some of our men succeeded but indifferently in the attempt, having never used them before; and the shoes, which we made the day before not being of the best description, materially impeded our progress. The shoes which the Indian had made for me at Jasper House were particularly good ones, and I found little difficulty in their use. Mrs. Lane had also taken the precaution to bring a pair with her, and as she had been accustomed to them from her childhood at Red River, where they are a great deal used, she proved one of our best pedestrians. We encamped early, making for the first time what is called a regular winter encampment. This is only made where the snow is so deep that it cannot be removed so as to reach the ground. The depth to which the snow attains can be calculated by the stumps of the trees cut off at its former level for previous camp fires; some of these were twelve or fifteen feet above us at the present time, and the snow was nine or ten feet deep under us. Some of the old voyageurs amused themselves by telling the new hands or *Mangeurs du Lard*, that the Indians in those parts were giants from thirty to forty feet high, and that accounted for the trees being cut off at such an unusual height.

It is necessary to walk repeatedly with snow shoes over the place chosen for the encampment until it is sufficiently beaten down to bear a man without sinking on its surface. Five or six logs of green timber, from eighteen to twenty feet long, are laid down close together, in parallel lines, so as to form a platform. The fire of dry wood is then kindled on it, and pine branches are spread on each side, on which the party, wrapped in their blankets, lie down with their feet towards the fire. The parallel logs rarely burn through in one night, but the dropping coals and heat form a deep chasm immediately under the fire, into which the logs are prevented from falling by their length. Into this hole an Iroquois, who had placed himself too near the fire, rolled a depth of at least six or seven feet, the snow having

melted from under him while asleep. His cries awoke me, and after a hearty laugh at his fiery entombment, we succeeded in dragging him out.

Nov. 12th.—To-day we attained what is called the Height of Land. There is a small lake at this eminence called the Committee's Punch-bowl; this forms the head waters of one branch of the Columbia River on the west side of the mountains, and of the Athabasca on the east side. It is about three quarters of a mile in circumference, and is remarkable as giving rise to two such mighty rivers; the waters of the one emptying in the Pacific Ocean, and of the other into the Arctic Sea. We encamped on its margin, with difficulty protecting ourselves from the intense cold. [Fig. 116; crIV-269]

Nov. 13th.—The lake being frozen over to some depth, we walked across it, and shortly after commenced the descent of the grand côte, having been seven days continually ascending. The descent was so steep, that it took us only one day to get down to nearly the same level as that of Jasper's House. The descent was a work of great difficulty on snow shoes, particularly for those carrying loads; their feet frequently slipped from under them, and the loads rolled down the hill. Some of the men, indeed, adopted the mode of rolling such loads as would not be injured down before them. On reaching the bottom, we found eight men waiting, whom M'Gillveray and the guide had sent on to assist us to Boat Encampment, and we all encamped together.

Nov. 14th.—I remained at the camp fire finishing one of my sketches, the men having made a very early start in order to reach Boat Encampment, where they would get a fresh supply of provisions, ours being nearly exhausted. [crIV-270 to 274] As soon as I had finished my sketch I followed them, and soon arrived at a river about seventy yards across, and with a very rapid current.

Having followed their track in the snow to the edge of the river, and seeing the strength of the current, I began to look for other tracks, under the impression that they might possibly have discovered a way to get round it. But I was soon undeceived by seeing in the snow on the other side the path they had beaten down on the opposite bank; nothing, therefore, remained but for me to take off my snow shoes, and make the traverse. The water was up to my middle, running very rapidly, and filled with drift ice, some pieces of which struck me, and nearly forced me down the stream. I found on coming out of the water my capote and leggings frozen stiff. My difficulties, however, were only beginning, as I was soon obliged to cross again four times, when, my legs becoming completely benumbed, I dared not venture on the fifth, until I had restored the circulation by running up and down the beach. I had to cross twelve others in a similar manner, being seventeen in all, before I overtook the rest of the party at the encampment. The reason of these frequent crossings is, that the only pass across the mountains is the gorge formed by the Athabasca at one side, and the Columbia at the other; and the beds of these torrents can only be crossed in the spring before the thaws commence, or in the fall after the severe weather has set in. During the summer the melting of the mountain snow and ice renders them utterly impracticable.

Nov. 15th.—It will be easily imagined with what regret we left a warm fire and comfortable encampment, to plunge at once into one of the deepest crossings we had yet encountered, covered like the preceding with running ice. Here, as in many other of the crossings, our only means of withstanding the force of the current was for all to go abreast shoulder to shoulder, in a line parallel with it, each man being supported by all below him. Mrs. Lane, although it was necessary to carry her in the arms of two powerful men across the river, acquitted herself in other respects as well as any of us. One of the greatest annoyances accompanying the use of snow shoes, is that of having to take them off on entering a river, and replacing them over the wet and frozen moccasins on coming out of it.

Before stopping to breakfast this morning, we crossed the river twenty-five times, and twelve times more before camping; having waded it thirty-seven times in all during the day.

The Columbia here makes long reaches, to and fro, through a valley, in some parts three miles wide, and backed with stupendous mountains, rearing their snowy tops above the clouds, and forming here and there immense glaciers, reflecting the rays of the sun with extreme brilliancy and prismatic beauty. The last part of the route lay through a slimy lake or swamp, frozen over, but not with sufficient solidity to bear us, so that we had to wade above our knees in a dense mass of snow, ice, and mud, there being no such thing as a dry spot to afford a moment's respite from the scarcely endurable severity of the cold, under which I thought I must have sunk exhausted.

At length, however, we arrived at Boat Encampment, about 5 P.M., almost perishing with cold and hunger, having tasted nothing since what I have already termed breakfast, which consisted only of a small supply of soup made of pemmi-kon, this being the mode of making the most of a small quantity of it.

On our arrival we found a good fire blazing, and some soup made from pork and corn, brought from Fort Vancouver, boiling in the pot, which I attacked with so much avidity, that one of the men, fearing I might take too much in my present exhausted state, politely walked off with the bowl and its contents.[4]

The men had been here waiting our arrival for thirty-nine days, and would have returned to Fort Vancouver the next day, had not the guide and M'Gillveray opportunely arrived in time to prevent them, as they thought we had either been cut off by the Indians, or that we had found it impossible to cross the mountains. In fact, they were clearing the snow out of the boats preparatory to starting. Had our messengers not arrived in time, it would most likely have proved fatal to us all, as we could not have re-crossed the mountains without provisions.

On leaving Boat Encampment, I did not take any sketches, although the scenery was exceedingly grand; the rapidity with which we now travelled, and the necessity for doing so owing to the lateness of the season, prevented me; and as I was determined to return by the same route, I knew that I should then have plenty of time and opportunity. I shall therefore give a mere outline of my rapid journey to Fort Vancouver, a distance of 1200 miles down the Columbia River, which we accomplished in fifteen days, and which afterwards took me four months to ascend.

[Indians in the mountains: crIV-280, 281]

Nov. 16th.—Our two boats were by this time ready; they were formed canoe fashion, with round bottoms of boards, clinker built. On leaving Boat Encampment the scene is exceedingly grand; immense mountains receding further and further in the distance on every side. Few who read this journal, surrounded by the comforts of civilised life, will be able to imagine the heartfelt satisfaction with which we exchanged the wearisome snow-shoe for the comfortable boats, and the painful anxiety of half-satisfied appetites for a well-stocked larder. True it was, that the innumerable rapids of the Columbia were filled with dangers of no ordinary character, and that it required the constant exercise of all our energy and skill to escape their perils, but we now had health and high spirits to help us. We no longer had to toil on in clothes frozen stiff from wading across torrents, half-famished, and with the consciousness ever before us, that

---

[4] KJ: "The men were so glad to see us that they sang and danced and cut up all manner of capers."

whatever were our hardships and fatigue, rest was sure destruction in the cold solitudes of those dreary mountains.

About three hours after our departure, we shot the celebrated "Dalle de Mort." It is about three miles long and is the most dangerous of all the rapids on the Columbia.[5]

17th and 18th.—We passed through the two lakes, and were obliged to work night and day to avail ourselves of the calm weather, although the snow fell without ceasing.

19th.—We again entered the current of the river, where the men were enabled to rest for a few hours.

Nov. 20th.—About noon we ran through the Little Dalle, which, though short, is a series of dangerous whirlpools, which can only be passed with the greatest precaution, and arrived safe at Colville at 6 o'clock in the evening. Colville is beautifully situated about a mile above the falls of the Chaudière or Kettle Falls; it exceeds in height any other fall on the Columbia, and derives its name from the round holes that the water has hollowed out in the rocks, resembling cauldrons of various sizes. Here we were most hospitably entertained by Mr. Lewis, who was in charge. To avoid this fall we had to carry our boats a distance of two miles over a hill two or three hundred feet high. We remained here three days, during which time the men did little else but eat and sleep. The rapidity with which they changed their appearance was astonishing. Some of them became so much improved in looks, that it was with difficulty we could recognise our voyageurs.

Nov. 23rd.—We encamped in the evening a few miles below the falls. During the night some Indians, who had been prowling about, crept into the boats and stole some wearing apparel, which proved very annoying to us, as our wardrobes were rather limited.

Nov. 24th.—We arrived at the Grand Rapid, which the boats were obliged to run. I, however, preferred getting out to walk, with the object of making some sketches. [Fig. 121; crIV-290] I had proceeded nearly three miles along the shore, and felt somewhat astonished at not seeing the boats following, when I observed something in the water, which I at first took to be the head of an Indian swimming across. I accordingly prepared my gun in case of an attack, as the Indians about here are considered some of the worst on the Columbia. On close observation, however, I made out the object to be the hood which I had noticed Mrs. Lane to wear in the morning, and soon afterwards I perceived the paddles and oars of one of the boats. I now began to feel alarmed for the safety of some of the party, and immediately returned to the rapid as fast as possible. There I saw one

of the boats, in which Mr. and Mrs. Lane were, in a most dangerous situation, having struck in the midst of the rapids upon a rock, which had stove in her side. The conduct of the men evinced great presence of mind. The instant she struck, they had sprung on the gunwale next the rock, and by their united weight kept her lying upon it. The water foamed and raged around them with fearful violence. Had she slipped off, they must all have been dashed to pieces amongst the rocks and rapids below; as it was, they managed to maintain their position, until the crew of the other boat, which had run the rapids safely, had unloaded and dragged the empty boat up the rapids again. They then succeeded in throwing a line to their hapless companions. But there was still considerable danger, lest in hauling the empty boat towards them they might pull themselves off the rock; they at length, however, succeeded by cautious management in getting the boat alongside, and in embarking in safety. In a moment afterwards their own boat slipped from the rock, and was dashed to pieces. Everything that floated we picked up afterwards, but still we lost a great many useful and necessary articles. We had, in consequence of this mishap, to send back overland to Colville for another boat. This detained us until the morning of the 26th. We now continued our journey rapidly and safely, and arrived at Okanagan on the evening of the 28th November. Our provisions had run short, and we were compelled to shoot one of the horses of the establishment, which we roasted, and found very palatable. In our emergency the men partook of it so voraciously that some of them were unable to work the next day.

Nov. 29th.—We continued our course, and in four days arrived at Fort Walla-Walla. Here we remained till December 4th, when we entered that part of the country which is annually visited by an almost continuous rain for five months of the year, and during the remainder of our voyage to Fort Vancouver, which we reached on the 8th December, we were exposed in our open boats to an incessant shower. Mr. Douglas and Mr. Ogden,[6] the two chief factors in charge of the fort, came down to

---

[5] KJ: "There were 2 men killed and eaten here from starvation, their canoe having been lost and their provisions run out. One killed two of his companions and the fourth one escaped. Our guide's father was one of the men killed. About 8 years ago there was [*sic*] 14 passengers drowned here by the upsetting of a canoe."

[6] Sir James Douglas (1803–1877), a British Guianan, joined the North West Company in 1820, then transferred to the Hudson's Bay Company, and retired as a chief factor in 1858. He was appointed governor of Vancouver Island in 1851 and of British Columbia in 1858. See *Dictionary of Canadian Biography*, vol. X.

Peter Skene Ogden (1794–1854), a Quebecker, had joined the North West Company in 1811 and became a chief trader of the Hudson's Bay Company in 1823 and chief factor in 1835. Most of his life after 1818 was spent on the Pacific slope, and he died in Oregon City.

the landing, a distance of about half a mile, to welcome us on our arrival, all hopes of which they had given up, and conducted us up to the fort, where we were entertained with the most liberal hospitality.[7]

Chapter XII.

Fort Vancouver.—The Flatheads.—Hereditary Names.—Casanov. —Ravages of Fever.—The Evil Genius.—How to flatten the Head. —The Sign of a Slave.—An impracticable Tongue.—"Clark, how are you?"—Revolting Habits.—Chinook Costume.—Baskets Water-tight.—How they cook the Camas.—Chinook Olives.—Chinook Lodges.—Good-tempered Gamblers.

Fort Vancouver, the Indian name of which is Katchutequa, or "the Plain," is the largest post in the Hudson's Bay Company's dominions, and has usually two chief factors, with eight or ten clerks and 200 voyageurs, residing there. [Figs. 150, 151; crIV-397 to 401] Our society was also enlivened by the addition of the officers of Her Majesty's ship of war the "Modeste," which had been on this station for two years, and lay in the river opposite the establishment. The buildings are enclosed by strong pickets about sixteen feet high, with bastions for cannon at the corners. The men, with their Indian wives, live in log huts near the margin of the river, forming a little village—quite a Babel of languages, as the inhabitants are a mixture of English, French, Iroquois, Sandwich Islanders [Fig. 154; crIV-416, 417], Crees and Chinooks.

The Columbia is here, ninety miles from its mouth, a mile and a quarter wide; the surrounding country is well wooded and fertile, the oak and pine being of the finest description. [Fig. 155; crIV-409 to 413, and ? 441, 442] A large farm is cultivated about eight miles up the river, producing more grain than the fort consumes; the surplus being sent to the Sandwich Islands and the Russian dominions. They have immense herds of domestic horned cattle, which run wild in unknown numbers; and sheep and horses are equally numerous. [crIV-406] When first introduced from California, Dr. M'Laughlin, the gentle-

man then in charge, would not allow any of the horned cattle to be killed for the use of the establishment until their numbers had reached 600, by which means they have multiplied beyond calculation. During the five months' autumn and winter, it rains almost continuously, with very little frost or snow. The river, however, was frozen over for a short time during the winter I spent there, but it was remarked as the coldest season ever experienced; during the other seven months the weather is dry and sultry.

[Mount Hood: crIV-402 to 405]

The Flat-Head Indians are met with on the banks of the Columbia River, from its mouth eastward to the Cascades, a distance of about 150 miles; they extend up the Walhamette River's mouth, about thirty or forty miles, and through the district between the Walhamette and Fort Astoria, now called Fort George. To the north they extend along the Cowlitz River, and the tract of land lying between that and Puget's Sound. About two-thirds of Vancouver's Island is also occupied by them, and they are found along the coasts of Puget's Sound and the Straits of Juan de Fuca. The Flatheads are divided into numerous tribes, each having its own peculiar locality, and differing more or less from the others in language, customs, and manners. Those in the immediate vicinity of the fort are principally Chinooks and Klickataats, and are governed by a chief called Casanov. This name has no translation, the Indians on the west side of the Rocky Mountains differing from those on the east in having hereditary names, to which no particular meaning appears to be attached, and the origin of which is in many instances forgotten.

Casanov is a man of advanced age, and resides principally at Fort Vancouver. I made a sketch (No. 8) of him while staying at the fort. [Pl. XXXVI; crIV-418, 419] Previously to 1829 Casanov was considered a powerful chief, and could lead into the field 1000 men, but in that year the Hudson's Bay Company and emigrants from the United States introduced the plough for the first time into Oregon; and the locality, hitherto considered one of the most healthy, was almost depopulated by the fever and ague. His own immediate family, consisting of ten wives, four children, and eighteen slaves, were reduced in one year to one wife, one child, and two slaves. Casanov is a man of more than ordinary talent for an Indian, and he has maintained his great influence over his tribe chiefly by means of the superstitious dread in which they held him. For many years, in the early period of his life, he kept a hired assassin to remove any obnoxious individual against whom he entertained personal

[7] KJ contains at this point an insertion evidently intended as an appendix: "This winter so cold in Oregon that 317 horses died at Colvil out of 320 leaving only 3 alive. Horned cattle not so great a proportion of deaths. The Indians suffered greatly. Some of the chiefs owned as much as 1000 to 1500 horses.

"Accidents on the Columbia River: Drowned at the Rapid St. Martin 2 / Dalles des Morts 2 / 2 grose point [*sic*] 11 / Rappid de Prate 5 / La Shute 1 / Little Dalles 26 / Grand Dalles 15 / Cascades 4 / Portage New 2 / [Total:] 68."

enmity. This bravo, whose occupation was no secret, went by the name of Casanov's scoocoom, or, "the Evil Genius." He finally fell in love with one of Casanov's wives, who eloped with him. Casanov vowed vengeance, but the pair for a long time eluded his search; until one day he met his wife in a canoe near the mouth of the Cowlitz River, and shot her on the spot, and at last procured also the assassination of the lover.

A few years before my arrival at Fort Vancouver, Mr. Douglass, who was then in charge, heard from his office the report of a gun inside the gates. This being a breach of discipline he hurried out to inquire the cause of so unusual a circumstance, and found one of Casanov's slaves standing over the body of an Indian whom he had just killed, and in the act of reloading his gun with apparent indifference, Casanov himself standing by. On Mr. Douglass arriving at the spot, he was told by Casanov, with an apology, that the man deserved death according to the laws of the tribe, who as well as the white man inflicted punishment proportionate to the nature of the offence. In this case the crime was one of the greatest an Indian could be guilty of, namely, the robbing the sepulchre canoes. Mr. Douglass, after severely reprimanding him, allowed him to depart with the dead body.

Sacred as the Indians hold their burial places, Casanov himself, a short time after the latter occurrence, had his only son buried in the cemetery of the Fort. He died of consumption—a disease very common amongst all Indians—proceeding no doubt from their constant exposure to the sudden vicissitudes of the climate. The coffin was made sufficiently large to contain all the necessaries supposed to be required for his comfort and convenience in the world of spirits. The chaplain of the Fort read the usual service at the grave, and after the conclusion of the ceremony, Casanov returned to his lodge, and the same evening attempted, as narrated below, the life of the bereaved mother, who was the daughter of the great chief generally known as King Comcomly, so beautifully alluded to in Washington Irving's "Astoria." She was formerly the wife of a Mr. McDougall,[1] who bought her from her father for, as it was supposed, the enormous price of ten articles of each description, guns, blankets, knives, hatchets, &c., then in Fort Astoria. Comcomly, however, acted with unexpected liberality on the occasion by carpeting her path from the canoe to the Fort with sea otter skins, at that time numerous and valuable, but now scarce, and presenting them as a dowry, in reality far exceeding in value the articles at which she had been estimated. On Mr. McDougall's leaving the Indian country she became the wife of Casanov. [Fig. 167; crIV-478]

It is the prevailing opinion of the chiefs that they and their sons are too important to die in a natural way, and whenever the event takes place, they attribute it to the malevolent influence of some other person, whom they fix upon, often in the most unaccountable manner, frequently selecting those the most dear to themselves and the deceased. The person so selected is sacrificed without hesitation. On this occasion Casanov selected the afflicted mother, notwithstanding she had during the sickness of her son been one of the most assiduous and devoted of his attendants, and of his several wives she was the one he most loved; but it is the general belief of the Indians on the west side of the mountains, that the greater the privation they inflict on themselves the greater would be the manifestation of their grief, and the more pleasing to the departed spirit. Casanov assigned to me an additional motive for his wish to kill his wife, namely, that as he knew she had been so useful to her son and so necessary to his happiness and comfort in this world, he wished to send her with him as his companion on his long journey. She, however, escaped into the woods, and next morning reached the Fort imploring protection; she was accordingly secreted for several days until her own relations took her home to Chinook Point. In the meantime a woman was found murdered in the woods, and the act was universally attributed to Casanov or one of his emissaries.

I may here mention a painful occurrence which took place on Thompson's River, in New Caledonia, as illustrative of this peculiar superstition.

A chief dying, his widow considered a sacrifice as indispensable, but having selected a victim of rather too much importance, she was unable for some time to accomplish her object; at length the nephew of the chief, no longer able to bear the continual taunts of cowardice which she unceasingly heaped upon him, seized his gun and started for the Company's Fort on the river, about twenty miles distant. On arriving he was courteously received by Mr. Black,[2] the gentleman in charge of the Fort, who expressed great regret at the death of his old friend the chief. After presenting the Indian with something to eat and giving him some tobacco, Mr. Black turned to leave the room, and while opening the door was shot from behind by his treacherous guest and immediately expired. The murderer succeeded

---

[1] Duncan McDougall was a fur trader working with the Pacific Fur Company of John Jacob Astor as a partner in 1810. He joined the Nor'Westers and died at Fort William after 1817.

[2] Samuel Black (c. 1785–1841) was a Nor'Wester but joined the Hudson's Bay Company in 1823. He had been in charge of Walla Walla and Kamloops before his murder by the Indian.

in escaping from the Fort, but the tribe, who were warmly attached to Mr. Black, took his revenge upon themselves and hunted him down. This was done more to evince their high esteem for Mr. Black than from any sense of impropriety in the customary sacrifice.

Amongst the Chinooks I have never heard any traditions as to their former origin, although such traditions are common amongst those on the east side of the Rocky Mountains. They do not believe in any future state of punishment, although in this world they suppose themselves exposed to the malicious designs of the scoocoom or evil genius, to whom they attribute all their misfortunes and ill luck. The Good Spirit is called the *Hias Soch-a-li Ti-yah,* that is the Great High Chief from whom they obtain all that is good in this life, and to whose happy and peaceful hunting grounds they will all eventually go, to reside for ever in comfort and abundance.

The Chinooks and Cowlitz Indians carry the custom of flattening the head to a greater extent than any other of the Flathead tribes. The process is as follows:—The Indian mothers all carry their infants strapped to a piece of board covered with moss or loose fibres of cedar bark, and in order to flatten the head they place a pad on the infant's forehead, on the top of which is laid a piece of smooth bark, bound on by a leathern band passing through holes in the board on either side, and kept tightly pressed across the front of the head,—a sort of pillow of grass or cedar fibres being placed under the back of the neck to support it. This process commences with the birth of the infant, and is continued for a period of from eight to twelve months, by which time the head has lost its natural shape, and acquired that of a wedge: the front of the skull flat and higher at the crown, giving it a most unnatural appearance. [Fig. 170; crIV-490]

It might be supposed, from the extent to which this is carried, that the operation would be attended with great suffering to the infant, but I have never heard the infants crying or moaning, although I have seen the eyes seemingly starting out of the sockets from the great pressure. But on the contrary, when the lashings were removed, I have noticed them cry until they were replaced. From the apparent dulness of the children whilst under the pressure, I should imagine that a state of torpor or insensibility is induced, and that the return to consciousness occasioned by its removal, must be naturally followed by the sense of pain.

This unnatural operation does not, however, seem to injure the health, the mortality amongst the Flathead children not being perceptibly greater than amongst other Indian tribes; nor does it seem to injure their intellect. On the contrary, the Flatheads are generally considered fully as intelligent as the surrounding tribes, who allow their heads to preserve their natural shape, and it is from amongst the round heads that the Flatheads take their slaves, looking with contempt even upon the white for having round heads, the flat head being considered as the distinguishing mark of freedom.

The Chinooks, like all other Indians, pluck out the beard at its first appearance. Slavery is carried on to a great extent among them, and considering how much they have themselves been reduced, they still retain a large number of slaves. These are usually procured from the Chastay tribe, who live near the Umqua, a river south of the Columbia, emptying near the Pacific. They are sometimes seized by war parties, but children are often bought from their own people. They do not flatten the head, nor is the child of one of them (although by a Chinook father) allowed this privilege. Their slavery is of the most abject description. The Chinook men and women treat them with great severity, and exercise the power of life and death at pleasure. I took a sketch of a Chastay female slave, the lower part of whose face, from the corners of the mouth to the ears and downwards, was tattooed of a blueish colour. [crIV-440] The men of this tribe do not tattoo, but paint their faces like other Indians.

I would willingly give a specimen of the barbarous language of this people, were it possible to represent by any combination of our alphabet the horrible, harsh, spluttering sounds which proceed from their throats, apparently unguided either by the tongue or lip. It is so difficult to acquire a mastery of their language that none have been able to attain it, except those who have been born among them. They have, however, by their intercourse with the English and French traders, succeeded in amalgamating, after a fashion, some words of each of these tongues with their own, and forming a sort of patois, barbarous enough certainly, but still sufficient to enable them to communicate with the traders. This patois I was enabled after some short time to acquire, and could converse with most of the chiefs with tolerable ease; their common salutation is Clak-hoh-ah-yah, originating, as I believe, in their having heard in the early days of the fur trade, a gentleman named Clark [3] frequently addressed by his friends, "Clark, how are you?" This salutation is now applied to every white man, their own language affording no

[3] John Clarke (1781–1852), a fur trader born in Montreal, had worked for the North West Company in 1800–10, for the Pacific Fur Company of John Jacob Astor in 1810–14, and as a factor of the Hudson's Bay Company in 1821–30.

appropriate expression. Their language is also peculiar in containing no oaths, or any words conveying gratitude or thanks.

Their habits are extremely filthy, their persons abounding with vermin, and one of their chief amusements consists in picking these disgusting insects from each other's heads and eating them. On my asking an Indian one day why he ate them, he replied that they bit him, and he gratified his revenge by biting them in return. It might naturally be supposed that they are thus beset from want of combs, or other means of displacing the intruders; but this is not the case, as they pride themselves on carrying such companions about them, and giving their friends the opportunity of amusing themselves by hunting and eating them.

The costume of the men consists of a musk-rat skin robe, the size of our ordinary blanket, thrown over the shoulder, without any breech-cloth, moccasins, or leggings. The dress which Casanov is represented as wearing, in the picture, being one that was presented to him by a friend from Walla-Walla. Painting the face is not much practised amongst them, except on extraordinary occasions, such as the death of a relative, some solemn feast, or going on a war party. The female dress consists of a girdle of cedar-bark round the waist, with a dense mass of strings of the same material hanging from it all round, and reaching almost to the knees. This is their sole summer habiliment. They, however, in very severe weather, add the musk-rat blanket. They also make another sort of blanket from the skin of the wild goose, which is here taken in great abundance. The skin is stripped from the bird with the feathers on and cut in strips, which they twist so as to have the feathers outwards. This makes a feathered cord, and is then netted together so as to form a blanket, the feathers filling up the meshes, rendering it a light and very warm covering. In the summer these are entirely thrown aside, not being in any case worn from feelings of delicacy. The men go quite naked, though the women always wear the cedar petticoat. [CRIV-437]

The country which the Chinooks inhabit being almost destitute of furs, they have little to trade in with the whites. This, coupled with their laziness, probably induced by the ease with which they procure fish, which is their chief subsistence, prevents their obtaining ornaments of European manufacture, consequently anything of the kind is seldom seen amongst them.

The Chinooks evince very little taste, in comparison with some of the tribes on the eastern side of the Rocky Mountains, in ornamenting either their persons, or their warlike or domestic implements. The only utensils I saw at all creditable to their decorative skill were carved bowls and spoons of horn, and baskets made of roots and grass, woven so closely, as to serve all the purposes of a pail, in holding and carrying water. In these they even boil their fish. This is done by immersing the fish in one of the baskets filled with water, into which they throw red hot stones until the fish is cooked; and I have seen fish dressed as expeditiously by them in this way, as if done in a kettle over the fire by our own people. The only vegetables in use among them are the camas and wappatoo. The camas is a bulbous root, much resembling the onion in outward appearance, but is more like the potato when cooked, and is very good eating. The wappatoo is somewhat similar, but larger, and not so dry or delicate in its flavour. They are found in immense quantities in the plains in the vicinity of Fort Vancouver, and in the spring of the year present a most curious and beautiful appearance, the whole surface presenting an uninterrupted sheet of bright ultramarine blue, from the innumerable blossoms of these plants. They are cooked by digging a hole in the ground, then putting down a layer of hot stones, covering them with dry grass, on which the roots are placed, they are then covered with a layer of grass, and on the top of this they place earth, with a small hole perforated through the earth and grass down to the vegetables. Into this water is poured, which, reaching the hot stones, forms sufficient steam to completely cook the roots in a short time, the hole being immediately stopped up on the introduction of the water. They often adopt the same ingenious process for cooking their fish and game.

There is another article of food made use of amongst them, which, from its disgusting nature, I should have been tempted to omit, were it not a peculiarly characteristic trait of the Chinook Indian, both from its extraordinary character and its use, being confined solely to this tribe. The whites have given it the name of Chinook olives, and it is prepared as follows:—About a bushel of acorns are placed in a hole dug for the purpose close to the entrance of the lodge or hut, covered over with a thin layer of grass, on the top of which is laid about half a foot of earth. Every member of the family henceforth regards this hole as the special place of deposit for his urine, which is on no occasion to be diverted from its legitimate receptacle. In this hole the acorns are allowed to remain four or five months before they are considered fit for use. However disgusting such an odoriferous preparation would be to people in civilised life, the product is regarded by them as the greatest of all delicacies.

During the season the Chinooks are engaged in gathering camas and fishing, they live in lodges constructed by means of a

Plate XVIII. Norway House. Stark POP14;CRIV-83.

few poles covered with mats made of rushes, which can be easily moved from place to place [Figs. 157, 160; crIV-426, 427, 429 to 432], but in the villages they build permanent huts of split cedar boards. Having selected a dry place for the hut, a hole is dug about three feet deep, and about twenty feet square. Round the sides square cedar boards are sunk and fastened together with cords and twisted roots, rising about four feet above the outer level; two posts are sunk at the middle of each end with a crotch at the top, on which the ridge pole is laid, and boards are laid from thence to the top of the upright boards fastened in the same manner. Round the interior are erected sleeping places, one above another, something like the berths in a vessel, but larger. In the centre of this lodge the fire is made, and the smoke escapes through a hole left in the roof for that purpose. [Pl. XXXVII; Figs. 158, 159; crIV-424, 425, 428]

The fire is obtained by means of a small flat piece of dry cedar, in which a small hollow is cut, with a channel for the ignited charcoal to run over; this piece the Indian sits on to hold it steady, while he rapidly twirls a round stick of the same wood between the palms of his hands, with the point pressed into the hollow of the flat piece. In a very short time sparks begin to fall through the channel upon finely frayed cedar bark placed underneath, which they soon ignite. There is a great deal of knack in doing this, but those who are used to it will light a fire in a very short time. The men usually carry these sticks about with them, as after they have been once used they produce the fire more quickly.

The only native warlike instruments I have seen amongst them were bows and arrows; these they use with great precision. Their canoes are hollowed out of the cedar by fire, and smoothed off with stone axes. Some of them are very large, as the cedar grows to an enormous size in this neighbourhood. They are made very light, and from their formation, are capable of withstanding very heavy seas.

The principal amusement of the Chinooks is gambling, which is carried to great excess amongst them. [crIV-433] You never visit the camp but you hear the eternal gambling song of *"he hah ha,"* accompanied by the beating of small sticks on some hollow substance. Their games are few. The one most generally played amongst them consists in holding in each hand a small stick, the thickness of a goose quill, and about an inch and a half in length, one plain, and the other distinguished by a little thread wound round it, the opposite party being required to guess in which hand the marked stick is to be found. A Chinook will play at this simple game for days and nights together, until

he has gambled away everything he possesses, even to his wife. They play, however, with much equanimity, and I never knew any ill feeling evinced by the loser against his successful opponent. They will cheat if they can, and pride themselves on its success; if detected, no unpleasant consequence follows, the offending party being merely laughed at, and allowed to amend his game. They also take great delight in a game with a ball, which is played by them in the same manner as the Cree, Chippewa, and Sioux Indians. Two poles are erected about a mile apart, and the company is divided into two bands, armed with sticks, having a small ring or hoop at the end, with which the ball is picked up and thrown to a great distance; each party then strives to get the ball past their own goal. There are sometimes a hundred on a side, and the play is kept up with great noise and excitement. At this game they bet heavily, as it is generally played between tribes or villages. The Chinooks have tolerably good horses, and are fond of racing, at which they also bet considerably. They are expert jockeys, and ride fearlessly.

[Indians: crIV-422, 423, 434 to 439]

Chapter XIII.

Leaving Fort Vancouver.—Seven degrees below Zero.—The Magic Bullet.—A Match for the Indians.—A Jesuit Mission.—Harmonious Gamesters.—A Wild Calf Chase.—The Swallow-tailed Coat.—The Haunted Volcano.—The Cocked Hat.—Dead Men's Canoes.—Filching a Good Name.—The Prairie de Bute.

I continued at Fort Vancouver for about a month, and left on the 10th of January 1847, with Mr. Mackenlie, a chief trader, for Oregon City, where the company has an establishment. After going down the Columbia about five miles, we entered the mouth of the Walhamette River, and ascended it twenty-five miles to Oregon City, passing two cities that are to be. One of them contained but two houses, and the other was not much more advanced. Oregon City contains about ninety-four houses, and two or three hundred inhabitants. There are a Methodist and a Roman Catholic church, two hotels, two grist mills, three saw mills, four stores, two watchmakers, one gunsmith, one lawyer, and doctors *ad libitum*. [Pl. XXXVIII; Fig. 161; crIV-443 to 450] The city stands near the Falls of the Walhamette which is here about thirty-two feet high. [Fig. 162; crIV-451, 452, 453]

The water privileges are of the most powerful and convenient description. Dr. M'Laughlin, formerly a chief factor in the Hudson's Bay Company, first obtained a location of the place, and now owns the principal mills. A great drawback, however, to its prosperity, is, that vessels cannot ascend the river nearer to it than fifteen miles, on account of the rapids. At the head of the navigation a city is building, which must eventually rival, if not eclipse Oregon in commercial prosperity. The morning after our arrival the thermometer stood at 7° below zero. Such intense cold had not been felt by the oldest inhabitants of these regions. It had the effect of killing nearly all the cattle that had become acclimated, as they are never housed. The Columbia, too, was frozen over, an unprecedented circumstance, so that my travels were for a time interrupted. I was, however, very comfortably quartered at Mr. Mackenlie's residence, who amused me in the long winter evenings over a good fire by his interesting tales of Indian life, with which he was well conversant. I will relate a couple of his anecdotes.

While he was in charge of a fort in New Caledonia, which is situated south of the Columbia River, he had a carat of tobacco, or three pounds, stolen from him. It was all that he had at that time, and of course was a serious loss. Supposing it to have been taken by some of the Indians, who were trading in large numbers about the establishment at that time, he requested the chief to call a council of all the tribe, as he had something to say to them. On this they all assembled and squatted down, leaving an open space in the centre, into which he walked with his fowling piece; this he loaded with two balls in the presence of the assembly, after which he related the circumstance of his loss, and stated his belief that some one of the Indians then present had taken it. He then told them that he wished that every one present would place his mouth to the muzzle of the gun, and blow into it, assuring them that it would injure no one innocent of the theft; but, on the other hand, if the guilty party should attempt to do so, it would inevitably kill him. He himself set the example of blowing into the piece, standing muzzle upwards on the ground; the chief followed, as well as the whole tribe, with the exception of one man, who sat hanging down his head, and when called upon by the chief to follow the example of the rest refused, saying, that he would not tempt the Great Spirit, for that he had taken the tobacco, and would return it, which he accordingly did.

Whilst Mr. Mackenlie was in charge of Walla-Walla he exhibited an instance of great presence of mind under very trying circumstances. His clerk had a quarrel and fight with the son of the chief, whom he beat. The Indian thereupon collected a large party of the tribe, and rushed with them into the yard of the fort, and attempted to seize the offender for the purpose of taking his life. Mr. Mackenlie kept them off for some time, but finding he could do so no longer, he ordered one of the men to bring him out a keg of powder, the head of which he knocked in, and taking a flint and steel from his pocket, he stood over it as if about to ignite it, telling the Indians that if they did not immediately depart he would show them how a white chief could die and destroy his enemies. The Indians took the alarm, and fled through the gates, which he immediately barred against them, secretly sending the clerk the next day to another post out of their reach.

After remaining at Mr. Mackenlie's house for about three weeks, I ascended the Walhamette River, in company with Father Acolti, a Jesuit missionary, for about thirty miles. We then disembarked and proceeded on horseback about eight miles to the Roman Catholic mission, where there is a large establishment of religieuses for the purposes of education, as well as a good brick church, situated in a beautiful prairie, surrounded with woods. [Pl. XXXIX; cRIV-454] It has also a nunnery occupied by six Sisters of Charity, who employ themselves in teaching the children, both white and red, amounting to forty-two pupils.

Father Acolti's residence is three miles from here, the Jesuit mission being distinct from the Roman Catholic; at least they are under separate authorities. Besides this one under Father Acolti, there are three Jesuit missions near the Rocky Mountains, and one in New Caledonia. This part of the country contains the largest tract of good land that is to be met with in Oregon. I enjoyed the hospitality of Père Acolti's establishment for three or four days, when I again returned to the Walhamette; and previously to embarking in the canoe, I ascended a high mountain, and made a sketch of the windings of the river, with the Umqua Mountains, where it takes its rise, in the distance. [Fig. 163; cRIV-455, 456, 457]

After visiting Mr. Mackenlie at Oregon City for a few days, I once more started for Fort Vancouver. About four miles below Oregon the Klackamuss enters the Walhamette; and, seated on the banks at its mouth, I saw a party of Indians of the Klackamuss tribe, and I put ashore for the purpose of taking a sketch of them. [Pl. XL; cRIV-458, 459] They were busy gambling at one of their favourite games. Two were seated together on skins, and immediately opposite to them sat two others, several trinkets and ornaments being placed between them, for which they played. The game consists in one of them having his hands covered with a small round mat resting on the ground. He has four small sticks in his hands, which he disposes under the mat in certain positions, requiring the opposite party to guess how he has placed them. If he guesses right, the mat is handed round to the next, and a stick is stuck up as a counter in his favour. If wrong, a stick is stuck up on the opposite side as a mark against him. This, like almost all the Indian games, was accompanied with singing; but in this case the singing was peculiarly sweet and wild, possessing a harmony I never heard before or since amongst Indians.

This tribe was once very numerous; but owing to their close vicinity to Oregon City, and the ease with which they can procure spirits, they have dwindled down to six or eight lodges.

We arrived late that evening at Fort Vancouver, having paddled on all day through heavy rain and cold. This, however, is thought little of in the Columbia during the rainy seasons, as no one troubles himself with making vain attempts to avoid wet at these periods. I remained here until the 25th of March; and although the weather was very wet, I found plenty of amusement with the officers of the "Modeste," who had built stables, and selected some very good horses. [Fig. 153; crIV-407, 408, 465?, 466?] With these we ran races, and chased the wild calves; the object of which latter exercise consisted principally in showing the dexterity of the rider, in stooping from his saddle and throwing the calf head-over-heels by the tail.

[Theatrical entertainments: Fig. 152; crIV-414, 415?]

These sports we occasionally varied by shooting and fishing, ducks and geese and seal being in great quantities in the neighbourhood of the fort. One day, a tall, large-boned Indian came on board the "Modeste" while I was sitting below with some of the officers. The Indian was dressed, as usual, in full costume, as they would call it in California (where, it is said, a shirt collar and spurs are considered the only clothing indispensably necessary); that is to say, he had his paddle in his hand, and walked about the deck with great gravity, examining the cannon, and other things equally incomprehensible to him, much to the amusement of the idle sailors. The purser, no doubt from a feeling of delicacy, took the Indian below, and gave him an old swallow-tailed coat of his, which was adorned with numerous brass buttons. The Indian, highly delighted, struggled into the garment with the greatest difficulty, as it was infinitely too small for him, the cuffs reaching but little below the elbow, and the front not meeting within a foot. Having, however, succeeded in getting into it, he perambulated the deck with tenfold dignity,

and the whole ship's crew yelled with laughter. The extraordinary noise brought us all on deck, and, amongst others, the captain came up. Even his dignity could not withstand the absurdity of the figure, to which he immediately added, by sending his steward down for an old cocked hat of his, which was given to the Indian. When this was mounted the figure was complete; and seldom has the deck of one of Her Majesty's ships been the scene of such uproarious and violent laughter. I made several efforts to make a sketch of the Indian before I could succeed; and though I at length did so, yet I fear that the picture would give but a faint idea of the cause of all our merriment. [crIV-415?]

March 25th.—I started from the Fort for Vancouver's Island in a small wooden canoe, with a couple of Indians, and encamped at the mouth of the Walhamette.[1]

March 26th.—When we arrived at the mouth of the Kattlepoutal River, twenty-six miles from Fort Vancouver, I stopped to make a sketch of the volcano, Mount St. Helen's, distant, I suppose, about thirty or forty miles. This mountain has never been visited by either Whites or Indians; the latter assert that it is inhabited by a race of beings of a different species, who are cannibals, and whom they hold in great dread; they also say that there is a lake at its base with a very extraordinary kind of fish in it, with a head more resembling that of a bear than any other animal. These superstitions are taken from the statement of a man who, they say, went to the mountain with another, and escaped the fate of his companion, who was eaten by the "Skoo-cooms," or evil genii. I offered a considerable bribe to any Indian who would accompany me in its exploration, but could not find one hardy enough to venture. It is of very great height, and being eternally covered with snow, is seen at a great distance. There was not a cloud visible in the sky at the time I commenced my sketch, and not a breath of air was perceptible: suddenly a stream of white smoke shot up from the crater of the mountain, and hovered a short time over its summit; it then settled down like a cap. This shape it retained for about an hour and a-half, and then gradually disappeared. [Pl. XLI; Figs. 164, 165; crIV-460 to 464, 467]

About three years before this the mountain was in a violent state of irruption for three or four days, and threw up burning stones and lava to an immense height, which ran in burning torrents down its snow-clad sides.[2] About ten miles lower down

---

[1] KJ states that they left at 4 P.M. and only travelled five miles the first day.

[2] KJ records Kane's making a sketch of the mountain from "Chalifour's Lake."

we encamped for the night near Coffin Rock,[3] much against the inclination of my men, whose superstition would have led them to avoid such a place. This rock gets its name from its being the place in which the Indians deposit their dead. I took a sketch of the rock before the night set in. [Fig. 166; crIV-470 to 473]

There is another rock lower down, on which were deposited two or three hundred of their burial canoes; but Commodore Wilkes having made a fire near the spot, it communicated to the bodies, and nearly the whole of them were consumed. The Indians showed much indignation at the violation of a place which was held so sacred by them, and would no doubt have sought revenge had they felt themselves strong enough to do so. [See p. 99, note 6.]

March 27th.—As usual, the rain came down in torrents. As we neared one of the points on the river, we perceived a naked Indian watching us; as we came up he ran away to his lodge, and, to my astonishment, reappeared in the cocked hat and purser's coat aforesaid. He received me with great friendship, having recognised me, before landing, as one of the party he had seen on board the "Modeste." He took me to his lodge and gave me some boiled salmon. He seemed to take great care of his uniform; but, unfortunately, the coat would not stretch, and it now burst wide open all the way up the back, which, I have no doubt, added considerably to his comfort. [Chinook: crIV-468, 469] After leaving him we entered the Cowlitz River, and proceeded up about eight miles and encamped on its banks. We saw a family of emigrants winding their toilsome way in quest of a spot to make their home. Their condition appeared miserable in the extreme.[4]

March 28th.—One of my Indians falling sick here, I procured another Indian and proceeded up the river at a very slow rate, owing to the rapidity of the current. The pine trees here are the largest I have ever seen. I measured one, which had drifted down the stream, and which had apparently a third of its length broken off. It was still 180 feet long, and 26 feet in circumference 5 feet from its root. [Trees with moss: crIV-482 to 487]

March 29th.—We came to another Indian burial ground, which seemed to be highly decorated. I wished my Indians to put ashore, but they would not do so. I was obliged, therefore, to put them out of the canoe on the opposite side of the river, and paddle the canoe over by myself. I have no doubt that they would have opposed my doing so had it not been for the name

[3] KJ says that Coffin Rock is four miles above the entrance to the Cowlitz River.
[4] KJ adds that the pines at the camping place were very large, and that the emigrant family was bound for Nisqually.

which I had already acquired amongst the Indians, of being a great medicine-man, on account of the likenesses which I had taken. My power of pourtraying the features of individuals was attributed entirely to supernatural agency, and I found that, in looking at my pictures, they always covered their eyes with their hands and looked through the fingers; this being also the invariable custom when looking at a dead person. On arriving at the place I found it lavishly decorated with numerous articles, of supposed utility and ornament, for the convenience of the defunct in the journey to the world of spirits. These articles consisted of blankets, tin cups, pots, pans, kettles, plates, baskets, horn bowls, and spoons, with shreds of cloth of various colours. One canoe, which was decorated more highly than the rest, I examined particularly. All the articles appended to it were rendered useless for this world by either tearing, breaking, or boring holes in them, the Indians believing that they would be made whole again by the Great Spirit. On examining the interior of a canoe I found a great number of ioquas and other shells, together with beads and rings: even the mouth of the deceased was filled with these articles. The body itself was carefully enveloped in numerous folds of matting made of rushes. At the bottom of the canoe lay a bow and arrow, a paddle, a spear, and a kind of pick, made of horn, for digging the camas roots; the top of the canoe, immediately over the body, had a covering of bark, and holes were bored in the bottom to allow the water to run out. These canoes are always placed on wooden supports, suspended in the branches of trees, or placed upon isolated rocks in the river, to keep them beyond the reach of ravenous animals. Sketch No. 9 represents this burial place. [Pl. XLII; Figs. 167, 168; crIV-474 to 478]

During my stay the Indians watched me closely from the opposite bank, and, on my return, they examined me as minutely as they well could with their eyes to see that I had not brought anything away with me. Had I been so imprudent as to have done so I should probably have answered for the sacrilege with my life, death being the certain penalty to the most trifling violation of the sanctity of a coffin canoe. I endeavoured to discover who was buried in the richly decorated canoe, but the only information I could get from them was that the deceased was the daughter of a Chinook chief. The Indians here have a superstitious dread of mentioning the name of any person after death, nor will they tell you their own names, which can only be found out from a third party. One of the men asked me if my desire to know his name proceeded from a wish to steal it. It is not an uncommon thing for a chief, when he wishes to pay you a very high compliment, to give and call you by his own name, and adopt some other for himself.

March 30th.—We landed at the Cowlitz farm, which belongs to the Hudson's Bay Company.⁵ Large quantities of wheat are raised at this place. I had a fine view of Mount St. Helen's throwing up a long column of dark smoke into the clear blue sky. Here I remained until the 5th of April, and took the likeness of Kiscox, the chief of the Cowlitz Indians, a small tribe of about 200. [CRIV-488] They flatten their heads and speak a language very similar to the Chinooks. They were very friendly to me and I was a good deal amongst them. [CRIV-479, 480, 481] Sketch No. 10 is Caw-wacham, a woman of the tribe, with her child under the process of having its head flattened. It was with some difficulty that I persuaded her to sit, as she seemed apprehensive that it would be injurious to her. [Figs. 169, 170, 171; CRIV-489 to 493] On the 5th of April I procured horses to cross to Nasquala at Puget's Sound, and rain poured down in torrents the whole day, making the swamps nearly impassable. We encamped in the evening near a small village of Cowlitz Indians, whom we found unusually kind and civil.

April 6th.—We passed over what is called the Mud Mountain. The mud is so very deep in this pass that we were compelled to dismount and drag our horses through it by the bridle; the poor beasts being up to their bellies in mud of the tenacity of bird-lime. This evening we encamped in the Prairie de Bute. This is remarkable for having innumerable round elevations, touching each other like so many hemispheres, of ten or twelve yards in circumference, and four or five feet in height. I dug one of them open, but found nothing in it but loose stones, although I went four or five feet down.⁶ The whole surface is thickly covered with coarse grass. I travelled twenty-two miles through this extraordinary looking prairie. [Fig. 172; CRIV-494 to 497]

April 7th.—We found some difficulty in crossing the Nasqually River, as the rains had flooded it, and we were obliged to adopt the usual plan where canoes cannot be obtained, that is,

---

⁵ Burpee, in the 1925 edition of *Wanderings*, gives this note: "Simon Plomondeau was advised by McLoughlin to settle on Cowlitz Prairie. Others followed, and in 1839 a large farm was surveyed by Charles Ross, John Work and James Douglas as a company settlement." KJ notes that there was a Catholic mission here.

⁶ KJ notes that the "Wilks Party" dug into some of the mounds but found nothing but round stones. This is a reference to Lt. Charles Wilkes who led an expedition in the west in 1838–42.

⁷ KJ notes here that a canoe and six Indians awaited Kane at Nisqually to take him to Fort Victoria.

⁸ KJ names the farm superintendent as "Dr. Tolmey." This would be William Fraser Tolmie (1812–1886).

swimming at our horses' tails, and floating our things over in skin baskets. A couple of hours brought us to Nasqually,⁷ which was established by a company called the Puget's Sound Company, for grazing and farming.⁸ When I visited it, it had about 6000 sheep and 2000 horned cattle. Its site is beautiful, on the banks of the eastern end of Puget's Sound. [Fig. 173; CRIV-498] The land is inferior to that in some other parts of the same district, the soil being gravelly; the grass, however, grows luxuriantly, and the mildness of the climate adapts it well for grazing purposes, as it is never necessary to house the animals. The wool, which is good, finds its way to the English market by the Company's ships, and the cattle are slaughtered and salted for the Sandwich Islands and the Russian dominions. The Indians about here are of very large stature; indeed, the largest that I have met with on the continent. The women are particularly large and stout. The tribe numbers between five or six hundred. They flatten their heads, but use a language different from the Chinooks. [Fig. 174; CRIV-499, 500] I made a sketch of Lach-oh-lett, their head chief, and his daughter, who wore a cap made of grass of different colours, much used by the women. [Pl. XLVIII; CRIV-501, 502]

Chapter XIV.

Fort Victoria.—Accidental Clover.—Blankets of Dog's Hair.—Aprons of Bark.—A Chief's Inauguration.—Monstrous Sturgeon.—Crows which Feed on Fish.—The Domestic Institution.—The Dead Slave.—Frightening a Native.—Washing the Dead.—The Game of Lehallum.—An Expensive Feast.—Medicine Caps.

April 8th.—I left Nasqually this morning with six Indians in a canoe, and continued paddling on the whole day and the following night, as the tide seemed favourable, not stopping till 2 P.M., when we reached Fort Victoria on Vancouver's Island, having travelled ninety miles without stopping.¹ Fort Victoria stands upon the banks of an inlet in the island about seven miles long and a quarter of a mile wide, forming a safe and convenient harbour, deep enough for any sized vessel. [Figs. 188, 189; CRIV-535, 536, 537] Its Indian name is the Esquimelt, or, Place for gathering Camas, great quantities of that vegetable

---

¹ The Fort Victoria "Journal" (Hudson's Bay Co. Archives B226a) states for April 8 that about 5 P.M. Mr. Côté arrived with a canoe which had left the fort with the English packet on March 23 and that it brought Mr. Sangster and Kane as passengers from Nisqually.

being found in the neighbourhood. On my arrival I was kindly welcomed by Mr. Finlayson, the gentleman in charge. He gave me a comfortable room, which I made my headquarters during the two months I was occupied in sketching excursions amongst the Indians in the neighbourhood and along the surrounding coasts.

The soil of this locality is good, and wheat is grown in considerable abundance. Clover grows plentifully, and is supposed to have sprung from accidental seeds which had fallen from the packages of goods brought from England; many of which are made up in hay.

The interior of the island has not been explored to any extent except by the Indians, who represent it as badly supplied with water in the summer, and the water obtained from a well dug at the fort was found to be too brackish for use. The appearance of the interior, when seen from the coast, is rocky and mountainous, evidently volcanic; the trees are large, principally oak and pine. The timbers of a vessel of some magnitude were being got out. The establishment is very large, and must eventually become the great depôt for the business of the Company. They had ten white men and forty Indians engaged in building new stores and warehouses. On the opposite side of the harbour, facing the fort, stands a village of Clal-lums Indians. [Pl. XLIII; Figs. 184, 185, 186, 187; crIV-526? to 534] They boast of being able to turn out 500 warriors, armed chiefly with bows and arrows. The lodges are built of cedar like the Chinook lodges, but much larger, some of them being sixty or seventy feet long. [Pl. XLV; Figs. 192, 194, 195, 198; crIV-545 to 551, 555, 557]

The men wear no clothing in summer, and nothing but a blanket in winter, made either of dog's hair alone, or dog's hair and goosedown mixed, frayed cedar-bark, or wildgoose skin, like the Chinooks. They have a peculiar breed of small dogs with long hair of a brownish black and a clear white. These dogs are bred for clothing purposes. [crIV-558, 559] The hair is cut off with a knife and mixed with goosedown and a little white earth, with a view of curing the feathers. This is then beaten together with sticks, and twisted into threads by rubbing it down the thigh with the palm of the hand, in the same way that a shoemaker forms his waxend, after which it undergoes a second twisting on a distaff to increase its firmness. [Fig. 197; crIV-553, 554] The cedar bark is frayed and twisted into threads in a similar manner. These threads are then woven into blankets by a very simple loom of their own contrivance. A single thread is wound over rollers at the top and bottom of a square frame, so

as to form a continuous woof through which an alternate thread is carried by the hand, and pressed closely together by a sort of wooden comb; by turning the rollers every part of the woof is brought within reach of the weaver; by this means a bag is formed, open at each end, which being cut down makes a square blanket. [Fig. 196; crIV-552, 556] The women wear only an apron of twisted cedar-bark shreds, tied round the waist and hanging down in front only, almost to the knees. They however, use the blankets more than the men do, but certainly not from any feeling of delicacy.

This tribe flatten the head, but their language varies very much from the Chinook; however, the same patois used on the Columbia is spoken by many of them, and I was thus enabled to communicate easily with them. I took a sketch of Chea-clach, their head chief [crIV-566, 567], of whose inauguration I heard the following account from an eye-witness. On his father becoming too old to fulfil the duties of head chief, the son was called upon by the tribe to take his place; on which occasion he left [for?] the mountains for the ostensible purpose of fasting and dreaming for thirty days and nights; these Indians, like all other tribes, placing great confidence in dreams, and believing that it is necessary to undergo a long fast whenever they are desirous of inducing one of any importance. At the end of the period assigned, the tribe prepared a great feast. After covering himself with a thick covering of grease and goosedown, he rushed into the midst of the village, seized a small dog, and began devouring it alive, this being a customary preliminary on such occasions. The tribe collected about him singing and dancing in the wildest manner, on which he approached those whom he most regarded and bit their bare shoulders or arms, which was considered by them as a high mark of distinction, more especially those from whom he took the piece clean out and swallowed it. Of the women he took no notice.

I have seen many men on the North-west coast of the Pacific who bore frightful marks of what they regarded as an honourable distinction; nor is this the only way in which their persons become disfigured. I have myself seen a young girl bleeding most profusely from gashes inflicted by her own hand over her arms and bosom with a sharp flint, on the occasion of losing a near relative. After some time spent in singing and dancing, Chea-clach retired with his people to the feast prepared inside a large lodge, which consisted principally of whale's blubber, in their opinion the greatest of all delicacies, although they have salmon, cod, sturgeon, and other excellent fish in great abundance.

All the tribes about here subsist almost entirely upon fish, which they obtain with so little trouble during all seasons of the year, that they are probably the laziest race of people in the world. Sturgeon are caught in considerable numbers, and here attain an enormous size, weighing from four to six hundred weight; this is done by means of a long pointed spear handle seventy to eighty feet in length, fitted into, but not actually fastened to, a barbed spear-head, to which is attached a line, with which they feel along the bottom of the river where the sturgeon are found lying at the spawning season. Upon feeling the fish the barbed spear is driven in and the handle withdrawn. The fish is then gradually drawn in by the line, which being very long, allows the sturgeon to waste his great strength, so that he can with safety be taken into the canoe or towed ashore. Most of their fishing lines are formed of a long seaweed, which is often found 150 feet long, of equal thickness throughout the whole length, and about as thick as a black-lead pencil; while wet it is very strong. Their fish-hooks are made of pine-roots, made something in the shape of our ordinary hooks, but attached differently to the line; the barb is made of bone.

Clams are in great plenty, and are preyed on in great numbers by the crows, who seize them in their claws and fly up with them to some height, and then let them drop on the rocks, which of course smashes the shell to pieces. I have watched dozens of them at this singular employment. A small oyster of a fine flavour is found in the bays in great plenty. Seal, wild ducks and geese, are also in great numbers.

The Indians are extremely fond of herring-roe, which they collect in the following manner:—Cedar branches are sunk to the bottom of the river in shallow places by placing upon them a few heavy stones, taking care not to cover the green foliage, as the fish prefer spawning on anything green. The branches are all covered by the next morning with the spawn, which is washed off into their waterproof baskets, to the bottom of which it sinks; it is then squeezed by the hand into small balls and dried, and is very palatable.

The only other vegetable besides the camas and wappatoos that the Indians use, are the roots of fern roasted, which here grow to a very large size.

[Clallam travelling lodges: Pl. XLVI; crIV-560 to 563]

Slavery in its most cruel form exists among the Indians of the whole coast, from California to Behring's Straits, the stronger tribes making slaves of all the others they can conquer. In the interior, where there is but little warfare, slavery does not exist. On the coast a custom prevails which authorises the seizure and enslavement, unless ransomed by his friends, of every Indian met with at a distance from his tribe, although they may not be at war with each other. The master exercises the power of life and death over his slaves, whom he sacrifices at pleasure in gratification of any superstitious or other whim of the moment.

One morning while I was sketching, I saw upon the rocks the dead body of a young woman, thrown out to the vultures and crows, whom I had seen a few days previously walking about in perfect health. Mr. Finlayson, the gentleman in charge of Fort Victoria, accompanied me to the lodge she belonged to, where we found an Indian woman, her mistress, who made light of her death, and was doubtless the cause of it. She told us that a slave had no right to burial, and became perfectly furious when Mr. Finlayson told her that the slave was far better than herself. "I," she exclaimed, "the daughter of a chief, no better than a dead slave!" and bridling up with all the dignity she could assume, she stalked out, and next morning she had up her lodge and was gone. I was also told by an eye-witness, of a chief, who having erected a colossal idol of wood, sacrificed five slaves to it, barbarously murdering them at its base, and asking in a boasting manner who amongst them could afford to kill so many slaves.

These Indians also flatten their heads, and are far more superstitious than any I have met with. They believe, for instance, that if they can procure the hair of an enemy and confine it with a frog in a hole, the head from which it came will suffer all the torments that the frog endures in its living grave. They are never seen to spit without carefully obliterating all traces of their saliva. This they do lest an enemy should find it, in which case they believe he would have the power of doing them some injury. They always spit on their blankets, if they happen to wear one at the time.

I was indebted to the superstitious fears which they attached to my pictures for the safety and ease with which I mingled amongst them. One of them gave me a great deal of annoyance by continually following and watching me wherever I went, for the purpose of warning the other Indians against my sketching them, telling them that it would expose them to all sorts of ill luck. I repeatedly requested him to desist, but in vain. At last I bethought me of looking steadily at himself, paper and pencil in hand, as if in the act of taking his likeness; when he became greatly alarmed, and asked me what I was about. I replied, "I am taking a sketch of you." He earnestly begged of me to stop, and promised never to annoy me again.

These Indians have a great dance, which is called "The

Medicine Mask Dance;" this is performed both before and after any important action of the tribe, such as fishing, gathering camas, or going on a war party, either for the purpose of gaining the goodwill of the Great Spirit in their undertaking, or else in honour of him for the success which has attended them. Six or eight of the principal men of the tribe, generally medicine-men, adorn themselves with masks cut out of some soft light wood with feathers, highly painted and ornamented, with the eyes and mouth ingeniously made to open and shut. In their hands they hold carved rattles, which are shaken in time to a monotonous song or humming noise (for there are no words to it) which is sung by the whole company as they slowly dance round and round in a circle. [Pl. XLIV; Figs. 190, 191, 193; CRIV-538 to 544]

Among the Clal-lums and other tribes inhabiting this region, I have never heard any traditions as to their former origin, although such traditions are common amongst those on the east side of the Rocky Mountains. They do not believe in any future state of punishment, although in this world they suppose themselves exposed to the malicious designs of the skoocoom, or evil genius, to whom they attribute all their misfortune and ill luck.

The good spirit is called Hias-Soch-a-la-Ti-Yah, that is, the great high chief, from whom they obtain all that is good in this life, and to whose happy and peaceful hunting-grounds they will all eventually go to reside for ever in comfort and abundance. The medicine-men of the tribe are supposed to possess a mysterious influence with these two spirits, either for good or evil. They form a secret society, the initiation into which is accompanied with great ceremony and much expense. The candidate has to prepare a feast for his friends and all who choose to partake of it, and make presents to the other medicine-men. A lodge is prepared for him which he enters, and remains alone for three days and nights without food, whilst those already initiated keep dancing and singing round the lodge during the whole time. After this fast, which is supposed to endue him with wonderful skill, he is taken up apparently lifeless and plunged into the nearest cold water, where they rub and wash him until he revives: this they call "washing the dead." As soon as he revives, he runs into the woods, and soon returns dressed as a medicine-man, which generally consists of the light down of the goose stuck all over their bodies and heads with thick grease, and a mantle of frayed cedar bark, with the medicine rattle in his hand. He now collects all his property, blankets, shells, and ornaments, and distributes the whole amongst his friends, trusting for his future support to the fees of his profession. The

dancing and singing are still continued with great vigour, during the division of the property, at the conclusion of which the whole party again sit down to feast, apparently with miraculous appetites, the quantity of food consumed being perfectly incredible.

Their lodges are the largest buildings of any description that I have met with amongst Indians. They are divided in the interior into compartments, so as to accommodate eight or ten families, and are well built, considering that the boards are split from the logs with bone wedges; but they succeed in getting them out with great smoothness and regularity. I took a sketch one day while a party were engaged in gambling in the centre of the lodge. The game is called lehallum, and is played with ten small circular pieces of wood, one of which is marked black; these pieces are shuffled about rapidly by the player between two bundles of frayed cedar bark. His opponent suddenly stops his shuffling, and endeavours to guess in which bundle the blackened piece is concealed. They are so passionately fond of this game that they frequently pass two or three consecutive days and nights at it without ceasing. [Fig. 199; CRIV-564, 565]

Saw-se-a the head chief of the Cowitchins,[2] from the Gulf of Georgia, an inveterate gambler, was engaged at the game. [Fig. 200; CRIV-568, 569] He had come to the Esquimelt on a friendly visit. This chief was a great warrior in his younger days, and received an arrow through the cheek in one of his battles. He took many captives, whom he usually sold to the tribes further north, thus diminishing their chance of escaping back through a hostile country to their own people, the northern tribes making slaves only of those living south of them. He possessed much of what is considered wealth amongst the Indians, and it gradually accumulated from tributes which he exacted from his people. On his possessions reaching a certain amount it is customary to make a great feast, to which all contribute. The neighbouring chiefs with whom he is in amity are invited, and at the conclusion of the entertainment, he distributes all he has collected since the last feast, perhaps three or four years preceding, among his guests as presents. The amount of property thus collected and given away by a chief is sometimes very considerable. I have heard of one possessing as many as twelve bales of blankets, from twenty to thirty guns, with numberless pots, kettles, and pans, knives, and other articles of cutlery, and great quantities of beads, and other trinkets,

[2] The Victoria "Journal" for May 20 states: "A large number of Indians are now encamped in the vicinity, some of whom arrived in the course of the day, but traded little or no furs."

Plate XIX. Muck-Cranium, a Cree from Fort Carlton. Stark POP6; CRIV-103.

Plate XX. The Man that Always Rides. ROM912.1.44; crIV-105.

as well as numerous beautiful Chinese boxes, which find their way here from the Sandwich Islands. The object in thus giving his treasures away is to add to his own importance in the eyes of others, his own people often boasting of how much their chief had given away, and exhibiting with pride such things as they had received themselves from him.

I also took a sketch of his son, No. 11, Culchillum. He had a medicine cap on, to which he attached great importance. It was made of human hair, taken from the heads of persons killed in battle, and ornamented with feathers. This, he told me, he only wore on great occasions, such as his present visit to the Clal-lums. On my expressing a wish to purchase it, he told me that he valued it too highly to part with it; nor would he allow me to take it to my tent to finish this sketch without himself accompanying it, for fear it might be deprived of some of its magical properties. [Pl. XLVII; cRIV-570, 571]

[Mount Baker: cRIV-525]

Chapter XV.

A Coasting Trip.—Indian Curiosity.—Rather Violent Quacks.—An Awkward Hint.—Fighting for a Whale.—A Warm Siege.—Running a Deadly Muck.—Catching Wild Ducks.—A Great Unknown.—The Fate of the "Tonquin."—Fishing for Money.—Shawstun the Ugly. —Caledonian Suttee.—Beautiful Biglips.—Price of a Second Spouse.

As I was desirous to coast round the Straits of De Fuca and visit the tribes on its shores, I employed Chea-clach the head chief and four of his people to take me and the interpreter of the fort round the straits in his canoe; and on the morning of the 6th of May we started about 10 o'clock, running up the east side of Vancouver's Island, and crossed the canal De Aro to the main land.[1] On nearing an Indian village, which contained, as I afterwards found, between five or six hundred Indians, they came rushing down to the beach in an attitude apparently hostile, and as the boats of the exploring expedition had been attacked the year before at the same place, we naturally felt some apprehensions for our safety.

We had no sooner approached the shore than a dense crowd surrounded us, wading up to their middles in water, and seizing our canoe dragged us all high and dry upon the shore, and inquired what we wanted. I replied, that I would explain my business to their chief, who immediately stepped forward in a friendly manner. Having told him that my business was to visit all the Indians, and to take likenesses of the head chiefs and

great warriors, he took me to his lodge, where I seated myself on a mat with him in front of me and commenced my drawing. [cRIV-503] In a few minutes the place was crowded, and when it could hold no more, the people clambered to the top of the lodge and tore off the mats from the supports, to which they clung, one upon another, like a swarm of bees, peering down upon us. Look which way I could it seemed one solid mass of hideous faces, daubed with red and white mud.

I hastily finished my sketch and hurried away, first giving the chief a plug of tobacco for his civility. His name was Chea-clach, chief of the Clallums.[2] On coming over I found the wind so strong that I thought it advisable to risk an encampment, and pitched my tent about two hundred yards from the village. We were soon surrounded by hundreds of Indians, the chief among the rest. I gave the latter some supper, and all the news, which he eagerly inquired after, and on my telling him I was tired and wished to go to sleep, which I could not do while so many of his people were about, he instantly arose and desired them to retire, which was promptly obeyed, he going away with them.

About 10 o'clock at night I strolled into the village, and on hearing a great noise in one of the lodges I entered it, and found an old woman supporting one of the handsomest Indian girls I had ever seen. She was in a state of nudity. Cross-legged and naked, in the middle of the room sat the medicine-man, with a wooden dish of water before him; twelve or fifteen other men were sitting round the lodge. The object in view was to cure the girl of a disease affecting her side. As soon as my presence was noticed a space was cleared for me to sit down. The officiating medicine-man appeared in a state of profuse perspiration from the exertions he had used, and soon took his seat among the rest as if quite exhausted; a younger medicine-man then took his place in front of the bowl, and close beside the patient. Throwing off his blanket he commenced singing and gesticulating in the most violent manner, whilst the others kept time by beating with little sticks on hollow wooden bowls and drums, singing continually. After exercising himself in this manner for about half an hour, until the perspiration ran down his body, he darted

---

[1] The Fort Victoria "Journal" states that Kane with the fort's interpreter crossed the straits on the morning of April 23 to the "Tlalum" (Clallam) village in a "Sangh" canoe. It records that he returned about 10 A.M. on the 30th. *Wanderings* gives May 6 as date of departure and May 14 as date of return.

KJ states that the crossing was 10 miles and that the village at which he arrived was "Cawa Chin" (Cowichan). The published version states that it was Clallam (see note 2). KJ does not have the phrase "to the main land."

[2] The preceding sentence does not occur in KJ or KWMS. The introduction of it here in the published version bestows on the chief the name Chea-clach which has already been given as the name of Kane's guide on the tour of the straits.

suddenly upon the young woman, catching hold of her side with his teeth and shaking her for a few minutes, while the patient seemed to suffer great agony. He then relinquished his hold, and cried out he had got it, at the same time holding his hands to his mouth; after which he plunged them in the water and pretended to hold down with great difficulty the disease which he had extracted, lest it might spring out and return to its victim.

At length, having obtained the mastery over it, he turned round to me in an exulting manner, and held something up between the finger and thumb of each hand, which had the appearance of a piece of cartilage, whereupon one of the Indians sharpened his knife, and divided it in two, leaving one end in each hand. One of the pieces he threw into the water, and the other into the fire, accompanying the action with a diabolical noise, which none but a medicine-man can make. After which he got up perfectly satisfied with himself, although the poor patient seemed to me anything but relieved by the violent treatment she had undergone.

[Straits Indians: crIV-504, 505, 506, 572?, 573]

May 7th.—We this morning left our encampment before daylight, without waiting to pay our respects to the chief. In the afternoon we touched at Whitby's Island, which divides the Straits of De Fuca from Puget's Sound. [crIV-507] A Catholic mission had been established on the island some few years before, but was obliged to be given up, owing to the turbulent disposition of the Indians, who, though friendly to the Hudson Bay Company as traders, look with great suspicion upon others who attempt to settle there, fearing that the whites would attempt to dispossess them of their lands.

On approaching the village of Toanichum, we perceived two stout bastions of logs, well calculated for defence in Indian warfare, and built with considerable skill. As our canoe neared the land, I observed them hurrying towards these bastions, and shortly afterwards we heard several shots. Supposing this to be intended as a salute, we drew still nearer, and were astonished at hearing more discharges, and seeing the balls fall near our canoe. My Indians immediately ceased paddling, and it was with the utmost difficulty that I could prevail on them to proceed. Had we shown the least inclination to retreat, I have no doubt that the firing would have been continued, and with better aim. However, on my landing and asking what they meant, they said it was only done for the purpose of letting me know that they were in the possession of fire-arms. [Fig. 176; crIV-511]

They afterwards treated me very hospitably. Lock-hi-num, the chief, offered us all the supplies at his command. It was, however, with the greatest difficulty that I could prevail on him to let me take his likeness; but at last I succeeded, by showing him the likenesses of several other chiefs, and telling him that they were intended to be shown to his Great Mother, the Queen, who no doubt would be much disappointed if his was not amongst the rest. [Fig. 175; crIV-508] I remained amongst them two or three hours, and sketched the village. I also succeeded in getting a very good-looking woman, the wife of the second chief, to sit for me. [crIV-509, 510] She had the flattest head of any I had seen in that vicinity. We then crossed over to the south side of the strait, and encamped for the night.

May 8th.—Proceeded up the south side of the straits in our canoe, and encamped on a long sand spit, projecting into the straits three or four miles.

May 9th.—Made a portage across the spit, and by the evening reached I-eh-nus, a Clallum village or fort. It was composed of a double row of strong pickets, the outer ones about twenty feet high, and the inner row about five feet, enclosing a space of 150 feet square. The whole of this inner space is roofed in, and divided into small compartments, or pens, for the use of each separate family. There were about 200 of the tribe in the fort at the time of my arrival. Their chief, Yates-sut-soot, received me with great cordiality. [crIV-514?] I remained with them three days, and all the tribe treated me with kindness, with one solitary exception, proceeding from a superstitious fear that the presence of a white man in a lodge would produce sickness in the family. Yates-sut-soot was very apprehensive of an attack from the Macaw Indians, and believing my powers and influence as a medicine-man to be of much importance, eagerly asked me which side I would take, in the event of their coming. I replied, that as long as they treated me well I would be their friend.

A few months before my arrival a great battle had been fought with the Macaws, in which the Clallums had suffered very severely. It originated in the Clallums having taken possession of the body of a whale which had been killed by the Macaws, but had got away, and was drifted by the current to the village. The Macaws demanded a share of the spoil, and also the return of their spears, some fifteen or twenty in number, which were sticking in the carcase; both demands were refused, and a feeling of animosity sprang up beween the tribes.

There are few whales now caught on the coast, but the Indians are most enthusiastic in the hunt, and the blubber is highly prized amongst them; it is cut into strips about four inches wide and two feet long, and eaten generally with dried fish.

Their manner of catching the whale is ingenious, and from the description which I received of the hunt must be very exciting. Upon a whale being seen blowing in the offing, they rush down to their large canoes, and push off with ten or twelve men in each. Each canoe is furnished with a number of strong seal-skin bags filled with air, and made with great care and skill, capable of containing about ten gallons each. To each bag is attached a barbed spear-head, made of bone or iron, when they can get it, by a strong string, eight or nine feet long, and in the socket of the spear-head is fitted a handle, seven or eight feet in length. Upon coming up with the whale, the barbed heads with the bags attached are driven into him and the handles withdrawn. The attack is continually renewed, until the whale is no longer able to sink from the buoyancy of the bags, when he is despatched and towed ashore. They are sometimes led twenty or thirty miles out to sea in the chase, but such is the admirable construction of their canoes, and so skilfully are they managed, that an accident rarely happens.

A few months after the quarrel about the whale, the brother of Yellow-cum, the head chief of the Macaws, went to Fort Victoria to trade for ammunition and other necessaries, and on his return was attacked by the Clallums. He and one of his men were killed, but three others escaped, and succeeded in getting to Cape Flattery, where Yellow-cum resided. Immediately upon hearing of the death of his brother, Yellow-cum fitted out twelve of his largest canoes, with twenty warriors in each, and made a sudden descent upon I-eh-nus; but he soon perceived that he had little chance of success while the Clallums remained within their enclosure completely protected by the logs, while his men were exposed without any shelter to the galling fire which was kept up through the openings between the pickets. He accordingly sent some of his party to the westward side of the fort, who set fire to the grass and wood, which soon communicated with the buildings, while he and the rest of his party kept watch to prevent any from escaping. The Clallums were soon forced to rush out and cover the retreat of their women and children into the mountains. Yates-sut-soot and Yellow-cum fought with great bravery hand to hand, with nothing but their knives, until they were separated in the mêlée. I saw one of the Clallums who had been shockingly gashed in the battle, having had to run through a long line of the Macaws, each of whom made a cut at him as he passed. The buildings were only partly

consumed. Yellow-cum took eighteen prisoners, mostly females, who were made slaves, and he had eight heads stuck on poles placed in the bows of the canoes on his return. These heads are carried to their village, and placed in front of the lodge of the warriors who had killed them as trophies. These Indians do not scalp their enemies. [Figs. 177, 180; crIV-515, 517]

Near the village are numerous singular graves with different erections over them, on which the Indians place the offerings for the dead. [Fig. 179; crIV-516]

May 12th.—We left with the intention of returning to Vancouver's Island, but the wind being very violent we had to put back to the shore, which we coasted for twelve or fourteen miles, until we came to the mouth of a river. The land to the south of us rises in one continuous range of high mountains far as the eye can reach, the peaks of many of which are covered with snow, even at this period of the year. We ascended the river about a mile to an Indian fishing station called Suck. The whole breadth of the stream is obstructed by stakes and open work of willow and other branches, with holes at intervals leading into wicker compartments, which the fish enter in their way up the river from the sea. Once in they cannot get out, as the holes are formed with wicker work inside shaped something like a funnel or a wire mouse-trap. In this preserve they are speared without trouble when required, and the village has thus a constant supply of food. They were catching great quantities at the time of my arrival, and we obtained an abundant supply for a small piece of tobacco. [Fig. 182; crIV-520, 521, 522]

These Indians also take a great many ducks by means of a fine net stretched between two posts about thirty feet high, and fifty or sixty feet apart. This is erected in a narrow valley through which the ducks fly in the evening. A smoky fire is made at the bottom of the net, which prevents the ducks from seeing it, and when they fly against it they become confused and fall down, when they are seized by the Indians.

The wind being still too strong for us to venture, we remained until the 14th. Chaw-u-wit, the chief's daughter, allowed me to take her likeness. Whilst she was sitting a great many of the Indians surrounded us, causing her much annoyance, as their native bashfulness renders all squaws peculiarly sensitive to any public notice or ridicule. She was, perhaps, about the best-looking girl I had seen in the straits, which is certainly no very high compliment to the rest of the female population. [Fig. 178; crIV-518, 519]

Chea-clack considering that our canoe was too small, succeeded in changing it for a larger one, and at 3 o'clock A.M. we embarked and proceeded to make a traverse of thirty-two miles in an open sea. When we had been out for about a couple of hours the wind increased to a perfect gale, and blowing against an ebb tide caused a heavy swell. We were obliged to keep one man constantly baling to prevent our being swamped. [Fig. 183; crIV-524]

The Indians on board now commenced one of their wild chants, which increased to a perfect yell whenever a wave larger than the rest approached; this was accompanied with blowing and spitting against the wind as if they were in angry contention with the evil spirit of the storm. It was altogether a scene of the most wild and intense excitement: the mountainous waves roaming round our little canoe as if to engulph us every moment, the wind howling over our heads, and the yelling Indians, made it actually terrific. I was surprised at the dexterity with which they managed the canoe, all putting out their paddles on the windward side whenever a wave broke, thus breaking its force and guiding the spray over our heads to the other side of the boat.

It was with the greatest anxiety that I watched each coming wave as it came thundering down, and I must confess that I felt considerable fear as to the event. However, we arrived safely at the fort at 2 P.M., without further damage than what we suffered from intense fatigue, as might be expected, from eleven hours' hard work, thoroughly soaked and without food; but even this soon passed away before the cheerful fire and "hearty" dinner with which we were welcomed at Fort Victoria. One of the Indians told me he had no fear during the storm, except on my account, as his brethren could easily reach the shore by swimming, even should the distance have been ten miles.

[Olympics: crIV-523]

A couple of days after my arrival at the fort, I was engaged in taking the likeness of an Indian. The door of my room was suddenly thrown open, and an Indian entered of a very plain and unprepossessing appearance. As I was unwilling to be disturbed, I rather unceremoniously dismissed the intruder, and closed the door on him, supposing him to be some common Indian; for were I to admit all comers, I should have been annoyed from morning till night. About half an hour afterwards, Mr. Finlayson came in, and told me that the great Yellow-cum, the head chief of the Macaws at Cape Flattery, had arrived at the fort. I had heard so much of this chief, both from his enemies, the Clallums at I-eh-nus, and the Indians at

Fort Vancouver, that I had determined to go to Cape Flattery, a distance of sixty miles, to see him. I was therefore very glad of his coming, as it would save me the journey; and I immediately went out in search of him, and was not a little astonished and vexed to find in him the visitor I had so rudely sent out of my room. I of course apologised, by stating my ignorance of who he was, and told him how anxious I had been to see him, and of my intention of going to Cape Flattery for that purpose. He said that he willingly acquitted me of any intentional insult; but he had felt extremely mortified at being treated so before so many Indians.

He accompanied me to my room, where I made a sketch of him, and had from him a recital of much of his private history. [crIV-580?] Yellow-cum's father was the pilot of the unfortunate "Tonquin," the vessel sent out by John Jacob Astor to trade with the Indians north of Vancouver's Island, mentioned in Washington Irving's "Astoria." He was the only survivor who escaped from the vessel previous to her being blown up, the rest of the unfortunate crew having been butchered on board, or blown up with the ship. It was impossible to obtain a clear narrative of this melancholy event, as no white man lived to tell the tale.

Yellow-cum is the wealthiest man of his tribe. His property consists principally of slaves and ioquas, a small shell found at Cape Flattery, and only there, in great abundance. These shells are used as money, and a great traffic is carried on among all the tribes by means of them. They are obtained at the bottom of the sea, at a considerable depth, by means of a long pole stuck in a flat board about fifteen inches square. From this board a number of bone pieces project, which, when pressed down, enter the hollow ends of the shells, which seem to be attached to the bottom by their small ends. The shells stick on the pieces, and are thus brought to the surface. They are from an inch and a half to two inches in length, and are white, slender, and hollow, and tapering to a point; slightly curved, and about the size of an ordinary tobacco-pipe stem. They are valuable in proportion to their length, and their value increases according to a fixed ratio, forty shells being the standard number to extend a fathom's length; which number, in that case, is equal in value to a beaver skin; but if thirty-nine be found large enough to make the fathom, it would be worth two beavers' skins; if thirty-eight, three skins; and so on, increasing one beaver skin for every shell less than the standard number.

Yellow-cum presented me with a pair of ear ornaments of

these shells, consisting of seventy or eighty shells in each. His wealth also partly consisted of sea otter skins, which are the most valuable fur found on the North American coast, their usual value in the tariff being twelve blankets; two blankets being equal to a gun; tobacco and ammunition and other things in proportion. The blanket is the standard by which the value of all articles on the north-west coast is calculated. Independent of his wealth, he possesses vast influence over all the tribes, and has become head chief from his own personal prowess and ability, and not from any hereditary claim to that dignity. It may be adduced, as a proof of the courage of this chief, and of his personal confidence, that I saw him at the fort surrounded by, and in cheerful conversation with, several of the chiefs of the Clallums, with whom he had often been engaged in deadly conflict. His prudence, however, led him to remain inside the fort after nightfall.

I visited the lodges of the Eus-ā-nich Indians, who were on a visit. The chief was very rich, and had eight wives with him. I made him understand, by showing him some sketches, that I wished to take his likeness. This was, however, opposed so violently by his ladies, that I was glad to escape out of reach of their tongues, as they were all chattering together, while he sat like a Grand Turk, evidently flattered by the interest they showed for his welfare. A few days afterwards, I met the chief some distance from his camp, and alone, when he willingly consented to let me take his likeness upon my giving him a piece of tobacco. [crIV-574?]

In one of my daily excursions, I was particularly struck by the ugliness of an Indian whom I met. Upon inquiry, I found he was Shawstun, the head chief of the Sinahōmās. He inquired very earnestly if my sketching him would not involve the risk of his dying; and after I had finished the sketch, and given him a piece of tobacco, he held it up for some moments, and said it was a small recompense for risking his life. He followed me afterwards for two or three days, begging of me to destroy the picture; and at last, to get rid of him, I made a rough copy of it, which I tore up in his presence, pretending that it was the original. [Fig. 181; crIV-512, 513]

I remained on Vancouver's Island until the 10th of June; and perhaps it would be as well, before my taking leave of it, to give a general summary of the information I acquired, from personal observation, and from the gentlemen of the Hudson's Bay Company, respecting the characteristics of the different tribes inhabiting these regions.

The Indians south of the Columbia River tattoo themselves below the mouth, which gives a light blue appearance to the countenance. Those at the mouth of the Columbia, and for a hundred miles up it, as well as those at Puget's Sound, and the Straits of De Fuca, and at the southern part of Vancouver's Island, have their heads flattened down in their infancy, as represented in the sketches of the Chinook tribe. [crIV-579] Those inhabiting the north part of the island have their heads compressed into a conical shape during infancy. This is done by means of a bandage, which is wound round the forehead, and gradually tightened, until the head becomes of the required shape. [Fig. 201; crIV-575 to 578]

The next tribe lying north of these on the continent are called by the voyageurs "Babines," or Big-lips, from the fact of the females having their under lips enlarged by the insertion of a piece of wood. [Figs. 203, 204, 205; crIV-585, 586, 587, 589, 590] A small, slender piece of bone is inserted through the under lip of the infant, from below upwards, and is gradually enlarged, until a flat piece of wood three inches long, and an inch and a half wide, has caused the lip to protrude to a frightful extent, the protrusion increasing with age. Great importance is attached to the size of the lip, as it constitutes the standard of female beauty; it also marks the difference between native free women and their slaves.

When the stick is removed on any occasion the lip drops down to the chin, presenting one of the most disgusting spectacles imaginable.

The men sometimes wear a ring through the nose, formed of bone, or brass if they can get it; but the practice is not universal. [Fig. 202; crIV-583, 584] They wear a cap made of the fibres of cedar-bark, woven very finely together, and a blanket made from the wool of the mountain sheep; they are very valuable, and take years in making. For one [blanket] which I procured with great difficulty, I had to pay five pounds of tobacco, ten charges of ammunition, one blanket, one pound of beads, two check shirts, and one ounce of vermilion. [crIV-588]

The next tribes, still more north than the last, insert beads of various colours, two-thirds of their depth, into the whole length of the upper lip, giving it the appearance of so much bead work. [Haida: crIV-581. Kwakiutl: Pl. XLVIII; crIV-582]

In the interior of New Caledonia, which is east of Vancouver's Island and north of the Columbia, among the tribe called "Taw-wa-tins," who are also Babines, and also among other tribes in their neighbourhood, the custom prevails of burning the bodies, with circumstances of peculiar barbarity to the widows of the deceased. The dead body of the husband is laid naked upon a large heap of resinous wood, his wife is then placed upon the body and covered over with a skin; the pile is then lighted, and the poor woman is compelled to remain until she is nearly suffocated, when she is allowed to descend as best she can through the smoke and flames. No sooner, however, does she reach the ground, than she is expected to prevent the body from becoming distorted by the action of the fire on the muscles and sinews; and whenever such an event takes place she must, with her bare hands, restore the burning corpse to its proper position; her person being the whole time exposed to the scorching effects of the intense heat. Should she fail in the due performance of this indispensable rite, from weakness or the intensity of her pain, she is held up by some one until the body is consumed. A continual singing and beating of drums is kept up throughout the ceremony, which drowns her cries. Afterwards she must collect the unconsumed pieces of bone and ashes and put them into a bag made for the purpose, which she has to carry on her back for three years; remaining for the time a slave to her husband's relations, and being neither allowed to wash nor comb herself for the whole time, so that she soon becomes a most disgusting object. At the expiration of the three years, a feast is given by her tormentors, who invite all the friends and relations of her and themselves. At the commencement they deposit with great ceremony the remains of the burnt dead in a box, which they affix to the top of a high pole, and dance around it. The widow is then stripped naked and smeared from head to foot with fish oil, over which one of the by-standers throws a quantity of swan's down, covering her entire person. She is then obliged to dance with the others. After all this is over she is free to marry again, if she have the inclination, and courage enough to venture on a second risk of being roasted alive and the subsequent horrors. [crIV-591]

It has often happened that a widow who has married a second husband, in the hope perhaps of not outliving him, committed suicide in the event of her second husband's death, rather than undergo a second ordeal. I was unable to learn any explanation of the motive for these cruel rites, and can only account for them in the natural selfishness, laziness, and cruelty of the Indians, who probably hope by these means to render their wives more attentive to their personal ease and comfort; whilst, at the same time, it secures them from assassination either by a jealous or an errant spouse.

Chapter XVI.

June 9th.—The Company's vessel which annually brings out goods and despatches for the interior having arrived, Mr. Finlayson was anxious to forward the letters on, and knowing that I was soon to start on my return, he asked me if I would take them to Fort Vancouver.[1] I was very anxious to do anything in my power in return for the hospitality and kindness I had received, and accordingly commenced my preparations for starting on the following morning. An old Nasqually chief had come down to the coast to look for a favourite wife who had been carried off by some of his predatory neighbours, and, as he supposed, had been sold somewhere in Vancouver's Island. But not being successful in his search, he was now returning, and I engaged to go with him. He was very glad of my company, as my being the bearer of despatches would be a certain protection for the whole party from whatever Indians we might meet. I asked him how he had managed to escape on coming down, and he showed me an old piece of newspaper, which he said he held up whenever he met with strange Indians, and that they, supposing it to be a letter for Fort Victoria, had allowed him to pass without molestation.

The gentlemen in charge of the various posts, have frequent occasion to send letters, sometimes for a considerable distance, when it is either inconvenient or impossible for them to fit out a canoe with their own men to carry it. In such cases the letter is given to an Indian, who carries it as far as suits his convenience and safety. He then sells the letter to another, who carries it until he finds an opportunity of selling it to advantage; it is thus passed on and sold until it arrives at its destination, gradually increasing in value according to the distance, and the last possessor receiving the reward for its safe delivery. In this manner

[1] The Fort Victoria "Journal" for June 5, 1847, records the departure of Kane, bearing a packet of letters received from England by the *Mary Dare*, for Nisqually in the company of Indians from that area who had been visiting. This date differs from the date in *Wanderings*, above.

letters are frequently sent with perfect security, and with much greater rapidity than could be done otherwise.

June 10th.—Early in the morning I embarked with the chief, a wife he had brought with him, and two slaves: we paddled on all day, and made good progress. In the evening we encamped under a high rock, where we found some goose eggs, of which we made a hearty supper.

June 11th.—We came to a rocky island, which was covered with thousands of seal, playing and basking in the sun. We shot several of them, as the Indians highly prize the blubber as food; but it was far too oily for my stomach. I, however, shot a white-headed eagle, and roasted him for my supper, and found him particularly good eating.

June 12th.—In the evening we arrived at an Indian village, where we stopped for the night; the whole surface of the water at this place seemed to be alive with the gambles of a small silvery fish, dancing and glistening in the rays of the setting sun. This fish is about the size of our sardines, and is caught in immense numbers; it is called there ulé kun, and is much prized on account of its delicacy and extraordinary fatness. When dried this fish will burn from one end to the other with a clear steady light like a candle.

There were several canoes out fishing in the evening, and they caught them with astonishing rapidity: this is done by means of an instrument about seven feet long, the handle is about three feet, into which is fixed a curved wooden blade about four feet, something the shape of a sabre, with the edge at the back. In this edge, at the distance of about an inch and a half, are inserted sharp bone teeth, about an inch long. The Indian stands in the canoe and, holding it as he would a paddle, draws it edgeways with both hands rapidly through the dense mass of fish, which are so thick that every tooth will strike a fish. One knock across the thwarts safely deposits them in the bottom of the canoe. This is done with such rapidity that they never use nets for this description of fishing.

June 13th.—To-day as we neared the shore we perceived two deer grazing, which the Indians were anxious to go after, but as we had already lost some time on the way I was more anxious to proceed. While at a very long distance I fired my double-barrelled gun at them, more in the hopes of driving them away than of killing them, when, much to the astonishment of both myself and the Indians, one of them fell dead. The chief looked very hard at me and then examined the gun, apparently in doubt whether the magic was in the gun or myself. I said

nothing, but took it all as a matter of course, whilst the Indians evidently looked upon me as a person not to be trifled with. We had a splendid supper that evening on our venison, and I took good care not to test the qualities of my gun again before them, although they often asked me.

June 14th.—Whilst passing an isolated rock, standing six or seven feet high above the water, and a little more than four feet in circumference, the old chief asked me if I knew what it had originally been. On my replying in the negative, he told me the following legend:—

"It is many moons since a Nasqually family lived near this spot. It consisted of a widow with four sons,—one of them was by her first husband, the other three by the second. The three younger sons treated their elder brother with great unkindness, refusing him any share of the produce of their hunting and fishing; he, on the contrary, wishing to conciliate them, always gave them a share of his spoils. He, in fact, was a great medicine-man, although this was unknown to them, and, being tired of their harsh treatment, which no kindness on his part seemed to soften, he at length resolved to retaliate. He accordingly one day entered the lodge, where they were feasting, and told them that there was a large seal a short distance off. They instantly seized their spears and started in the direction he pointed out, and, coming up to the animal, the eldest drove his spear into it. This seal was 'a great medicine,' a familiar of the elder brother, who had himself created him for the occasion. The foremost of them had no sooner driven in his spear than he found it impossible to disengage his hand from the handle, or to draw it out; the two others drove in their spears with the like effect. The seal now took to the water, dragging them after it, and swam far out to sea. Having travelled on for many miles they saw an island in the distance, towards which the seal made. On nearing the shore they found, for the first time, they could remove their hands from their spears. They accordingly landed, and supposing themselves in some enemy's country, they hid themselves in a clump of bushes from observation. While lying concealed, they saw a diminutive canoe coming round a point in the distance, paddled by a very little man, who, when he came opposite to where they were, anchored his boat with a stone attached to a long line, without perceiving them. He now sprang over the side, and diving down, remained a long time under water. At length he rose to the surface, and brought with him a large fish, which he threw into the boat: this he repeated several times, each time looking in to count the fish he had caught. The three brothers being very hungry, one of them offered to swim out while the little man was under water, and steal one of the fish. This he safely accomplished before the return of the fisherman; but the little fellow no sooner returned with another fish than he discovered that one of those already caught was missing, and, stretching out his hand, he passed it slowly along the horizon, until it pointed directly to their place of concealment. He now drew up his anchor and paddled to the shore, and immediately discovered the three brothers, and being as miraculously strong as he was diminutive, he tied their hands and feet together and, throwing them into his canoe, jumped in and paddled back in the direction from whence he had come. Having rounded the distant point, where they had first descried him, they came to a village inhabited by a race of people as small as their captor, their houses, boats, and utensils being all in proportion to themselves.

"The three brothers were then taken out and thrown, bound as they were, into a lodge, while a council was convened to decide upon their fate. During the sitting of the council an immense flock of birds, resembling geese, but much larger, pounced down upon the inhabitants, and commenced a violent attack. These birds had the power of throwing their sharp quills like the porcupine, and although the little warriors fought with great valour, they soon became covered with the piercing darts and all sunk insensible on the ground. When all resistance had ceased the birds took to flight and disappeared.

"The brothers had witnessed the conflict from their place of confinement, and with much labour had succeeded in releasing themselves from their bonds, when they went to the battle ground, and commenced pulling the quills from the apparently lifeless bodies; but no sooner had they done this, than all instantly returned to consciousness. When all of them had become well again they wished to express their gratitude to their preservers, and offered to grant whatsoever they should desire. The brothers requested to be sent back to their own country. A council was accordingly called to decide on the easiest mode of doing so, and they eventually determined upon employing a whale for the purpose. The brothers were then seated on the back of the monster, and proceeded in the direction of Nasqually. However, when they had reached about half way, the whale began to think what a fool he was for carrying them instead of turning them into porpoises, and letting them swim home themselves. Now the whale is considered as a 'Soch-a-li-ti-yah,' or Great Spirit, although not the same as the 'Hias-Soch-a-li-ti-yah,' or Great High Spirit, possessing greater powers than all

other animals put together, and no sooner had he thought upon the matter than he carried it into effect. This, accordingly, is the way that the porpoises first came into existence, and accounts for their being constantly at war with the seals, one of which species was the cause of their misfortunes. After the three brothers had so strangely disappeared, their mother came down to the beach and remained there for days, watching for their return and bewailing their absence with tears. Whilst thus engaged one day the whale happened to pass by, and, taking pity on her distress, turned her into that stone."

I could not observe any very special peculiarity in the formation of this rock while paddling past it in a canoe; and, at least from the points of observation presented to my eye, no resemblance to the human figure, such as the conclusion of the legend might lead us to anticipate, appeared to be traceable. Standing, however, as this rock does, entirely isolated, and without any other being visible for miles around, it has naturally become an object of special note to the Indians, and is not uncalculated, from its solitary position, to be made the scene of some of the fanciful creations of their superstitious credulity.

June 15th.—We arrived at Nasqually, where I procured horses to take me to the Cowlitz River. I again crossed Prairie de Bute and Mud Mountain, and arrived at my old friend Kiscox's lodge on the evening of the third day; but, to my astonishment, I found him and his family unusually distant in their manners, and the children even running away from me and hiding. At last he asked if I had not taken the likeness of a woman when last among them. I said that I had, and mentioned her name, Caw-wacham, alluding to the portrait of a woman and child, No. 10 [crIV-491]; a dead silence ensued, nor could I get the slightest answer to my inquires. Upon leaving the lodge, I met a half-breed, who told me that Caw-wacham was dead, and that I was supposed to be the cause of her death. The silence was occasioned by my having mentioned a dead person's name, which is considered disrespectful to the deceased, and unlucky.

I immediately procured a canoe, and started for Fort Vancouver, down the river, paddling all night, well knowing the danger that would result from my meeting with any of her relations, and arrived safely at Fort Vancouver on the 20th of June,[2] with my budget of news from the civilised world. Here I had to remain until the 1st of July, waiting for the boats, which were daily arriving from New Caledonia and the Upper Columbia with furs, and reloading again with their winter outfits

---

[2] KJ states that Kane arrived at Fort Vancouver on June 11 after a nine-day passage from Fort Victoria.

a Cree War cap.

Paul Kane - 1846

Plate XXI. Otisskun or "The Horn," a Cree, Fort Pitt. Stark POP17; crIV-127.

for their posts in the interior. During this time I amused myself in hunting and sketching. I took a sketch of a Chinook boy with a singular headdress of beads; the design seemed to be entirely original with him, as I had never before met with any resembling it. [Fig. 156; crIV-420, 421]

July 1st.—The nine boats composing the brigade had now completed their outfit, and were all prepared for their different destinations. Mr. Lewis[3] was to command until he arrived at his own post, Colville; but we had great difficulty in collecting the men, between sixty and seventy in number: some wanted their allowance of rum, or regale, before they started, given to the Company's men only preparatory to a long voyage. Others were bidding farewell to their Indian loves, and were hard to be found; in fact, all hesitated to give up the life of idleness and plenty in which they had been luxuriating for the last two or three weeks, for the toils and privations which they well knew were before them. However, towards evening we succeeded in collecting our crews, and Mr. Lewis promised them their regale on the first fitting opportunity. The fort gave us a salute of seven guns, which was repeated by the Company's ship lying at the store-house. The occupants of the fort crowded round us; and at last, amidst cheers and hearty wishes for our safety, we pushed off. Owing to the lateness of the hour at which we started, we only got to the Company's mills, eight miles from the fort, that evening.

July 2nd.—We started very early this morning, and the men plied their oars with unusual vigour, as they were to get their regale this evening. [crIV-389, 390] By 2 o'clock P.M. we had reached the Prairie de Thé, a distance of twenty-eight miles. Here we landed to let the men have their customary debauch. In the Hudson's Bay Company's service no rations of liquor are given to the men, either while they are stopping in fort or while travelling, nor are they allowed to purchase any; but when they are about commencing a long journey, the men are given what is called a regale, which consists of a pint of rum each. This, however, they are not allowed to drink until they are some distance from the post, where those who are entitled to get drunk may do so without interfering with the resident servants of the establishment.

Immediately on landing, the camp was made, fires lit, and victuals cooked; in short, every preparation for the night was completed before the liquor was given out. As soon as the men got their allowance, they commenced all sorts of athletic games; running, jumping, wrestling, &c. We had eight Sandwich Islanders amongst the crews, who afforded great amusement by a

sort of pantomimic dance accompanied by singing. The whole thing was exceedingly grotesque and ridiculous, and elicited peals of laughter from the audience; gradually, as the rum began to take effect, the brigades, belonging to different posts, began to boast of their deeds of daring and endurance. This gradually led on to trying which was the best man. Numberless fights ensued; black eyes and bloody noses became plentiful, but all terminated in good humour.[4] The next day the men were stupid from the effects of drink, but quite good-tempered and obedient; in fact, the fights of the previous evening seemed to be a sort of final settlement of all old grudges and disputes. We did not get away until 3 o'clock P.M., and only made a distance of about fourteen miles.[5] We encamped at the foot of the Cascades, where the first portage in ascending the Columbia commences. [Figs. 146, 149; crIV-388, 396]

July 4th and 5th.—We were engaged both days in carrying the parcels of goods across the portage, and dragging the empty boats up by lines.[6] This is a large fishing station, and immense numbers of fish are caught by the Hudson's Bay Company and the Cascade Indians, who congregate about here in great numbers at the fishing season, which happened at the time of our passing. They gave us a good deal of trouble and uneasiness, as it was only by the utmost vigilance that we could keep them from stealing. On the evening of the 5th we got over the portage; and, although the men were tired, we proceeded seven miles further up the river before we encamped, so as to get clear of the Indians. [Fig. 145; crIV-384 to 387]

In strolling about while the men were engaged in carrying the goods across the Cascades, I discovered a large burying-ground of Flatheads, and I was very anxious to procure a skull. To do this, however, I had to use the greatest precaution, and ran no small risk, not only in getting it, but in having it in my possession afterwards; even the voyageurs would have refused to travel with me, had they known that I had it in my collection, not only on account of the superstitious dread in which they hold these burial-places, but also on account of the danger of discovery, which might have cost the lives of the whole party. I, however, took advantage of the men being busy watching the Indians to keep them from stealing, and the Indians being

---

[3] John Lewes, chief trader and chief factor of the Hudson's Bay Company, who was active in the Columbia Department, and whom Kane had already met on his outward trip; see also Appendix 10, Letter 11. KJ states that Donald Manson, then stationed in New Caledonia, was second in command of the party.

[4] In KJ Kane complains that the noise kept him awake all night.

[5] KJ states that they travelled three, not fourteen, miles.

[6] KJ notes that they carried 450 parcels each weighing 65 pounds across the portage.

equally busy in watching for an opportunity to steal, and succeeded in getting a very perfect skull smuggled in among my traps without the slightest suspicion.

At the place where we encamped on the evening of the 5th, there were a great many stumps of trees standing in the river; it is supposed to be a landslip. I made a sketch of it. [Fig. 144; crIV-382, 383]

During the night, two of our Sandwich Islanders deserted. A boat was immediately unloaded, and sent back, with the view of intercepting them at the Cascades. They had received 10*l.* sterling each in goods as their outfit, and, in passing the Cascades, had hid their bags in the woods, and hoped to get back again to the coast with their booty. Their pursuers, however, discovered their track, and found the goods, though they did not find the men; but knowing they must be near the place, they got Tomaquin to look after them. [Fig. 147; crIV-391] The next morning, Tomaquin with three of his tribe, brought them in: each of the Indians, while paddling, carried his knife in his mouth, ready to strike should the Islanders make any resistance. It appeared that they had visited his camp in the night, on which he assembled his tribe and surrounded them; when the Islanders, thinking they were going to be killed, surrendered and begged for mercy. Tomaquin was rewarded with four blankets and four shirts.[7] The next thing was to punish the deserters, and very little time was wasted in either finding a verdict or carrying it out. Our guide, a tall powerful Iroquois, took one of them, and Mr. Lewis seized the other, as they stepped from the canoe: the punishment consisted in simply knocking the men down, kicking them until they got up, and knocking them down again until they could not get up any more, when they finished them off with a few more kicks. Mr. Lewis, although a very powerful man, had only his left hand, a gun having exploded in his right, shattering it so dreadfully that he was obliged to have it cut off at the wrist; but the operation having been performed in the roughest backwood fashion, it often pained him, and the doctors wanted him to let them cut it off again, so as to make a good stump, but he would not let them. On this stump he usually wore a heavy wooden shield, but, luckily for the poor Islanders, it was not on when they landed, or, as he said himself, he might have killed them. The punishment of those men must of course appear savage and severe to persons in civilised life, but it is only treatment of this kind that will keep this sort of men in order; and desertion or insubordination, on journeys through the interior, is often attended by the most dangerous consequences to the whole party.

July 6th.—It rained heavily all day, and the wind became so high, that we were obliged to put ashore, although the ground was very low and swampy, and the mosquitoes were in myriads.

July 7th.—Passed a Methodist mission,[8] and came to the Portage of the Dalles. We employed the Indians here to make the portage, thirty to each boat, for which each man receives five balls and powder. The Indians at the Dalles do not distort the head. The country begins to look barren, and is entirely destitute of wood. Salmon in great abundance is caught in these rapids. [crIV-392]

July 8th.—Arrived at the Chutes: we found no difficulty as to the carriage of our boats, as the Indians were very numerous and willing to be employed. In former times these people were more troublesome than any other tribes on the Columbia River. In making this portage, it was then necessary to have sixty armed men for the protection of the goods. It was here that the man with the tin box was shot, mentioned in Washington Irving's "Astoria." We were on the present occasion obliged to buy wood from the Indians, to cook our supper, not a tree nor even a bush being visible in any direction. The Indians, who obtain drift-wood for their own use when the river is high and brings it within their reach, of course prize it highly from its scarcity. The Indians who reside and congregate about the Chutes for the purpose of fishing, are called the Skeen tribe; they do not flatten their heads, and appear to be a hardy, brave people, at this time particularly friendly to the Hudson's Bay Company people, and at peace with their Flathead neighbours. The Indians hereabouts catch a few deer and some other game, out of whose skins they make whatever dresses they wear, which are, however, very scanty. I give, in Sketch No. 12, the likeness of Mancemuckt, the chief; he wore a fox-skin cap and a leather deerskin shirt at the time. [Fig. 148; crIV-393, 394, 395]

July 9th.—Left the Chutes with a strong fair wind, running up the rapids under sail, while the water curled over the bows of the boats, which we only prevented from filling by shortening the sail. We encamped in the neighbourhood of a very thievish tribe of Indians, according to report, and were obliged to make

[7] KJ recounts that Kane asked Tomaquin if he were not afraid of the Sandwich Islanders. Tomaquin replied that it was only the whites of whom he was afraid.

[8] The Methodist station at the Dalles had been founded among the Wasco Indians in April 1838 by the Rev. H. K. W. Perkins at a place called Wascopam. It was under the auspices of the Oregon Missionary Society, a Methodist organization. The mission was taken over by the American Board of Commissioners for Foreign Missions in 1847. See Gustavus Hines, *Oregon, Its History, Conditions and Prospects* (New York 1859), pp. 30–31.

use of one of the burial canoes for fuel, taking the bones out and depositing them carefully near some of the others. We had not got our pot to boil, before some of the tribe made their appearance, and gave us to understand that we had destroyed the grave of a relative of one of the men. After a great deal of arguing and trouble, and our party being too strong for the Indians to attempt any open violence, this man consented, at last, to receive some tobacco, ammunition, and other little presents, as an indemnity for our sacrilege. This we willingly gave him, as, had we not done so, in all probability they would have killed the first white man they could have laid their hands on with impunity; having, however, received compensation for the insult, there was no fear of anything further being done about it.

July 10th.—Saw great quantities of rattlesnakes to-day, some few of which we killed; the men, while tracking (that is hauling the boats along the edge of the shore by a line, in places where the river is too rapid to row), were in great dread of them as they had no shoes, but fortunately no one was bitten. It is said by the Indians, that salt applied plentifully and immediately to the wound will effect a cure, also that drinking copiously of ardent spirits as soon as the bite has been inflicted will avert the danger. I have, however, never seen either of them tried, and should much suspect the latter cure to be merely a piece of Indian cunning, to overcome the great difficulty of getting liquor, on any terms, from the Company's servants and officers.

July 11th.—Many Indians followed us for a long distance on horseback along the shore. I obtained one of their horses, and, accompanied by an Indian, took a gallop of seven or eight miles into the interior, and found the country equally sterile and unpromising as on the banks of the stream. The bend in the river, which the boats were, of course, obliged to follow, enabled me to come up with them a very few miles further; the ride, although uninteresting as regarded landscape—for not a tree was visible as far as the eye could reach—was still a delightful change to me from the monotony of the boats. As we approached the place where the Walla-Walla debouches into the Columbia river, we came in sight of two extraordinary rocks projecting from a high steep cone or mound about 700 feet above the level of the river. These are called by the voyageurs the Chimney Rocks, and from their being visible from a great distance, they are very serviceable as landmarks. Sketch No. 13 represents one of them and the cone, but, owing to the position in which I stood while taking the sketch, the other rock or chimney is not visible, being immediately in rear of the one represented. [Fig. 135; crIV-358 to 361]

The Walla-Walla Indians call these the "Rocks of the Ki-use girls," of which they relate the following legend, which was told to me by an Indian, whilst I was sketching this extraordinary scene. It must be borne in mind that all Indian tribes select some animal to which they attribute supernatural, or, in the language of the country, *medicine* powers: the whale, for instance, on the north-west coast; the kee-yeu, or war eagle, on the east side of the Rocky Mountains, supposed to be the maker of thunder; and the wolf on the Columbia River. Now the great medicine wolf of the Columbia River—according to the Walla-Walla tradition, the most cunning and artful of all manitous—having heard that a great medicine grasshopper was desolating the whole of the country which of right belonged to himself, and was especially under his protection, immediately resolved to trace him out, and have a personal encounter with him. With this view, he proceeded down the banks of the river, and soon fell in with the object of his search. Each of these formidable manitous thought it best to resort to stratagem to overcome his opponent. Being afraid of each other's "medicine" powers, they accordingly commenced by exchanging civilities, and then, with a view of terrifying each other, began boasting of their wonderful exploits, and the numbers they had killed and eaten. The grasshopper said to the wolf that the best way to ascertain who had devoured the largest numbers would be to vomit up the contents of their respective stomachs, and he who threw up the most hair—that being an indigestible substance—by showing who had swallowed the most animals, should be considered as the superior. To this proposal the wolf consented, and they commenced retching and vomiting up all in their stomachs. The grasshopper, in the violence of his exertions, naturally closed his eyes, and the wolf, perceiving this, adroitly drew a great part of his opponent's share over to his own side without being detected. The grasshopper, when he perceived how much larger the pile before the wolf was than his own, gave up the contest, and proposed to the wolf an exchange of shirts in token of amity and forgiveness. To this also the wolf consented, but requested the grasshopper to take off his shirt first as he was the first proposer; but the grasshopper refused, and wished the wolf to commence the ceremony.

The wolf finally even agreed to this, and striking himself suddenly on the breast, his shirt immediately flew off; the grasshopper was greatly astonished, and not being possessed of any charm by which he could strip himself so expeditiously, was obliged to take off his shirt in the common way of drawing it over his head; the wolf now watched his opportunity, and while the grasshopper had his head and arms entangled in the shirt, he killed him.

The wolf having thus got rid of his troublesome and dangerous rival, commenced his return home. On arriving within a few miles of the Walla-Walla, he saw three beautiful Ki-use girls, with whom he fell desperately in love: they were engaged in carrying stones into the river, in order to make an artificial cascade or rapid, to catch the salmon in leaping over it. The wolf secretly watched their operations through the day, and repaired at night to the dam and entirely destroyed their work: this he repeated for three successive evenings. On the fourth morning, he saw the girls sitting weeping on the bank, and accosted them, inquiring what was the matter: they told him they were starving, as they could get no fish for want of a dam. He then proposed to erect a dam for them, if they would consent to become his wives, to which they consented sooner than perish from the want of food. A long point of stones running nearly across the river is to this day attributed to the magic of the wolf-lover.

For a long time he lived happily with the three sisters (a custom very frequent amongst Indians, who marry as many sisters in a family as they can, and assign as a reason that sisters will naturally agree together better than strangers); but at length the wolf became jealous of his wives, and, by his supernatural power, changed two of them into the two basalt pillars, on the south side of the river, and then changed himself into a lark rock, somewhat similar to them, on the north side, so that he might watch them for ever afterwards. I asked the narrator what had become of the third sister. Says he, "Did you not observe a cavern as you came up?" I said that I had. "That," he replied, "is all that remains of her!"

Chapter XVII.

Fort Walla-Walla.—Salmon the Staff of Life.—Burrows for the Winter.—Ride to see a Cataract.—Splendid Fall of Water.—Desert of burning Sand.—A jealous Spouse.—Respect to a dead Chief.

July 12th.—I arrived at Walla-Walla. It is a small fort, built of *dobies*, or blocks of mud baked in the sun, which is here intensely hot. Fort Walla-Walla is situated at the mouth of the river of the same name, in the most sandy and barren desert that can be conceived, and is about 500 miles from the mouth of the Columbia. Little or no rain ever falls here, although a few miles

lower down the river it is seen from hence to pour down in torrents. Owing to its being built at the mouth of a gully, formed by the Columbia River through high mountainous land leading to the Pacific Ocean, it is exposed to furious gales of wind, which rush through the opening in the hills with inconceivable violence, and raise the sand in clouds so dense and continuous as frequently to render travelling impossible. I was kindly received by Mr. M'Bain, a clerk in the Hudson's Bay Company's service, who, with five men, had charge of the fort. The establishment is kept up solely for trading with the Indians from the interior, as those about the post have few or no peltries to deal in. [Figs. 134, 136; crIV-354 to 356, 357?]

The Walla-Walla Indians live almost entirely upon salmon throughout the whole year. In the summer season they inhabit lodges made of mats of rushes spread on poles. [crIV-374] Owing to the absence of trees in their vicinity, they have to depend for the small quantity of fuel which they require, upon the drift-wood, which they collect from the river in the spring. In the winter they dig a large circular excavation in the ground, about ten or twelve feet deep, and from forty to fifty feet in circumference, and cover it over with split logs, over which they place a layer of mud collected from the river. A hole is left at one side of this roofing, large enough for one person to enter at a time. A stick with notches reaches to the bottom of the excavation, and serves as a ladder, by means of which they ascend and descend into the subterranean dwelling. Here twelve or fifteen persons burrow through the winter, having little or no occasion for fuel; their food of dried salmon being most frequently eaten uncooked, and the place being excessively warm from the numbers congregated together in so small and confined a space. They are frequently obliged, by the drifting billows of sand, to close the aperture, when the heat and stench become insupportable to all but those accustomed to it. The drifting of the sand is a frightful feature in this barren waste. Great numbers of the Indians lose their sight, and even those who have not suffered to so great an extent have the appearance of labouring under intense inflammation of these organs. The salmon, while in the process of drying, also become filled with sand to such an extent as to wear away the teeth of the Indians, and an Indian is seldom met with over forty years of age whose teeth are not worn quite to the gums.

July 13th.—Procured three horses and a man, and left for the Paluce or Pavilion River; traversed a sandy country, where we could find no water until we arrived at the Fouchay River, when we met with Pere José, a Jesuit missionary, who had left

Walla-Walla on the night before, on the way to his mission of the Cœur de Laine.[1] Here we encamped.

July 14th.—Started at five o'clock in the morning. Weather intensely hot, and no water procurable all day.[2] Found some Indians, who ferried ourselves and baggage over the Nezperees River, in a canoe, which is here about 250 yards wide. We swam our horses at the mouth of the Pelouse River, where it empties itself into the Nezperees. The Chief of this place is named Slo-ce-ac-cum. [crIV-353] He wore his hair divided in long masses, stuck together with grease. The tribe do not number more than seventy or eighty warriors, and are called Upputup-pets. He told me that there was a fall up the Pelouse that no white man had ever seen, and that he would conduct me up the bed of the river, as it was sufficiently shallow for our horses. I accepted his proposal, and rode eight or ten miles through a wild and savage gorge, composed of dark brown basaltic rocks, heaped in confusion one upon another to the height of 1000 and 1500 feet, sometimes taking the appearance of immense ruins in the distance. [Pl. XXXIV; crIV-341, 351?, 352?] At one place the strata assumed the circular form, and somewhat the appearance, of the Colosseum at Rome. [crIV-338, 339, 340] Our path, at the bottom of this gorge, was very difficult, as it lay through masses of tangled brush and fallen rocks.

The chief now halted,[3] and refused to go further unless I gave him a blanket in payment; but as this was unreasonable I urged on my horse, desiring my own man, who accompanied me, to follow with the jaded nag. I had not advanced more than a mile when the chief came up to us and guided us to the falls through one of the boldest and most sublime passes the eye ever beheld. At the foot of the falls we made our encampment, and our guide left us, quite satisfied with his present of tobacco and ammunition. The water falls in one perpendicular sheet of about 600 feet in height, from between rocks of a greyish-yellow colour, which rise to about 400 feet above the summit of the fall. The water tumbles into a rocky basin below, with a continuous hollow echoing roar, and courses with great velocity along its bed, until it falls into the Nezperees. There was a constant current of air around our encampment, which was delightfully cool and refreshing. When I was there it was low water, and the

Indian told me, that during the rainy season the falls were much increased in volume, and of course in grandeur of effect. [Fig. 132; crIV-342 to 346]

July 15th.—Having finished my sketches of this magnificent scene, we left our encampment for a fall fifteen or twenty miles higher up the river, and it was necessary for us to leave the bed of the river and attain the top of the banks, which being at least 1000 feet above us, would have been impracticable, had we not found a ravine, which, although steep and difficult, we managed to lead our horses up. In this hollow we found great quantities of wild currants, of delicious flavour, which proved most refreshing. [cr-IV-347]

At length we gained the summit. The country around, as far as the eye could reach, seemed to be a perfect desert of yellow, hot sand, with immense masses of broken rock jutting up abruptly here and there over the surface. No trees or shrubs of any kind relieved the monotony of the barren waste. A few patches of tuft-grass, thinly scattered here and there, were the only representatives of vegetation, while animal life seemed to be entirely extinct, and during my whole journey through this place I never met with an animal or bird,—not even a mosquito or a snake.

We now followed the course of the river, and encamped at the upper fall, where I remained until the 17th sketching, much gratified with the surrounding magnificent scenes. The fall of water is only about fifteen feet. Along the margin of the river high bushes and grass grow, whose bright green contrasts vividly with the high hills of yellow sand which enclose them. [Pl. XXXV; crIV-348, 349]

I was anxious to have remained in this neighbourhood for a week or ten days longer, to have made some more sketches of the curious and strange region in which I found myself, but the half-breed whom I had with me became so anxious to return, and so importunate and sulky about it, that he made me quite uncomfortable, and I consented to return. I found out afterwards that it was on account of his wife, of whom he was jealous, being left at the fort. Had I known this sooner I would have chosen another man; as it was, it was with great regret that I commenced retracing my steps down the river on the 17th, and in the evening again encamped on the banks of the Nezperees.

During the day we saw a large band of fine horses running wild; they had belonged to a chief who was much honoured by his tribe, and as a mark of respect, at his death, they determined not to use or touch his horses, which had, accordingly, kept

---

[1] Father Joseph Joset came to America in 1843 and went directly to the far west where he spent the balance of his life. Cœur d'Alene mission was founded in 1843 on the Spokane River in what is now upper Idaho.

[2] KJ: "14th. Left at 5 this morning for the River Nez Perces and arrived at 12, a distance of 30 m. No water all day. A good place for a person with the hydrophobia."

[3] The chief had halted at a ford. KJ notes that the chief thought he had Kane in his power and that Kane could not find his way out.

increasing in numbers. I took a sketch of the Nezperees, near the mouth of the Pelouse River, showing the singular formation of the basaltic rocks. [Fig. 133; crIV-350]

Chapter XVIII.

The Stream dried up.—American Presbyterian Mission.—A perfect Savage.—Scorched to death by the Sun.—Disastrous Expedition.— The Messenger of Woe.—The "Yellow Serpent."—A Father of Sorrow.—A Grave-side Address.—The Living and the Dead.—The lost Cup.—Taken for a Scoocoom.—A dreadful Disappointment.

July 18th.—Started for Dr. Whitman's mission, a distance of sixty miles, neither myself nor my man knowing anything of the road. I inquired of one of the Indians here: he pointed out the direction, but told us that we would be sure to die before we reached it for want of water; nor could we prevail on any of them to guide us. However, we started in the direction pointed out: the weather was intensely hot, and we had nothing to shelter us from the scorching rays of the sun, which were reflected back by the hot yellow sand.[1] Towards the middle of the day we observed a bush in the distance, and in our line of march; we eagerly rushed forward, hoping to find water, for want of which both ourselves and our horses were now suffering severely; but had the mortification to find the stream dried up, if ever there had been one there. Our only hope was now to struggle on as fast as possible, but our horses soon began to fail, and we were obliged to lead them many a weary mile tottering with exhaustion, before we arrived at the mission house. This we at length accomplished about 6 o'clock in the evening, and I was received very kindly by the missionary and his wife. [Figs. 137, 138; crIV-362, 363]

Dr. Whitman's duties included those of superintendent of the American Presbyterian missions on the west side of the Rocky Mountains. He had built himself a house of unburnt clay, for want of timber, which, as stated above, is here extremely scarce. He had resided at this locality, on the banks of the Walla-Walla River, upwards of eight years, doing all in his power to benefit the Indians in his mission. He had brought forty or fifty acres of land in the vicinity of the river under cultivation, and had a great many heads of domestic cattle, affording greater comfort to his family than one would expect in such an isolated spot. I remained with him four days, during which he kindly accompanied me amongst the Indians. These Indians, the Kye-use, resemble the Walla-Wallas very much. They are always allies in

war, and their language and customs are almost identical, except that the Kye-use Indians are far more vicious and ungovernable.

Dr. Whitman took me to the lodge of an Indian called To-ma-kus, that I might take his likeness. We found him in his lodge sitting perfectly naked. His appearance was the most savage I ever beheld, and his looks, as I afterwards heard, by no means belied his character. He was not aware of what I was doing until I had finished the sketch. He then asked to look at it, and inquired what I intended doing with it, and whether I was not going to give it to the Americans, against whom he bore a strong antipathy, superstitiously fancying that their possessing it would put him in their power. I in vain told him that I should not give it to them; but not being satisfied with this assurance, he attempted to throw it in the fire, when I seized him by the arm and snatched it from him. He glanced at me like a fiend, and appeared greatly enraged, but before he had time to recover from his surprise I left the lodge and mounted my horse, not without occasionally looking back to see if he might not send an arrow after me. [Fig. 139; crIV-364?, 365, 366]

Usually, when I wished to take the likeness of an Indian, I walked into the lodge, sat down, and commenced without speaking, as an Indian under these circumstances will generally pretend not to notice. If they did not like what I was doing they would get up and walk away; but if I asked them to sit they most frequently refused, supposing that it would have some injurious effect upon themselves. In this manner I went into the lodge of Til-au-kite, the chief, and took his likeness without a word passing between us. [Fig. 140; crIV-367, 368, 369]

[Plateau Indian: crIV-370]

Having enjoyed the kind hospitality of Dr. Whitman and his lady for four days, on

July 22nd[2] I left for Walla-Walla, after breakfast, taking with me, at the Doctor's desire, a dog belonging to Mr. M'Bain. The weather continued intensely hot, and I had not ridden more than an hour when I observed the poor animal in a state of such extreme exhaustion that I requested my man to place him on his horse, but the man, feeling inconvenienced by him, put him down on the ground, and in a few minutes afterwards the poor brute lay down and died, actually scorched to death by the burning sand.

On the day after my arrival at the fort, a boy, one of the sons of Peo-Peo-mox-mox, the chief of the Walla-Wallas, arrived at

[1] KJ says that they went 30 miles without water, rested at the "Tuchay" (Fuchay?) for an hour, and then went another 20 miles.
[2] KJ gives the date of departure as July 20.

the camp close to the fort. [Fig. 143; crIV-377] He was a few days in advance of a war party headed by his father, and composed of Walla-Walla and Kye-use Indians, which had been absent eighteen months, and had been almost given up by the tribes. This party, numbering 200 men, had started for California for the purpose of revenging the death of another son of the chief, who had been killed by some Californian emigrants; and the messenger now arrived bringing the most disastrous tidings, not only of the total failure of the expedition, but also of their suffering and detention by sickness. Hearing that a messenger was coming in across the plains, I went to the Indian camp and was there at his arrival. No sooner had he dismounted from his horse than the whole camp, men, women, and children, surrounded him, eagerly inquiring after their absent friends, as they had hitherto received no intelligence, beyond a report, that the party had been cut off by hostile tribes. His downcast looks and silence confirmed the fears that some dire calamity must have happened, and they set up a tremendous howl, while he stood silent and dejected, with the tears streaming down his face. At length, after much coaxing and entreaty on their part, he commenced the recital of their misfortunes.

After describing the progress of the journey up to the time of the disease (the measles) making its appearance, during which he was listened to in breathless silence, he began to name its victims one after another. On the first name being mentioned, a terrific howl ensued, the women loosening their hair and gesticulating in a most violent manner. When this had subsided, he, after much persuasion, named a second and a third, until he had named upwards of thirty. The same signs of intense grief followed the mention of each name, presenting a scene which accustomed as I was to Indian life, I must confess, affected me deeply. I stood close by them on a log, with the interpreter of the fort, who explained to me the Indian's statement, which occupied nearly three hours. After this the excitement increased, and apprehensions were entertained at the fort that it might lead to some hostile movement against the establishment. This fear, however, was groundless, as the Indians knew the distinction between the Hudson's Bay Company and the Americans. They immediately sent messengers in every direction on horseback to spread the news of the disaster among all the neighbouring tribes, and Mr. M'Bain and I both considered that Dr. Whitman and his family would be in great danger. I, therefore, determined to go and warn him of what had occurred. It was six o'clock in the evening when I started, but I had a good horse, and arrived at his house in three hours. I told him of the arrival

of the messenger, and the excitement of the Indians, and advised him strongly to come to the fort, for a while at least, until the Indians had cooled down; but he said he had lived so long amongst them, and had done so much for them, that he did not apprehend they would injure him. I remained with him only an hour, and hastened back to the fort, where I arrived at one o'clock, A.M. Not wishing to expose myself unnecessarily to any danger arising from the superstitious notions which the Indians might attach to my having taken some of their likenesses, I remained at Fort Walla-Walla four or five days, during which the war party had returned, and I had an opportunity of taking the likeness of the great chief Peo-Peo-mox-mox, or, "the Yellow Serpent," who exercises great influence, not only over his own people, but also among the neighbouring tribes.[3] [Fig. 142; crIV-375, 376]

While at the fort one of the gentlemen of the establishment, who had been amongst the Indians for forty years, and who had resided for the most part of that time amongst the Walla-Wallas, related to me the following story, which I shall introduce, as nearly as possible, in the manner in which it was told to me; as it is strongly illustrative of the Indian character, of their love for their children, and the firmness with which they meet the approach of death, and their belief in a future state.

Several years back, when the Walla-Wallas used to go in annual buffalo hunts, and herds of these immense animals frequented the west side of the mountains, though now rarely seen, the tribe was governed by a chief adored by his own people, and respected and feared by all the surrounding tribes for his great wisdom and courage. This chief had many sons, who, in childhood, all promised to resemble their father both in mind and body, but one by one, as they arrived at manhood, and as the proud father hoped to see them take their place amongst the warriors and leaders of the tribe, they withered and sank into untimely graves, and as each loved one passed away, the stern chief soothed his silent sorrow with hopes of those still left. At last his hair grew white with sorrow and with age, and he had but one boy left—his youngest—but apparently the strongest, the bravest, and the best: at least to the old warrior's heart he was all this; for in him still seemed to live all the most cherished virtues of his dead brothers.

The old man now devoted his whole time to the instruction of this boy: he taught him to hunt the buffalo and the moose, to

---

[3] For Peo-Peo-mox-mox, see Richard Dillon, *Fool's Gold: The Decline and Fall of John Sutter of California* (New York 1967).

snare the lynx and trap the bear, to draw the bow and poise the spear with unerring aim. Young as the boy was, he yet made him head the warriors of his tribe, and led him on himself, the foremost to surprise the enemy and secure the bloody trophies of victory; already had he become the theme of the war-chant, and his name was known far and wide for all the virtues that could adorn an Indian brave.

But the Great Spirit took this one too; and the lonely and desolate father shut himself up in the solitude of his lodge, and no one saw him nor spoke to him, nor was there any sound of wailing or of grief heard from that sad abode. At length the appointed day arrived upon which the body was to be laid in its last resting-place, where the chief had ordered a large grave to be made; and the funeral procession being formed, the chief came forth and placed himself at their head, but, to the astonishment of all, instead of being dressed in the shabby garments indicative of mourning, he came forth arrayed in full war costume, fully equipped as if for some distant hostile excursion, painted with the most brilliant war paints, and hung round with the trophies of his many bloody and successful wars.

Calmly and sternly he marched to the grave, and the body of his loved son having been laid in it, with all the Indian treasures supposed to be useful to him in the next world, the bereaved father stood on the verge, and addressed his tribe: "From my youth upwards I have ever sought the honour and welfare of my tribe, and have never spared myself either in the battle or the chase. I have led you from victory to victory, and, instead of being surrounded by hostile tribes, you are now feared by all, and your friendship is sought, and your enmity dreaded, wherever the hunters of the tribe may roam. I have been a father to you, and ye have been as children to me, for more moons than I am able to count, until my hairs have become as hoar frost upon the mountains. You have never withheld your obedience from me, nor will you deny it to me now. When the Great Spirit was pleased to call my children one by one, to His blessed hunting grounds, I saw them borne to the sepulchre of their fathers without murmuring against His will, so long as one was left me. I toiled on for him, taking pride in his pride, glorying in his glory, and living in his life, fondly hoping that when I should go to join his loved brothers in the other world that I should leave him to perpetuate my deeds amongst you; but the Great Spirit hath called him also,—this last prop of my declining years,—this hope of my old age,—endeared to me by so many fond recollections of his worth, his manly strength, his courage, skill, and prowess in war. Alas! he lies in the cold ground, and I

am left alone, like the sapless trunk of a tree whose branches have been scathed by the lightning. I tracked that loved form, now cold, from its childhood's gambols to its manly acts of daring. I it was who first placed in his hands the bow and the tomahawk, and taught him how to use them; and often have you witnessed and praised his skill and courage in wielding them. And shall I now forsake him, and leave him alone and unaided, to take the long and toilsome journey in the Spirit's hunting grounds? No! his spirit beckons me to follow, and he shall not be disappointed; the same grave shall contain us, the same earth shall cover us; and as in this world, his father's arm was ever near to assist him in every toil and danger, so shall his spirit find him by his side in the long and toilsome journey to the plenteous and everlasting hunting grounds of the Great Spirit. You, my people, have never disobeyed me, and will not fail to fulfil my last commands. I now leave you, and when I lie extended at his side[,] heap the earth over us both: nothing can change my purpose." He then descended into the grave, and clasped the corpse in his arms. His people, after in vain endeavouring to change his resolution, obeyed his commands, and buried the living and the dead. A stick, with a piece of ragged red cloth, was the only monument erected over the warriors, but their names will form the theme of many an Indian *talk* as long as the Walla-Walla tribe exists.

July 29th.—I had determined to go to Colville by the Grand Coulet: this, from the appearance of the two extremities, seemed to have been a former bed of the Columbia River, but no person could tell me anything about it, nor could I hear of any one, either Indian or White, who had penetrated any considerable distance up it; the place was, however, so much talked of as the abode of evil spirits and other strange things, that I could not resist the desire of trying to explore it. I accordingly sent on everything by the boats, except what I usually carried about my own person, but I could not get an Indian guide, as none of them would venture an encounter with the evil spirits.

At last a half-breed, called Donny, although ignorant of the route, agreed to accompany me. We procured two riding horses, and one to carry our provisions, consisting of two fine hams, which had been sent to me from Fort Vancouver, and a stock of dried salmon, cured by the Indians. About ten miles from the fort, we swam our horses across the Nezperees River, where it enters the Columbia, and then proceeded along the banks of the Columbia, about ten miles further, where we encamped for the night.

During the day we passed a large encampment of Nezperees,

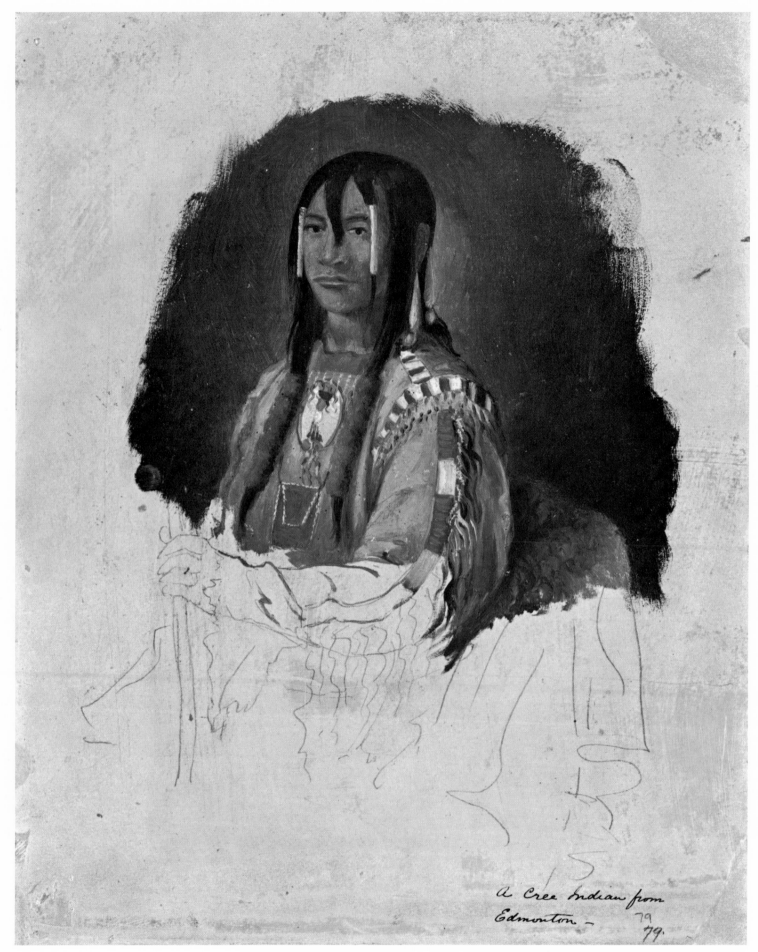

A Cree Indian from Edmonton — 79 79.

Plate XXII. Cree Indian. Stark POP16; crIV-139.

Medicine Pipe Stem Dance.   Black feet & Blood Indians

Paul Kane. 1846

Plate XXIII. Medicine pipe-stem dance (Blackfoot). Stark POP10; CRIV-157.

who were very kind to us, but stole a tin cup (a valuable article in that part of the world) I suppose as a souvenir of my visit. I took a sketch of a man, and might have frightened the chief into getting the cup restored to me by means of this sketch, but I had been so warned of the treachery and villany of these Indians, that I considered it too dangerous an experiment. [Fig. 141; crIV-371 to 373]

July 30th.—Proceeded along the shore for eight or ten miles,[4] when I discovered that I had left my pistols and some other articles at our last night's encampment. I had, therefore, to send my man back for them, while I sat by the river, with horses and baggage, under a burning sun, without the slightest shelter. Whilst sitting there, a canoe approached with four Indians, streaked all over with white mud (the ordinary pipe-clay). On landing, they showed much surprise, and watched very cautiously at a distance, some creeping close to me, and then retreating. This continued for about three hours, during which not a sound broke through the surrounding stillness. I had commenced travelling very early, and this, combined with the heat and silence, made me intensely drowsy. Even the danger I was in scarcely sufficed to keep my eyes open, but the Indians were evidently at fault as to what to make of me.

As I sat upon the packs taken from the horse, nodding in silence, with a fixed stare at them whichever way they turned, my double-barrelled gun, cocked, across my knees, and a large red beard (an object of great wonder to all Indians) hanging half way down my breast, I was, no doubt, a very good embodiment of their ideas of a scoocoom, or evil genius. To this I attributed my safety, and took good care not to encourage their closer acquaintance, as I had no wish to have my immortality tested by them.

At length my man returned with the missing articles, and the Indians hastily took to their canoe and crossed the river. We now continued our course along the river until evening, when we encamped, and as we were very hungry, and expected a hard journey next day, we determined upon attacking one of our hams. I accordingly seized hold of the bone to pull it from the bag with which it was covered, when, alas! the bare bone slipped out, leaving a living mass of maggots, into which the heat had turned the flesh, behind. Upon examination, we found the other in the same state, and had to satisfy our hunger on the salmon, which, as usual, was full of sand.

---

[4] KJ states that he went 30 miles, not eight or ten, before he missed his pistols.

Chapter XIX.

The Horrors of Thirst.—The Lake of Pelicans.—A queer Bedfellow. —Steering by the Sun.—Sweet Water at Last.—Rather a hardy Horse.—Losing each Other.—Wonderful natural Walls.—The Grand Coulet.—A Great Treat.—The River Columbia.—Indians again.

July 31st.—Owing to the great bend which the Columbia takes to the northward, I thought I should save a considerable distance by striking across the country, and intersecting the Grand Coulet at some distance from its mouth. We accordingly left the river early in the morning, and travelled all day through a barren, sandy desert, without a drop of water to drink, a tree to rest under, or a spot of grass to sit upon. Towards evening, we saw in the distance a small lake, and to this we accordingly pushed forward: as soon as our horses perceived it, wearied and exhausted as they were, they rushed forward and plunged bodily into the water. No sooner, however, had they tasted it, than they drew their heads back, refusing to drink. On alighting, I found the water was intensely salt, and never shall I forget the painful emotion which came over me, as it became certain to my mind that I could not satisfy my thirst. Our horses were too weary, after our long and rapid ride, to proceed further; and though it was tantalising to look at the water which we could not drink, the vegetation which surrounded it was refreshing to the horses, and we remained here all night, though we enjoyed scarcely any sleep owing to our thirst.

August 1st.—We started at 4 o'clock this morning, and travelled steadily on without getting water, until about noon, when we fell in with a narrow lake, about a mile long, very shallow, and swarming with pelicans, whose dung had made the water green and thick. Bad as this was, added to its being also rather salt, yet our thirst was so great, that we strained some through a cloth and drank it. Leaving this Lake of Pelicans, we now entered upon a still more discouraging route: the country, as far as the eye could reach, was covered with loose fine sand, which the violent winds of this region had drifted into immense mounds, varying from 80 to 120 feet in height. [crIV-378] This was very toilsome to us, as our horses had become so exhausted that we were obliged to lead them, and we sank deep at every step in the hot sand. Had the wind risen while we were crossing this place, we must have been immediately buried in the sand. Towards evening we arrived at a rock, and in a small cleft we discovered three or four gallons of water almost as black as ink, and abounding in disgusting animalcula. The horses no sooner saw it, than they made a spring towards it, and it was with the greatest difficulty we drove them back, fearing that they would drink all, and leave us to our misery. After satisfying our thirst, we strained a kettleful for our supper, and allowed the horses to drink up the remainder, which they did to the last drop, showing how necessary was the precaution we had taken. Here we passed the night.

Aug. 2nd.—I awoke in the morning, and felt something cold and clammy against my thigh, and on throwing off my blanket, perceived a reptile of the lizard species, eight or ten inches long, which had been my companion during the night. I cannot say whether it was venomous or not, but I found no ill effects from it. We proceeded on, and about noon emerged from these mountains of sand; the country was still sandy and barren, but here and there we found tufts of grass sufficient to support our horses. The country was intersected with immense walls of basaltic rock, which continually threw us out of our direct course, or rather the course I had determined on, for of the actual route I had no information. These interruptions added considerably to our difficulties, as I had no compass, and it was only by noticing the sun at mid-day by my watch, and fixing on some distant hill, that I guided my course. We still suffered from the want of water, and my man was getting disheartened at our wandering thus almost at random through this trackless desert.

Aug. 3rd.[1]—After riding a few hours, we came to an immense gully or dried-up water-course crossing our route. The banks rose seven or eight hundred feet high from the bottom on each side, and its width was nearly half a mile. At first it seemed impossible to pass it; however, after many difficulties, we succeeded in leading our horses to the bottom, which we crossed, and clambered up the rocks on the opposite side for about 200 feet, when we came to one of the most beautiful spots that can well be conceived: at least, it appeared to us all that was beautiful, amongst the surrounding desolation.

It was a piece of table land, about half a mile in circumference, covered with luxuriant grass, and having in its centre a small lake of exquisitely cool fresh water. The basaltic rock rose like an amphitheatre, from about three-quarters of its circuit to the height of about 500 feet, while the precipice up which we had toiled sank down at the other side. We remained here three hours, luxuriating in the delicious water, so sweet to us after suffering the torments of thirst for so long. My man seemed as

if he never could have enough of it, for when he could swallow no more, he walked in, clothes and all, and actually wallowed in it, the horses following his example. How much longer we might have been tempted to stay here, it is impossible to say, but we accidentally set fire to the grass and were obliged to decamp; this was accomplished with considerable difficulty, and in getting up the precipitous rocks, the pack-horse lost his footing and fell to the bottom, but pitching, fortunately, on his back with the packs under him, he escaped with a few cuts on his legs only. Had he been anything but an Indian horse, he would doubtless have paid the forfeit of his life for the insecurity of his feet.

As soon as I arrived at the level of the country once more, I saw in the distance another vast wall of rock, and leaving my man to bring up the unfortunate pack-horse, I rode briskly forward to endeavour to find a passage over this formidable barrier, considering it to be like many others that we had already passed, an isolated wall of basalt. I therefore rode backwards and forwards along its front, exploring every part that presented any opening, but without finding one that our horses could traverse. At last I came to the conclusion that we must go round it, but my man not having come up, it was necessary for me to return and seek him, which proved for several hours unavailing, and I began to fear that he and my provisions were inevitably lost; however, after riding a long way back, I fell upon his track, which I followed up with care.

I soon perceived that he had taken a wrong direction. After some time, I saw him mounted on a high rock in the distance, shouting and signalling with all his might till I got up to him: he was very much frightened, as he said that if he had lost me he never could have got on. Though the day was by this time pretty far advanced, we succeeded in making a circuit of the basaltic wall, and struck a deep ravine which in the distance so much resembled the banks of the Columbia, that I at first thought I had missed my way, and had come upon the river.

When we reached the edge, I saw that there was no water at the bottom, and that there could be no doubt of my having at last arrived at the Grand Coulet.[2] With great difficulty we descended the bank, 1000 feet; its width varies from one mile to a mile and a half; and there can be no doubt of its having been previously an arm of the Columbia, which now flows four or five hundred feet below it, leaving the channel of the Coulet dry,

---

[1] KJ gives the date as August 2.
[2] KJ states that they went through the Grand Coulee for ten miles, and went in all 35 miles.

and exposing to view the bases of the enormous rocky islands that now stud its bottom, some of them rising to the elevation of the surrounding country. [CRIV-379, 380, 381]

This wonderful gully is about 150 miles long, and walled-in in many places with an unbroken length twenty miles long of perpendicular basalt 1000 feet high.[3] The bottom of this valley is perfectly level, and covered with luxuriant grass, except where broken by the immense rocks above mentioned: there is not a single tree to be seen throughout its whole extent, and scarcely a bush; neither did we see any insects, reptiles, or animals. Having found a beautiful spring of water gushing from the rocks, we encamped near it. After we had rested ourselves, we commenced an examination of our provisions of dried salmon, for we saw no chance of adding anything to our larder, and of course what we had was of great importance. Much to our regret, we found that it was perfectly alive with maggots, and every mouthful had to be well shaken before eating; so full of life indeed had the fish become, that my man proposed tying them by the tails to prevent their crawling away. Bad as the salmon was, our prospects were made still more gloomy by the fact that there was but a very small supply left, and that we had a long and unknown road to travel before we could hope for any help. A thunderstorm came on during the night, and in the whole course of my life I never heard anything so awfully sublime as the endless reverberations amongst the rocks of this grand and beautiful ravine. There is hardly another spot in the world that could produce so astounding an effect.

Aug. 4th.—We followed the course of the Coulet, lost in admiration of its beauty and grandeur assuming a new aspect of increased wildness and magnificence at every turn. I shot the first bird we had seen since leaving Walla-Walla, except the pelicans, which are never eaten, even by the Indians, who are far from particular. This bird proved to be what is here called a wild turkey, but resembling in nothing the wild turkeys of the south. Its plumage resembles that of a pheasant, it is not larger than a domestic hen, and its flesh, though very white, is dry and unpalatable; to us, however, it proved a great treat, as we were enabled to make one meal without the usual accompaniments of sand and maggots. Our journey now would have been delight-ful, if we had anything like good food. We had plenty of grass of the best quality for our horses, delicious springs gushing from the rocks at every mile or two, and camping grounds which almost tempted us to stay at the risk of starvation.

Aug. 5th.[4]—Towards evening we began to see trees, principally pine, in the heights and in the distance, and I concluded that we were now approaching the Columbia River. I now pressed forward and before sundown emerged from the gorge of this stupendous ravine, and saw the mighty river flowing at least 500 feet below us, though the banks rose considerably more than that height above us on each side. This river exceeds in grandeur any other perhaps in the world, not so much from its volume of water, although that is immense, as from the romantic wilderness of its stupendous and ever-varying surrounding scenery, now towering into snow-capped mountains thousands of feet high, and now sinking in undulating terraces to the level of its pellucid waters.

Two Indians were floating down the river, on a few logs tied together. They were the first we had encountered for many days[5]; and on our hailing them, they landed, and climbed up to us. They told me we were ten days' journey from Colville. This I did not believe, although I could not tell why they wished to deceive me. I gave them a little tobacco, and hoped to get some provisions from them, but they said they had none, so we were obliged to make our supper on the salmon as usual. We descended the bank, and camped for the night on the margin of the river.

Chapter XX.

August 6th.[1]—We continued along the shore for twelve or fifteen miles, under the rocky banks, which towered over our heads fourteen or fifteen hundred feet. In some places, immense ledges hung over our path, seemingly ready to crush all beneath them. At length we came to a high perpendicular rock jutting out into the river; and as the water was too deep and too rapid to allow us to wade round its base, we attempted to ascend the

---

[3] KJ: "Every 5 or 6 miles I found a cold spring of water, quite refreshing after what I had suffered. My man set fire to the prairie where we had breakfasted which came very near burning our horses had we not got it under control. We were at the time walled in by high rocks and only one narrow pass to get out."

[4] KJ reads August 3.

[5] KJ mentions four days.

[1] KJ reads August 4.

bank over loose rocks and stones that slipped from under us at every step, and rolled thundering to the bottom. Having led our horses up about three hundred feet, I stopped, and sent Donny a-head on foot to seek for an opening to the top. The pack-horse could with great difficulty preserve his footing under his load. One of the other horses, with incredible sagacity, now walked up past me, until he reached his burdened companion; and, putting his shoulder under one side of the load, actually assisted him in sustaining it, until the man's return. Finding that we could not possibly ascend, we were obliged to turn back; and we did not find a practicable place to ascend until we had nearly reached the place from which we had started in the morning.

At last, with great difficulty, we succeeded in gaining the upper bank, and entered upon a wild and romantic district, studded here and there with small clumps of trees, which gradually increased in thickness, until we became surrounded with dense woods, having made a circuit of about twenty-five miles, traversing gullies of prodigious depth and steepness. We again struck the river opposite the mouth of a small stream, on whose banks we saw a couple of Indians. As soon as we were perceived, they sent a canoe over to us, offering to assist in swimming the horses across, as they assured us that the shortest and best route to Colville was on the other side. We accepted their friendly offer, and camped alongside them on the other side. Both Donny and myself were dreadfully fatigued from the length of our day's travel, the labour we had gone through, and the weakness under which we suffered from the want of sufficient food. These Indians, as I afterwards learned, were generally very unfriendly to the whites, and had often given trouble to small parties passing, generally levying a pretty heavy toll for a free passage through their territory. But to me they were all kindness, presenting me with plenty of fresh salmon and dried berries, which were most acceptable, after the disgusting fare on which we had been so long struggling to support life; and one of them proposed to accompany me as a guide to Colville. My last day's experience made me gladly accept of this offer; and long before darkness set in, I found myself as sound asleep as the most weary of dyspeptic patients could wish himself to be.

August 7th.—Started very early in the morning with the guide, and made, what is called in those parts, a long day. We were continually ascending and descending, and found it very fatiguing. It was quite dark when we encamped on the banks of the river.

August 8th.—Started again very early for the purpose of reaching Colville before night. Came to a high hill overlooking the Columbia for many miles of its course, and sat down on its summit to enjoy the magnificent prospect, and give a short rest to the horses. [crIV-332?] As I was lying under the trees, the wind sprang up, and, much to my astonishment, I felt the whole sod moving under me. At first I imagined it to be an earthquake, and expected to see the whole hillside move off; but on examination, I found that it proceeded from the roots of the immense trees being interlaced one within another in the shallow soil. This alone prevented their being blown over, as the rocks are everywhere close to the surface; and as the wind bends the tops of the trees, the roots rise and fall with the surface in a rolling motion like a dead swell. We proceeded on until we were within a mile of Kettle Falls, where we swam across in the usual way, holding on by the tails of our horses; and just at dusk we were kindly received by Mr. Lewis.

Fort Colville stands in the middle of a small prairie, about one mile and a half wide by about three miles long, surrounded by high hills. This little prairie is extremely valuable for agricultural purposes, as it is, in fact, an island of fertility, surrounded by barren rocks, sandy plains, and arid mountains, to the distance of three or four hundred miles along the river, the Spokan valley to the south being the nearest land fit for cultivation. [crIV-330] I remained here until the 9th of September, when I made an excursion of sixty miles, accompanied by Mr. Lewis, to Walker and Eales' [Eells'] Presbyterian mission, where I was most hospitably received by these worthy people. [Fig. 131; crIV-336]

Each of the missionaries had a comfortable log-house, situated in the midst of a fertile plain, and, with their wives and children, seem to be happily located. There are numerous Indian *caches* of dried salmon in the vicinity, which are very seldom robbed, although left in isolated spots for months without any person in charge. I enjoyed for a week the kind hospitality of my hosts, who were most attentive in accompanying me in my visits to the Spokan River and the Indians in the vicinity. [Pl. XXXII; crIV-334, 335]

The Spokan Indians are a small tribe, differing very little from the Indians at Colville either in their appearance, habits, or language. They all seemed to treat the missionaries with great affection and respect; but as to their success in making converts, I must speak with great diffidence, as I was not sufficiently acquainted with the language to examine them, even had I wished to do so. I have no doubt that a great number have been baptised; but I also am aware that almost all Indians will take a name from a man whom they esteem, and give him one in return; and the more ceremony there is about the transaction, the more importance will be attached to it, and the greater the inducement to others to be equally honoured. No influence, however, seems to be able to make agriculturists of them, as they still pursue their hunting and fishing, evincing the greatest dislike to anything like manual labour. [Pl. XXXIII; crIV-331, 337]

On the 17th [2] of September I returned again to Colville. The Indian village is situated about two miles below the fort, on a rocky eminence overlooking the Kettle Falls. These are the highest in the Columbia River. They are about one thousand yards across, and eighteen feet high. The immense body of water tumbling amongst the broken rocks renders them exceedingly picturesque and grand. [Plate XXX; crIV-297, 298, 299, 307] The Indians have no particular name for them, giving them the general name of Tum-tum, which is applied to all falls of water. The voyageurs call them the "Chaudière," or "Kettle Falls," from the numerous round holes worn in the solid rocks by loose boulders. These boulders, being caught in the inequalities of rocks below the falls, are constantly driven round by the tremendous force of the current, and wear out holes as perfectly round and smooth as in the inner surface of a cast-iron kettle. The village has a population of about five hundred souls, called, in their own language, Chualpays. [crIV-294?] They differ but little from the Walla-Wallas. The lodges are formed of mats of rushes stretched on poles. A flooring is made of sticks, raised three or four feet from the ground, leaving the space beneath it entirely open, and forming a cool, airy, and shady place, in which to hang their salmon to dry. [Pl. XXXI; Fig. 124; crIV-308 to 312, 315]

These people are governed by two chiefs, Allam-māk-hum Stole-luch, the "Chief of the Earth." [*sic*] This chief exercises great power over the tribe except as regards the fishing, which is under the exclusive control of See-pays, the "Chief of the Waters." He [Allam-mak-hum Stole-luch] dispenses justice strictly, and punishes with rigour any cheating or dishonesty among his subjects. [crIV-295] He opposes the gambling propensities of his tribe to the utmost, even depriving the victorious gamblers of their share of the fish received annually from the Chief of the Waters; but still the passion for gambling continues, and an instance occurred during my stay here of a young man committing suicide by shooting himself, having lost everything he possessed by indulging in this habit. I may here remark

[2] KJ gives the date as 16th, not 17th.

that suicide prevails more among the Indians of the Columbia River than in any other portion of the continent which I have visited.

A curious case occurred, about a year before my visit, of two sisters, wives of one man, each jealous of the other, who went into the woods and hung themselves, as was supposed, unknown to each other, as they were found dead a long distance apart.

The principal game played here is called Al-kol-lock, and requires considerable skill. A smooth level piece of ground is chosen, and a slight barrier of a couple of sticks placed lengthwise, is laid at each end of the chosen spot, being from forty to fifty feet apart and only a few inches high. The two players, stripped naked, are armed each with a very slight spear about three feet long, and finely pointed with bone; one of them takes a ring made of bone, or some heavy wood, and wound round with cord; this ring is about three inches in diameter, on the inner circumference of which are fastened six beads of different colours at equal distances, to each of which a separate numerical value is attached. The ring is then rolled along the ground to one of the barriers, and is followed at the distance of two or three yards by the players, and as the ring strikes the barrier and is falling on its side, the spears are thrown, so that the ring may fall on them. If only one of the spears should be covered by the ring, the owner of it counts according to the coloured bead over it. But it generally happens, from the dexterity of the players, that the ring covers both spears, and each counts according to the colour of the beads above his spear; they then play towards the other barrier, and so on until one party has attained the number agreed upon for game. [Figs. 125, 126; crIV-316 to 321]

The other chief is called See-pays, the "Chief of the Waters," or the "Salmon Chief." [Fig. 122; crIV-292, 293, 296?] No one is allowed to catch fish without his permission. His large fishing basket or trap is put down a month before anyone is allowed to fish for themselves. This basket is constructed of stout willow wands woven together, and supported by stout sticks of timber, and is so placed that the salmon, in leaping up the falls strike against a stick placed at the top, and are thrown back into the confined space at the bottom of the trap, which is too narrow to allow them to attempt another jump.

The salmon commence their ascent about the 15th of July, and continue to arrive in almost incredible numbers for nearly two months; in fact, there is one continuous body of them, more resembling a flock of birds than anything else in their extraordinary leap up the falls, beginning at sunrise and ceasing at the approach of night. The chief told me that he had taken as many as 1700 salmon, weighing on an average 30 lbs. each, in the course of one day. Probably the daily average taken in the chief's basket is about 400. The chief distributes the fish thus taken during the season amongst his people, everyone, even to the smallest child, getting an equal share.

By the time the salmon reach the Kettle Falls, after surmounting the numerous rapids impeding their journey from the sea, a distance of between 700 and 800 miles, they become so exhausted, that in their efforts to leap these falls, their strength often proves unequal to the task, and striking against the projecting rocks they batter their noses so severely, that they fall back stunned and often dead, and float down the river, where they are picked up some six miles below by another camp of Indians, who do not belong to the Salmon Chief's jurisdiction, and of course have no participation in the produce of his basket. None of these salmon coming up from the sea ever return, but remain in the river and die by thousands; in fact, in such numbers that in our passage down the river in the fall, whenever we came to still water, we found them floating dead or cast up along the shore in such vast numbers as literally to poison the atmosphere.

The young fish return to the sea in the spring. Strange to say, nothing has ever been found in the stomachs of the salmon caught in the Columbia River; and no angler, although frequent trials have been made by the most expert in the art, has yet succeeded in tempting them to take any description of fly or other bait.

After the expiration of one month, the Salmon Chief abandons his exclusive privilege, as the fish are then getting thin and poor, and allows all who wish it to take them. For this purpose some use smaller baskets made like the chief's; others use the spear, with which they are very expert, and an ordinary spearsman will take easily as many as 200 in a day; others use a small hand-net in the rapids, where the salmon are crowded together and near the surface. These nets are somewhat like our common landing-nets, but ingeniously contrived, so that when a fish is in them, his own struggles loosen a little stick which keeps the mouth of the net open while empty; the weight of the salmon then draws the mouth close like a purse, and effectually secures the prey.

Salmon is almost the only food used by the Indians on the Lower Columbia River, the two months' fishing affording a sufficient supply to last them the whole year round. The mode in which they cure them is by splitting them down the back,

after which each half is again split, making them sufficiently thin to dry with facility, a process occupying in general from four to five days.[3] The salmon are afterwards sewed up in rush mats, containing about ninety or one hundred pounds, and put up on scaffolds to keep the dogs from them. Infinitely greater numbers of salmon could be readily taken here, if it were desired; but, as the chief considerately remarked to me, if he were to take all that came up, there would be none left for the Indians on the upper part of the river; so that they content themselves with supplying their own wants. [Fig. 123; crIV-300 to 306, 313, 314]

A few days before leaving Colville I was informed that the Chualpays were about to celebrate a scalp dance, and accordingly I took my sketch-book and went down to their encampment, where I learned that a small party had returned from a hunting expedition to the mountains, bringing with them, as a present from a friendly tribe, the scalp of a Blackfoot Indian. This to them was a present of inestimable value, as one of their tribe had been killed by a Blackfoot Indian two or three years before, and they had not been able to obtain any revenge for the injury. This scalp, however, would soothe the sorrows of his widow and friends. Accordingly, it was stretched upon a small hoop, and attached to a stick as a handle, and thus carried by the afflicted woman to a place where a large fire was kindled: here she commenced dancing and singing, swaying the scalp violently about and kicking it, whilst eight women, hideously painted, chanted and danced round her and the fire. The remainder of the tribe stood round in a circle, beating drums, and all singing. [Figs. 127 to 130; crIV-322 to 329]

Having witnessed the performance for about four or five hours, seeing no variation in it, nor any likelihood of its termination, I returned, deeply impressed with the sincerity of a grief which could endure such violent monotony for so long a period. My kind host, Mr. Lewis, was now obliged to give up rambling about with me, as he had to see to the preparations for the further progress of the return brigade. Both himself and his Cree wife were most attentive in adding every little thing to my outfit which they could supply. Mrs. Lewis was a most excellent wife for a trader, possessing great energy and decision, combined with natural kindness of disposition. Several years before I became acquainted with her she had amputated her husband's arm, a little below the elbow, with a common knife, and tied it up so well, that he soon recovered without any other assistance.

[3] w59: "I have never seen salt made use of by any tribe of Indians for the purpose of preserving food, and they all evince the greatest dislike to salt meat."

Her surgical aid had been called in requisition by the accidental discharge of his gun, which had shattered the limb so much that it was hopeless to try and save it.

[Chinewoss: crIV-333]

Chapter XXI.

Dreadful Tidings.—Horrible Tragedy.—A devoted Husband.—A joyful Surprise.—Perilous Pass.—Walk on Shore.—The Rapid of the Dead.—The detected Cannibal.—A Western Honeymoon.—The Last Embrace.—Capote Blanc.—Boat Encampment.—A bothered Steed.—Forest swept away.—The Flooded Athabasca.—Shoes long as yourself.—Crossing Jasper's Lake.—In for it everyway.—Rising of the River.—Starving of the Dogs.—Waiting for a Frost-Bridge.—Too Thin to be Eaten.—Fort Assiniboine.—Pleasure after Pain.

Sept. 21st.—This evening two men arrived from Walla-Walla, and my grief and horror can be well imagined when they told me the sad fate of those with whom I had so lately been a cherished guest.[1] It appeared that the war party before mentioned had brought the measles back with them, and that it spread with fearful rapidity through the neighbouring tribe, but more particularly among the Key-uses. Dr. Whitman, as a medical man, did all he could to stay its progress; but owing to their injudicious mode of living, which he could not prevail on them to relinquish, great numbers of them died. At this time the doctor's family consisted of himself, his wife, and a nephew, with two or three servants, and several children whom he had humanely adopted, left orphans by the death of their parents who had died on their way to Oregon, besides a Spanish half-breed boy, whom he had brought up for several years. There were likewise several families of emigrants staying with him at the time, to rest and refresh themselves and cattle.

The Indians supposed that the doctor could have stayed the course of the malady had he wished it; and they were confirmed in this belief by the Spanish half-breed boy, who told some of them that he had overheard the doctor say to his wife after they had retired for the night, that he would give them bad medicine, and kill all the Indians, that he might appropriate their

land to himself. They accordingly concocted a plan to destroy the doctor and his wife, and all the males of the establishment. With this object in view, about sixty of them armed themselves and came to his house. The inmates, having no suspicion of any hostile intention, were totally unprepared for resistance or flight. Dr. and Mrs. Whitman and their nephew, a youth about seventeen or eighteen years of age, were sitting in their parlour in the afternoon, when Til-au-kite, the chief, and To-ma-kus entered the room, and, addressing the doctor, told him very coolly that they had come to kill him. The doctor, not believing it possible that they could entertain any hostile intentions towards him, told them as much; but while in the act of speaking, To-ma-kus drew a tomahawk from under his robe and buried it deep in his brain. The unfortunate man fell dead from his chair. Mrs. Whitman and the nephew fled up stairs, and locked themselves into an upper room.

In the meantime Til-au-kite gave the war whoop, as a signal to his party outside to proceed in the work of destruction, which they did with the ferocity and yells of so many fiends. Mrs. Whitman, hearing the shrieks and groans of the dying, looked out of the window, and was shot through the breast by a son of the chief, but not mortally wounded. A party then rushed up stairs, and, despatching the nephew on the spot, dragged her down by the hair of her head, and, taking her to the front of the house, mutilated her in a shocking manner with their knives and tomahawks.

There was one man who had a wife bedridden. On the commencement of the affray he ran to her room, and, taking her up in his arms, carried her, unperceived by the Indians, to the thick bushes that skirted the river, and hurried on with his burden in the direction of Fort Walla-Walla. Having reached a distance of fifteen miles, he became so exhausted, that, unable to carry her further, he concealed her in a thick hummock of bushes on the margin of the river, and hastened to the fort for assistance. On his arrival, Mr. M'Bain immediately sent out men with him, and brought her in. She had fortunately suffered nothing more than fright. The number killed, including Dr. and Mrs. Whitman, amounted to fourteen. The other females and children were carried off by the Indians, and two of them were forthwith taken as wives by Til-au-kite's son and another. A man, employed in a little mill, forming a part of the establishment, was spared to work the mill for the Indians.

The day following this awful tragedy, a Catholic priest, who had not heard of the massacre, stopped, on seeing the mangled corpses strewn round the house, and requested permission to

---

[1] Kane's date for receiving word of the Whitman massacre is curious. The incident actually occurred on November 27–29. His memory must have been faulty when he came to set down the date of the event itself and a date and place for receipt of the news. KJ makes no mention of the receipt of news of the massacre; it also refers to Kane's party reaching Boat Encampment in October 1847, thus long before the date of the massacre.

bury them, which he did with the rites of his own church. The permission was granted the more readily as these Indians are friendly towards the Catholic missionaries. On the priest leaving the place, he met, at a distance of five or six miles, a brother missionary of the deceased, a Mr. Spalding, the field of whose labours lay about a hundred miles off, at a place on the River Coldwater.[2] He communicated to him the melancholy fate of his friend, and advised him to fly as fast as possible, or in all probability he would be another victim. He gave him a share of his provisions, and Mr. Spalding hurried homeward full of apprehensions for the safety of his own family; but unfortunately his horse escaped from him in the night, and, after a six days' toilsome march on foot, having lost his way, he at length reached the banks of the river, but on the opposite side to his own house.

In the dead of the night, and in a state of starvation, having eaten nothing for three days, everything seeming to be quiet about his own place, he cautiously embarked in a small canoe and paddled across the river. But he had no sooner landed than an Indian seized him and dragged him to his house, where he found all his family prisoners, and the Indians in full possession. These Indians were not of the same tribe with those who had destroyed Dr. Whitman's family, nor had they at all participated in the outrage; but having heard of it, and fearing that the whites would include them in their vengeance, they had seized on the family of Mr. Spalding for the purpose of holding them as hostages for their own safety. The family were uninjured, and he was overjoyed to find that things were no worse.

Mr. Ogden, the chief factor of the Hudson's Bay Company on the Columbia, immediately on hearing of the outrage, came to Walla-Walla, and, although the occurrence took place in the territory of the United States, and of course the sufferers could have no further claim to the protection of the Company than such as humanity dictated, he at once purchased the release of all the prisoners, and from them the particulars of the massacre were afterwards obtained. The Indians, in their negotiations with Mr. Ogden, offered to give up the prisoners for nothing, if he would guarantee that the United States would not go to war with them; but this, of course, he could not do.

On the 22nd September our two boats, with their crews of

six men each, being all ready, we bade farewell to our kind host and his family and again embarked on the river.[3] As usual, on leaving a fort, we did not start till evening, and stopped again for the night at ten miles distant, at Day's Encampment. We had no regale, as these men were not going into the interior. They only carried the express to Boat Encampment, where they exchange boxes with the express from the east side of the mountains, with whom I was to recross.

Sept. 23rd.—To-day we succeeded in getting past the Little Dalles in safety. They are about twenty miles from Kettle Falls, and are the narrowest part of the Columbia River for full one thousand miles. It is here contracted into a passage of one hundred and fifty yards by lofty rocks on each side, through which it rushes with tremendous violence, forming whirlpools in its passage capable of engulphing the largest forest trees, which are afterwards disgorged with great force. This is one of the most dangerous places that the boats have to pass. In going up the river the boats are all emptied, and the freight has to be carried about half a mile over the tops of the high and rugged rocks. One man remains in each boat with a long pole to keep it off from the rocks, whilst the others drag it by a long tow-rope up the torrent. [Fig. 119; crIV-286, 287]

Last year a man, who was on the outside of the rope, was jerked over the rocks by some sudden strain, and was immediately lost. In coming down, however, all remain in the boats; and the guides in this perilous pass, display the greatest courage and presence of mind at moments when the slightest error in managing the frail bark would hurl its occupants to certain destruction. On arriving at the head of the rapids, the guide gets out on to the rocks and surveys the whirlpools. If they are filling in "or making," as they term it, the men rest on their paddles until they commence throwing off, when the guides instantly re-embark, and shove off the boat, and shoot through this dread portal with the speed of lightning. Sometimes the boats are whirled round in the vortex with such awful rapidity that it renders the management impossible, and the boat and its hapless crew are swallowed up in the abyss.

Sept. 24th.—We had fine weather and made good progress. I shot the largest wolf to-day I had ever seen; he was swimming away from us across the river.

Sept. 25th.—The morning broke dark and cloudy, and soon turned to heavy rain; but the wind was fair, so we hoisted our sail, and soon scudded into an open lake, about three miles wide and twelve long.

Sept. 26th.—It continued raining heavily all night, and heavy

[2] The Rev. Henry Spalding came with his wife to the Oregon in 1836 along with the Whitmans, but established his mission station at Lapwai Creek two miles from its junction with the Clearwater River among the Nez Percé Indians.
[3] KJ states that Kane was placed in charge of the two Hudson's Bay Company boats with instructions to meet the express coming from the other side of the mountains.

Plate XXIV. A lake in the plains, between Fort Pitt and Fort Edmonton. ROM946.15.138; crIV-181.

mists hung over us during the day; but we continued our journey and got into what is called another lake.

Sept. 27*th.*—Still in the lakes. The day was clearer, and we could distinguish the surrounding scenery, which seemed to consist of immense mountains, towering peak on peak above the clouds. The land appeared barren and unfit for cultivation. The cedars are of enormous magnitude, some of them measuring not less than thirty or forty feet in circumference. I was told of one fifty feet, but did not see it. I attempted to reach the upper side of one which had been uprooted and lay on the ground, with the end of my gun stretched out at arm's length, and could but just attain it. [Fig. 122; crIV-283 to 285, 288, 289]

Sept. 28*th.*—We had an exciting chase after a mountain goat, which showed himself in the distance, on a point of land jutting out into the lake. Putting the boat ashore, I started in pursuit, accompanied by three or four Indians, and after a long hunt succeeded in killing him. He afforded us a most delicious repast. In size and shape he somewhat resembled the domestic goat, but was covered with white wool resembling that of a sheep; the horns are straight, small, pointed, and black.

Sept. 29*th.*—Got through the lakes by 5 o'clock P.M., and again entered into what may be more properly called the river. The rain was pouring heavily on us almost all day, whilst in the distance we could see the tops of the mountains becoming white with snow down to a well-defined line, where it seemed to change to rain.

Sept. 30*th.*—Started at 6 A.M., during a pouring rain, which soon soaked us to the skin. We stopped here to make some paddles,[4] in a forest abounding with birch, the only wood fit for this purpose, and which is not met with lower down the Columbia; large cedar-trees were also very abundant.

Oct. 1*st.*—The morning was fine and clear, and the temperature was agreeable: I was enabled to leave the boat for a walk for a few miles along the shore, much to the relief of my legs. The place is a sandbank, extending for miles in a direction parallel with the shore, and generally but a few furlongs from it; it is called the "Grand Batteur." The steepness of the banks of the river, and the density of the under-brushwood, had confined us to the boats for the last three days; it was therefore no wonder that I should enjoy a walk. We saw some very large piles of drift-wood, called by the Canadians "Aumbereaux." These piles consist of trees of all sizes, but usually very large, which are drifted down the river, and are piled high up upon one another by the force of the ice when they meet with any obstruction. I amused myself by setting fire to some of them *en*

passant, and leaving an immense fire burning, the smoke of which we could see for days in our rear.

Oct. 2*nd.*—It again rained heavily all day. Towards the evening we encamped. It is difficult to imagine the pleasure of an encampment round a large fire, after sitting in an open boat on the Columbia River, with the rain pouring down in torrents all day; but though the rain may not have ceased, yet the cheerful warmth of the fire dispels all the annoyance of mere moisture in this uncivilised state of life. We passed the Upper Little Dalle, a very long and rapid shoot of three or four miles. One of the Indians brought in some white berries, which he ate eagerly, but which I found very nauseous. I never saw any berry in the course of my travels which the Indians scruple to eat, nor have I seen any ill effect result from their doing so.

Oct. 3*rd.*—Saw four carriboos, a species of deer of the ordinary size, which we followed, but without success, as they got the wind of us before we could approach them within gunshot. We fell in with the Indian chief of the lakes, and procured some bear's and deer's meat from him, of which he seemed to possess a plentiful supply.[5] A small species of dog was tied to the bushes near his lodge, to prevent them from hunting on their own account, and driving away all the deer. The chief told me that when disposed to hunt with them, he had only to find a fresh deer-track, set his dogs on it and lie down to sleep, as they never fail to find the deer, and turn them back to the place where they had left him lying. We saw some of these dogs, apparently on the track of some deer, full twelve or fifteen miles from the chief's lodge.

Oct. 4*th.*—The chief, with wife and daughter, accompanied us in their canoe, which they paddled with great dexterity, from ten to fifteen miles. They make their canoes of pine bark, being the only Indians who use this material for the purpose; their form is also peculiar and very beautiful. These canoes run the rapids with more safety for their size, than those of any other shape. The chief and his ladies breakfasted with us, and then bid us good bye. [Figs. 120, 121; crIV-290, 291]

We camped at night below the "Dalle des Morts," or the Rapid of the Dead, so called from the following circumstance. About twenty-five or thirty years ago, an Iroquois, a half-breed, and a French Canadian, having charge of a boat, had to descend this frightful rapid. Fearful of running it, they affixed a long

---

[4] KJ mentions stopping for six hours to make paddles, the first time that the crews had had an opportunity to walk for three days.

[5] KJ: The chief "had a long range to hunt in—from Colville to Boat Encampment. I admired his dogs. . . . I saw that at all the lodges that they kept their dogs tied for fear that they will go hunting on their own account."

line to the bow, and being themselves on the shore, they attempted to lower her gradually by means of it down the foaming torrent. The boat took a sheer and ran outside of a rock, and all their efforts to get her back, or reach the rock themselves through the boiling surge were unavailing. The rope, chafing on the sharp edge of the rock, soon broke, and she dashed down among the whirling eddies, and broke to pieces, with their whole stock of provisions on board.

They then continued to follow on foot, along the rugged and difficult banks of the river, without food, guns, or ammunition; nor had they been able to save even a blanket, to protect them from the inclement weather. At night they encamped in a shivering and famishing condition, not having been able to surmount more than three miles of the obstacles that obstructed their passage at every step along the banks. The next day they proceeded with no better success. They well knew that if they constructed a raft it would not live an hour in this part of the Columbia River, owing to the quick succession of rapids that here beset the navigation. In this starving condition they continued their slow progress till the third day, when the half-breed, fearing his companions would kill him for their food, left them, and was never after heard of, falling, in all probability, a prey to the wolves. The other two lay down, and the Iroquois watching his opportunity, got up at night, and beat his companion's brains out with a stick, and going to work in a methodical manner, after first satisfying his craving hunger with a portion of the body, cut the remainder in thin slices and dried them in the sun, after the manner in which buffalo meat is prepared. Here he remained three days drying his meat, which he made into a pack, and continued his journey with it down the river bank, until he came to the commencement of the Upper Lake, where he made a raft, on which he placed his dried meat, and covered it over with pine-bark, seating himself upon it, and paddling down the lake.

He had not proceeded very far, before he met a canoe, which had been sent from one of the forts below, on the Spokan River, in quest of them, owing to their long absence. The new comers immediately inquired what had become of his two companions; he replied, that they had deserted him, giving at the same time an account of the loss of the boat. They took him on board their canoe, and one of the men seeing the bark on the raft, and desirous of getting it to place under him in the canoe, the Iroquois shoved off the raft, with evident signs of confusion, on which the man, who noticed his embarrassment, paddled up to it, and lifting the bark, discovered the dried meat beneath it,

among which was a human foot. He was asked how he had obtained the dried meat, and replied, that he had killed a wolf, swimming across the river.

The foot with the meat was slyly deposited in a bag, belonging to one of the men, but not without the act being perceived by the murderer, who, while they were asleep during the night, threw the bag and its contents into the river. Appearing not to notice its loss, they went on to Fort Spokan, and delivered him up to Mr. M'Mullan, the person in charge, detailing the particulars. The Indian was shortly afterwards sent to a distant post in New Caledonia, both as a punishment, and also in order to get rid of him, as no voyageur will willingly associate with any one known to have eaten human flesh. I had previously travelled several hundreds of miles with the son of this very man, who always behaved well, although there certainly was something repulsive in his appearance, which would have made me dislike to have had him for a companion in a situation such as above described.

Oct. 5th.—It rained so hard throughout the day and night, and the river was swollen so much, that we despaired of hauling the boats up the rapids, and therefore remained until the following morning at our encampment.

Oct. 6th.—It was a lovely morning. Saw some carriboos, but could not approach them near enough for a shot. We had a magnificent view of the Rocky Mountains in the distance, in all their azure grandeur. The flood soon subsided sufficiently to allow our ascending the rapids, although it took us the whole day to haul the boats up—the distance is not more than three miles—but the boats were so strained and tossed about in the operation, that we were obliged to haul them ashore and grease their bottoms with the resin which exudes from the pine.

Whilst the men were engaged in these operations, I took advantage of the delay, and made a sketch, looking down the rapids. [CRIV-282] As I was sketching, our steersman, who was present at the time, told me a melancholy occurrence, which took place at this spot, and which I will give as nearly as possible in his own words. "About four years ago," said he, "I crossed the Rocky Mountains with a party of forty. When we got to Boat Encampment, we embarked in two boats; the one which I was steering had twenty-two on board, amongst whom was a gentleman sent into the interior for the purpose of botanical research. On his way to Saskatchawan, he had fallen in with a young lady, a half-breed, who was travelling to cross the mountains and go down the Columbia on a visit to some of her friends. They had not travelled far, before a mutual attachment induced them to become man and wife, at Edmonton, though few couples, I think, in the world would choose a trip across the mountains for a honeymoon excursion; but they bore all their hardships and labours cheerfully, perfectly happy in helping each other, and being kind to their companions.

"We had two or three other women with us, and I had my own daughter, about ten years old, whom I was taking home to my wife at Fort Vancouver. I had left her two or three years before, on the east side of the mountains, with some of her relations, as I was unable to bring her over at the time I had come with my wife. We had also a young man of the name of M'Gillveray, belonging to the Company, with a small dog; the remainder was principally voyageurs.

"When I came to the head of the rapids, I found that the other boat, which contained the principal guide, had passed on, and I thought, therefore, that the rapids were in a proper state for running them, that is, that the whirlpools were throwing out and not filling, which they do alternately. I therefore went on without stopping, and when in the midst of the rapids, where there was no possibility of staying the downward course of the boat, I discovered to my dismay that the whirlpools were filling. One moment more and the water curled over the sides of the boat, immediately filling her. I called out for all to sit still and hold on steadily to the seats, as the boat would not sink entirely owing to the nature of the cargo, and that I could guide them to shore in this state. We ran more than a mile in safety, when the boat ran close by a ledge of rocks. The botanist, who held his wife in his arms, seeing the boat approach so near the rock, made a sudden spring for the shore; but the boat filled with water, yielded to the double weight of himself and wife, and they sank clasped in each other's arms. The boat was suddenly turned completely bottom upwards; but I and another man succeeded in getting on the top of her, and were thus carried down safely. We thought we heard some noise inside the boat, and the man who was with me, being a good swimmer, dived under, and soon, to my unexpected joy, appeared with my little daughter, who almost miraculously had been preserved by being jammed in amongst the luggage, and supported by the small quantity of air which had been caught by the boat when she turned over. We soon got ashore: M'Gillveray and four others saved themselves by swimming, the remaining fourteen were drowned; we immediately commenced searching for the bodies, and soon recovered all of them, the unfortunate botanist and his wife still fast locked in each other's arms,—an embrace which we had not the hearts to unclasp, but buried them as we found them, in one grave. We afterwards found M'Gillveray's little dog thrown up dead on a sandbank, with his master's cap held firmly between his teeth."

Oct. 7th.—We embarked in the morning, and continued our journey through a continual drizzle of rain, which was anything but pleasant.

Oct. 8th.—The weather cleared up, and we saw carriboos in great numbers; but, as usual, they were too wary for us to get a shot at them. Passed the rapids of St. Martin before night.

Oct. 9th.—Travelled but a short distance to-day, having to cut our way through the numerous fallen trees which, projecting into the stream, obstructed the course close to the shore, which we were obliged to take owing to the violence of the current in mid-channel.

Oct. 10th.—In the forenoon we perceived tracks of human feet in the sand on the shore, which astonished us very much, as no Indians come near these parts; and on approaching Boat Encampment, which we did about 2 P.M., we perceived smoke rising, which made us hope that the brigade from the east with the express had arrived, but were much disappointed at finding that it was only my old friend Capote Blanc, the Sho-shawp chief from Jasper's House, and two Indians who had come over to hunt. Here we made a suitable encampment, and hauled up our boats high and dry on the sand. Capote Blanc had been very successful in his hunt, and had a large stock of dried moose meat and beavers' tails, with which he supplied us abundantly, receiving a few small articles and ammunition in exchange.

We now had nothing to do but to try and pass the time pleasantly as we could under the circumstances, until the arrival of the brigade from the east side of the mountains. [Pl. XXIX; Figs. 117, 118; crIV-275 to 279] The men spent the day principally in gambling, and performing charms which they supposed would hasten the arrival of the brigade, such as erecting crosses, with one of the arms pointing to the direction from which it was expected. They also prepared what they call a "lobstick." [6] For this purpose a high tree is chosen which has thick branches at the top, and all the lower limbs are carefully trimmed off; a smooth surface is then cut on one side of the tree, on which the person in whose honour it has been trimmed is invited to cut his name; this being done, three rounds of blank-charges are fired, and three cheers given, and the spot

---

[6] KJ for October 12 reads: "The men cut a lobstick of 111 feet and I am requested to put my name on it as it was intended for me. Our little party then turned out and fired 3 rounds, and gave 3 cheers in honour of their Bushway as I was called." "Bushway" is a version of *bourgeois*, and evidently a term applied to a leader of a party in the fur trade; see Richard Dillon, *Fool's Gold*, p. 45.

afterwards bears the name of his encampment. On this occasion I had the honour of carving my name upon the "lobstick." We had almost constant rain, accompanied by immense snow-flakes, which obscured our view of the mountains nearly the whole time of our remaining here. I, however, managed to pick out some few bright hours for sketching.

We found very little game about here; the men only succeeded in trapping a few martens, and we began to be very uneasy, fearing that some disaster must have befallen the brigade which was to meet us.[7] I endeavoured to prevail on some of the men to accompany me across the mountains; but they would not go with me, so that I was forced to stay with the rest. Boat Encampment derives its name from its being the head of the navigable water. Three rivers here unite, forming the commencement of the north branch of the Columbia, so that the enlargement of the river is very sudden.

Oct. 28th.—About three o'clock in the afternoon a clerk in the company's service arrived,[8] and announced that he had come in advance of the eastern brigade, which would arrive next day under the command of Mr. Low: this was indeed joyful news to us, as we were all heartily tired of our gloomy situation.

Oct. 29th.—Mr. Low and party arrived this morning with between fifty and sixty horses loaded with provision, and the furs destined for Russia. They had been nine days crossing from Jasper's House. Mr. Low seemed doubtful about our being able to recross with the horses; but I cared little whether we had horses or not, so that I got away, for I was completely wearied with my long inaction. My provisions, too, were getting short, and the person in charge did not offer to replenish my stock, so that I had no choice but to cross as quickly as possible.

Oct. 30th.—This day Mr. Low left for Fort Vancouver with the boats [9] which had brought me up, leaving me with four Indians [10] who had accompanied him from the east side for the purpose of taking the horses back, and of guiding me over the mountains.

Oct. 31st.—It was a beautiful morning, and we started about ten o'clock, after loading fifteen horses out of the fifty-six which Mr. Low had brought with him, and got the first day as far as the Grande Batture, where we encamped.

Nov. 1st.—We passed through the Pointe des Bois, a distance of ten miles, by about the worst road I had ever travelled, it being cut up by so many horses having passed it a short time previously. My horse stuck in a mud hole until he sank up to his head, and it was with the greatest difficulty that one of the men and myself extricated him alive. What with the horses sticking

in the mud, the packs falling off, the shouting to the animals in Cree, and swearing at them in French, there being no oaths in the Indian languages, I never passed such a busy, tiresome, noisy, and disagreeable day in my life. This was in a great measure owing to having so few men to look after so large a number of horses, which would not keep the road, but ran helter skelter through the thick woods. At last we arrived at the bottom of the Grande Côte, and there encamped for the night, thoroughly wearied out and disgusted with horse-driving.

Nov. 2nd.—We started an hour before daybreak to ascend the stupendous Grande Côte, and soon found the snow becoming deeper at every step. One of our horses fell down a declivity of twenty-five to thirty feet with a heavy load on his back, and, strange to say, neither deranged his load nor hurt himself. We soon had him on the track again as well as ever, except that he certainly looked a little *bothered*. The snow now reached up to the horses' sides as we slowly toiled along, and reached the summit just as the sun sank below the horizon; but we could not stop here, as there was no food for the horses, we were therefore obliged to push on past the Committee's Punch Bowl,[11] a lake I have before described.

It was intensely cold, as might be supposed, in this elevated region. Although the sun shone during the day with intense brilliancy, my long beard became one solid mass of ice. It was long after dark before we arrived at the Campment de Fusei, having met with no other place which afforded any food for the horses,[12] and even here they had to dig the snow away with their hoofs to enable them to get at it.

A distressing occurrence took place here some years previously. Whilst a party were ascending this mountain, a lady, who was crossing to meet her husband, was in the rear, and it was not noticed until the party had encamped that she was not come up. Men were instantly sent back to seek her. After some

---

[7] There are many indications of frustration in the KJ entries. Those for October 24–26 read:

"24th: Prew, Sanslay and Le Frambeys agree to start with me to-morrow across the mountains on foot.

"25th: The men have declined to start for want of moccasins.

"26th: Cold ice made two inches in the night. The men have tried every expedient to bring the brigade such as making a cross and directing its arms in the way they are expected. Another sign, if the moon passes close to such and such a star, the brigade will be here tomorrow and according to the distance so they gauge the time they will arrive."

[8] KJ identifies the new arrivals as Mr. Mackenzie and a guide.

[9] KJ reads that they left with four boats.

[10] KJ calls the men who were left with Kane half-breeds and not Indians.

[11] KJ adds ironically: "Rather cold punch at present."

[12] KJ says the snow was too deep higher up for the horses to get food.

hours' search, they found her tracks in the snow, which they followed until they came to a perpendicular rock overhanging a roaring torrent; here all traces of her were lost, and her body was never found, notwithstanding every exertion was made to find it. Little doubt, however, could exist but that she had lost her way, and had fallen over the precipice into the torrent, which would have quickly hurried her into chasms where the foot of man could not reach.

Nov. 3rd.—Last night was the coldest (according to my feelings) that I had ever experienced; [13] but not having a thermometer with me, I do not know what was the intensity. I am, however, confident that it was colder on that night than it was on a subsequent night, when the spirit thermometer indicated 56° below zero, a temperature at which mercury would have become frozen and useless. I endeavoured to thaw myself by melting some snow over the fire; but the water froze upon my hair and beard, although I stood as close as I well could to a blazing fire, and I actually had to scorch my face before I could thaw the ice out. We now passed through the Grande Batture, and, much to our relief, found the snow decreasing in depth as we descended. We succeeded in reaching the Campment de Regnalle in the evening, and camped there for the night.

Nov. 4th.—We got our breakfast and started long before day.[14] We made good progress until about noon, when we came to a wild tract of country which appeared to have been visited years before by some terrible hurricane, which had uprooted the whole forest for miles round, not leaving a tree standing; a younger growth of trees were now pushing their heads up through the fallen timber of the ancient forest. We all got so hungry with our violent exercise in such a cold clear atmosphere, that we could not resist the temptation of stopping and cooking something to eat, before we entered the tangled maze before us. This was the first time we had done so, as daylight was too valuable to be wasted in sitting down, and the danger of being caught in one of the tremendous snow storms, which are so frequent in these regions, was too imminent for us not to push on to the utmost of our power. The snow often lies here to the depth of twenty or thirty feet, and one storm might have caused us the loss of the horses and baggage at least, even if we had been able to save ourselves by making snow shoes. It was, therefore, no slight temptation which could induce the men who knew the country to stop for dinner; but hunger is a good persuader, and carried the question. After dinner we pushed on with renewed strength; but it was with great difficulty that we were enabled to get the horses through the fallen and tangled

woods, and it was not until after nightfall that we reached the "Grand Traverse," where we found three men, who had been sent out to meet us and assist in driving in our sixty horses, which were as yet all safe.

Nov. 5th.—In the morning we found the Athabasca River in a flooded state, and a heavy snow storm had set in; we, however, proceeded to ford the rapid stream, although the snow was driving with such fury in our faces that we could not distinguish the opposite bank. The water almost covered the backs of the horses, and my pack, containing sketches and curiosities, &c., had to be carried on the shoulders of the men riding across, to keep them out of the water. After fording the river we crossed La Rouge's Prair[i]e, and encamped on the very spot that I had slept at exactly a year previously, to the very day.

Nov. 6th.—The wind blew intensely cold, and we had to pass along the margin of a frozen lake, seven or eight miles long, over which the snow drifted furiously in our faces. It became so cold that we could no longer sit on the horses, but were obliged to dismount and drive them on before us. My beard, the growth of nearly two years, gave me great trouble, as it became heavy with ice from the freezing of my breath; even my nostrils became stopped up, and I was forced to breathe through my mouth.

Fortunately I fell in with an Indian lodge,[15] and had an opportunity of thawing myself, so that I rode the remainder of the way to Jasper's House with comparative comfort. There we soon forgot our trouble over a good piece of mountain sheep, which is really delicious, even when not seasoned by such hardships as we had undergone.

This place is completely surrounded by lofty mountains, some of them close to the house, others many miles distant, and is subject to violent tornadoes, which sweep through the mountain gorges with terrific fury. A great number of mountain sheep had been driven down into the valleys by the intensity of the cold, which had set in this winter with unusual severity. I have counted as many as five large flocks of these animals grazing in different directions from the house at one time, and the Indians brought them in every day, so that we fared most sumptuously. These sheep are those most commonly called the "big horn." [crIV-257, 263]

---

[13] KJ reads that this was the coldest night in which Kane had ever camped out rather than the coldest he had ever experienced.

[14] KJ reads: "It is strange I have not taken a meal in daylight since leaving Boat Encampment. We have to travel both late and early for fear of being set fast by the snow as it sometimes falls to a depth of 25 feet."

[15] KJ points out that the lodge belonged to one of the men in Kane's party.

I made a sketch of a ram's head of an enormous size; [16] his horns were similar in shape to those of our domestic ram, but measured forty-two inches in length. [Fig. 113; crIV-256] They are considerably larger than our domestic sheep; their coat somewhat resembles in texture and colour the red deer, but a little darker. We were now obliged to set our men to work to make snow-shoes, as our further journey had to be made over deep snow. The birch wood of which they are made does not grow near Jasper's House, and the men had to go twenty miles off to get it. At last, by the 14th, our snow shoes and a sledge were completed, and with much difficulty I obtained two wretched dogs from the Indians, and one Mr. Colin Frazer lent me, to drag the sledge with my packs, provisions, and blankets. I had two men, one an Indian, the other a half-breed. They had come with Mr. Low from Edmonton, with seven others, and ought to have waited for me; but we had been so long coming, and the weather had got so cold, that the seven got afraid of waiting any longer, and departed without me. Had these two followed the example of their companions, I should have been obliged to spend a most dreary winter in the wretched accommodation which Jasper's House afforded.

Nov. 15th.—Early in the morning we equipped ourselves for the journey, putting on snow shoes between five and six feet long,—the pair I wore were exactly my own height, five feet eleven inches. Owing to our having so few dogs, we could not carry many provisions, but trusted to our guns to provide more on the way.

About fifteen or sixteen miles from Jasper's House, we came to an Indian lodge, which we found tenanted by a woman and her five children, her husband being out on a hunt. She was so civil and kind, and the lodge was so comfortable, that we were induced to stop, particularly as it was our first day on snow shoes, and stopping there saved us the trouble of making a camp for ourselves. The hunter returned late in the evening, having killed four sheep, one of which he brought home on his back. This we all set to work to cook, the squaw boiling as much as her kettle would hold, and the men sticking the rest upon sticks and roasting it. The whole party then set resolutely to work, and ate the whole sheep, and it was not a small one either. The hunter told us that he had seen thirty-four sheep that day, and that he never remembered a winter in which so many sheep had come down from the mountains. He proved a most agreeable host,

and entertained me with stories of his hunting exploits during the whole evening. My kind hostess prepared me a bed of sheep skins for the night, the most comfortable bed I had slept in for many months.

Nov. 16th.—At an early hour before daylight we got our breakfast and harnessed our dogs, and made our way through some very thick woods. We entered on Jasper's Lake, twelve miles long, the wind blowing a perfect hurricane, as it always does here when it blows at all. Fortunately the wind always comes from the mountains: had it been otherwise, we should not have been able to pass along the lake on the glare ice against such a storm of wind and sleet; as it was, we were blown along by the wind, and could only stop ourselves by lying down; our sledge sometimes flying in front of the dogs, while we were enveloped in a cloud of snow that prevented our seeing more than a few yards before us.

When we were about half way over the lake, we perceived two Indians, who were making their way across in a course intersecting our own route, and evidently had hard work to keep in the right direction. On coming up to them, we all sat down and had a smoke. The Indians, when they come to ice or hard frozen snow, where the snow shoe has to be taken off, always take off their moccasins also, and travel barefooted; by this means they preserve their moccasins, and when they sit down they put them on dry and wrap their feet in their furs. This walking barefooted on ice in such intense cold would seem dangerous to the inexperienced, but, in fact, the feet of those who are accustomed to it suffer less in this way than they do from the ice which always forms on the inside of the moccasin in long and quick travelling, as the ice thus formed cracks into small pieces and cuts the feet. After we had crossed the lake, we proceeded about five miles down the river, and encamped.

Nov. 17th.—The night had been intensely cold, but all felt well and in high spirits when we started in the morning. These feelings were, however, soon damped by the painful difficulties which we soon encountered. Where the river is rapid, the ice becomes rough, craggy, and unsafe, and is raised in hillocks to a considerable height, by the masses being forced by the current on the top of each other. Some of those hillocks we met were so formidable, that we at first doubted the possibility of surmounting them; even in the hollows we were obliged to move slowly, feeling our way with long sticks, to ascertain if the ice was solid. This was rendered necessary by the frequent occurrence of flat fields of ice, which, being formed high above the usual level of the water, and having nothing to support them underneath,

---

[16] The sketch is evidently crIV-256; it is now in the Stark Collection. κj notes that he intended the sketch for Sir George Simpson. The Simpson collection has been dispersed and no trace of a painting based on this sketch has been found.

easily give way, and the traveller falls either into the torrent far below, or upon another layer of ice. These dangerous places are formed by the large masses of ice getting jammed together against the rocks, or in some bend of the river, and damming the water up, on the top of which a thin coating is formed. As soon as the weight of water becomes too heavy for the dam, it is carried away, and the water sinks, leaving the coat formed on the top without support from beneath, which, when covered with snow, it is impossible to distinguish from good ice, except by feeling it with a stick.

We had not proceeded very far, before one of the men fell through one of these places; luckily he did not come to water, and we soon got him out. Our dogs were now almost useless, as they were unable to drag the sledge over the uneven surface, and we were obliged to push the sledge after them with our poles, and often to lift the dogs, sledge, and baggage up and down the perpendicular ice ridges (or *bourdigneaux*, as the voyageurs call them) with which our path was constantly intersected. At this place it was impossible to leave the river, as the ground on both sides was so broken, and the forest was so dense and tangled, that we should have starved long before we could have made our way through it. About an hour before sundown I unfortunately broke through, and it was with the utmost difficulty that I saved myself from being carried under by the current, which here ran with the velocity of a mill race: happily, I neither lost my pole nor my presence of mind, so the men had time to come up and help me out; but the moment I was out of the water my clothes became perfectly stiff, and we were obliged to make a fire and encamp for the night.

Nov. 18th.—Our trials seemed now to be increasing at every step, but the struggle was not optional now; so cheering ourselves with the idea that none know what they can bear until they are tried, we prepared for an early start. Our first trouble was that the dog Mr. Frazer lent me (the best dog we had) was gone; he had gnawed the cord asunder with which he was tied, and bolted off home.[17] This was a serious loss, as besides his use in drawing the sledge, we did not know but that we might want to eat him, our provisions were getting so scarce, and we met with very few rabbits, the only thing to be found on the route at this season.

Our next difficulty was to pass the Grand Rapid, where we found the river obstructed for nearly four miles by bourdigneaux, from ten to fourteen feet high. Over this continuous mass

[17] KJ emphasizes Kane's concern at the loss of the dog: it resulted in his trunk having to be left behind to be sent on later.

of icy pinnacles we scrambled with incredible labour, our limbs bruised with repeated falls, and our feet wounded and cut by treading on the sharp edges of fractured ice. At last, overpowered by fatigue and pain, we made our camp for the night, almost disheartened with our slow progress, as we had not made more than ten or twelve miles through the whole day.

During the night we were awoke by a tremendous roaring amongst the masses of ice, caused by a rising in the river. I could not help feeling apprehensive lest we should be crushed amongst it, from our camp being so near; but the men were too tired to move, and I was too tired to argue with them; so we slept on.

Nov. 19th.—When we got up in the morning, we found that the water had overflowed the ice, and we were compelled to make a circuit through the woods. We found the brush and fallen timber so thick, that we had to cut a road through it to enable our two dogs and the sledge to get along. It took us three hours to make an advance of one mile, before we again got back to the bourdigneaux, glad even to get to them, in preference to the tangled and almost impassable growth of trees and underwood which follows the course of the river through its whole length. This day I suffered a great deal; my feet were so severely cut by the frozen strings of my snow-shoes, that I left a track of blood behind me on the snow at every step. At night, when we encamped, it became so cold that we could only sleep for a few minutes at a time: no matter how large we made the fire, it would only keep that part warm which was immediately next to it, so that we were obliged to keep turning round and round to save ourselves from freezing.

Nov. 20th.—This morning I found I had what the voyageurs call *mal de racquet*. This complaint attacks those who are unaccustomed to the use of snow-shoes, if they walk far on them at first. It is felt at the instep. I do not know how to convey an idea of the intense pain, except by saying that it feels as if the bones were broken, and the rough edges were grinding against each other at every motion.

Nov. 21st.—In the morning we found that the river had become dammed up a short distance below our encampment, and was throwing the ice up in mountainous heaps with tremendous noise. This forced us again to make a short détour through the woods, which we effected with a great deal of trouble. By the time we got to the river again it snowed very hard, and continued without intermission all day; notwithstanding all this, and the mal de racquet, from which I suffered very severely, we pushed on, and, impelled by dire necessity, for our supply of food was fast diminishing, we made rather a good day's journey. We had, up to this, always given our dogs food every day, but my guide advised us not to do so any more, as he had known dogs travel twenty days without food, and every ounce we now had was too precious to give to them, even if they died; so the poor brutes were tied up supperless, and we tried to content ourselves with about half of what was our usual allowance.

Nov. 22nd.—The snow still continued, and was getting very deep and light, adding considerably to the labour of our journey; but we toiled on manfully, and succeeded in getting across Baptiste River before we stopped for the night, which did not seem to me as cold as usual, I suppose on account of the falling snow and stillness of the atmosphere.

Nov. 23rd.—The snow had ceased falling, but lay very deep and feathery on the ground, so that it fell over on to the snow-shoes, adding to their weight. This to me became very distressing, after two or three hours' walking, owing to the state of my ankles; but the weather was clear and fine, and the bright sun, while it lasted, seemed to cheer us on, so that at night, when we stopped, we calculated that we had made at least thirty-five miles. Not having met with any rabbits, we were obliged to stint ourselves in food, and starve our dogs.

Nov. 24th.—To-day we again came to open water, and had to make another détour through the woods of about a mile and a half, but it was not such a bad place as we had encountered before, the woods being a little more open. When we came to the river again, we found ourselves on the top of a high bank, down which we lowered our sledge and baggage, and then pitched the poor dogs after. As for ourselves, we scrambled at the commencement of the descent, then rolled a little by way of variety, and fell the rest of the way; however, the snow was so deep, that we did not get hurt, and after some trouble in unburying ourselves at the bottom, we continued our route along the river.

Nov. 2[5]th.—We had not travelled more than twenty miles, when we came to a part of the river in which the current was so rapid, that the ice was all tumbling about in broken masses. On each side we were encompassed by high banks rising into hills, which it was impossible for us to ascend; and as it is a rule, in travelling in the interior, never to go back, we had nothing for it but to encamp under the shelter of the hill, in hopes that the intense cold of the night would sufficiently unite the masses of ice to enable us to cross in the morning.

After our camp was made, the men, seeing me suffer so much from the mal de racquet, recommended me to scarify my in-

steps, and kindly offered to perform the operation, which is done with a sharp gun-flint; but I was afraid of the frost getting into the wounds, and refused, although I had every confidence in their knowledge of what would be the best remedy in a case like mine. We had not succeeded in shooting a single animal on our route, and it was with melancholy forebodings we looked at our diminished stock of provisions. Our poor dogs looked so savage and starved, that we had to tie their heads close up to the trees, fearing lest they might gnaw the strings, and make off.

Nov. 26th.—In the morning we found the ice sufficiently strong to induce us to proceed, but we had to use great caution, as it was still very weak. Our long snow shoes covering such a large surface, supported us safely; but the ice was so thin, that the dogs and sledge went through, and we should have lost everything we had, had not the Indian held a string fastened to the sledge, and by this means hauled them up. When we surmounted this difficulty, we found the ice better than usual, and were enabled to make in all forty miles before we encamped.

Nov. 27th.—We got on to-day very well till about noon, when the mal de racquet became so painful to me, that I thought I would try to walk without my snow-shoes. But I had not waded through the snow very far before I fell through the ice. Luckily, I got out easily enough, but I was wet through; and as our provisions were nearly all gone, and we were all hungry, I pushed on in my wet clothes, trusting to the violent exercise to keep me warm. I certainly did not suffer from cold, but the freezing of my leathern trowsers chafed my legs and made me very uncomfortable. We encamped after a very hard day's work, and as we were in great hopes of reaching Fort Assiniboine next day, we finished the last of our provisions.

Nov. 28th.—We started early in the morning, about three o'clock: this was an hour earlier than we usually got away, but we had nothing to cook and no breakfast to eat. I began to feel that my hardships were telling seriously on me. The mal de racquet tortured me at every step; the soles of my feet were terribly cut and wounded from the ice, which formed inside of my stockings as much as an eighth of an inch thick every day, occasioned by the freezing of the perspiration. It breaks in small pieces, and is like so much sharp gravel in the shoes; and I was weak from the want of food: but the hope of reaching a place of safety kept me up, and I toiled on over the bourdigneaux, which were very numerous to-day, steadily but slowly. At last, overcome with fatigue and weakness we had to encamp still far from the fort. We had a long consultation over our camp fire, as to whether we should eat the dogs or not, but their thinness saved

Edmonton House

Paul Kane
1846

Plate XXV. Fort Edmonton. Stark pwc22; crIV-188.

Plate XXVI. Winter Travelling (a wedding party leaving Fort Edmonton). ROM 912.1.48; CR IV-201.

them—the two would not have furnished us with a sufficient meal; besides, they could draw the sledge still, and that was a great consideration to us in our weak state; and we knew that if we met with no accident, we must reach the fort next day; still, if the dogs had been young, and in anything like condition, they would most assuredly have gone into the pot.

Nov. 29th.—We again started very early in the morning, hunger waking us up earlier than usual. It is the general rule of travelling in these northern regions, to start as soon as awake, and to continue until fagged out. Daylight is of such short duration (not more than four or five hours) at this time of the year, that it is taken little into account, the light of the snow and the Aurora enabling the traveller to see at all hours. Our way was not very bad, in comparison with what we had come over; still we had to move on slowly from weakness, and it was not until four o'clock P.M., that we arrived at Fort Assiniboine, having travelled 350 miles in fifteen days.

No sooner had we arrived, than all hands set to work cooking; luckily for us, this post is plentifully supplied with white fish—indeed, it is almost the only thing they ever have to eat here—which are caught in immense numbers in a small lake near the fort, called M'Leod's Lake.[18] I never saw such large ones as those caught here. They average six and seven pounds; and one of them which I saw weighed had actually attained to the enormous weight of eighteen pounds.

Whether it was the hunger from which I was suffering, or the real goodness of the fish, I know not now; but certainly they seemed to be the most delicious I had ever tasted, and the memory of that feast hung over me, even in my dreams, for many a day afterwards. One of the women devoted herself to the rather arduous task of satisfying my appetite, whilst my two men cooked on their own account, thinking that nobody else would do it quick enough; and no cook who cared for his reputation would have dished-up fish in the raw state in which they devoured the first two or three. I, however, controlled myself, and gave the woman a little time to prepare mine. Having wrapped my feet up in clean pieces of blanket (the only stockings worn in the interior) and put on a pair of clean dry moccasins, I bethought me of the poor dogs, and taking down some raw fish, went out to feed them. It was almost miraculous to see the big lumps of fish which they gulped down, without even an attempt at mastication. Their appearance after the repast was singularly ridiculous, as their bellies were paunched

[18] KJ adds: "Made a hearty meal on white fish which Mrs. Brazeau got ready for us."

out like full bladders, whilst the rest of their bodies retained still all the scraggy symptoms of prolonged hunger.

On returning from my charitable errand, I found that the good woman had lost no time, and soon, seated on a pile of buffalo skins before a good fire, I commenced the most luxurious repast of which it had ever been my fate to partake. I had no brandy, spirits, nor wine, neither had I tea, or coffee—nothing but water to drink. I had no Harvey's sauce, or catsup, or butter, or bread, or potatoes, or any other vegetable. I had nothing but fish; no variety, save that some were broiled on the hot coals and some were boiled. But I had been suffering for days from intense cold, and I now had rest; I had been starving, and I now had food; I had been weary and in pain, without rest or relief, and I now had both rest and ease. But, to sum up all, I had come through a long and serious peril, where for days I had been haunted with the idea that I must camp alone in that solitary forest, and let the men go on, with no food to support me but what I might obtain by the chance snaring of rabbits. It was, in fact, the dread of this almost hopeless alternative, that urged me to exertions upon which I cannot look back except with wonder, and thus brought me at last to the safety and comfort in which I now luxuriated. How many fish the men ate, I do not know; but having satiated themselves, they all lay down to sleep. In the middle of the night they woke me up, to ask me if I would not join them in another feast, but I did not; much to their astonishment, as the woman had told them that she was afraid I was sick, as I only ate four fish out of the seven she had prepared for me. However, in the morning, about five o'clock, I commenced again, and made another hearty meal; and then how happy I was when I lay down and slept again, instead of clambering over the rugged bourdigneaux!

Chapter XXII.

An easy Time.—Clever Rabbit-snare.—Fort Edmonton.—Buffalo Ice-pits.—The Horse and its Keeper.—A tame Battue.—Saving the Credit of the Herd.—Harnessing the Dogs.—My Big Head.—Sober Mirth.—Christmas-day in the Wilds.—Our Fare.—The Feast and the Dance.—"One that looks at the Stars."—Fighting to the Death. —The better part of Valour.—Making a Calf.—An affectionate Bull. —The Aurora Borealis.

Nov. 30th and Dec. 1st.—I remained at Fort Assiniboine to allow my feet to recover, which they did rapidly, as I did little but sleep before the fire and eat fish. On the evening of the 1st we all felt so well, that we prepared to proceed next morning to Edmonton, which we calculated to reach easily in four days.

Dec. 2nd.—We started early in the morning on snow-shoes,[1] taking with us very little provisions, as we were assured that we should find plenty of rabbits on the road. Our route lay through the woods, which were very thick and encumbered with fallen trees: this rendered our progress slow and very fatiguing; but our renewed strength, and the certainty of a good supper when we stopped kept up our spirits and enabled us to make a very good day's journey.[2] When we encamped for the night, we set to work cooking the rabbits which we had killed on the way, of which we had more than enough. The whole evening they were running across our path. This year they were much more numerous than had been remembered for a long time previously, and the woods were filled with traps set by the Indians, from which we might have helped ourselves if we pleased; but this would not have been considered right as long as we had our guns to shoot them. These snares are fastened to the top of young saplings in such a manner as to spring up when the rabbit is caught, and so suspend him in the air; if this was not done, the wolves and the lynxes, who always follow the rabbits in great numbers, and whose tracks we perceived all round us, would eat them as fast as they were caught.

The lynx is caught by a slip noose made of sinew, simply fastened to a small movable log, which the ensnared animal can drag with difficulty after him. Strange to say, they never attempt to gnaw the string which holds them, although, from the shape of their teeth, they evidently could do so with the greatest ease.

Dec. 3rd, 4th, and 5th.—Our route was mostly through woods, but the weather was pleasant, and we had abundance of rabbits, so that the journey seemed like a mere pleasure trip in comparison with what we had gone through.

On the evening of the 5th we arrived at Fort Edmonton, where I was most kindly received by Mr. Harriett,[3] and provided with a comfortable room to myself—a luxury I had not known for many months. This was to be my head-quarters for the winter; and certainly no place in the interior is at all equal to it, either in comfort or interest. All the Company's servants,[4] with their wives and children, numbering about 130, live within the palings of the fort in comfortable log-houses, supplied with abundance of fire-wood.

Along the banks of the river in the vicinity of the fort, about twenty feet below the upper surface, beds of hard coal are seen protruding, which is, however, not much used, except in the blacksmith's forge, for which purpose it seems to be admirably adapted. The want of proper grates or furnaces in those distant regions, where iron is at present so scarce, prevents its general use as fuel.

Provisions are in the greatest plenty, consisting of fresh buffalo meat, venison, salted geese, magnificent white fish, and rabbits in abundance, with plenty of good potatoes, turnips, and flour. The potatoes are very fine, and the turnips do well here. Of wheat, they can of course have only one crop; but with very indifferent farming they manage to get from twenty to twenty-five bushels per acre. The crop, however, is sometimes destroyed by early frost. The corn is ground in a windmill, which had been erected since my last visit, and seemed to make very good flour. Indian corn has been tried, but it did not succeed, owing to the very short summer.[5]

Outside, the buffaloes range in thousands close to the fort; deer are to be obtained at an easy distance; rabbits run about in all directions, and wolves and lynxes prowl after them all through the neighbouring woods. As for seeing aborigines, no place can be more advantageous. Seven of the most important and warlike tribes on the continent are in constant communication with the fort, which is situated in the country of the Crees and Assiniboines, and is visited at least twice in the year by the Blackfeet, Sur-cees, Gros-Vents, Pay-gans, and Blood Indians, who come to sell the dried buffalo meat and fat for making pemmi-kon, which is prepared in large quantities for the supply of the other posts.

The buffaloes were extremely numerous this winter, and several had been shot within a few hundred yards of the fort. The men had already commenced gathering their supply of fresh meat for the summer in the ice-pit. This is made by digging a square hole, capable of containing 700 or 800 buffalo carcases. As soon as the ice in the river is of sufficient thickness, it is cut into square blocks of a uniform size with saws; with these blocks the floor of the pit is regularly paved, and the blocks cemented together by pouring water in between them, and allowing it to freeze solid. In like manner, the walls are solidly built up to the surface of the ground. The head and feet of the buffalo, when

---

[1] KJ states that he left for Edmonton by horseback, not snowshoe.

[2] KJ notes that they found the road very thick despite the fact that sleds had passed a few days before.

[3] This is John Edward Harriott, appointed a chief factor of the Hudson's Bay Company in 1846.

[4] KJ puts the number of the Company's servants in the fort at 50.

[5] KJ adds: "It supplies to other forts about 1000 bags of pemmican."

killed, are cut off, and the carcase, without being skinned, is divided into quarters, and piled in layers in the pit as brought in, until it is filled up, when the whole is covered with a thick coating of straw, which is again protected from the sun and rain by a shed. In this manner the meat keeps perfectly good through the whole summer, and eats much better than fresh killed meat, being more tender and better flavoured.

Shortly after my arrival, Mr. Harriett, myself, and two or three gentlemen of the establishment, prepared for a buffalo hunt. We had our choice of splendid horses, as about a dozen are selected and kept in stables for the gentlemen's use from the wild band of 700 or 800, which roam about the fort, and forage for themselves through the winter, by scraping the snow away from the long grass with their hoofs. [Fig. 104; crIV-203] These horses have only one man to take care of them, who is called the horsekeeper; he follows them about and encamps near them with his family, turning the band should he perceive them going too far away. This would appear to be a most arduous task; but instinct soon teaches the animals that their only safety from their great enemies, the wolves, is by remaining near the habitations of man; and by keeping in one body they are enabled to fight the bands of wolves, which they often drive off after severe contests. Thus they do not stray far away, and they never leave the band. These horses are kept and bred there for the purpose of sending off the pemmi-kon and stores to other forts during the summer; in winter they are almost useless, on account of the depth of snow.

In the morning we breakfasted most heartily on white fish and buffalo tongues, accompanied by tea, milk, sugar, and *galettes*, which the voyageurs consider a great luxury. These are cakes made of simple flour and water, and baked by clearing away a place near the fire; the cake is then laid on the hot ground, and covered with hot ashes, where it is allowed to remain until sufficiently baked. They are very light and pleasant, and are much esteemed. We then mounted our chosen horses, and got upon the track the men had made on the river by hauling wood. This we followed for about six miles, when we espied a band of buffaloes on the bank; but a dog, who had sneaked after us, running after them, gave the alarm too soon, and they started off at full speed, much to our disappointment. We caught the dog, and tied his legs together, and left him lying in the road to await our return.

After going about three miles further, we came to a place where the snow was trodden down in every direction, and on ascending the bank, we found ourselves in the close vicinity of an enormous band of buffaloes, probably numbering nearly 10,000. An Indian hunter started off for the purpose of turning some of them towards us; but the snow was so deep, that the buffaloes were either unable or unwilling to run far, and at last came to a dead stand. We therefore secured our horses, and advanced towards them on foot to within forty or fifty yards, when we commenced firing, which we continued to do until we were tired of a sport so little exciting; for, strange to say, they never tried either to escape or to attack us.

Seeing a very large bull in the herd, I thought I would kill him, for the purpose of getting the skin of his enormous head, and preserving it. [crIV-204, 205, 206] He fell; but as he was surrounded by three others that I could not frighten away, I was obliged to shoot them all before I could venture near him, although they were all bulls, and they are not generally saved for meat. The sport proving rather tedious, from the unusual quietness of the buffaloes, we determined to return home, and send the men for the carcases, and remounted our horses. But, before we came to the river, we found an old bull standing right in our way, and Mr. Harriett, for the purpose of driving him off, fired at him and slightly wounded him, when he turned and made a furious charge. Mr. Harriett barely escaped by jumping his horse on one side. So close, indeed, was the charge, that the horse was slightly struck on the rump. The animal still pursued Mr. Harriett at full speed, and we all set after him, firing ball after ball into him, as we ranged up close to him, without any apparent effect than that of making him more furious, and turning his rage on ourselves. This enabled Mr. Harriett to reload, and plant a couple more balls in him, which evidently sickened him. We were now all close to him, and we all fired deliberately at him. At last, after receiving sixteen bullets in his body, he slowly fell, dying harder than I had ever seen an animal die before.

On our return, we told the men to get the dog-sledges ready to go in the morning to bring in the cows we had killed, numbering twenty-seven, with the head of the bull I wanted; whereupon the squaws and half-breed women, who have always this job to do, started off to catch the requisite number of dogs. About the fort there are always two or three hundred who forage for themselves like the horses, and lie outside. These dogs are quite as valuable there as horses, as it is with them that everything is drawn over the snow. Two of them will easily draw in a large cow; yet no care is taken of them, except that of beating them sufficiently before using them, to make them quiet for the time they are in harness.

It would be almost impossible to catch these animals, who are almost as wild as wolves, were it not for the precaution which is taken in the autumn of catching the dogs singly by stratagem, and tying light logs to them, which they can drag about. By this means the squaws soon catch as many as they want, and bring them into the fort, where they are fed—sometimes—before being harnessed. This operation is certainly (if it were not for the cruelty exhibited) one of the most amusing scenes I had witnessed. Early next morning I was roused by a yelling and screaming that made me rush from my room, thinking that we were all being murdered; and there I saw the women harnessing the dogs. Such a scene! The women were like so many furies with big sticks, threshing away at the poor animals, who rolled and yelled in agony and terror, until each team was yoked up and started off.

During the day the men returned, bringing the quartered cows ready to be put in the ice-pit, and my big head, which, before skinning, I had put in the scales, and found that it weighed exactly 202 lbs. The skin of the head I brought home with me.

The fort at this time of the year presented a most pleasing picture of cheerful activity: every one was busy; the men, some in hunting and bringing in the meat when the weather permitted, some in sawing boards in the saw-pit, and building the boats, about thirty feet long and six feet beam, which go as far as York Factory, and are found more convenient for carrying goods on the Saskatchawan and Red River than canoes. They are mostly built at Edmonton, because there are more boats required to take the peltries to York Factory than is required to bring goods back; and more than one-half of the boats built here never return. This system requires them to keep constantly building.

The women find ample employment in making mocassins and clothes for the men, putting up pemmi-kon in ninety-pound bags, and doing all the household drudgery, in which the men never assist them. The evenings are spent round their large fires in eternal gossiping and smoking. The sole musician of the establishment, a fiddler, is now in great requisition amongst the French part of the inmates, who give full vent to their national vivacity, whilst the more sedate Indian looks on with solemn enjoyment.

No liquor is allowed to the men or Indians; but the want of it did not in the least seem to impair their cheerfulness. True, the gentlemen of the fort had liquor brought out at their own expense; but the rules respecting its use were so strict and so well known, that none but those to whom it belonged either expected, or asked, to share it.

On Christmas-day the flag was hoisted, and all appeared in their best and gaudiest style, to do honour to the holiday. Towards noon every chimney gave evidence of being in full blast, whilst savoury steams of cooking pervaded the atmosphere in all directions. About two o'clock we sat down to dinner. Our party consisted of Mr. Harriett, the chief, and three clerks, Mr. Thebo,[6] the Roman Catholic missionary from Manitou Lake, about thirty miles off, Mr. Rundell, the Wesleyan missionary, who resided within the pickets, and myself, the wanderer, who, though returning from the shores of the Pacific, was still the latest importation from civilised life.

The dining-hall in which we assembled was the largest room in the fort, probably about fifty by twenty-five feet, well warmed by large fires, which are scarcely ever allowed to go out. The walls and ceilings are boarded, as plastering is not used, there being no limestone within reach; but these boards are painted in a style of the most startling barbaric gaudiness, and the ceiling filled with centre-pieces of fantastic gilt scrolls, making altogether a saloon which no white man would enter for the first time without a start, and which the Indians always looked upon with awe and wonder.

The room was intended as a reception room for the wild chiefs who visited the fort; and the artist who designed the decorations was no doubt directed to "astonish the natives." If such were his instructions, he deserves the highest praise for having faithfully complied with them, although, were he to attempt a repetition of the same style in one of the rooms of the Vatican, it might subject him to some severe criticisms from the fastidious. No table-cloth shed its snowy whiteness over the board; no silver candelabra or gaudy china interfered with its simple magnificence. The bright tin plates and dishes reflected jolly faces, and burnished gold can give no truer zest to a feast.

Perhaps it might be interesting to some dyspeptic idler, who painfully strolls through a city park, to coax an appetite to a sufficient intensity to enable him to pick an ortolan, if I were to describe to him the fare set before us, to appease appetites nourished by constant out-door exercise in an atmosphere ranging at 40° to 50° below zero. At the head, before Mr. Harriett, was a large dish of boiled buffalo hump; at the foot smoked a boiled buffalo calf. Start not, gentle reader, the calf is very

[6] The Rev. Jean-Baptiste Thibault (1810–1879), who became vicar-general of the diocese of St. Boniface in 1843. See *Dictionary of Canadian Biography*, vol. X.

small, and is taken from the cow by the Cæsarean operation long before it attains its full growth. This, boiled whole, is one of the most esteemed dishes amongst the epicures of the interior. My pleasing duty was to help a dish of mouffle, or dried moose nose; the gentleman on my left distributed, with graceful impartiality, the white fish, delicately browned in buffalo marrow. The worthy priest helped the buffalo tongue, whilst Mr. Rundell cut up the beavers' tails. Nor was the other gentleman left unemployed, as all his spare time was occupied in dissecting a roast wild goose. The centre of the table was graced with piles of potatoes, turnips, and bread conveniently placed, so that each could help himself without interrupting the labours of his companions. Such was our jolly Christmas dinner at Edmonton; and long will it remain in my memory, although no pies, or puddings, or blanc manges, shed their fragrance over the scene.

In the evening the hall was prepared for the dance to which Mr. Harriett had invited all the inmates of the fort, and was early filled by the gaily dressed guests. Indians, whose chief ornament consisted in the paint on their faces, voyageurs with bright sashes and neatly ornamented mocassins, half-breeds glittering in every ornament they could lay their hands on; whether civilised or savage, all were laughing, and jabbering in as many different languages as there were styles of dress. English, however, was little used, as none could speak it but those who sat at the dinner-table. The dancing was most picturesque, and almost all joined in it. Occasionally I, among the rest, led out a young Cree squaw, who sported enough beads round her neck to have made a pedlar's fortune, and having led her into the centre of the room, I danced round her with all the agility I was capable of exhibiting, to some highland-reel tune which the fiddler played with great vigour, whilst my partner with grave face kept jumping up and down, both feet off the ground at once, as only an Indian can dance. I believe, however, that we elicited a great deal of applause from Indian squaws and children, who sat squatting round the room on the floor. Another lady with whom I sported the light fantastic toe, whose poetic name was Cun-ne-wa-bum, or "One that looks at the Stars," was a half-breed Cree girl; and I was so much struck by her beauty, that I prevailed upon her to promise to sit for her likeness, which she afterwards did with great patience, holding her fan, which was made of the tip end of swan's wing with an ornamental handle of porcupine's quills, in a most coquettish manner. [Fig. 107; crIV-212, 213, 214]

After enjoying ourselves with such boisterous vigour for several hours, we all gladly retired to rest about twelve o'clock, the guests separating in great good humour, not only with themselves but with their entertainers.

A few days afterwards, when we had recovered from the effects of our Christmas festivities, I went out with François Lucie, the half-breed voyageur [Pl. XXVII; crIV-215, 216], of whom Sir George Simpson, in his "Journey round the World," tells the following story:—

"A band of Assiniboines had carried off twenty-four horses from Edmonton, and, being pursued, they were overtaken at the small river Boutbière. One of the keepers of the animals, a very courageous man, of the name of François Lucie, plunged into the stream, grappling in the midst with a tall savage, and, in spite of his inferiority of strength, he kept so close that his enemy could not draw his bow; still, however, the Indian continued to strike his assailant on the head with the weapon in question, and thereby knocked him off his horse into the water. Springing immediately to his feet, Lucie was about to smite the Assiniboine with his dagger, when the savage arrested his arm by seizing a whip, which was hanging to his wrist by a loop, and then turning round the handle, with a scornful laugh, he drew the string so tight as to render the poor man's hand nearly powerless. François continued nevertheless to saw away at the fellow's fingers with his dagger till he had nearly cut them off, and when at length the Assiniboine of necessity relaxed his grasp, François, with the quickness of thought, sheathed the weapon in his heart." François told me the story himself, much as related above, except, he said, that the savage did not die immediately, although he had ripped his breast so open that he could see his heart throbbing, and that he never let go the lasso of the stolen horses until it ceased, which was for some minutes, though he tried to pull it from his hand.

We had not left the fort more than five or six miles behind us, when we fell in with an enormous grisly bear, but François would not fire at him, nor allow me to do so, although I told him I had helped to kill one before. A younger man than he, who had his character to make, might have been foolish enough to have run the risk, for the sake of the standing it would have given him amongst his companions; but François had a character established, and would not risk attacking so formidable an animal with only two men. In fact, their enormous strength, agility, and wonderful tenacity of life, make them shunned even by large numbers, and few are killed, except by young men, for the sake of proudly wearing the claws—one of the most esteemed ornaments to an Indian chief—round their necks.

The bear walked on, looking at us now and then, but seeming

to treat us with contempt. My fingers were itching to let fly at him: it seemed so easy, and his skin was in such fine condition. But though my gun had two barrels, and François was by my side, with the almost certainty of putting three balls well in; yet we well knew that it was ten chances to one that three balls would [not] kill him quick enough to prevent a hand-to-hand encounter, a sort of amusement that neither were Quixotic enough to desire. After we had proceeded a few miles further, we fell in with a small band of buffaloes, and François initiated me into the mysteries of "making a calf."

This ruse is generally performed by two men, one covering himself with wolf skin, the other with buffalo skin. They then crawl on all fours within sight of the buffaloes, and as soon as they have engaged their attention, the pretended wolf jumps on the pretended calf, which bellows in imitation of a real one. The buffaloes seem to be easily deceived in this way. As the bellowing is generally perfect, the herd rush on to the protection of their supposed young with such impetuosity that they do not perceive the cheat until they are quite close enough to be shot; indeed, François' bellowing was so perfect, that we were nearly run down. As soon, however, as we jumped up, they turned and fled, leaving two of their number behind, who paid the penalty of their want of discernment with their lives.

We shortly afterwards fell in with a solitary bull and cow, and again "made a calf." The cow attempted to spring towards us, but the bull seeming to understand the trick, tried to stop her by running between us: the cow, however, dodged and got round him, and ran within ten or fifteen yards of us, with the bull close at her heels, when we both fired and brought her down. The bull instantly stopped short, and bending over her, tried to raise her up with his nose, evincing the most persevering affection for her in a rather ridiculous manner; nor could we get rid of him so as to cut up the cow, without shooting him also, although bull flesh is not desirable at this season of the year, when the female can be procured.

Having loaded our horses with the choice parts of the three cows we had killed, we proceeded home, François having taken particular care to secure the mesenteries or monyplies, as he called them, a part much esteemed in the interior, although I must confess I did not like it myself.

Another mode of hunting buffaloes, which we often practised with great success at Edmonton, was accompanied however with considerable fatigue: it consisted in crawling on our bellies and dragging ourselves along by our hands, being first fully certain that we were to the leeward of the herd, however light the wind, lest they should scent us until we came within a few yards of them, which they would almost invariably permit us to do. Should there be twenty hunters engaged in the sport, each man follows exactly in the track of his leader, keeping his head close to the heels of his predecessor: the buffaloes seem not to take the slightest notice of the moving line, which the Indians account for by saying that the buffalo supposes it to be a big snake winding through the snow or grass.

Tired as I was at night after my day's hunt, I was kept long from my bed, fascinated by the appearance of the heavens, which presented to the view one of the most splendid meteoric phenomena I had ever witnessed. Soon after dark a zone of light began to appear, increasing rapidly in brilliancy until about nine or ten o'clock, when it attained its greatest intensity. It was about four degrees in breadth, and extended from the east to the west across the zenith. In its centre, immediately overhead, appeared a blood-red ball of fire, of greater diameter than the full moon rising in a misty horizon; from the ball emanated rays of crimson light, merging into a brilliant yellow at the northern edges. The belt also on the northern side presented the same dazzling brightness; while the snow and every object surrounding us was tinted by the same hues. I continued lost in admiration of this splendid phenomenon until past one in the morning, when it still shone with undiminished, if not increased, brilliancy. Tired out at last, I was compelled to retire to bed, but those who still sat up told me that it faded away about three o'clock in the morning, without varying its position or form. The Indians have a poetical superstition in regard to the Aurora Borealis, which is in this high latitude remarkably brilliant, shooting up coruscations of surprising splendour. These, they think, are "the spirits of the dead dancing before the Manitou, or Great Spirit."

Chapter XXIII.

A pleasant Wedding.—Sledges and Carioles.—Useful but Dangerous Dogs.—The Hunter's Bravado.—Journey through the Snow.—An unwilling Chase.—A Tumble in a Drift.—Indian Etiquette.—The Spotted Leg.—The Indian in Heaven.—Battle of the Dogs.—Arrival at Fort Pitt.—The Medicine Pipe-stem and its Carrier.—Ceremony of opening Pipe-stems.—Exhibition of Medicine Dresses.—Digging up the Hatchet.—Crying for War.—Invoking the Great Spirit.—Preparing for the March.—Eating a Warrior's Heart.

On the 6th of January 1848, we had a wedding at Edmonton; the bride was the daughter of the gentleman in charge, the bridegroom Mr. Rowand, junior, who resided at Fort Pitt, a distance of 200 miles from the establishment. [crIV-202?] After the ceremony, which was performed by the Rev. Mr. Rundell, the Methodist missionary, we spent a pleasant evening, feasting and dancing until midnight. Having received an invitation to accompany the happy pair on the journey home, I gladly accepted it, as I began to find my amusements rather monotonous. Next morning I was awoke by the yelping of the dogs and the ringing of the bells on the dog-collars, accompanied by the shouts of the men thrashing the brutes into something like discipline, as they harnessed them to the sledges and carioles. [Fig. 100; crIV-195] On coming out into the yard, I found our party nearly ready to start. It consisted of Mr. Rowand and his bride, with nine men.[1] We had three carioles and six sledges, with four dogs to each, forming when on route a long and picturesque cavalcade: all the dogs gaudily decorated with saddle-cloths of various colours, fringed and embroidered in the most fantastic manner, with innumerable small bells and feathers, producing altogether a pleasing and enlivening effect (sketch No. 14).

Our carioles were also handsomely decorated, the bride's more particularly, which had been made expressly for the occasion, and was elaborately painted and ornamented, and was drawn by a set of dogs recently imported from Lower Canada by Mr. Rowand. The cariole is intended for carrying one person only; it is a thin flat board, about eighteen inches wide, bent up in front, with a straight back behind to lean against; the sides are made of green buffalo hide, with the hair scraped completely off and dried, resembling thick parchment; this entirely covers the front part, so that a person slips into it as into a tin bath. [Pl. XXVI; Figs. 101 to 103; crIV-194, 196 to 201]

We started as the day dawned, the dogs running at a furious rate, as they invariably do at first starting, and require all the strength and agility of the men to keep the sledges and carioles from upsetting, which they manage to do as well as they can by holding on to a cord attached to each side from behind. Two men go before on the run in snow shoes to beat a track, which the dogs instinctively follow: these men are relieved every two hours, as it is very laborious. The dogs generally used are of a breed peculiar to the country, and partake largely of the character and disposition of the wolf, which they often so resemble in appearance as sometimes to have been shot in mistake. Their ferocity is so great that they are often dangerous. Some of them

this winter attacked a horse belonging to Mr. Harriett, harnessed to a sledge. Mr. Harriett had tied him to a stake and left him; on his return, in about half an hour, he found the dogs tearing him to pieces; nor would the dogs leave their prey until he had shot five of them: the horse died almost immediately.

Mr. Rundell was himself attacked one evening, while walking a short distance from the fort, by a band of these brutes belonging to the establishment; they got him down, and, but for his cries bringing the assistance of a squaw, they would have served him in a similar manner.

Immediately on leaving the fort, we got on the ice of the Saskatchawan River, and travelled down it all day, having, in the true voyageur style, trusted to our prowess as hunters for a supply of food on our journey, although of 200 miles; and, having literally brought nothing with us but the kettles,[2] we were unable to break our fast until we had killed a fat cow, which was soon demolished by ourselves and the dogs. This apparent absence of foresight is, in reality, often affected by the voyageurs out of bravado, for they are quite as much disinclined to hunger and abstinence as other people. In our case we might certainly have brought plenty of food if we liked, but, on the other hand, buffaloes were plentiful, and there was almost a certainty of obtaining them.[3]

Jan. 9th.—Left our encampment three hours before day, and about daylight we killed two buffaloes and stopped to breakfast. The wind blew very cold and strong all day, with continued snow. After breakfast we left the circuitous windings of the river, and the friendly shelter of its banks and woods, to cut across the bleak and open plains, where we were exposed to the full fury of the chill blast; but this shortened our journey by many miles. In the evening we killed two more buffaloes, and encamped in a clump of pines, the last sheltered spot we might expect on our journey.

Jan. 10th.—Our spirit thermometer stood this morning at 47° below zero, Fahr.[4] Finding it impossible to keep myself warm in my cariole, in spite of plenty of skins and blankets, I put on a pair of snow shoes and walked all day. The snow was three feet deep on an average, and was drifted by the wind with such

[1] KJ says that the party which left on January 8 was accompanied for the first day by Mr. Prudence, the bride's uncle, and François Lucie on sleds. The number of dogs with the party is given as 46.

[2] KJ adds: "Not even a pinch of salt. This family think it quite unvoyageurlike to travel with anything like comfort." There was plenty of food to be had for the hunting since they saw six large herds of buffalo on the first day.

[3] KJ: "We camped early as we had had no breakfast on leaving the fort."

[4] KJ notes that the reason it was so cold was because there were no woods to protect them.

violence in our faces as to nearly blind us; notwithstanding which our guides seemed to find no difficulty in pursuing their course—such is the instinctive faculty of these men in tracing their way over this trackless desert, where not a stick or a shrub is to be met with to guide them. Towards evening we arrived at a sort of enclosure, which had evidently been erected by the Blackfoot Indians as a protection from the Crees, whose country this is, but where the Blackfeet sometimes come to steal horses. In the evening we only got one cow, which seemed barely to satisfy our dogs.[5]

Jan. 11th.—Started as usual this morning three hours before daylight, the days being short: this early starting is necessary to allow the men to stop and make the encampment before dark. We met two of the Company's men on their way from Carlton to the place we had so recently left. We killed only one buffalo to-day, and were obliged to sleep on the snow, no pine branches being within reach to make our beds.[6] These we missed much, as they add much to the comfort of an encampment.

Jan. 12th.—We again got on the river. Having brought a small quantity of meat from our last night's supper with us, but not sufficient for all, some of our party went on in advance to hunt, whilst we stopped to take a scanty breakfast. About two hours afterwards we came up to them, sitting round a good fire cooking a fine fat cow, the delicate pieces of which they were demolishing with considerable rapidity, owing to the lateness of their meal.

During the day a diverting occurrence took place, although it might have turned out very serious. A herd of buffaloes had come down the bank on to the ice, and did not perceive our approach until the foremost sledge was so near them as to excite the dogs, who rushed furiously after them, notwithstanding all the efforts of the men to stop them. The spirit of the hunt was at once communicated through the whole line, and we were soon all, carioles and sledges, dashing along at a furious rate after the buffaloes. The frightened animals made a bold dash at last through a deep snow bank, and attempted to scramble up the steep bank of the river, the top of which the foremost one had nearly reached, when, slipping, he rolled over and knocked those behind, one on top of another, down into the deep snow-drift amongst the men and dogs, who were struggling in it. It would be impossible to describe the wild scene of uproar and confusion that followed. Some of our sledges were smashed, and one of the men was nearly killed; but at last we succeeded in getting clear and repairing damages. We continued on our wedding tour.

Jan. 13th.—Started at half-past 1 A.M. We followed a buffalo track along the river, in the deep ruts of which our carioles were frequently upset, rolling us into the snow. Having killed three buffaloes on the banks of the river, we stopped to breakfast; two calves, evidently belonging to the slaughtered animals, remained within a hundred yards of our fire the whole time.[7]

Leaving the river, we passed over a succession of hills and valleys until dark, when we arrived at a camp of Cree Indians, consisting of about forty lodges. We went to the lodge of the chief named "Broken Arm," who received us very kindly, spreading buffalo robes in the best part of his tent for us to sit on, and placing before us the best his stock afforded. After supper, the chief having cut some tobacco and filled a handsome stone pipe, took a few whiffs from it himself, and then presented it to me. On my doing the same, and offering it to him again, as is the custom, he told me that he wished me to accept it as a gift.

The lodge was soon filled with Indians, anxious to learn the news, which they are always eager to hear from strangers. Amongst our visitors was the son-in-law of the chief; and, according to the Indian custom, he took his seat with his back towards his father and mother-in-law, never addressing them but through the medium of a third party, and they preserving the same etiquette towards him. This rule is not broken through until the son-in-law proves himself worthy of personally speaking to him, by having killed an enemy with white hairs; they then become entitled to wear a dress trimmed with human hair, taken from the scalps of their foes. I remarked that one of the leggings of the young man was spotted with some red earth, and the other not: on inquiring the reason, I was told that the spotted leg had been wounded, and the red earth was intended to indicate blood.

We sat up very late, talking to the chief, who seemed to enjoy our society very much. Amongst other topics of discourse, he began talking about the efforts of the missionaries amongst his people, and seemed to think that they would not be very successful; for though he did not interfere with the religious belief of any of his tribe, yet many thought as he did; and his idea was, that as Mr. Rundell had told him that what he preached was the only true road to heaven, and Mr. Hunter told him the same thing, and so did Mr. Thebo, and as they all three said that the other two were wrong, and as he did not know which was right, he thought they ought to call a council amongst

---

[5] KJ states that they killed three buffalo all day without leaving their straight course.
[6] KJ notes that they slept on dry willows.
[7] KJ says that the dogs were tied at the time.

Plate XXVII. François Lucie, a Cree half-breed guide, Fort Edmonton. Stark POP9; CRIV-215.

Plate XXVIII. Assiniboin chiefs, Rocky Mountain House. *Left:* Mah-Min or "The Feather," head chief. *Right:* Wah-he-joe-tass-e-neen or "The half-white Man," second chief. Stark pwc1; crIV-221.

themselves, and that then he would go with them all three; but that until they agreed he would wait. He then told us that there was a tradition in his tribe of one of them having become a Christian, and was very good, and did all that he ought; and that when he died he was taken up to the white man's heaven, where everything was very good and very beautiful, and all were happy amongst their friends and relatives who had gone before them, and where they had everything that the white man loves and longs for; but the Indian could not share their joy and pleasure, for all was strange to him, and he met none of the spirits of his ancestors, and there was none to welcome him, no hunting nor fishing, nor any of those joys in which he used to delight, and his spirit grew sad. Then the Great Manitou called him, and asked him, "Why art thou sad in this beautiful heaven which I have made for your joy and happiness?" and the Indian told him that he sighed for the company of the spirits of his relations, and that he felt lone and sorrowful. So the Great Manitou told him that he could not send him to the Indian heaven, as he had, whilst on earth, chosen this one, but that as he had been a very good man, he would send him back to earth again, and give him another chance.

Jan. 14th.—We travelled to-day through a hilly country until we arrived at another encampment of about thirty lodges. Our dogs rushed down amongst the lodges, dragging the sledges and carioles after them, and were immediately attacked by all the dogs in the Indian camp, barking, howling, and fighting, until all the sledges were upset, and some of them broken to pieces. It was half an hour before we could separate the enraged brutes.[8]

These Indians had a buffalo pound within a short distance of their encampment, which was literally crammed with the dead frozen carcases they had slaughtered in it. On nearing Fort Pitt we fell in with two buffaloes, immediately in our track, and as we did not want the meat, they might have been allowed to escape, but for the large development of the bump of destructiveness in our men's heads.

We reached the fort soon after dark, having been seven days on our route from Edmonton. We had killed seventeen buffaloes in this journey, for feeding ourselves and dogs. The animals had, we were told, never appeared in such vast numbers, nor shown themselves so near the Company's establishments; some have even been shot within the gates of the fort. They killed with their horns twenty or thirty horses in their attempt to drive them off from the patches of grass which the horses had pawed the snow from with their hoofs for the purpose of getting at the grass, and severely gored many others, which eventually recovered.

These remarks convey but a faint idea of the astonishing numbers of these animals: within the whole distance we had travelled on this journey we were never out of sight of large herds of them, and we had not found it necessary to go a step out of our direct course to find more than we required for our use. They were probably migrating northwards, to escape from the human migrations which are so rapidly filling up the southern and western regions, which were formerly their pasture grounds.

I spent a very pleasant and interesting month at Fort Pitt,[9] surrounded by Cree Indians, this being one of their principal places of resort, and had ample opportunity of studying their habits and manners. [Pl. XXII; crIV-139 to 142] I took an elaborate sketch of a pipe-stem carrier with his medicine pipe-stem. The pipe-stem carrier is elected every four years by the band of the whole tribe to which he belongs, and is not allowed to retain the distinction beyond that period, all being eligible for the situation who have sufficient means to pay for it. But the expense is considerable, as the new officer elect has to pay his predecessor for the emblems of his dignity, which frequently are valued at from fifteen to twenty horses. Should he not possess sufficient means, his friends usually make up the deficiency, otherwise the office would in many cases be declined. It is, however, compulsory upon the person elected to serve if he can pay. The official insignia of the pipe-stem carrier are numerous, consisting of a highly ornamental skin tent, in which he is always expected to reside; a bear's skin upon which the pipe-stem is to be exposed to view when any circumstance requires it to be taken out from its manifold coverings in which it is usually wrapped up, such as a council of war, or a medicine pipe-stem dance, or on a quarrel taking place in the tribe, to settle which the medicine-man opens it for the adverse parties to smoke out of,—their superstitions leading them to fear a refusal of the reconciling ceremony, lest some calamity should be inflicted on them by the Great Spirit for their presumption;—a medicine rattle, which is employed in their medicine dances, and a wooden bowl, from which the dignitary always takes his food,—this he always carries about his person, sometimes in his hand, and often on his head;—besides numerous small articles.

It requires two horses to carry them when on the move. The pipe-stem itself is usually carried by the favourite wife of the

---

[8] KJ estimates that there were in all about 200 dogs.
[9] KJ states that Kane remained at Fort Pitt for 20 days.

official, and should it under any circumstances fall on the ground, it is regarded as a bad omen, and many ceremonies must be gone through to reinstate it. A young man, a half-breed, assured me that he had once a pipe-stem committed to his charge by an official who had gone out on a hunting excursion, and that being well aware of the sanctity attributed to it by the Crees, he was determined to try himself the effect of throwing it down and kicking it about, and that shortly after this act of desecration, as it would be considered, the pipe-stem carrier was killed by the Blackfeet. From that time he became a firm believer in the sanctity of the pipe-stem, and, as may be supposed, told me this story as a great secret.

A pipe-stem carrier always sits on the right side of his lodge as you enter, and it is considered a great mark of disrespect to him if you pass between him and the fire, which always occupies the centre of the lodge. He must not condescend to cut his own meat, but it is always cut for him by one of his wives, of whom he usually has five or six, and placed in his medicine bowl, which, as before said, he has always with him. One of the greatest inconveniences attached to the office, particularly to an Indian, who has always innumerable parasitical insects infesting his person, is, that the pipe-stem carrier dares not scratch his own head without compromising his dignity, without the intervention of a stick, which he always carries for that purpose. The pipe-stem, enclosed in its wrappers, always hangs in a large bag, when they can procure it, of party-coloured woollen cloth, on the outside of the lodge, and is never taken inside either by night or by day, nor allowed to be uncovered when any woman is present.

About a fortnight after my arrival, Kee-a-kee-ka-sa-coo-way, "the Man who gives the War-whoop," whom I mentioned before as having met on the Saskatchawan on my journey out, arrived at Fort Pitt with his sub-chief, Muck-e-too, "Powder." [crIV-133?]

Kee-a-kee-ka-sa-coo-way is the head chief of all the Crees, and was now travelling through all their camps to induce them to take up the tomahawk and follow him on a war excursion in the following spring. He had eleven medicine pipe-stems with him, ten of which belonged to inferior chiefs, who had already consented to join in the expedition. Being curious to witness the opening of these pipe-stems and see the ceremonial accompanying it, I travelled with him to the camp, situated a few miles from Fort Pitt. On our arrival, the wrappers of the stems were removed and carried in procession, headed by the chief in person, through the camp. The procession, halted in front of nearly

every lodge, where he delivered a continuous harangue, the burden of which was to rouse them to take up arms and revenge the death of the warriors who had been killed in former wars. During the whole of this address the tears continued to stream down his face as if at his entire command. This the Indians call crying for war.

The weather was most intensely cold, notwithstanding which, and his being half naked, so strongly was every feeling concentrated on the subject, that he appeared altogether insensible to its severity, although the thermometer must have indicated at least thirty to forty degrees below zero. On the day following, I endeavoured to prevail on him to open the pipe-stems, in order that I might sketch some of them; this he at first declined, until he had been told that I was a great medicine-man, and that my sketching them would very much increase their efficiency when opened on the field of battle. He thereupon opened them with the following ceremonies. He first took a coal from the fire, and sprinkled upon it the dried leaves of a plant collected on the Rocky Mountains, the smoke of which filled the place with a fragrant odour resembling that of the incense burned in Catholic churches; while this was burning, he filled the bowls of these pipes with tobacco and some other weed, after which he took off all his clothes, with the exception of the breechcloth.

On my looking rather suspiciously at the clothes he had taken off, seeing they were rather old and filthy, he took notice of my doing so, and remarked, that although he possessed better, he was not allowed by the customs of his tribe to wear them, as he was then mourning the death of four of his relations who had been killed by the Blackfeet the year before. (He, however, put on his good clothes for me afterwards, when I took sketch No. 15, as I told him that the picture would be shown to the queen.) [Figs. 85, 86; crIV-130, 131, 132] He then threw over his shoulders the skin of a wolf highly ornamented after the Indian fashion, and immediately removed the wrappers of leather, &c., that covered one of the stems, and inserting it into one of the bowls he had previously filled with tobacco, commenced a song which I could not understand.

On finishing, he lighted the pipe, and inhaled a mouthful of smoke; then turning his face upwards and pointing in the same direction with the stem, he blew upwards a long stream of smoke, and called on the Great Spirit to give them success in war, to enable them to take many scalps, and set their enemies asleep whilst they carried off their horses; that their own wives might continue virtuous and never grow old. He then turned the stem to the earth, after blowing out another puff of smoke, and called upon the earth to produce abundance of buffalo and roots for the coming season. He then pointed the stem towards me, and requested that, if I possessed any influence with the Great Spirit, I would intercede with him for the supply of all their wants. A half-breed woman happening to look into the lodge at this moment, the ceremony was instantly suspended, and she as instantly shrunk back; a woman never being allowed to be present when the medicine pipe-stem is exposed to view.

After some little prolonged ceremony, consisting principally of all present smoking from each stem as it was opened, he permitted me to sketch them, but never left the lodge until I had finished and he had carefully recovered and removed them. He told me he had been on this war mission to nearly every camp in his tribe, and intended to visit the whole of them; the distance he would have to travel in snow shoes to accomplish this would not be less than six or seven hundred miles. It is the custom of the Indians after such a call to assemble at a place appointed on the Saskatchawan River, where they continue feasting and dancing three days previously to their starting for the enemy's country. Here all their pipe-stems and medicine dresses are exhibited, and they decorate themselves with all the finery they can command, in which they continue their advance until they reach the enemy. But no sooner are they in view, than their ornaments and their whole clothing are hastily thrown aside, and they fight naked. [Figs. 87, 88; crIV-134 to 138]

A year before my arrival amongst them, a war party of 700 left for the Blackfeet country, which nation the Crees regard as their natural enemies, and are never at peace with them. After travelling for some fifteen or twenty days, a sickness broke out among them, affecting numbers and carrying off a few. This was considered by some of their great men a judgment upon them from the Great Spirit for some previous misconduct, and they, therefore, returned home without having accomplished anything. On another occasion a similar party fell in with a great warrior among the Blackfeet, named "Big Horn," and six of his tribe, who were out on the legitimate calling of horse stealing, —for the greater the horse thief the greater the warrior. This small band, seeing their inferiority to their enemies, attempted flight; but finding escape impossible, they instantly dug holes sufficiently deep to intrench themselves, from which they kept up a constant fire with guns and arrows, and for nearly twelve hours held at bay this large war party, bringing down every man who ventured within shot, until their ammunition and arrows were entirely exhausted, when they of course fell an easy prey to their enemies, thirty of whom had fallen before their

fire. This so enraged the Crees that they cut them in pieces, and mangled the dead bodies in a most brutal manner, and carried their scalps back as trophies.

It is said that Big Horn frequently sprang out from his intrenchment, and tried to irritate his foes by recounting the numbers of them he had destroyed, and boasting his many war exploits, and the Cree scalps that then hung in his lodge. So exasperated were they against him, that they tore out his heart from his quivering body, and savagely devoured it amongst them.

I returned to Edmonton by the same route, and in the same manner I had come from it,[10] and as nothing material occurred in the route, I omit the details.

Chapter XXIV.

I remained at Edmonton until the 12th of April, when, having heard that a large band of Blackfeet were shortly expected to visit Rocky Mountain House, situated about 180 miles southwest of Edmonton, on the Saskatchawan, for the purpose of trading, and being anxious to see them, I started with a small party of six men and about twenty horses, ten of which were loaded with goods. The snow had not left the ground, and our horses were in very bad condition, from living out all the winter, except the one which I rode, which had been kept in, and was the most vicious brute I ever met. When I dismounted from him the first evening, he tried to get away from me, and when he found that I held on to the lasso, he attacked me with open mouth, and had not one of the men knocked him down with a stick, he might have seriously injured me. Our progress was, therefore, necessarily slow, as I would not ride away from the party.

We found buffaloes in places where the Indians said they had never been seen before, and remained two days at a place called

---

[10] KJ notes that on this occasion he was at Fort Edmonton for six days.

Battle River, to rest our horses, as we had plenty of food for ourselves and grass for the horses. I went out with an Indian and killed a cow, which was followed by her calf. Wishing to take the calf alive, so that it might carry itself to the camp, I pursued and caught it, and, tying my sash round its neck, endeavoured to drag it along; but it plunged and tried so violently to escape that I was about to kill it, when the Indian took hold of its head, and turning up its muzzle, spat two or three times into it, when, much to my astonishment, the animal became perfectly docile, and followed us quietly to the camp, where it was immediately cooked for supper.

Finding three of the rivers in our route much flooded, we were obliged to make rafts to cross upon, so as to keep the goods dry. At the fourth river we were fortunate to find a raft formed by nature, in the shape of a large mass of floating ice, which one of the men swimming out dragged ashore. It was sufficiently buoyant to support two or three men, and by attaching our lassoes to it, and drawing it backwards and forwards, we soon got all our goods over dry. The horses we made swim.

Some of the men suffered severely from what is called "snow blind," which is a species of inflammation, brought on by the strong glare of the sun reflected from the snow. The pain in the eyeballs is excessive, and resembles the feeling produced by having sand in the eyes; the sufferers are sometimes blinded by it for weeks. This can be prevented by wearing a veil, which I did, and is generally adopted when they can be procured.

We arrived at Rocky Mountain Fort on the 21st of April. This fort is beautifully situated on the banks of the Saskatchawan, in a small prairie, backed by the Rocky Mountains in the distance. In the vicinity was a camp of Assiniboine lodges, formed entirely of pine branches. [Fig. 108; crIV-217, 218, 220?] It [Rocky Mountain House] was built for the purpose of keeping a supply of goods to trade with the Blackfoot Indians, who come there every winter, and is abandoned and left empty every summer. It is built like most of the other forts, of wood, but with more than ordinary regard to strength, which is thought necessary on account of the vicious disposition of the Blackfoot tribe, who are, without exception, the most warlike on the northern continent. I may state that beds of coal are seen protruding here along the banks of the river, similar to that of Edmonton.

[Cree: crIV-227]

There is also a small band of Assiniboines in the neighbourhood of the fort. The Blackfeet attacked them last year, and carried off two girls captives. One of them, after having been carried away a long distance, was stripped naked, and told to find her way back as best she could, and as she was never heard of afterwards, it was supposed that she perished from cold and hunger; the other girl was taken charge of by a chief, who sent her relations word that she should be returned safe, which promise he fulfilled.

We found a man at the establishment, called Jemmy Jock, a Cree half-breed, who had temporary charge of it; he had obtained much Blackfoot celebrity. He was sent out when a clerk of Hudson's Bay Company, by them, to the Blackfoot Indians, in order to learn their language, for the purpose of facilitating the trade with them. He then married a daughter of one of their chiefs, and taking a fancy to their mode of life, he left the Company's service, and stayed with them. He afterwards became one of their chiefs, and being a man of singular acuteness, soon acquired great influence. The missionaries entertained very little respect for him, and have spoken very badly of him throughout the whole country; but as far as my intercourse with him went, I always found him trustworthy and hospitable. I learned much from him relative to the customs of the Blackfoot tribe, of which, owing to his long residence amongst them, thirty or forty years, he possessed a greater knowledge probably than any other man with the same education.

Shortly after my arrival a report was brought in that the Blackfoot Indians had killed a party of Crees, and that amongst the slain was a pipe-stem carrier, whom they had skinned and stuffed with grass; the figure was then placed in a trail which the Crees were accustomed to pass in their hunting excursions. The Assiniboines, who reside in the vicinity of this fort, I found the most kind and honourable of any tribe that I met with. They constitute a very small part (say forty or fifty families) of a very large tribe who live in a more easterly direction. Mah-Min, "The Feather," their head chief, permitted me to take his likeness, and after I had finished it, and it was shown to the others, who all recognised and admired it, he said to me, "You are a greater chief than I am, and I present you with this collar of grizzly bear's claws, which I have worn for twenty-three summers, and which I hope you will wear as a token of my friendship." This collar I have, of course, brought home with me. [Pl. XXVIII; Fig. 109; crIV-221 to 224]

The second chief, Wah-he-joe-tass-e-neen, "The half-white Man," seeing that I was so successful with his head chief's likeness, and probably feeling a little jealous, came and requested me to take his also, which I willingly did, as he had one of the most extraordinary countenances I had met with for some time. [Pl. XXVIII; crIV-221, 225, 226] He was a man, however, noted as a great hunter, and as an evidence of his tremendous powers of endurance, it was related to me that one morning he had started on snow shoes in pursuit of two moose, and pursued them until they separated. He then followed one track until he killed his prey, cut it up, and put it on scaffolding to secure it from the wolves. He then returned to where the tracks separated, and followed the other; this he also killed, and placed, as he had done the former, returning to his lodge late in the evening. In the morning he sent off three men with dog sledges to bring in the game, and they were three days following his tracks before they got home.

Mah-Min gave one of the missionaries who was up here last summer a very long and serious lecture upon lying. It seems the missionary, who did not smoke himself, had brought with him a carat of tobacco for the purpose of purchasing horses and food from the Indians, should he require them. Immediately on his arrival, the Indians, who had exhausted their stock, eagerly inquired if he had any tobacco, but he was afraid that if he acknowledged he had any they would want it all, and leave him without anything to barter with them, and denied that he had any. Shortly afterwards, when he was about to return, he went to Mah-Min, and told him that he wanted horses and some provisions to return, and that he would pay him for them in tobacco, when Mah-Min said to him, "You preach to the Indians many things, and tell them not to steal or lie; how can they believe or listen to you? You are the father of lies. You said you had no tobacco, and now you say you have plenty."

We had nothing to eat at Rocky Mountain House but rabbits, and even of those we could not get as much as we wanted; this was in consequence of the *cache*, in which the dried meat was placed, having been robbed by the Assiniboines, who, if they could not be honest against the temptations of hunger, at least tried to be as much so as they could, for they placed furs of considerable value in the place of the meat they had stolen. This was the second year they had played the same game; but however satisfactory the arrangement might be to the Hudson's Bay Company, it certainly was anything but pleasant either to their servants or myself; so that after being half starved for ten days, and seeing no signs of the Blackfoot Indians coming in, I persuaded Jemmy Jock to come back with me to Edmonton. This he agreed to do, and he said he had a *cache* of dried meat on the road which would supply us with plenty, so that all we had to do was to ride fast until we came to it.

Early in the morning, we started, taking four extra horses

with us as relays. This is done by one man riding in front, then the loose horses, and the other man follows and drives them on; the horses seldom stray or give trouble in this way, and, as they carry no weight, are comparatively fresh when the horse you ride has broken down. We rode the whole day at a tremendous pace, stimulated by hunger, and arrived at the *cache* towards dusk. Having tied our horses, Jemmy went to the *cache*, which was made of logs built together, something like a loghouse, but not very closely fitted together, and began throwing off the heavy logs which covered the top and concealed it. [cr-IV-219] He heard a regular rumpus within, so he called to me to fetch the guns; when I got up, he removed part of the top, and a fine fat wolverine jumped out, which I immediately shot down. The brute must have been starved and desperately thin to have squeezed himself through the openings between the logs, and no doubt impelled by hunger, and the smell of the meat inside, had not thought much of a slight squeeze. However, when he was once in, and had had a good meal, he could not get out again, and the idea of starving himself as long as the meat lasted, did not seem to have occurred to him. This was a great disappointment to us, as there was very little left, and that mangled, torn, and tossed about in the dirt by the animal. We, however, contrived to make a supper, and saved some for the future; but it was so little, that instead of taking our time on the road as we had intended, we had nothing for it but to ride as fast as we could.

The next day was most uncomfortable, as we had a heavy snow storm blowing in our faces the whole day; but we pushed on gallantly, and finished our provisions between supper and breakfast next morning, and on the afternoon of the third day we got into Edmonton, but only with two horses, the others having been fagged out and left behind.

May 22nd.—Mr. Low arrived from the east side of the Rocky Mountains, in company with Mr. de Merse,[1] the Roman Catholic Bishop of Vancouver, and Mr. Paul Frazer. The boats and their cargoes had been long prepared, and we only waited for a favourable break in the weather to commence our journey home.

May 25th.—The weather having cleared up, we embarked with the before-mentioned gentlemen for Norway House. We had twenty-three boats, and 130 men, with Mr. Harriett as our chief. We saw great numbers of dead buffaloes along the shore of the river, which, from the long continuance of the snow

[1] Modeste Demers (1809–1871), appointed first bishop of Victoria in 1847. See *Dictionary of Canadian Biography*, vol. X.

covering the herbage, had become so exhausted, that they were drowned in attempting to swim across the river, in their accustomed migration to the south every spring, and now lay in thousands along the banks.[2] At night we drifted down with the current, the men tying several boats together, so as to be under the guidance of one man, whilst the rest lay down and slept.

May 26th.—We saw several large herds of buffaloes swimming across the river, all going south.[3]

May 27th.—What with the strong current, the men pulling all day, and our drifting all night, we again arrived at Fort Pitt, where we got an addition to our party of two more boats. These boats are all loaded with the furs and pimmi-kon of the Saskatchawan district. The furs are taken down to York Factory, in the Hudson's Bay, where they are shipped to Europe; the pimmi-kon is intended for those posts where provisions are difficult to be procured. We remained at Fort Pitt for two days whilst the other boats were getting ready, and I took advantage of the delay to sketch a Cree chief. He was dressed in full costume, with a pipe-stem in his hand. [See pp. 143–45, above]

May 29th.—We left Fort Pitt, quite filling the river with our fleet of boats, presenting a most imposing and animated appearance, considering that we were navigating inland waters so far from the boundaries of civilisation. We saw great numbers of wolves busily employed in devouring the carcases of the drowned buffaloes, and had some amusing hunts with our boats after them, our men greatly enjoying the sport.[4] We continued our course in great humour and comfort, without meeting with anything which I considered particularly worthy of recording at the time, until

June 1st, when we saw a large party of mounted Indians, riding furiously towards us. On their nearer approach they proved to be a large war party, consisting of Blackfoot Indians, Blood Indians, Sur-cees, Gros Ventres, and Pay-gans.[5] We had a Cree Indian in one of our boats, whom we had to stow away under the skins which covered the goods, lest he should be discovered by the party, who were expressly bound on an expedition against his tribe, and whom our disproportionate number could not have opposed had they sought to take him from us. We instantly put ashore to meet them, and Mr. Harriett and myself met them on the banks of the river, leaving strict orders

with the men to keep the boats afloat sufficiently near the shore for us to re-embark promptly in case of danger. They received Mr. Harriett, however, in a most friendly manner, he being personally known to numbers of them. They immediately spread a buffalo skin for us to sit down upon, depositing all their arms, consisting of knives, guns, and bows and arrows, on the ground in front of us, in token of amity.

There was, however, one exception to this pacific demonstration, in the case of an Indian I had frequently heard spoken of before, named Omoxesisixany, "Big Snake." [crIV-146, 147] This chief walked round the party, cracking and flourishing a whip, and singing a war song, evidently desirous of getting up a fight, and refusing to lay down his arms with the rest, although frequently requested to do so. At length, however, he put them down, and sat with the rest, and taking (though with evident reluctance) a few puffs from the pipe which was going the round of the party, in token of peace, he turned to Mr. Harriett and said, that as he had smoked with the white man, he would present him with his horse, at the same time leading up a beautiful brown animal which I had seen him alight from on our arrival, he handed Mr. Harriett the lasso. Mr. Harriett declined his gift, explaining that it was impossible for him to take it with him in the boats.

They told us they were a party of 1500 warriors, from 1200 lodges, who were then "pitching on" towards Fort Edmonton; that is, they were making short journeys, and pitching their tents on towards Edmonton, leaving few behind capable of bearing arms. They were in pursuit of the Crees and Assiniboines, whom they threatened totally to annihilate, boasting that they themselves were as numerous as the grass on the plains. They were the best mounted, the best looking, the most warlike in appearance, and the best accoutred of any tribe I had ever seen on the continent during my route. As Mr. Harriett was very anxious to cultivate the acquaintance and friendship of such questionable characters, he accepted of their invitation to "camp" with them until the following morning, which was exceedingly acceptable to me, as it enabled me to make several sketches, and to hear something about them. After our smoke several of the young Braves engaged in a horse race, to which sport they are very partial, and at which they bet heavily; they generally ride on those occasions stark naked, without a saddle, and with only a lasso fastened to the lower jaw of the horse as represented in Sketch No. 16. [Fig. 89; crIV-143, 144, 145] I had some difficulty at first in getting the chiefs to let me take

[2] KJ notes: "Thousands died of starvation. I counted in sight at one time no less than 18."

[3] KJ adds: "As they do every spring and return in fall to the woods."

[4] KJ notes that they shot several wolves swimming across the river.

[5] KJ places the number in the party at 500.

their likenesses, but after they comprehended what I wanted, they made no objections.

Big Snake's brother was the first who sat to me [CRIV-153], and while I was sketching, he told me the following anecdote of his brother, of whom he seemed to be very proud. Mr. Harriett understood the language and acted as interpreter. Some time back, Big Snake had the free admission to one of the American forts near the Rocky Mountains. Coming up one day with two other Indians, to enter the gate, it was shut rudely in his face by the orders of the commander, who had only lately arrived in the country. This his pride led him to regard as a direct insult; he rode away, and falling in with some cattle that he knew belonged to the fort, he commenced firing on them, and killed thirteen. As soon as the sentinel, who had given the offence, heard the shots, he suspected the reason, and informed the superintendent, who immediately collected his men, and sallied out with them well armed, in the direction of the firing. Big Snake being on the watch, hid himself with his two companions behind a small hill.

The party from the fort apprehending there might be a large number of Indians hid, hesitated to advance within gun-shot; but a negro of the party offered to proceed and reconnoitre. Approaching the hill with great caution, and seeing no one, he began to think they had escaped; but, when within about twenty yards of the top, Big Snake sprang up from his lair and fired, bringing him down, and the next moment bore off his scalp, and waved it in derision towards the Americans.

A short time afterwards Big Snake met a large party of Blackfeet, "pitching" towards the fort on a trade. On his arrival amongst them, he stated what he had done, and dared any one to censure his conduct on peril of making him his enemy. Although the band well knew that what he had done amounted to an open declaration of war, and would of course cut off any communication or trade with the establishment, unless they actually gave up Big Snake as a prisoner, yet they suffered their disappointment in silence rather than incur the anger of one whom they so much feared. Another band of the same tribe, ignorant of the circumstance, arrived at the fort a few days afterwards. The Americans, thinking this a good opportunity of chastising the aggressors, loaded one of their cannons with musket-balls, and while the unsuspecting Indians were standing huddled together at the gate, waiting for admittance, applied the fusee. Fortunately it did not explode, and the Indians, seeing the unusual stir and the flash, became alarmed, and fled.

On a second application of the fusee, it discharged its murderous projectiles amongst the fugitives, and killed ten persons, principally women and children.

Some time after, Big Snake heard that one of the most influential Indians of the tribe had blamed him, in a speech, for involving the tribe in much inconvenience and destroying their trade. On hearing these remarks, he directly went in search of the censurer, armed with a scalping-knife, and, on coming up with him, attempted to stab him; his foot, however, slipped in the attempt, which saved the other's life, although he received a severe wound in the side. These two continued for some time after in a state of deadly hostility, until Big Snake was persuaded by many of his friends to make peace, to which he at length consented, and proceeded towards his lodge for that purpose. In the meantime he had told his wife, if she saw any disturbance, to move her lodge instantly to the top of a small hill, a few hundred yards distant, which might be more easily defended. On his arrival at the man's lodge, he found him seated with his wife and children around him, and, taking up one of the children, he began to caress it, and asked it to intercede with its father for the injury he had done him. The man, however, moodily held down his head without any reply, whilst Big Snake again asked the child to take pity on him still. The father remained silent. On which Big Snake, getting enraged at the rejection of the friendly overtures he had condescended to make to one whom he regarded so much as an inferior, and feeling himself humiliated by the refusal, rushed from the tent, seized his gun, which he had taken the precaution of placing within reach in case of emergency, and commenced firing through the skin covering of the tent, killing two of its inmates, and wounding a third; after which he returned to the hill, where his wife was pitching the tent, according to his orders, where he remained and defied the whole camp to molest him.

After I had finished this picture, and the others had examined it with great attention, a general impression seemed to prevail amongst them all that I must be a great medicine-man. And as we encouraged the idea, which afforded us no inconsiderable protection from any treachery on their part, I had no trouble in getting as many sitters as I could possibly manage. Amongst others, I sketched group No. 17 [Fig. 92; CRIV-154, 155, 156], consisting of Big Snake, the centre figure; Mis-ke-me-kin, "The Iron Collar," a Blood Indian chief, with his face painted red [CRIV-149]; to the extreme left of the picture, is a chief called "Little Horn," with a buffalo robe draped round him, and between him and Big Snake is Wah-nis-stow, "The White Buffalo," principal chief of the Sur-cee tribe. [Fig. 91; crIV-150, 151] In the background stand two chiefs of inferior quality, one of them has his face painted half black, being in half-mourning for some friend. [crIV-152?] As they were expecting to have a fight with the Crees next day, they got up a medicine dance in the afternoon, and I was solemnly invited to attend, that I might add my magical powers in increasing its efficacy. Amongst all the tribes here assembled, the sacredness of the medicine pipe-stem is held in very high estimation, and it was with much solemnity that I was placed in the best position, to work my incantations; that is to say, to make the sketch No. 18. [Plate XXIII; Figs. 93, 94, 95; crIV-157 to 164]

Next morning we embarked, after having presented the chiefs with eight or ten pounds of tobacco [6] to be distributed amongst the rest, and had not proceeded many miles, when we had to put ashore again [7] to gratify an old Blood Indian chief, who had arrived at the camp shortly after our departure, and had galloped immediately after us, for the purpose of having a talk with Mr. Harriett, whom he had known many years before, and for whom he entertained the warmest friendship. After the talk, he stripped himself naked, excepting his breech-cloth. Mr. Harriett, not to be behindhand with him, gave him everything but his shirt and pantaloons: it was rather a losing operation for him; although the chief's leather shirt and leggings were quite new and highly ornamented, yet they were not exactly what Mr. Harriett would like to wear, so he gave them to me to add to my stock of Indian costumes. One of the Indians who had accompanied the old chief, noticing I had a new capote on, thought he would try what could be done by an interchange of civilities with me. He accordingly took off a dirty old greasy shirt he had on, and laid it down before me; but as I had no other clothes with me but what I had on, I was forced to decline this most endearing mark of friendship, much to his disappointment, although the scamp could not help grinning as I shook my head in token of refusal.

June 3rd.—We were obliged to lie by the whole of this day, on account of the violence of the wind and snow, which rendered any attempt at proceeding very uncomfortable, and almost useless.

June 4th.—Early in the forenoon, we arrived at Carlton,

[6] KJ describes the gift as 25 or 30 pounds of tobacco.
[7] KJ states that they put ashore to meet another party of Indians that had been following them about 20 miles behind.

and Bishop De Merse immediately took horses to cross by land to Red River Settlement, a distance of sixteen days' journey.

Chapter XXV.

Fort Carlton.—Battle of the Indians.—Death of a Hero.—Cumberland House.—An Unwieldy Wife.—Shooting the Grand Rapids.—Norway House.—Child Suckled by a Man.—"Big Snake's" Fate.—Storm on the Winnipeg.—"The Constant Sky."—A Midnight Incantation.—Powers of the Medicine.—Fort Alexander.—The Grand Bonnet.—The Plague of Mosquitoes.—Stopped by a Fog.—Deserted Mission.—Two Days' Feast.—The Lake of the Woods.—Watermen indeed.—Fort Frances.—An Express Canoe.—Lake Superior.—Sault St. Marie.—Conclusion.

The Crees around this post all took to the woods on hearing of the large party of Blackfeet in their vicinity, and, as we heard, were collecting in large numbers in a camp, about fourteen miles off, for the purpose of opposing the invasion of the hostile tribes.

June 5th.—We remained at Carlton during the day, as Mr. Harriett was anxious to hear of the proceedings of the hostile tribes; indeed, he felt rather apprehensive of the treachery of the Blackfeet, and knew that the large numbers of our party would check them from attempting anything which might hereafter call for redress.

June 6th.—In the morning a fugitive arrived, bringing news of a battle between the hostile Indians. It appears that the Crees had a medicine dance, and had, according to their custom, erected an ornamental pole, around which they hang their medicine bags, &c., whilst dancing. After the conclusion of their dance, they returned to their camp, a distance of about three miles, which consisted of ninety lodges, leaving the medicine pole standing; shortly after, the invading war party we had met discovered the pole, and on one of their number climbing to the top, to tear off the ornaments, he from the height perceived the Cree camp in the distance, upon which the party prepared themselves for battle.

One of the Cree scouts had also perceived them, but had formed a very erroneous idea of their numbers, and had mentioned them only as a small party. Upon this the Crees immediately proceeded to the attack, thinking to overwhelm them by their superior numbers, and did not discover their error until

Encampment Foot of the Rocky Mountains

Plate XXIX. Boat Encampment, Columbia River. Stark wwc100; crIV-276.

Plate XXX. Kettle Falls, Fort Colvile. Stark wop19; crIV-298.

they were actually engaged. When they perceived that they were so much outnumbered, they retreated to their camp; all but one chief, Pe-ho-this, who, disdaining to fly, dashed madly into the midst of his enemies, dealing death around him with his poke-a-mau-gun or war club. On every side, bullet and arrow pierced his body; but he continued the unequal conflict, until his bridle arm was shattered by a ball, when his wounded and frightened horse, no longer under control, dashed with him from the tumult, and carried him still living to his lodge, but with only just sufficient strength to enable him to beg his tribe to take care of his wives and children for his sake, when he fell dead from his charger.

The whole camp now fled with their women and children, leaving their lodges standing; except two old and enfeebled chiefs, who, as is not unusual amongst Indians under such circumstances, remained in the best lodge, and having dressed themselves in their gayest clothes and ornaments, painted their faces, lit their pipes, and sat singing their war songs, until the Blackfeet came up and soon despatched them.

The Crees had nineteen killed and forty wounded, besides losing their lodges and a good deal of property, which they could not carry with them. The Sur-cees lost Wah-nis-stow, before mentioned, and having taken six scalps, thought they had done enough, and returned from the battle to have a dance with the scalps. The Blood Indians, after losing three of their party, also retired after taking a few scalps, leaving the Blackfeet, who had lost six, to bear the brunt of the battle; the Pay-gans and Gros Ventres not having arrived until the fight was over, of course suffered no loss.

Immediately after hearing this, Mr. Harriett ordered us to embark, as he knew that the Blackfeet and their allies would immediately return to their own country after meeting with any success, and having a few scalps to take home, according to the invariable custom of the Indians. We embarked early in the forenoon, and glided quickly down the rapid stream, aided by our oars. We now were out of the buffalo country altogether, and had no fresh meat but some little that we had brought with us for the use of the gentlemen of the party; the men, however, were plentifully supplied with pemmi-kon.

June 10th.—We arrived at Cumberland House, which we left next morning, having received an addition to our party of three more boats and their crews.[1]

June 12th.—We arrived at the Paw, where my old friend Mr. Hunter gave me a most hearty welcome. Mrs. Hunter had died during my absence, and he had been waiting for us for the purpose of going down to Norway House. We met here Sir John Richardson and Dr. Rae, *en route* to Mackenzie River, with two canoes in search of Sir John Franklin. From them we first heard of the events that had recently occurred in Europe, the flight of Louis Philippe from Paris, and the revolutionary movements then agitating the Continent.

Whilst walking past the small trading post established here, Mr. Hunter asked me to go in, and we were received very kindly by a little shrivelled up French Canadian, married to a Cree squaw, one of the most extraordinary looking women I had ever seen. She was so fat that she was obliged to sit on a small waggon, in which they drew her about, and her mode of going to bed was by rolling off this on to a buffalo skin. She had not been able to use her legs for many years. I have generally noticed that all Indian women, when brought into the forts, and when relieved from the toils and exposures of their native life, become fat, lazy, and unwieldy.

We left the same evening, bringing Mr. Hunter with us. Few incidents worth noticing occurred on our route. Mr. Harriett's boat, in which I sat, was generally a-head of the party, being lighter and rather better built than the rest. One evening we got to the place Mr. Harriett selected for encampment considerably before any of the others, and I got out my drawing materials and took a sketch of the brigade, as it was coming up with a fair breeze, crowding on all sail to escape a thunder storm rolling fast after them. [Figs. 73, 74; crIV-92 to 95]

June 17th.—We arrived at the Grand Rapids, and the whole brigade shot down them, a distance of three and a half miles; this is the same rapid where Paulet Paul achieved his herculean feat before mentioned. No rapid in the whole course of the navigation on the eastern side of the mountains is at all to be compared to this in point of velocity, grandeur, or danger to the navigator. The brigade flies down as if impelled by a hurricane, many shipping a good deal of water in the perpendicular leaps which they often had to take in the descent. The whole course is one white sheet of foam, from one end to the other.

We passed here the brigade of boats[2] bound upwards for Mackenzie River; they were laboriously making the portage up, whilst we were shooting down with lightning speed. The heavily laden men, as they toiled along the banks, cast many an

---

[1] kj for June 10: "Cumberland, crossed over 3 miles to see the Fort. Got a keg of beer from Mr. de Shambo [?] which [I] passed. Soon left on the same day."

[2] kj identifies Mr. Kinsey as being in charge of the brigade.

envious look at our flying company, who yelled and shouted with excitement whilst plunging down the foaming cataract. Having run the rapids in safety, we arrived in a few minutes more at Lake Winnipeg, and encamped on the shore, where we cooked and ate our supper. From this point we had to make a traverse of seventy miles as the crow flies to Mossy Point, the entrance to Jack Fish River; but as the wind was against us, we lay down to sleep.

About 1 o'clock in the morning we were all aroused, and found the wind blowing fresh and fair, so that we put off immediately to take advantage of the fortunate occurrence. I was soon asleep again in the boat, and did not awake till after sunrise, when I found we were far out of sight of land and the wind blowing a heavy gale. About 2 o'clock P.M. we rounded Mossy Point, and at 5 o'clock arrived at Norway House, where the brigade left me, they going on to York Factory, and I remaining to meet Major McKenzie, who was expected soon to pass on his way to Fort Francis.

The annual council of chief factors, which is usually held at Red River, was this year held at Norway House, and I had the pleasure of again meeting with Sir George Simpson, and several gentlemen to whose kindness I had before been deeply indebted. I was detained here for more than a month, and though the weather was clear and fine, yet we could not sit in the house in comfort without having the stove lighted. I amused myself in fishing and shooting. I speared a good many sturgeon, which are here very fine and numerous, and also great lots of gold eyes, which are a peculiar species of fish, like the herring, though larger and thicker, but not worth catching. Mr. Rowand said that they eat like mud. I certainly never tasted them but once, and I was not tempted to repeat the experiment.

I was often accompanied in the canoe by Ogemawwah Chack, "The Spirit Chief" (sketch No. 19), an Esquimaux from the Hudson's Bay who had attained to an extreme old age. [Fig. 76; crIV-90, 91] According to received opinion, he was 110 years old, and the events which he related as having witnessed seemed to warrant the belief. He had an only son, whom I often met, quite elderly in appearance. The mother of this boy had died very shortly after his birth, and there being no woman giving suck near at the time, the father, to soothe the cries of the starving infant, placed the child's mouth to his own breast, and finding that the child derived some benefit from it, he continued the practice for some days, and, strange to say, milk flowed from his nipple, and he brought up the child without the assistance of any woman.

Before leaving Norway House, some Cree Indians arrived, and boasted that one of their war chiefs had vanquished the great Blackfoot chief, Big Snake, in single combat. [Fig. 90; crIV-148] Big Snake had ridden away from the main body of his tribe, in hopes of stealing some horses, as he thought that the Crees in their precipitate flight were likely to have left them behind; and, hoping to have all he got for himself, he took no comrades with him. The Cree chief discovered him from behind a hill, riding alone on the plain beneath, and, burning with vengeance, rushed at him, without waiting for his other warriors, who were not, however, far off. Big Snake did not see the others, and disdaining to fly from a single foe, he boldly galloped to meet his enemy; but the fight was short, as the Cree succeeded in piercing him with his spear at the first meeting, and he was scalped and dead before the others came up.

July 24th.—Major McKenzie at last arrived with five boats, manned principally with Indians; he only remained a few hours, when I embarked with him; but we only proceeded about six miles when it became dark, and we encamped for the night.

July 25th.—We stopped to breakfast at a picturesque little island near the outlet of Lake Winnipeg, after which we passed the Spider Islands, so called from the countless myriads of these insects which infest them. In the evening we encamped at Point de Tremble, on Poplar Point.

July 26th.—We left in the morning with a strong breeze, which changed into a perfect gale, making many of our Indians sea-sick. The swells of Lake Winnipeg, from the shallowness of this wide expanse of water when set in motion by a heavy wind, are far more abrupt and dangerous for boats than those of the Atlantic; and I could not but feel very apprehensive for our safety,—a feeling which was evidently shared by Major McKenzie, for he kept a signal flying from his mast-head, which the guide well knew meant for him to put ashore, but which he would not obey, as he considered it a most dangerous alternative to change his course; and the shore, from its rocky character, being very difficult of approach in stormy weather.[3] We, however, by dint of constant baling, continued our course in safety until we arrived at the mouth of Behring's River, which we entered in safety, much to the relief of the Major's anxiety for both cargoes and crews. Here we remained windbound for the rest of the day and part of the following.

By way of passing the time, I took my gun and strolled up

[3] KJ notes that Major McKenzie had been able to stand the battle of Corunna when he was wounded, but that the swells of Lake Winnipeg completely upset him.

the river, accompanied by the guide, and fell in with a solitary Sotto woman and child sitting under a tree. She was quite alone, as her husband had gone up the river fishing in the morning. She did not appear to be at all alarmed or confused at our approach, and freely entered into conversation with the guide, to whom she told her name, Caw-kee-ka-keesh-e-ko, "The Constant Sky." Tempted by the beauty of the scene, and she seeming to be in no wise unwilling, I sketched her likeness and the surrounding landscape with considerable care. [CRIV-87, 88]

July 27th.—We started rather late,[4] and being only able to make Rabbit Point, we encamped. We here found immense flocks of wild pigeons, and killed a good supply. Our Indians killed several skunks, which they prize very much as delicate eating, preferring them to the pigeons, although the bare smell of them in our vicinity almost took away my appetite for the former.

July 28th.—About 2 o'clock P.M., we endeavoured to proceed, but only got as far as the Dog's Head, the wind being so strong and unfavourable, that it was thought useless to run any risk for the short distance that we would be able to make against it. In the evening our Indians constructed a jonglerie, or medicine lodge, the main object of which was to procure a fair wind for next day. For this purpose they first drive ten or twelve poles, nine or ten feet long, into the ground, enclosing a circular area of about three feet in diameter, with a boat sail open at the top. The medicine-man, one of whom is generally found in every brigade, gets inside and commences shaking the poles violently, rattling his medicinal rattle, and singing hoarse incantations to the Great Spirit for a fair wind. Being unable to sleep on account of the discordant noises, I wrapped a blanket round me, and went out into the woods, where they were holding their midnight orgies, and lay down amongst those on the outside of the medicine lodge, to witness the proceedings. I had no sooner done so than the incantations at once ceased, and the performer exclaimed that a white man was present. How he ascertained this fact I am at a loss to surmise, as it was pitch dark at the time, and he was enclosed in the narrow tent, without any apparent opening through which he could espy me, even had it been light enough to distinguish one person from another.

The Major, who, with many other intelligent persons, is a firm believer in their medicine, told me that a Canadian once had the temerity to peep under the covering which enclosed the jonglerie, but that he got such a fright that he never fairly recovered from it, nor could he ever be prevailed upon to tell what it was that had so appalled him. After about two hours'

shaking and singing, the medicine-man cried out that he saw five boats with the sails set running before the wind, which communication was greeted by the whole party with their usual grunt of satisfaction and assent.

After this, many questions were asked him by the Indians, some inquiring after the health of their families at home, whom they had not seen for many months. Upon putting the question, the inquirer threw a small piece of tobacco over the covering of the tent, upon which the medicine-man agitated the tent, and shook his rattle violently, and then replied that he saw one family enjoying themselves over a fat sturgeon, another engaged in some pleasing employment, &c., &c. I then put a question to him myself, accompanying it with a double portion of tobacco, for which I got a double portion of noise. I asked about my curiosities which I had left at Norway House (for want of room in our boats), to be brought on by the canoes which had taken up Sir John Richardson on their return, they not being engaged to carry him further than Prairie River. The medicine-man told me that he saw the party with my baggage encamped on a sandy point, which we had ourselves passed two days before.

However singular the coincidence may appear, it is a fact, that on the next day we had a fair wind, for which the medicine-man of course took all the credit; and it is no less true, that the canoes with my baggage were on the sandy point on the day stated, for I inquired particularly of them when they came up to us.

July 29th.—We started very early in the morning, with a fair wind, and stopped to breakfast at the Loon Narrows. We reached Otter Head [5] in the evening, and then encamped.

July 30th.—We breakfasted at Point Mille-lac, and arrived at 10 o'clock A.M. at Fort Alexander, where we found a great number of Saulteaux Indians, who come in large numbers about this season of the year, and disperse themselves among the small lakes, where they gather great quantities of wild rice, resembling our own in taste, but much larger and black.[6] The scarcity of other provisions in these parts renders the rice very valuable, but the Indians are so lazy, that they will not collect much more than they want for themselves without being bribed to do so, and the clerk in charge of the establishment is obliged to give

---

[4] KJ: "They breakfasted at Sturgeon River."

[5] KJ reads Buffalo Head.

[6] KJ notes that they purchased 250 bushels from the Indians. The price was one-third of a pint of rum for a bushel of rice. Kane adds that rice cannot be got without rum.

them, for that purpose, a certain quantity of rum to induce them to go to collect rice for the establishment, and also to give them some on their return, besides paying them in goods for the quantity they bring in. Major McKenzie here met his wife and two daughters, who had been on a visit to Red River. We remained at Fort Alexander four days, changing our crews, the Indians who had been with us belonging here.

Before leaving Lake Winnipeg, I would remark that the whole of its eastern shore, which I had just coasted, presented a most wild, rocky, rough, hilly, and almost impassable country, and several of the Indians who had been through, described it as being of the same character far back from the lake, and interspersed with innumerable lakes and swamps.

August 3rd.—We left with four boats, manned with thirty men, twenty-seven of whom were Indians, two French Canadians, and one Orkney man, and commenced the ascent of the Winnipeg River. Mrs. McKenzie and her two daughters were to follow us in a light canoe, with a crew of Indians. We had to make several portages during the day, and in the evening got over the portage of the Prancing Horses, a cascade about twenty feet high. We had a whole fleet of light canoes following us, containing the Indian wives and children. Two of them contained brides, who had been married in the morning without any ceremony that I heard of.

Aug. 4th.—In the morning,[7] we made the White Mud Portage, which was very picturesque, and of which I took a sketch, No. 20, with the Indians and squaws who were following us, carrying their canoes across [Pl. XIII; crIV-19, 20, 21]; and in the course of the day made another called Little Rock, about seven feet high, and camped at the upper end of it.

Aug. 5th.—Left at 4 o'clock A.M., and arrived at the Grand Bonnet, a portage of a mile in length, which it took us the whole day to drag the boats across; the weather was burning hot, and the mosquitoes in legions. The canoes, containing the women and children, kept close at our heels, and always came up to our encampment for provisions; this so reduced our stock, that out of regard to our own safety, we were obliged to put them upon short allowance.[8]

Aug. 6th.—We crossed the Second Bonnet, and met some Indians, who sold us a few sturgeon, and crossing Lac de Bonnet, where several of our Indian followers left us for the rice-grounds, we encamped for the night on the banks of the river Malaine. Owing to the low marshy state of the country hereabouts, we were dreadfully tormented with mosquitoes. The poor Orkney man, in particular, seemed to be an especial fa-

vourite, and there had been evidently an attempt made to eat him up altogether. In the morning, his face presented the appearance of a person in the smallpox.

Aug. 7th.—Passed six portages to-day, one of which is called the Wooden Horse, and encamped at the Grande Gullete. The chief's son,[9] of Rat Portage, who was one of our engaged men, here deserted us, and stole off in a canoe with his two wives. [Fig. 53; crIV-30, 31]

Aug. 8th.—To-day we had to make several portages,[10] and in the evening encamped three miles above the Grand Rapid of this river, having still thirteen canoes of Indians paddling in our wake. This evening we found some smooth flat rocks, which the voyageurs always prefer to grass or earth to make their bed on, and I can say, from experience, that they have formed a judicious estimate of the superior comfort they afford after a hard day's travel; for grass or sand is certainly the worst surface to sleep upon, however soft it may feel at first.

Aug. 9th.—We breakfasted at the Barrière Portage, and arrived about noon at the Slave Falls, of which I made a sketch. [Fig. 51; crIV-14 to 17] Three military officers, Captain Moody, Mr. Brown, and Mr. Constable, caught up to us in their light canoes; they were on their way from Red River to Canada, and pushed on after a very short stay. We had hardly bid them good-bye, when Mrs. McKenzie and her two lovely daughters came up, and stayed with us until next morning. Our Indians now refused to proceed further, unless they received an allowance of rum; and the Major was obliged to promise them a supply as soon as he arrived at Rat Portage.

Aug. 10th.—Our starting[11] was delayed this morning in consequence of a dense fog, and we only got as far as the Rochers Boules before breakfast; after which, the ladies left us for their residence at Rat Portage. During the day we passed the Aux Chênes, and encamped about four miles below the Point of Woods.

Aug. 11th.[12]—Our provisions were now getting very low, and we had still further to restrict our distributions to the women

---

[7] KJ notes that they made a portage of the Silver Falls before the portages of the White Mud Falls and the Little Rock Falls. They thus made three portages in one day. He notes the second falls were ten feet high.

[8] KJ states that they crossed both the First and the Second Bonnet. The weather was intensely hot and the mosquitoes were in myriads.

[9] KJ identifies the chief's son as Cashi-Cabit, the Long Tooth, or "The Tooth of the Glutton."

[10] KJ adds: "One of the 2 women that got married at Fort Alexander had fits. I gave her some peppermint and told her sister to rub her. She had eaten too much."

[11] KJ notes that they had to wait until 6 A.M. before setting out.

[12] KJ for August 11 states that they made an early start and breakfasted at Chute à Jacques. He adds that canoes were leaving for Winnipeg.

and children. On each side of the river for a long distance are innumerable small shallow lakes, bearing usually large quantities of rice; but the water in them had sunk so low this season, that the Indians were apprehensive of a failure in the crop, which would be attended with the most serious consequences, as upon it was placed their whole dependence for food. When we arrived at the Grand Equerre we stopped for the night.

Aug. 12th.—We passed to-day the deserted Catholic mission called Wabe-samung, "White Dog," from the name of the portage next above it. This was established by Mr. Belcour,[13] a Catholic priest, but he had left it the year before, as he found there was not enough of land near it that would pay for cultivation. The whole country between this and Fort Alexander was rocky and barren, so that no mission could hope to get any Indians to settle permanently near it. In the evening we encamped at the White Dog Portage.[14]

Aug. 13th.—We got to the Yellow Mud Portage by breakfast-time, and afterwards crossed the "Grande Décharge," so called from its being the place where the boats are hauled up after the goods are discharged from them, in distinction from a portage, at which latter place, as I have already observed, it is necessary to carry the boats as well as the cargoes. In the evening we encamped at what is called the Fishery, or the place where the people from Rat Portage come to fish. It was with great difficulty we could find a place to sleep on free from ants, whose hillocks we disturbed at every step. I made several attempts to lie down, but they annoyed me so much, that at last I got into one of the boats.[15]

Aug. 14th.—Left our encampment at 3 A.M., and arrived at Rat Portage at 10, where we were received by Mrs. McKenzie with the greatest hospitality and kindness. The Indians here subsist on sturgeon and white fish in the summer, and rice and rabbits in the winter. We rested ourselves here two days, and employed ourselves principally in feasting on white fish, to make up for the short allowance of food under which we had lately been suffering.

Aug. 16th.—It was with great regret that I parted with the kind Major and his family. The men having made the portage from which this post is named, we left about 2 in the afternoon, and soon entered the Lake of the Woods, where we chose a comfortable little island, and encamped for the night.

Aug. 17th.—We threaded our way among innumerable islands, many of them thickly covered with woods, from which circumstance the lake takes its name. We saw on one of them about five acres of cultivated corn, the only instance of the kind

I had seen since I left Norway House. There is another island called Garden Island, which lay to the west of our route, about six miles long and about three wide, on which I was told some Indians raised yearly a few bushels of corn and potatoes. At night we again chose an island for our resting place.

Aug. 18th.—We were wind-bound until 5 P.M., during which time we were visited by a large party of Saulteaux Indians; we embarked in the evening, but only succeeded in getting on about six miles before we were again obliged to stop, and remained all the next day.

Aug. 20th.—Made an early start with a fair wind, which carried us into the mouth of the River La Pluie. Here we found some Indians who were gathering snow-berries and sand-berries; the latter are the size of large grapes, of a reddish blue colour. They grow on long vines trailing upon the sand, and are very good eating when washed free of the particles which adhere to them. We encamped about four miles up the river, and were again tortured by our old enemies the mosquitoes, aided by detachments of black flies.

Aug. 21st.—Roused by the flies, we started early.[16] Our route up the river was much enlivened by the antics of the Indians when tracking, that is, hauling the boats up the current, which they do for days together whenever the banks, or indeed the bed of the river, will admit of it; for they seemed to be perfectly amphibious, wading about in the water, and swimming from side to side as a matter of course, without thinking of getting into the boat, and making great fun of one of our Canadians who had got into a canoe with two squaws, to cross.[17]

Aug. 22nd.—The men woke me up at 2 o'clock in the morning from my warm blankets, for the purpose of getting under way; but when just ready to start, we were prevented by a violent storm of rain, which continued until about 6 o'clock, when we immediately set off. The country about here is very swampy, but, from its height, I think much of it might be drained, and adapted for cultivation. I noticed all along the banks of this river, that wherever pine trees had been burned

---

[13] The Rev. Georges-Antoine Bellecourt (1803–1874) served as a missionary in the northwest from 1831 to 1858. He operated the mission of Notre Dame de Merci at Wabassimong in 1843–44. See *Dictionary of Canadian Biography*, vol. X.

[14] KJ states that they camped at the White Mud Portage. He had mentioned it earlier, and evidently corrected his entry for the book.

[15] KJ: "We received the Chief of Rat Portage on board while his 2 wives paddled a canoe alongside. He seemed rather proud of sitting with white chiefs. We took them to Rat Portage."

[16] Kane was a great admirer of the canoemen. He entered in his journal: "Never saw such water dogs as our men."

[17] KJ notes of the one exception, "a small Canadian who would not risk it."

down, poplars invariably sprung up in their places, although no other poplars could be seen in the vicinity.

Aug. 23rd.—We left our encampment at 1 A.M., so as to make sure of arriving at Fort Frances before night. The Indians tracked with the line the whole day, frequently up to their middles in the water, and often swimming; this wearisome toil they kept up for sixteen hours, with the exception of one hour, during which we stopped for breakfast, never for one moment losing their cheerfulness and good humour. I scarcely think that any other race of people could go through such fatigue with the same alacrity and energy.[18]

At 5 o'clock P.M. we reached Fort Frances, so named after the sister of Lady Simpson. [Figs. 49, 50; crIV-10, 11] Here the annual three months' voyage terminates, that being the time which it takes to convey the furs to York Factory, in Hudson's Bay, and bring back the outfit of goods.[19] The fort is situated near where Rainy Lake disembogues into a river of the same name, forming a beautiful cascade. [crIV-12] The Indians catch great quantities of sturgeon at the foot of these falls in the month of June.[20] The sturgeon here are very small—seldom weighing more than 40 or 50 lbs.—at least in comparison with those taken at the mouth of Frazer's River on the west side of the mountains, which often weigh from 5 to 7 cwt.

Fort Frances has usually about 250 Indians in its neighbourhood, who have a half-breed missionary of the Methodist church resident amongst them;[21] but I understood he was about to leave them, disheartened by the small success attendant upon his exertions. The Indians live here as at Rat Portage, on rice, fish, and rabbits. The last are so numerous in the winter, that one man caught eighty-six in one night, being only unsuccessful with fourteen snares out of the 100 he had set in the evening.

The skins, like the Canadian, are far inferior to the European rabbits': the only use to which I have seen them applied has been in the manufacture of rabbit-skin robes, which are made by cutting the skin with the hair on into strips, which are twisted and netted together in such a manner as to keep the hair outwards on both sides of the robe. The people of the fort grow some wheat and potatoes, but though there is some very good land about, they find it impossible to induce the Indians to cultivate it. The crop of wheat which they got in while I was there, was almost entirely spoiled by smut, and they were obliged to wash it before they could turn it to any account. I remained here eighteen days waiting for the passing of the express canoe which annually carries the letters from the interior posts to Lachine.

Sept. 10th.—The express canoe arrived in the evening with Mr. M'Tavish.[22] He was come direct from York Factory, where he had been stationed for fourteen years, and gave a most dismal account of the climate and country; he was now going to the Sault St. Marie, to the charge of which post he had been recently appointed by way of giving him a little taste of civilisation, of which he rather stood in need.

Sept. 11th.—We started at 6 o'clock in the morning, and got through Lac la Pluie by 5 in the afternoon; after this we had to make two portages, and encamped just before dark at the second.

Sept. 12th.—Started at 3 o'clock A.M., the morning was very cold and foggy; and we had a severe frost during the night. We breakfasted at the Grand Chute, and had a very severe day's work afterwards, as we had to make four bad portages, and did not encamp until 9 o'clock at night; the men having worked eighteen hours steadily. We were lucky enough to meet some Indians after dark,[23] from whom we obtained a good supply of delicious white fish. We now exerted all our energies to hasten our journey as the danger of ice setting in was becoming imminent, and with great labour we arrived at the Mountain Portage on the evening of the 18th.

Sept. 19th.—I got up at the first appearance of day, that I might have the opportunity whilst the men were making the portage, of again visiting the Kakabakka falls. As the day dawned the magnificent spectacle gradually cleared to my view in all its mighty grandeur and magnificence, and I felt more impressed than ever with the opinion that these falls far surpass the Niagara in beauty and picturesque effect, and would have much liked to have taken another sketch of them; but my admiring contemplations were hastily cut short by a peremptory summons from the canoes, which were waiting for me. I hastily

---

[18] KJ, noting that they went until 5 P.M., says: "There are not many men in the world that could stand it."

[19] KJ states that when the men had carried their packs to the stores, their three month's voyage was over.

Kane was wrong about the naming of Fort Frances, which commemorates Lady Simpson herself.

[20] KJ goes into detail about obtaining caviar from the sturgeon at this place, stating: "They have received 18 packs of sturgeon sands [caviar] in one year, 90 pounds per pack, 12½ sands to the pound. There will be 20,450 sands in the 18 packs, and as there is but one sand taken from a sturgeon, there will be 20,450 sturgeon caught here in the month of June."

[21] The missionary was the Rev. Peter Jacobs, who was highly critical of the Hudson's Bay Company management at the Fort Frances post.

[22] With them as passenger was William Mactavish (d. 1870), at the time a Hudson's Bay Company clerk, but appointed a chief factor in 1851, Governor of Assiniboia in 1858, and Governor of Rupert's Land in 1864.

[23] According to KJ, the Indians were met at Grand Rapids.

rejoined them, and we dashed down the uninterrupted current forty miles to Fort William, where we arrived early in the afternoon. On leaving Fort William, we suffered a great deal the next five days from the high cold wind, which frequently stopped our progress.

Sept. 24th.—We were wind-bound at the mouth of a small river, and as there seemed no prospect of a change, I followed the stream up about ten miles until I came to a cascade. The interior of the country as far as I went seemed to be of the same character as the coast, high mountain rocks, interspersed with a few trees of stunted growth and scanty herbage. I was lucky enough to shoot four ducks, which proved a most acceptable addition to the pemmi-kon and fish which we had brought with us. We got off next day, although the weather was still bad, but we were anxious to get to Michipicoton, as there is a post there, and we might obtain some little comfort at least, if we were detained.

Sept. 27th.—We arrived at the post about 9 o'clock in the evening, and remained there the whole of next day. The post is situated in a deep bay at the mouth of the river, and is sur-rounded by some of the best land to be found on the British shores of Lake Superior. The head chief of the Ojibbeways, who resides near the post, sat for me in his red coat trimmed with gold lace. These coats are given by the Company to such Indian chiefs as have been friendly and serviceable to them, and are very highly prized by their possessors. His name was Maydoc-game-kinungee, "I hear the Noise of the Deer." [Pl. XI; crIV-1, 2]

Sept. 29th.—We started very early in the morning, and encamped that evening opposite to Montreal Island.

Sept. 30th.—We got to Montreal River, where we stopped for two hours for breakfast, passed Micah Bay at 1 o'clock, and encamped at night at the Isle aux Sables.

Oct. 1st.—We stopped to breakfast at 4 o'clock near Gros-Cap, a porphyry rock rising 1500 feet above the level of the lake, and got to the post at Sault St. Marie by 2 o'clock P.M. Here I consider that my Indian travels finish, as the rest of my journey home to Toronto was performed on board steam-boats; and the greatest hardship I had to endure, was the difficulty I found in trying to sleep in a civilised bed.

PART THREE   Paul Kane's Sketches and Paintings

For an explanation of the capitalization and spelling used in the captions, please refer to the introduction to Part Four, where a list of abbreviations for the collections will also be found.

Fig. 1. Paul Kane, a photograph. Collection of Mrs. Paul Kane III.

Fig. 2. Mrs. W. S. Conger, painted *c.* 1834. Collection of
S. E. Weir; cr I-13.

Fig. 4. The riverboat *Norma* with her captain.
Stark op26; cr I-25.

Fig. 3. Eliza (Clench) Armour,
painted *c.* 1836. Collection of
Mrs. R. J. Shirley; cr I-24.

Fig. 5. Roman youth, from one of Kane's European sketchbooks.
Collection of Mrs. T. M. Willet; CRII-6.

Fig. 6. Trees in a Roman landscape, from one of Kane's European sketchbooks.
Collection of Mrs. T. M. Willet; CRII-6.

Fig. 7. Rubens, self-portrait, as copied
by Kane. Private collection; CRII-9.

Fig. 8. Mayor George Gurnett of Toronto. Corporation of the City of Toronto; CRV-26.

Fig. 9. James Richardson, of Cobourg and St. Catharines. ROM964.185; CRV-28.

113.

Drying Salmon at the Dalles - Columbia River

166.

Plate XXXI. Drying salmon at the Dalles, Columbia River. Stark wwc50; crIV-310.

Plate XXXII. Spokane River. ROM946.15.189; crIV-334.

Fig. 10. Bloor's Brewery, Toronto. ROM946.15.254; CRV-12.

Fig. 11. Thomas Daly, city clerk
of Toronto, an artist.
ROM946.15.142; CRV-33.

165

Fig. 12. Niagara Falls. ROM946.15.335; CRV-3.

Fig. 13. Homewood, the early residence of the Hon. G. W. Allan. Collection of G. P. H. Vernon; CRV-13.

Fig. 14. Kwa-qua-dah-bon-niva-skung or "Dawn of Day," a chief of the Saugeen. Stark EOP9; crIII-3.

Fig. 15. Maska-nonga or "Big Fish," an Ojibwa, Saugeen village. Stark EOP19; crIII-5.

Fig. 16. A page of sketches made on Georgian Bay. ROM946.15.53; CRIII-6.

Fig. 17. An Ojibwa chief's daughter from Lake St. Clair. Stark EOP5; CRIII-7.

Fig. 18. Wappoose (Wah-pus or "The Rabbit"), Saugeen village. ROM912.1.1; CRIII-11.

168

Fig. 19. Indian encampment on Big Bay, Owen Sound. Stark EOP13; CRIII-12.

Fig. 20. An Indian Encampment on Lake Huron. Art Gallery of Ontario 2121; CRIII-19.

Fig. 21. Indian Bivouac. Public Archives of Canada, Kane I-1; crIII-24.

Fig. 22. French River Rapids.
rom912.1.2; crIII-26.

90,

Spokan Chief Spokan River

202

Plate XXXIII. Tum-se-ne-ho or "The Man without Blood," a Spokan chief. Stark wwc43; crIV-337.

Fig. 24. Manitowaning, with wigwams of Indians assembled for the receipt of presents. David Mitchell Gallery; crIII-39.

Fig. 23. From a page of sketches, Georgian Bay. *Upper*, rocky islands; *lower*, Ojibwa grave house opposite Manitowaning. ROM946.15.51; crIII-36.

Fig. 25. Manitowaning and the assembly of tribes for the receipt of presents. ROM946.15.30; crIII-41.

Fig. 26. Shawwanossoway or "One with his Face towards the West," an Ojibwa medicine man sketched at Manitowaning. Stark EOP2; crIII-44.

Fig. 27. Indian from Michipicoten. Stark EOP6; crIII-50.

Fig. 28. Muck-koze or "Young Bear," Ottawa chief, Manitoulin Island. Stark EOP24; crIII-52.

Fig. 29. Awbonwaishkum, Ottawa chief, Manitowaning. Stark EOP12; CRIII-53.

Fig. 31. Captain George Ironsides or "Walk on the Water," Indian agent, Manitowaning. Stark EOP16; CRIII-56.

Fig. 30. Stone pipe carved by Awbonwaishkum. Stark EOP21; CRIII-55.

Fig. 33. Asabonish or "The Raccoon," Ottawa chief, with his daughter, sketched at Wikwemikong. Stark EOP28; CRIII-63.

Fig. 32. Pipe and club, sketched at Manitowaning(?). ROM946.15.33; CRIII-62.

Fig. 34. Sault Ste Marie, with the Ermatinger grist mill. ROM946.15.25; CRIII-74.

Fig. 35. Fort and Indian village at Mackinac.
ROM946.15.255; crIII-78.

Fig. 36. The natural bridge at Mackinac.
Stark EOP20; crIII-82.

Fig. 37. Rocky headland with wigwams, Mackinac.
Stark EOP29; crIII-84.

Fig. 38. Wampum belts, from Mackinac.
Stark A4-43; crIII-95.

Fig. 39. Ke-wah-ten or "The North Wind"(?). Stark POP3; CRIII-107.

Fig. 40. Iwa-toke or "The Serpent,"
a Menominee, Lake Winnebago.
Stark ᴇᴏᴘ26; ᴄʀIII-106.

Fig. 41. Fishing by Torch Light (Fox River).
ʀᴏᴍ912.1.10; ᴄʀIII-112.

Fig. 42. Oscosh or "The Bravest of the Brave," Menominee chief, Fox River. Stark A4-38; crIII-113.

Fig. 43. Match-o-kee-maw or "Big Chief," Menominee chief, Fox River. Stark POP4; crIII-117.

Fig. 44. Muck-a-ta, Fox River. Stark EOP17; crIII-122.

Fig. 46. Mauza-pau-Kan or "Brave Soldier," a Winnebago chief, Fox River. National Gallery of Canada 6457; crIII-129.

Fig. 45. Muck-a-ta, Fox River. ROM912.1.12; crIII-123.

181

Fig. 47. Kakabeka Falls. ROM946.15.66; crIV-3.

182

Fig. 48. Pin Portage. Stark POP25; crIV-7.

Plate XXXIV. Looking down the Pelouse River. ROM946.15.182; crIV-341.

Fort Frances

Paul Karre 1846

Fig. 49. Fort Frances. Stark PWC2; crIV-10.

160

Fig. 50. Fort Frances. Stark PWC3; crIV-11.

Dalle des Morts

Fig. 51. Slave Falls, Winnipeg River. Stark WWC19; CRIV-15.

Winnipeg River   Paul Kane 18

184

Fig. 52. Winnipeg River. Stark POP13; CRIV-24.

Fig. 53. Two Indian heads, Cash-a-cabut (*left*) and Each-a-quip (*right*), Saulteaux from the Fort Frances region. ROM946.15.273; CrIV-30.

Fig. 55. Peter Jacobs, Wesleyan Indian missionary. Stark PWC14; CrIV-33.

185

Fig. 54. Sho-ne-ah or "Silver," a Saulteaux
chief, Fort Alexander. Stark POP5; CrIV-32.

Fig. 56. Red River Settlement. Stark POP1; CrIV-36.

Fig. 57. Red River Settlement. ROM946.15.68; CrIV-35.

Fig. 58. A Sioux Indian (apparently sketched south of Fort Garry).
ROM912.1.29; crIV-41.

Fig. 59. Na-taw-waugh-cit or "The Man that was born," Saulteaux, sketched south of Fort Garry. Stark EOP22; crIV-43.

Fig. 60. Half Breeds Travelling. ROM912.1.24; CrIV-54.

Plate XXXV. Falls, upper Pelouse River. Stark woP22; crIV-349.

Chinook Indian — Columbia River

93.

Plate XXXVI. Casanov, noted warrior, Fort Vancouver. Stark WOP4; CRIV-418.

ig. 61. Red River cart and ox. ROM946.15.74; CRIV-55.

Fig. 62. Dog with travois. ROM946.15.84; CRIV-58.

Fig. 63. Métis setting up camp on the prairies. ROM946.15.71; CRIV-66.

Fig. 64. Half Breed Encampment.
ROM912.1.25; CRIV-68.

Fig. 65. Half Breed Encampment
(a detail of Fig. 64).

Fig. 66. Métis camp and hunters. ROM946.15.70; CrIV-69.

191

Fig. 67. Half Breeds Running Buffalo. ROM912.1.26; CrIV-73.

Fig. 68. Wounded buffalo bull, shot by Kane. ROM946.15.87; crIV-78.

Fig. 69. Wounded buffalo bull, shot by Kane. Stark PWC8; crIV-79.

Fig. 70. Donald Ross, Chief Factor,
Norway House. Provincial Archives,
British Columbia, 3760; crIV-89.

Fig. 71. Wesleyan mission station, Jack River. Stark pwc17; crIV-84.

Wesleyan Methodist Station Playgreen Lake 44

193

Fig. 72. Two portrait studies: a Saulteaux girl and an Assiniboin. ROM946.15.61; CRIV-86.

Fig. 73. Brigade of boats, near Le Pas. ROM946.15.83; CRIV-92.

Plate XXXVII. Interior of a ceremonial lodge, Columbia River. Stark wop13; crIV-425.

Fig. 74. Brigade of Boats. ROM912.1.31; CRIV-95.

Fig. 75. Fort Carlton from a distance. Stark PWC18; CRIV-96.

Fig. 76. Ogemawwah Chack or "The Spirit Chief," an Eskimo, Norway House. Stark WOP2; CRIV-90.

Fig. 77. Studies of the buffalo hunt near Fort Carlton. ROM946.15.103; CRIV-99.

Fig. 78. A Buffalo Pound. ROM912.1.33; CrIV-101.

Fig. 79. "The Man that Shot the Wolf with an Arrow," a Cree, Fort Carlton. ROM946.15.96; crIV-104.

Fig. 80. Cree Indians travelling. ROM946.15.102; crIV-106.

Fig. 81. The Serpentine Valley, Saskatchewan River. ROM946.15.139; CRIV-119.

Fig. 82. The Golden Valley, Saskatchewan River. ROM946.15.108; CRIV-120.

Fig. 83. Fort Pitt, with bluff. Stark pwc23; crIV-122.

Fig. 84. Prairie antelope.
Stark pwc11; crIV-123.

Fig. 86. Kee-akee-ka-saa-ka-wow, "The Man that gives the War Whoop" (Fort Pitt). ROM912.1.42; crIV-132.

Fig. 85. Kee-a-kee-ka-sa-coo-way or "The Man who gives the War-whoop," a Cree, Fort Pitt. Peabody Museum, Harvard University—Bushnell 41-72/395; crIV-131.

201

Fig. 87. Cree pipe-stem. ROM946.15.99; CRIV-135.

Fig. 88. Cree pipe-stems. ROM946.15.100; CRIV-136.

Fig. 89. Indian Horse Race. National Gallery of Canada 6921; crIV-145.

Fig. 90. The Death of Big Snake; contemporary print made in Toronto. Collection of A. A. H. Vernon; crIV-148.

Fig. 91. Wah-nis-stow or "The White Buffalo," a Sarsi chief, sketched near Fort Pitt. Stark pwc5; crIV-150.

Fig. 92. Big Snake, a Blackfoot Chief, recounting his War Exploits. National Gallery of Canada 22; crIV-155.

Fig. 93. Medicine Pipe Stem Dance (Blackfoot). ROM912.1.56; crIV-158.

Fig. 94. Jacket ornamented with a crow (military society regalia). ROM946.15.313; crIV-162.

Part of Oregon City

Plate XXXVIII. The mills of Oregon City. Stark WOP16; CRIV-449.

Fig. 95. Buffalo robe depicting adventures of Sa-co or "The Sinew Piece," a Blood. Stark wwc82; cr-164.

Fig. 96. Studies of buffalo, near Fort Pitt.
ROM946.15.90; CRIV-174.

Fig. 97. Buffalo bulls fighting, near Fort Pitt.
Stark PWC9; CRIV-175.

208

Fig. 98. Buffalo Bulls Fighting. ROM912.1.28; CRIV-176.

Fig. 99. A Prairie on Fire. ROM912.1.39; CrIV-187.

Fig. 100. Sled dogs of the plains. Stark PWC13; CrIV-195.

Fig. 101. Sled dogs decorated for a wedding party, Fort Edmonton.
Stark pwc12; crIV-194.

Fig. 103. Decorated sled for wedding party, Fort Edmonton. rom946.15.129; crIV-199.

Fig. 102. Snow on trees.
Stark wwc40; crIV-196.

211

Fig. 104. Catching Wild Horses. ROM912.1.45; CRIV-203.

Plate XXXIX. St. Paul's Mission, Willamette valley. ROM946.15.264; CRIV-454.

Willamette Indians

Plate XL. Clackama Indians, Willamette valley. Stark WOP11; CrIV-459.

Fig. 105. Assiniboine Hunting Buffalo. National Gallery of Canada 6920; crIV-209.

213

Fig. 106. Italian youths chasing a bull, a print used by Kane in painting the canvas of which Fig. 105 is a replica. Collection of Mrs. Paul Kane III; crIV-208.

214   Fig. 107. Cunnawa-bum or "One that looks at the stars" (Cree half-breed girl, Fort Edmonton). ROM912.1.41; CRIV-214.

Fig. 108. Rocky Mountain House. ROM912.1.57; CRIV-218.

Fig. 109. Mah-Min or "The Feather" (Assiniboin chief, Rocky Mountain House). Montreal Museum of Fine Arts 47.992; crIV-223.

Fig. 110. Buffaloes at Sunset. National Gallery of Canada 6919; crIV-243.

Fig. 111. Jasper House. Stark pwc25; crIV-250.

Fig. 114. Rocky Mountain goat. Stark wop18; crIV-262.

Fig. 112. Pack horses, in the mountains. rom946.15.133; crIV-253.

Fig. 113. Bighorn Rocky Mountain ram. Stark wwc98A; crIV-256.

Mount St Helens with smoke from
the crater hovering in a peculiar form
over the top of the mountain

Plate XLI. Mount St. Helens, with smoke cone. Stark WOP10; CRIV-461.

Fig. 115. Athabasca River in the mountains. ROM946.15.238; CRIV-264.

219

Fig. 116. The Committee's Punch Bowl, Rocky Mountains. ROM946.15.239; CRIV-269.

Fig. 117. Mountain peaks as seen from Boat Encampment, Columbia River. ROM946.15.236; CRIV-277.

220

Fig. 118. A photograph of the view sketched by Kane in Fig. 117. Photograph by Mrs. E. Dickey, Revelstoke, B.C.

Fig. 119. The Little Dalles, Columbia River. Stark wwc6; crIV-286.

Fig. 120. Studies among the Kutenai Indians, Columbia River. ROM946.15.202; CRIV-291.

Fig. 121. Columbia River near Grand Rapids. ROM946.15.174; CRIV-290.

Fig. 122. Ask-a-weelish (*left*) and See-pays or "Chief of the Waters" (*right*), Fort Colvile. Stark wwc80; crIV-288, 292.

223

Fig. 123. Catching salmon on the Columbia River. Stark wwc87; crIV-306.

Fig. 124. Indians smoking salmon near the
Columbia River. ROM946.15.206; CRIV-309.

224

The Game of Al-kol-lock Chualpay Indians
Columbia River

Fig. 125. The Chualpays game of Al-kol-lock, Fort Colvile. Stark wwc78; crIV-316.

g. 126. Indians Playing at Alcoloh (Al-kol-lock).
tional Gallery of Canada 60; crIV-321.

Fig. 127. Chualpays scalp dance, Fort Colvile. Stark wwc31; crIV-322.

Fig. 128. Painted faces of Chualpays women dancers, Fort Colvile. Stark wwc72; crIV-324.

Fig. 129. Scalp Dance by Spokane (?) Indians. National Gallery of Canada 103; crIV-329.

Fig. 130. Studies of a Chualpays scalp dance, with a medicine man. Stark wwc63; crIV-327.

Mission Station Spakan River

156.

Fig. 131. Mission station of the Rev. Elkanah Walker and the Rev. Cushing Eells, Tshimakain. Stark wwc69; crIV-336.

99.

Fall on the Pelouse River

Fig. 132. Lower falls, Pelouse River. Stark wwc49; crIV-343.

Fig. 133. A river view near Fort Walla Walla. ROM946.15.186; CRIV-350.

Fort Wallawalla Paul Kane 1846

Fig. 134. Fort Walla Walla. Stark WWC62; CRIV-355.

Pyramid Rock Koos Kooskee River

Fig. 135. Chimney Rocks, Columbia River. Stark wwc65; crIV-358.

230

Fig. 136. Landscape, near Fort Walla Walla (?). rom946.15.173; crIV-357.

65.

Burial Canoes *170*

Plate XLII. Chinook grave, Cowlitz River. Stark wwc29; crIV-475.

Fig. 137. The Whitman Mission, Waiilatpu. ʀᴏᴍ946.15.318; ᴄʀIV-362.

Fig. 138. Mrs. Whitman's fan. ʀᴏᴍ946.15.207; ᴄʀIV-363.

Fig. 139. To-ma-kus, a Cayuse, at the Whitman Mission. Peabody Museum, Harvard University—Bushnell 41-72/393; crIV-365.

Fig. 140. Til-au-kite or "Act of Lightning," a Cayuse, Whitman Mission. Stark wwc59; crIV-367.

Fig. 141. Nez Percé Indian. rom912.1.72; crIV-372.

. 142. Peo-Peo-mox-mox (or "The Yellow Serpent"; a Walla Walla chief).
M912.1.69; crIV-376.

Fig. 143. Son of Peo-Peo-mox-mox, a Walla Walla. rom946.15.196; crIV-377.

Fig. 144. Landslip above the Cascades, Columbia River. Stark wwc30; crIV-382.

234

Fig. 145. The Cascades, Columbia River. Stark wop9; crIV-387.

Fig. 146. Below the Cascades, Columbia River, with Indian fishing. Stark wwc92; crIV-388.

Fig. 147. Tomaquin, Cascade chief, Columbia River. ROM946.15.195; crIV-391.

Fig. 148. Mancemuckt, chief of the Skinpah, Columbia River. Stark wwc102-I; crIV-393.

Fig. 149. A Cascade Indian, Columbia River. Stark wwc55; crIV-396.

Plate XLIII. Northwest canoes. ROM946.15.231; CRIV-531.

Medicine Masks   North West Coast   B.C.

Paul Kane
1847

Plate XLIV. Medicine masks of the northwest coast tribes. Stark wwc27; crIV-538.

COURTESY ROYAL ONTARIO MUSEUM, TORONTO

Fig. 150. Fort Vancouver. ROM946.15.211; crIV-397.

COURTESY STARK FOUNDATION, ORANGE, TEXAS

Fig. 151. Fort Vancouver, west end. Stark WOP17; crIV-400.

Fig. 154. Old Cox, a Sandwich Islander of the Hudson's Bay Company. ROM946.15.271; CRIV-416.

Fig. 152. A handbill for a theatrical performance at Fort Vancouver, a souvenir kept by Kane. Collection of Mrs. Paul Kane III.

Fig. 153. Man with saddle horse, near Fort Vancouver. ROM946.15.251; CRIV-408.

Fig. 155. Well in the woods, near Fort Vancouver.
Stark wop8; crIV-409.

Fig. 156. Indian (girl?) on a race course near Fort Vancouver. Stark wwc35; crIV-420.

Fig. 157. Bundle of rushes used for making mats. ROM946.15.321; CRIV-427.

Fig. 158. Interior of a Chinook lodge, Fort Vancouver. Stark WWC41; CRIV-424.

Fig. 159. A Klikitat lodge, Fort Vancouver. ROM946.15.221; CrIV-428.

Chinook Lodge - Mount Hood in the distance

Fig. 160. A Chinook travelling lodge, with a view of Mount Hood. Stark WWC101; CrIV-429.

Fig. 161. Oregon City. ROM946.15.164; CRIV-448.

Fig. 162. Falls near Oregon City. ROM946.15.269; CRIV-452.

Claïen Indian woman basket making

181

Plate XLV. Clallam woman weaving basket, and other studies. Stark wwc45; crIV-555.

Fig. 163. Willamette valley at Champoeg. ROM946.15.193; CRIV-455.

243

Fig. 164. Mount St. Helens erupting. ROM912.1.78; CRIV-462.

Fig. 165. Mount St. Helens. Stark WOP21; CRIV-464.

244

Fig. 166. Coffin Rock, lower Columbia River. Stark WWC91; CRIV-470.

Fig. 167. King Comcomly's burial canoe. Stark wwc86; crIV-478.

Fig. 168. Indian graves, Cowlitz River. Stark wwc32; crIV-476.

Fig. 169. Flathead woman, Cowlitz River.
Stark wwc102G; crIV-489.

Fig. 170. A child having its head flattened.
Stark wwc10; crIV-490.

Chinook child undergoing process
of flattening the head. 191

Fig. 171. Flathead Woman and Child, Caw-wacham. Montreal Museum of Fine Arts 47.991 crIV-492.

Fig. 172. Prairie de Bute. Stark wwc64; crIV-494.

248

Fig. 173. Nisqually, a village on Puget Sound. Stark wwc47; crIV-498.

Fig. 174. Indian lodge at Nisqually.
ROM946.15.322; crIV-499.

Fig. 175. Lock-hi-num, a chief of Whidbey Island.
Stark wwc56; crIV-508.

249

Fig. 176. Indian village of Toanichum, Whidbey Island. Stark wwc3; crIV-511.

Fig. 177. Battle between Clallam and Makah at I-eh-nus, Strait of Juan de Fuca. Stark wwc54; crIV-515.

Fig. 178. Chaw-u-wit, daughter of the chief at Suck, Strait of Juan de Fuca. Stark wwc8; crIV-518.

Fig. 180. A Battle of I-eh-nus. rom912.1.84; crIV-517.

Fig. 179. Graves at I-eh-nus, Strait of Juan de Fuca. Stark wwc89; crIV-516.

Fig. 181. Shawstun, Snohomish chief from Puget Sound.
Stark wwc37; crIV-512.

Fig. 182. Salmon trap at Suck.
Stark wwc26; crIV-520.

Salmon Trap. Du Fuca Straits 1847

Paul Kane

252

Crossing the Straits of de Fuca
Paul Kane 1847

Fig. 183. Crossing the Strait of Juan de Fuca in a storm. Stark wwc70; crIV-524.

Fig. 184. An Indian village, Esquimalt. Stark wwc66; crIV-526.

Paul Kane 1846 *The Return of a War Party - Pacific Coast*

Fig. 185. War party, Juan de Fuca. Stark wwc90; crIV-527.

Travelling Lodges   Paul Kane   1846

Plate XLVI. Clallam travelling lodges. Stark wwc4; crIV-560.

Fig. 186. An Indian village, Esquimalt, with canoes returning from gathering camas. Stark wwc58; crIV-529.

Fig. 187. Northwest canoes. Stark wwc71A; crIV-533.

Fig. 188. Fort Victoria, with an Indian village. ROM946.15.212; CRIV-535.

Fig. 189. Fort Victoria. Stark wwc104; CRIV-536.

Fig. 190. Medicine man with mask, from Strait of Juan de Fuca. Stark WOP7; CRIV-539.

Fig. 191. Medicine Mask Dance. ʀᴏᴍ912.1.92; ᴄʀIV-541.

Fig. 192. Interior of a Winter Lodge of the Clallams. National Gallery of Canada 6923; CRIV-550.

Fig. 194. Interior of a Clallam lodge, Vancouver Island. Stark wwc81; crIV-545.

Fig. 193. Indian medicine rattle, northwest coast. Stark wwc99A; crIV-544.

Fig. 195. Carved house post, Fort Victoria (?). rom946.15.248; crIV-551.

Plate XLVII. Culchillum, a Cowichan, wearing a medicine cap, Fort Victoria. Stark wwc102H; crIV-570.

Plate XLVIII. A Ucaltas man and a Nisqually girl. Stark wwc83; crIV-582, 502.

Fig. 196. Indian woman weaving a blanket, Fort Victoria. Stark wwc73; crIV-552.

Fig. 197. Woman spinning yarn, Fort Victoria. Stark wwc97; crIV-553.

Fig. 198. Studies of figures inside a lodge, Fort Victoria. ROM946.15.227; CRIV-557.

Fig. 199. Game of lehallum, Vancouver Island. Stark WWC25; CRIV-564.

Fig. 200. Saw-se-a (a Cowichan chief, Strait of Georgia). ROM912.1.94; crIV-569.

Fig. 201. A Nootka chief, northern Vancouver Island. Stark wwc16; crIV-575.

Fig. 202. Ma-cheek-e-a-wis, a Chimmesyan Indian. Stark wop6; crIV-584.

Fig. 203. A Babbine Chief. ROM912.1.87; CrIV-587.

Fig. 204. A Babine woman. Stark woᴘ12; cʀIV-585.

Fig. 205. Babine pipe-stem. Stark wwc1; cʀIV-589.

PART FOUR   *A Catalogue Raisonné*

Introduction

Paul Kane's works divide themselves logically into several groups. These are made up of works he painted before going to Europe; sketches and canvases from the years of his study in Europe, 1841–43; works relating to his Indian travels in the Great Lakes region during 1845; those relating to his travels between Lake Superior and the Pacific during 1846–48; and works completed in the Toronto area, both portraits and landscapes, after 1845. The *catalogue raisonné* has therefore been divided into the following sections:

I: Works done before 1841.
II: Works done in Europe 1841–43.
III: Portraits and landscapes of the Great Lakes region, 1845.
IV: Portraits and landscapes of the west, 1846–48.
V: Portraits and landscapes, done chiefly in the Toronto region, following 1845.

Within each of these sections works are grouped in various ways to provide a pattern for the presentation. In sections III and IV, for instance, there are subordinate headings for stages of the western travels; the divisions they introduce may originate in his visits at Hudson's Bay Company posts, in routes of travel from post to post, etc. These divisions are often broken into sub-groups for such subject-matter as landscape, portraits of Indians from particular tribes, ceremonials, and hunting scenes, the works within a sub-group relating to the stage of the journey indicated by the heading for the division. Within any group are listed canvases, sketches on which they were based, and sketches of related subjects. For example, all sketches and canvases of the buffalo hunt south of Fort Garry have been placed in one sub-group; studies and canvases for the encampment of the Métis buffalo hunters in another. Sub-groups usually have a preliminary paragraph intended to provide identification or background information for them.

Within each item in the *catalogue*, whether it is sketch or canvas, are included: (1) title, if any has been assigned previously to the picture (in capital and lower-case letters), or a phrase (in lower-case letters) briefly identifying the subject-matter; (2) explanatory notes if required; (3) reference to a list or lists in which the work may have been noted at some time (i.e. Kane's own logs, an exhibition list, a collector's list); (4) the medium in which the work was done; (5) its over-all size; (6) plate or figure number if it is illustrated in this book; (7) the collection in which it is now held. References to *Wanderings of an Artist* give page numbers of the text reprinted here; they also indicate when an item has appeared as an illustration in the 1859 edition.

As has been noted in the preliminary pages of this book, Kane's spelling of names of Indians and their tribes varies considerably. In this *catalogue raisonné* names of individual Indians are normally given in the spelling used by Kane in the printed version of *Wanderings of an Artist*; alternative spelling found in his manuscripts or elsewhere appears in a following parenthesis. Names of tribes and geographical names are in modern style, but where Kane's spelling may be significant it is provided.

The titles by which Kane's Indian canvases have been known have varied through the years. The earliest complete listing of his much publicized cycle of one hundred Indian works is that in the hand of the Honourable George W. Allan, made when they were turned over to him by Kane in 1856 (see Appendix 5). The title of 1856 has been assigned here to the appropriate works. The majority of these canvases are, however, now in the Royal Ontario Museum collections, and have been entered in several previously published lists; the first was a catalogue published about 1903 when the canvases were the property of E. B. Osler, and another list appeared in the Radisson Society edition of *Wanderings* (1925; reprinted 1968). Later titles by which these canvases are known follow the original titles, within brackets. For other collections, the titles given are those by which the owner now knows the paintings.

Abbreviations

A4	Stark Foundation Collection, Paul Kane, Artifact no. 4
AG	Allan Gift: Sketches given by the Allan family to Mrs. Paul Kane following the artist's death in 1871 (see Appendix 7)
Bushnell	David I. Bushnell Collection, Peabody Museum, Harvard University
Coe	Coe Collection, Yale University
CR	*Catalogue raisonné*
Glenbow	Glenbow–Alberta Institute, Calgary
GS	Paintings delivered by Kane to Sir George Simpson (see Appendix 4)
GWA	Paintings delivered by Kane to the Honourable George W. Allan, 1856 (see Appendix 5)
KLL	Kane's landscape log kept on his 1846–48 travels, now in the Stark Foundation (see Appendix 1)
KPL	Kane's portrait log kept on his 1846–48 travels, now in the Stark Foundation (see Appendix 2)

LP   Paintings delivered by Kane to the Parliament of Canada, 1855 (see Appendix 6) for its Library

NGC   National Gallery of Canada collections, Ottawa

PAC   Public Archives of Canada, Ottawa

ROM   Royal Ontario Museum (Ethnology Department) collections, Toronto

Stark   Nelda C. and H. J. Lutcher Stark Foundation collections, Orange, Texas

TCH   *Catalogue of Sketches of Indians, and Indian Chiefs, Landscapes, Dances, Costumes, &c, &c by Paul Kane;* for the exhibition at the Toronto City Hall, 1848 (see Appendix 3)

*   An asterisk indicates the item has not been seen by the present author.

Section I

Paintings and sketches executed by Kane before he went to Europe in 1841

LANDSCAPES

Kane exhibited nine paintings, principally copies, at the exhibition in Toronto of the Society of Artists and Amateurs, 1834. None has been traced. The following list has been extracted from the printed catalogue, and follows its wording.

I-1   Harlech Castle and distant view of Snowdon, North Wales, copy. SAAT1834, no. 112.*

I-2   Lake George, after (Thomas) Drury. SAAT1834, no. 113.*

I-3   Residence of John Gamble, Esq., Mimico Creek. SAAT1834, no. 116.* There is a remote possibility that this landscape is the one listed as V-14.

I-4   Elm Park, from a print. SAAT1834, no. 121.*

I-5   View of Niagara Falls, from a print. SAAT1834, no. 140.*

I-6   Falls of Tivoli, from a print. SAAT1834, no. 151.*

I-7   A Mameluke, from a print. SAAT1834, no. 152.*

I-8   Hardraw Force, from a print. SAAT1834, no. 173.*

I-9   Landscape, from a print. SAAT1834, no. 174.*

PORTRAITS

The following portraits have been attributed to Kane. Not all have been located and examined by the author.

I-10   Young girl (naïve style). Possibly *c.* 1830. Oil on canvas. 2'10" x 2'7". (Colln Mrs. Paul Kane III)

I-11   Michael Peter Empey. The subject, who was a friend of Kane, was born *c.* 1811 and lived at Bradford, Ont. The painting must date from the early 1830s. Oil on paper mounted on wooden panel. 8" x 7¼". (Colln Mrs. S. Trivett)

I-12   W. S. Conger. For a biography of the subject see G. W. Craw, *The Peterborough Story* (Peterborough 1967). Illustrated in E. C. Guillet's *The Valley of the Trent* (Toronto 1957), Plate 103. Painted *c.* 1834. Oil on canvas. 12" x 10". (Colln Peterborough Centennial Museum) *

I-13   Mrs. W. S. Conger. Painted *c.* 1834. Oil on canvas. 12" x 9⅞". Fig. 2. (Colln S. E. Weir) *

I-14   F. S. Clench (Kane's father-in-law). Illustrated in Guillet, *The Valley of the Trent*, Plate 102. Possibly *c.* 1836. Oil on canvas. (Private colln) *

I-15   Mrs. F. S. Clench (Kane's mother-in-law). Illustrated in Guillet, *The Valley of the Trent*, Plate 101. Possibly *c.* 1836. Oil on canvas. (Private colln)*

I-16   William Weller. Illustrated in Guillet, *The Valley of the Trent*, Plate 99. Oil on canvas. (Private colln) *

I-17   Mercy (Willcox) Weller. Illustrated in Guillet, *The Valley of the Trent*, Plate 100. Oil on canvas. (Private colln) *

I-18   The Hon. Henry Ruttan (1791–1871). For a biography of the subject see *Dictionary of Canadian Biography*, vol. X. Illustrated in Guillet, *The Valley of the Trent*, Plate 104. Oil on canvas. (Private colln) *

I-19   Henry Richard Norton. Norton was a partner of W. S. Conger (see I-12), and operated a cabinet-making shop in Cobourg, Ont. See also K. E. Kidd, "Notes on scattered works of Paul Kane," in the 1962 *Annual* of the Art and Archaeology Division, Royal Ontario Museum, Toronto. Oil on wooden panel. 1'11½" x 1'7". (ROML965.1.1)

In this same article Kidd attributes a portrait of Charles Fothergill, now in the collection of the ROM, to Kane. Information which has come to light subsequently proves that this portrait is the work of George S. Gilbert.

I-20   Brayley Norton (wife of H. R. Norton). See Kidd, 1962 *Annual*, Art and Archaeology Division, ROM. Oil on wooden panel. 1'11½" x 1'7". Plate II. (ROML965.1.2) This portrait, on loan to the Sigmund Samuel Gallery of Canadiana of the ROM through the courtesy of Mr. E. C. Guillet, is reproduced with his kind approval.

I-21   The Hon. Zaccheus Burnham (1777–1857). Burnham, born at Dumbarton, N.J., lived in Cobourg and its district. He was a militia captain in charge of shipping on Lake Ontario, 1812, a member of both the Legislative Assembly and the Legislative Council, and treasurer of the Newcastle District. Oil on canvas. 2'6¼" x 2'2¼". (Colln N. Nickels) *

I-22   George Hetherington. Exhibited at the Art Gallery of Toronto in 1934, and then the property of T. S. Lawson.*

I-23   Mrs. Perry (sister of Mrs. W. S. Conger). Referred to in the notes on Kane made by F. S. Challener, now in the Art Gallery of Ontario.*

I-24 Eliza (Clench) Armour, younger sister of Harriet (Clench) Kane. Born in Cobourg 1831. Painted *c.* 1836. Oil on canvas. (Oval) 2′ x 1′8″. Fig. 3. (Colln Mrs. R. J. Shirley)

I-25 The riverboat *Norma* with captain (or owner). This ship was built at Louisville, Ky., 1839, 188 44/95 tons, and then transferred to New Orleans. The figure is probably that of George Washington Haygood of New Orleans, at various times both master and part owner. Probably painted at New Orleans 1839–41. Oil on canvas. 2′10½″ x 1′9½″. Fig. 4. (Stark op26)

I-26 Queen Victoria. Full length portrait copied from an engraving of a portrait by H. B. Chalon. Painted 1840–41. Not located; referred to in the *Commercial Register* (Mobile, Alabama), March 20, 1841.* (See Appendix 11.)

I-27 President Harrison. Portrait, probably half length. Painted 1840–41. Not located. Referred to in the *Commercial Register* (Mobile, Alabama), March 20, 1841.* (See Appendix 11.)

Section II

Paintings and sketches executed in Europe 1841–1843

Kane regretted having lost some of the notes and sketches completed in Italy, particularly sketchbooks of the work done in Rome and Naples. These appear to have been lost before his return to Canada in 1845. Section II contains some paintings which he is known to have executed but which have since disappeared.

ROMAN PERIOD

Kane was in Rome from September 17, 1841, to February 17, 1842, when he left for Naples. He seems to have spent much of his time in the Borghese Gallery copying paintings. The following are works known to have been copied or sketched in Rome.

II-1 A Madonna, by Murillo (1617–1682). The title appears on a shipping list but the work has not been located. Owned by Kane at his death, 1871.*

II-2 A Mary Magdalene, by Andrea del Sarto (1486–1531). The title appears on a shipping list but the work has not been located.*

II-3 A head, by Raphael (1483–1520). There are two Raphael heads in the Borghese Gallery. The title appears on a shipping list but the work has not been located.*

II-4 A head, by J. Palma Il Vecchio (1480–1528). There is such a portrait in the Borghese Gallery. The title appears on a shipping list but the work has not been located.*

II-5 A portrait of Gregory XV, by Giovanni Busato (1806–1886). The head has been taken as a detail from a celebrated picture of the time. Oil on canvas. (Colln Mrs. Paul Kane III)

II-6 A Roman sketchbook. This book has 23 pages with pencil sketches of Roman views including the Claudian Aquaduct and tombs of the emperors, and 3 pages with sepia water-colour figure studies. 5½″ x 4″. Figs. 5, 6. (Colln Mrs. T. M. Willet)

FLORENTINE PERIOD

Kane was in Florence from May 27 to August 12, 1842, when he left for Venice. He made application on June 14 to paint in the Pitti Palace. He seems to have worked chiefly among the self-portraits now in the Uffizi Collection.

II-7 Pope Julius II, by Raphael. Copy of a portrait now in the Uffizi Collection. Oil on canvas. (Colln Mrs. R. W. Thurston)

II-8 A Florentine sketchbook. In this book are 28 pencil sketches, including landscapes, architectural subjects, Ariosto's chair, and studies of paintings in the Uffizi including the self-portraits of C. Dolci and F. Lippi, and the portrait of Daniel Barbaro by Veronese. 4″ x 5½″. (Colln Mrs. Paul Kane III)

II-9 Self-portrait, by Peter Paul Rubens (1577–1640), from the painting in the Uffizi. Originally part of sketchbook, II-8. Pencil. 5½″ x 4″. Fig. 7. (Private colln)

II-10 Self-portrait, by Rembrandt (1609–1669). Copy of a portrait in the Uffizi Collection. The title appears on a shipping list but the work has not been located. Owned by Kane at his death, 1871.*

II-11 Portrait, by Leonardo da Vinci (1452–1519). Copy of a portrait, probably in the Uffizi. The title appears on a shipping list but the work has not been located. Owned by Kane at his death, 1871.*

FLORENTINE AND VENETIAN PERIODS

Kane reached Venice from Florence about August 15, 1842, and remained until September 28, 1842, when he left for France and England via Milan. He received a permit to sketch in the Accademia, Venice, on September 15, 1842.

II-12 A section of a sketchbook. The Italian section comprises 15 sketches in pencil completed in Florence and Venice. (The balance of the book includes studies of Indians made on Georgian Bay, which are entered in crIII.) Italian studies include those of the marble statue of St. George by Donatello from Or San Michele, Florence, architectural details, chairs, a bridge over a Venetian canal, a gondola, and a general view of Venice. 5¾″ x 8¾″. (ROM946.15.3 to ROM946.15.17)

MISCELLANEOUS PAINTINGS

II-13 Italian youth. Oil on paper. (Colln Mrs. R. W. Thurston)

II-14 Pilgrims at a Shrine. Oil on canvas. (Colln M. O'Brien, on loan to ROM)

II-15 "Una Donna alla Fontana (Girl at Fountain)." Sketch, probably a copy of a painting in Rome or Florence. The title appears on a shipping list but the work has not been located.*

II-16 "Piperani." Sketch, probably a copy of a painting in Rome or Florence. The title appears on a shipping list but the work has not been located.*

II-17 "Donna di Frescati." Sketch, probably a copy of a painting in Rome or Florence. The title appears on a shipping list but the work has not been located.*

II-18 "Donna di Mola de Gaeta." Sketch, probably a copy of a painting in Rome or Florence. The title appears on a shipping list but the work has not been located.*

II-19 Martyrdom of St. John the Baptist. Original not located; owned by Kane at his death in 1871.*

Section III

Paintings, sketches and drawings of Indians and landscapes relating to the 1845 expedition to Georgian Bay, Lakes Huron and Michigan, and adjoining regions

Kane left Toronto on June 17, 1845. He travelled to the Saugeen Indian reservation on Lake Huron where he made his first Indian sketches. From there he passed through the Thirty Thousand Islands of Georgian Bay to Manitoulin Island, Sault Ste Marie and Mackinac Island at the entrance to Lake Michigan. Proceeding down Lake Michigan to Green Bay, he visited the Lake Winnebago and Fox River regions in Wisconsin. He executed no sketches on his return journey to Toronto that autumn. Sketches made on the trip and paintings based on them have been arranged geographically following the route of his travels.

No log of Kane's 1845 sketches has been located, making identification of several particularly difficult. It seems fairly certain that a log for some of these sketches once existed. Identification has been based principally on the catalogue of the 1848 exhibition in the Toronto City Hall, in which many were shown, on notes made either by a member of the George W. Allan family or possibly by Kane's grandson, and on references to sketches in *Wanderings*. Identification of a number is tentative; fortunately most of these are of minor importance.

Kane's tribal designations have been followed. Chippewa and Ojibwa are actually synonomous terms which apply to one large tribal group. This can be subdivided into the Ojibwa of Lake Superior, the Missisauga of Manitoulin Island and the mainland around the Mississaga River, the Ottawa of Georgian Bay and the Potawatomi of Michigan. Missisauga are not mentioned in Kane's writings.

SAUGEEN

Kane remained at the Saugeen Indian village from June 22 to June 30. It is situated near Chief's Point on Lake Huron towards the base of the Bruce Peninsula. The Saugeen were settled in two bands, one at the mouth of the Saugeen River and the other on Sydenham Bay. They moved to these sites after surrendering their territories by treaty to the British government in 1836. Kane refers to them as "Saugeens," "Saguenays," and "Ojibwas."

III-1 Ojibwa (Ojibbeway) Chief (?). It has been suggested that this is Maticwaub or "The Bow," principal Saugeen chief, whom Kane mentions sketching (*Wanderings*, p. 52). No field sketch has been located. No such title or name appears in the list of canvases turned over by Kane to Allan; however GWA 70, designated as a portrait of "Maun-qua-dous," is apparently this canvas. Oil on canvas. 2'3" x 1'8½". (ROM912.1.4)

III-2 Kwa-qua-dah-bon-niva-skung or "Dawn of Day," chief of the "Saguenays" (Saugeen). This is possibly one of three or four lesser chieftains subsidiary to Maticwaub (see III-1). Sketched June 24, 1845. (See III-3.) w.c. 5¾" x 8¾". (ROM946.15.56)

III-3 Kwa-qua-dah-bon-niva-skung or "Dawn of Day." Identification has been based on an inscription, pre-dating Kane's death, on the sketch. (See III-2; see also IV-394.) AG72. Oil on paper. 12⅛" x 9¾". Fig. 14. (Stark EOP9)

III-4 An Ojibwa chief. It has been suggested, without apparent foundation, that this is a portrait of Maskuhnoonjee or "Big Pike" (*Wanderings*, p. 52). The chieftain bears no resemblance to the one in III-5, also identified as Maskuhnoonjee (but note change in spelling). See also III-6 for another sketch identified as of "The Pike." AG90. Oil on paper. 8⅛" x 6⅛". (Stark EOP4)

III-5 Sketch bearing double inscription of Maska-nonga or "Big Fish" and Shewans-u-ne-bin or "Alias 8 Summers." It is evidently a portrait of Maskuhnoonjee or "Big Pike," an Ojibwa: it was so exhibited in 1848 and so listed after Kane's death. (See III-4 and III-6.) TCH2. AG76. Oil on paper. 12⅜" x 9¾". Fig. 15. (Stark EOP19)

III-6 Page of studies. *Top* (left to right): 1/ Indian head in profile; 2/ European wearing beaver hat; 3/ Indian head inscribed Oogemsh-wah-be-zee or "Chief Young Swan"; 4/ Indian head inscribed Mus-Kosh or "Pike" (see III-4 and III-5). *Bottom* (left to right): 1/ overturned canoe; 2/ standing woman holding child; 3/ two standing women holding children. The inscriptions are evidently in Kane's hand. Pencil. 5¾" x 8¾". Fig. 16. (ROM946.15.53)

III-7 A chief's daughter from Lake St. Clair. An early inscription on the sketch, not in Kane's hand, identifies her as an Ojibwa. Kane refers to her (*Wanderings*, pp. 52–53). TCH238. AG6. Oil on paper. 9⅝" x 6⅛". Fig. 17. (Stark EOP5)

III-8 A Woman from Manitooawning (The Daughter of Asabonish). This canvas is obviously based on III-7, a portrait of a chief's daughter from Lake St. Clair, rather than on the girl in III-63, as has been claimed. GWA85. Oil on canvas. 2'1" x 1'10". (ROM912.1.7)

III-8A The Daughter of Asabonish. Replica of III-8. Oil on canvas. (Oval) 1′11½″ x 1′6¼″. (Colln Mr. and Mrs. Jules Loeb)

III-9 Wah-pus (Waugh-bi-see) or "The Rabbit," an Indian chieftain from Owen Sound who was at Saugeen during Kane's visit (*Wanderings*, p. 53). Crude sketches of canoes in margin. Pencil. 4¾″ x 3″. (Stark A4-1)

III-10 Sketches of Wah-pus or "The Rabbit" (three-quarter view), and (on reverse) white woman wearing bonnet. Pencil. 3″ x 4″. (ROM946.15.311)

III-11 Wappoose (Wah-pus or "The Rabbit"). Painting based probably on III-9. GWA76. Oil on canvas. 2′1″ x 1′8″. Fig. 18. (ROM912.1.1)

OWEN SOUND

Kane visited this town both in going to and in returning from Saugeen.

III-12 Indian encampment on Big Bay at Owen Sound. Identified from an early inscription, not in Kane's hand. AG8. Oil on paper. 6¾″ x 11⅛″. Fig. 19. (Stark EOP13)

GEORGIAN BAY

Thirty Thousand Islands

Kane and a companion, Dillon, canoed for two weeks among these islands. Locale of the sketches is not documented, but all evidently relate to the canvas of an Indian village (III-18 and III-19) which Kane says is among the islands.

III-13 Indian encampment with four bark wigwams and canoe. Pencil. 5¾″ x 8¾″. (ROM946.15.37)

III-14 Indian encampment of bark wigwams. Pencil. 5¾″ x 8¾″. (ROM946.15.39)

III-15 Indian encampment with ten bark wigwams and eight canoes in foreground. Pencil. 5¾″ x 8¾″. (ROM946.15.40)

III-16 Indian encampment with two bark wigwams. Pencil. 5¾″ x 8¾″. (ROM946.15.43)

III-17 Indian encampment with three bark wigwams and tent (possibly that of Kane). w.c. 5¾″ x 8¾″. (ROM946.15.32)

III-18 A Sketch on Lake Huron (Encampment among the Islands of Lake Huron). No sketch of this village has been located and the canvas is based presumably on sketches III-13 to III-17. (*Wanderings*, p. 53; woodcut, Fig. 1.) GWA42. Oil on canvas. 1′6″ x 2′5″. (ROM912.1.8)

III-19 An Indian Encampment on Lake Huron. Replica of III-18. Oil on canvas. 1′7″ x 2′5″. Fig. 20. (Art Gallery of Ontario 2121)

GEORGIAN BAY REGION

Conical Ojibwa wigwams

Conical wigwams of poles covered with birch bark appear in a number of sketches such as III-12 to III-19. The following isolated sketches cannot

be assigned to any particular locale but are presumably from the Georgian Bay region.

III-20 Wigwam, evidently covered with matting. Sketch has inscription, not in Kane's hand, reading "Indian wigwam on Lake Ontario"; it is more probably from Georgian Bay. AG35. Oil on paper. 9⅝″ x 11⅝″. (Stark EOP15)

III-21 Wigwam, evidently covered with matting and birch bark. Bears an inscription, not in Kane's hand, reading "Wigwam, Lake Huron." TCH43. AG42. Oil on paper. 9¾″ x 12⅛″. (Stark EOP32)

Indian life

III-22 Page of studies: Indian head with feather in hair; two Indians grinding corn in mortar (see *Wanderings*, p. 53); fishing net; dog; tripod of oars. Pencil. 5¾″ x 8⅞″. (ROM946.15.1)

III-23 Page of studies, principally of Indians reclining and of canoes. Pencil. 5¾″ x 8¾″. (ROM946.15.2)

III-24 Indian Bivouac. Painting of romantic character incorporating items from III-22 and III-23 including tripod of paddles, mortar, dog, reclining figure and canoes, and introducing a gun as mentioned by Kane (*Wanderings*, p. 53). Oil on canvas. 2′2⅞″ x 3′2⅛″. Fig. 21. (PAC Kane I-1)

See also III-128

FRENCH RIVER

Although his narrative does not mention the French River, Kane presumably visited it while canoeing through the Thirty Thousand Islands.

III-25 French River rapids. A party of military men or fur traders halt along the river. KLL7. TCH50. AG14. Oil on paper. 8⅛″ x 13½″. Plate III. (Stark POP22)

III-26 French River Rapids. Painting based on III-25. GWA19. Oil on canvas. 1′8″ x 2′5″. Fig. 22. (ROM912.1.2)

SPIDER ISLANDS

Kane reports the breaking of a sudden thunderstorm when he was approaching Manitowaning Bay, Manitoulin Island, from the northeast. He went ashore on an island where he found a single lodge and an Indian woman with two children (*Wanderings*, p. 53). The following works cannot all be assigned with certainty to Spider Islands but were evidently sketched either there or nearby.

III-27 Tent pitched beneath pine tree on island. Pencil. 5¾″ x 8¾″. (ROM946.15.46)

III-28 Ojibwa Camp (Ojibwa Camp on Spider Islands). Painting based on III-27 but substituting wigwam for tent. GWA2. Oil on canvas. 1′3¾″ x 1′7″. Plate IV. (ROM912.1.3)

III-29 Conical wigwam beneath trees on island. By report the locale is Spider Islands. Pencil. 5¾″ x 8¾″. (ROM946.15.47)

III-30 Ojibwa Camp. Painting based on III-29. Oil on canvas. 1′5½″ x 2′4½″. (Colln Mrs. T. M. Willet)

III-31 Ojibwa camp, Spider Islands. Bushnell identified this sketch without stating reasons (see D. I. Bushnell, *Sketches by Paul Kane in the Indian Country*, Smithsonian Institution 1940, pp. 4–5). Oil on paper. 8½″ x 14″. (Bushnell 41-72/391)

III-32 Shoreline and islands, probably either Spider Islands or Thirty Thousand Islands. Pencil. 5¾″ x 8¾″. (ROM946.15.48)

III-33 Small rocky islands and wigwam, probably either Spider Islands or Thirty Thousand Islands. Pencil. 5¾″ x 8¾″. (ROM946.15.50)

III-34 Small rocky islands, probably either Spider Islands or Thirty Thousand Islands. Pencil. 5¾″ x 8¾″. (ROM946.15.49)

III-35 Indian standing on rocky headland. Georgian Bay region. Pencil. 5¾″ x 8¾″. (ROM946.15.52)

III-36 Page of sketches. *Upper:* rocky shoreline, designated as "Rock 1." *Centre:* rocky islands. *Bottom:* Indian grave house of Ojibwa type on shoreline. The landscape is that of the Georgian Bay region, distant village in lower frame is Manitowaning. Pencil. 5¾″ x 8¾″. Fig. 23. (ROM946.15.51)

III-37 Two low-lying islands. Pencil. 3″ x 4¾″. (Stark A4-2)

MANITOULIN ISLAND

Manitowaning

Manitowaning (spelled "Manetouawning" by Kane), an Indian village situated on Manitowaning Bay towards the western end of Manitoulin Island, was visited by Kane during July 1845 (*Wanderings*, p. 54). At this time Indians of several tribes had gathered at Manitowaning to receive presents (*Wanderings*, p. 55). Settlement of Manitoulin Island by the Indians began in 1836; by 1844 the population on the whole island, chiefly Ottawa and Chippewa, numbered some 700. Distribution of presents by the British government began in 1836; it was discontinued in 1860.

TOPOGRAPHY

III-38 Manitowaning as seen from across Manitowaning Bay. Pencil. 5¾″ x 8¾″. (ROM946.15.45)

III-39 View of Manitowaning with Indian wigwams during the 1845 assembly for the receipt of presents. Pencil. 8¼″ x 1′2″. Fig. 24. (Colln David Mitchell Gallery)

III-40 View of Manitowaning with Indian wigwams and groups of Indians during the assembly of tribes. Pencil. 8¼″ x 1′2″. (Colln David Mitchell Gallery)

III-41 View of bands arranged for receipt of presents. Pencil. 5¾″ x 8¾″. Fig. 25. (ROM946.15.30)

OJIBWA

Kane took the assembly of tribes for receipt of presents as an opportunity to sketch Indian chiefs from the whole region. The MS of *Wanderings*

before revision for publication indicates that, in addition to the individuals whom he mentions as having sketched, there were "many other chiefs of lesser note, of most of whom I made sketches." Evidently among these were a number of Ojibwa chieftains from Lake Superior. The following sketches are apparently of Ojibwa at Manitowaning.

III-42 Sigennok or "The Blackbird," head chief. He was paid by the British government as an "interpreter" (*Wanderings*, pp. 54, 55). (See III-58.) Presumably this is the same individual as "As,si,ke,nack (The Blackbird)" described by Anna Jameson as a remarkable man and the most celebrated orator of his nation when she met him in 1838. She quotes his translation of the governor's address at Manitowaning during the treaty ceremony in that year. (See Mrs. Anna Jameson, *Sketches in Canada and Rambles among the Red Men*, London 1852, part II, pp. 276, 278–82.) TCH1. AG82. Oil on paper. 9¾″ x 6¼″. (Stark EOP14)

III-43 Page of portrait studies. *Left:* profile head inscribed "Now-qua-ke-glick, Noon day." *Centre:* boy, head and shoulders, inscribed "Sig-in-nock-ence" (son of Sigennok, III-42). *Right:* head in profile, unidentified. Pencil. 5¾″ x 8¾″. (ROM946.15.44)

III-44 Shawwanossoway or "One with his Face towards the West." Kane points out that he was a great medicine man (*Wanderings*, pp. 55–56). TCH16. Oil on paper. 12¼″ x 9⅝″. Fig. 26. (Stark EOP2)

III-45 Shah-wah-nas-ha-wa (Shaw-wan-osso-way). Painting based on sketch III-44. GWA99. Oil on canvas. 2′1″ x 1′8″. (ROM912.1.6)

III-46 Ojibwa from Lake Superior. Probably sketched at Manitowaning. TCH5. AG59. Oil on paper. 11½″ x 9¼″. (Stark EOP23)

III-47 Ojibwa Indian boy from Lake Superior. Probably sketched at Manitowaning. TCH6. AG10. Oil on paper. 6¾″ x 5⅝″. (Stark EOP3)

III-48 She-bah-ke-zhick or "Hole in the Sky," an Ojibwa chief from Lake Superior (Fort William?). Probably sketched at Manitowaning. (See also IV-45, 47.) TCH3. Oil on paper. 11⅜″ x 9¼″. (Stark EOP33)

III-49 Indian from Michipicoten. Probably an Ojibwa, sketched at Manitowaning. TCH10. AG78. Oil on paper. 11″ x 6½″. (Stark EOP18)

III-50 Indian from Michipicoten. Probably an Ojibwa, sketched at Manitowaning. TCH9. Oil on paper. 12¼″ x 9¾″. Fig. 27. (Stark EOP6)

III-51 Saw-gun. Probably an Ojibwa, sketched at Manitowaning. TCH7. Oil on paper. *c.* 5″ x 5″. (Colln Mrs. T. M. Willet)

See also IV-1, 2.

OTTAWA

Five or six wandering families of the Ottawa tribe, originally from Lake Michigan, lived on Manitoulin Island in 1835. Others who had been living on lands in the United States arrived shortly after, and evidently by 1844 a sizeable number of Ottawa Indians were among the 700 residents of the island.

III-52 Muck-koze or "Young Bear," chief of the Ottawa of Manitoulin Island. His Anglicized name is sometimes given as "Black Bear." (See IV-133.) TCH13. AG87. Oil on paper. 12⅜″ x 9⅝″. Fig. 28. (Stark EOP24)

III-53 Awbonwaishkum, Ottawa chief from Manitowaning. (*Wanderings*, p. 54; woodcut, Fig. 2.) TCH12. AG45. Oil on paper. 9¾″ x 7¾″. Fig. 29. (Stark EOP12)

III-54 Awbonwaishkum. Painting based on III-53. Oil on canvas. (Over-all) 2′1″ x 1′8″; (oval) 2′ x 1′6½″. (ROM912.1.5)

III-55 Stone pipe carved by Awbonwaishkum. Sketch of a pipe now in the ROM collections. It has been stated, without supporting evidence, that this pipe comes from Lake Superior. (*Wanderings*, p. 54; woodcut, Fig. 3). Oil on paper. 7¼″ x 12¼″. Fig. 30. (Stark EOP21)

WYANDOT

A group of Huron Indians known as Wyandot moved about 1750 to the Ohio valley and there exerted considerable influence. They were always pro-British in their dealings.

III-56 Captain George Ironsides or "Walk on the Water." Kane states that he was a descendant of Tecumseh, a Shawnee chief from the Ohio River valley killed by the Americans in a bloody battle on the Thames River in Upper Canada (Ontario), 1812. Ironsides arrived in Manitowaning during Kane's visit to take over as Indian agent for the British (*Wanderings*, p. 57). Oil on paper. 11⅝″ x 9⅜″. Fig. 31. (Stark EOP16)

NO TRIBAL DESIGNATION

The following sketches of Indians, presumably either Ojibwa or Ottawa, were made at Manitowaning.

III-57 Sha-nu-oh-ke-zhick or "Against the Heavens" (an inscription on the sketch, not in Kane's hand, reads Sha-Neu-Oh-Rigits or "The Heron"), an Indian from Lake Nipissing. TCH8. AG21. Oil on paper. 11¼″ x 9½″. (Stark EOP11)

III-58 Ma-cheek-e-wis. This portrait was formerly identified as that of Sigennok (III-42). The new attribution is based on the TCH catalogue. It should be noted that the man in III-42 wears an Indian chief's medal, appropriate to Sigennok. TCH4 (see IV-584). Oil on paper. 10⅞″ x 8¼″. (Stark EOP1)

III-59 Two Indian portrait heads. *Left:* man wearing chief's medal and identified by totem of a catfish. *Right:* man identified by inscription Cath-a-nish-a-na-bay or "Black Indian." These sketches are tentatively assigned to Manitowaning, but it is possible the subjects were Saulteaux from the Fort Frances area. w.c. 5¾″ x 8¾″. (ROM946.15.19)

III-60 Page of sketches. *Left:* studies of two carved stone pipes. *Right:* full-face portrait head of Indian. Possibly sketched at Manitowaning. Pencil and w.c. 5¾″ x 8¾″. (ROM946.15.36)

See also III-76, 77.

ARTEFACTS

The following sketches have been assigned provisionally to Manitowaning but with little supporting evidence.

III-61 Sketches of drums. *Left:* drums with insignia of pair of facing animals and figure above. *Right:* unfinished sketch of drum. w.c. and pencil. 5¾″ x 8¾″. (ROM946.15.31)

III-62 Sketch of pipe and club. *Upper:* club with bird's head finial on grip. *Lower:* black stone pipe with lead inlay and elaborate feather decoration on stem. Pencil and w.c. 5¾″ x 8¾″. Fig. 32. (ROM946.15.33)

Wikwemikong (Wequimecong)

Wikwemikong is a village six miles from Manitowaning (*Wanderings*, pp. 56–57). The manuscript version of Kane's book states that he remained there for a fortnight and "made sketches of the two principal chiefs of this village and many others." It is possible that some portraits here assigned to Manitowaning may actually have been sketched at Wikwemikong.

OTTAWA

III-63 Asabonish or "The Raccoon," principal Ottawa chief at Wikwemikong, with his daughter (*Wanderings*, p. 57). Burpee states that the daughter is the subject of a canvas, III-8. However III-8 is obviously based on III-7 rather than on the girl's head in this sketch, despite the fact that GWA85 lists the III-8 canvas as "A Woman from Manitooawning." TCH11. AG49. Oil on paper. 12¼″ x 9¾″. Fig. 33. (Stark EOP28)

SAULT STE MARIE

Sault Ste Marie straddles the international boundary on the St. Mary's River. Kane visited the place during August 1845, May 1846 and October 1848. He states in *Wanderings* (p. 57) that in 1845 he remained a few days (the manuscript version states two weeks). He sketched on both the American and the Canadian side of the river. All sketches executed at Sault Ste Marie are included here in the 1845 section; it is possible a few were done during later visits.

Indian village on American shore

III-64 Indian encampment with two domed wigwams, Ojibwa type, covered with matting and birch bark. Pencil. 5¾″ x 8¾″. (ROM946.15.21)

III-65 Sault Ste Marie. Painting based on III-64 but with an added wigwam. GWA30. Oil on canvas. 1′7″ x 2′6″. Plate V. (ROM912.1.9)

III-66 Dome-shaped wigwam with three birch-bark canoes. Pencil and w.c. 5¾″ x 8¾″. (ROM946.15.22)

III-67 Dome-shaped wigwam. Pencil. 5¾″ x 8¾″. (ROM946.15.27)

III-68 Dome-shaped wigwam with camp-fire shelter. Pencil. 5¾″ x 8¾″. (ROM946.15.34)

III-69 Two dome-shaped wigwams with fish net. Pencil. 5¾″ x 8¾″. (ROM946.15.24)

III-70 Dome-shaped wigwam. Pencil. 5¾″ x 8¾″. (ROM946.15.28)

St. Mary's River

III-71 Two Indians in a canoe paddling in rapids. View from the American shore. (*Wanderings*, p. 62.) Pencil. 5¾″ x 8¾″. (ROM946.15.29)

III-72 Two Indians with fish net paddling a canoe in rapids. View from the Canadian shore. Pencil. 5¾″ x 8¾″. (ROM946.15.38)

III-73 Two Indians with fish net paddling a canoe in rapids. View from the American shore. Pencil. 5¾″ x 8¾″. (ROM946.15.26)

III-74 View of the Canadian shore with ruined grist mill and dome-shaped wigwam. The former is the remains of a mill built by Charles Oakes Ermatinger (1780–1853), an Indian trader who was agent of the North West Company at Sault Ste Marie for several years. Through construction of the mill at what became known as Windmill Point he hoped to encourage wheat growing in the area. Pencil. 5¾″ x 8¾″. Fig. 34. (ROM946.15.25)

Portraits

A locale for III-76 and III-77 cannot be ascertained with any certainty. It is probable they were executed at either Manitowaning or Sault Ste Marie.

III-75 Susan Belo, a half-breed girl (*Wanderings*, p. 62). TCH17. AG23. Oil on paper. 12⅛″ x 9¾″. (Stark EOP8)

III-76 Page of studies including five heads, standing figure of a woman and an Indian spear. Pencil. 5¾″ x 8¾″. (ROM946.15.23)

III-77 Two Indian portrait studies. *Left:* young man wearing Indian chief's medal; inscribed C-dah-mak-Skuash. *Right:* girl wearing beads. Pencil and w.c. 5¾″ x 8¾″. Plate VI. (ROM946.15.35)

MACKINAC

Kane visited Mackinac Island, at the entrance to the straits leading from Lake Huron to Lake Michigan, in 1845. As at Manitowaning, he found many Indians assembled here to receive treaty money and presents, this time from the United States government (*Wanderings*, pp. 57–58). He used the opportunity to make several portrait sketches. The published *Wanderings* states that he remained at Mackinac for three weeks; his manuscript version reads six weeks.

Topography

III-78 General view of the fort and Indian village. A fort was built on the island by Capt. Patrick Sinclair of the American army in 1780–81. It was the scene of considerable action between the Americans and British during the war of 1812–14, and **was** captured by the British on July 27, 1812. The fort was responsible for the development of Mackinac Island as a fur-trading centre. Pencil. 7″ x 9¾″. Fig. 35. (ROM946.15.255)

III-79 The natural bridge at Mackinac. Kane points out that this picturesque spot (known today as Arch Rock) was visited by "all strangers" (*Wanderings*, p. 58). Pencil. 5¼″ x 8¾″. (ROM946.15.20)

III-80 The natural bridge at Mackinac. Pencil. 4¾″ x 3″. (Stark A4-13)

III-81 The natural bridge at Mackinac. Pencil. 4¾″ x 3″. (Stark A4-14)

III-82 The natural bridge at Mackinac. TCH45(?). AG1. Oil on paper. 12⅜″ x 9⅞″. Fig. 36. (Stark EOP20)

III-83 The natural bridge at Mackinac. TCH47. AG66. Oil on paper. 11½″ x 9⅝″. (Stark EOP31)

III-84 Rocky headland with wigwams in foreground. This sketch has been described as a "Landscape near Spider Island, Lake Superior" and as "Lake Superior." Colouring and terrain are similar to those in III-82 and III-83. It is almost certainly one of the Mackinac Island sketches exhibited in 1848. TCH46(?). Oil on paper. 12¼″ x 9⅝″. Fig. 37. (Stark EOP29)

III-85 Wooded shoreline, possibly on Mackinac Island. Pencil. 3″ x 4¾″. (Stark A4-12)

III-86 Sketch of rocky pinnacle on Mackinac Island (now known as Sugar Loaf). Pencil. 8¼″ x 1′2″. (Private colln)

III-87 Page of studies, probably made on Mackinac Island. *Left:* seated Indian. *Right:* rocky headland. Pencil. 5¾″ x 8¾″. (ROM946.15.41)

Ojibwa and Ottawa

III-88 Mani-tow-wah-bay (Man-a-to-wa-bay) or "He-Devil," an Ojibwa from Lake Michigan (*Wanderings*, p. 58). TCH239. Oil on paper. 11¾″ x 8⅞″. Plate VII. (Glenbow)

III-89 Now-on-dhu-go, an Ottawa chief from Lake Michigan. TCH15. AG22. Oil on paper. 11⅝″ x 9⅜″. Plate VIII. (Stark EOP27)

III-90 Page of studies. *Left:* birch-bark box decorated with quill work (see IV-88, 469). *Centre:* head of Indian wearing medal around neck. *Right:* rocky headland suggesting Mackinac Island landscape. Pencil. 5¾″ x 8¾″. (ROM946.15.42)

Potawatomi

The following sketches may well be associated with the Mackinac Island material, judging from their position in the sketchbook (an uncertain criterion). Kane also met Potawatomi at Fox River.

III-91 Studies of three Indian heads in profile; labelled "Potawatomi." Pencil. 3″ x 4¾″. (Stark A4-4)

III-92 Studies of three Indian heads in profile and a horse. One head is obviously that of the individual pictured in III-90. Pencil. 3″ x 4¾″. (Stark A4-5)

III-93 Two Indian heads, with silver ornaments, in profile. Pencil. 4¾″ x 3″. (Stark A4-3)

III-94 Page of studies. *Left:* group of standing figures. *Right:* head in profile. Pencil. 3″ x 4¾″. (Stark A4-11)

Wampum belts

III-95 Sketches of four wampum belts evidently associated with the Indians at Mackinac: 1/ belt with inscription dated 1764 (possibly a wampum belt given by Sir William Johnson to the Indians at the Niagara conference of 1764); 2/ belt, undated; 3/ belt with inscription STTIB 1786; 4/ belt with inscription LIEUT COL. R. MC DOUALL COMM. MACKINAC (McDouall was British commander at Fort Mackinac during the war of 1812–14). Pencil. 3″ x 4¾″. Fig. 38. (Stark A4-43)

III-96 Sketches of three wampum belts (a fourth roughed in), evidently associated with the Indians of Mackinac. These are a second version of nos. 1, 2 and 3 in III-95. Pencil. 4½″ x 1′2″. (Private colln)

Studies of Indian life

Locale of the following sketches is uncertain. Association in the sketchbook with other Mackinac Island material seems to indicate that they were done there, but the subjects are typical of the whole general region.

III-97 Page of studies: group of Indians by wigwam, group of five Indians, and a large canoe with nine passengers. Pencil 4¾″ x 3″. (Stark A4-6)

III-98 Page of studies: seated figure, with boat under sail. Pencil. 3″ x 4¾″. (Stark A4-7)

III-99 Shoreline with birch-bark canoe and domed wigwam. Pencil. 3″ x 4¾″. (Stark A4-8)

III-100 Studies of two wigwams and overturned canoe. Pencil. 3″ x 4¾″. (Stark A4-9)

III-101 Studies of two wigwams. Pencil. 3″ x 4¾″. (Stark A4-10)

III-102 Studies of shoreline with domed wigwam, canoe and standing figure. Pencil. 3″ x 4¾″. (Stark A4-15)

III-103 Study of an adult figure and a boy holding bow. Pencil. 4¾″ x 3″. (Stark A4-16)

III-104 Sketch of birch-bark canoe. Pencil. 4¾″ x 3″. (Stark A4-17)

III-105 Bay with low shoreline and domed wigwam in foreground. Pencil. 3″ x 4¾″. (Stark A4-18)

LAKE WINNEBAGO

Kane visited Lake Winnebago during the autumn of 1845 while travelling along the Fox River (in the state of Wisconsin). From Green Bay he accompanied three American government officials on their way to pay treaty moneys to Indians living west of Lake Michigan.

Menominee

Kane sketched two sisters living on the lakeshore (*Wanderings*, p. 58); this is traditionally Winnebago territory, but Kane specifically states in the catalogue of 1848 that the girls were Menominee.

III-106 Iwa-toke or "The Serpent." (See also IV-251.) TCH20. AG86. Oil on paper. 12¼″ x 9⅝″. Fig. 40. (Stark EOP26)

III-107 Ke-wah-ten or "The North Wind." This sketch was exhibited at the Toronto City Hall in 1848 as a portrait of Iwa-toke's sister. It bears a notation, not in Kane's hand, "Menomenee Tribe, Lake Winnebago." It has also been described as a portrait of "Kee-wa-a-tin 'North Wind,' an Indian girl from the Menomenee tribe on Winnipeg River." Unlike Iwa-toke, this girl is decked out with elaborate silver ornaments and ear-rings. (See also III-108.) TCH21. AG61. Oil on paper. 12¼″ x 9½″. Fig. 39. (Stark POP3)

III-108 Portrait of a girl, bearing an inscription, not in Kane's hand, reading "Indian Woman, Fox River, Winnebago." The sketch is so similar in feeling to that of Iwa-toke, III-106, that one would assume that this girl was Iwa-toke's sister rather than the girl in III-107 who has been called Ke-wah-ten. AG50. Oil on paper. 12⅛″ x 9⅞″. (Stark EOP25)

Winnebago(?)

III-109 Wah-bannim (Wah-bo-nim) or "The White Dog." This sketch bears an inscription, not in Kane's hand, reading "Indian from Lake Winnebago." Kane describes Wah-bannim as wearing black paint in mourning for his wife (*Wanderings*, p. 58). (See also IV-365.) TCH22. AG4. Oil on paper. 12¼″ x 10″. (Stark POP21)

III-110 Waugh-be-nim (Wah-bannim). Painting based on III-109. Face is painted black for mourning and eyebrows are plucked. This painting has been described as that of a Menominee Indian but there is no documentary evidence as to tribe and the area is traditionally Winnebago. GWA98. Oil on canvas. 2′1″ x 1′8″. (ROM912.1.13)

FOX RIVER

Spearing fish

The evening before Kane reached a Menominee camp on Fox River (*Wanderings*, p. 58) he watched Indians spearing fish by torch light as he had himself done in "boyish days" on Toronto Bay. Kane states that the fish were salmon. In this he was mistaken; no salmon were known in the Great Lakes above Niagara Falls.

III-111 Spearing by torch light on Fox River (*Wanderings*; woodcut, Fig. 4). Oil on paper. (Colln Major R. W. Willis)

III-112 Fishing by Torch Light (Spearing salmon by torch light). Painting based on III-111. GWA39. Oil on canvas. 1′6″ x 2′5″. Fig. 41. (ROM912.1.10)

Menominee

Kane made a two-day journey up the Fox River from Lake Winnebago to visit a Menominee camp. He found 3,000 Indians assembled for the annual payment of treaty moneys by the American government (*Wanderings*, pp. 59–61). The site is known today locally as the "Poygan" Pay Ground. As at Manitowaning and Mackinac, Kane used the opportunity to sketch various Indians.

III-113   Oscosh (Oshkosh) or "The Bravest of the Brave." Kane describes him as head chief of the Menominee (*Wanderings*, p. 59). Oscosh (1795–1850) as a young man assisted the British in capturing Michilimackinac in the war of 1812. He represented his people in negotiations with the Americans in 1827; they recognized him on that occasion as head chief of the Menominee. An extant portrait by Samuel M. Brookes shows him in European garb. His name is perpetuated in that of the town of Oshkosh, Wisconsin. Pencil. 4¾″ x 3″. Fig. 42. (Stark A4-38)

III-114   Two sketches of portrait heads. *Upper:* Indian with silver hair ornaments, braided hair queues on side of face, and feather hair ornament. *Lower:* Sketch labelled "O" with a figure identical to that in III-113 except for a head ornament. Pencil. 4¾″ x 3″. (Stark A4-22)

III-115   Pipe of Peace. Evidently this is the pipe which, Kane says, Oscosh was sending to President John Tyler of the United States (*Wanderings*, p. 59). Two figures hold hands in friendship at the base of the richly decorated stem. Pencil. 4¾″ x 3″. (Stark A4-23)

III-116   Pipe of Peace. This is possibly the pipe used at the opening of the annual treaty money ceremony; Kane describes how Oscosh first lit it and then passed it on to the other chieftains. Pencil. 3″ x 4¾″. (Stark A4-24)

III-117   Match-o-kee-maw or "Big Chief"; inscription, possibly in Kane's hand. This may be a form of the name of an Indian Kane sketched whom he refers to as Kitchie-ogi-maw or "the Great Chief" (*Wanderings*, p. 60). See III-120. AG62. Oil on paper. 12⅜″ x 9¾″. Fig. 43. (Stark POP4)

III-118   Three studies of Indian heads. *Upper:* slight sketch with head dress. *Lower left:* three-quarter head with face painting similar to that in III-117; *Lower right:* full-face head with single-feather head dress. Pencil. 4¾″ x 3″. (Stark A4-25)

III-119   Study of head with face painting and features similar to those in III-117 and III-118. 4¾″ x 3″. (Stark A4-27)

III-120   Kitchie-ogi-maw. It is difficult to reconcile this portrait with the sketches III-117 to III-119. The roach, feather in hair and sheathed knife around the neck are similar to those pictured in III-121. GWA90. Oil on canvas. 2′6″ x 2′1″. (ROM912.1.11)

III-121   Page of sketches: profile head with elaborate head ornament; detached head ornament; knife in suspended sheath; head with knife in sheath suspended around neck. The knife is similar to that in III-120. Pencil. 4¾″ x 3″. (Stark A4-37)

III-122   Muck-a-ta. The TCH catalogue describes him as a Menominee although the sketch bears an inscription "Potowattamie." Kane refers to a visit from him (*Wanderings*, p. 61). TCH23. AG43. Oil on paper. 12¼″ x 9⅝″. Fig. 44. (Stark EOP17)

III-123   Muck-a-ta. Painting based on III-122 but with embellishments. This canvas does not appear in the list of Kane's paintings received by Allan in 1856. Presumably it was delivered later and substituted for a canvas which Kane took back. Oil on canvas. 2′1″ x 1′8″. Fig. 45. (ROM912.1.12)

III-124   Muck-e-tah-kin-ne-u, or "Black Eagle." TCH19. AG38. 12¼″ x 9¾″. (Stark EOP10)

[There is no III-125.]

Potawatomi

III-126   Coe-coosh or "The Hog," described by Kane as a Potawatomi "black-leg" (*Wanderings*, p. 59). A sketch IV-225 and a canvas IV-226 have been identified incorrectly as of Coe-coosh, a mistake which resulted from a framing error. TCH14. Oil on paper. 11¾″ x 9½″. Plate IX. (Stark EOP30)

III-127   A Potawatomi Indian. This painting has generally been known as a portrait of Coe-coosh, but the face in it does not correspond in any particular with the features in III-126. It has also been published incorrectly as a portrait of Wah-he-joe-tass-e-neen (IV-226), a mistake resulting from a framing error. (See also III-128.) GWA75. Oil on canvas. 2′1″ x 1′8″. (ROM912.1.14)

III-128   "Pine Tree." Replica of III-127. This replica was identified in recent years by an Indian of the Lake Huron–Georgian Bay region as a portrait of his grandfather. Oil on canvas. 2′6″ x 2′1″. (ROML957.11)

Winnebago

III-129   Mauza-pau-Kan, or the "Brave Soldier." Chief of the Winnebago. Kane refers to making his portrait (*Wanderings*, p. 61; it seems clear from the sketch and the context in the book that the sentence referring to Mauza-pau-Kan actually belongs at the end of the preceding paragraph). TCH18 (where the subject is designated as from Wolf River). Oil on paper. 12⅜″ x 9″. Fig. 46. (NGC6457)

Unidentified Indians, chiefly Menominee

III-130   Page of sketches. Three heads, two in profile, and one full face with face painted in quarter segments. Pencil. 3″ x 4¾″. (Stark A4-21).

III-131   Page of studies. Five heads and a leg. Pencil 4¾″ x 3″. (Stark A4-26)

III-132   Oke-a-sa. Study of head, full face, with painted cheeks and cheek ornaments, silver ear decorations, roach and many strands of beads. Pencil. 4¾″ x 3″. (Stark A4-28)

III-133   Page of four head studies, some with silver ornaments. Pencil. 4¾″ x 3″. (Stark A4-30).

III-134   Page with two portrait studies. *Upper:* full-face head study with hair ornamentation, painted face and strands of beads; inscribed Ac-o-namy. *Lower:* profile head inscribed In-na-quwa. Pencil. 4¾″ x 3″. (Stark A4-31)

III-135   Page with six head studies. Pencil. 4¾″ x 3″. (Stark A4-33)

III-136   Page with three head studies. *Upper:* painted face with head ornament. *Lower left:* profile head with feather head dress. *Lower right:* unfinished sketch. Pencil. 4¾″ x 3″. (Stark A4-34)

III-137   Profile study of head with single-feather head dress, silver hair ornaments and silver ear ornament. Pencil. 4¾″ x 3″. (Stark A4-35)

III-138   Two profile head studies. *Upper:* head with elaborate facial painting and two braided queues on each side of face. *Lower:* head with silver ornaments, elaborate silver ear ornaments and three feathers in roach. Pencil. 4¾″ x 3″. (Stark A4-36)

III-139   Studies of two heads. *Upper:* three-quarter view. *Lower:* profile head with hair queue and feather head dress. Pencil. 4¾″ x 3″. (Stark A4-39)

III-140   Sketch of single head. Pencil. 4¾″ x 3″. (Stark A4-40)

FORT SNELLING

Sioux scalp dance

There is no evidence that Kane visited For Snelling, site of Minneapolis, while he was in the region west of Lake Michigan in 1845. He probably went through Minneapolis on his westward trip to Fort Garry in 1849, at which time he may have seen the fort. However his preliminary studies for a canvas showing a Sioux scalp dance and the fort do not appear to have been made on the site. Bushnell (*Sketches*, p. 24) quotes a letter from Henry Lewis to Kane from Montreal July 4 (1850?), in which Lewis sends Kane a sketch of Fort Snelling.

III-141   Sketch of figure bearing scalp trophies in each hand. Pencil. 5½″ x 9½″. (ROM946.15.58)

III-142   Standing figure with robe falling on ground. 5″ x 8″. (ROM946.15.276)

III-143   Pencil study for Sioux scalp dance. Presumably the Lewis sketch of the fort was used in preparing the background for this study. Pencil. 5½″ x 9″. (ROM946.15.155)

III-144   Sioux Scalp Dance. Fort Snelling is in the background. Painting is based on studies III-141 to III-143. GWA50. Oil on canvas. 4′ x 2′5″. Plate X. (ROM912.1.15)

Section IV

Paintings, sketches and drawings relating to Kane's 1846–48 expedition from Toronto to Fort Victoria by the Hudson's Bay Company routes across the Canadian plains and through the Oregon territory

Kane left Toronto for his second major sketching trip among the Indians on May 9, 1846. He joined the Hudson's Bay Company spring brigade beyond Fort William, travelling with it by way of Norway House and Fort Edmonton, crossing the Rockies and reaching Fort Vancouver in the Oregon territory, on the Columbia River, December 8, 1846. *En route* he made a detour to Fort Garry to observe the annual spring buffalo hunt of 1846. Kane sketched during the winter of 1846–47 in the Fort Vancouver region and during the following spring at Fort Victoria and its environs. Leaving Fort Vancouver on July 1, 1847, he started eastward on his homeward trip, halting to do much sketching in the plateau region of the Oregon country. He reached Fort Edmonton on December 5. Using this post as his base of operations, he sketched extensively on the western plains during the first months of 1848. Kane left Fort Edmonton with a returning fur trade brigade on May 25, 1848, travelling by way of Norway House and reaching Toronto the following October.

This section has been arranged geographically, moving from east to west. Divisions within it include works related to both the outward and the return journey.

SAULT STE MARIE

Sault Ste Marie material has been listed in section III. Despite Kane's remarks in *Wanderings* (p. 62), it is clear from other evidence, including his sketchbook, that most if not all of it was executed in 1845 rather than in 1846 or 1848.

MICHIPICOTEN

Ojibwa

This Lake Superior island is traditionally Ojibwa territory. Items III-46 to III-51 are portraits of Ojibwa evidently from this island and its adjacent regions but they were sketched at Manitowaning in 1845. Kane visited Michipicoten September 27–29, 1848, on his return trip to Toronto.

IV-1   Maydoc-game-kinungee or "I hear the Noise of the Deer." This Ojibwa chief was painted on Michipicoten Island but may have been there on a visit from the Kaministiquia River (*Wanderings*, p. 157). TCH81. W.C. 4½″ x 5¼″. (Bushnell H-72/402)

IV-2   Chief from Fort William (Maydoc-gan-kinungee). Painting based on IV-1. GWA91. Oil on canvas. 2′6″ x 2′1″. Plate XI. (ROM12.1.16)

FORT WILLIAM TO LAKE WINNIPEG

On May 24, 1846, Kane joined the Hudson's Bay Company fur brigade under Mr. Lane 35 miles beyond Fort William. He accompanied it as far as Fort Alexander which was reached June 11. He retraced this route in 1848, with Major McKenzie's party from Norway House, leaving Fort Alexander on August 3 and reaching Fort William September 19, 1848.

Topography

IV-3　Kakabeka Falls. Kane describes making a sketch of it on May 25, 1846 (*Wanderings*, p. 63). He points out that the table rock had fallen some time between 1848 and the date of the publication of *Wanderings*, 1859. Pencil. 5¼″ x 8½″. Fig. 47. (ROM946.15.66)

IV-4　Kakabeka Falls (Kakkabakka Falls). Painting based on IV-3. GWA53. Oil on canvas. 1′9½″ x 2′5½″. (ROM912.1.17)

IV-5　Kakabeka Falls. Replica of IV-4. GS12 (?). Oil on canvas. 12⅛″ x 18¼″. (Coe)

IV-6　The Mountain Portage. This has sometimes been referred to as "The By-pass at Kakabeka Falls." Kane sketched Kakabeka Falls while the men were portaging (*Wanderings*, p. 63). No preliminary sketch has been located for this painting. Possibly it was inspired by some European painting or engraving; the composition is unusual for Kane. GWA54. Oil on canvas. 2′1½″ x 1′8″. Plate XII. (ROM912.1.18)

IV-6A　Lost Men's Portage, west of Kakabeka Falls, sketched May 25, 1846 (*Wanderings*, p. 63). The sketch is on the same sheet as IV-301, at the upper right. KLL5. w.c. 5″ x 7¼″. (ROM946.15.-332)

IV-7　Pin Portage. Kane describes passing over the portage on May 25, 1846; this sketch was probably executed then rather than on the return journey (*Wanderings*, p. 63). TCH49. AG30. Oil on paper. 8⅛″ x 13¼″. Fig. 48. (Stark POP25)

IV-8　Dog Portage. Kane reports making a sketch of the waterfall at the upper end of Big Dog Portage on May 26, 1846 (*Wanderings*, p. 63). This sketch was probably made at that portage rather than at Dog Portage proper. KLL1. AG41. TCH48. Oil on paper. 8″ x 13⅜″. (Stark POP24)

IV-9　Hunting Ducks (at Lake of the Thousand Islands, Winnipeg River). Kane describes in detail the hunting methods witnessed here May 29, 1846 (*Wanderings*, p. 64). The painting is probably based on a sketch, not located. GWA40. Oil on canvas. 1′6″ x 2′5″. (ROM912.1.22)

IV-10　Fort Frances. General view with water mill in foreground and fort in rear. Kane was at Fort Frances from August 23 to September 11, 1848, at which time this sketch was probably executed. (*Wanderings*, p. 156.) TCH199. AG131. w.c. 5½″ x 9¼″. Fig. 49. (Stark PWC2)

IV-11　Fort Frances. View of the water mill from the fort. (See IV-10.) AG152. w.c. 5½″ x 9⅛″. Fig. 50. (Stark PWC3)

IV-12　Falls near Fort Frances. Kane seems to have made two sketches of these falls, either between June 1 and June 5, 1846, or between August 30 and September 10, 1848. He refers in his manuscript journal to sketching rapids, where Rainy River empties out of Rainy Lake on its way to the Lake of the Woods, during the 1846 trip (also *Wanderings*, p. 65); the resulting sketch, unlocated, may have been the one exhibited as TCH198. The second sketch, IV-12, was made on the same spot; it has been exhibited as "Coffin Rock" (see IV-470). (See *Wanderings*, p. 156.) TCH180. AG170. w.c. 5½″ x 9⅛″. (Stark PWC4)

IV-13　Unidentified view. There is a slight possibility that this is the mission post of Wabassimong seen by Kane on June 8, 1846, and August 12, 1848 (*Wanderings*, pp. 66, 155). Pencil. 5½″ x 6½″. (ROM946.15.317)

IV-14　Slave Falls, Winnipeg River. Sir George Simpson had particularly requested Kane to note this, the highest falls on the Winnipeg River (letter of May 31, 1846; Appendix 10, Letter 3). Evidently Kane made not only this sketch but also IV-15 and IV-16 on August 9, 1848 (*Wanderings*, p. 154). Pencil. 5″ x 7½″. (ROM946.15.67)

IV-15　Slave Falls, Winnipeg River. Sketch formerly identified as of "Dalles des Morts." AG179. w.c. 5½″ x 9⅜″. Fig. 51. (Stark WWC19)

IV-16　Slave Falls, Winnipeg River. (See IV-14 and IV-15.) TCH200. AG158. w.c. 5⅜″ x 9½″. (Stark PWC20)

IV-17　Slave Falls, Winnipeg River. Painting based on IV-16. GWA17. Oil on canvas. 1′6″ x 2′5″. (ROM912.1.20)

IV-18　Chute-de-Jacques, Winnipeg River. Kane was here on June 9, 1846, and August 11, 1848 (*Wanderings*, pp. 66, 154). KLL2. TCH52. Oil on paper. 8″ x 13⅜″. (Stark POP19)

IV-19　White Mud Portage, Winnipeg River. This sketch was made on August 4, 1848 (*Wanderings*, p. 154). TCH201. AG97. w.c. 5¼″ x 9⅜″. Plate XIII. (Stark PWC7)

IV-20　White Mud Portage. Painting based on IV-19. (*Wanderings*; coloured litho.) GWA6. Oil on canvas. 1′6″ x 2′5″. (ROM912.1.21)

IV-21　White Mud Portage. Replica of IV-20. LP10. Oil on canvas. 1′5½″ x 2′4½″. (NGC138). A second replica of IV-20 was sold by Knoedler & Co., New York, in 1952 *; see R. H. Hubbard, *The National Gallery of Canada: Catalogue of Paintings and Sculptures*, vol. III.

IV-22　An encampment on the Winnipeg River. Sketched June 10, 1846 (*Wanderings*, p. 67). Kane reports that the visiting Indians were Saulteaux. KLL8. TCH51. Oil on paper. 8⅛″ x 13⅜″. Plate XIV. (Stark POP15)

IV-23　Encampment, River Winnipeg. Painting based on IV-22. GWA31. Oil on canvas. 1′7″ x 2′6″. (ROM912.1.19)

IV-24   Winnipeg River. KLL4. AG92. Oil on paper. 8″ x 13⅜″. Fig. 52.
(Stark POP13)

[There is no IV-25.]

IV-26   Large Smith's Rock Portage. Identified from an inscription, not
in Kane's hand. w.c. 5½″ x 9¼″. (ROM946.15.257)

IV-27   Oke Falls. Identified from an inscription, not in Kane's hand.
w.c. 5½″ x 9¼″. (ROM946.15.258)

IV-28   Two canoes on a rocky shoreline. Topography is similar to that
in the region but the locale has not been identified. Pencil.
4⅞″ x 7¼″. TCH202. AG204. (Stark 3)

Saulteaux

"Saulteaux" is a term given occasionally to the Ojibwa of the Lake Superior region. Kane refers to them also as "Soto" and mentions meeting
a number between Fort William and Lake Winnipeg. In addition to the
following sketches, he pictures Saulteaux in IV-19 to IV-23.

IV-29   Iacaway (Ias-a-way), or "The Loud Speaker." Sketched at Fort
Frances June 4, 1846 (*Wanderings*, p. 66). This sketch was formerly published as one of "Little Rat," Rainy River (see also
IV-46, 221); no sketch of Little Rat (or Waw-gas-kontz), KPL2,
has been located. (See also IV-130.) Probably KPL1. TCH24. Oil
on paper. 8″ x 7″. (Agnes Etherington Art Gallery, Kingston,
0-89).

IV-30   Two Indian portrait heads. Inscription on reverse reads: (*left*)
Cash-a-cabut or "Greedy Tooth"; (*right*) Each-a-quip or "One
who sits with his feathers on." The names are in the Ojibwa
tongue. Sketched in the Fort Frances region. (*Wanderings*, p.
154) Pencil. 5½″ x 9¼″. Fig. 53. (ROM946.15.273)

IV-31   Head-and-shoulder portrait study of Indian. An inscription in
Ojibwa, evidently referring to this sketch, reads: Tipich-la-ga-
sheck or "The Spirit Sky." Probably sketched at the same time
as IV-30. Pencil. 4½″ x 5½″. (ROM946.15.274)

IV-32   Sho-ne-ah or "Silver." A Saulteaux chief from Fort Alexander.
Kane visited his village June 11, 1846 (*Wanderings*, pp. 67–68).
AG46. Oil on paper. 12¼″ x 9¾″. Fig. 54. (Stark POP5)

LAKE WINNIPEG TO FORT GARRY

Kane left Fort Alexander on June 11, 1845, and arrived at Lower Fort
Garry two days later. He went to Upper Fort Garry on June 15 in the
company of the Rev. Peter Jacobs (*Wanderings*, p. 68).

IV-33   Peter Jacobs, Wesleyan Indian missionary. AG161. w.c.
5″ x 4⅝″. Fig. 55. (Stark PWC14)

IV-34   Peter Jacobs, Wesleyan Indian missionary. Oil sketch based on
IV-33. 8⅝″ x 6⅞″. (Colln S. E. Weir)

FORT GARRY

Upper Fort Garry (built 1835, demolished 1882) was the Hudson's
Bay Company's headquarters in western Canada and its chief provision
depot. It formed the focal point of a settlement on the Red River which
grew up in the area following the first arrival of Lord Selkirk's Highland
immigrants in 1812. Kane spent a short time here on his arrival June 15,
1845, leaving almost immediately for the Métis buffalo hunt. He remained for a few days at the upper fort on his return from the hunt before leaving from the lower fort for Norway House on July 5. (*Wanderings*, pp. 68–69, 74.)

Topography

IV-35   Red River Settlement. General view. *Left to right:* St. Boniface
Cathedral, blockhouse, Upper Fort Garry. Pencil. 5½″ x 9″.
Fig. 57. (ROM946.15.68)

IV-36   Red River Settlement. General view. *Left to right:* Bishop's palace, cathedral and Grey Sisters' Hospital in St. Boniface, and the
windmill and Upper Fort Garry across the river. TCH210. AG88.
Oil on paper. 9″ x 13⅞″. Fig. 56. (Stark POP1)

IV-37   Red River Settlement. Painting based on IV-36. (*Wanderings*;
woodcut, Fig. 5). GWA3. Oil on canvas. 1′6″ x 2′5″. (ROM912.-
1.23)

IV-38   Red River Settlement. Replica of IV-37. LP9. Oil on canvas.
1′6″ x 2′5″. (NGC102)

IV-39   River scenery. Possibly a view along the Red or the Saskatchewan
River. 5″ x 6½″. (ROM946.15.118)

SOUTH OF FORT GARRY

Kane spent the latter part of June 1846 with Métis hunters on their
annual buffalo hunt southwest of Fort Garry. (*Wanderings*, pp. 69–72.)
He made sketches of Indians he met on the way, of the landscape, the
Métis hunters, and various phases of the buffalo hunt proper. Items IV-40
to IV-80 all relate to this expedition.

Sioux

The Sioux or Dakota, a large tribe, occupied territory from east of the
Mississippi River to the head of Green Bay, and north beyond the Canadian border towards Lake Winnipeg. Kane says he met twelve Sioux
chieftains after passing Dry Dance Mountain (*Wanderings*, p. 70). He
makes no mention of sketching them, but at no other time in his journeys
does he appear to have met members of this tribe; see, however, note 9
to chapter VI of *Wanderings*. His paintings of Sioux at Fort Snelling
(III-140 to III-143) were not done from life.

IV-40   Two portraits. w.c. 5¼″ x 8¼″. Plate XV. (ROM946.15.57)

IV-41   A Sioux Indian. Painting is based on the sketch of a Sioux in
IV-40 (*left side*). The robe seems to be based on a specimen in
Kane's ethnological collection. GWA87. Oil on canvas. 2′8″ x 1′8″;
(oval) 2′ x 1′7″. Fig. 58. (ROM912.1.29)

IV-42   Three portrait studies. Pencil. 5½″ x 8½″. (ROM946.15.64)

Saulteaux

A small band of Saulteaux accompanied the Métis during the buffalo
hunt. Evidently the following sketches were made during the hunt.

IV-43 Na-taw-waugh-cit (Na-too-waw-sit) or "The Man that was born." Full figure portrait with an otter robe. KPL4. TCH240. Oil on paper. 11¼″ x 7¾″. Fig. 59. (Stark EOP22)

IV-44 Na-taw-waugh-cit or "The Man that was born." KPL4. w.c. 7″ x 5″. (ROM946.15.277)

IV-45 Peccothis (Pe-ca-dhis) or "The Man with a Lump on his Navel." Profile study. Kane describes sketching him (*Wanderings*, p. 70). This item was formerly identified as a portrait of She-bah-ke-zhick or "Hole in the Sky" (see III-48). KPL3. Pencil. 5″ x 3″. (ROM946.15.63)

IV-46 Peccothis (Pe-ca-dhis) or "The Man with a Lump on his Navel." Formerly this sketch was identified as one of Waw-gas-kontz (see IV-29). KPL3. TCH25. AG89. Oil on paper. 8⅛″ x 6½″. (Stark POP2)

IV-47 Two portrait studies. The one at the left seems to relate to KPL3, "Peccothis" (IV-45, 46) but this is conjectural: Kane used, it would appear, three different number series and the "3" may relate to a lost series. This person has also been identified as She-bah-ke-zhick (III-48 and see IV-45), but without supporting evidence. The figure on the right is unidentified. w.c. 5¼″ x 7¼″. (ROM946.15.62)

See also IV-48 to IV-51.

Unidentified Indians

A group of sketches for which there is no documentary identification were evidently completed at this time. A roach suggests that the subjects may be Saulteaux, but this suggestion is without substantiation.

IV-48 Unidentified head. Oil on paper. 8″ x 9½″. AG51. (Stark WWC74)

IV-49 Unidentified head. This is the same individual as the one in IV-48. w.c. 3¾″ x 4½″. (ROM946.15.78)

IV-50 Unidentified head. w.c. 3¾″ x 4½″. (ROM946.15.79)

IV-51 Unidentified head. w.c. 3¾″ x 4½″. (ROM946.15.80)

Camp scenes

IV-52 Sketch on the prairies. Kane describes camping with a companion 30 miles south of Fort Garry *en route* to the hunt (*Wanderings*, p. 69). This sketch has been inscribed, but not in Kane's hand, as "Scratching River." TCH209. Oil on paper. 8⅛″ x 11⅜″. Plate XVI. (Stark POP18)

IV-53 Pembina River. Kane reported finding the main body of hunters along this river, a two-day journey from Fort Garry (*Wanderings*, p. 69). TCH233. AG167. w.c. 5¼″ x 8⅞″. (Stark PWC 15)

IV-54 Half Breeds Travelling. Painting is possibly based on an unlocated sketch which Kane mentions as having made three days after he left Fort Garry (*Wanderings*, p. 70). GWA35. Oil on canvas. 1′6″ x 2′5″. Fig. 60. (ROM912.1.24)

IV-55 Red River cart and ox. Kane describes the cart's construction (*Wanderings*, p. 69). Pencil. 5″ x 7″. Fig. 61. (ROM946.15.74)

IV-56 Page of sketches, showing Red River cart and ox; standing Métis smoking; Métis loading poles on cart. Described by Kane (*Wanderings*, p. 69). Pencil. 5″ x 7″. (ROM946.15.75)

IV-57 Baby in dog travois. w.c. 5″ x 6½″. (ROM946.15.85)

IV-58 Dog with travois. w.c. 4¾″ x 6½″. Fig. 62. (ROM946.15.84)

IV-59 Dog with travois. Pencil. 5″ x 6½″. (ROM946.15.146)

IV-60 Packhorse and drag. Pencil. 4¾″ x 6½″. (ROM946.15.144)

IV-61 Cow with pack on back. Pencil. 4¾″ x 6½″. (ROM946.15.144)

IV-62 Study of dog and bird. Pencil. 5½″ x 9¼″. (ROM946.15.83)

IV-63 Panoramic view of Métis travelling on prairie with camping equipment (*Wanderings*, p. 70). Pencil. 5½″ x 9″. (ROM946.15.69)

IV-64 Panoramic view of Métis travelling on prairie with equipment (*Wanderings*, p. 70). Pencil. 5″ x 7″. (ROM946.15.76)

IV-65 Métis encampment. This has also been described as an Ojibwa encampment. TCH208. AG181. w.c. 5¼″ x 8⅞″. (Stark PWC6)

IV-66 Panoramic view of Métis setting up camp on the prairies. w.c. 5½″ x 9″. Fig. 63. (ROM946.15.71)

IV-67 View of section of a Métis encampment. w.c. 5″ x 7″ (ROM946.15.72)

IV-68 Half Breed Encampment. Composite painting, evidently based on IV-65 to IV-67 and other studies. GWA27. Oil on canvas. 1′6″ x 2′5″. Figs. 64, 65. (ROM912.1.25)

The buffalo hunt

IV-69 Métis camp and hunters on hilltop. This scene is probably that described by Kane when the group were waiting for the hunt to begin (*Wanderings*, p. 71). w.c. 5¼″ x 8¾″. Fig. 66. (ROM946.15.70)

IV-70 Studies of Métis hunters on hilltop awaiting signal to charge the buffalo herd, and a downed buffalo. Pencil. 5″ x 7″. (ROM946.15.77)

IV-71 Panoramic view of Métis chasing the main buffalo herd (*Wanderings*, pp. 71–72). w.c. 5⅛″ x 8⅞″. Plate XVII. (Stark PWC16)

IV-72 Panoramic view of Métis chasing the main buffalo herd. A second and unfinished version of IV-71. AG74. Oil on paper. 8½″ x 13¾″. (Stark POP23)

IV-73 Half Breeds Running Buffalo. No preliminary study seems to have been executed for this work. Note remarks by Sir George Simpson advising adjustment of Kane's original version (Appendix 10, Letter 12). GWA34. Oil on canvas. 1′6″ x 2′5″. Fig. 67. (ROM912.1.26)

IV-74 Half Breeds Running Buffalo. Replica of IV-73. Probably GS13. Oil on canvas. 12⅛″ x 18¼″. (Coe)

IV-75 Page of buffalo hunt studies: Métis slaughtering buffalo, standing buffalo, buffalo head. Pencil and w.c. 5″ x 7″. (ROM946.15.93)

Wounded buffalo

While Kane was sketching during the hunt on June 26, 1845, a wounded buffalo charged him (*Wanderings*, p. 72). Kane shot him.

IV-76   Standing buffalo bull. Pencil. 5½″ x 6½″. (ROM946.15.86(1))

IV-77   Standing buffalo bull. Pencil. 5½″ x 6½″. (ROM946.15.86(2))

IV-78   Standing buffalo bull, wounded. Pencil. 5½″ x 6½″. Fig. 68. (ROM946.15.87)

IV-79   Wounded buffalo bull. TCH172. AG106. w.c. 4⅛″ x 5⅜″. Fig. 69. (Stark PWC8)

IV-80   Wounded Buffalo Bull. Painting based on IV-79. GWA43. Oil on canvas. 1′6″ x 2′5″. (ROM912.1.27)

FORT GARRY TO NORWAY HOUSE

Kane left Fort Garry July 5, 1846, arriving at Norway House July 12. He was forced to remain at Norway House until August 14. The brigade with which he was to travel was bringing trade goods from York Factory for the interior and otter skins which were to be carried to the Pacific as annual payment for the Russians (*Wanderings*, p. 76). On his return Kane retraced part of this ground, leaving Norway House July 24, 1848, and arriving at Fort Alexander on the 30th.

Topography

IV-81   Lake with rocky shoreline. It has been suggested, without supporting evidence, that this is a shore on Lake Winnipeg. w.c. 5″ x 6″. (ROM946.15.95)

IV-82   Norway House. Norway House, on Little Playgreen Lake at the north end of Lake Winnipeg, was established in 1814 as a staging post on the road from York Factory to the Red River Settlement. The first building was burned in 1824 and it was immediately reconstructed on a modest scale. A new and more extensive fort was commenced in 1831, which gradually assumed greater importance as a stopping place for traffic going to the Red River and for the fur brigades using the Saskatchewan River. It was this fort which Kane visited; parts of it still stand today (*Wanderings*, pp. 74, 152). (See W. B. Ready, "Norway House," *The Beaver*, Winnipeg, March 1949, pp. 30–34.) Pencil. 5½″ x 9″. (ROM-946.15.213)

IV-83   Norway House. KLL9. TCH78. Oil on paper. 8″ x 13½″. Plate XVIII. (Stark POP14)

IV-84   Wesleyan mission station, Jack River (Playgreen Lake). Kane visited the station July 12, 1846 (*Wanderings*, p. 76). The Rev. Wm Mason, resident missionary, reported from this place (known at the time as Rossville) on August 20, 1844, stating that the church, then under construction and shown in the sketch, soon would be finished. (Methodist Missionary Society Archives, London, Eng.) Mason had arrived in 1843; by 1847 he had established a printing press where he was publishing tracts in Cree, and in 1848 the *Rules of the Methodist Missionary Society*.

KLL19. TCH196. AG182. w.c. 5⅜″ x 8⅞″. Fig. 71. (Stark PWC17)

IV-85   Wesleyan mission station, Jack River. Pencil. 5″ x 7″. (ROM-946.15.73)

Saulteaux

IV-86   Two portrait studies. *Right:* young girl. In his portrait log Kane refers to a sketch of a Saulteaux girl whose mother "wanted to know if it would hurt her to sit for her picture." The same incident is recorded in *Wanderings* (p. 75) as occurring on his outward journey. In the log Kane calls this girl Caw-ce-cu-che-cock (Cawkeekaikeedje-ekoke), "Constant Sky." However, in the published book he uses this name for a woman met on his return journey; see IV-87, 88. KPL5. *Left:* Portrait study with note in Kane's hand "Assinboine." w.c. 5¼″ x 7¼″. Fig. 72. (ROM-946.15.61)

IV-87   Caw-kee-ka-keesh-e-ko or "The Constant Sky." Kane sketched this woman at the mouth of Behring River, Lake Winnipeg, on July 26, 1848, and he gives this name to her in *Wanderings* (p. 153). (See also IV-237.) Probably TCH26. Oil on paper. *c.* 5½″ x 5½″. (Colln Paul Kane IV)

IV-88   The Constant Sky (Caw-kee-kee-keesh-e-ko). Painting evidently based on IV-87. The quillwork box on which the woman rests her hand is based on one in a sketch, III-90, and reappears in IV-469. GWA59. Oil on canvas. 2′1″ x 2′6″. (ROM912.1.30)

NORWAY HOUSE

Portraits

IV-89   Donald Ross, Chief Factor, Norway House (*Wanderings*, p. 76). Mrs. R. B. Ross, a member of the subject's family, wrote in 1920 of this painting: "This picture was painted by the artist PAUL KANE 13th August 1846 and is a portrait of DONALD ROSS, Esq., Chief Factor of the Hudson's Bay Co. (and founder of Norway House). . . . Mr. Kane was to leave Norway House the next day. He met Mr. Ross going to hold service in the big hall (on Sunday) and said that if he wanted his portrait painted he (Mr. Kane) must do it that day. Mr. Ross agreed and it was painted on Sunday and is a very good likeness. . . ." Oil on paper. 7″ x 6″. Fig. 70. (Provincial Archives, British Columbia, 3760)

IV-90   Ogemawwah Chack (Oke-maw-wah-jack) or "The Spirit Chief." This Eskimo went out with Kane from Norway House to fish and shoot in 1848 (*Wanderings*, p. 152). Formerly this sketch was identified as that of Tomaquin, chief of the Cascade, Columbia River (see IV-391). TCH33. AG58. Oil on paper. 10⅛″ x 9⅛″. Fig. 76. (Stark WOP2)

IV-91   An Esquimaux (Oge-maw-waw-chawk). Painting based on IV-90 and probably using an Eskimo fur jacket from Kane's ethnological collection. (*Wanderings*; coloured litho.) GWA89. Oil on canvas. 2′6″ x 2′1″. (ROM912.1.32)

NORWAY HOUSE TO FORT CARLTON

Kane left Norway House with the fur trade brigade under the charge of Mr. Rowand on August 14, 1846, arriving at Fort Carlton, on the North Saskatchewan River, September 7. On his return journey in 1848, he left Fort Carlton June 6 and reached Norway House June 18.

Topography

IV-92   Brigade of boats. Kane completed this sketch on his return journey in 1848 when he hurried ahead of the brigade near Le Pas to sketch it; as he was doing so, a sudden thunderstorm threatened (*Wanderings*, p. 151). Pencil. 5½″ x 9¼″. Fig. 73. (ROM-946.15.83)

IV-93   Brigade of boats. Study of three boats. Pencil. 4″ x 5″. (ROM-946.15.334)

IV-94   York boats on the river. This is evidently the study for IV-95. AG206. Pencil. 5⅜″ x 9⅜″. (Stark 4)

IV-95   Brigade of Boats. Painting based on IV-93 and IV-94. GWA1. Oil on canvas. 1′6″ x 2′5″. Fig. 74. (ROM912.1.31)

IV-96   Fort Carlton from a distance (*Wanderings*, p. 78). When Henry J. Warre visited the fort a year before Kane's outward trip, he wrote: it "is miserable as a defensive building—is octagonal & built of wood, at every angle two large Blunderbusses are mounted and kept ready loaded to intimidate the enemy (on the Chinese plan I suppose). The numbers of Dogs, Children, Indians and cattle around make the place very dirty, and the mosquitoes are more troublesome than I ever remember them. The Valley of the River is wild and pretty and in winter the Buffalo surround the Fort. Bears are very abundant, also Elk. . . ." (Public Archives of Canada, Henry J. Warre Papers.) KLL20. TCH231. AG202. w.c. 5⅜″ x 8⅞″. Fig. 75. (Stark PWC18)

FORT CARLTON

A buffalo pound

Kane accompanied Indians, almost certainly Cree, on a buffalo hunt on September 12, 1846. This hunt took place six miles from Fort Carlton, which he had been visiting (*Wanderings*, p. 79).

IV- 97   Buffalo pound as prepared for the hunt by Indians. Sketch shows pound with funnel-like entrance of sticks and brush. Pencil. 5½″ x 9½″. (ROM946.15.104)

IV- 98   Driving buffalo into pound. General view of the hunt with mounted rider leading buffalo into pound, men rising behind posts ("dead men") to wave buffalo robes as the buffalo approach, and various gifts to the Great Spirit hanging in tall trees at the entrance to the pound. Pencil. 5⅜″ x 9¼″. AG208. (Stark 1)

IV- 99   Page of buffalo hunt studies: Indian standing with buffalo robe; hunters running buffalo into pound; running buffalo, Indian in tree waving medicine pipe-stem at entrance to pound. Pencil. 3″ x 5″. Fig. 77. (ROM946.15.103)

IV-100   Prairie landscape. This view has been introduced into the background of the canvas IV-101. w.c. 5″ x 7″. (ROM946.15.107)

IV-101   A Buffalo Pound. Painting based on IV-97 to IV-100. GWA7. Oil on canvas. 1′6″ x 2′5″. Fig. 78. (ROM912.1.33)

Cree

The Cree, an important Algonquian tribe, lived in Manitoba and Saskatchewan between the Red and Saskatchewan rivers. They were much reduced by smallpox in 1786 and 1838. The tribe, split into bands, had dispersed to many parts of the prairies for the purpose of trading with the Hudson's Bay Company.

Kane spent much time with the Cree. He first encountered them during the several days after his arrival at Fort Carlton on September 7, 1846. He sketched Cree also at Fort Pitt, Fort Edmonton, Rocky Mountain House and intermediate points.

IV-102   Us-koos-koosish (Uskoosekoosis/ Hus-kus-coo-sish) or "Young Grass." Kane sketched this Cree brave at Fort Carlton (*Wanderings*, p. 78). KPL7. TCH29. Oil on paper. 11¾″ x 8¼″. (Colln C. M. McCallister)

IV-103   Muck-Cranium, a Cree from Fort Carlton. AG52. Oil on paper. 11⅛″ x 6¾″. Plate XIX. (Stark POP6)

IV-104   "The Man that Shot the Wolf with an Arrow," a Cree sketched at Fort Carlton. Kane describes an incident which appears to relate to this man (*Wanderings*, p. 80) and refers to him as "A Perfect Centaur" (*Wanderings*, p. 74). Burpee follows a catalogue of the Allan collection canvases published *c.* 1900 in identifying this description with the canvas IV-105. KPL11. TCH86. w.c. 5½″ x 9″. Fig. 79. (ROM946.15.96)

IV-105   The Man that Always Rides. This man's identity is uncertain. A possibility for an identification is a man whom Kane lists in his notes as Eikutope, "The man that always rides," and whom he describes as a Blackfoot (later killed by a Cree in one of their forays); a sketch has not been found. (See also IV-104.) As in other cases, the composition for this canvas would appear to have a European prototype (or possibly to be after a painting by George Catlin). GWA79. Oil on canvas. 2′ x 1′6¼″. Plate XX. (ROM912.1.44)

IV-106   Cree Indians travelling. A note on the reverse, not in Kane's hand, reads: "Cree Indians on the March, Fort Carlton." Pencil. 4½″ x 8¾″. Fig. 80. (ROM946.15.102)

IV-107   Cree Indians Travelling. Painting based on IV-106. GWA49. Oil on canvas. 1′6″ x 2′5″. (ROM912.1.49)

IV-108   Cree tent with women gambling, Fort Carlton. KLL10. Pencil. 5″ x 6½″. (ROM946.15.152)

IV-109   Two portrait studies of Cree. *Right:* Pe-pa-ka-chos-a (Pe-pa-ka-chos). *Left:* Achu-wish-a-ma-hy or "The Grizzly Bear Standing." Probably sketched at Fort Carlton. TCH87 and TCH88. 5½″ x 9″. (ROM946.15.97)

FORT CARLTON TO FORT PITT

Kane, in company with the Rev. Mr. Rundle and Mr. Rowand, left Fort Carlton on September 12, 1846. On September 19 they reached Fort Pitt, on the North Saskatchewan River, encountering numerous Cree on the way. Kane remained at Fort Pitt until September 23. In 1848 he was again in Fort Pitt for a month after January 14, and from May 27 to 29 during his return journey to Toronto.

Topography

The exact location for most of the sketches of the North Saskatchewan valley has not been determined. All have been entered here although some may actually be of landscapes beyond Fort Pitt.

IV-110   Scene on the Saskatchewan River. Formerly identified as a view near Lethbridge, Alta., or on the Belly River. KLL13. w.c. 5½″ x 9″. (ROM946.15.119)

IV-111   Scene on the Saskatchewan River. Formerly identified as a view near Lethbridge, Alta., or on the Belly River. KLL14. w.c. 5½″ x 9″. (ROM946.15.125)

IV-112   Scene on the Saskatchewan River. A second version of IV-111. Formerly identified as Bow River valley. w.c. 5½″ x 9″. (ROM946.15.126)

IV-113   Scene on the Saskatchewan River. KLL15. Pencil. 5½″ x 8¾″. (ROM946.15.110)

IV-114   Scene on the Saskatchewan River. A second version of IV-113. Pencil. 5½″ x 9″. (ROM946.15.111)

IV-115   Scene on the Saskatchewan River. Formerly identified as possibly the Belly River. KLL16. w.c. 5½″ x 9″. (ROM946.15.120)

IV-116   Scene on the Saskatchewan River. On the reverse is a small sketch of a tent and a Red River cart. KLL17. AG160. w.c. 5½″ x 9⅞″. (Stark PWC19)

IV-117   Scene on the Saskatchewan River. KLL18. w.c. 5″ x 7″. (ROM946.15.109)

IV-118   Scene on the Saskatchewan River. On the reverse is a slight sketch of a horse drawing poles. Pencil. 5″ x 6½″. (ROM946.15.116)

IV-119   The Serpentine Valley. KLL25. w.c. 5½″ x 9″. Fig. 81. (ROM946.15.139)

IV-120   The Golden Valley. Kane describes making this sketch on September 14, 1846 (*Wanderings*, p. 80). KLL26. w.c. 4½″ x 9″. Fig. 82. (ROM946.15.108)

IV-121   A Valley in the Plains. Painting based on IV-120. GWA57. Oil on canvas. 1′6″ x 2′5″. (ROM912.1.34)

IV-122   Fort Pitt, with bluff. Warre, on a visit to Fort Pitt in 1845, wrote: "it is beautiful; as we ascended the north branch of the river the Fort appears like a Gentleman's seat surrounded by magnificant [*sic*] timber, but alas! The reality disappointed our expectations. The trees dwindled into small poplars and the fort itself is a mere wooden building 120 ft square with walls 20 ft high and two blockhouses at the angles of the river front

and one in the rear. As at Carlton, Blunderbusses are kept ready loaded and if we may believe the account given by the Interpreter in charge of the fort, not without some reason [because of the Blackfoot]. . . . The interior of the Fort is crowded with wooden buildings, rendering fire extremely probable, and almost impossible to put a stop to should it once gain a head." (Public Archives of Canada, Henry J. Warre Papers.) (See *Wanderings*, pp. 81–82.) KLL27. TCH205. AG218. w.c. 5⅜″ x 9″. Fig. 83. (Stark PWC23)

FORT PITT

Wild life

IV-123   Heads of prairie antelope (*Wanderings*, pp. 80, 81). TCH171. AG186. w.c. 4⅞″ x 7″. Fig. 84. (Stark PWC11)

IV-124   Wolf's head (*Wanderings*, p. 81). An inscription, not in Kane's hand, describes this animal as Mah-i-cum or Prairie Dog. TCH237. AG91. Oil on paper. 6½″ x 8⅛″. (Stark POP11)

IV-125   Deer (*Wanderings*, p. 80). Pencil. 5″ x 6½″. (ROM946.15.59)

Chipewyan

The Chipewyan lived in the Lake Athabasca region. In September 1846 Kane discovered a single member of this tribe living at Fort Pitt.

IV-126   Chimaza (Chin-i-a-sa) or "The Little Slave" (*Wanderings*, p. 82). KPL12. TCH92. w.c. 7″ x 4⅞″. (Stark PWC21)

Cree

Kane met Cree at Fort Pitt and vicinity on three different occasions. Most of the following group were apparently sketched during the month after January 14, 1848 (other times for sketches are noted). Kane's manuscript journal states that the Indians sketched at Fort Pitt were Assiniboin; this is evidently an error on his part.

IV-127   Otisskun (O-this-skun) or "The Horn." A Cree chieftain with war-cap and bag sketched September 16, 1846 (*Wanderings*, p. 81). An inscription, not in Kane's hand, calls him a Cree. KPL15. TCH28. Oil on paper. 13¼″ x 8⅛″. Plate XXI. (Stark POP17)

IV-128   The War Cap (The War Cap of Otiskun). Painting based on IV-127 but with a ceremonial pipe, based on IV-135, added. GWA97. Oil on canvas. 2′6″ x 2′1″. (ROM912.1.35)

IV-129   Studies of two figures. *Left*: seated figure, inscribed in Kane's hand "The Horn, U-thay-skun." *Right*: standing figure. KPL15. w.c. and pencil. 5″ x 6½″. (ROM946.15.151)

IV-130   Kee-a-kee-ka-sa-coo-way (Caw-ke-ka-saw-k-way) or "The Man who gives the War-whoop." Kane mentions meeting this man at Fort Pitt during January 1848 (*Wanderings*, pp. 81, 144–45). Sketch is inscribed in Kane's hand "The man that always speaks," and his journal gives the same English equivalent. This sketch was identified formerly as one of Iacaway, Saulteaux chieftain at

Fort Frances (see IV-29). KPL14. w.c. 5″ x 6½″. (ROM-946.15.60)

IV-131 Kee-a-kee-ka-sa-coo-way (Ka-ah-ke-ka-sahk-a-wa-ow), or "The Man who gives the War-whoop." A portrait study of the individual pictured in IV-130. (See Bushnell, *Sketches*, pp. 12–14.) KPL14. TCH84. w.c. Fig. 85. (Bushnell 41-72/395)

IV-132 Kee-akee-ka-saa-ka-wow, "The Man that gives the War Whoop" (Kee-a-kee-ka-sa-coo-way). The facial features are evidently based on IV-131. An elaborate hair ornament may be inspired by hair pins collected by Kane (now in Manitoba Museum of Science and History). Although the chief's medicine pipe-stem is similar to the one on the left in IV-136, it is more probably based on an actual specimen collected by Kane (also in Manitoba Museum of Science and History). (See *Wanderings*, p. 144; coloured litho.) GWA69. Oil on canvas. 2′6″ x 2′1″. Fig. 86. (ROM912.1.42)

IV-133 Muck-e-too or "Powder"(?) second chief of the Cree, met at Fort Pitt. Kane mentions meeting this man with Kee-a-kee-ka-sa-coo-way (IV-130). (*Wanderings*, pp. 81, 144.) The sketch itself has been identified as of Muck-koze or "Young Bear," an Ottawa chieftain (III-52). Both IV-133 and III-52 have been keyed to TCH13. KPL13. w.c. 3½″ x 4¾″. (ROM946.15.54)

IV-134 Cree pipe-stem. Presumably this is one of eleven pipe-stems which Kane saw in the possession of Kee-a-kee-ka-sa-coo-way (*Wanderings*, p. 145). w.c. 5½″ x 9½″. (ROM946.15.101)

IV-135 Cree pipe-stem (see IV-134) and pencil studies of two Indian heads. w.c. 5½″ x 9¼″. Fig. 87. (ROM946.15.99)

IV-136 Two Cree pipe-stems (see IV-134). *Left:* pipe-stem with golden eagle head. *Right:* decorated pipe-stem. Pencil and w.c. 5¾″ x 9½″. Fig. 88. (ROM946.15.100)

IV-137 Cree pipe-stems (see IV-134). (See Bushnell, *Sketches*, p. 14). w.c. 9¼″ x 5½″. (Bushnell 41-72/396)

IV-138 Cree pipe-stem (see IV-134). TCH41? (which states, incorrectly, that this pipe-stem is from the Pacific coast near the Strait of Juan de Fuca; see also IV-160). AG15. Oil on paper. 11⅝″ x 9¼″. (Stark POP7)

IV-139 Cree Indian. This sketch was exhibited in Toronto in 1848 as that of an Indian of the Cree tribe from the Saskatchewan River near Fort Pitt. Subsequently it was listed, without apparent basis, as "Cree Indian, Edmonton." TCH27. AG73. Oil on paper. 12¼″ x 9¾″. Plate XXII. (Stark POP16)

IV-140 Cree Pipe-Stem Bearer. Painting based on IV-139 (for face) and IV-135 (for pipe-stem). (See *Wanderings*, pp. 143–44.) The painting does not appear to have been turned over by Kane to Allan in 1856 and was probably given to him at a later date. Oil on canvas. 2′6″ x 2′1″. (ROM912.1.36)

IV-141 A Cree woman. Probably sketched at Fort Pitt. KPL18. w.c. 5½″ x 2¾″. (ROM946.15.300)

IV-142 Five standing figures, almost certainly sketched at Fort Pitt. *Upper:* Three-quarter view of standing male, tribe not specified; standing woman with child on back, labelled "Cree"; back view of standing woman, labelled "Cree." *Lower:* standing figure, Musk-ku-thay-ka-ou-mu-thay or "The man that always runs in the plains," an Assiniboin; seated figure, Mis-cu-pa-puck-we or "Red Shirt," an Assiniboin. KPL16 and KPL17. w.c. 5″ x 7″. (ROM946.15.150)

Blackfoot and allies

During the 18th century the Blackfoot were the strongest and most aggressive of all prairie tribes. Their territory extended from present-day Saskatchewan to the Rockies and from the North Saskatchewan River to the upper Missouri. They were divided into three tribal units, each under its own chieftain: the Blackfoot proper, the Blood, and the Piegan. The Sarsi, who originally occupied territory from the Peace River to the Red Deer River, affiliated themselves wholeheartedly with the Blackfoot.

On his return trip to Toronto, Kane left Fort Pitt with the Hudson's Bay Company fur brigade on May 29, 1848. They met a large party of Indians east of the fort on June 1 (*Wanderings*, pp. 148–50), and camped with them for a day during which Kane made several sketches. The party consisted of Blackfoot and their allies, from the Blood, Sarsi, Gros Ventres and Piegan.

IV-143 Indian Horse Race. Kane describes the race (*Wanderings*, p. 148; woodcut, Fig. 16). No preliminary sketches have been located. GWA9. Oil on canvas. 1′6″ x 2′5″. (ROM912.1.51)

IV-144 Indian Horse Race. Replica of IV-143. Oil on canvas. (Colln Mrs. James A. Grant)

IV-145 Indian Horse Race. Replica of IV-143. LP11. Oil on canvas. 1′6½″ x 2′5¼″. Fig. 89. (NGC6921)

IV-146 Omoxesisixany or "Big Snake" (*Wanderings*, pp. 148–50). An identification has evidently been based on an inscription not in Kane's hand. (See Bushnell, *Sketches*, pp. 20–21.) TCH90(?). w.c. 4½″ x 5½″. (Bushnell 41-72/399)

IV-147 Big Snake, Blackfoot Chief from the Western Prairies. Painting is supposedly based on IV-146. GWA73. Oil on canvas. 2′1″ x 1′8″. (ROM912.1.52)

IV-148 The Death of Big Snake. Kane heard an erroneous report of the death of Big Snake when he got to Norway House in June 1848 (*Wanderings*, p. 152). Big Snake actually died in 1858. Kane painted this imaginary view of the incident after reaching Toronto. No preliminary sketches have been located and the composition suggests that the canvas was based on a European prototype. The painting was made into a large coloured lithograph in Toronto *c.* 1856 (Fig. 90). GWA41. Oil on canvas. 1′8″ x 2′1¼″. (ROM912.1.53)

IV-149 Mis-ke-me-kin or "The Iron Collar." Kane says that this Blood Indian had his face painted red (*Wanderings*, p. 149). (See Bushnell, *Sketches*, pp. 20–21). TCH89. w.c. (Bushnell 41-72/400)

IV-150 Wah-nis-stow or "The White Buffalo"; according to Kane's narrative, principal chief of the Sarsi (*Wanderings*, p. 150). This sketch was labelled as that of a Blackfoot when exhibited in Toronto in 1848. TCH91. AG192. w.c. 5¼″ x 5¼″. Fig. 91. (Stark PWC5)

IV-151 Insignia. Study of a detail introduced into IV-150. Pencil. 5¼″ x 7¼″. (ROM946.15.272)

IV-152 Indian chieftain. No certain identification has been established for this figure. Kane refers to a lesser chieftain at the Blackfoot camp with his face partially painted black for mourning (*Wanderings*, p. 150). Evidently the face in this sketch was introduced into IV-154; however, the figure with the blackened face in IV-154 does not wear the same clothing as the man in this sketch. An inscription on the sketch, not in Kane's hand, identifies the subject as Red Vest or "The Feather," a Cree. 11″ x 8¼″. AG57. (Stark POP26)

IV-153 Big Snake's Brother. Kane mentions sketching this man (*Wanderings*, p. 149). No preliminary sketch for this canvas has been located. GWA65. Oil on canvas. 2′6″ x 2′1″. (ROM912.1.54)

IV-154 Six Blackfoot Chiefs (Six Indian Chiefs). Kane describes making the original sketches for this group portrait (*Wanderings*, pp. 149–50; coloured litho.). He identifies the chieftains (*left to right*) as Little Horn; a lesser chieftain; Wah-nis-tow; Big Snake; another lesser chieftain; Mis-ke-me-kin. Three of the portraits are presumably based on sketches IV-146, IV-149, IV-150 and possibly IV-152, but there is little actual resemblance. The clothes are seemingly based on items in Kane's ethnological collection, but there are variations from surviving specimens. GWA72. Oil on canvas. 2′1″ x 2′6″. (ROM912.1.50)

IV-155 Big Snake, a Blackfoot Chief, recounting his War Exploits to Five of His Subordinate Chiefs (Blackfoot Chief and Subordinates). Replica of IV-154. LP1. Oil on canvas. 2′1″ x 2′6″. Fig. 92. (NGC22)

IV-156 Staff of Big Snake. Study for IV-154 and IV-155. Pencil, 4½″ x 7½″. (ROM946.15.105)

IV-157 Medicine pipe-stem dance. Kane says that the Indians assigned him a good position for viewing the ritual while he was executing his sketch (*Wanderings*, p. 150). TCH59. Oil on paper. 9¾″ x 12¼″. Plate XXIII. (Stark POP10)

IV-158 Medicine Pipe Stem Dance. Painting based on IV-157. The eagle head pipe-stem is probably sketched from a specimen (now in Manitoba Museum of Science and History) similar to one drawn by Kane earlier; see IV-132, 136 left. (*Wanderings*;

coloured litho.). GWA37. Oil on canvas. 2′5″ x 4′7″. Fig. 93. (ROM912.1.56)

IV-159 Blackfoot pipe-stem carrier. Single figure holding eagle head pipe-stem in the reverse position to that in IV-132. Pencil. 7½″ x 5½″. (ROM946.15.106A)

IV-160 Blackfoot pipe-stem (fragment of original sketch). Detail study. This object was at one time described as the feathers of an Indian ceremonial head dress. The sketch has been inscribed TCH41 (see also IV-138). AG54. Oil on paper. 9⅝″ x 8″. (Stark EOP7)

IV-161 Blackfoot Pipe Stem Carrier. Painting based on IV-159 and IV-160. GWA80. Oil on canvas. 1′8″ x 1′2″. (ROM912.1.55)

IV-162 Jacket ornamented with a crow. Evidently part of a military society regalia. w.c. 5″ x 7¼″. Fig. 94. (ROM946.15.313)

IV-163 Head dress ornamented with a weasel. Evidently part of a military society regalia. Pencil. 5¾″ x 9½″. (ROM946.15.314)

IV-164 Painted buffalo robe recording the adventures of Sa-co or "The Sinew Piece," a Blood Indian. KLL30. TCH148. AG210. 5⅜″ x 8⅞″. Fig. 95. (Stark WWC82)

Buffalo

Kane describes seeing many buffalo on the prairie before he reached Fort Pitt on his westward trip during 1846; he continued to see these animals until he reached Fort Edmonton. Studies, evidently of this region, are grouped together here, but the majority cannot be dated.

IV-165 Studies of two buffalo. Pencil. 5¼″ x 6½″. (ROM946.15.92)

IV-166 Studies of three buffalo. Pencil. 5¼″ x 6½″. (ROM946.15.88)

IV-167 Studies of three buffalo. Pencil. 5″ x 7¼″. (ROM946.15.89)

IV-168 Studies of three buffalo. Pencil. 5¼″ x 6½″. (ROM946.15.91)

IV-169 Buffalo skull on the prairies. w.c. 2¾″ x 5½″. (ROM-946.15.153)

IV-170 Indian Summer on the Saskatchewan. Evidently painted from a sketch, unlocated, made September 13, 1846 (*Wanderings*, p. 80). Details have been introduced from IV-166 to IV-169. GWA44. Oil on canvas. 1′6″ x 2′5″. (ROM912.1.37)

IV-171 Buffalo trail. w.c. 5½″ x 9″. (ROM946.15.147)

IV-172 Long Grass Valley with dead man's hill in the distance. This was possibly sketched in the region of Long Grass Prairie (*Wanderings*, p. 82), where, Kane reports on September 24, 1846, buffalo were so numerous as to impede progress. KLL28. w.c. 5½″ x 9″. (ROM946.15.148)

IV-173 Buffalo in the Saskatchewan River valley. Pencil. 5″ x 4″. (ROM946.15.334)

IV-174 Page of studies of buffalo. These include a preliminary study of two fighting bulls (see also IV-175 to IV-177). w.c. 5″ x 6½″. Fig. 96. (ROM946.15.90)

IV-175 Buffalo bulls fighting. Painting study based on sketch in IV-174. w.c. 4⅞″ x 6½″. Fig. 97. (Stark PWC9)

IV-176 Buffalo Bulls Fighting. Painting based on IV-175. GWA10. Oil on canvas. 1′6″ x 2′5″. Fig. 98. (ROM912.1.28)

IV-177 Buffalo Bulls Fighting. Replica of IV-176. (Colln Mrs. Ralph D. Baker)

FORT PITT TO FORT EDMONTON

Topography

In 1846 Kane, accompanied by the Rev. Mr. Rundle and Mr. Rowand, left Fort Pitt on September 23 and arrived in Fort Edmonton September 26. The following sketches form an extension of the series IV-110 to IV-121; it is possible that some were executed before Kane reached Fort Pitt.

IV-178 Scene on the Saskatchewan River. KLL22. Pencil. 5½″ x 9″. (ROM946.15.114)

IV-179 Scene on the Saskatchewan River. Pencil. 5½″ x 9.″ (ROM946.15.115)

IV-180 Salt lake. Described by Kane (*Wanderings*, pp. 82–83). Probably sketched September 24, 1846. KLL23. w.c. 5¾″ x 6½″. (ROM946.15.149)

IV-181 A lake in the plains. This may be the lake beside which Kane says he camped on the evening of September 24, 1846 (*Wanderings*, p. 82). KLL24. TCH204. w.c. 5¼″ x 9″. Plate XXIV. (ROM946.15.138)

IV-182 Prairie landscape. Pencil. 5½″ x 9″. (ROM946.15.121)

IV-183 Prairie landscape. Locale said to be between Edmonton and Prince Albert. w.c. 5½″ x 9¼″. (ROM946.15.140)

IV-184 Rolling hillside and prairie. Pencil. 5½″ x 9.″ (ROM946.15.143)

IV-185 Prairie fire. This is presumably the fire seen by Kane on September 26, 1846, from Fort Edmonton (*Wanderings*, p. 83). Unfinished w.c. 7½″ x 12″. (ROM946.15.319)

IV-186 A prairie on fire. Presumably another view of the fire sketched in IV-185. KLL21. TCH203. w.c. 5½″ x 9″. (ROM946.15.124)

IV-187 A Prairie on Fire. Painting based on IV-186 but changed from a day to a night view. GWA55. Oil on canvas. 1′6″ x 2′5″. Fig. 99. (ROM912.1.39)

FORT EDMONTON

Kane was at Fort Edmonton from September 26 to October 6, 1846, when he left for the Pacific. He returned December 5, 1847, remaining until January 7, 1848, when he left for a visit to Fort Pitt. He returned again during February, leaving on April 12 for Rocky Mountain House. He went back to Fort Edmonton, and left there for Norway House with the spring fur brigade on May 25, 1848. (*Wanderings*, pp. 83, 136, 138–39.)

Fort and environs

Fort Edmonton, on the North Saskatchewan River, was the Hudson's Bay Company's principal post on the western prairies. The building pictured in IV-188 is the last of several built by the Company. The first was erected at Sturgeon River in 1795. A second stood within the limits of the present city of Edmonton from 1802 to 1810. Concurrently the North West Company had a fort nearby. A new main fort was built after the union of the two companies in 1821, but in 1830 floods forced its abandonment as it stood on low ground. The final Fort Edmonton, visited by Kane, was built betwen 1830 and 1832. This stood until 1915 when it was dismantled for the construction of the Legislative Building of the Province of Alberta.

IV-188 Fort Edmonton. KLL29. TCH206. AG183. w.c. 5⅜″ x 9″. Plate XXV. (Stark PWC22)

IV-189 Edmonton. Painting based on IV-188. GWA20. Oil on canvas. 1′6″ x 2′5″. (ROM912.1.38)

IV-190 Fort Edmonton. General view of the high ground overlooking the plain and the fort. Pencil. 5½″ x 9″. (ROM946.15.122)

IV-191 Fort Edmonton. Pencil. 2½″ x 5¾″. (ROM946.15.113)

IV-192 Eroding banks of the Saskatchewan River, evidently in the vicinity of Fort Edmonton. Pencil. 2½″ x 5¾″. (ROM946.15.112)

IV-193 View of the Saskatchewan River, evidently upstream from Fort Edmonton. Unfinished w.c. 5″ x 6½″. (ROM946.15.117)

Wedding party

Kane describes the wedding of Miss Harriott, daughter of John Edward Harriott, the chief factor at Fort Edmonton, to Mr. Rowand Jr., "who resided at" Fort Pitt. This took place on January 6, 1848 (*Wanderings*, p. 141). Kane recounts that he accompanied the bridal party which left the fort the next day and travelled in their company to Fort Pitt.

IV-194 Sled dogs decorated for the wedding party. Described on reverse as "Contines dogs." Kane points out that the bride's cariole was pulled by dogs brought recently from Lower Canada (Quebec) (*Wanderings*, p. 141). TCH174. w.c. 5½″ x 9½″. Fig. 101. (Stark PWC12)

IV-195 Sled dogs of the plains (Indian dogs). Kane makes particular reference to their ferocity (*Wanderings*, p. 141). TCH156. AG164. w.c. 5½″ x 9½″. Fig. 100. (Stark PWC13)

IV-196 Study of snow on trees. This sketch is included here because it was incorporated into the composite painting of the wedding party, IV-201, although there is no proof that it was done at Fort Edmonton. TCH146. AG140. w.c. 6⅞″ x 4⅞″. Fig. 102. (Stark WWC40)

IV-197 Evergreen laden with snow, a sketch included here because of its similarity to IV-196. w.c. 5″ x 7″. (ROM946.15.286)

IV-198 Evergreen laden with snow, a sketch included here because of its similarity to IV-196. w.c. 5″ x 7″. (ROM946.15.287)

IV-199 Decorated sled. Kane says that it was especially ornamented for the bride (*Wanderings*, p. 141). w.c. 5¼″ x 9¼″. Fig. 103. (ROM946.15.129)

IV-200 Winter travelling with dog sleds. Preliminary study for IV-201. Pencil. 5⅝″ x 9¼″. (Stark 2).

IV-201 Winter Travelling (Winter Travelling in Dog Sleds). View of the Rowand wedding party leaving Edmonton for Fort Pitt on January 7, 1848 (*Wanderings*, p. 141; woodcut Fig. 14). The painting is based on the studies in IV-194, IV-196, IV-199, IV-200. GWA38. Oil on canvas. 1′7″ x 2′5″. Plate XXVI. (ROM912.1.48)

IV-202 Sketch of young man and woman. There is no documentary identification of this couple, but it seems possible that they may be Miss Harriott and Mr. Rowand Jr. at the time of the wedding in Fort Edmonton. Pencil. (Stark, sketch in Kane's journal)

Catching wild horses

IV-203 Catching Wild Horses. No preliminary sketches exist for this painting nor does Kane make direct reference to the incident. He does refer to roaming bands of horses in the Edmonton area during December 1847, and this painting probably pictures a locale west of the city (*Wanderings*, p. 137). GWA11. Oil on canvas. 1′6″ x 2′5″. Fig. 104. (ROM912.1.45)

Gigantic buffalo head

Kane killed an enormous buffalo for its head while hunting near Fort Edmonton *c.* December 5, 1847 (*Wanderings*, p. 137). This trophy is now in the Manitoba Museum of Science and History. The following sketches appear to be studies of it.

IV-204 Buffalo head. Pencil. 4¾″ x 5½″. (ROM946.15.94)

IV-205 Buffalo head. TCH55. AG68. Oil on paper. 6½″ x 8″. (Stark POP12)

IV-206 Two buffalo heads. AG178. w.c. 4⅞″ x 6⅞″. (Stark PWC10)

Assiniboin

The Assiniboin, a branch of the Sioux, lived during the 17th century in the Lake of the Woods region. They had moved into the central prairies by the mid 19th century, but introduction of firearms drove them even farther west. The tribe had divided into two groups by the 1860s. The northern Assiniboin, with whom Kane came in contact, were on the western branches of the Saskatchewan and Assiniboine rivers towards the Rocky Mountains. The southern group were in American territory. The tribe, who were nomads, were closely allied to the Cree.

IV-207 Potika-poo-tis or "The Little Round Man," nicknamed "The Duke of Wellington." Kane sketched him at Fort Edmonton in September 1846 (*Wanderings*, p. 83), and calls him an Assiniboin chief. This sketch has been referred to, incorrectly, as "Cree Chief from Fort Edmonton." KPL10. AG83. Oil on paper. 11⅜″ x 9½″. (Stark POP8)

IV-208 Running Buffalo (Two Assiniboine Indians Running a Buffalo). Kane describes how he saw Assiniboin hunting while he was at Fort Edmonton (*Wanderings*, p. 84). He makes no mention of sketching them at the time, and no sketches have been located. The painting is based on an Italian print by Pinelli engraved in Rome in 1815, entitled "Cavalcatura che conducona le bestie bovine in Rome per macellare." The print comes from a volume *Nuova Raccolta di cinquanta Costumi pittoreschi incisi all' acqua forte da Bartolomeo Pinelli* (Roma 1816), which was in Kane's library (Fig. 106). GWA58. Oil on canvas. 1′6″ x 2′5″. (ROM-912.1.46). A replica of this painting was sold by Knoedler & Co. in New York in recent years; it has not been traced.*

IV-209 Assiniboine Hunting Buffalo. Replica of IV-208. LP6. Oil on canvas. 1′6½″ x 2′5¾″. Fig. 105. (NGC6920)

IV-210 Assiniboine Running Buffalo. Replica of IV-209. Oil on canvas. 1′5½″ x 2′4″. (Colln H. R. Milner)

Cree

IV-211 A Cree from Edmonton. No preliminary sketches for this painting have been located. GWA71. Oil on canvas. 2′6″ x 2′1″. (ROM912.1.43)

IV-212 Cun-ne-wa-bum. Four compositional studies for IV-214. Pencil. 3¾″ x 4½″. (ROM946.15.79)

IV-213 Cun-ne-wa-bum. Three compositional studies for IV-214. Pencil. 3¾″ x 4½″. (ROM946.15.80)

IV-214 Cunnawa-bum (Cun-ne-wa-bum) or "One that looks at the stars." Half-breed Cree girl who danced with Kane at the 1847 Christmas evening ball at Fort Edmonton (*Wanderings*, p. 139; coloured litho., frontispiece). The dress is in the Manitoba Museum of Science and History. IV-212 and IV-213 are compositional studies for this painting, but no actual study for the head has been located. GWA60. Oil on canvas. 2′1″ x 1′8″; (oval) 2′ x 1′7″. Fig. 107. (ROM912.1.41)

IV-215 François Lucie, a Cree half-breed guide. Kane hunted with him and refers to him on several occasions (*Wanderings*, p. 139 *et al.*). TCH31. AG16. Oil on paper. 10⅞″ x 8¾″. Plate XXVII. (Stark POP9)

IV-216 François Lucie. Painting based on IV-215. GWA100. Oil on canvas. 2′6″ x 2′1¾″. (ROM912.1.40)

ROCKY MOUNTAIN HOUSE

Kane left Fort Edmonton April 12, 1848, and reached Rocky Mountain House on the 21st. He returned to Fort Edmonton early in May. Much of his stay at Rocky Mountain House was spent in sketching Assiniboin and Cree.

Topography

Rocky Mountain House had been established as a post by the North West Company in 1799, and was chosen by the Hudson's Bay Company to replace its own post after the union of the two companies in 1821. It was operated from 1828 to 1861 as a winter post only. This fort was completely rebuilt in 1864 but abandoned in 1875 in favour of the Calgary post.

IV-217 Rocky Mountain House with Assiniboin lodges in the foreground. (*Wanderings*, p. 146.) (Bushnell, *Sketches*, p. 15.) TCH211. w.c. 5½″ x 9⅛″. (Bushnell 41-72/397)

IV-218 Rocky Mountain House. Painting based on IV-217. GWA48. Oil on canvas. 1′6″ x 2′5″. Fig. 108. (ROM912.1.57)

IV-219 Log cache for food storage between Rocky Mountain House and Fort Edmonton. Kane describes finding a wolverine in it (*Wanderings*, p. 147). Pencil. 5½″ x 9″. (ROM946.15.302)

Assiniboin

IV-220 Assiniboin lodge at Rocky Mountain House (?). This lodge resembles those pictured in IV-217 and IV-218, but evergreen lodges are known to have existed in other parts of the west. This particular lodge appears to be of birch bark with a covering of evergreen. w.c. 5½″ x 9½″. (ROM946.15.217)

IV-221 Assiniboin chiefs at Rocky Mountain House. *Left:* Mah-Min or "The Feather," head chief. *Right:* Wah-he-joe-tass-e-neen or "The half-white man," second chief. (*Wanderings*, pp. 146–47.) Formerly these sketches were incorrectly identified as portraits of Iacaway and Little Rat (see IV-29). TCH82 and TCH83. AG100. w.c. 5¼″ x 8⅞″. Plate XXVIII. (Stark PWC1)

IV-222 Head Chief of the Assiniboins (Mah-Min). The portrait is based on that in IV-221, but there are variations in the dress. The club, roach and quiver were evidently suggested by those in IV-224 (which have not definitely been established as Assiniboin). GWA62. Oil on canvas. 2′6″ x 2′1″. (ROM912.1.58)

IV-223 Mah-Min or "The Feather" (Head Chief of the Assiniboine). Replica of IV-222. This portrait has on occasion been referred to as that of a Blackfoot. Oil on canvas. 2′6″ x 2′1″. Fig. 109. (Montreal Museum of Fine Arts 47.992)

IV-224 War clubs. Evidently these clubs and a quiver have been introduced into IV-222 and IV-223, but there is no documentary proof that they are Assiniboin. TCH155. AG125. w.c. 5¼″ x 9½″. (Stark WWC75)

IV-225 Wah-he-joe-tass-e-neen or "The half-white man." This is evidently a preliminary sketch. It was formerly identified as a sketch of Coe-coosh (see III-126). w.c. 4½″ x 5″. (ROM946.15.55)

IV-226 Second Chief of the Assiniboins (Wah-he-joe-tass-e-neen). Painting based on IV-221, and formerly identified as a portrait of Coe-coosh (III-127). GWA63. Oil on canvas. 2′6″ x 2′1″. (ROM912.1.59)

Cree

IV-227 Pe-a-pus-qua-hum or "One that passes through the sky." This Cree lived among the Assiniboin at Rocky Mountain House.

(See Bushnell, *Sketches*, pp. 17–18.) TCH85. w.c. 5½″ x 4½″. (Bushnell 41-72/398)

PRAIRIE INDIAN ENCAMPMENTS

No locale or tribe can be identified for the following sketches. A number of the figures are evidently Cree but lack of documentary evidence would make any attribution conjectural.

IV-228 Group of Plains Indians with tepee and horse. Pencil. 4½″ x 6½″. (ROM946.15.308)

IV-229 Group of Plains Indians with tepee and horse. Pencil. 4½″ x 6″. (ROM946.15.309)

IV-230 Group of three seated women. w.c. 5½″ x 9″. (ROM946.15.312)

IV-231 Seated woman. It has been suggested that she is an Ojibwa girl from the Georgian Bay Region (Kathleen Wood, "Paul Kane Sketches," *Rotunda*, Winter 1969, p. 9, illus.). It seems equally possible that she is related to the group pictured in IV-230. Pencil. 5″ x 7½″. (ROM946.15.291)

IV-232 Group of Plains Indians smoking. Pencil. 3¾″ x 5½″. (ROM946.15.315)

IV-233 Seated Indian with pipe. Evidently this is a more detailed study of one of the group in IV-232. Pencil. 3¾″ x 5½″. (ROM946.15.316)

IV-234 Two standing figures: man with trade gun, possibly a Hudson's Bay Company employee, and an Indian. Pencil. 6½″ x 10″. (ROM946.15.303)

IV-235 Page of sketches, probably all completed on the plains. *Left to right:* standing European boy holding spear; profile head of Indian with forelock similar to that worn by the Cree at Fort Carlton (see, e.g., IV-103); profile head of Indian with beads on side of face. Numbers have been associated with each of the three sketches in a recent hand; they do not correspond with Kane's log. Pencil. 5½″ x 6½″. (ROM946.15.294)

IV-236 Indian woman with papoose and cradle board on her back. An inscription on the reverse, possibly in Kane's hand, reads: "Bay-je-gi-she-quish, The Striped Cloud," and "Og-sah-wah-nah-quoch-ogue, The Golden Cloud." Pencil. 4″ x 4¾″. (ROM946.15.154)

IV-237 Seated Indian girl leaning on a post. It has been suggested, without confirmation, that this is a crude study of the Saulteaux girl in IV-87. w.c. 5″ x 7¼″. (ROM946.15.81)

IV-238 Indians grouped around a tepee; a crude sketch. Pencil. 5½″ x 9¼″. (ROM946.15.219)

IV-239 Indian encampment on shoreline. An inscription in sepia ink on the reverse, possibly in Kane's hand, reads: "Edmonton, Mar. 5th." The paper is watermarked Whatman 46. Pencil. 3½″ x 5″. (ROM946.15.123)

FORT EDMONTON TO FORT ASSINIBOINE

Kane left Fort Edmonton for the Pacific on October 6, 1846, and arrived at Fort Assiniboine, Athabasca River, on the 10th. He notes seeing buffalo on this outward journey. He retraced the route during the late autumn of 1847, but does not mention sketching on the return journey.

IV-240 Group of Buffalo. Kane describes sketching a group at "Sturgeon Creek" sixteen miles west of Fort Edmonton (*Wanderings*, p. 84; woodcut, Fig. 6). No preliminary sketches have been located. GWA32. Oil on canvas. 1'7½" x 2'5"; (oval) 1'5½" x 2'3¼". (ROM912.1.47)

IV-241 Buffaloes at Sunset. Replica of IV-240. Oil on canvas; (oval) 1'4½" x 2'½". (Colln Mr. and Mrs. Jules Loeb)

IV-242 Buffaloes reposing near Sturgeon Creek. Replica of IV-240. Oil on canvas; (oval) 1'2¾" x 2'1". (Glenbow)

IV-243 Buffaloes at Sunset. Replica of IV-240. LP4. Oil on canvas; (oval) 1'4½" x 2'3½". Fig. 110. (NGC6919)

IV-244 Buffaloes at Sunset. Replica of IV-240. The Coe collection, which contains this replica, allegedly came from Sir George Simpson's collection, but this canvas is not in the list of paintings ordered by Sir George from Kane. Oil on canvas. 10¾" x 16½". (Coe)

FORT ASSINIBOINE TO JASPER HOUSE

Kane left Fort Assiniboine October 11, 1846, and arrived at Jasper House November 3, where he remained for two days. On his return journey, he was at Jasper House November 5–15, 1847, and reached Fort Assiniboine on November 29. He encountered many difficulties on his return journey; the sketches in this group were probably all completed on the outward trip.

Jasper House, on the Athabasca River, was an important supply depot for horses and canoes carrying freight to the west coast by way of the Athabasca and Yellowhead passes. A post was built by the North West Company at Jasper, near the outlet of Brulé Lake, about 1813. It was rebuilt by the Hudson's Bay Company between 1827 and 1829 near the mouth of the Miette River and was maintained until 1884. (*Wanderings*, p. 87.)

IV-245 Athabasca River with mountains in the distance. Probably sketched October 31, 1846 (*Wanderings*, p. 86). An inscription on the reverse reads "Jasper's Lake." KLL31. w.c. 5" x 7". (ROM946.15.131)

IV-246 Athabasca River with mountain in the distance. Close-up view of terrain in IV-245. Pencil. 5" x 6½". (ROM946.15.268)

IV-247 Athabasca River. Pencil. 5" x 6½". (ROM946.15.234)

IV-248 Jasper House and Jasper Lake. Pencil. 5" x 6½". (ROM-946.15.267)

IV-249 Jasper Lake with Miette's Rock. KLL32. TCH190. w.c. 5" x 7". (ROM946.15.130)

IV-250 Jasper House. (*Wanderings*; woodcut, Fig. 7.) KLL33. TCH189. AG139. w.c. 5¼" x 8⅞". Fig. 111. (Stark PWC25)

JASPER HOUSE

Shuswap and Carrier

The Shuswap were the most important of the Salishan tribes in British Columbia; they held much territory between the Columbia and Fraser rivers including the basin of the Thompson River above Ashcroft. The Carrier (their formal name is Takulli) were a tribe of British Columbia living on the upper Fraser and the Blackwater rivers and in the vicinity of Stuart and Babine lakes.

IV-251 As-in-a-chap (Assannitchay) or "Capote Blanc." Kane met this Shuswap at Jasper on November 5, 1846, and again at Boat Encampment on October 10, 1847 (*Wanderings*, pp. 87, 129). This sketch was identified formerly as one of Iwa-toke, the Menominee from Lake Winnebago (III-106). (See Bushnell, *Sketches*, p. 6.) KPL20. w.c. 5½" x 4½". (Bushnell 41-72/392)

IV-252 A-chis-a-lay or "The Call of the Wind." This sketch was evidently made at Jasper House. Kane describes the man in his log as a member of the "As-ick-an-a" tribe from the Peace River, and says Sir Alexander Mackenzie called its people the "Carriers." KPL21. TCH93. AG216. w.c. 5⅜" x 9". (Stark PWC24)

JASPER TO BOAT ENCAMPMENT

Kane left Jasper on November 5, 1846. He crossed over to Boat Encampment on the Columbia River by way of the Committee's Punch Bowl and reached it on November 14. Returning a year later, he left Boat Encampment on October 31 and arrived at Jasper on November 6, 1847.

IV-253 Four pack horses. These are probably horses in the cavalcade which was with Kane's party when it left Jasper on November 5, 1846 (*Wanderings*, p. 87). Pencil. 5¼" x 6½". Fig. 112. (ROM946.15.133)

IV-254 Sketch of pack horse and detail study of horse's head. Pencil. 5" x 7". (ROM946.15.249)

IV-255 LaRocque's Prairie with wild horses. Kane camped at this spot on the night of November 6, 1846, and exactly a year later on his way home (*Wanderings*, pp. 87, 131). The sketch was formerly identified incorrectly as of "The Cascade Mountains, B. Columbia." KLL35. TCH191. w.c. 5½" x 8¾". (Stark wwc79)

IV-256 Bighorn Rocky Mountain ram. Kane made this sketch on November 6, 1847, just before reaching Jasper on his homeward journey, and reports the horns as having a length of 42 inches (*Wanderings*, pp. 131–32). TCH175. AG103. w.c. 5" x 7¼". Fig. 113. (Stark wwc98A)

IV-257 Bighorn Rocky Mountain sheep (ewe). w.c. 5" x 7". (ROM-946.15.135)

IV-258 Rocky Mountain goat (*Wanderings*, pp. 87, 127). Pencil. 5" x 7". (ROM946.15.136)

IV-259 Rocky Mountain goat. Pencil. 5″ x 7″. (ROM946.15.137)

IV-260 Rocky Mountain goat (head). Pencil. 5″ x 7″. (ROM-946.15.134)

IV-261 Rocky Mountain goat. TCH145. AG201. w.c. 5″ x 7¼″. (Stark wwc94)

IV-262 Rocky Mountain goat. Presumably this is the sketch for a canvas, unlocated, painted for Sir George Simpson (GS14). AG96. Oil on paper. 9″ x 14″. Fig. 114. (Stark WOP18)

IV-263 Prairie with mountain sheep. KLL34. w.c. 5½″ x 9″. (ROM946.15.237)

IV-264 Athabasca River in the mountains. KLL37. TCH194. w.c. 5½″ x 9″. Fig. 115. (ROM946.15.238)

IV-265 Athabasca River in the mountains. KLL36. w.c. 5½″ x 9″. (ROM-946.15.328)

IV-266 A winter scene in the Rockies: Athabasca River. KLL36. w.c. 5¼″ x 9″. (Stark wwc18)

IV-267 Snow in the Rockies. Possibly painted November 10–12, 1846, when Kane experienced very heavy snow in the mountains (*Wanderings*, p. 88). w.c. 5″ x 7″. (ROM946.15.132)

IV-268 Tree laden with snow. w.c. 5½″ x 4½″. (ROM946.15.289)

IV-269 The Committee's Punch Bowl. Probably sketched November 12, 1846 (*Wanderings*, p. 88). KLL39. w.c. 5½″ x 9″. Fig. 116. (ROM946.15.239)

IV-270 A sketch of the falls at the headwaters of the Columbia River. This is probably the sketch Kane refers to under the date November 14, 1846 (*Wanderings*, p. 88). KLL40. w.c. 5″ x 7″. (ROM946.15.278)

IV-271 A sketch on the upper Columbia River (?). Pencil. 5½″ x 9″. (ROM946.15.241)

IV-272 A sketch on the upper Columbia River (?). Pencil. 5½″ x 9″. (ROM946.15.240)

IV-273 Mountain landscape. An earlier suggestion that this is a view of Mount St. Helens is incorrect. Pencil. 5¼″ x 9″. (ROM-946.15.160)

IV-274 A river in the mountains, possibly the Columbia River. AG150. w.c. 4⅞″ x 7″. (Stark wwc12)

IV-275 Camping scene in the woods, possibly near Boat Encampment. Pencil. 5″ x 7″. (ROM946.15.296)

IV-276 Boat Encampment. Sketch with Kane's tent and luggage. Kane was here on November 15, 1846, and October 10–31, 1847 (*Wanderings*, pp. 89, 129–30). TCH230. w.c. 5¼″ x 8¾″. Plate XXIX. (Stark wwc100)

IV-277 Study of mountain peaks as seen from Boat Encampment. w.c. 5½″ x 9½″. Fig. 117. (ROM946.15.236)

IV-278 Boat Encampment. Painting based on IV-276 and IV-277. GWA26. Oil on canvas. 1′6″ x 2′5″. (ROM912.1.60)

IV-279 Boat Encampment. Replica of IV-278. Oil on canvas. 1′1¾″ x 1′8¼″ (Glenbow)

MOUNTAINS

Plains Indians

IV-280 Party of three Indians in birch-bark canoe. Pencil. 5½″ x 9½″. (ROM946.15.301)

IV-281 Party of Indians in two canoes on mountain lake. Evidently this is a representation of an Indian legend. IV-280 is possibly a preliminary sketch. Oil on canvas. 1′6″ x 2′5″. (Colln P. Winkworth)

BOAT ENCAMPMENT TO FORT COLVILE

IV-282 Dalles des Morts, or the Rapid of the Dead (probably based on a sketch to which Kane refers in *Wanderings*, p. 128). GWA13. Oil on canvas. 1′6″ x 2′5″. (ROM912.1.61)

IV-283 Sailing on Upper Arrow Lakes. Probably sketched September 25–29, 1847 (*Wanderings*, p. 127). Pencil. 5″ x 7″. (ROM946.15.82)

IV-284 Shoreline of Upper Arrow Lakes. Formerly described as "View on the Columbia River." Pencil. 5″ x 6¼″. (ROM946.15.333)

IV-285 Shoreline of Upper Arrow Lakes. Pencil. 5½″ x 9″. (ROM-946.15.176)

IV-286 The Little Dalles, twenty miles above Kettle Falls near Fort Colvile. Probably sketched September 23, 1847 (*Wanderings*, p. 126). KLL115. AG209. wc.. 5½″ x 9½″. Fig. 119. (Stark wwc6)

IV-287 The Little Dalles. Painting based on IV-286. Oil on canvas. 1′7¾″ x 2′5″. (Stark WOP24)

COLUMBIA RIVER

Kutenai

The Kutenai Indians, of a distinct linguistic stock, lived in the southeastern part of British Columbia and on the lakes near the source of the Columbia River. The lower Kutenai group in particular were distinguished for their unusual bark canoes. (*Wanderings*, p. 127)

IV-288 Ask-a-weelish. A chief of the lakes 60 miles above Colvile. TCH95. AG99. w.c. 5¼″ x 8⅞″. Fig. 122. (Stark wwc80, left)

IV-289 An Indian of the lakes above Colvile. KPL22. TCH106. AG185. w.c. 4⅞″ x 3⅝″. (Stark wwc38)

IV-290 Columbia River near Grand Rapids. A Kutenai-type canoe is in the water. KLL41. w.c. 5½″ x 9″. Fig. 121. (ROM946.15.174)

IV-291 Page of sketches: Kutenai canoe, sweathouse, tepee, and a mat lodge of the upper Columbia River. Pencil. 5½″ x 9½″. Fig. 120. (ROM946.15.202)

FORT COLVILE

Chualpays

Kane identifies the Indians whom he met at Fort Colvile as Chualpays and remarks that they are similar to the Spokan and not much different from the Walla Walla. A division of Salish, they are referred to in modern terminology as "Colville." (The Hudson's Bay Company post on the Columbia had been named "Colvile" for a governor of the Company and this spelling is used in the present book where appropriate.)

IV-292   See-pays, or "Chief of the Waters." Sketch was probably made September 17, 1847 (*Wanderings*, p. 123). KPL83. TCH96. AG99. w.c. 5¼″ x 8⅞″. Fig. 122. (Stark wwc80, right)

IV-293   Chief of the Salmon (See-pays). Painting based on IV-292. GWA92. Oil on canvas. 2′6″ x 2′1″. (ROM912.1.63)

IV-294   El-ko-ka-shin, a "Shawalloway Indian, from the Cascades." This designation, from the TCH catalogue, evidently refers to this sketch. An inscription on it, not in Kane's hand, reads "The Blue Jay from Kettle Falls." Both names may apply to this individual. A "Blue Jay" is a man set apart among Salishan tribes because of his dealings with the supernatural; see R. G. Conn, "The Rarest Kind of Blue Jay," *Blue Jay* (Regina, Sask.), XXV, 1, March 1967. TCH98. AG104. w.c. 5¼″ x 8⅞″. (Stark wwc20, left)

IV-295   Allam-mak-hum Stole-luch (Elle-a-ma-cum-stuck) or "Chief of the Earth." Kane describes him in his book as a Chualpays (*Wanderings*, p. 123), but in his manuscript portrait log as a Spokan. It was formerly suggested that this sketch might be a portrait of Casanov (see IV-418). KPL23. w.c. 7″ x 5″. (ROM-946.15.215)

IV-296   Unidentified portrait. The treatment of hair is similar to that for See-pays, chief of the Chualpays (see IV-293). AG159. w.c. 4¾″ x 3¾″. (Stark wwc39)

SALMON FISHING

Kane discusses in detail the methods used by Chualpays in salmon fishing near Fort Colvile, which he observed on his return trip across the continent (*Wanderings*, pp. 123–24). Sketches associated with this type of fishing are gathered together below, although some may have originated at other points along the Columbia since Kane mentions salmon fishing at Fort Walla Walla and Fort Vancouver; only those sketches which can definitely be associated with other areas are not included here.

IV-297   Kettle Falls, Spokane River. KLL112. TCH182. AG151. w.c. 5⅜″ x 9½″. (Stark wwc68)

IV-298   Kettle Falls. KLL111. AG7. Oil on paper. 8⅛″ x 13⅜″. Plate XXX. (Stark wop19)

IV-299   Kettle Falls. Inscribed, but not in Kane's hand, "Salmon Falls, Koos-koos-kia River." AG156. w.c. 5½″ x 9⅞″. (Stark wwc46)

IV-300   Weir on Columbia River at Colvile. Pencil. 5¼″ x 9½″. (ROM946.15.161)

IV-301   Platform for fishermen at Kettle Falls. (In the upper right is a small landscape, Lost Men's Portage; see IV-6a). w.c. 5″ x 7¼″. (ROM946.15.332)

IV-302   Indian with fish spear poised on platform. Pencil 5¼″ x 9½″. (ROM946.15.203)

IV-303   Salmon weir at Kettle Falls. Study of the central portion of the waterfalls. w.c. 5½″ x 9⅜″. (ROM946.15.205)

IV-304   Indians spearing salmon on the Columbia River. TCH166. AG133. w.c. 5½″ x 9½″ (Stark wwc84)

IV-305   Indians spearing salmon. AG168. w.c. 5⅜″ x 9½″. (Stark wwc85)

IV-306   Catching salmon on the Columbia River. *Left:* elaborately decorated quiver with bow. *Lower right:* Indian with speared fish and club; study of woman with tump line and a papoose on her back. AG105. w.c. 5⅜″ x 9½″. Fig. 123. (Stark wwc87)

IV-307   Falls at Colville. Painting based on sketches IV-299 to IV-306. GWA5. Oil on canvas. 1′7″ x 2′5″. (ROM912.1.64)

IV-308   Fish houses, Columbia River. Indian lodges: 1/ the head chief's lodge; 2/ the second chief's; 3/ the salmon chief's. (See IV-310, 328.) The third lodge is evidently that of See-pays (IV-292). KLL114. AG191. w.c. 5½″ x 9⅜″. (Stark wwc60)

IV-309   Indians smoking salmon near the Columbia River. On reverse, seated woman. w.c. and pencil. 5½″ x 9″. Fig. 124. (ROM946.15.206)

IV-310   Drying salmon at the Dalles, Columbia River. Indian lodges: 1/ the head chief's lodge; 2/ the second chief's. (See IV-308.) KLL113. AG180. w.c. 5½″ x 9¼″. Plate XXXI. (Stark wwc50)

IV-311   Indian Camp, Colville. Painting based on IV-310. The woman with tump line and papoose has probably been suggested by the sketch in IV-306, and the horse with woman's saddle by IV-370. GWA15. Oil on canvas. 1′7″ x 2′5½″. (ROM912.1.62)

IV-312   Drying salmon at the Dalles, Columbia River. Oil version of IV-310. Oil on paper. 8½″ x 13½″. (Colln H. R. Milner)

IV-313   Three standing fishermen with dip nets. Pencil. 5½″ x9″. (ROM946.15.325)

IV-314   Spearing fish. Pencil. 5¼″ x 10½″. (ROM946.15.244)

IV-315   Fish-drying camp on the Columbia River. Pencil. 6¾″ x 9¾″. (ROM946.15.198)

GAME OF AL-KOL-LOCK

Kane witnessed this game of the Chualpays during his stay at Fort Colvile September 17–22, 1847 (*Wanderings*, p. 123). He describes the method of playing; a ring falls on thrown spears and scores are determined by means of coloured balls on the ring, each of which has a different value.

IV-316   Game of Al-kol-lock, Columbia River. AG116. w.c. 5½″ x 9″. Fig. 125. (Stark wwc78)

IV-317   Study of the ring used in Al-kol-lock; it includes colour notations for beads. Pencil. 5½″ x 9½″. (ROM946.15.204)

IV-318 Study of ring and of bone-tipped wand used in the game of Al-kol-lock. w.c. 4½″ x 6½″. (ROM946.15.210)

IV-319 Study of two figures playing Al-kol-lock, and the backs of two observers seated on right. Pencil. 5½″ x 9½″. (ROM-946.15.209)

IV-320 Game of Alcoloh (Al-kol-lock). Painting based on IV-316, and with background based on IV-332. GWA21. Oil on canvas. 1′6″ x 2′5″. (ROM912.1.65)

IV-321 Indians Playing at Alcoloh. Replica of IV-320. LP12. Oil on canvas. 1′6″ x 2′5″. Fig. 126. (NGC60)

SCALP DANCE

Kane witnessed a scalp dance during his stay at Fort Colvile, September 17–22, 1847 (*Wanderings*, p. 124). He sketched various aspects of the ritual.

IV-322 Chualpays scalp dance. TCH60. AG115. w.c. 5⅜″ x 9½″. Fig. 127. (Stark wwc31)

IV-323 Studies of the scalp dance. *Left:* medicine man and widow holding hoop with Blackfoot scalp. *Right:* eight faces of women dancers, with colour notations. Pencil. 5½″ x 9½″. (ROM-946.15.230)

IV-324 Painted faces of eight attendant women dancers. TCH94. AG127. w.c. 5½″ x 9⅜″. Fig. 128. (Stark wwc72)

IV-325 Sketches of two standing figures. *Left:* medicine man. *Right:* figure holding hoop. Pencil. 5½″ x 9½″. (ROM946.15.229)

IV-326 Studies of scalp dance. *Left:* three heads with painted faces, and details of scalp attached to stick held by the widow. *Centre:* medicine man with body painting. *Right:* two studies of widow holding scalp. Pencil. 5½″ x 9¼″. (ROM946.15.208)

IV-327 Studies of scalp dance. *Left:* unidentified figure of an Indian. *Centre:* standing figure holding hoop and a medicine man with painted stripes on body. *Right:* woman with cradle board. AG165. w.c. 5⅜″ x 9½″. Fig. 130. (Stark wwc63)

IV-328 Scalp Dance, Colville. Painting based on sketches IV-322 to IV-327, and on buildings in IV-308. GWA22. Oil on canvas. 1′7″ x 2′5″. (ROM912.1.66)

IV-329 Scalp Dance by Spokane [*sic*] Indians. Replica of IV-328. LP5. Oil on canvas. 1′7″ x 2′5″. Fig. 129. (NGC103)

Miscellaneous sketches

IV-330 Hudson's Bay mill, Fort Colvile. Pencil. 5¼″ x 9″. (ROM-946.15.159)

IV-331 Painted horse, Colville. This has been described incorrectly as a Blackfoot horse (see Bushnell, *Sketches*, pp. 18–19). KLL116. TCH154. w.c. 5⅜″ x 9⅛″. (Bushnell 41-72/401)

IV-332 Sketch on the Columbia River 50 miles below Colvile. Identified

from a notation on the sketch, not in Kane's hand. (See IV-320.) AG145. w.c. 5⅜″ x 9½″. (Stark wwc42)

See also IV-290.

Flathead

Authorities usually describe this tribe as living in the western part of what is now the state of Montana; their formal name is given as Salish, and they are placed as a division of the Salishan family. There were small bodies of Salish in the area around the Spokane River, and they are usually identified as Spokan.

It is not clear to what group Kane is referring in connection with the sketch listed below. He points out in a manuscript note related to it that the Flatheads were closely related to the Spokan (see IV-337). He also says that the name Flathead is a misnomer as the heads of these Indians were not artificially flattened like those of the Chinook. (The name likely arises because their heads were not distorted but left flat on top.) He refers elsewhere (*Wanderings*, p. 111) to a Flathead burial ground at the Cascades on the Columbia River.

IV-333 Chinewoss, a Flathead or "Sheach-a-way" Indian from west of the Rockies. Identification has been made from an inscription on the reverse. KPL Addendum. TCH97. AG104. w.c. 5¼″ x 8⅞″. (Stark wwc20, right)

SPOKANE RIVER

Topography

IV-334 Sketch on the Spokane River. KLL117. TCH216. w.c. 5½″ x 9″. Plate XXXII. (ROM946.15.189)

IV-335 Falls on the Spokane River (?). This highly tentative identification has been made from a recent inscription on the reverse of the sketch. Pencil. 5½″ x 9″. (ROM946.15.190)

IV-336 Mission station of Walker and Eells, Spokane River. Kane arrived at the mission for a week's visit on September 9, 1847 (*Wanderings*, p. 122). The station had been established by the Rev. Elkanah Walker and the Rev. Cushing Eells as a mission to the Spokan Indians at Tshimakain in 1834, and was abandoned in 1848; it was supported by the American Board of Commissioners for Foreign Missions. KLL118. TCH197. AG187. w.c. 5⅜″ x 9⅜″. Fig. 131. (Stark wwc69)

Spokan

The Spokan were Salish Indians living in several small groups on and near the Spokane River in the northeastern part of what is now the state of Washington. Kane, in company with Mr. Walker and Mr. Eells, the Presbyterian missionaries, visited there between September 9 and 17, 1847 (*Wanderings*, pp. 122–23).

IV-337 Tum-se-ne-ho, or "The Man without Blood," a Spokan chief of the Spokane River. TCH109. w.c. 9⅜″ x 5½″. Plate XXXIII. (Stark wwc43)

PELOUSE RIVER

Topography

Kane left Walla Walla on July 13, 1847, to visit the Pelouse River. He was particularly impressed by its upper and lower falls.

IV-338 Coliseum-like formation near the lower falls. Sketch formerly identified as "Walls of the Columbia." Kane saw the formation on July 14, 1847 (*Wanderings*, p. 115). KLL101. w.c. 5½" x 9½". (ROM946.15.180)

IV-339 Coliseum-like formation near the lower falls, a second view, w.c. 5½" x 9½". (ROM946.15.181)

IV-340 The amphitheatre near the lower falls. Sketched July 14, 1847 (*Wanderings*, p. 115). An inscription on the sketch, not in Kane's hand, reads: "Grand Coulee near Walla-Walla River." KLL100. w.c. 5½" x 9⅜". (Stark WWC5)

IV-341 Looking down the Pelouse River with its basaltic rock. Sketched July 14, 1847 (*Wanderings*, p. 115). KLL104. w.c. 5½" x 9½". Plate XXXIV. (ROM946.15.182)

IV-342 Rocky gorge. It has been suggested that this is the entrance to the lower falls region. Pencil. 5" x 7¼". (ROM946.15.187)

IV-343 The lower falls on the Pelouse River. Sketched July 14, 1847 (*Wanderings*, p. 115). KLL99. TCH220. AG146. w.c. 5½" x 9½". Fig. 132. (Stark WWC49)

IV-344 The lower falls on the Pelouse River, the same view as in IV-343. AG75. Oil on paper. 9⅛" x 14". (Stark WOP20)

IV-345 Peluce [Pelouse] Falls. Painting based on sketches IV-343 and IV-344. GWA16. Oil on canvas. 1'6" x 2'5¼". (ROM912.1.70)

IV-346 Pelouse Falls. Replica of IV-345. GS11. Oil on canvas. 11¾" x 18¼". (Coe)

IV-347 A Sketch on the Peluce [Pelouse]. Possibly this is the ravine which Kane ascended July 15, 1847 (*Wanderings*, p. 115). GWA56. Oil on canvas. 1'7¼" x 2'6". (ROM912.1.71)

IV-348 Falls on the upper Pelouse River. Visited by Kane July 15 to 17, 1847 (*Wanderings*, p. 115). KLL102. AG163. w.c. 5½" x 9¾". (Stark WWC44)

IV-349 Falls on the upper Pelouse River. TCH61. Oil on paper. 8⅛" x 13⅜". Plate XXXV. (Stark WOP22)

IV-350 Nez Percé River or south branch of the Columbia River or Snake River (*Wanderings*, p. 116). The locale was identified formerly as "Rock called the Too-He-Pu-See-Girls" (see IV-358). KLL105. w.c. 5½" x 9½". Fig. 133. (ROM-946.15.186)

IV-351 River scenery. It has been suggested, but without supporting evidence, that the river is the Pelouse. w.c. 5½" x 9". (ROM-946.15.188)

IV-352 River scenery. It has been suggested, but without supporting evidence, that the river is the Pelouse. w.c. 5" x 7¼". (ROM946.15.179)

Paloos Indians

The Paloos are a Shahaptian tribe who occupied the Pelouse River valley in the present states of Washington and Idaho, and the north bank of the Snake River as far as its junction with the Columbia River. They numbered 500 in 1854. The tribe has always had close relations with the Nez Percé Indians.

IV-353 Slo-ce-ac-cum, chief of the "Upputuppets." Sketched July 14, 1847 (*Wanderings*, p. 115). Reverse bears an inscription, not in Kane's hand, reading "How-e-ago-sun-upet-uppet." KPL73. w.c. 5" x 7". (ROM946.15.197)

FORT WALLA WALLA

Kane visited Fort Walla Walla on July 12, 1847, and again on the 22nd after returning from a visit to the Pelouse River and the Whitman Mission (*Wanderings*, pp. 114, 117). Fort Walla Walla, often called Fort Nez Percé, comprised the following buildings in 1847: 1 dwelling house 38' x 28'; 1 range of houses occupied by men of the establishment 48' x 18'; 1 dwelling house 17' x 18'; 1 range of stores 46' x 21'; a second 40' x 13'; 1 powder magazine 7' x 10'; 1 pigeon house 9' x 7'; 1 poultry house 10' x 9'; 2 stone bastions each 16' x 16'; wall of fort 12' high, 1½' thick, 113' x 113', with stone foundations. Outbuildings comprised 1 stable 33' x 18'; 1 house 14' x 10' for smoking meat; 1 root house 20' x 15'; 1 pig sty 30' x 16'; 1 horse park 56' x 54', 6' high. A farm had a dwelling 20' x 15', 1 dairy built of logs 20' x 15', with 30 acres of cultivated land. The buildings were all of adobe construction except the dairy. (Hudson's Bay Company Archives, London, D5/18.) The fort was abandoned in 1856 as a result of the Indian wars.

Topography

IV-354 Fort Walla Walla. Pencil. 5½" x 9½". (ROM946.15.172)

IV-355 Fort Walla Walla. KLL98. TCH183. AG47. w.c. 5⅜" x 9½". Fig. 134. (Stark WWC62)

IV-356 The Rock of the Nez Percé Girl (Scene near Walla Walla). View as described by Kane, with Indian fishing (*Wanderings*, p. 114). No preliminary sketch has been located. GWA33. Oil on canvas. 1'6" x 2'5". (ROM912.1.68)

IV-357 Landscape. It is said to be near Walla Walla, according to a recent notation which is not confirmed. w.c. 5½" x 9½". Fig. 136. (ROM946.15.173)

Chimney Rocks

Kane arrived on July 11, 1847, at the junction of the Columbia and Walla Walla rivers and was much impressed by the "Chimney Rocks," a formation known to the Walla Walla Indians as the "Rocks of the Ki-use Girls" (*Wanderings*, pp. 113–14).

IV-358 Chimney Rocks (*Wanderings*, p. 113; woodcut, Fig. 13). KLL97. TCH185. AG162. w.c. 5⅜" x 9½". Fig. 135. (Stark WWC65)

IV-359 Chimney Rocks. A detail study. Pencil. 5½″ x 9″. (ROM-946.15.177)

IV-360 Chimney Rocks. A detail study. Pencil. 5″ x 6½″. (ROM-946.15.245)

IV-361 Castle Rocks, Columbia River (Chimney Rocks). The painting is based on IV-358. GWA14. Oil on canvas. 1′6″ x 2′5¼″. (ROM912.1.67)

WHITMAN MISSION

Kane visited the mission July 18–22, 1847 (*Wanderings*, p. 116). It had been founded at Waiilatpu among the Cayuse in 1836 by Marcus and Narcissa Whitman. They carried on mission work there under the auspices of the American Board of Commissioners for Foreign Missions for eleven years. They were massacred shortly after Kane's visit.

IV-362 The Whitman Mission. This building was finished in 1839. It was a T-shaped structure with a wooden frame, walls of adobe bricks, and a roof of poles, straw and earth. The walls were smoothed and whitewashed with a solution made from river mussel shells; later the Hudson's Bay Company supplied green paint for the doors and window frames, grey for the interior woodwork, and yellow for the pine floors. The main section of the house was at first of a storey-and-a-half construction with three rooms on the ground floor and space for bedrooms above. A long single-storey wing contained a kitchen, a bedroom and a classroom. To this an out-kitchen, storeroom and other facilities were added at a later date. The house was burned in 1872. (E. N. Thompson, *Whitman Mission, National Historic Site*, National Park Service, Historical Handbook Series no. 37, Washington, 1964.) This sketch by Kane is the only known surviving view of the mission. Pencil. 5½″ x 9½″. Fig. 137. (ROM946.15.318)

IV-363 Mrs. Whitman's fan. TCH153. w.c. 5½″ x 9½″. Fig. 138. (ROM946.15.207)

Cayuse

At the time of Kane's trip, the Cayuse, a Waiilatpuan tribe, occupied territory in the present-day states of Washington and Oregon around the headwaters of the Walla Walla, Umatilla and Grand Ronde rivers. In the mid-1830s they numbered 400 individuals and were noted horse traders. They were always closely associated with the Nez Percé tribe, and by 1851 had so intermarried with them that there were few remaining pure-blood members of the tribe.

IV-364 To-ma-kus, an Indian at Dr. Whitman's mission (?). Kane describes sketching the man after his arrival on July 18, 1847; he found him sitting naked in his lodge (*Wanderings*, p. 116). Kane reports later that he was the murderer of Dr. Whitman (*Wanderings*, p. 125). This tentative identification has been made from an inscription on the sketch, not apparently in Kane's hand. AG118. w.c. 7⅛″ x 5⅛″. (Stark wwc77)

IV-365 To-ma-kus, the murderer of Dr. Whitman (see IV-364). This sketch was formerly identified as one of Wah-bannim (III-109) (see Bushnell, *Sketches*, p. 6). The new attribution is made on the basis of Kane's portrait log. KPL79. TCH101(?). w.c. 4½″ x 5½″. Fig. 139. (Bushnell 41-72/393)

IV-366 Tomakus. Portrait based on IV-365. GWA82. Oil on canvas. 2′ x 1′7″; (oval) 1′8″ x 1′2″. (ROM912.1.73)

IV-367 Til-au-kite (Te-law-cite-an) or "Act of Lightning." This man was a chief of the Cayuse and one of Dr. Whitman's murderers. Sketched between July 19 and 21, 1847 (*Wanderings*, p. 116). KPL78. TCH99. AG177. w.c. 5¼″ x 4⅜″. Fig. 140. (Stark wwc59)

IV-368 Tilli-koit (Til-au-kite). This canvas does not appear to be based on IV-367. GWA78. Oil on canvas. 2′1″ x 1′8″. (ROM-912.1.74)

IV-369 The wife of Til-au-kite. KPL74. TCH100. w.c. 7¼″ x 5¼″. (Stark wwc28)

IV-370 Page with two sketches. *Right:* woman wearing hat of the Plateau region. *Left:* study of a woman's saddle of this general region (see also IV-311). Tribe unidentified. Possibly sketched either among the Cayuse or at Fort Colvile. w.c. 5½″ x 9½″. (ROM946.15.162)

WALLA WALLA REGION

Nez Percé

The Nez Percé, or Sahaptin as they were later called, lived in the early 19th century in what is now western Idaho, northeastern Oregon, and in southeastern Washington, on the lower Snake River and its tributaries. They were neighbours of the Cayuse and Walla Walla on several branches of the Snake.

IV-371 Nez Percé Indian. Bushnell considers that this is the sketch Kane refers to as having made on July 29, 1847 (*Sketches*, pp. 9–11; see *Wanderings*, p. 119). w.c. 4½″ x 5½″. (Bushnell 41-72/394)

IV-372 Nez Percé Indian. Painting based on IV-371, but with variations. GWA74. Oil on canvas. 2′1″ x 1′8″. Fig. 141. (ROM912.1.72)

IV-373 Nach-a-wish, a Nez Percé Indian. This attribution is made on the basis of an entry in Kane's portrait log. The sketch bears an inscription "Portrait of the Indian who murdered Dr. Whitman" but this is not in Kane's hand. KPL77. AG130. w.c. 5¼″ x 4½″. (Stark wwc36)

Walla Walla

The Walla Walla Indians, a Shahaptian tribe, lived on the lower Walla Walla River and the eastern bank of the Columbia River from the Snake River to the Umatilla River in the present states of Washington and Oregon. They are closely related to the Nez Percé but have a distinct dialect. Kane was in contact with them during his stay at Fort Walla Walla in July 1847.

IV-374 A Walla Walla lodge. KLL52. TCH179. w.c. 5″ x 7″. (ROM-946.15.222)

IV-375 Tam-at-a-pa, brother of Chief Peo-Peo-mox-mox of the Walla Walla Indians. KPL76. TCH103. w.c. 5¼″ x 8⅞″. (Stark wwc15, left)

IV-376 Peo-Peo-mox-mox (or "The Yellow Serpent"), chief of the Walla Walla Indians. Kane sketched him at Fort Walla Walla between July 22 and 26, 1847 (*Wanderings*, p. 117). No sketch for this painting has been located. GWA94. Oil on canvas. 2′1″ x 1′8″. Fig. 142. (ROM912.1.69)

IV-377 Son of Peo-Peo-mox-mox. Kane has numbered this sketch as KPL80, but the numbering evidently relates to a lost portion of the log. TCH102. w.c. 4½″ x 5¼″. Fig. 143. (ROM-946.15.196)

GRAND COULEE REGION

Kane left Fort Walla Walla on July 29, 1847, and travelled by way of the Grand Coulee to Fort Colvile which he reached on August 8, 1847 (*Wanderings*, pp. 118–22). The following sketches were evidently completed during this trip.

IV-378 Sketch of sand dune country. Inscription on the reverse, not in Kane's hand, reads "Alakpowa, a tributary of the Columbia R." The locale is possibly the sand dune country described by Kane (*Wanderings*, p. 119). w.c. 5½″ x 9″. (ROM946.15.192)

IV-379 Grand Coulee. KLL107. TCH218. AG157. w.c. 5⅜″ x 9½″. (Stark wwc51)

IV-380 Grand Coulee. KLL108. w.c. 5½″ x 9½″. (ROM946.15.178)

IV-381 Grand Coulee. KLL109. TCH219. w.c. 5⅜″ x 9½″. (Stark wwc7)

LOWER COLUMBIA RIVER

Topography

On his return journey in 1847, Kane describes passing the portages of the Cascades, the Dalles, and the Chutes on July 3 to July 8 (*Wanderings*, pp. 111–12). These sketches were probably completed at that time. When he had descended the Columbia River late in 1846 the brigade was moving quickly and he does not mention this region.

IV-382 "Landslip" six miles above the Cascades on the Columbia River (*Wanderings*, p. 112). KLL95. TCH186. AG33. w.c. 5¼″ x 8⅞″. Fig. 144. (Stark wwc30)

IV-383 "Landslip" six miles above the Cascades on the Columbia River. Rough sketch for IV-382. Pencil. 4″ x 5¼″. (ROM946.15.297)

IV-384 At the head of the Cascades. KLL94. w.c. 5″ x 7¼″. (ROM-946.15.331)

IV-385 The Cascades. This sketch was earlier identified as a sketch on the Spokane River. KLL93. TCH187. AG149. w.c. 5⅜″ x 9½″. (Stark wwc53)

IV-386 The Cascades. KLL42. Pencil study. 5½″ x 9″. (ROM-946.15.183)

IV-387 The Cascades. Sketch based on IV-386. AG32. Oil on paper. 8¼″ x 13¼″. Fig. 145. (Stark wOP9)

IV-388 Below the Cascades. Indian fishing on the Columbia River (*Wanderings*, p. 111). KLL92. AG169. w.c. 5½″ x 9½″. Fig. 146. (Stark wwc92)

IV-389 Cape Horn, twenty miles above Fort Vancouver, 200 feet high and subject to high winds. Pencil. 5½″ x 9½″. (ROM-946.15.266)

IV-390 Cape Horn. Same view as in IV-389. KLL90. TCH184. AG184. w.c. 5⅜″ x 9¼″. (Stark wwc67)

Cascade, Dalles, Skinpah, Tenino

The Cascade (the formal name is Watlala) were a division of the Chinookan family, who lived at the Cascades or farther up the Columbia River towards the Dalles. The Dalles Indians were Chinookan tribes who lived at the Dalles and on the opposite side of the Columbia River. The Tenino, a Shahaptian tribe, inhabited the valley of the Deschutes River in what is now the state of Oregon, and their dialect was spoken on the Columbia from the Dalles to the Umatilla River. The Skinpah (or Skeen, Skein, Shutes), for example, who lived on the north bank of the Columbia opposite the mouth of the Deschutes, spoke the Tenino dialect. Distinctions among the tribes of this region were not easy for white observers and were further complicated by seasonal visits of other Indians on fishing expeditions.

IV-391 Tomaquin (Tamaquin), chief of the Cascade on the Columbia River (*Wanderings*, p. 112). (See also IV-90.) KPL24. TCH110. w.c. 7″ x 5″. Fig. 147. (ROM946.15.195)

IV-392 So-wall-o-way (Saw-wollo-wa), "a Dall or Tenimo Indian," a chief of the Dalles. KPL70. TCH108. AG109. w.c. 7⅛″ x 5″. (Stark wwc9)

IV-393 Mancemuckt, chief of the Skeen or Shutes. Sketched on July 8, 1847 (*Wanderings*, p. 112). KPL72. w.c. 5½″ x 3⅞″. Fig. 148. (Stark wwc102-I)

IV-394 Mancemuckt, chief of the Skeen or Shutes. Formerly this sketch was identified as one of Kwa-qua-dah-bon-niva-skung, a chief of the Saugeen Indians (see III-2, 3). KPL72. w.c. 7½″ x 5″. (ROM946.15.56)

IV-395 An Indian of the Dalles, Columbia River (Mancemuckt). Painting is based on IV-393 (*Wanderings*; coloured litho.). GWA77. Oil on canvas. 2′1″ x 1′8″, (oval) 2¼″ x 1′7½″. (ROM912.1.75)

IV-396 A Cascade Indian, sketched about 40 miles above Fort Vancouver. KPL34. w.c. 7″ x 5″. Fig. 149. (Stark wwc55)

FORT VANCOUVER

The Fort and environs

Fort Vancouver was founded by the Hudson's Bay Company in 1825–26 as a fur-trade supply depot, and for at least twenty years was headquarters for its operations west of the Rockies and its principal centre in the Pacific Northwest. The original fort had been erected a mile back from the Columbia River. It was rebuilt on the final site closer to the river in 1829. This second structure was the one which Kane visited and where he lived intermittently from December 8, 1846, to July 1, 1847. The fort was abandoned by the Hudson's Bay Company in 1860 as a result of American penetration into the area, which had become part of the United States in June 1846.

At the time of Kane's visit (*Wanderings*, p. 91), there were from 60 to 75 buildings in the village west of the fort's stockade where lesser employees of the fort such as tradesmen, artisans, boatmen and labourers lived. North of the stockade the framework for two new schoolhouses, each measuring 50 by 40 feet, had been erected in 1844; in 1848 they were said to be without floors and to be used for shearing sheep. The first large-scale agricultural operations had been begun in 1826 on 300 acres. (See John A. Hussey, *A History of Fort Vancouver and its Physical Structure*, Washington State Historical Society, 1957, for a detailed history of the fort.)

IV-397 Fort Vancouver. General view in 1847 looking south towards the Columbia River. *At left*, two unfinished school buildings; *at right*, village outside the stockade; *centre*, the fort proper, with the east and south stockade walls; *in left distance*, ship in dock, almost certainly H.M.S. *Modeste*; *at upper right*, detail of redoubt at southeastern angle of the bastion. This view is similar to that in an oil painting of *c.* 1845 in the Coe Collection, Yale University, by an unidentified artist (see Hussey, *History of Fort Vancouver*, frontispiece). Kane's sketch was formerly identified as one of Fort Victoria. Pencil. 5½″ x 9″. Fig. 150. (ROM946.15.211)

IV-398 Fort Vancouver. General view in 1847 looking southeast towards the west and south walls of the stockade, and with Mount Hood on the horizon. Pencil. 5½″ x 9″. (ROM946.15.141)

IV-399 Fort Vancouver. Village area to the west of the fort proper, looking south towards Mount Hood. *Upper right:* detail of log building and fence. Pencil. 5½″ x 9″. (ROM946.15.169)

IV-400 Fort Vancouver. A sketch taken from the west end of the plain in front of the fort. The same view as in IV-399 but with additional details. KLL57. TCH62. AG95. Oil on paper. 8″ x 13⅜″. Fig. 151. (Stark WOP17)

IV-401 Fort Vancouver. Corner of stockade with tepee. Pencil. 5″ x 7″. (ROM946.15.270)

IV-402 Mount Hood. View from north bank of the Columbia River near Fort Vancouver. Buildings in foreground. Pencil. 5½″ x 9″. (ROM946.15.167)

IV-403 Mount Hood. View from north bank of the Columbia River near Fort Vancouver. Pencil. 5½″ x 9″. (ROM946.15.168)

IV-404 Mount Hood. View from north bank of the Columbia River, probably near Fort Vancouver. Trees in foreground. Pencil. 5¼″ x 9″. (ROM946.15.199)

IV-405 Mount Hood. View from north bank of the Columbia River, probably near Fort Vancouver. Pencil. 5½″ x 9½″. (ROM946.15.185)

IV-406 Studies of pasturing cattle. They are possibly part of the herds of cattle at Fort Vancouver (*Wanderings*, p. 91). Pencil. 4¾″ x 7¼″. (ROM946.15.256)

IV-407 Groups around a camp fire. Possibly at Fort Vancouver. Pencil. 8″ x 9½″. (ROM946.15.259)

IV-408 Man with saddle horse. A semi-caricature. Probably one of Kane's friends at Fort Vancouver. (*Wanderings*, p. 97.) w.c. 5″ x 7″. Fig. 153. (ROM946.15.251)

IV-409 Well in the woods (a burned-out tree stump) northeast of Fort Vancouver. KLL59. TCH72. AG79. Oil on paper. 11½″ x 9¼″. Fig. 155. (Stark WOP8)

IV-410 Well in the woods. Another version of IV-409. w.c. 5″ x 7″. (ROM946.15.285)

IV-411 Stump with whimsical doodle. Another version of IV-409. w.c. 5½″ x 3″. (ROM946.15.284)

IV-412 Mud puppy. w.c. 5½″ x 9½″. (ROM946.15.265)

IV-413 Valley with fields. No definite locale has been determined for this sketch. The neighbourhood of Fort Vancouver has been suggested. The sketch bears a number 48, which in KLL is the number assigned to the falls of the Willamette at Oregon City. Could this possibly be a view of the new farms at Champoeg? It is also possible that the sketch is a view in southern Ontario and has no connection with Kane's western tour. AG81. w.c. 5¾″ x 11⅛″. (Stark PWC26)

See also IV-429, 430, 431, 450, 465 for other sketches related to Mount Hood.

Theatrical studies

The crew of H.M.S. *Modeste* presented a series of theatrical evenings during 1846–47. Kane attended on at least one occasion. The following were possibly sketched at one of these performances.

IV-414 Heads of two harlequins. Pencil. 5″ x 7¼″. (ROM946.15.263)

IV-415 Military figure with tricorne hat and gun. (*Wanderings*, p. 97?) Pencil. 5¼″ x 6½″. (ROM946.15.294, reverse).

Sandwich Islanders

Sandwich (Hawaiian) Islanders were among the staff at various Hudson's Bay Company establishments on the Pacific coast. The Company maintained a post in the Sandwich Islands, and there was considerable traffic back and forth between it and the west coast of the American continent. Kane refers to eight Islanders in the party with which he started up the Columbia in July 1847, two of whom tried to desert on one occasion (*Wanderings*, pp. 111, 112).

IV-416 Old Cox, Sandwich Islander. KPL39. TCH122. w.c. 5″ x 7″. Fig. 154. (ROM946.15.271)

IV-417 Study of a head, possibly that of a Sandwich Islander, and a parrot. Pencil. 5″ x 6½″. (ROM946.15.235)

Chinook, Klikitat and Calapooya

Kane points out that the Indians living in the vicinity of Fort Vancouver were chiefly "Chinooks and Klickataats" (*Wanderings*, p. 91). Tribes of the Chinookan linguistic family lived on the Columbia River from the Dalles to the coast, and on the Willamette River as far up as the present site of Oregon City; it is probable that Kane is referring to these tribes when he uses the term "Chinook." The Chinook proper claimed territory on the north side of the Columbia River for about fifteen miles from its mouth and north along the seacoast as far as the northern part of Shoalwater Bay.

The Klikitat were of the Shahaptian linguistic stock and lived at the headwaters of the Cowlitz, Lewis, White Salmon and Klickitat rivers, north of the Columbia. The Calapooya (the name is given to a division of the Kalapooian family but the term often means the whole family) occupied a large territory in the present state of Oregon running south from that of the Chinook and cut off from the sea by the coastal tribes, but extending east to the Deschutes River.

IV-418 Casanov (Ca-is-no-of), noted warrior chief from Fort Vancouver. Kane states in his log that the man was a "Kalupanet" (Calapooya) chief but in the TCH catalogue he is identified as a Chinook. *Wanderings*, p. 91, states that Casanov governed the Indians in the region of Fort Vancouver, mainly "Chinooks and Klickataats." (*Wanderings*; woodcut, Fig. 8). (See also IV-295.) KPL29. TCH34. AG17. Oil on paper. 9⅝″ x 8⅛″. Plate XXXVI. (Stark WOP4)

IV-419 Casanov. Painting based on IV-418. GWA67. Oil on canvas. 2′6″ x 2′1″. (ROM912.1.76)

IV-420 Indian on a race course near Fort Vancouver, sketched with a head dress of beads. Identified as a boy in the TCH catalogue, this figure is more probably a girl wearing a special band to hide her eyes during menstruation. The belief that it was harmful magic for her to look at people during this particular time necessitated this precaution. (See *Wanderings*, p. 111.) KPL38. TCH116. AG138. w.c. 4⅞″ x 7″. Fig. 156. (Stark WWC35)

IV-421 Study of figure in IV-420. Pencil. 5″ x 7¼″. (ROM946.15.323)

IV-422 Klikitat Indian. KPL26. TCH117. AG174. w.c. 7″ x 4⅞″. (Stark WWC13)

IV-423 Indian head. Possibly sketched at Fort Vancouver. Pencil. 5″ x 7″. (ROM946.15.330)

Indian lodges

IV-424 Lodge interior. Kane describes this as the interior of a Chinook lodge at Fort Vancouver; the lodge appears to be constructed of split cedar boards (*Wanderings*, pp. 94–95), and matting is hung in the interior. This was formerly identified, incorrectly, as a Blackfoot lodge. KLL49. TCH159. AG69. w.c. 5″ x 7″. Fig. 158. (Stark WWC41)

IV-425 Lodge interior, described as being on the Columbia River. This is evidently a ceremonial lodge, with a special screen at one end. Oil on paper. 9½″ x 11½″. Plate XXXVII. (Stark WOP13)

IV-426 Temporary lodge of the Chinook, covered with woven rush mats, probably on the Columbia River (*Wanderings*, p. 95). A note on the reverse, not in Kane's hand, suggests that the lodge was on Vancouver Island. Pencil. 4¾″ x 6¾″. (ROM946.15.223)

IV-427 Bundle of rushes. These are evidently rushes cut for the construction of lodges (*Wanderings*, p. 95). w.c. 5″ x 7¼″. Fig. 157. (ROM946.15.321)

IV-428 Klikitat lodge. KLL44. TCH214. w.c. 5″ x 7″. Fig. 159. (ROM-946.15.221)

IV-429 Chinook travelling lodge with view of Mount Hood. These lodges were used while fishing and gathering camas (*Wanderings*, p. 95). TCH177. 5½″ x 9″. Fig. 160. (Stark WWC101)

IV-430 Chinook Lodge, Mount Hood in the distance. Painted from sketch IV-429, but with additional figures. GWA24. Oil on canvas. 1′6″ x 2′5″. (ROM912.1.99)

IV-431 Mount Hood. Replica of IV-430. This version was delivered to the Library of Parliament early in 1856, at which time Kane described it as a painting of "Chinooks, a Branch of the Flat Head Tribes of the N.W. Coast." The painting is entered in volume III of the *Catalogue* of the National Gallery of Canada as "Mount Hood with Spokane Indians," but there is no apparent reason for the alteration from "Chinook" to "Spokane." LP3. Oil on canvas. 1′7″ x 2′6″. (NGC6918)

IV-432 West Coast Indian Encampment. Replica of IV-430. Oil on canvas. 1′5½″ x 2′4½″. (Beaverbrook Art Gallery)

Indian groups

Locale of the following cannot be determined conclusively. Possibly they are sketches of Chinook at Fort Vancouver.

IV-433 Lodge interior with six Indians seated in foreground, presumably gambling, and two others reclining in background (*Wanderings*, p. 95). Pencil. 5″ x 7″. (ROM946.15.246)

IV-434 Indian head. Pencil. 5″ x 8″. (ROM946.15.276)

IV-435 Three nude figures dancing. 5″ x 8″. Pencil. (ROM946.15.275)

IV-436 Studies of figures from Columbia River region, executed either at Fort Vancouver or near Fort Colvile. The sketch is numbered "87," the number referring, presumably, to a lost portion of Kane's log which seems to have covered the upper Columbia

River region. TCH112. AG176. w.c. 5⅜″ x 9½″. (Stark wwc61)

IV-437 Group of seated and standing Indians. These include a woman with cedar-bark string skirt (*Wanderings*, p. 94). Probably sketched at Fort Vancouver. Pencil. 6½″ x 8½″. (ROM-946.15.306)

IV-438 Three Indians holding dip nets, sketched at Fort Vancouver or Fort Colvile. Pencil. 5½″ x 9″. (ROM946.15.325)

IV-439 Indian, identified by inscription, not in Kane's hand, as "Cowlitz Indian." w.c. 5⅛″ x 4¼″. (Stark wwc102D)

Chasta

Kane describes the prevalence of slavery among the Indians of the Fort Vancouver region (*Wanderings*, p. 93). The Chasta were probably an Athapascan tribe: in 1867 they resided on the Siletz Reservation in Oregon. Kane says that they lived near the Umpqua River, and others mention the Rogue River.

IV-440 A slave of the Chasta tribe, found among the Chinook of the Fort Vancouver region (*Wanderings*, p. 93). TCH121. AG107. w.c. 6⅞″ x 4⅞″. (Stark wwc57)

COLUMBIA RIVER VALLEY (?)

IV-441 Sketch of lake with low shoreline. Pencil. 5″ x 6½″. (ROM-946.15.145)

IV-442 Sketch of lake surrounded by evergreens. Pencil. 5″ x 7″. (ROM946.15.295)

WILLAMETTE VALLEY

Kane left Fort Vancouver on January 10, 1847, with Mr. Mackenlie, a chief trader, for Oregon City. He remained with him at Oregon City for three weeks, during which time there was unprecedented frost (*Wanderings*, pp. 95–96). From Oregon City he continued on up the river with Father Acolti to visit the Roman Catholic mission of St. Paul (*Wanderings*, p. 96). On his return he again stayed with Mr. Mackenlie for a few days (*Wanderings*, p. 96) before setting out for Fort Vancouver. He stopped to sketch some Clackamas River Indians about four miles below Oregon City on this journey.

Topography

IV-443 Oregon City. Upper end, showing mills and Methodist church from the opposite shore of the river. Pencil. 5½″ x 9″. (ROM-946.15.163)

IV-444 Oregon City. Kane's landscape log notes: "Oregon from below: it has 2 watch makers, 1 blacksmith, 1 gunsmith, 1 tailor, 3 saw mills and 2 grist mills." KLL56. TCH66. AG11. Oil on paper. 8⅛″ x 13½″. (Stark wop14)

IV-445 Oregon City. Painting executed from IV-444. Oil on canvas. GWA4. 1′6″ x 2′5″. (ROM912.1.82)

IV-446 Oregon City. Two views from the shore. *Upper:* general view of town with details of buildings. *Lower:* general view. Pencil. 5½″ x 9″. (ROM946.15.326)

IV-447 Oregon City: a second view. KLL45. TCH67(?). AG44 (incorrectly given as "Mackinaw"). Oil on paper. 8″ x 13¼″. (Stark wop15)

IV-448 Oregon City. General view looking downstream from shore opposite the town and beside waterfall. Pencil. 5½″ x 9″. Fig. 161. (ROM946.15.164)

IV-449 The mills of Oregon City. KLL47. TCH65. AG94. Oil on paper. 8½″ x 13⅜″. Plate XXXVIII. (Stark wop16)

IV-450 Oregon City (?) Two sketches of groups of buildings, presumably at the lower end of Oregon City; one has Mount Hood in the distance. Alternatively, these may possibly be buildings in the environs of Fort Vancouver. Pencil. 5½″ x 9″. (ROM-946.15.171)

IV-451 Falls near Oregon City. Kane exhibited several sketches of waterfalls in this area; TCH68 and TCH69 are described as "Falls near Oregon City," and TCH212 as "Falls on the Wilhamet River." This sketch does not seem to be any of the items exhibited. Pencil. 5½″ x 9″. (ROM946.15.175)

IV-452 Falls near Oregon City. Possibly TCH68 or TCH69. w.c. 5½″ x 8½″. Fig. 162. (ROM946.15.269)

IV-453 Falls near Oregon City (?). Pencil. 5½″ x 8½″. (ROM-946.15.65)

See also IV-413.

IV-454 St. Paul de Wallamette, Willamette valley. Kane describes visiting the mission with Father Acolti (*Wanderings*, p. 96). It was about 32 miles from Oregon City, and was established early in the decade by a group of nuns from Quebec who opened classes immediately on their arrival for Indian and white children. The brick chapel was under construction in February 1845 and was evidently completed at the time of Kane's visit; it is said to have been the first brick building erected on the upper Pacific coast. (For details of mission work in the area see *Notices & Voyages of the famed Quebec Mission to the Pacific Northwest . . . 1838 to 1847*, Portland, Oregon Historical Society, 1956.) TCH195. w.c. 5½″ x 9½″. Plate XXXIX. (ROM946.15.264)

IV-455 Willamette valley from the high hill in front of Champoeg (*Wanderings*, p. 96). Champoeg, site of an Indian village and a trading post of the Astor company, was settled by farmers in the 1830s. The first organized government in the region was set up here in 1843. Buildings pictured in Kane's sketch include the Hudson's Bay Company house and store, the André Longtain and Robert Newell properties and others. Several residents were former Hudson's Bay Company employees. (For full details of the Champoeg settlement see J. A. Hussey, *Champoeg: Place of*

Transition, Portland, Oregon Historical Society, 1967.) KLL62. w.c. 5¼″ x 8¾″. Fig. 163. (ROM946.15.193)

IV-456 Willamette valley. Presumably this is KLL62, but the mission to which the artist makes reference in his log cannot be distinguished. TCH213. AG190. w.c. 5½″ x 9⅜″. (Stark wwc24)

IV-457 The Willamette River from the Mountain (The Walhamette River from a Mountain). Painting based on IV-455. GWA52. Oil on canvas. 2′4½″ x 1′6″. (ROM912.1.81)

Clackama

Kane visited this tribe during early February 1847 (*Wanderings*, pp. 96–97). The Clackama were a Chinookan tribe occupying several villages on the Clackamas River in Oregon. Their entire population was said to be only 88 in 1851, whereas in 1806 they had numbered 1,800.

IV-458 Indian head in profile. KPL28. w.c. 5⅞″ x 4¼″. (Stark wwc102(A))

IV-459 Four Clackama Indians with painted faces. Kane points out that they had been gambling when he met them. The face in IV-458 is that of one of the group. KPL28. TCH36. AG63. Oil on paper. 11½″ x 9⅜″. Plate XL. (Stark wop11)

MOUNT ST. HELENS

Mount St. Helens, a 9,671 foot peak, is approximately 50 miles northeast of present-day Portland, Oregon. Although its volcano is now dormant, it erupted from vents in the sides between 1841 and 1857. Kane sketched the erupting volcano in March 1847, while *en route* from Fort Vancouver to Fort Victoria (*Wanderings*, p. 97). (See Kenneth L. Holmes, "Mount St. Helens' Recent Eruptions," *Oregon Historical Society Quarterly*, LVI, 3, 1955, 197–200.)

IV-460 View of Mount St. Helens from the mouth of what Kane calls the "Cattlepoutal" or "Kattlepoutal" River. Evidently this is the field sketch which Kane describes having made on March 26, 1847 (*Wanderings*, p. 97). Holmes (p. 206) points out that the sketch was made from the mouth of the Lewis River. KLL63. w.c. 5″ x 7″. (ROM946.15.329)

IV-461 View of Mount St. Helens with smoke cone. The foreground of the sketch is evidently based on IV-460. Kane reports watching this phenomenon for an hour and a half (*Wanderings*, p. 97). Holmes (p. 205) notes that Josiah L. Parrish, a Methodist missionary, saw a similar phenomenon in 1842. TCH63. AG19. Oil on paper. 8⅛″ x 13⅜″. Plate XLI. (Stark wop10)

IV-462 Mount St. Helens. This night view is evidently based on IV-460 for foreground and on IV-463 for the erupting volcano in the distance. GWA18. Oil on canvas. 1′6″ x 2′5″. Fig. 164. (ROM-912.1.78)

IV-463 View of Mount St. Helens from the Cowlitz farm. Kane made this sketch on March 30, 1847 (*Wanderings*, p. 99). KLL69. w.c. 5½″ x 9″. Fig. 165. (ROM946.15.184)

IV-464 View of Mount St. Helens erupting. Presumably this sketch is based on IV-463, but a more elaborate foreground has been added. KLL69. TCH64. AG37. Oil on paper. 8″ x 13⅜″. Fig. 164. (Stark wop21)

IV-465 Fourth plain, to the rear of Fort Vancouver, with three saddle horses and riders resting. Presumably this sketch shows the north side of Mount St. Helens although it has been suggested that the mountain is Hood. KLL51. 3½″ x 5″. (ROM946.15.165)

IV-466 Fourth plain, to the rear of Fort Vancouver. A second version of IV-465, with one horse. Pencil. 5″ x 6¼″. (ROM946.15.166)

IV-467 Mouth of "Cattlepoutal" (Lewis) River. Sketch of the foreground of IV-460, but omitting the mountain. Pencil. 7″ x 10″. (ROM946.15.298)

FORT ASTORIA

Chinook

Astoria, located on the south side of the Columbia River, was adjacent to the territory of the Chinook on the north side at the river's mouth. The post had originally been established by Astor's Pacific Fur Company in 1811 for trading purposes, and was re-established in 1843 by overlanders. Kane makes no reference to visiting Astoria either during his trip from Fort Vancouver to Fort Victoria, when he came down the Columbia River to the mouth of the Cowlitz River, or while he was staying at Fort Vancouver during the winter of 1846–47. However, he specifies that the two following sketches portray women from Fort Astoria and his log states that IV-478 was done there.

IV-468 A Chinook woman from Astoria. KPL36. w.c. 7″ x 5″. (Stark wwc21)

IV-469 Chinook girl from Fort Astoria. No sketch for this girl has been located. The box she holds is apparently based on a sketch executed at Mackinac (III-90; see also IV-88). Oil on canvas. 2′6″ x 2′1″. (Stark wop23)

LOWER COLUMBIA AND COWLITZ RIVERS

Indian burials

Kane visited several canoe burial grounds, examining the first of them on March 29, 1847. He discusses the practice at length (*Wanderings*, p. 98).

IV-470 Coffin Rock. Kane writes that this site is on the Columbia River ten miles downstream from the mouth of the "Kattlepoutal" (Lewis) River, which in turn is 26 miles from Fort Vancouver. He camped there on the night of March 26, 1847 (*Wanderings*, p. 98). KLL64. AG119. w.c. 5¼″ x 8⅞″. Fig. 166. (Stark wwc-91)

IV-471 Coffin Rock. Painting based on IV-470. GWA12. Oil on canvas. 1′6″ x 2′5″. (ROM912.1.77)

IV-472 Rocky shoreline. This landscape is similar to the shoreline in the vicinity of Coffin Rock. Pencil. 5½″ x 9″. (ROM946.15.191)

IV-473 Shoreline similar to that in the region of Coffin Rock. Unfinished w.c. 5½″ x 9″. (ROM946.15.170)

IV-474 Chinook canoe grave on the Cowlitz River. Presumably this is the burial place Kane saw March 29, 1847 (*Wanderings*, p. 98; woodcut, Fig. 9). KLL66. TCH161. AG132. w.c. 5″ x 7″. (Stark wwc22)

IV-475 Chinook grave on the Cowlitz River. KLL65. TCH163. AG193. w.c. 5¼″ x 8⅞″. Plate XLII. (Stark wwc29)

IV-476 Graves near the farm on the Cowlitz River. These may be near the group pictured in IV-475. KLL68. TCH164. AG207. w.c. 5¼″ x 8⅞″. Fig. 168. (Stark wwc32)

IV-477 Burying Place on the Cowlitz River. Painting is based on sketches IV-473 and IV-474, and possibly also on other sketches not located. GWA47. Oil on canvas. 1′6″ x 2′5″. (ROM912.1.79)

IV-478 King Comcomly's burial canoe. Although Kane, as noted above, makes no mention of visiting Astoria in his published narrative or manuscript diary, his landscape log specifies that this is "the grave of Com-comly at Astoria, Chief of the Chinooks." Comcomly received the Lewis and Clark expedition in 1805. After the Astoria expedition arrived at the mouth of the Columbia River to commence a permanent fur trade, he gave his daughter in 1813 as a bride to Duncan McDougall, the Canadian then at their head; she married Casanov, IV-418, when McDougall left the area (*Wanderings*, p. 92). Comcomly is said to have been preceded by 300 slaves when he visited Fort Vancouver. KLL89. AG110. w.c. 5⅜″ x 9¼″. Fig. 167. (Stark wwc86)

Canoes

IV-479 Cowlitz canoe. Identified from an inscription in Kane's hand. This canoe has a vertical prow and stem. It is ornamented with two carved animal heads, one attached to the prow facing forward and the other attached to the inside of the stern, similarly facing forward. Paddle above. This form of canoe is similar to the one in IV-480 which bears an identification, uncorroborated, on the mat reading "Klick-a-tat." Pencil. 3½″ x 12″. (ROM-946.15.201)

IV-480 Three canoes and paddles of the Columbia River. The canoes have been identified, but by a hand other than Kane's, as: *upper*, Klick-a-tat; *centre*, Chinook; *lower*, Cowlitz. However the upper of these three canoes is identical with the one pictured in IV-479, which is labelled as "Cowlitz" in Kane's hand. AG120. w.c. 5⅜″ x 9″. (Stark wwc2)

IV-481 Two canoes of the Columbia River region. The upper is identical to the lower of the three in IV-480, which is identified as "Cowlitz" (but see note on IV-480). The lower canoe has a shark's head painted on the prow and is identical with the centre canoe of the three in IV-480, identified as "Chinook." Pencil. 5½″ x 9″. (ROM946.15.200)

Tree studies

It has been suggested that Kane made these sketches while travelling from Fort Vancouver to Puget Sound during April 1847. They were obviously done in the Pacific coast region.

IV-482 Study of tree covered with moss. TCH170. w.c. 5½″ x 9½″. (ROM946.15.279)

IV-483 Study of tree covered with moss. TCH158. w.c. 9½″ x 5½″. (ROM946.15.280)

IV-484 Tree stump and windfall. w.c. 3¾″ x 7″. (ROM946.15.281)

IV-485 Study of a tree covered with moss. w.c. 5″ x 7¼″. (ROM-946.15.282)

IV-486 Study of a tree covered with moss. w.c. 5½″ x 3″. (ROM-946.15.283)

IV-487 Study of a tree covered with moss. w.c. 5½″ x 3″. (ROM-946.15.284, reverse).

COWLITZ RIVER

Cowlitz

The Cowlitz Indians were a Salish tribe living on the Cowlitz River in the southwestern portion of the present state of Washington. Once powerful, their numbers in 1847 were, Kane states, 200. Kane made the following sketches when he met members of the tribe during his visit to the Cowlitz farm which was operated by the Hudson's Bay Company. He was there from March 30 to April 5, 1847, on his way to Fort Victoria. He encountered members of the tribe on his return journey to Fort Vancouver between June 15 and June 20, but did not linger because of their hostility. He says that the tribe spoke a language similar to that of the Chinook, and flattened their heads.

IV-488 Kiscox (Kiss-cox), a Cowlitz River chief (*Wanderings*, p. 99). KPL40. TCH119. AG102. w.c. 7″ x 4⅞″. (Stark wwc11)

IV-489 A Flathead woman. She is possibly Caw-wacham, referred to by Kane (*Wanderings*, pp. 99, 110) and listed as KPL33. w.c. 5¾″ x 4¼″. Fig. 169. (Stark wwc102G)

IV-490 A child in the process of having its head flattened (*Wanderings*, pp. 93, 99). This sketch was used by Daniel Wilson in the preparation of a coloured lithograph of a "Flathead Woman and Child" (*Prehistoric Man*, 1862, II, frontispiece). KPL35. TCH167. AG114. 4⅞″ x 7″. Fig. 170. (Stark wwc10)

IV-491 Flathead Woman and Child, Caw-wacham (Caw-wacham). Painting based on sketches IV-489 and IV-490 (*Wanderings*; coloured litho.). GWA68. Oil on canvas. 2′6″ x 2′1″. (ROM-912.1.80)

IV-492 Flathead Woman and Child, Caw-wacham. Replica of IV-491. Oil on canvas. 2′6″ x 2′1″. Fig. 171. (Montreal Museum of Fine Arts 47.991)

IV-493 Flathead child. No documentation has been found for this sketch. It may have been made in the Cowlitz area, or it may be

TCH115, described as "Child's head—Chinook." w.c. 5½″ x 4″. (Stark wwc102F)

See also IV-439.

PRAIRIE DE BUTE

Kane passed over a 22-mile stretch of plain on his way from the Cowlitz farm to the Nisqually River. It was dotted with peculiar mounds, and he describes seeing them on April 6, 1847, and again on June 15, 1847, when he was returning to Fort Vancouver (*Wanderings*, pp. 99, 110).

IV-494 Prairie de Bute. KLL70. TCH217. w.c. 5⅜″ x 9⅜″. Fig. 172. (Stark wwc64)

IV-495 Prairie de Bute. Pencil. 4¾″ x 7″. (ROM946.15.156)

IV-496 Prairie de Bute. Pencil. 5″ x 6½″. (ROM946.15.158)

IV-497 Prairie de Bute. Painting based on IV-494. GWA36. Oil on canvas. 1′6″ x 2′5″. (ROM912.1.83)

PUGET SOUND

Topography

IV-498 Nisqually, a village on Puget Sound. The Hudson's Bay Company had formed the Puget's Sound Agricultural Company to promote land settlement. Kane visited the area on April 7, 1847 (*Wanderings*, p. 99). KLL83. TCH215. AG166. w.c. 5⅜″ x 9¼″. Fig. 173. (Stark wwc47)

Nisqually

Kane refers to the Nisqually Indians at the time of his visit to the Nisqually area on April 7, 1847 (*Wanderings*, p. 99).

IV-499 Indian lodge at Nisqually. KLL71. w.c. 3¾″ x 7″. Fig. 174. (ROM946.15.322)

IV-500 Indian lodge of Lach-oh-lett, head chief of the Nisqually. KLL72. w.c. 5″ x 7″. (ROM946.15.324)

IV-501 Lach-oh-lett (Lach-a-lit), a Nisqually chief living on the shores of Puget Sound. KPL41. w.c. 5″ x 7″. (ROM946.15.277)

IV-502 Nisqually girl. KPL67. TCH125. AG142. w.c. 5¼″ x 8⅞″. Plate XLVIII. (Stark wwc83, right; see also IV-582)

STRAITS OF GEORGIA AND JUAN DE FUCA

In his published narrative (p. 103) Kane says he hired five natives from the Indian village adjoining Fort Victoria to accompany him on a tour of the straits region. He also took with him the fort's interpreter. According to *Wanderings*, they departed May 6 and returned to Fort Victoria on May 15, 1847; Kane notes that he left again for Fort Vancouver on June 10. From Fort Victoria he and his party travelled east around the lower end of Vancouver Island and through the Haro Strait. On "the main land" they visited a village apparently near the mouth of the Fraser River. Subsequently they travelled southwest along the mainland and called at "Toanichum" on Whidbey Island, and at "I-eh-nus" and "Suck" on the south shore of Juan de Fuca. They returned to Fort Victoria by canoe across the open straits. (The notes provided for chapters XIV, XV, and XVI of *Wanderings*, above, record variations elsewhere in some details of this itinerary.)

Sketches IV-503 to IV-524 were almost all completed on this tour.

Mainland village

Kane stopped on May 6 at a village he describes as occupied by the Clallam. They are a Salish tribe closely related to the Songish. In *Wanderings* this village is sited on the mainland, but see note 1 for chapter XV of *Wanderings*.

IV-503 Cloll-uck, chief of the Clallam, "entrance to the Canal de Arrow" (Haro Strait). KPL47 (Kane's additional notes identify him as the Indian referred to in *Wanderings*, p. 103; see also note 2 for *Wanderings*, chapter XV). w.c. 5″ x 7″. (ROM946.15.98, left)

IV-504 E-a-cle, "a Cathi chief on the south side of the straits." Kane reports that he came from a neighbouring village, which Kane apparently did not visit. KPL48. 5″ x 7″. (ROM946.15.98, right)

IV-505 Rough sketch of a woman with a bowl and a fire-making stick, inscribed "south side of strait." Probably sketched in the region of Haro Strait. Pencil. 5″ x 7″. (ROM946.15.224)

IV-506 "A Quatlin from the mouth of Fraser's River." "Quatlin" refers to Kwantlen, who were a Cowichan tribe in the area at the mouth of the south Fraser River (see also IV-568 to IV-573). KPL52. TCH141. AG144. w.c. 7″ x 5⅛″. (Stark wwc33)

Skagit River or Whidbey Island: Skagit

Kane uses a variety of names (Shatchet, Sca-chet, Suchet) for what is evidently the Skagit, a Salish group. Their lands were at the mouth of the Skagit River in the present state of Washington and on the central part of Whidbey Island.

IV-507 A "Shatchet" Indian. This man is referred to in the catalogue of the 1848 exhibition, evidently incorrectly, as being from the Fraser River. KPL43. TCH142. AG175. w.c. 7″ x 5″. (Stark wwc76)

Whidbey Island, Toanichum: Clallam (?)

Kane visited this village on May 7 (*Wanderings*, p. 104). He identifies the village by name but not by tribe. It is in the traditional territory of the Clallam.

IV-508 Lock-hi-num, a chief of Whidbey Island (*Wanderings*, p. 104). KPL42. TCH123. AG199. w.c. 7″ x 4⅞″. Fig. 175. (Stark wwc56)

IV-509 A Flathead woman, wife of a Clallam chief, Whidbey Island. Evidently this is the wife of the second chief of Toanichum whom Kane mentions sketching (*Wanderings*, p. 104). TCH134. w.c. 6⅛″ x 4¼″. (Stark wwc102G)

IV-510 A Flathead Woman, Whidbey Island (A Flathead Woman).

Painting based on IV-509. GWA93. Oil on canvas. 2'1" x 1'8". (ROM912.1.85)

IV-511 Indian village of Toanichum, Whidbey Island. KLL73. TCH223. AG211. w.c. 5⅜" x 9". Fig. 176. (Stark WWC3)

Puget Sound: Snohomish

The Snohomish were a Salish tribe who lived on Whidbey Island, and on the mainland at the mouth of the Snohomish River.

IV-512 Shawstun (Shouts-ton), head chief of the "Sinna-hamus" Indians. Sketched at Fort Victoria (*Wanderings*, p. 107). Kane points out in his log that this man's tribe lived on Puget Sound. KPL55. TCH129. AG197. w.c. 6¾" x 4¾". Fig. 181. (Stark WWC37)

IV-513 Ona-put (Onepa), a "Sinna-hamus chief," Puget Sound. KPL54. TCH133. w.c. 5¼" x 4½". (Stark WWC102E)

South shore of Juan de Fuca

I-EH-NUS: CLALLAM

Kane remained at I-eh-nus village May 9 to May 12 (*Wanderings*, pp. 104–5).

IV-514 Probably Yates-sut-soot (Yeats-sut-sute), chief of the Clallam at I-eh-nus. Formerly this portrait was identified as that of "Old Bear," a Spokan Indian. It was exhibited by Kane in 1848 as of a "Chinook" Indian. KPL49. TCH120. AG123. w.c. 7" x 4⅞". (Stark WWC52)

IV-515 Battle between Clallam and Makah at I-eh-nus. The Makah were a Nootka tribe living at Cape Flattery to the west of I-eh-nus. This is evidently an imaginary sketch based on an account of the battle (*Wanderings*, p. 104). The sketch was formerly identified as the "Battle of Walula encampment." KLL77. AG155. w.c. 5¼" x 9⅜". Fig. 177. (Stark WWC54)

IV-516 Graves at I-eh-nus (*Wanderings*, p. 105). KLL78. TCH152. AG194. w.c. 5¼" x 8⅞". Fig. 179. (Stark WWC89)

IV-517 A Battle of I-eh-nus (A Battle). Painting based on sketches IV-515, IV-516, IV-551. GWA23. Oil on canvas. 1'6" x 2'5". Fig. 180. (ROM912.1.84)

SUCK: CLALLAM

Strong winds forced Kane and his party to remain at Suck, which he states is west of I-eh-nus, from May 12 to 14. Did he confuse the name of this village with that of Sooke on the south end of Vancouver Island? Or did the inhabitants of this village migrate to Sooke shortly after Kane's visit? Suttles ("Economic Life of the Coast Salish of Haro and Rosaria Straits," Ph.D. thesis, University of Washington, 1951) refers to Sooke Indians of Sooke Bay making a treaty with Sir James Douglas in 1850 and implies that they were then newly arrived at that village site.

IV-518 Chaw-u-wit, daughter of the chief at Suck (*Wanderings*, p.

105). KPL50. TCH137. AG173. w.c. 7" x 4¾". Fig. 178. (Stark WWC8)

IV-519 A Clallum Girl (Chau-u-wit). Burpee and others have identified this painting as a portrait of Chaw-u-wit. It is not based on the sketch of her (IV-518) nor on any other sketch which has been located. There is always the possibility that it is from a lost sketch. GWA88. Oil on canvas. 2'1" x 1'8". (ROM912.1.86)

IV-520 Salmon trap at Suck (*Wanderings*, p. 105). TCH224. AG124. w.c. 5¼" x 8⅞". Fig. 182. (Stark WWC26)

IV-521 A Weir for Catching Salmon. Painting based on IV-520. Originally this canvas was in the Allan collection, and presumably was given back to Kane in return for another canvas. GWA51. Oil on canvas. 1'6" x 2'5". (Stark WOP25)

IV-522 Landscape, with bundles of sticks marked as being four feet long. Evidently these stakes were prepared for use in the construction of the salmon trap at Suck. w.c. 7½" x 10¼". (ROM-946.15.320)

IV-523 Mountain landscape. Tentatively this landscape has been identified as a view of the Olympics seen from Beecher Bay near Race Rocks. Pencil. 5" x 6½". (ROM946.15.242)

Strait of Juan de Fuca

IV-524 Crossing the Strait of Juan de Fuca. Apparently this sketch, which shows Kane and his party returning to Fort Victoria by canoe in a storm, was completed from memory (*Wanderings*, p. 106). KLL79. TCH229. AG111. w.c. 5½" x 9⅜". Fig. 183. (Stark WWC70)

MOUNT BAKER

This prominent peak is in the state of Washington south of the 49th parallel and due east of Victoria.

IV-525 Mount Baker from Gordon Head, Vancouver Island, with the mountain rising above San Juan Island. This sketch was formerly known as one of Mount Hood. KLL76. TCH228. AG135. w.c. 5½" x 9¼". (Stark WWC48)

ESQUIMALT, INDIAN VILLAGE

The sketches in this group seem all to be associated with an Indian village which was on the east side of the Esquimalt harbour. Kane's published narrative does not mention an Indian village by this name specifically, but it is referred to in his manuscript notes.

IV-526 A "Sangeys Village on the Esquimault"(?) This was formerly known as a sketch of the village of Sooke, and in fact the topography is similar to that at Sooke. The Songish were a Salish tribe of the southern end of Vancouver Island, around Victoria. KLL84. TCH225. AG200. w.c. 5¼" x 8⅞". Fig. 184 (Stark WWC66)

IV-527 War party, Juan de Fuca. The sketch pictures the upper reaches of Esquimalt harbour with the rocky area called Gibraltar Point. (See also IV-537.) KLL87. TCH151. AG134. w.c. 5½″ x 8⅞″. Fig. 185. (Stark wwc90)

IV-528   Details of canoe in IV-527. Pencil. 4¾″ x 7¼″. (ROM-946.15.250)

IV-529   Indian village at Esquimalt with canoes returning from gathering camas. Apparently this is the village pictured in IV-526 and IV-527. KLL80. TCH226. AG113. w.c. 4⅞″ x 7″. Fig. 186. (Stark wwc58)

IV-530   Northwest canoes. KLL85. TCH149. AG188. w.c. 5⅜″ x 9½″. (Stark wwc93)

IV-531   Northwest canoes. KLL85. TCH150. w.c. 5½″ x 9½″. Plate XLIII. (ROM946.15.231)

IV-532   Northwest canoes. w.c. 5½″ x 9″. (ROM946.15.232)

IV-533   Northwest canoes. AG153. w.c. 4⅞″ x 7″. Fig. 187. (Stark wwc71A)

IV-534   The Esquimalt, Indian Village (The Esquimalt). Composite painting with a village and canoes in left foreground based on IV-529, and a village on the distant shore suggested by IV-526 and IV-527. Early sources record only one Indian village at Esquimalt, indicating that Kane may have introduced two villages for compositional reasons. There are records of two Indian villages adjoining Fort Victoria before 1861; however this painting is said to be a view of Esquimalt rather than Fort Victoria. GWA45. Oil on canvas. 1′6″ x 2′5″. (ROM912.1.90)

FORT VICTORIA

The Fort

Kane stayed at Fort Victoria intermittently between April 8 and June 9, 1847. Fort Victoria was established by the Hudson's Bay Company as a base for fur trade operations in New Caledonia. The original fort was built by a party of 50 men and 3 officers under James (later Sir James) Douglas. Construction was started on March 16, 1843. The work was especially urgent since the new fort was expected to replace Fort Vancouver as the centre for the Company's operations on the Pacific; from 1840 on, the Company was much aware of the imminent transfer of the Oregon territory to the United States. The fort straddled the present Fort Street in Victoria. Its bastions were destroyed in 1861, and the fur storehouse, constructed in 1846, was then turned into the Theatre Royal; this, the last of the fort's buildings left standing, was destroyed in 1892.

IV-535   Fort Victoria with Indian village (*Wanderings*, pp. 99–100). The Indian village was on Singhees Road, Victoria West, until 1911 when the residents were moved to the Esquimalt Reserve. w.c. 5½″ x 9¼″. Fig. 188. (ROM946.15.212)

IV-536   Fort Victoria, sketched from a spot called today Hospital Rock on the Industrial Reserve, the site of the Indian village during Kane's visit. *Upper:* whimsical portrait sketch and interior of

an Indian house. AG128. w.c. 5½″ x 8⅞″. Fig. 189. (Stark wwc104)

IV-537   The Return of a War Party. Painting based on sketch of Fort Victoria (IV-535) and with two war canoes suggested by the sketch of the war party in IV-527. GWA46. Oil on canvas. 1′6″ x 2′5″. (ROM912.1.91)

Northwest dance rituals

All the principal tribes of the northwest Pacific Coast organized their society according to social rank. The elaborate activities of the potlach were centred around the establishment of social claims and marked by the ceremonial distribution of hospitality and gifts. At certain times totem poles would be erected and there were dances, songs and theatrical performances, designed to demonstrate the special privileges of those giving the potlach. These performances were witnessed by invited guests. Masks and rattles played a large part in the performances, and were among the most elaborate art work of these peoples.

Kane makes no attempt to distinguish the masks and rattles of the different tribes; those he sketches are evidently representative of a variety of tribal groups. Most sketches were probably made at Fort Victoria where members of a number of west coast tribes came as visitors.

IV-538   Medicine masks of the northwest coast tribes. Presumably this sketch was made at Fort Victoria but presents masks of different tribes. In the Kane papers there is, for instance, a reference to a male mask from Fort Simpson (farther up the mainland of British Columbia). The mask at the upper left of this sketch is similar to the "Man with a moustache" mask collected in 1806 by the Russians along the Pacific northwest coast. (Erna Siebert and Werner Forman, *North American Indian Art*, London, 1967, Plates 25 and 30.) The mask in the centre of the upper row is a "Moon Mask," possibly carved by a member of the Bellacoola tribe. KLL86. TCH165. w.c. 5½″ x 8¾″. Plate XLIV. (Stark wwc27)

IV-539   Medicine man with mask from Strait of Juan de Fuca. TCH37. AG53. Oil on paper. 7¾″ x 5½″. Fig. 190. (Stark wop7)

IV-540   Medicine man with mask. TCH38. Oil on paper. 12½″ x 9¾″. (Stark wop5)

IV-541   Medicine Mask Dance. Such dances were normally performed at night in special houses rather than outdoors by daylight. The painting incorporates three of the masks pictured in IV-538. (According to Kenneth Kidd, a version of this subject, probably the sketch for the painting, is in the Eberstadt Collection of Western American Art, New York.*) GWA8. Oil on canvas. 1′6″ x 2′5″. Fig. 191. (ROM912.1.92)

IV-542   Medicine Mask Dance. Replica of IV-541. Said to be in a private Toronto collection.*

IV-543   Carved west coast mask and war club. Pencil. 5¾″ x 9½″. (ROM946.15.128)

IV-544 Indian medicine rattle with west coast motif. AG212. w.c. 5″ x 7″. Fig. 193. (Stark wwc99A)

Domestic life of Clallam and other Indians

Kane is the principal authority for the Clallam having a village in the Fort Victoria region. A few evidently found their way to the southern end of Vancouver Island. Kane, who met and sketched members of the tribe on his tour of the straits, states that they had a large village on Victoria harbour (*Wanderings*, p. 100). In connection with this group of sketches there are references to the Songish (see also IV-526) and to the Sanetch (Eus-a-nich), a Salish tribe occupying the Saanich peninsula adjoining the present city of Victoria (see also IV-574).

IV-545 Interior of a Clallam lodge, Vancouver Island (*Wanderings*, pp. 100, 102). KLL88 (?). TCH169. AG108. w.c. 5¼″ x 8⅞″. Fig. 194. (Stark wwc81)

IV-546 Interior of a lodge with a family group and dogs arranged around a camp fire. The sketch evidently shows a unit in a multiple family dwelling. AG172. w.c. 5½″ x 9¼″. (Stark wwc88)

IV-547 Interior of a lodge, Vancouver Island. Family group arranged around a camp fire, and baby suspended in a cradle. A marginal note, not in Kane's hand, states that this is a Clallam travelling lodge. AG203. w.c. 5″ x 7⅛″. (Stark wwc96)

IV-548 Indian cradle. AG219. w.c. 4⅞″ x 6¾″. (Stark wwc95)

IV-549 Interior of a Lodge, Vancouver's Island (Interior of a Lodge). This composite painting is based on IV-545, IV-546 (for the group in the right middle distance), IV-548 (for suspended cradle). GWA29. Oil on canvas. 1′7″ x 2′6″. (ROM912.1.97)

IV-550 Interior of a Winter Lodge of the Clallams. Replica of IV-549. LP9. Oil on canvas. 1′6½″ x 2′5¼″. Fig. 192. (NGC6923)

IV-551 Carved house post. Probably sketched at Fort Victoria. w.c. 5″ x 7″. Fig. 195. (ROM946.15.248)

IV-552 Interior of a lodge with Indian woman weaving a blanket (*Wanderings*, p. 100). Kane in his log refers to the woman as being a "Eus-a-nich." KPL64. TCH168. AG141. w.c. 5½″ x 9¼″. Fig. 196. (Stark wwc73)

IV-553 Woman spinning yarn (*Wanderings*, p. 100). Kane calls her a "Sangas" in his log. KPL63. TCH144. AG220. w.c. 4⅞″ x 7″. Fig. 197. (Stark wwc97)

IV-554 Girl spinning in a lodge. Kane's log describes her as a "Sangeys." KPL45. w.c. 5″ x 7″. (ROM946.15.226)

IV-555 Clallam woman weaving a basket, and studies of carved argillite dish, storage box, and white-haired dog. AG117. w.c. 5⅜″ x 8⅞″. Plate XLV. (Stark wwc45)

IV-556 A Woman Weaving a Blanket (Clal-lum Woman Weaving a Blanket). Composite painting based on IV-552, IV-553 and IV-555. GWA28. Oil on canvas. 1′6″ x 2′5″. (ROM912.1.93)

IV-557 Page of studies of figures inside a lodge. *Upper, left to right:* suspended cradle covered with bear skin, storage box, woven hat.

Centre: five seated figures, one a mother feeding a child on cradle board. *Lower:* two women gambling. w.c. 5½″ x 9½″. Fig. 198. (ROM946.15.227)

IV-558 Sketch of dog after being clipped for wool (*Wanderings*, p. 100), and of a canoe being launched. Pencil. 4¾″ x 7″. (ROM-946.15.157)

IV-559 Study of two dogs, and of a bed shelf in a lodge interior. Pencil. 5″ x 7″. (ROM946.15.225)

IV-560 Clallam travelling lodges. KLL74. AG122. w.c. 5¼″ x 9⅞″. Plate XLVI. (Stark wwc4).

IV-561 Lodges on Vancouver's Island (Fishing Lodges of the Clallams). Painting based on IV-560. GWA25. Oil on canvas. 1′6″ x 2′5″. (ROM912.1.96)

IV-562 Fishing Lodges of the Clallums. Replica of IV-561. LP8. Oil on canvas. 1′6½″ x 2′5¼″. (NGC6922)

IV-563 Clallam Indian Travelling Lodges. Painting with same subject-matter as IV-561. Probably TCH77. Oil on paper. 8½″ x 13½″. (Colln H. R. Milner)

IV-564 The game of lehallum, Vancouver Island (*Wanderings*, p. 102). TCH227. AG136. w.c. 5⅜″ x 9⅜″. Fig. 199. (Stark wwc25)

IV-565 Study of a group in a lodge interior, probably gambling. Pencil. 4⅞″ x 7″. (Stark wwc71B)

IV-566 Chea-clach, head chief of the Clallam. He accompanied Kane on a tour of the region and the Strait of Juan de Fuca (*Wanderings*, pp. 100, 103). KPL44. TCH35. AG56. Oil on paper. 12¼″ x 9⅞″. (Stark wop3)

IV-567 Chee-ah-clak (Chea-clach). Portrait based on IV-566. GWA83. Oil on canvas. 2′6″ x 2′1¼″. (ROM912.1.89)

Indian visitors to the Fort

Many visitors at Fort Victoria belonged to other tribes of the northwest coast area and came to the Hudson's Bay Company post to trade. Kane used the opportunity to augment his collection of paintings of the various Indian tribes. Portraits he secured in this way would appear to be IV-568 to IV-590. See also IV-512.

COWICHAN

Kane was in the territory of this tribe during his tour of the straits (see IV-506), but the following sketches were of visitors to Victoria.

IV-568 Saw-se-a, head chief of the Cowichan, from the Gulf of Georgia (*Wanderings*, pp. 102–3). KPL60. TCH139. w.c. 5¼″ x4⅛″. (Stark wwc102C)

IV-569 Saw-se-a (San-ce-a). Painting based on IV-568. GWA95. Oil on canvas. 2′1″ x 1′8″. Fig. 200. (ROM912.1.94)

IV-570 Culchillum, the son of Saw-se-a, wearing a medicine cap (*Wanderings*, p. 103; woodcut, Fig. 11). KPL61. TCH140. w.c. 5¼″ x 4½″. Plate XLVII. (Stark wwc102H)

IV-571 Medicine Man, Vancouver's Island (Culchillum). Painting based on IV-570. GWA64. Oil on canvas. 2′6″ x 2′1″. (ROM912.1.95)

IV-572 A "Whellamay" girl. Exhibited in 1848 as a Cowichan Indian from the Strait of Juan de Fuca. KPL58. TCH127. w.c. 5″ x 7″. (Stark WWC23, left)

IV-573 A Cowichan woman. KPL59. TCH127. w.c. 5″ x 7″. (Stark WWC23, right)

SANETCH

Kane visited their lodges to make sketches while they were visiting at Fort Victoria (*Wanderings*, p. 107). (See also IV-552 and heading above it.)

IV-574 A "U-Saanich"; from Haro Strait. KPL51. TCH131. w.c. 5″ x 7″. (ROM946.15.194)

NOOTKA

Nootka was a term originally applied to a tribe of Nootka Sound on the west coast of Vancouver Island, but eventually it was extended to all tribes speaking the same language. They occupied the island's west coast with the exception of the northerly tip. The Makah (see IV-515, 580) are sometimes included as part of the Nootka group. (*Wanderings*, p. 107)

IV-575 A New-a-tay (Nootka) chief. Kane would seem to be incorrect in stating in his log that the chief is from the north end of Vancouver Island; the extreme northern tip is Kwakiutl territory (see Wilson, *Prehistoric Man*, 1862, II, 317). KPL65. TCH143. AG198. w.c. 7″ x 4⅞″. Fig. 201. (Stark WWC16)

IV-576 A Conical Shaped Headed Indian (A New-a-tee). It has been suggested that this is the same man as the one in IV-575. The two are not strikingly similar, but the painting was probably inspired by the sketch. GWA86. Oil on canvas. 2′1″ x 1′8″. (ROM912.1.98)

IV-577 Page of five studies demonstrating conical head deformations. These Indians are possibly Nootka. Pencil. 5½″ x 2¼″. (ROM946.15.217)

IV-578 Indian child with head deformation, evidently of a conical type. w.c. 7″ x 5″. (ROM946.15.216)

IV-579 Indian child from south of Juan de Fuca. Inscription, not in Kane's hand, reads "Chinook Child." (See Wilson, *Prehistoric Man*, 1862, II, 320.) KPL68. AG213. w.c. 5″ x 3½″. (Stark WWC14)

MAKAH

The Makah (Macaw) belong to the Nootka group and live on Cape Flattery, in the present state of Washington.

IV-580 Cape Flattery Indian. The inscription on the sketch is not in Kane's hand. Kane describes sketching Yellow-cum, wealthiest of the Cape Flattery Indians (*Wanderings*, pp. 106–7), and records his sketch as KPL53. No such sketch has been positively identified. This is possibly the item in question. KPL53(?). TCH132(?). w.c. 5¼″ x 4⅝″. (Stark WWC102J)

See also IV-515.

HAIDA

Haida is the native and popular name for the Indians of the Queen Charlotte Islands and for those from the southern end of Prince of Wales Island. Cumshaw was a Haida town at the northern entrance to Cumshaw Inlet, Queen Charlotte Islands. Its population in 1836–41 was estimated at 286 people, living in 20 houses.

IV-581 Slum-a-chusset, a Cumshaw chief. KPL57. TCH130. w.c. 5″ x 7″. (ROM946.15.214)

KWAKIUTL

The Kwakiutl, a group of closely related tribes, lived in the neighbourhood of Prince Rupert, B.C. During the 1850s and 1860s a large tribe of the group, the Lekwiltok (or Ucaltas), lived between Knight and Bute inlets.

IV-582 A "You-call-tee" (Ucaltas) Indian. KPL66. TCH126. AG142. w.c. 5¼″ x 8⅞″. Plate XLVIII. (Stark WWC83, left; see also IV-502)

CHIMMESYAN

The Chimmesyan (Tsimshian), a small linguistic family, lived on the Nass and Skeena rivers and the neighbouring coast to the south. A number of remote groups moved to the vicinity of Fort Simpson when it was built by the Hudson's Bay Company in 1834 on the mainland opposite the Queen Charlotte Islands. Members of the tribe were periodic visitors to Fort Victoria.

Evidently Kane confused the Chimmesyan and the Babine (Big Lips), a branch of the Takulli living in the interior of British Columbia north of Babine Lake. Babine were known to have copied the customs of the coastal tribes, including use of labrets (*Wanderings*, pp. 107–8). The following entries seem to refer to Chimmesyan rather than to the Babine.

IV-583 Chief of the Chimmesyan Indians with a ring in his nose. Queen Charlotte Islands, Chatham Sound. (For the custom of the ring in the nose see *Wanderings*, p. 107.) KPL69. TCH136. AG129. w.c. 7″ x 5″. (Stark WWC34)

IV-584 Ma-cheek-e-a-wis, Chimmesyan Indian. KPL69. TCH4(?). There may be an error in the TCH catalogue, since another sketch also bears the number TCH4. AG48. Oil on paper. 10⅛″ x 9½″. Fig. 202. (Stark WOP6)

IV-585 A Babine woman. TCH80. Oil on paper. 11½″ x 9¼″. Fig. 204. (Stark WOP12)

IV-586 A Babbine Woman (A Babbine or Big-lip Woman). The woman in this painting is evidently based on the sketch IV-585, with the child added. GWA84. Oil on canvas. 2′6″ x 2′1″. (ROM-912.1.88)

IV-587　A Babbine Chief. This canvas is probably based on an unlocated sketch. When lithographed for the frontispiece in the Wilson book, *Prehistoric Man*, the title was changed to "Chimseyan Chief." GWA61. Oil on canvas. 2'6" x 2'1". Fig. 203. (ROM-912.1.87)

IV-588　Chimmesyan (or Babine) blanket. This is probably the blanket which Kane says he bought (*Wanderings*, p. 107). It was used as an accoutrement in the painting IV-587. On occasion, it has been described, but incorrectly, as Clallam. w.c. 5½" x 9". (ROM946.15.228)

IV-589　Babine pipe-stem of carved slate. TCH173. AG147. w.c. 4⅜" x 8⅞". Fig. 205. (Stark WWC1)

IV-590　Babine pipe-stem of carved slate. AG148. w.c. 5½" x 9". (Stark WWC17)

TAUTIN

Kane refers to the "Taw-wa-tin" (Tautin), who are a branch of the Takulli living on the mainland, opposite Vancouver Island. Kane may be confused in the tribal terminology.

IV-591　Cremation rites, evidently drawn from imagination (*Wanderings*, pp. 107–8). Pencil. 5½" x 9". (ROM946.15.327)

UNIDENTIFIED LOCALE

Gambling scenes

A wide range of suggestions have been advanced about the locale for the following group of sketches. They include the Georgian Bay region, Rocky Mountain House (Assiniboin), and Fort Vancouver or Fort Victoria. The bear's claw collar suggests the figures may be Assiniboin, but of course other tribes also wore these collars.

IV-592　Group of three seated Indians gambling. Pencil. 5" x 7". (ROM-946.15.260)

IV-593　Group of seven Indians gambling. Pencil. 5" x 7". (ROM-946.15.261)

IV-594　Group of five seated Indians gambling. Pencil. 5" x 7". (ROM-946.15.262)

GUIDES AND VOYAGEURS

IV-595　Tommskarrohoto, an Iroquois guide from Caughnawaga near Montreal. This identification is tentative. The sketch was previously identified as that of a Kwantlen chief. KPL87(?). AG44. Oil on paper. 9⅓" x 5⅞". (Stark WOP1)

IV-596　A voyageur. This sketch has been identified, without firm evidence, as the head of Sir George Simpson; the identification is obviously incorrect. w.c. 6½" x 5". (ROM946.15.252)

PERSONAL SKETCHES

IV-597　Self-portrait made during the course of his western tour. Oil on paper. 8⅛" x 6⅝". Plate I. (Stark WWC103)

IV-598　Sketch of a house inscribed "Paul Kane's Wigwam," and with an Indian head inscribed "Design for Knocker." w.c. 8" x 12½". (ROM946.15.253)

IV-599　Architectural design of a cottage, and an Indian caricature. Pencil. 8" x 10". (ROM946.15.259)

PORTRAITS OF WHITES FROM KANE'S WESTERN TOURS

No identification in Kane's notes has been made for the following sketches. He mentions a number of people whom he met during the tour including missionaries, Hudson's Bay Company officials and (in letters) local residents of Fort Vancouver.

IV-600　Bust of woman. Pencil. 5" x 7". (ROM946.15.247)

IV-601　Bearded man's head. Pencil. 5" x 7". (ROM946.15.288).

IV-602　Head of woman in a classical pose. Pencil. 4½" x 5½". (ROM-946.15.290)

IV-603　Head of bearded man wearing a hat. Pencil. 5" x 3½". (ROM-946.15.292)

IV-604　Head of a woman with kerchief tied over her head. This sketch and IV-603 appear to be a pair. Pencil. 5" x 3½". (ROM-946.15.293)

IV-605　Three-quarter length sketch of woman seated at a table. Pencil. 4" x 5¼". (ROM946.15.299)

IV-606　Profile study of head of woman wearing a sunbonnet. Pencil. 3" x 4". (ROM946.15.311)

Section V

Landscapes, portraits and other sketches and paintings executed by Kane following his return to Canada in 1845 but evidently not related to his travels in western North America

NIAGARA FALLS AND DISTRICT

Kane frequently visited Niagara Falls, which could be reached easily by means of the steamer running from Toronto to Queenston. On May 6, 1846, he halted at Niagara Falls while travelling west with Sir George Simpson, "to admire for the hundredth time the Falls of Niagara." His drawing master, Thomas Drury, spent much time in sketching at Niagara. The following undated sketches and paintings were probably executed after 1845.

V-1　Niagara Falls. Panoramic view of the Canadian and American falls from the heights on the Canadian side. AG154. w.c. 5½" x 9⅛". (Stark EWC1)

V-2　Niagara Falls. Panoramic view identical to that in V-1 but with suggestions of autumn colouring. Oil on canvas. (Oval) 1'6" x 2'5". (Colln Mrs. Paul Kane III)

V-3 Niagara Falls. The Canadian falls from the edge of the ravine on the Canadian side. Pencil. 5½″ x 9″. Fig. 12. (ROM946.15.335)

V-4 Niagara Falls. The American falls from the edge of the ravine on the Canadian side. Pencil. 5½″ x 9″. (ROM946.15.336)

V-5 Niagara Falls. The Canadian falls from the Canadian shore. Pencil. 2½″ x 5½″. (ROM946.15.337)

V-6 Niagara Falls. The 45-foot tower was built on the American side of the Canadian falls in 1833. It was joined to Goat Island by the Terrapin Bridge. Pencil. 5½″ x 9″. (ROM946.15.338)

V-7 Niagara Falls. The American falls from the shoreline on the American side. Pencil. 5½″ x 9″. (ROM946.15.339)

V-8 Niagara Falls. The Canadian falls from the edge of the ravine on the Canadian side. Pencil. 3″ x 5½″. (ROM946.15.340)

V-9 Niagara Falls. The brow of the Falls. Attributed to Kane. w.c. (Colln Maj.-Gen. M. P. Bogart)*

V-10 Queenston. View of the ruins of Brock's Monument after being blown up by a sympathizer with William Lyon Mackenzie, in 1840. The monument had been erected to commemorate Sir Isaac Brock, British general, who was killed during the battle in which American forces were defeated in their attack on the heights, October 13, 1812. The monument was rebuilt in 1854. Pencil. 5½″ x 9″. (ROM946.15.341)

V-11 Sketch of a stereoscopic view for tourist entertainment, probably at Niagara Falls. Pencil. 5½″ x 9″. (ROM946.15.342)

TORONTO

V-12 Bloor's Brewery, Rosedale Ravine. The brewery was established by Joseph Bloor in 1830, and he eventually turned it over to John Rose. The latter operated it as Castle Frank Brewery until 1864. The building was torn down in 1875. The blockhouse on the hill to the right stood in the middle of Bloor Street at the head of Sherbourne Street. It had been built to protect Toronto from the north during the 1837–38 uprising and was torn down in the same year as the brewery, 1875. w.c. 5½″ x 9″. Fig. 10. (ROM946.15.254)

V-13 "Homewood," first residence of George W. Allan, Toronto (built 1846, demolished in 1940s). Mrs. Allan's diary reads in an entry of February 9, 1849: "I went to George's office and we went to Kane's rooms, to see his sketches and a view he is taking of 'Homewood.'" Oil on canvas. 10⅞″ x 15¾″. Fig. 13. (Colln G. P. H. Vernon)

LANDSCAPES, MISCELLANEOUS

V-14 Rural Ontario farmhouse with bridge. There is a remote possibility that this is the residence of John Gamble (see I-3). w.c. 5½″ x 9″. (ROM946.15.310)

V-15 Rural landscape with autumn colouring. w.c. (Oval) 3½″ x 4½″. (ROM946.15.304)

V-16 Church spire, unidentified; (on reverse) man with curling broom. Pencil. (Oval) 4½″ x 3½″. (ROM946.15.305)
See also IV-413.

PAINTINGS RELATING TO INDIANS

V-17 Joseph Brant. This painting is identical in subject-matter to a painting by George Catlin also in the ROM collections. Both are evidently based on a portrait of Brant by Ezra Ames, an engraved reproduction of which was used as the frontispiece in a two-volume work by W. L. Stone, *Life of Joseph Brant—Thayendanegea* (New York 1838). The book was in Kane's library. GWA66. Oil on canvas. 2′6″ x 2′1″. (ROM912.1.100)

V-18 Columbus Meeting the Indians at His Landing at San Salvador. Formerly in the Perkins Bull Collection, Brampton, and sold in Montreal in 1953.*

V-19 Portrait of an Indian. Said to have been in the collection of a Toronto mayor c. 1870. Oil on canvas. (Colln Harold E. Groves) *

V-20 Scene in the Northwest, a Portrait. Unlocated, this portrait may actually have been a painting, done in the winter of 1845–46 from a sketch executed during the previous summer, which entered the Allan collection. Shown at the exhibition of the Toronto Society of Artists, 1847, no. 26.*

V-21 Indian Summer on Lake Superior. (See remarks on V-20.) Shown at the exhibition of the Toronto Society of Artists, 1847, no. 88.*

V-22 Group of Indians. Said to have been suggested by a plate in a book by Sir John Richardson, *Arctic Searching Expedition* (London 1851), vol. I, Plate IX. w.c. 5¼″ x 9¼″. (ROM946.15.218)

PORTRAITS

It is virtually impossible to determine whether certain portraits were executed by Kane before or after his European tour. The following, for documentary or stylistic reasons, are presumed to date from after 1844. There are likely a number of portraits of the pre-1841 and post-1843 period which have survived unidentified in the region of Mobile, Alabama.

V-23 Self-Portrait. Probably executed immediately after Kane's return from Europe. Used as a frontispiece in the 1925 edition of *Wanderings of an Artist*. Oil on canvas. (Colln S. E. Weir) *

V-24 Unidentified man. Oil on canvas. 2′5″ x 2′. (Colln Mrs. Paul Kane III, 49/PK)

V-25 Portrait of a mother and child. Unlocated work, shown in Toronto at the exhibition of the Society of Artists, 1847, no. 24.*

V-26 George Gurnett (1792?–1861). Gurnett was Mayor of Toronto 1837, 1848 and 1849. See W. S. Wallace, *Macmillan Dictionary of Canadian Biography*. Shown in Toronto at the exhibition of the Toronto Society of Artists, 1847, no. 39. This painting was presumably done in the 1844–46 period although the style is tight and it has an archaic character which is related to that of I-11. Oil on paper. 2′10″ x 2′2″. Fig. 8. (Colln of mayors' portraits, Corporation of the City of Toronto)

V-27 Portrait of a Gentleman. Shown in Toronto at the exhibition of the Society of Artists, 1847, no. 117.*

V-28 James Richardson (d. 1853). As a young man, Richardson lived in Cobourg; he edited the *St. Catharines Constitutional*, 1850–53. Oil on canvas. 29¼″ x 24¾″. Fig. 9. (ROM964.185)

V-29 Allan MacNab (presumably Sir Allan MacNab, 1798–1862, although there is some controversy as to whether this may actually be a portrait of Sir Allan's father; see K. E. Kidd, ROM, Art and Archaeology Division, *Annual*, 1962, pp. 64–73). In reference to the attribution to Kane, it should be noted that James Bowman, Kane's artist friend, painted Sir Allan MacNab, Sir Allan's mother-in-law, and other members of the family in 1831; could this canvas and V-30 actually be by Bowman rather than Kane? Oil on canvas. (ROM, on loan to Dundurn Castle Museum, Hamilton) *

V-30 Archibald MacNab, brother of Sir Allan MacNab. (See K. E.

Kidd, and V-29 above.) Oil on canvas. (ROM, on loan to Dundurn Castle Museum, Hamilton) *

V-31 A French-Canadian Notary. This is a copy of a portrait by Cornelius Krieghoff dated 1848 (Beaverbrook Art Gallery). Oil on canvas. 2′3″ x 1′9″. (Colln Mrs. Paul Kane III, 55/PK)

V-32 Study of the back of a girl. Oil on canvas. 2′¼″ x 1′7″. (Stark OP27)

V-33 Thomas Daly, Toronto city clerk and an amateur artist. Kane may have done this sketch at the time he was exhibiting his western sketches late in 1848 in the old Toronto City Hall at the request of the Toronto City Council. Pencil. 5½″ x 9″. Fig. 11. (ROM946.15.142)

V-34 Mackenzie through the Mountains. This is an imaginary sketch of Sir Alexander Mackenzie, famous trader and explorer, going across the Rocky Mountains to the Pacific in 1793. Pencil and ink. 5¼″ x 10½″. (ROM946.15.243)

APPENDICES

Appendix 1

Paul Kane's Landscape Log, Kept on His 1846–48 Journey *

No. 1. The Dog Portage on the Dog Ravene.

No. 2. Portage de Gock. It derives its name from the following circumstance. There is an Indian by the name of Gock who was taunted by one of his companions to run it with his canoe. He went round the small island and took the shote but was dashed to pieces, canoe and all.

No. 3. Portage de Boar on the R. Winnipeg. Its Indian name is Carneshawsing the two carrying places.

No. 4. Is a sketch on the R. Winnipeg.

No. 5. The Lost Man's Portage on the Fort William R. 2 men lost themselves for 4 days.

No. 6. A carrying place, Fort William R.

No. 7. The brigade stopping to have breakfast at French R. Rapids.

No. 8. Visited by a party of Sotos at our evening encampment.

No. 9. Norway House.

No. 10. A Cree Tent with woman gaming. Carlton.

No. 11. See notes on Saw-waughten.

No. 12. Ft. Garry, Red River.

No. 13, 14, 15, 16, 17, 18 are sketches on the Saskatchewan.

No. 19. The Methodist Mission at Jack River.

No. 20. Carlton.

No. 21. Burnt Prairie.

No. 22 and 23. Salt Lakes.

No. 24. A Lake in the Planes.

No. 25. The Serpentine Valley.

No. 26. The Golden Valley.

No. 27. Fort Pitt with Bluff. Also crossing the river.

No. 28. Long Grass Valley with the Dead Men's Hill in the distance. Buffalo feeding.

No. 29. Edmonton.

No. 30. A Buffalo robe with the war adventures of Sa-Co—the Sinnew. Piece. A Blood Indian.

No. 31. Athabaska River with the Rocky Mountains in the distance.

No. 32. Jasper's Lake with Miette's Rock.

33. Jasper's House.

34. A prairie with mountain sheep.

35. Le Rocque's prairie with wild horses.

36. The Athabaska in the Mountains.

37. A sketch in the mountains.

38. A snow scene in the mountains.

39. The committee's punch bowl.

40. A sketch of a fall at the head waters of the Columbia.

41. Columbia River, the grand rapid.

42. The Cascades.

43. No. 1. Click-a-tat. 2. Chinook. No. 3. Cowlitz Canoe.

44. Click-a-tat lodge.

45. Oregon the City. There is about 94 houses and 200 inhabitants. The Hudson's Bay Co. has an establishment here. There are 4 other stores here, 2 hotels and 2 churches, Catholic and Methodist.

46. Main Street in Oregon City.

47. The mills of Oregon.

48. Falls of the Willamette, 30 feet high.

49. A Chinook Lodge interior painted at Vancouver. These lodges are made of split cedar and mats.

50. Click-a-tat lodge on the Columbia near Vancouver.

51. The Fourth plain eight miles back of Vancouver.

52. A Walla Walla Lodge.

53. The lower plain near Vancouver with Mount Hood in the distance.

54. A sketch of Mount Hood above Vancouver.

56. Oregon from below. It has 2 watch makers, 1 blacksmith, 1 gunsmith, 1 tailor, 3 saw mills and 2 grist mills.

57. A sketch taken from the west end of the plain in front of Fort Vancouver.

58. A Cascade Indian lodge taken on the south side of the Columbia.

59. The well in the woods, a hollow burnt stump which keeps water good for a long time from the wood being charred. No water near this spot. It is north east from Ft. Vancouver.

60. Fort Vancouver, one of the largest forts in the H. B. Co. territory, it has 2 chief factors, 14 clerks and 200 men. Keep a large stock of cattle.

61. The Catholic mission about 32 miles above Oregon City. Mr. Demers, Superior, Mr. Bolduc, Assistant. It has a nunnery attached to it with 6 Nuns or Sisters of Charity. They have 42 pupils. It is near the River Willamette. There is near here also a Jesuit Mission, Father Acolti, Superior. They have 3 Missions in the Rocky Mountains and one in New Caledonia. I was treated with a great deal of kindness here by Father Acolti.

* The Landscape Log is preserved as a manuscript held by the Nelda C. and H. J. Lutcher Stark Foundation, Orange, Texas. The wording and spelling of Kane's original are followed; material in the log which appears in *Wanderings of an Artist* has been omitted. Kane prepared a manuscript for a second book which would be largely illustrations (see section VI of Part One); much of the text merely duplicates *Wanderings of an Artist*; the occasional note about a sketch is new, and this material has been added at appropriate points in this appendix and in Appendix 2.

62. 2 sketches taken from the top of a high hill in front of Champoeg showing the country for 20 miles with Champoeg in the foreground of one and the mission in the other. This is the character of the country in this part of Oregon.

63. The mouth of the Cattle-putle River with Mount St. Helens in the distance, a cloud on top of it, and the sky clear in every direction. Taken from the Columbia.

64. Coffin Rock. This is the mode of burial in this part of the Columbia down to the mouth of the river.

65. A Chinook grave on the Cowlitz River. . . .

66. A Chinook grave on the Cowlitz.

67. A Cowlitz grave.

68. Graves near the farm on the Cowlitz. They bury in canoes also.

69. Mount St. Helens as seen from the Cowlitz farm. This is a burning mountain about 40 miles from the farm. . . .

70. Prairie de Bute or Hill Prairie between the Cowlitz and Nisqually. These hills were thought to be the burial place of the Indians but on examination they were found to contain nothing but stones. Commodore Wilkes examined some of them. It is 20 miles from Nisqually.

71. A Nisqually Indian lodge.

72. The lodge of Loch-o-let at Nisqually.

73. The Indian village of To-an-e-chum on Whidbey's Island in the Straits. When we arrived near here, the Indians flew to their bastions and fired off several guns to intimidate us from landing if we were hostile and to let us know that they had guns. When we got on shore they treated us with much kindness. They live here in constant fear of one another for if an unfortunate individual is caught out alone, he is made a slave of by the next tribe though they are not at war with one another.

74. Clallum travelling lodges. These are only used when they go fishing for a short time.

75. A place for catching salmon on the south side of the S. called Suck. . . .

76. Mount Baker taken from Vancouver's Island looking across the Canal de Arrow.

77. The battle of I. Eanus on the south side of the straits. . . . They do not scalp the dead here as in other parts. They cut off the head and stick it on a pole which they place in front of their canoes or near their lodges.

78. Graves at I Enis.

79. Crossing the Dungeness in the Straits of De Fuca to Vancouver's Island in a heavy blow. . . . [The crew] kept up their medicine song all the time. The old man in the stern kept up one continual howl like a dog but when one wave bigger than the rest would threaten to engulf us, then there was one great shout to drive it back and stay its progress. . . .

80. The canoes returning from gathering camas to the Esquimault.

81. Canal de Arow.

82. Fort Victoria.

83. Nisqually.

84. Sangeys Village on the Esquimault.

85. North West Canoes.

86. North West Masks.

87. A war party in the Straits of de Fuca.

88. The inside of a Clallum Lodge.

89. The grave of Com-comly at Astoria, Chief of the Chinooks.

90. Cape Horn, 20 m. above Vancouver on the Columbia, 200 feet high and subject to high winds.

91. The Grand Prairie and big rock some call the Castle.

92. Below the Cascades 3 m.

93. The Cascades.

94. At the head of the Cascades.

95. The land slip. Some suppose these trees to have grown where they are and the water to have risen from an avalanche of rock falling across the Cascade 6 m. below. This is incorrect as the rocks are worn smooth by the action of the water at the Cascades.

96. The Shutes where the man with the tin box was shot (Astoria).

97. The Rocks of the 2 Crausegeeves near Walla Walla. . . .

98. Fort Walla Walla.

99. The Pelouse Falls 400 feet. The rock is about 650 feet composed of basalt.

100. The amphitheatre near the lower falls.

101. The Coliseum near the lower falls.

102. The upper fall 15 feet.

103. A front view of the same.

104. Looking down the Pelouse River, the rocks all basaltic.

105. The Nezperse or south branch of the Columbia or Snake River.

106. Kause [Cayuse?] fan given to Mrs. Whitman at an Indian feast.

107. The Grand Coulee.

108 and 109. Grand Coulee.

110. A sketch on the Columbia 50 m. below Colville.

111. The Kettle Falls. 1700 salmon have been taken from this basket in one day. I weighed three. One was 35, the other 2, 32 pounds each. One man has the whole of control of this fishery. There is one spot where if a basket was placed they might catch 3 or 4000 a day. It is called the Kettle Falls by the whites from the water coming round holes in the rocks. This sketch is from the south side of the river.

112. A sketch of the Kettle Falls from the north shore. . . . The fall is about 19 feet. . . .

113 and 114. Indian lodges. No. 1, the Head Chief's lodge. 2. The Second Chief's. 3. The Salmon Chief's in Sketch No. 113 at Colville.

115. The Little Falls 20 m. above Colville. . . . The lives of 14 persons out of 30 were lost near here. . . .

116. A painted horse, Colville. The Indians are very fond of painting their horses before going to run a race.

117. A sketch on the Spokane.

118. Walker and Eells mission with cachés in the foreground. . . .

Appendix 2

Paul Kane's Portrait Log, Kept on His 1846–48 Journey *

1. I.as-a-way (Iacaway). The Loud Speaker. A Soto chief taken at Fort Frances on Rainy Lake.
2. Wayus-Rons (Wawgaskontz). The Little Rat. A chief taken at the same place.
3. Pe-ca-dhis (Peccondiss). The man with the lump on his navel. Taken on the Plains with the half breeds. A Soto.
4. Na-taw-waugh-cit (Natawassit). A Soto. The man that was born. This man wanted 2 horses for his robe.
5. Caw-ce-cu-che-cock (Cawkeekaikeedje-ekoke). A Soto. The Constant Sky. Her mother wanted to know if it would hurt her to sit for her picture. (I saw at this camp a rather good-looking girl whom I tried to persuade to wash the grease and dirt from her face and sit to me. With this however the customs of the tribe forbade her acquiescence as she was then in mourning for the loss of a relative and not allowed to cleanse her person or apparel for a year. She had not then washed herself for 3 months. Although her then apparel was disgustingly filthy she showed me a number of handsome Indian female dresses.)
6. Ogemaw-waugh-juck. The Spirit Chief. He is so old that he remembers when the French took Churchill.
7. Hus-Kuss-coo-sish (Uskoosekoosish). Young Grass. A Cree who has been in a great many battles with the Blackfeet. He has a ball through the shoulder and was shot in the belly.
8. Nicaway (Nickaway). The man that goes on a hunting party without rousing camp. A Musk-e-gaw (Muskaigow or Swampy Indian) from Norway House.
9. Do. (Musk-e-gaw from Norway House). Young woman.
10. An Assiniboine. Pe-tic-o-low-this. The little round man. . . . A bear was in the practice of coming to his tent to steal meat. He made a stage and put some meat under it and laid down on top in the night. The bear came and he shot him. . . . He was painted at Edmonton.
11. A Cree taken at Carlton, name not known. This is the man that shot the wolf with an arrow.
12. Chiniaza. The little slave. A Chipeway-an. Taken at Fort Pitt. (This tribe lives near the Athabasca lake. His prowess and dexterity in hunting wild animals of all kinds won him a degree of notoriety among the traders. He had when I saw him a hundred moose skins besides furs to a considerable amount.)
13. Muck-e-too.

14. Caw-Ke-Ka-saw-K-Way. For these two look at the journal.
15. O-this-skun. The Horn. He carries the bones of his brother in a bag on his back, handsomely ornamented.
16. Musk-ku-thay-ka-ou-mu-thay (Muskoothay-Capoomonthay). The man that always runs in the Plains. (An Asnaboyne or Stonee Indian so called from the river Asnaboyne which has a very rocky channel.)
17. Mis-cu-pa-puck-we (Mascoupay Pochawyon). Red Shirt. Assiniboine.
18. A Cree Woman.
19. Ka-Kee-se-guce-na-may-ed (Cawkeesaykeijenawmeed). The man that gives the day. (This man is a Cree and a great warrior.) He wished to know why I did not show the place in his shoulder where the Blackfeet wounded him.
20. As-in-a-chu. The white cappa or Waugh-be-gin-a. A Shuswap chief. Taken at Jaspers.
21. A·Chis·a·lay (Atchisalay). The Call of the Wind. The As-ick-an-a tribe from Peace River, called by Sir A. Mackenzie the Carriers (for their carrying great burthens on their backs having no beasts of burthen to substitute). Their teeth are worn down by eating dried salmon, his food being full of sand.
22. Taken on the lakes above Colville. (A boy paddling a canoe sketched on one of the Columbia Lakes.)
23. Elle-a-ma-coum-staluck (Allamahkum Stoolach). The Chief of the Earth. A Spokane Chief. (The head chief of the Shooalpay tribe at the Kettle Falls.) A Man of a great deal of influence.
24. Ta-ma-quin-a-tum (Tamaquin). Water Chief of Cascade Indians with a beard which you seldom see. These Indians live on fish (salmon) caught in great abundance on the Columbia. Waugh-Cla-Ca is the name of this tribe. They take their name from a lake that is near their village.
25. A Chinook woman taken at Vancouver. (This was a large tribe and the locality healthy previous to 1829 in which year the plow was first introduced by the Hudson's Bay Co. and immigrants from the United States. In that year fever and ague first made its appearance among them and depopulated large tracts of country, nearly all the following villages which previous to that time contained a large population are now extinct. Their principal settlement is Chinook Point at the mouth of the Columbia River, where King Cumcumly ruled in 1810. The Clatsup village contains very small remnant of its former inhabitants. Wasiackum is entirely extinct. Catlamut is the same. Kullowith the same, and the mouth of the Cowletts River the same. Kullimo, Katlepootle and Walkumup are also in the same condition. On Sovey's Island there were formerly four villages viz—Namenum, Mucknoma, Mamme-with and Naquaick—and at the present day scarcely a lodge remains on the island. They died of this disease in such numbers that their bodies lie unburied on the river's bank by scores—and numbers were met with floating down the river. The Hudson's Bay Company supplied the sick liberally with Quinine and other appropriate medicines, but their efforts were counteracted by the Indian mode of living, and the injurious system they obstinately pursued of treating the complaint—this consisted

* See note for Appendix 1, which applies also to Appendix 2. In the Portrait Log manuscript there are jottings of names of Indians whom Kane had sketched in 1845, but these scrawled names are omitted here. He also made some small identification sketches of heads and landscapes; these have been listed in the *catalogue raisonné* and their source given as Stark A4.

principally in flinging into the river without reference to the particular periods of the disease at which only cold bathing could be beneficial or safe.)

26. A Click-a-tat taken at Vancouver. This is the manner that they wear their hair when they are offended. (The Sotos on the contrary loosen their hair from all confinement and allow it to fall down over the face when they wish to evince a similar irritated feeling. The Klickatats most generally reside at the Cascades.)

27. A woman of the Chai-to tribe near the Umqua.

28. 4 Clackamus Indians taken on the Clackamus River near the City of Oregon. (Their lodges were formerly very numerous, but owing to the fatal effects of ardent spirits, which in spite of prohibition and fines against selling it to the Indians, they manage to obtain from their close vicinity to Oregon City where whiskey or a poisonous compound called there blue ruin, is illicitly distilled. Their numbers have so greatly diminished that there are not now more than 6 or 8 lodges in this river, and little doubt can be entertained that in a few years these also will melt away.)

29. Casenove, Chief of the Kalupanet Nation.

30. Waslameth (the only remaining) wife of Casenove, Kalapanet tribe, belonging to the neighborhood of Vancouver.

[There is no number 31 in Kane's log.]

32. Chief by the name of Cut-tell-tow (Kutteltoo) lives near the Pisk-ca-kuse River between Wallawalla and Okanagon. This is one of the most celebrated thieves (of horses) in the country. He is commonly known as the tall young man. (Chief of the Piscocoose Indians.)

33. Caw-we-chum (Cawitcham), a woman of the Caw-we-licks (Cowlitz), on Cowlitz River that flows into the Columbia 60 miles below Vancouver on the south side.

34. Cascade Indian about 40 miles above Vancouver.

35. A child (Chinook) under the process of having its head flattened.

36. A Chinook woman from Astoria.

37. A Masset (Shatchet) Indian from Queen Charlotte Islands.

38. An Indian taken on the Indian race course near Vancouver taken with a head dress of beads.

39. Old Cox from the Sandwich Islands who was present at the death of Capt. Cook. He does not know his age. (He accompanied Prince Tamihami to England, and after his death returned to the Sandwich Islands and from there he came to the Columbia River in one of the Hudson's Bay Co. ships and entered their service. I met him as well as many of his countrymen at Fort Vancouver where they were employed in the company's service.)

40. Ciss-Cox (Kisscox), a Cowlitz Chief lives on a river of the same name. Amount to about 200. Live on camess and fish. Flatten their heads and wear the rat blanket.

41. Loch-o-let (Lacholett), Nisqually Chief, lives on the shores of Puget's Sound. These are the largest Indians I have ever met with. (The women are particularly tall and stout.)

42. Loch-hinum (Lochinum), Chief of the Tu-an-a-chun, on Whidbey's Island. I had some difficulty in getting him to set until he heard that all the other chiefs had set.

43. A Shatchet Indian.

44. Che-a-clack, Chief of the Sangeys, number about 500 warriors, live on the south end of Vancouver's Island in the Straits of de Fuca.

45. A Sangeys girl spinning. (A Songas girl twisting yarn.)

46. Ska-tel-san—a Samas tillacum with a (grass) hat that is much worn here south of de Fuca.

47. Cloll-uck (Claluch). Chief of the Clallums, entrance to the Canal de Arrow. There are about 20 lodges here. This man was a chief of a good deal of influence among his people.

48. E·a-cle-a (Eaclach), a Cath-i (Cathay) chief on the south side of the straits. I met him in his canoe with 3 of his wives. He wanted me to go to his village where he said he had plenty of salmon and good things to eat. I made a sketch of him while in his canoe.

49. Yeats-sut-sute (Yates-sut-sook). Chief of the Clallums. The name of the village is I·Eanus (Hienus), population 500, with 40 large canoes.

50. Chaw-you-wit (Chawuwit), the daughter of a chief of a place called Suck, the handsomest girl I have ever seen on the coast south side of the straits.

51. A U-Sanich (Eusanitch) Indian . . . Canal de Arrow.

52. A Quatlin from the mouth of Fraser's River. This tribe is at war with the Sangeys. He had some beautiful shells in his ears. (The favourite food of this tribe is the sturgeon which here attain an enormous size, some having been taken of 700 lbs. weight.) . . .

53. Yellow-cum or Cape Flattery Jack.

54. Ona-put-a—Sinna-hamus chief lives in Puget's Sound. His tribe is war like.

55. Head chief of the Sinna-hamus Indians. This is a large tribe and lives in Puget's Sound. His name is Shouts-ton (Shawtstun).

56. A Clallum woman making a basket which they make very handsome. (These baskets are made like those of the Chinooks to hold water and are handsomely formed of grass dyed of different colors.)

57. Slam-a-chusset (Slamahkusset), a Cum-shaw chief. I could not find out where his tribe lived. Taken at F. Victoria.

58. A Whellamay (Walmah) girl.

59. A Cawitchen woman.

60. Saw-see-a, head chief of the Cawitchans. He is a great gambler at the game called le-halem and lives in the Gulf of Georgia.

61. Cull-chillam, the son of Saw-see-a, with a medicine cap on.

62. The wife of a Clallum chief on Whidby's Island.

63. A Sangas woman twisting yarn.

64. A You-Sanish (Eusanitch) woman weaving a blanket.

65. A New-a-tay Chief. (This tribe lives on the north end of Vancouver's Island and compress the head in infancy into a conical shape bringing the vertex nearly to a point. . . .)

66. A You-calltee (Eucaltee) Indian. These Indians are the dread of all the neighbouring tribes. They live in Johnston's St. They watch their opportunity and when the Indians of the Gulf of Georgia entered for

the purpose of fishing, they pounce upon them and woe be to the poor devil that is caught alone. They frighten their children with the name of a You-call-tee.

67. A Nesqually girl with (coloured) grass cap on her head.

68. Child of the S. of De Fuca.

69. Chim-see-an (Chimseyan). Slaves are not allowed to wear a ring in their nose. Rings in the nose is a mark of freedom.

70. Saw-wollo-wa (Soowallowa). A Dall or Tenimo Indian. (An Indian of the Tenimo.)

71. Qua-w-tus (Kuatus). A Wishcum Indian (living in the vicinity of the Dalls).

72. Mani-nucht (Mancemuckt) the chief of the Skene or Shutes.

73. Slam-e-ass-sun (Slooassun). The Chief of the Pelouse or Pavilion River. The name of this tribe is the Uppet Uppets and but small (not numbering more than 70 or 80 warriors).

74. The wife of Tilaukaikt. A (head chief) Waulupu or Kyuse Chief, a man of influence and lived near Dr. Whitman's Mission and are a large tribe, 1,000.

75. I-e-ash-an (Ieash) the foolish, a Cham-nass-am (Chamnapam), at the mouth of the Nezperce River. A small tribe, a branch of the Nezperces.

76. Tam-at-a-pa, a brother of the great Walla Walla Chief Pe-a-pe-o-macks-macks (Peo-peo-mox-mox) or the Yellow Serpent, a man of great influence in his tribe. He is feared for he will horsewhip a man for the most trifling offence. This tribe numbers 3,500 (Mr. McKinley). (I took a sketch of the boy, son of Peo-peo-mox-mox, whose name was Tuchnoot or the Man without Medicine.)

77. Nach-a-wish, a Nezpercé Indian. This tribe is large and live on the Nezperce River.

78. Te-law-cite-an (Teilochikt), the man that is in the act of lighting. The head chief of the Waulpa Kyuse lives near Dr. Whitman's and has given him a great deal of trouble. He has slapped his face and pulled his ears which the Dr. took without a murmur.

79. Ta-mach-hus (Tamakus). The greatest savage I have ever met with. (I had no sooner finished the sketch than Tamakus asked to look at it, and enquired what I intended doing with it, whether I was not going to give it to the Americans against whom he bore a strong antipathy and superstitiously fancied that their possessing it would put him in their power. I in vain told him that I should not give it to them, but not being satisfied with this assurance, he was going to throw it in the fire when I seized his arm and snatched it from him. He glared at me like a fiend and appeared greatly annoyed but before he had time to recover from his surprise, I left the lodge and mounted my horse, not without occasionally looking behind to see if he were following.)

80. Keishawellish, Head Chief of the Senechastey Indians, living on the lakes on the Columbia River 60 miles above the Kettle Falls, numbering 300 souls. These people hunt between this and the Rocky Mountains, where game is abundant, particularly the Cariboo, a species of deer. They occupy the whole range between here and the Rocky Mountains.

81. Achewishamahigh, or "The Grisly Bear Standing," head chief of the Callaspellums living on a lake of the same name, south of the Columbia River. Their numbers are about 650. There is a Jesuit mission established among the Indians.

82. Tumsinniho, "The man without blood," a Spokane Indian living on the Spokan River.

83. A Spokan Indian.

84. A Sketch of Indians playing the game of Alkoloch. This game is one of skill and more difficult to acquire than any Indian game I have seen. . . . This game is played by all the Indians on the Columbia River, and the present sketch was taken among the Scualpees. The stakes were played for two horses.

85. Paikachose, a Cree, a most expert horse thief, having just brought in 7 of these animals which he has taken from the Blackfeet.

86. Eikeetopee, "The man that always rides," a Blackfoot Indian, who I afterwards learned was killed by the Crees in one of their excursions.

87. Tommskarrohoto, an Iroquois. He has been a guide in the employ of the Hudson's Bay Company for the last 25 or 30 years. This tribe resides principally at Cochnawaga (Caughnawaga) near Montreal. This man I met with on Lake Winnipeg on his return from accompanying Sir John Richardson into the interior in the capacity of a guide. There are no people perhaps so dextrous in the management of a canoe as the Iroquois. Nearly all the guides on the Columbia River and other waters in the Hudson's Bay territory belong to this tribe.

88. Maydoigamekinungee, "I hear the noise of the deer," is head chief of the Ojibbeways on the Camonanestaquay river.

Appendix 3

Catalogue for Paul Kane's Exhibition, 1848 *

1 Sig-in-nock—Blackbird—Head Chief of Ma-ni-too-awning, Ojibwah tribe.

2 Mas-kuh-noon-ge—Big Fish—An Indian of the Ojibwah tribe.

3 She-bah-ke-zhick—Hole in the Sky—An Indian Chief of Ojibwah tribe, from Lake Superior.

4 Ma-cheek-e-wis.

5–6 Indians of the same tribe from Lake Superior.

7 Saw-gun.

8 Sha-nu-oh-ke-zhick—Against the Heavens—from Lake Nipissing.

9–10 Indians from Michipicaton.

11 As-a-bo-nish—Racoon—Indian Chief of the Attawah tribe, from the Manitoulin Islands.

* Catalogue of Sketches of Indians, and Indian Chiefs, Landscapes, Dances, Costumes, &c. &c. by Paul Kane. Toronto: Printed by Scobie and Balfour, Adelaide Buildings, King Street. November, 1848.

A copy of this Catalogue is in the Metropolitan Toronto Central Library. It is referred to as TCH in the catalogue raisonné above.

12 Indian from Manitooawning.

13 Muck-koze—The Young Bear—Chief of Ottawah tribe, from the Manitoulin Islands.

14 Co-cosh—The Hog—a Pot-a-wat-o-me Indian.

15 Now-on-dhu-go—of Attawah tribe from Lake Michigan.

16 Shaw-way-nos-soway—a great Medicine Man, from the Manitoulin Islands.

17 A half-breed Indian Girl, from the Sault St. Mary.

18 Maw-za-pau-kau—The Brave Soldier—from Wolf River.

19 Muck-e-tah-kin-ne-u—Black Eagle—Manomone tribe, from Fox River, Lake Winnibago.

20 I-o-we-to-ke—The Serpent—an Indian Woman of the Manomone tribe, from Fox River, Lake Winnibago.

21 Ke-wah-tin—The North Wind—Man[o]mone tribe, Lake Winnibago.

22 Wah-bo-nim—The White Dog—Manomone tribe, Lake Winnibago.

23 Muck-a-too—same as above.

24 I-a-co-way—The Loud Speaker—Chief of the Soto Indians, from Fort Francis lac la pluie.

25 Pe-co-dhis—same as above.

26 Ka-ke-ka-ki-ji-koe—The Constant Sky—a Soto girl from the Red River Settlement.

27 ⎱ Indians of the Cree tribe, from the Saskachawan River, near
28 War Cap. ⎰ Fort Pitt.

29 Hus-kus-coo-sish—The Young Grass—of the Cree tribe, on the Saskachawan River.

30 Pe-tic-o-paw-this—The Little Round Man—of the Cree tribe, on the Saskachawan River, near Carlton.

31 Francis Lucie—a half-breed Cree, from Edmonton House.

32 A blood Indian Chief—from the Western prairies.

33 Oke-maw-wah-jack—The Spirit Chief—an Esquimaux.

34 Ca-is-no—of the Chi[n]ook tribe, from Columbia River.

35 Chi-a-clah—Chief of the Songes, from Vancouver's Island.

36 Wilhamet Indians.

37–8–9–40 Medicine Men on the Pacific Coast, near the Straits de Fuca.

41 A Medicine Pipe, do. do.

42–3–4 Indian Wigwams.

45–6–7 Sketches on the Island of Mackinaw.

48 The Dog Portage.

49 The Pin Portage.

50 French River Rapids.

51 Encampment on River Winnipeg.

52 Chûte à Jacko, on do. do.

53 Pointe des Bois, do. do.

54 Blackfoot Chief, from the Western prairies.

55 Buffalo head.

56 Group of Buffaloe.

57 Saskachawan River.

58 A Buffalo Pound.

59 A Medicine Pipe Stem Dance.

60 A Scalp Dance.

61 Falls on the Peluce River.

62 View near Fort Vancouver (Mount Hood)

63–4 Sketches of Mount St. Helen, near Fort Vancouver.

65 Mills in Oregon City.

66 Oregon City.

67 Main Street, Oregon City.

68–9 Falls near Oregon City.

70 Fort Vancouver.

71 Interior of a Click-a-tat Lodge on Columbia River.

72 A Well in the Woods.

73 Lodges on the Columbia River—drying Salmon.

74 Catching Salmon on the Falls near Colville, Columbia River.

75 Castle Rock, Columbia River.

76 Sketch of Mount Hood, Columbia River.

77 Lodges on Vancouver's Island.

78 Norway House.

79 Sketch on River Winnipeg.

80 Babeen Woman, North West Coast.

Sketches in Water Colours.

81 May-dwi-ga-mi-ki-nun-ge—I hear the noise of the deer—The head chief of the Ojibwah tribe, on the Kaministaquoiah River.

82 Mah-min—The Feather—Head Chief of the Asseneboine tribe, Rocky Mountain House.

83 Wah-ke-jo-e-tass-a-neen—The white half man—second chief of the Asseneboine tribe, Rocky Mountain House.

84 Ka-ah-ke-ka-sahk-a-wa-ow—The man that gives the war whoop—The head chief of the Cree tribe.

85 Pe-a-pus-qua-hum—One that passes through the sky—a Cree Indian living among the Asseneboines, Rocky Mountain House.

86 A Cree Indian.

87 Pe-pa-ka-chos—A Cree Indian.

88 Achu-wish-a-ma-hy—The Grisly Bear standing—a Cree Indian.

89 Iron Collar—Blood Indian Chief from the Western prairies.

90 Big Snake—Blackfoot Chief from do.

91 White Buffalo Calf—Blackfoot Indian do.

92 Chin-i-a-sa—The Little Slave—a Chippawayan Indian, on the Athabasca River.

93 Achi-sa-lay—The call of the Wind—of the Assickanay tribe, on the Rocky Mountains.

94 Collection of Painted Heads.

95 A Chief of the Lakes, Columbia River.

96 See-pase—Chief of the Salmon, Columbia River.

97 Chin-oo-as—A Flathead Indian, from the West side of the Rocky Mountains.

98 El-ko-ka-shin—A Shawalloway Indian, from the Cascades.

99 Tillu-ko-ikt—A Chief of the Kyoos tribe. This man was one of the party of Indians who murdered Dr. & Mrs. Whitman, and 12 other individuals of the Missionary Station at Wy-al-poo, on the Walla Walla River.

100 The Wife of Tillu-ko-ikt.

101 Tamachus—also one of Dr. W.'s murderers.

102 Son of the great Walla Walla Chief, Pe-o-pe-o-maux-maux.

103 Brother to the same.

104–5 Nepersee Indians, Nepersee River.

106 Indian of the Lakes.

107 Ku-ar-tos—An Indian of the Wishkum tribe, from the Shoots on the Columbia River.

108 So-wall-o-way—a Chief of the Dalles.

109 Tum-se-ne-ho—The Man without Blood—a Spokan Chief, on the Spokan River.

110 To-ma-quin—a Cascade Chief, Columbia River.

111 A Cascade Indian, Columbia River.

112 Studies of Figures, do.

113–14 Chin-ook Women, from Astoria.

115 Child's head—Chinook, do.

116 Boy with head dress, do.

117 A Click-a-tat Indian, Columbia River.

118 Cow-we-cham—Cow-we-litcks—River Cow-we-litcks.

119 Kiss-cox—Chief of do. do.

120 A Chinook Indian.

121 A Slave of the Chastay tribe, south of the Columbia River, on the Sea Coast.

122 Old Cox—a Sandwich Islander, who was present at the murder of Capt. Cook.

123 Law-hi-num—Chief of Whidbey's Island, Paget Sound.

124 Sca-tel-son—a Songhes Indian, Vancouver's Island.

125 A Girl from Pagit Sound.

126 Ukultee Indian, Johnson's Straits.

127 A Cow-i-chin Indian, from the Straits de Fuca.

128 Yate-sut-soot—Chief of the Chalms, south side of the Straits de Fuca.

129 A Chief of the Sin-no-ho-mas, Puget Sound.

130 Slam-ma-hur-set—Chief of the Cum-sin-no-ho—taken at Fort Victoria, Vancouver's Island.

131 A U-sa-nich Indian, from the Gulf of Georgia.

132 Yallocum, Chief of Cape Flattery.

133 Onepa—A Sinnohomas, Puget Sound.

134 Wife of Clalm Chief, Whidbey Island.

135–6 Chiefs of the Chimpseyans, Chatham Sound.

137 A daughter of a Clalm Chief, south of the Straits de Fuca.

138 A Clalm Woman making a basket.

139 Saw-sea-a, the Head Chief of the Cow-i-chin tribe.

140 Son of Saw-se-a—Medicine Man—north of Fraser's River.

141 A Quat-lin Indian, on Fraser's River.

142 A Sca-chet Indian, do.

143 A Nu-et-tee Chief, north end of Vancouver's Island. The Nuettee Indians have conical-shaped heads.

144 A Songhes Woman twisting yarn.

145 A Mountain Goat.

146 Study of Snow on a tree.

147 Study of a Carved Stone Pipe.

148 Buffalo War Robe.

149–50 North West Canoes.

151 War Party in Canoes, in the Esquimelt.

152 Indian Graves—Puget's Sound.

153 Sketch of Indian Fan—belonged to the late Mrs. Whitman, murdered by Tillukoikt, Tamachus and others.

154 A Painted Horse.

155 War Clubs.

156 Indian Dogs.

157 A Sketch.

158 Moss Tree.

159 Interior of Lodge.

160 Canoes on Columbia River.

161-2-3 Indian Graves on Columbia River.

164 Indian Graves on Cowlet's River.

165 Medicine Masks—North West Coast.

166 Indians spearing Fish—Columbia River.

167 Method of flattening the head among the Chinook Indians.

168 Indian Woman weaving a blanket.

169 Interior of a Clalm Lodge.

170 Pine Tree.

171 Heads of Prairie Antelopes.

172 A Buffalo Bull.

173 Carved Stone Pipe.

174 Sled Dogs.

175 A Mountain Ram's Head.

Sketches on the Columbia River.

176 Dalle des Morts.

177 Mount Hood.

178 Columbia River.

179 Indian Lodge.

180 Coffin Rock.

181 The Little Dalles.

182 The Kettle Falls.

183 Fort Walla-Walla.

184 Cape Horn.

185 Rock called the Too-ne-per-see-girls.

186 Supposed Land Slip.

187 Cascades.
188 Sketch near Fort Vancouver.

Sketches in the Rocky Mountains.

189 Jasper's House.
190 Jasper's Lake.
191 Laroque's Prairie.
192 Snow Scene in the Mountains.
193–4 Mountain Scenery.
195 Roman Catholic Mission Station, near the Wilhamet River, 30 miles from Oregon City.
196 Wesleyan Methodist Station, Play Green Lake.
197 Presbyterian Mission Station, near the Spokan River.
198 Falls near Fort Francis—Rainy Lake.
199 Fort Francis.
200 Slave Falls.
201 White Mud Portage.
202 Canoes.
203 Prairie on Fire.
204 Lake in the Prairie.
205 Fort Pitt.
206 Edmunton House.
207 Indian Grave.
208 Encampment of Half-breeds, near Red River Settlement.
209 Sketch in the Prairie.
210 Fort Gary, Red River.
211 Rocky Mountain House.
212 Falls on the Wilhamet River.
213 Bird's Eye View of Wilhamet River.
214 A Click-a-tat Lodge.
215 Puget Sound Establishment.
216 Sketch on Spokan River.
217 Prairie de Bute.
218–19 Sketches on the Grande Coulé south of the Columbia River.
220–1–2 Sketches on the Peluce River, a branch of the Nepersee River.
223 Indian Forts on Whidbey's Island.
224 A Barrière for catching salmon, south of the Straits de Fuca.
225 A Songhes village at the Straits de Fuca.
226 Indians returning from gathering Camas, Vancouver's Island.
227 Indians gambling—the game of Le-hal-lum.
228 Mount Baker, from Vancouver's Island.
229 Crossing the Straits de Fuca.
230 Boat Encampment, head of the North Branch of the Columbia River.
231–2 Carlton, Saskachawan River.
233 Pambino River.
234 Columbia River.

235 Lodges on Prairie, near Fort Vancouver.
236 Carved Pipe.
237 A wolf's head.
238 A Chief's Daughter from Lake St. Clair.
239 Man-a-to-wa-bay—The *He-devil*—Ojibwah tribe, Lake Michigan.
240 Na-too-waw-sit—The man that was born—a Soto Indian.

Appendix 4

Paintings Delivered by Paul Kane to Sir George Simpson, 1849 *

1. A buffalo Pound; 2. An Indian Lodge near Fort Vancouver, Mount Hood in the Distance; 3. Catching Salmon at Colville; 4. Indian Lodges near Colville; 5. Castle Rock on the Columbia River; 6. Indian Lodges on Vancouver Island; 7. A Scalp Dance near Colville; 8. A Sketch on the Saskatchewan; 9. Portrait of a Cree taken at Edmonton; 10. A Blackfoot on Horseback.

[Kane states that an injury to his hand has prevented him from completing an additional four sketches, namely, The Falls of Pelouse, The Kaministaquoiah Falls, A Buffalo Hunt, and Mountain Goat. For Sir George's acknowledgment see Appendix 10, Letter 17.]

* This list is referred to in the *catalogue raisonné* as GS.

Appendix 5

Canvases Sent by Paul Kane to George W. Allan, 1856 *

Brigade of boats	1
Ojibbeway Camp	2
Red River Settlement	3
Oregon City	4
Falls at Colville	5
White Mud Portage	6
A Buffalo pound	7
Medicine Mask dance	8
Indian Horse race	9
Buffalo bulls fighting	10

* The original of this list is in the collections of the Royal Ontario Museum, Toronto. It is referred to in the *catalogue raisonné* as GWA.

Appendices

follow it throw each a dart under it, the object being that the ring should fall and rest upon the darts & the beads which happen to rest on the darts count towards the game according to their color. This game is played by all the Indians on the Columbia River.

Appendix 6

Paul Kane's Draft of Notes for Paintings Delivered to the Parliament of Canada, 1856 *

1. Big Snake, A Blackfoot Chief, recounting his war exploits to 5 of his subordinate chiefs.
2. *"Boat Encampment,"* situated at the head of the N. Branch of the navigable waters of the Columbia River (for canoes). Derives its name from its being the terminus of all boat navigation & the commencement of the land carrier across the Mountains, consequently the spot at which all parties going or returning must necessarily encamp.
3. *"Mount Hood"*—A Mountain about 7000 feet high situated near the South side of the Columbia River & at about 120 yards from its mouth. The figures in the foreground are "Chinooks," a Branch of the Flat Head Tribes of the N.W. Coast.
4. *Buffaloes at Sunset*—taken near Edmonton at a small lake near the Saskatchewan River.
5. *Scalp Dance*—by a party of "Spokane" Indians taken on the Upper Columbia.
6. "Assineboines" Indians—hunting or "running Buffalo" on horseback —taken in the plains situate on the East of the Rocky Mts. & in their vicinity.
7. *Fishing Lodges of the "Clallums"*—on Vancouver's Island. These Lodges are constructed of a coarse description of matting which is taken down and carried in Canoes when travelling.
8. *Interior of a Winter Lodge* of "Clallums" on Vancouver's Island. These lodges are constructed of split cedar & are consequently not portable—are frequently large enough to accommodate 100 *individuals*.
9. *Part of Red River Settlement* with a view of Fort Garry on the right & the Catholic Church at the left of the River.
10. *The White Mud Portage*—situate on River Winnipeg. The picture represents "Saulteaux" Indians carrying their canoes & baggage, called *"Making the Portages."*
11. *A Horse Race*—Among the Blackfeet Indians on the Prairies. An amusement of very frequent occurrence & consists generally of a 4 mile Race, viz: two miles to & from a given point.—the Riders being invariably in a state of nudity.
12. Two Indians playing the Game "Alcoloh." This sketch was taken among the Shualpees near the Falls of the Columbia.—The game consists in rolling a ring of iron 3 inches in diameter with 6 beads of different colors bound by strings to the inner edge of the circle. The Ring is rolled along the ground until it strikes agst. a stick intercepting its progress.—At the moment of its devolution the two competitors who

* The original of this draft is in the Kane family papers. It is referred to in the *catalogue raisonné* as LP.

Appendix 7

Works of Paul Kane Given to Mrs. Kane by the Allan Family, 1871 *

1. Mackinaw.
2. Upper Pelluce Falls.
3. River Scene.
4. Wah-Be-Num (White Dog), Lake Winebago.
5. Vue d'un Belvidere.
6. An Ojjibeway Girl from St. Claire.
7. Salmon Spearing.
8. Wigwams, Owen Sound.
9. Scene near Fort Vancouver.
10. Ojibiway Indian Boy Lake Superior.
11. Oregon City.
12. Norway House.
13. Chute à Jacque, Winnipeg River.
14. French River Rapids.
15. Medicine Pipe Stem.
16. François Lucie.
17. Chinook Indian, Columbia River.
18. She-bah-ke-zhick—Hole in the Sky. Ojibwah Indian, Ft. William, Lake Superior.
19. Mt. St. Helens with smoke from crater.
20. Indian Boy.
21. Sha-new-di-kigik—The Heavens. Indian, Lake Nipissing.
22. Ottawa Tribe, Lake Nipigne, Naw-on-do-go.
23. Susan Belo, Half Breed Girl, Sault de St. Marie.
24. Coo-Coosh, The Hog. Potawatamie Indian.
25. Sig-in-nock—Black Bird, Ojibwah Chief.
26. Encampment, Winnipeg River.
27. Cree War Cap.
28. Medicine Man with Mask, Vancouver Island.
29. Soto Indian.
30. Pin Portage.
31. Babbene Woman, Pacific Coast.
32. Waterfall.
33. River Scene.

* The list is available in the collections of the Royal Ontario Museum. It is referred to in the *catalogue raisonné* as AG.

34. Mackinaw.
35. Wigwam.
36. Prairie de Bute.
37. Mt. St. Helens.
38. Muck-e-tah-kin-new, Black Eagle, Fox River, Lake Winnipeg.
39. Interior of Lodge, Columbia River.
40. Pointe aux Bois.
41. Dog Portage.
42. Wigwam, Lake Huron.
43. Muck-a-ta, Potawatamee Indian.
44. Indian man.
45. Aw-bon-wuish-kum, Indian from Manitowaning.
46. Sho-ne-ah, Silver.
47. Ft. Walla Walla.
48. Mo-chuke-e-nis, Indian Portrait.
49. Indian Chief, Manitoulin Island.
50. Indian Girl.
51. Indian Boy.
52. Indian Man.
53. Medicine Men, Straits de Fuca.
54. Indian Pipe.
55. Prairie Encampment.
56. Chee-u-clak, Head Chief of the Songees, Vancouver Is.
57. Indian Portrait.
58. Indian Portrait.
59. Indian from Lake Superior.
60. Cottage Scene.
61. Ke-wah-tin, The North Wind, Manamane Tribe, Lake Winnipeg.
62. Match-o-ke-man, Big Chief.
63. Group of Willamette Indians.
64. Paul Kane.
65. Indian Girl.
66. Mackinaw.
67. Cashto.
68. Buffalo Head.
69. Interior of Blackfoot Lodge.
70. Medicine Pipe Stem Dance, Blackfeet & Blood Indians.
71. Indian from Michipicoten.
72. Kaw-qua-dab-bow-nwa-skung, Dawn of Day, Chief of Saugene Indians, July 24, 45.
73. Cree Indian, Edmonton.
74. Buffalo Hunting.
75. Grand Coulet.
76. Mus-kuh-now-je, Big Fish, Ojjibewah Tribe.
77. River Scene.
78. Michipicoten Indian from Lake Superior.
79. A Well in the Woods.
80. Shah-wuk-nahsoowa, Great Medicine Man, Manitoulin.
81. Prairie Scene.
82. Head Chief, Ojibwah Indian, Manitowaning.
83. Cree Indian Chief.
84. Captain Ironside, descendent of Tecumseh.
85. Sabo(?).
86. Io-we-toke, Indian Woman, Fox River, Winnebago.
87. Muckose, Young Bear, Ahtaw-wah Chief.
88. River Scene.
89. Chief of Seto Indians, Fort Frances, Lake LePluie.
90. Ojibwah Indian.
91. Mah-he-cum, Indian Dog.
92. Winnipeg River.
93. Pipe from Lake Superior.
94. Part of Oregon City.
95. Mt. Hood from near Fort Vancouver.
96. Rocky Mountain Goat.
97. White Mud Portage, Winnipeg River.
98. Medicine Masks, North West Coast, B.C.
99. Columbia River Indians.
100. Indians.
101. Indians.
102. Indian.
103. Rocky Mt. Sheep head.
104. Indians.
105. Catching Salmon, Columbia River.
106. Wounded Buffalo.
107. Slave of the Chastay tribe, Pacific Coast.
108. Interior of Lodge, Vancouver Island.
109. Indian.
110. Burial Place.
111. Crossing the Straits of de Fuca.
112. Sledge Dogs.
113. Vancouver Island.
114. Chinook Child undergoing process of flattening the head.
115. Dance of the Women.
116. Game of Al-Kol-lock, Chucepay Indians, Columbia River.
117. Chalur Indian Woman basket making.
118. Indian.
119. Coffin Rock.
120. Canoes of Columbia.
121. Tilanpoikt Indian.
122. Wigwams, B. Columbia.
123. Indian.
124. Salmon Trap, de Fuca Straits.
125. Quivers, Pipes, &c.
126. Buffalos Fighting.
127. Indian heads.
128. Fort and interior of hut.

129. Chief of Chimpseyans, Chatham Sound.
130. Indian.
131. Windmill & Fort.
132. Burial Canoe, Cowlitzs Indians.
133. Indians spearing fish, Columbia River.
134. Return of War Party, Pacific Coast.
135. Mount Hood.
136. Game of Lihallum, Vancouver Island.
137. Fort Frances.
138. Chinook Indian Boy.
139. Jasper House, East side Rocky Mts.
140. Winter Scene.
141. Woman weaving a blanket.
142. Indians of Johnson's Straits.
143. Grand Coulet and near Walla Wallah River.
144. Fraser River Indian.
145. River Sketch.
146. Fall on Peluse River.
147. Pipe Stems.
148. Pipe Stem.
149. Water Fall.
150. River Scene.
151. Kettle Falls.
152. Water Fall.
153. Canoes.
154. Falls of Niagara.
155. Walulah Encampment.
156. Salmon Falls, Koos-koos-Kia River.
157. Upper Columbia.
158. Falls on Slave River.
159. Indian.
160. View of Saskatchewan.
161. Peter Jacobs.
162. Pyramid Rock, Koos-Koos-Kia River.
163. Falls on Upper Pelouse.
164. Dogs of the Plains.
165. Medicine Men.
166. Puget Sound.
167. Pembina River.
168. Spearing Salmon.
169. Fishing Columbia River.
170. Falls near St. Frances, Rainy Lake.
171. Wedding Party Travelling by Dog Sledge.
172. Interior of hut.
173. Indian.
174. Indian.
175. Suchal Indian.

176. Columbia River Indians.
177. Indian.
178. Buffalo Head.
179. Dalle des Meurtes.
180. Drying Salmon at the Dalles, Columbia River.
181. Ojibbeway Camp.
182. Wesleyan Methodist Station, Playfair Lake.
183. Edmonton House.
184. Cape Horn.
185. Indian of the Lakes.
186. Antelope Heads.
187. Mission Station, Spokane River.
188. Canoes, Pacific Coast.
189. Cascade Mts., B. Columbia.
190. Willamette River.
191. Fish House, B.C.
192. Blackfoot Indian.
193. Burial Canoes.
194. Idol & Graves, Vancouver Island.
195. Cowichin Indians, Straits of Fuca.
196. Half breeds running buffalo.
197. Indian Chief, Puget Sound.
198. Indian.
199. Indian Chief, Puget Sound.
200. Indian Village, Straits de Fuca.
201. Rocky Mountain Goat.
202. Saskatchewan River.
203. Lodge, Vancouver Island.
204. Canoe.
205. Study of Snow on Trees.
206. Naval Scene.
207. Indian Graves Calulle River.
208. Driving Buffalo into a pound.
209. The Little Dalles.
210. Picture writing on skin.
211. Huts.
212. Pipe Stem.
213. Chinook Child.
214. Chippeweyan Indian, Athabasca River.
215. Flathead Woman.
216. A-ches-a-lay, Call of the Wind, of the Asichuna Tribe of Peace River called by Mr. A. Mackenzie Carrier Indian.
217. ———
218. River Scene.
219. Indian Cradle.
220. Flathead Woman spinning yarn.
221. Prairie Scene.

Appendix 8

Pigments and Mediums Used by Paul Kane

The following analysis of pigments and mediums in Kane's studio sketch box (Colln Mrs. Paul Kane III) has been prepared by M. Ruggles, R. Boyer, J. Childs and J. Hanlan of the Conservation Laboratories of the National Gallery of Canada (November 1969)

Sample	Result of analysis	Method of analysis
1, White	White lead, 2 $PbCO_3 \cdot Pb(OH)_2$	X-ray diffraction
2, Red	Gypsum, $CaSO_4 \cdot 2H_2O$	X-ray diffraction
	Alizarin	Infra-red spectroscopy
3, Blue	Prussian Blue, $Fe_4(Fe(CN)_6)_3$	X-ray diffraction
	Alunite $(K,Na) Al_3(OH)_6(SO_4)_2$	X-ray diffraction
4, Pink	Calcium carbonate, $CaCO_3$	X-ray diffraction
	Alizarin	Infra-red spectroscopy
5, Brown	Hematite, $\times Fe_2O_3$	X-ray diffraction
	Magnesioferrite, $MgFe_2O_4$	X-ray diffraction
6, Blue	Cf. no. 3	
7, Brown	Van Dyck Brown	Infra-red spectroscopy
8, Red	Vermilion, HgS	X-ray diffraction
	Probably alizarin	
9, Brown	Mixed with sand and oxidized linseed oil	Infra-red spectroscopy
	Hematite, $\times Fe_2O_3$	X-ray diffraction
	Magnesioferrite, $MgFe_2O_4$	
10, Yellow	Yellow ochre	X-ray diffraction
11, Brown	Goethite, $Fe_2O_3 \cdot H_2O$	X-ray diffraction
	Arsenic impurity	X-ray fluorescence
12, Black	Bone or Ivory black	X-ray diffraction
	Calcium phosphate, $Ca_3(PO_4)_2$	
13, Yellow	White lead, $2PbCO_3 \cdot Pb(OH)_2$, and partially oxidized white lead, probably $2PbO \cdot PbCO_3$, which can be produced by calcination	X-ray diffraction
14, Dark brown resin	Mixture of Batavia Damar resin and Mastic resin most probable	Infra-red spectroscopy
15, Viscous amber liquid	Mastic resin	Infra-red spectroscopy
	Turpentine	Odour
16, Viscous yellowish brown liquid	Linseed oil	Infra-red spectroscopy
17, Red (plus medium)	Vermilion, HgS	X-ray diffraction
18, Not original	(not investigated)	
19, Amber pellets	Mastic resin	Infra-red spectroscopy

Appendix 9

Books in the Library of Paul Kane at His Death, 1871 *

Two years of "Illustrated Magazine of Art"
11 vols. Bell's British Theatre
6 vols. Shakespeare
3 vols. Waverley Novels
Italian Dictionary
Nugent's French-English Dictionary
2 vols. Pain's Sketchbook
1 vol. Polar Seas & regions
Diary of a late Physician
Remarks on Italy
The Sketchbook of Geoffrey Crayon, Esq.
Daily Communication with God
Matthew Henry
Tales from Blackwood
The Last Days of Pompeii
Life of Archbishop Cranmer
Prismatics
History of England—Macaulay
Sparks from a Locomotive
Book of 1000 Anecdotes
Queen of Hearts. Wilkie Collins
Life of Benvenuto Cellini
Michael Angelo & Raphael
Richardson's Arctic Expedition
Geographical view of the world
The Sparrowgrass Papers—Cozzens
Stack's Italy
Scenes and adventures as a soldier & settler—Moodie
Woman's right to labour—Mrs. Dall
9 vols. Chambers Journal
Dr. Chase's Receipts
Journal of Devotions
John Bull
Pollock's Course of Time
Young's Night Thoughts
Mason's Select Remains
Sheridan's Dictionary
Lemprieces(?) Classical dictionary

* This list was obtained from the Surrogate Court Office, County of York, Ontario. It has been reproduced without change.

Walke's Dictionary
India and its inhabitants
The Indian in his Wigwam, Schoolcraft
Report of the Commissioner of Indian Affairs
Powell on evidence
Aeroleuchius (?) in the principles of Composition
Prof. Wilson—2 vols. Prehistoric Man
2 vols. Life of Brant
Edmund Burke
4 vols. Animal Kingdom
Bacon Currier (?)
Burns' Works
Adams Geography
Cyclopedia of Medicine and Surgery
Culpepper's Herbal
Appleton's Cyclopedia of Biography
Byron's Works
Captain Back's Arctic Land Expedition
Tanner's Narrative
Thirty Years among the Indians
Canada at the Universal Exposition
Valentine McClutchy, The Fish Agent
The Comic History of Rome
Captain Ross's Second Voyage
Rennie's Supplement to the Shakespeare
Locke On the Understanding
3 vols. Otis
Cox's Adventures
Simpson's Journey Around the World
Good's Book of Nature
Origin of the North American Indians
4 vol. Wanderings of an Artist, Paul Kane
2 vols. Italian Costume, Camille Bonnard
Olieeve de Raphael 152 plates

Appendix 10
Letters, Principally to and from Paul Kane

Letter 1: Michael Kane, Toronto, to Paul Kane, Detroit

Toronto 4th Novr. 1836

My Dear Paul,

Yours of the 22nd ultimo I received on the 2nd Inst—The statement of your advantageous removal from hence is most gratifying—as you have begun, so I hope you will continue prosperous—

You say that Mr. Bowman has got married and that in all probability will prevent your Italian excursion. This I take to be a fortunate circumstance first in keeping you on the Continent where you ought to remain and

Secondly Mr. B. has given you a precedent which you would go well to imitate Viz—acquire long experience before you attempt the blind hazard of marriage.

Frederick has not been with me since you left Toronto—Dan and family are well and I remain

Dear Paul
Your Father
Michael Kane

[Kane family papers]

Letter 2: Stewart Watson, London, to Paul Kane, Toronto

My Dear Kane.

If I were near you I should see whether the length of my *cane* could measure your Kane. What a long time has passed since you left us and not one line of remembrance. I will not accuse you either of neglect nor forgetfulness for it is more in nature to deny the possession of these evil qualities to the friends we regard than to bring them in array against them as excuse for what after all may have been unavoidable. So I will not blame you but gratify my vanity by thinking that as I have a kindly recollection of you that sometimes you will think so of us. I wrote you a very long letter to the care of your father at Toronto and therein gave you a sort of statement of my hopes and prospects. In it I said that much would depend on the success of my picture of St. Peters in the Exhibition of the Royal Academy and if it sold. My cattle pictures sold in Edinburgh and since that time I have sold other two fancy Italian subjects. This together with painting some Portraits has been my means of living but just as I had placed my picture of St. Peters in the Exhibition and had the satisfaction to see it well hung and in the expectation of selling it, the Art Unions were declared illegal and fourteen thousand pounds which had been collected this year for the purchase of pictures to have been disposed of by lottery so I have no hopes from that quarter. Our friend Stewart was here last year and we had many delightful talk of Italy and our good friend Paul Kane. He is settled in Edinburgh and had some good pictures in the last Exhibition. Syme has been ill again and wrote me that he thought of going to the Water Doctor in Germany to be healed in His "seat of honour." Kennedy's large picture was quite a failure, a horrid thing. The Academy talk of doing away entirely with the sending out a pensioner to Italy as Kennedy and the three before him came home worse than they went out. Salter wrote me two or three months ago from Rome. He was scouting about as he was wont with you in Venice, and was to return to England this fall. Dunbar had married a girl in Trastevarino, so he is settled for life in Rome. There was a good joke happened with him and White and a young Italian, the result was a challenge from Dunbar and he was put in jail, but he said "I am of an English Noble family and claim the privilege of being placed in St. Angelo." Here he had to pay about ten times as much as he would have done in the other jail, so he now boasts of the last year being the most eventful of his life. He turned Catholic—was a week in jail and married. Since writing this, Mrs. Watson hints that *you* told us this piece of news of Dunbar, if so, you'll excuse it. Our old friend, a Mr. Handyside, arrived here from Montreal shortly after your departure. He came on business with the Secretary of the Colonies here about the cause of Canada. He was very anxious that we should come out to Canada and settle. Now I do not think either it or the States a good place for us artists, but I have a very warm side to your side of the water, and particularly to a Canadian comfortable country house with plenty of wood and freedom. It is an up hill business in this country to be an artist and there [is] so much opposition. The artists here have all got fresco mad from the idea that the government intend to decorate the new Houses of Parliament. My friend Newcombe of New York wrote me some time ago. He gives a sad picture of America. Henry Inman has sold off and come to London where Mr. Huntingdon (who was in Italy shortly before you came), has also come to settle. Waugh is *married* and settled in *Philadelphia*, and Paul Kane is where? Do write soon and tell me. I have commenced my costumes. They are splendidly published by Akerman in the Strand but they do not yield me much. I think I have done pretty well thus far and will not give you any further news till you write me. I hope you will continue in your promise to give me free quarters if and when we arrive. I am still in the determination to come to Canada and to paint Indians and hope that I'll meet you and work together for in truth I am tired of England. Mrs. Watson desires to be kindly remembered to you and with my best regards believe me ever your affectionate friend,

> Stewart Watson,
>> 91 Dean Street, Soho Square, London,
>>> 4 June 1844.

Mr. Martin with whom we staid at Russell St. was lost with his little son in a Steam Boat coming from Scotland.

[Kane family papers]

Letter 3: Sir George Simpson to Paul Kane

> Fort Frances, Lac à la Pluie,
>> 31 May 1846.

My dear sir,

I enclose, according to promise, a Circular to the gentlemen of the H.B. Co's. Service which will secure you every assistance & attention throughout the country.—As there will be a boat or canoe sent from Ft. Alexander to Red River Settlement as soon as you arrive there, I think a visit to that place might be agreeable to you, especially as I might be able to put you in the way of being a spectator of the grand Buffalo hunts made in the plains in that vicinity. Wishing you a safe and pleasant voyage, I am

> My dear sir,
>> Yours truly,
>>> G. Simpson.

P.S. I would strongly recommend you paying attention to the magnificent falls on the Winnipeg River.

P. Kane, Esq.,
> En Route,
>> Lac à la Pluie.

[Kane family papers]

Letter 4: Sir George Simpson to Hudson's Bay Co. Posts

> Fort Frances—Lac à la Pluie,
>> 31 May 1846.

Gentlemen,

I have the pleasure to introduce to you the bearer hereof Mr. P. Kane an Artist, who has come to the country on a professional tour; and I have to request the favor of your showing that gentleman your kind attentions and the hospitalities of such of the Company's posts as he may visit; and you will be pleased to afford Mr. Kane passages from post to post in the Company's craft—free of charge.

> I am,
>> Gentlemen,
>>> Your very obedt. sevt.,
>>>> G. Simpson.

The Gentlemen of the
> Hon. Hudsons Bay Co's. Service,
>> Ruperts Land and Elsewhere.

[Kane family papers]

Letter 5: Robert Cluston, Fort Garry, to Paul Kane

> Fort Garry, R. R. Settmts,
>> 15 Decr. 1846.

Mr. Kane,
> Edmonton House,
Sir,

While at St. Peter's last autumn I met Sir George Simpson on his way to Canada, and was requested by him to say that you would much oblige him, if you could send him a *Side* view of the Buffalo hunt, to match the one he has already got.—

> Believe me,
>> Yours very truly,
>>> Robt. Cluston.

[Kane family papers]

Letter 6: James Douglas, Fort Vancouver, to Paul Kane

Fort Vancouver 31 May 1847.

Paul Kane Esquire,

My Dear Sir

As there is an Express about to start for Victoria, I do myself the pleasure of dispatching a note, in quest of you, which will I presume find you somewhere on the road, safe and well.

I hope you have had a useful, if not over agreeable journey, and that you have been as well rewarded, for all your trouble, as you expected when you left this place.

I have no doubt you have found much of the beautiful and the sublime in the scenery of Nisqually and the Sound beyond, which it will be a great pleasure to see, in all the freshness of nature, indelibly fixed, on the glowing canvas. I hope you have met with every assistance and attention from the gentlemen at the several establishments you have visited in course of your present journey, and I beg to mention that the canoe, which takes the present express to Victoria, will return immediately to Nisqually, and is wholly at your service, if you wish to take a passage by it on your way home. The Cadboro, Modeste and Cowilitz are unfortunately all wind bound in Baker's Bay and it is quite uncertain when they may get to sea, as the weather continues unfavourable. We have had no foreign arrivals since your departure.

Wishing you a safe and pleasant return,
Yours very truly,
James Douglas.

[Kane family papers]

Letter 7: Certificate by Sir James Douglas respecting Kane's sketches

I have seen Mr. Kane's faithful and spirited sketches of Oregon Scenery, and have been perfectly delighted with these masterly delineations of places, rendered familiar by a residence of 20 years on the banks of the Columbia and N. West Coast.

The Indian Portraits and Costumes are perfect and it is impossible to give a better idea, than they Convey, of the dress and appearance of the Native inhabitants of this Country.

James Douglas,
C. Factor, Hudsons Bay Co.

Fort Vancouver,
30th June '47.

[Kane family papers]

Letter 8: Paul Kane to Peter S. Ogden, Fort Vancouver

Fort Colville, 20th 7 47

My dear Mr. Ogden,

I have just arrived from Mr. Walker & Eells where I have been most kindly received and hospitably entertained which I partly attribute to your letter having preceded me. I have to thank you for this, and many other marks of your kindness, which will be duly remembered and properly appreciated. I have made some valuable sketches on the Pavellion and in the Grand Coulie, the latter surpasses in grandeur and sublimity my fondest expectations. I thank you for your letter of the 2nd and the 4 Spectators. I am just packing up for my departure. Give my respects to Mr. Ogden, Mr. Cory and Mr. Douglas and all my old Friends. You will hear more from me the next time.

I remain,
Yours truly,
Paul Kane.

P.S. I am sorry you have not heard from Mr. Work. I hope in the Spring you may find it convenient to send me if not all at least a part of the Articles expected, Yours &.&. P. Kane.

[Kane family papers]

Letter 9: Certificate by William McBean respecting Kane's sketches

I have been favoured with the sight of Mr. Kane's Sketches of Landscapes and Portraits, some of which he drew while passing a few days here, and am happy to remark that the whole is admirably and happily executed —with an exact and strong similitude to the Original.

Heartily wishing him every success and with sentiments of the greatest possible Respect and Esteem, I beg to subscribe myself,
and am, his Most Obt. Hum. Servant,
William McBean.
In charge of Fort Nez Perces or Wallawalla.
30th July 1847.

[Kane family papers]

Letter 10: Peter S. Ogden, Fort Vancouver, to Paul Kane

Oregon,
Vancouver, September 2nd, 1847.

My dear Kain:

Since you took your departure little has taken place here to vary the dull monotony with the exception of a visit of four Americans, 1 East Indian and one French ship, the latter loaded with one Archbishop and 21

Priests, Fathers & Nuns, the latter for the salvation of the morals of the Country have been selected with more than usual precautions, being composed of old Women pass'd forty and beauty at a very low discount. We are indebted to the Oregon Spectator in being visited by so many Ships, but I regret to say they left the Settlement with only half loads. We have also had a reinforcement of two Missionary Methodist Gent. to replace those on hand who have been ordered home and have obeyed orders. But now comes sad news indeed alas poor *Mrs. Corry* has been entirely eclipsed and thrown into the *shade*. You artists understand the meaning of this latter word better than I can describe it and shall leave it to you, know then that Capt. Drury of the East India Ship was accompanied by Mrs. Drury and the all-beautiful and accomplished Miss D. aged 18[;] altho' invited and passed and repassed the Ship twice could not muster sufficient resolution to pay my respects, not so with David McLoughlin, he did and at first sight fell a victim. It is no exaggeration, she is all I can assure you as I have described her, in this one and all who have seen her fully agree in opinion. Proposals have been duly and *regularly* made, the Lady, her Father and Mother, have all duly given their consent, but the old Gent has enacted such I consider most *cruel* terms and that no Father has a right to demand, that before marriage they both become Members of the R.C. Church and take the Sacrament prior to being united, you perhaps differ in opinion with me in regard to a Father's rights. I should certainly like to argue the point with you, but knowing you so well scarcely suppose there would be a difference. However, let all this remain for the present undecided and let me tell you the Ship and the young Lady have now gone to California and will return in November when David's fate will be decided. Now from what I have stated do you not think with the assistance of the imagination there is a *sublime* field for a sketch and you who have already done so much justice to the wild scenery of Oregon in this quarter and in the N. West Coast, could easily assert one with your pencil and indeed for the benefit of your friends and no doubt the Public also—It is to be doubly regretted that the weather during the winter was so unfavourable to your pursuits and your stay so short in the Interior country. You have no doubt added largely to your stock and I trust one day and that not far distant I shall have the pleasure of seeing them—This indeed has been a very warm summer and to convey to you some idea from the 17 August to 21 the Thermometer in the shade averaged 106 and May, June, & July a fair average was 95. What then must it have been in the Interior Country in these arid Plains. I expect to hear you have been almost burned alive. I hope you have however succeeded in making a large collection of Sketches and that they will reach their destination in safety. Mr. & Mrs. Corry still continue to reside within our Stockades in the same house (East End) that you so often visited and would from what I have heard be inclined to remain for the winter and no doubt will as their new House is far, very far from being completed.

Mr. Stanley is now going up to the Interior in quest of Scenery. What with Artists, Archbishops, Bishops, Priests, Nuns, Deacons and Fathers, 22 having lately arrived direct from *Brest* the country will be lost forever. At the Dalles a few days since the Americans, say seven in number, had a squabble, one of the seven killed and two nearly murdered and one slightly —the Indians one killed and two slightly wounded. The Gov. has gone to settle this affair, he will I fear make bad worse. 500 Waggons are on their way here and 500 waggons of Mormons have commenced a location at the South side of Great Salt Lake. Many parts of this letter will be almost unintelligible to you, but in the tedious passages you will have in ascending the Columbia you will have full time to decipher it and I only wish I were with you to assist you. Thank God the time is drawing night and before I bid you a safe passage across the Mountains and a pleasant winter, let me add, remember your promise—I shall write you in the Spring. Our ship is not yet arrived from the Coast, altho it has been expected the last ten days, but rest assured I shall not forget my promise in sending you whatever may come from Work.

Yours sincerely and truly,
Peter Skeen Ogden.

Mr. Graham is to be married this week to Miss Susan Birnier. Stanley is employed by Catlin, a friend of yours, to sketch for him. Indian Chiefs are in great demand with him.

[Kane family papers]

Letter 11: Certificate by John Lee Lewes respecting Kane's sketches

Fort Colvile, Columbia River,
September 16th, 1847.

Mr. Paul Kane during a residence of about six weeks with me, at Fort Colvile, Columbia River, several times let me have the opportunity of examining the many Sketches he had taken West of the Rocky Mountains, consisting of Landscape scenery, Groups of Indian figures, and individual likenesses of many Aboriginees of these parts. A residence of four Years on the Banks of the Columbia in the Service of the Hudson's Bay Company and thirty six Years in the same Employment, East of the Rocky Mountains, making a total of Forty Years constant intercourse with the many different Tribes of Natives who inhabit these vast regions, has given me many opportunities of seeing Indian life as it actually exists among them, and from a perfect knowledge I have of them, I here beg leave to testify that the sketches which Mr. Kane has taken, representing Indian Groups are most true and striking, their manners and customs are depicted with a correctness, that none but a Master hand could accomplish.

The individual likenesses are also of a first rate class, personal acquaintance with the greater portion of the Individuals from whom these Sketches were taken, enables me to vouch for their correctness, which are most striking and perfect likenesses of the living Originals.

The Landscape Scenery representing many parts of the Columbia River, with which I am well acquainted are also most correctly delineated, and from their truth to nature, well adapted to convey a Just Idea of the many Picturesque and romantic spots of the Columbia.

John Lee Lewes,
Chief Factor of the Hudson's Bay Comp.

[Kane family papers]

Letter 12: Sir George Simpson to Paul Kane

[undated; 1847?]

Mr. Kane,
My dear Sir,

I am disappointed in not hearing from you by the Spring express but was glad to learn that you were well and hope to hear that you have passed an agreeable time of it across the mountains.

I understand you are expected back to this side the mountains in the Autumn, with the intention of passing the winter in the Saskatchewan: while there I should feel greatly obliged if you would take for me some sketches of buffalo hunts, Indian camps, Councils, feasts, Conjuring matches, dances, warlike exhibitions or any other scenes of savage life that you may consider likely to be attractive or interesting, with a view to their being coloured and framed, &, of equal size so as to match each other.—As you are likely to have a long winter before you, perhaps you could prepare a dozen and upon as large a scale in point of size as possible. In taking the sketch of the buffalo hunt you were good enough to send me last year, you must have stood in the rear of the herd; a side view would have given a better idea of the appearance of the animals, as from the hind view, it required a little explanation to make a stranger understand that the mass of dark objects before him, were intended either for buffalo or any other living animals.

I shall expect the pleasure of seeing you at Norway House next spring, meantime believe me,

My dear Sir,
Truly yours,
G. Simpson.

P.S. I intend the sketches applied for, if you would be good enough to provide them, to be framed and hung up in a room I design as a museum for Indian curiosities.

[Kane family papers]

Letter 13: Paul Kane to John Lee Lewes

Edmonton House, March 2nd, 1848

My Dear Sir;

You are aware before this that you are expected on this side of the Mountains. Had you come you would have had to walk to Fort Assiniboine or remain at Jaspers all winter, as the river set fast before I arrived there. I

was fourteen days, and suffered a good deal from "Mal des rakettes" and want of provisions. I arrived at Edmonton on the 6th December, being 75 days from your hospitable mansion. I left the two Boys to rusticate at Jaspers as it was impossible for them to walk so far, especially the fat one who got still fatter on the voyage. Your keg of sugar I left with Mr. Fraser in good order. I intended to open your Cassette at Fort Assinboine and found that the Keys you gave me which I enclose, would not fit the Lock. It was apparently dry and uninjured, so I left it. We had had a Wedding here lately, a Daughter of Mr. Harriott's by a former wife, to Mr. John Rowand. I accompanied them to Fort Pitt and have just returned.

Give my best respects to Mrs. Lewes, Frederick and Mr. McArthur.

I remain,
Yours truly,
Paul Kane.

To John Lee Lewes
Colville.

[Kane family papers]

Letter 14: Peter S. Ogden to Paul Kane

Vancouver, March 12, 1848

My dear Kane,

Many thanks for your friendly *notice* of me in yours from Colville which reached here on the 20th Nov. earlier than the year preceding as you can truly vouch for. Now friend before I proceed further I give you fair warning I am writing by candle light and intend to inflict on you a long letter and as my writing is at the best very unintelligible if you have not a good stock of patience, had better throw this sheet in the fire without even giving it a perusal or your patience a severe trial for only on it both must go through the ordeal so God help and assist and grant you a safe deliverance.—I was indeed glad to hear the wild scenery of the Interior of Oregon far exceeded your expectations and your time was amply repaid. In this opinion you agree with Stanley who has gone over from what he tells me privately the same Country and will now shortly leave this Country for the Islands. The only difference between your two cases, on his return to Walla Walla had a most narrow escape of his life but more of this before I finish my letter and let me in the interim proceed to transact business together. The memo. of curiosities you requested from the Coast came duly in the Fall 15th Oct. but by no means so complete as I had expected but my friend Work excuses himself on the plea of want of sufficent time to obtain more and this I verily believe to be true. I now forward you a copy of what was received and what is now forwarded and from the precautions I have taken trust will reach you in safety and shall only regret if they do not as I verily believe you did not expect I would have taken any interest in your affairs after you were gone, and so long as I remain shall be most happy to render you all the assistance in my power to promote your views.

We have had very dull and gloomy times since the Fall.—The American Immigration consisting four thousand Souls if they have any, brought in with them their pleasant travelling companions the Measles, Dysentry and Typhus Fever. All these found a fair field to employ themselves in, soon lost fourteen men. In this number was the Guide who you must have seen last Summer in Mr. Lewis boat, about forty Americans, Sixty five individuals in the French Settlement, but the Indian population as usual shared most conspicuous. On the occasion from the Col[umbia] River alone fifteen hundred died. You will remark this, the Cowlitz, Nisqually and Pugets Sound are not included but I am still in hopes to receive a report from them before the Express starts and if I do, you shall have it—The last account we had the Measles had reached Whidby Island and I presume will travel all over the Coast and you may easily imagine the Indians residing in villages what destruction it will make—At Walla Walla the Cayuse imputed their deaths to Dr. Whitman's medicines and in retaliation murdered not only him but his worthy wife and twelve Americans. This indeed was a cruel deed and [they] retained including Spalding Mission upwards of sixty Individuals, Men, Women and Children in captivity to redeem their unfortunate fellow beings, and fortunately surrendered. I made a trip to Walla Wala but you will find all particulars connected with this affair in the Paper I now forward you. I had rather an unpleasant trip but humanity dictated the propriety of going to their relief—and has also enabled me to write a sketch on this melancholy subject and as I *felt* the subject those who have perused it agree in saying I have done it every justice, even your particular friend Mrs. Corry agrees in opinion even as well as *Richard*— and I can assure you pleases *self*. Stanley has also employed his talents on the same subject which accompanies my sketch and also tends greatly to improve mine. I have already alluded to Stanley's *narrow* escape—two days after the Massacre on his return from Mr. Spaldings and when within five miles of the Drs. Mission an Indian from the latter place met him (a Cayuse) and with a Pistol cocked presented at his head in a threatening wise demanded to know if he was an American or French. Fortunately Stanley did not understand him but still more so he replied he was an Il lyena (A Frenchman), when he was ordered to lose no time in reaching the Fort, which advice he readily followed, and escaped a cruel death. Poor Barclay lost his eldest son, a most severe blow to them. This was the only death inside the Pickets. At one time for nearly four weeks there were not including Gent. six that were not laid low. During this period the Doctor's berth was no sinecure. As for myself I was about at the time and only came in for a slight attack of Dysentry. Mr. and Mrs. Corry still continue to occupy the same house and fill the most important situation. In April they propose leaving us as they have made *some* progress with their house. It is *now sound*. This has occupied the little Man's attention since you left this and he thinks he has made real progress. At present War is raging in the Interior. Four Hundred Americans have gone up to Walla Wala and we are uneasy about getting the Express up. It goes by a new *route* and Love has charge of it. The present War has already cost two hundred and fifty six thousand dollars and its present daily expense is equal to fifteen hundred per day. Do you think Uncle Sam will consent to all this? There are a variety of opinions on the subject—May I hope to hear from you. Recollect your promise. I know I can depend on you. May we hope to meet again in 49. I am making every preparation for it—

Yrs. Truly and Sincerely,
Peter Skeen Ogden.

[Kane family papers]

Letter 15: Hector E. McKenzie to Paul Kane

Lesser Slave Lake, March 24th, 1848

My Dear Sir,

I must now redeem the promise that I gave you in parting and endeavour to give you an account of our trip, altho this trip was like other trips in this country with the possession of little or no interest.—We found Mr. Brazeau with whom we remained for two and a half days, recounting the extraordinary success he had had in the way of being a Lynx catcher together with sundry other matters. The Weather for Voyaging was tolerably fine till we reached this Lake when a Storm caught us on the middle of a traverse accompanied by snow that you could not see the length of your nose if you were to be paid a thousand dollars more or less. The snow was so thick that we could not see land in any direction so that we did not know which way to go—for instead of going straight we were going in an opposite direction until Belleface undertook to guide up to the place we intended to reach, and performed it satisfactorily of which he was not a little vain. I must give the poor devil his due, there was not one of us who could have found the place we intended to cross to until the storm had been over. We reached this place on the 22nd Inst. and found Mr. McDougall together with the Mrs. & Miss with the rest of the bantlings in good Health. We are to start for Dunvegan tomorrow and Mr. McDougall is providing everything for our comfort for the journey because he wants us away from here. That accounts for the milk &—For I am persuaded that he would not have been so attentive to our comfort En Route to Dunvegan if the circumstances were otherwise—Mr. Priest Bourrassa come from Dunvegan on our arrival there and perhaps you will have the pleasure of seeing him at Edmonton.—He is another Beauty and will no doubt afford you a good subject for your art—How goes the *Backgammon Board* science versus Luck & *vice versa*.

I still remember the promise I made you of getting a Bow &c when I get to McKenzie River. Let me know what will be your address when you will be locating at Toronto—I have nothing particular to add more to this scroll so I will conclude in wishing you every blessing,

I am,
My Dear Sir
Your most obedient & Grateful Servt.
Hector E. McKenzie.

P.S. Please send me a copy of "Poor Lucy Neale".

H. McK.

Mr. Paul Kane,
    Edmonton.

[Kane family papers]

Letter 16: Sir George Simpson to Paul Kane

Hudson's Bay House,
Lachine 9 Nov. 1848.

My dear Sir,

The pressure of business has prevented my earlier acknowledging receipt of your letter of 22 October, by which I was happy to learn that you had reached home in safety, after your extended wanderings in the Indian country.

With reference to the mode of bringing out your proposed publication. I think the best plan would be to do it by subscription, and as it would be necessary to travel about to collect subscribers, you might, by giving attention to the portrait painting branch of your art in the principal towns you would visit, I should think make sufficient to clear your expenses.—I naturally feel a great interest in your undertaking, and if you decide on adopting the plan of publishing by subscription, I should do my best towards inducing my friends to enter their names upon your list.

I am sorry to hear that some of your paintings were damaged on the way down; I hope however, your collection has not sustained any material injury, which would indeed have been mortifying, after having expended so much time and labour upon them.

Your account which reached me by the last Canoe from the interior, is enclosed, showing a balance against you of £-14.6.9 Cy.

I remain,
My dear sir,
Yours very faithfully,
G. Simpson.

Paul Kane, Esq.,
Toronto.

[Kane family papers]

Letter 17: Sir George Simpson to Paul Kane

Hudson's Bay House,
Lachine, 19 January
1849.

My dear Sir,

I have to acknowledge your letter of 3 inst. accompanying the ten sketches [see Appendix 4], which came safely to hand and for which I am much obliged. I shall be glad to receive at your convenience the remaining 4 sketches you are preparing for me, accompanied by a Memo of what I am indebted to you for these pictures, which I prize very highly.

I am happy to hear your exhibition at Toronto fully answered your expectation. I think that the present would be a favourable time for you to open a similar exhibition in Montreal, when the town is full of strangers, owing to the meeting of Parliament—and I should have much pleasure in promoting your views here by any means in my power.—

The amount enclosed in your note was quite correct and has squared your little account from the interior.

I remain,
My dear Sir,
Yours very faithfully,
G. Simpson.

Paul Kane, Esq.,
Toronto.

[Kane family papers]

Letter 18: Sir E. Poore to Lady Poore

Datestamp: Galena, Illinois, May 4

Up the Mississippi,
May 2, 1849.

Dear Mother,

Here we are all safe and sound as yet, about 250 miles above St. Louis. On the Steamer Dr. Franklin No. 2 (coming down from Cincinnati) one man died on board of the cholera and we had 5 other cases of it. Philips has been very much frightened about it and was wishing every day to get away from St. Louis. We were 6 days getting down from Buffalo to Sandusky a 3 day passage, but taking the journey altogether we have got on very well. I expect I shall not be able to write to you again till we get to Vancouver's Island.

I called on the American Fur Company but I could not see them. This will be mailed at Galena, the great Lead mines of the West. It was a miserable thing to see a man die as that one I spoke of did away from home. He had left from home with $5000 to buy cattle, was taken sick and did not tell any one of it till 2 days after and in the middle of the 2nd day he died. They made a kind of a coffin for him and when about 7 miles above Cairo cut a cross on a tree and buried him under it, some kind of parson said a kind of a sermon over him and we left again. I should think we met and passed about 70 or 80 men going to California, everyone seemed to be mad after gold. Tell Stew I paid Kane for his pictures. Love to all.

Aff. Love,
E. Poore

[Poore family papers]

Letter 19: Sir E. Poore to Lady Poore

Red River,
June 18, [1849]

Dear Mother,

Since we left St. Peaters we have had nothing but bad luck. We left there on the 15 of May with one cart, 5 mules & 5 horses & one guide & his horse. On the road we got another cart & horse & a canoe. Philips one morn tied his horse up to the cart with the canoe on it (the canoe is to cross the rivers with, many very bad), some thing frightened him & he threw his head up & broke about 4 ft. off the end of it. All the way we have had mud, water, etc. for it has been a very wet season & the carts would stick & we had to get off into the water—Frank, the Guide, & myself often up to our waists in water, a thing Kane or Philips would never do if it was possible to avoid. I wish so much F. & I had come alone as we first intended. One evening we came to a large village of Indians who would not let us pass for some time so we made as tho we would camp but told the Chief that we had got a lot of papers &c which some of them were about them. & that they *might* be about presents which if they kept us *might be* withheld from them (They have only had presents once). In about 2 hours we were allowed to pass & we went on till 11 P.M. Two days after as we were helping the carts thro a river (Rice R.) the guide said he heard a shout, the horses and two pack mules with all our provisions (except tea) were over on this side the Hs., tied up; when we got the carts thro we went to get on our horses, my 3, the guides & the two pack mules were *gone*, hunted about for the trail, found it. I got on a black pony, took my rifle & F. his & off we started after them. Kane was on the pony but would not go because we thought the horses had been stolen by Indians & we might if we came up to them have to fight. I had run a stick up into my foot which was the reason I rode. F & I found the h[orses] had gone off full gallop, in going they had kept bushes between us & them the whole way & had gone nearly in a direct line E.N.E. The ground was in many places very swampy & full of rabbit holes in others, but they had not gone into a single swamp nor over one rabbit hole. In going on we thought we heard a hollow & when we came up to the place found the horses had stopped & walked about 100 yds. & started again full jump proving, all things taken together, no doubt they were in the hands of Indians. Left the trail at dark, got back to camp & as the rest had eaten what they could lay their hands on F. & I made supper off *Tea leaves they had used and sugar*. Started on next day. On the 5th of this month as I was driving one of the carts (we had to get on as we best could) now & eat what we could kill (i.e. such birds &c no large animals) I was turned out by having the horses hind foot put in my mouth (i.e. kicked). I spit out at once the tooth on the right side of the front ones & the front one next it was driven at an angle of 45 in my mouth, broke the roof & split my upper lip about an inch and a half down towards my chin right thro. F. & I started to ride here (it was about 60 miles from this). That night we swam one river (Rat R.) so I was wet all night having

got ½ dry by a fire we made. When we arrived here (started next morn at 4 A.M. and here at 10) the Dr. was sick with the gout & ten miles off so I doctored myself & am nearly well now. Philipps after we left him in trying to cut down a tree the axe slippped & he cut his foot ½ off & is now in bed. F. & I are going to start tomorrow on a buffalo hunt *by ourselves*. I suppose we will be away about 3 weeks, hope P. will be fit to go on by that time.

Affte. Love,
E. Poore

I shall not have another chance of writing till I get to the Columbia. I am going to send 2 Boxes from here with 150 Buffalo tongues & Bosses which will arrive in London about the end of September & be directed to you Care of the Hudson Bay Co. & you must send & fetch it.

[Poore family papers]

Letter 20: Sir E. Poore to Lady Poore

Fort Garry, Ruperts Land (i.e. Red River)

Dear Mother,

This morn Frank & myself start for the Columbia with *one old Indian & a half breed* of the place. Charley stays the winter here & I had intended to do so also but then I thought it would be a waste of time & money. Kane we found out is a regular imposter or humbug, he has only crossed the *mountains* in the *company's boats*, i.e. they go nearly all the way in them. Tell George that by incessant practice I can use the lasso like an Indian. When you get this send *Bill* down to the H'ble Hudsons Bay House (I think it is in Fenchurch Street No. 4 or 5) and ask for *3* boxes directed to you at Inverness Road to be left there till called for, one of them with myne & Frank's watch which have got broken. Will you have them mended & send them to Stuarts by the first opportunity. There is also all the odds and ends I could pick up in so short a time, in the nest of boxes there is a small piece of paper with Lady Poore on it in which is contained 3 pieces of E. Poore's upper jaw which have come out since his teeth were kicked by the pony's foot; the other two are full of Buffalo tongues and Bosses, they *must be soaked in water* 24 hours before being boiled to be good. The hair line in the small box is an Indian bridle and bit just like the one I use. I would have sent a saddle to match but it is too good a one to ride on but I will bring it or send it home some day. You ought to see me now with *long hair, earrings,* leather *trousers fringed* & all the other fixings belonging to a half breed. Kane we are going to send back for he is *of no use whatever* so I *suppose* all the drawing I shall ever do you might stick in your eye. It is likely when I get to Cali[fornia] that I shall try a little in the cattle line as I know a man that is there in it and I think I should make a very good *riding partner*. Tell George I think I have at last found a place for him to emigrate to *Pugets Sound*, no winter in fact everything he could want but more of that when I have seen to it. I will write an account of it from Fort Vancouver. We shall have to pass through the Black feet country, *the* worst in all America but I hope we shall get on all right (not get our hair lifted). Frank I like *more & more*. We pull so well together & I believe he would go thro thick & thin with me. With best love to all believe me dear Mother,

to be yr aff
Son (the wild)
E. Poore.

[Poore family papers]

Letter 21: Sir Edward Poore to Lady Poore

Fort Vancouver,
Nov. 19, 1849.

Dear Mother,

I suppose you will be anxious to here how yr. hopeful gets on so here he is in a state of high preservation but *very thin*, Do. Franklin. After I wrote to you finding Kane such a very disagreeable person, we gave him money to quit & poor Philip's foot was not in a fit state to travel (We waited 50 days) so I told him F & I had made up our minds to start. We had tried hard to get a passage by the boats but Sir G. Simpson would not give in and I found out after it was because of Kane. F. & I started from Red R. on the 27th of July with 7 horses, 8 mules, an Indian & a half breed (i.e. half Ind.). Mosquitoes very bad, in fact we and the poor animals were nearly eaten up with them. After various adventures not good enough to write here except our guide (the Ind.) lost the way twice, as we were riding along we saw a *Buffalo Bull*, didn't I feel queer just kind of all overish, changed horses on to *My Hunter*, a little blue poney, one that had come from the Blackfeet Ind., very fast, Do. F. & off we started. The beast had got scent of us & had started but we were bound to catch him. They have a most extraordinary gallop. After a long race I suppose it must have been 5 miles, I was about 100 yds. in front of F. I was putting in the best licks to get alongside to fire, the poney put his foot in a badger hole (it is quite extraordinary the number of them & their formation. They are made first by the ground squirrel and dug out & eaten by the badgers. They are about a foot over & 3 to 5 ft. deep straight down) & came over such a buster his nose was the first part that came to the ground & then his ears & then his tail. F. came up. Are you hurt? No, says I, go on. Got up & when I came up to him again he had fired & broke his shoulder. Two more shots finished him. The guide had told us to take the tenderloin & tongue out. The next thing was to do it. After cutting about ½ an hour got out about 20 lb. of meat which I thought was the loin & F. tried the tongue. He got hold of what we thought was the wind pipe but turned out to be the tongue. Next thing, where were the rest. Looked around for the tracks & when we came to them there were Crees with them. Went to their camp & found 30 tents of them, 14 Stonees & 10 Chipeways & stayed with them that night & next day. I felt very much shook when I got cool. Two days after we had to cross the South Branch R. We came and nooned there. The Ind. went down to a point to bind some willows together in that [oval framework] shape. The things were then put on the top & the oil clothes under & the ends or the sides brought to the top & drawn together with a string. It makes a first rate boat. Goulat said, well something is wrong for old hog back is running (he had not hurried himself before). When he came he said that he had seen eight Indian tracks & he said that he thought they were an advance guard of a party of B[lack]feet Indians. We expected them to fire on us as soon as we were in the water. We then made the oil cloth boats striped & tied the two boats to *2 horses tails* to swim over, but after three trials we found it would not act, so made two paddles and got on over and Goulat on the other. We then (the Ind. and me) swam the horses over. I got on one but he rolled so he struck my foot so I left him and swam on my own hook. It was a long swim & water *very* cold. By the time I got over I had had as much as I wanted & shook as if I had the ague. The next day July 14 we came to Carlton House, a dirty little fort. From there we took 6 fresh horses, left the Ind. & took 2 other men. Fort Pitt without anything of consequence. From there to Edmonton House saw plenty of buffalo. Great fun running them. I wrote to Philips who intended to stay at R. R. till next spring & come up by the boats. This country is *not what it is cracked up to be*. We were very nearly turning back from this to go back from this & I really did not think it was worth the trouble so far to see. Hunting there is next to none & little excitement excepting driving 10 loose & pack horses if that is any. About 300 B[lack]feet Ind. had just left. Some of them had fallen in with two tents of Crees & wounded two. If we had fallen in then it would have been bad for our health. They were so frightened at this that we could not get a guide across the mountains so we had to wait there 26 days for the boats. In going up the Athabasca R. one of the men fell in the water & I was the only one that went in after him. The water was bitter cold & current strong. Two days after F. shot two red deer. The day before I had had a little pain in my chest & that morn it was so bad I could hardly get to the place. It was about a mile from the R. It has worn nearly off now. In crossing the mountain portage a most melancholy accident happened the gentleman in charge, a very agreeable person by the name of Charles. One even after camp a raven came & set on a tree close by. F. took his rifle and missed it. I laughed at him when he said he could drive in any knot in a tree you like to show. I pointed out one. No, stop said Charles, let us all have a shot for a shilling apiece, the best to win. There was an oldish man of the name of Young who had an American rifle I had warned him as being a very dangerous one & apt to go off. C. said to him, come out & bring yr. old rifle (F. & I had plugged up the nipple partly thro fun & danger but he had got it off) & have a shot. He came out and fired & returned into the tent loaded. They were standing round the fire, C. with his back to it, F. with his face facing two other young clerks & the cook. I had been to make a mark. As Young came out of the tent the rifle went off and shot poor Charles in the right breast (F. was singed). He fell nearly into the fire which we put out and got the tent over him. He never spoke after. Once he appeared to be sensible but directly after his face resumed the same stupid look. He was in great pain, said "let me go" twice & "mercy" once.

He also spoke of what we took to be some words of Cree but we could not make them out. The only sentence he spoke was "that was well done, Mr. Young." He then sat up & looked round wildly & banged down & died. He suffered about two hours. Next morning we rolled him in 3 blankets & buried him making after a small log house over him.

At Boat Encampment we took the boats to come down the Columbia. Arrived at Colvil safe, started again & two days after running a rapid ours was the 2nd boat (there were two) we ran up agst. a rock and smashed, scrambled on the rock 10 of us. The boat broke in two and two persons sat on the part of the boat that was left. It was as much as the 10 of us could do to stand on the rock it was so small. The other boat knocked a hole in herself & was just sinking when she got to land. There we were for nearly 4 hours, the water nearly up to my knees, all the time very cold & the current about 15 miles per hr. They mended the other boat and with difficulty took us off. At Walla Walla they fired twice out of a cannon & the second time as the man was ramming down, it went off & nearly took his head off. It was an awful sight, the hand was only hanging by a few cords. I told them they had better cut it off, but none of them would do it. The Dr. here has taken his arm off today at the elbow. He is a Sandwich Islander. Fancy a common teamster or carter gets here *now $125 per month*, sailors $150, cook & steward $200, mate $350, capt. $500. By these you may judge of wages. The commonest board in California is from *$5 to $7 a day* cord trousers here $10, 3 point blanket $10, etc. potatoes $3 & 4 the bushel. What direction we are going now, dear mother, I do not know. They say here we ought to go back by Mexico but time will show. Give my best love to all the sisters at home '& abroad. The cholera is not in California yet. Tell Stewart when you write to him that we have often wished he could have seen us when we have been in a fix, how he would have laughed at us in many places. Over 3,000 people have come *over land across the Interior* to California. One man told me they had passed on an average 10 graves a day on the road. Nearly one half the people at the diggings have died & there they lay unburied, all are in such a hurry for gold. The seeds are small shrubs they grow in a sandy soil. I have not read this over. You must forgive mistakes.

Love,
E. Poore.

[Poore family papers]

Letter 22: James Douglas to Paul Kane

Fort Victoria,
16th Jany. 1851.

My dear Sir,

I had the pleasure of your communication from Toronto, in November last by our Express from York Factory. I was truly happy to hear of your welfare and of the great encouragement you had received both at home and from abroad, in publishing your Indian sketches, a work which I trust may prove as profitable in a pecuniary way, as I have no doubt, it will be honourable to your talents, as an artist.

I shall be very happy to contribute my mite towards the success and completeness of your work, though I am rather at a loss how articles of dress could be forwarded from this country to Canada without putting you to a serious expense. Probably the least objectionable plan would be to ship them to England by the Company's annual vessel—from thence to be forwarded to Canada. Pray inform me if that would answer. I regret that you have not received the Kodiak dress, which according to promise, I left at Vancouver, on my appointment to Fort Victoria, with Mr. Ogden, to forward by the express in the autumn. It must have remained by the way, as I have no doubt Ogden sent it on—and it may probably yet reach you. [The Kodiak dress must have, in fact, reached Kane. It is now in the collections of the Manitoba Museum of Science and History, Winnipeg.]

Sir Edward Poore spent the greater part of last winter at this place and left us in spring to recross the mountains. He was not much edified nor greatly charmed with his north western journey; our country in fact possesses few attractions except to men of business, and it is not likely to please the mere pleasure hunter.

I am sorry to observe that the fatal spirit of disunion has not yet been suppressed in Canada—there may be grievances as there must necessarily be imperfections in all human institutions, but it is not in annexation that I would seek for relief were I a Canadian. Had you as much of Yankee justice and liberality as we have in this quarter, the idea of annexation would soon lose its charm.

I shall be happy to hear from you as often as convenient.

With best wishes,
I remain,
Dear Sir,
Yours truly,
James Douglas.

[Kane family papers]

Letter 23: Peter S. Ogden to Paul Kane

Vancouver, March 18th, 1851.

My dear Kane,

Many thanks for your friendly letter dated Toronto March 26th 1850 which the Fall express safely delivered me at least six weeks earlier than you arrived here. I was disappointed in not seeing you here with Sir Edward. The latter did not make a *deep* impression with the *Vancouver Dandys* and still less with the military who often remarked he could be no Gent., having no regard to dress—so you see the external garment is their criterion of a Gent.—altho I am not overfond of dress, still I am of opinion the rules of propriety should in all things be strictly observed which I must say Sir Edward lost sight of. What has become of the Man and friend Franklin, truly a free young Man. Now Kane let me give you a little Vancouver news—Two years since Douglas was appointed to Vancouver's

Island & Depy. Governor Richard Blows Lane, appointed by the Queen. Did you ever read of [undecipherable] being Governor of [undecipherable], something very similar to the situation they hold there and so long as Gold Mines are in existence no one will be so rash as to land and settle there. In fact here the Oregonians are constantly in motion and their eyes and ears are open and at the slightest report all are ready to start. I regretted much to learn the fate of the curiosities. I had taken great care in packing them and strongly recommended the parcel to Mr. Lane who promised fair. I had also taken the same precaution with the Guide but as the latter is dead we cannot well call him to an account and as Love is no longer in the Company's service it is useless to say a word to him on the subject. Had they been in time to forward by the Fall Express would have reached you in safety. They were a fine collection—it is not impossible but I pay you a visit before many years. We have now regular Mails via Panama and we have monthly news from England and the States. This is a great change for the better but it adds greatly to my labours. Thank God for all, and except the fever I have no cause to complain on the score of health. Glad to learn your paintings and sketches give you full employment. I hope they may prove lucrative. I hear Stanley is massing a rich harvest from his travels in Oregon, the Islands and California. He did not visit Vancouver's Island so there in regard to wild scenery and Rocky Mountains you have decidedly the advantage over him. He is a worthy young Man and I heartily wish *you* every success. Mr. and Mrs. Compton reside at 4th Plain about seven Miles from this place. He finds farming on a gravelly soil not very lucrative and is gaining a livelihood by painting and Mrs. C. teaches the young ideas [?] how to shoot. She is as fascinating as ever and much admired by the Officers. Amongst the latter here there's one a great favourite of mine. Bales & Scriven are the order of the day. They have a splendid Brass band and good German musicians—we have (officers) a good billiard table—have Parties nightly in fact as gay as we would be if in Toronto for we have a Gov., also Judges, Atty. General, Sectys. Lawyers and Doctors by the Gross. In fact we have a general assortment but I trust you will make no further enquiries as to what kind of Gents they are. Should your inclination and interest ever again lead you again to this place rest assured of a hearty welcome from

Yrs. Truly and Sincerely,
Peter Skeen Ogden.

Write me when your inclination leads your thoughts towards an Exile. Lane, Mackinlay, Law & Allen have all become merchants on their own accounts.

[Kane family papers]

Letter 24: J. C. Taché to Paul Kane

5 Aoust, 1851.

My Dear Sir,

I am infinitely glad to inform you that Mr. Uniacke and me having brought your case before the House, we have entirely succeeded. Now no doubt will remain in one way or another you'll get at least £250. This day, mark it, is a day of reward for your exertions as an artist. The Legislature of your country have eulogized you, the most eminent men have praised your talents. Two hours have been expended in exalting your talents and your energy. This is not flattery, this is the truth.

Here are the names of the Gentlemen that have spoken with the more warmth in your favor, MM. Uniacke, Elmslie, Baldwin, Sherwood, Chairman, and

Your friend,
J. C. Taché.

Paul Kane, Esqr.
  Toronto.
[Kane family papers]

Appendix 11
Paul Kane in Alabama, 1841

"THE FINE ARTS—MR. KANE"

Commercial Register (Mobile, Alabama), March 20, 1841

Every body recollects the sneering remark of a Scotch reviewer, made twenty years since, "Who reads an American book?" The coxcomb would be mortified (were he alive) by being asked, "Who does not read American books?" Then, both literature and art, on this western continent, were in their infancy, now there is a hopeful prospect that we shall be able to pay back with interest, our obligations to Great Britain for the loan of her genius. In science and mechanics, she boasts little advantage of us. In literature we may not yet have sowed our wild oats. Like lusty youth, we often violate all rules, and begin to teach before we have learned anything ourselves; nevertheless we have names which will be coeval with the memory of English genius. Our greatest deficiency is in imaginative literature, or rather we are more prolific in imaginative trash, than our European mother:—but who is unwise enough to expect poetry from a nation in its apprenticeship? From men who are placed in a field where every thing invites them to labor for a competency, and among whom there is little of aristocratic habit and wealth, and none of that condition of society which marked the Augustan, Medicean and Elizabethan ages of literature! A nation must have some experience in luxury; the descent of property must be such as to ensure its accumulation and stability, giving leisure for idleness and engendering a habit of magnificence and display, before any adequate patronage can be imparted to literature and the fine arts. Either men must be liberally paid for their genius or society must be so constituted as to oblige genius to spin its silken web or languish in want and starve in obscurity. This was the condition of England when a hot roll secured, simultaneously, death, immortality, and a tomb in Westminster abbey to Otway.

In this country, if a genius cannot live by his poetry, he can learn a trade, serve as a clerk, or go out into the new country, seize the plough, and, like Cincinnatus "greatly independent live." Poetry is a starving and contemptible business among a hard working nation, and that is the main reason why it is so badly followed here.

In art we may soon be able to show John Bull specimens that will put Sir Arthur Shea and the whole Royal Academy to the blush. Sully has borne the palm from the best English portrait painters, and Alston, in Boston, is now engaged on a historical picture which is likely to rival Martin or Dubuffe's most celebrated works. In sculpture, Cincinatti has nourished artists who, although mere boys, have given a tone to our national character in Europe. The genius of Power, now languishing in poverty among the classical sculpture of Italy, has excited the wonder and admiration of the best European critics; and Greenough has just shipped from Florence a colossal statue of Washington, which probably could not be surpassed or reached by Thorwaldsen, the most eminent sculptor now living. We may yet (who knows?) rival Apelles and Praxiteles.

This, however, is a wandering from my purpose.—My object is to direct public attention to the paintings of Mr. PAUL KANE, an artist who has lived among us some ten or twelve months. This gentleman's full length VICTORIA, after the picture by *Chalons* [*sic*.] of the Royal Academy, is indicative of a high degree of talent. In point of merit, the work approaches that of the original artist from the fact that it is a full length copy of a *miniature engraving*.* The colouring and tone, with the masses of light and shade, are peculiar to himself. The drapery is so disposed as always to present, no matter how frequently examined, the most graceful and easy curvatures, and its tints are gorgeous and brilliant in the extreme. The flesh is clear and transparent, while the limbs and immediate adjuncts of the figure, are presented to the eye through a purity and silvery clearness of tone, which gives to them almost the distinctness of *bas relief*. There are besides, a dignity and a sort of aristocratic self-possession about the whole which one naturally expects to find in everything connected with royalty. This quality is by no means the least difficult part of the art. How far the work is a correct likeness, I am unable to judge; but it seems to me to embody my idea of Her Majesty, as drawn from reading the best descriptions of her personal appearance. Without much sweetness of character or femininity of expression, there is a great deal of benevolence of feeling in her portrait, resulting one would suppose, while looking at the round, lusty, rather Dutch-built figure, as much from high health and the activity of vivativeness, as from native disposition. The stock whence her Majesty comes was never remarkable for loftiness of character or genius, and Victoria seems to be no exception to the rule.

There is one objection in my mind to this picture, and that is the want of finish in the less essential parts of the work. I hold this to be a defect,

* NOTE. Although the copy of an engraving, I am assured that Mr. Kane's Victoria is as correct a likeness as the original painting itself. It differs somewhat from that of Sully in portraiture, and in attitude, is, as a picture (not a work of art), infinitely more imposing and interesting.

although in a measure recommended by that great master, Sir Joshua Reynolds, with Northcote among many other eminent men among his pupils.—Modern critics on the art, among whom is the acute Hazlett, have attributed a very prejudiced influence to this error. The most celebrated pictures of the greatest artists are those which are the most finished—in which the details are as complete as the superior parts of the work. A good painter, by a proper disposition of his details and the use of colors which heighten the contrast while preserving the harmony of the parts, need apprehend little danger of the less essential destroying the effect of the more essential parts. The theory of Reynolds has made many a man of genius a slovenly, careless dauber.

In half-length figures, Mr. Kane excels. His portraits are very striking, as much from their correct likeness as from the baldness of their outline, their softness and dignity, and the transparency of their coloring. His picture of General Harrison, painted at a very short notice, is exceedingly life-like, and the masses of light and shade and depth of coloring are as much like those described of Rembrandt as the works of any young artist I have seen. If there is any objection to his portraits, it is a little stiffness, which I am disposed to attribute to the constrained posture that most sitters maintain, rather than to the artist. Ease and grace are everything in a portrait. Even negligence is better than stiffness. This, however, will be found a capital defect, in almost all portraiture—a defect which can only be readily observed by seeing a great number of pictures together. There is a sameness in the attitude—a sort of holiday or Sunday appearance about the figures as though they had put on their best looks to suit the occasion. Variety in this department of the art is a great excellence and deserves a more attentive study from the fact that there is so little scope for its exertion.

Mr. Kane, however, has other merits beside those of an artist. He is a gentleman and a very clever fellow, and is always happy to see visitors to his studio, whether they come from mere curiosity or as visitors.

B.

Appendix 12

Paul Kane before the Parliament of Canada, 1856

(*Journals* of the Legislative Assembly of Canada, 1856, pp. 556–57)

Mr. *Paul Kane* begs leave to bring under the notice of the Contingent Committee the following circumstances connected with his agreement to furnish the House of Assembly with twelve Paintings, in consideration of receiving £500, which was paid to him in 1851:—

In the first place, Mr. *Kane* begs to state that the understanding arrived at between Mr. *Hincks*, Mr. *Malcolm Cameron*, and the other Gentlemen with whom he was in communication when the grant referred to was made, was that the Paintings should only be supplied to the House after Mr. *Kane* had finished his complete series, which he has now been exclusively engaged at for eleven years and has not yet accomplished. The object of his application to the House was for a gratuity to enable him to devote himself entirely to that work with a view to the publication of his Pictures, in illustration of a narrative of his travels and adventures in the North-West, which he intended, and still intends giving to the Press. It will be obvious to the Committee, and this view was at once admitted to be reasonable by the Committee in 1851, that out of a series of Paintings intended for publication under copyright, to make twelve choice selections and expose them in an apartment public as the Library of the Legislature, would effectively destroy his right, and in fact the necessity of securing such copyright, as nothing could prevent the public from obtaining access to them for any purpose they might desire. The arrangement, therefore, was that these Paintings should be presented to the House as soon as it could be done without any such danger.

In explanation of the period elapsed since the arrangement was effected, Mr. *Kane* begs the Members of the Committee to consider that he has been many years engaged at the work in question in his own interest, and that no delay that was not absolutely indispensable in so voluminous a work can reasonably be supposed to have been voluntarily incurred.

These remarks Mr. *Kane* offers in justification of himself and of the time transpired since he undertook that engagement; he has now, however, to inform the Committee that, anticipating the return of the Government to *Toronto* would be immediately followed by a demand of the nature now made upon him, he waived the consideration above set forth, and has now been for some months occupied in preparing the series intended for the House, which he hopes to complete by the close of the Summer. He, therefore, requests that the Committee will be good enough to withdraw their Report, which was prepared and presented without his being called upon to offer any explanations, and suspend action in the matter until the opening of the next Session, when Mr. *Kane* will be prepared to place the twelve Paintings in the hands of the proper Officer of the House, on the understanding that such precautions as he may suggest will be adopted to prevent his prospective copyright being infringed, in furtherance of the understanding on which was based as well Mr. *Kane*'s original application, as the liberal action of the Committee upon it.

BIBLIOGRAPHY AND INDEX

BIBLIOGRAPHY

This bibliography lists works directly related to the life and career of Paul Kane. The notes to Part One and Part Two contain references (with bibliographical information) to other works which have provided background for the present study; the names of their authors appear in the index.

WRITINGS BY THE ARTIST

Paul Kane, "The Chinook Indians," *Canadian Journal*, new ser., II (1857), 11–30.

——, "The Chinook Indians," *Daily Colonist* (Toronto), August 6, 7, 8, 9, 1855.

——, "Incidents of Travel on the North-West coast, Vancouver's Island, Oregon, etc.: The Chinook Indians," *Canadian Journal*, III (1854–55), 273–79.

——, "Notes of a Sojourn among the Half-Breeds, Hudson's Bay Company's territory, Red River," *Canadian Journal*, new ser., I (1856), 128–38.

——, "Notes of Travel among the Walla-Walla Indians," *Canadian Journal*, new ser., I (1856), 417–24.

——, *Wanderings of an Artist among the Indians of North America from Canada to Vancouver's Island and Oregon through the Hudson's Bay Company's Territory and Back Again* (London 1859); re-published with introduction and notes by L. J. Burpee (Master-works of Canadian authors, ed. J. W. Garvin, VII, Toronto 1925; repub. with intro. by J. G. MacGregor, Edmonton 1968).

Les Indiens de la baie d'Hudson, promenades d'un artiste parmi les Indiens de l'Amérique du Nord . . . , trans. by Edouard Delessert (Paris 1861).

Wanderungen eines Künstlers unter den Indianern Nordamerikas . . . , trans. by Louise Hauthal (Leipzig 1862).

En Kunstners Vandringer blandt Indianerne i Nordamerika . . . , by J. K. (Copenhagen 1863).

REVIEWS OF KANE'S WRITINGS

Charles Lavollée, "Un artiste chez les Peaux-Rouges," *Revue des deux mondes* (Paris), XXII (1859), 963–86.

Daniel Wilson, "*Wanderings of an Artist*," *Canadian Journal*, new ser., IV (1859), 186–94.

Athenaeum (London), July 2, 1859, pp. 14–15.

CATALOGUES IN WHICH KANE'S WORK IS MENTIONED

Catalogue of the First Exhibition of the Society of Artists and Amateurs of Toronto (Toronto 1834).

Catalogue of Sketches and Paintings by Paul Kane (Winnipeg 1922).

Catalogue, Pictures of Indians and Indian Life by Paul Kane (property of E. B. Osler, n.p., [1904]).

Paul Kane, *Catalogue of Sketches of Indians, Chiefs, Landscapes, Dances, Costumes, etc.* (Toronto 1848).

National Gallery of Canada, *Catalogue of Paintings and Sculpture*, ed. R. H. Hubbard (3v., Ottawa, 1959–61), III, *The Canadian School*, 151–56.

Toronto Society of Arts (Toronto 1847).

PUBLICATIONS WHICH DISCUSS KANE'S SKETCHES AND PAINTINGS

Anglo-American Magazine (Toronto), I, 1852, 372–74 (review of Kane's paintings at the Upper Canada Provincial Exhibition, 1852).

B., "The Fine Arts—Mr. Kane," *Commercial Register* (Mobile, Alabama), March 20, 1841.

D. I. Bushnell, Jr., *Sketches by Paul Kane in the Indian Country, 1845–1848* (Smithsonian Miscellaneous Collections, XCIX, Washington 1940).

Canadian Agriculturist (Toronto), III (1851), 228; IV (1852), 292–93.

W. G. Colgate, "An Early Portrait by Paul Kane," *Ontario History*, XL (1948), 23–25.

E. C. Guillet, *The Valley of the Trent*, Champlain Society, Ontario Series (Toronto 1957).

J. R. Harper, "Ontario Painters 1846–1867," National Gallery of Canada, *Bulletin*, I (Ottawa 1963), 16–31.

K. E. Kidd, "Notes on Scattered Works of Paul Kane," Royal Ontario Museum, Art and Archaeology Division, *Annual*, 1962, 64–73.

———, "Paul Kane—A Sheaf of Sketches," *Canadian Art* (Ottawa), VIII (1950–51), 166–67.

E. S. Rogers, *Paul Kane Sketch Pad* (Toronto 1969).

Kathleen Wood, "Paul Kane Sketches," *Rotunda* (Toronto), II (1969), 4–15.

PRINCIPAL PUBLICATIONS DEALING WITH KANE'S CAREER

W. G. Colgate, *Canadian Art, its Origin and Development* (Toronto 1943).

E. A. Corbett, "Paul Kane in Western Canada," *Geographical Magazine* (London), July 1947, 94–103.

N. F. Davin, *The Irishman in Canada* (London and Toronto 1877), 611–17.

J. R. Harper, *Painting in Canada, a History* (Toronto 1966).

———, "Paul Kane," *Dictionary of Canadian Biography*, vol. X (Toronto 1971).

Bertha L. Heilbron, "Artist as Buffalo Hunter: Paul Kane and the Red River Half-Breeds," *Minnesota History*, XXXVI (8), December 1959, 309–14.

K. E. Kidd, "Paul Kane, Painter of Indians," Royal Ontario Museum of Archaeology, *Bulletin* 23 (Toronto 1955), 9–13.

———, "The Wanderings of Kane," *Beaver*, Outfit 277 (December 1946), 3–9.

W. H. G. Kingston, *Western Wanderings; or, A Pleasure Tour in the Canadas* (2v., London 1856), II, 39, 42–47.

H. J. Morgan, *Sketches of Celebrated Canadians* (Quebec 1862), 731–33.

"Paul Kane," *Anglo-American Magazine* (Toronto), VI (May 1855), 401–6.

A. H. Robson, *Paul Kane* (Toronto 1938).

Daniel Wilson, "Paul Kane, the Canadian Artist," *Canadian Journal*, new ser., XIII (1871–73), 66–72.

———, *Prehistoric Man: Searches into the Origin of Civilization in the Old and the New World* (2v., Cambridge and London 1862).

INDEX

NOTE: K.: Kane; HBC: Hudson's Bay Company. Identification of place names is by present-day nomenclature: for example, the provinces of Ontario, Manitoba, Saskatchewan, Alberta, and British Columbia; the states of Oregon and Washington

Index